INSTRUCTOR'S MANUAL
to accompany

Western Civilizations

FIFTEENTH EDITION

Western Civilizations

FIFTEENTH EDITION

Judith Coffin and Robert Stacey

Instructor's Manual by

Steven Kreis

WAKE TECHNICAL COMMUNITY COLLEGE

W. W. NORTON & COMPANY • NEW YORK • LONDON

Copyright © 2005, 2002, 1998, 1993, 1988 by W. W. Norton & Company, Inc.

Printed in the United States of America.

ISBN 0-393-92563-3 (pbk.)

W. W. Norton & Company, Inc., 500 Fifth Avenue, New York, NY 10110
   www.wwnorton.com

W. W. Norton & Company, Ltd., Castle House, 75/76 Wells Street, London W1T 3QT

1 2 3 4 5 6 7 8 9 0

CONTENTS

INTRODUCTION TO THE *INSTRUCTOR'S MANUAL* AND ELECTRONIC MEDIA OFFERINGS

This manual is intended for use by college-level instructors of the Western civilization survey. The manual also reflects those revisions made in the fifteenth edition of the *Western Civilizations* textbook. Adjunct instructors and those coming to teach the Western civilization survey for the first time will find this manual especially useful. Seasoned professors who have taught this survey many times will also find that this manual will help them redefine the survey.

The manual includes extensive **Chapter Outlines** which are drawn directly from the textbook. While it is unlikely that every single feature of the textbook can be covered in any given semester, the outlines are detailed enough to suggest different approaches and interpretations. **General Discussion Questions** are also included in the manual and should be used to stimulate classroom discussion. They may also be used as starting or ending points of lectures as well as for exam or essay questions. Each chapter of *Western Civilizations* includes boxed documents and primary sources. Use the **Document Discussion Questions** included here as guidelines for classroom discussion or as homework assignments. The manual also includes full text **Sample Lectures**. In some cases the lectures cover the general theme of an entire chapter, in others they focus on one facet of a chapter. Adjunct instructors will find these lectures useful for the content they provide and as templates for writing lectures, which is perhaps the most overwhelming task facing those teaching the Western civilization survey for the first time. Every chapter of this manual ends with an annotated list of **Suggested Feature Films** and **Suggested Classroom Films**. It is to your advantage to prepare a handout that introduces each film you decide to screen and explains why you have chosen to show it. Include questions about the film so that students have a better idea of how it fits into their course of study. Finally, when dealing with feature films, be prepared to explain the significance of the film in its historical context—while the film may tell a story, it also tells us something about the period in which it was made.

While this manual is designed to be used in conjunction with the *Western Civilizations* textbook, there are additional electronic media included on the Web site at http://www.wwnorton.com/wciv. The Web site includes some new features that will help you integrate the textbook, this manual, images, maps, audio and video files, and quizzes. For instance, the Web site now contains twenty **Map Exercises** that you can use to raise the level of classroom discussion beyond matters specific to geography alone. In other words, these exercises raise numerous questions about each map that can be integrated into your lecture, homework assignments, and examination essays. You should ask your students to treat the maps as they would treat documents. In addition, there are now twelve **Digital History Features** included on the Web site. These represent specific topics that range across historical periods and chapters of the textbook, forcing students to recognize the continuities and discontinuities between different historical periods. The Digital History Features include a number of questions for review as well as images, documents, and audio and video files. For instance, in Part IV: From Medieval to Modern, there are four Map Exercises and two Digital History Features that are combined to demonstrate the profound effects of the transition from a medieval world of famine, war, and plague to the world of the Renaissance and Reformation. Map Exercise 6, "Fourteenth- and Fifteenth-Century Europe," will help students understand the speed at which the Black Death ravaged Europe while Digital History Feature 5, "After the Black Death," describes the effects of the plague on popular consciousness and highlights numerous peasant revolts that occurred in Europe in the mid-to-late fourteenth century. The *Instructor's Manual* includes eight headnotes that correspond to the eight parts of the textbook and offer advice on how the Map Exercises and Digital History Features can be integrated with the requirements of lecture, discussion, student feedback, and homework assignment.

The Web site also contains a **Quiz** for every chapter of the textbook. Instructors can use the quizzes for review or as the basis for their own examinations. Students can learn their test scores immediately or they can e-mail their instructor with their responses. The quizzes also contain page references to the textbook. Other student review materials on the site include **Flashcards**, which provide space to type the definition of a term before flipping the card to compare their definition with the book's. We have also added new **Interactive Chronologies** that require students to assemble a chapter timeline like an online jigsaw puzzle.

The Western civilization survey covers a broad expanse of time and challenges the instructor to balance adequate coverage with interpretation. It is difficult to master all the details of six thousand years of Western history over the course of two semesters. The instructor new to the Western civilization survey ought to keep in mind that total coverage is perhaps unlikely. Instead, use your lectures to focus on your strengths. Above all, strive for clarity of presentation. We hope that you use all the available resources at your disposal. With this in mind, both the student Web site and this manual are designed to help the student and instructor build connections between the lecture, the textbook, primary sources, and the online content.

Part I: The Ancient Near East

IDEAS FOR USING THE WESTERN CIVILIZATIONS DIGITAL HISTORY CENTER

The Map Exercise and Digital History Features at *www.wwnorton.com/wciv* will assist the instructor in helping students to better understand the origins of Western civilizations in the Ancient Near East, from the Neolithic Age to the period of Minoan and Mycenaean cultures.

- Map Exercise 1: The Ancient Near East, Egypt, and Archaic Greece (Chapters 1–2)
- Digital History Feature 1: Water—The Primary Element (Chapters 1–2)
- Digital History Feature 2: Women and Mystery Cults (Chapters 1–2)

Use Map Exercise 1 to focus lecture and classroom discussion on the importance of geography to the rise of Western civilizations. This Map Exercise is also important for highlighting similarities in the development of civilization in the Ancient Near East and Egypt, and also how those civilizations differed from developments in Archaic Greece, where the management of water was perhaps less significant. The Digital History Feature "Water—The Primary Element" serves as a reminder that the earliest civilizations were hydraulic and that the success of early empires depended on communities' ability to harness the life-giving waters of the Tigris and Euphrates Rivers in Mesopotamia and the Nile in Egypt. The Digital History Feature "Women and the Mystery Cults" illustrates the importance of mystery in the religious life of early humanity. Women played a key role in this development. Use this Digital History Feature to show how the earliest cult practices in Neolithic communities were based upon the *Magna Mater*, or mother goddess, and then compare this to the later development of mystery cults in the Hellenistic and Roman worlds.

CHAPTER 1 | The Origins of Western Civilizations

OUTLINE

I. Introduction
    A. Human history and the rise of civilizations
    B. The growth of the city
II. The Stone Age Background
    A. Prehistory: before written records appeared
        (c. 3000 B.C.E.)
    B. Paleolithic: Old Stone Age
        1. Upper Paleolithic Era, c. 40,000 B.C.E.
        2. Hunters and gatherers (nomads)
III. The Neolithic Revolution: New Stone Age,
    c. 11,000 B.C.E.
    A. Major characteristics
        1. Development of managed food
           production
        2. Permanent settlements
        3. Intensification of trade
        4. More complex society
        5. Specialization
        6. Social distinctions
    B. The origins of food production in the ancient
       Near East
        1. Domestication of plants and animals
        2. A gradual process with revolutionary
           consequences
        3. The Fertile Crescent (ancient western
           Asia/ancient Near East)
        4. Population increase
        5. Surplus and storage
        6. Why did the agricultural revolution
           take place?
    C. The great villages of the Near East
        1. Emergence of villages

        2. Jericho
           a. Spectacular building program
           b. Pottery
        3. Çatal Hüyük
           a. Earliest evidence of cattle herding
           b. Stratified society based on food
              surplus and storage
        4. Rise of a priestly class—a bridge to
           political forms of authority
        5. Trade and the exchange of commodities
           a. Accelerated exchange of
              commodities and new ideas
           b. Increasing social stratification
           c. Social elites
IV. The Development of Civilization in Mesopotamia
    A. Mesopotamia ("the land between the rivers")
        1. The Tigris and Euphrates
        2. Irrigation
    B. Ubaid culture
        1. Sophisticated irrigation systems
        2. Temple-building
        3. Religious structure
           a. Rise of a priestly class
           b. Managing economic resources
    C. Urbanism in the Uruk Period (4300–
       2900 B.C.E.)
        1. Transition to Sumerian city-states
           a. Temple architecture
           b. Urbanization
    D. The development of writing
        1. Record-keeping
        2. Pictographs
        3. Cuneiform ("wedge-shaped writing")
        4. Scribal schools ("Houses of the Tablet")

V. The Sumerians Enter History
  A. Sumerian writing
  B. The first "historical" society
  C. Sumerian cities: Uruk, Ur, Lagash, Eridu, and Kish
  D. Religion
    1. Pantheon of Sumerian gods (around 1500 of them)
    2. Each city-state protected by its own patron god
    3. Economic, political, and religious competition
  E. Redistributive economy and the temple/warehouse complex
  F. Slavery
    1. Prisoners of war
    2. Slaves as forms of property
  G. The Early Dynastic Period begins (2900–2500 B.C.E.)
    1. War leadership
    2. Conflict between city-states
    3. *Lugal* ("*big man*")
      a. Eclipsed power of priestly class
      b. Led the army and their positions became hereditary
      c. Increased tension between power of the temple and power of the palace
    4. *The Epic of Gilgamesh*
      a. Legendary king of Uruk
      b. Military conquest and heroism
      c. Gilgamesh v. Enkidu—city v. wilderness
      d. Pessimistic toward natural environment
  H. Sumerian religion
    1. Creation and the god Enlil
    2. Humanity created to serve the gods
    3. Ziggurats ("stepped temples")
    4. Festivals and sacrifices
    5. Fear and suspicion
    6. Appeasing the gods
    7. Grim view of the afterlife
    8. Resignation toward the futility of life
  I. Science, technology and trade
    1. High degree of self-reliance and ingenuity
    2. Produced copper weapons and tools
    3. Invention of the wheel (chariots and carts)
    4. Mathematics
      a. Lunar calendar
      b. Divided time into multiples of sixty
    5. Sailboats, textiles, paints, perfumes, and medicines
    6. Trade
      a. Acquired raw materials
      b. Interacted with Egyptians and Persians
  J. The end of the Early Dynastic Period (2500–2350 B.C.E.)
    1. Intensification of intercity warfare
    2. Politically and religiously unified elite
    3. Commoners fell into debt slavery
    4. Royal Tombs of Ur
      a. Increased power of the lugal
      b. Lugal perhaps had better afterlife
    5. Sumerian warfare grew as population increased
    6. Sumer remained a collection of independent city-states
VI. The Akkadian Empire (2350–2160 B.C.E.)
  A. Sargon of Akkad—aided Sumerian unification
    1. Lived north of Sumer
    2. Program of conquest—conquers Sumer in 2350 B.C.E.
    3. A new capital at Akkad
    4. From city-states to a kingdom united under Sargon
    5. Naram-Sin—extended Akkadian empire
  B. The Dynasty of Ur (2100–2000 B.C.E).
    1. Sumer and Akkad under attack—empire dissolves into rival city-states
    2. Ur-Nammu and Shulgi
      a. Pursued military conquests
      b. Commercial expansion
    3. A dying empire
    4. Ibbi-Sin and Ishbi-Irra
      a. Losing control of the empire
      b. Incessant warfare
    5. The Sumerian renaissance and the rise of the Amorites
VII. The Old Babylonian Empire
  A. Hammurabi
    1. Ascends throne in 1792 B.C.E.
    2. Used writing as a weapon
    3. Elevated Marduk, patron deity of Babylon
  B. Religion and law
    1. Interweaves political power with religious practice
    2. Wars of aggression
    3. United his people politically
    4. Ruled as king of Babylon, the city of Marduk
    5. Ritual intercourse and fertility

6. The *Code of Hammurabi*
    a. Actual rulings of Hammurabi
    b. Illustrates nature of Babylonian social classes
    c. Slaves
    d. Social stratification
    e. Women
C. The legacy
  1. A durable state
  2. Conception of kingship
  3. Importance of religion
VIII. The Development of Civilization in Egypt
  A. General observations
    1. Geography and the Nile
    2. Black Land–Red Land
    3. Egypt as center of the cosmos
    4. Powerful, centralized state controlled by pharaohs
    5. Kingdoms and periods
  B. Predynastic Egypt (c.10,000–3100 B.C.E.)
    1. Hunters and gatherers
    2. Increased population
    3. First settlement at Merimde Beni Salama (4750 B.C.E.)
    4. Upper Egyptian towns (3200 B.C.E.): Nekhen, Naqada, This, and Abydos
      a. High degrees of social specialization
      b. Sophisticated fortifications
      c. Elaborate temples
      d. Attracted industry and travelers
  C. The unification of Egypt: the Archaic Period (3100–2686 B.C.E.)
    1. Manetho's dynastic categorization
    2. "King Scorpion"
    3. Egypt unified by Narmer (legendary King Menes or Min)
    4. Administrative capital at Memphis (Lower Egypt)
    5. Pharaoh
      a. Pharaoh as divine
      b. Earthly manifestation of Horus (falcon-god)
  D. Language and writing
    1. Hieroglyphs ("sacred carvings")
    2. Champollion and the Rosetta Stone
    3. Writing as tool for Egyptian government and administration
    4. Hieratic scrip—used for everyday business of government and commerce
    5. Papyrus
  E. The Old Kingdom (c. 2686–2125 B.C.E.)
    1. Difficulty of interpreting records
    2. Centralized power of pharaoh—pharaoh was Egypt

    3. Appointed local governors (*nomarchs*)
    4. Extensive bureaucracy
    5. Imhotep—the greatest administrative official
      a. Right-hand man to Djoser (Third Dynasty pharaoh)
      b. Learned medicine, astronomy, theology, mathematics, and architecture
      c. "Step-pyramid"
        i. Built west of Memphis
        ii. Based on the mastaba, stacked one on top of the other
        iii. The symbol of pharaonic power
    6. Fourth Dynasty (2613–2494 B.C.E.)
      a. Great pyramids of Giza
      b. The account of Herodotus
      c. Pyramids built not by slaves, but by tens of thousands of peasant workers
      d. Tensions increase between pharaonic religion and local gods and leaders
  F. Society in Old Kingdom Egypt
    1. The elite: royalty and nobility
    2. The poor: everyone else
    3. Women in the Old Kingdom
      a. High degrees of legal status
      b. Rigidly patriarchal society
      c. Barred from state office
  G. Egyptian religion and world view
    1. The uniqueness of the Egyptians
    2. "Egyptian-ness"
    3. Life, re-creation, and renewal
    4. The myth of Osiris and Isis—life from death
    5. The Egyptian death cult
      a. Osiris as central deity
      b. Death was unpleasant but a necessary part of the cycle
      c. *Ka* (otherworldly existence) and *Duat* (the underworld)
      d. Embalming and mummification
      e. Coffin texts and "Books of the Dead"
      f. *Ma'at*—binding together the endless cycle of life, death, and the return of life
      g. Confidence and optimism
  H. The end of the Old Kingdom
    1. Fifth and Sixth Dynasties (2492–2181 B.C.E.)
    2. Less monumental architecture

GENERAL DISCUSSION QUESTIONS

1. What is civilization? How would you define it? How does it differ from culture or society?

2. Was the rise of kingdoms and empires a "natural" phenomenon? Do human beings need the leadership of a strong ruler to form a civilized society? Or were there special factors in the ancient Near East that favored monarchies?

3. What aspects of life in ancient Mesopotamia and Egypt made them the first Western civilizations? To what extent does civilization depend on urban life? What are the general characteristics of urban life that can be identified regardless of historical period?

4. Hydraulic theories emphasize the importance of water—access, control, and distribution—in forming the earliest governments and civilizations. Does the rise of ancient Near Eastern civilizations in river valleys support such theories? How can you argue against these theories?

5. Why is the concept of "Indo-Europeans" historically significant? Who were they and what did they do?

6. What ideas and factors made it possible for the ancients to believe in many different gods simultaneously? Why did monotheism tend to develop after polytheism?

7. We are fortunate that we have the Code of Hammurabi at our disposal. Does the Code have any modern aspects or does it seem like a specifically ancient document? Was the way justice was defined by the Code identical to the way it is defined today?

8. During his lifetime, every pharaoh was Horus-Ra; at death he became Osiris. How did the evolution of Egyptian funeral customs demonstrate a "democratization of death"?

9. How does ancient history suggest that progress is often the result of war or invasion?

10. What is the main contribution of ancient Near Eastern and Egyptian civilizations to western civilizations?

DOCUMENT DISCUSSION QUESTIONS

The Flood: Two Accounts

1. What is the significance of the *Epic of Gilgamesh*? Why was it written? What function did the *Epic of Gilgamesh* serve in ancient Mesopotamia?

2. How did the geography and climate of Mesopotamia influence this epic and Mesopotamians' attitudes toward the gods, kingship, civilization, and the afterlife?

3. How does the account of Noah in the Book of Genesis differ from that of Utanapishtim in the *Epic of Gilgamesh*? Compare both human and divine characters.

4. Is a myth a picturesque story that contains some spiritual truth? Is it history and/or a historical source that explores stories of human origins? How can we apply historical criticism to religious texts?

The Code of Hammurabi

5. Does the Code of Hammurabi sound harsh, fair, or lenient? Penalties such as exile and mutilation were less severe than death, but was harsh justice necessary in Babylonia? Based on your reading of the Code, was Hammurabi an enlightened ruler?

6. In what ways does the Code of Hammurabi exhibit the influences of the urban society from which these laws were imposed? What are the general characteristics of ancient Near Eastern urban society?

The Egyptian Book of the Dead

7. What was the purpose of the Egyptian Book of the Dead? How did individual Egyptians use the Book to gain immortality?

8. What is striking about the emphasis on judgment after death in the Egyptian Book of the Dead? Why was the Mesopotamian view of death generally gloomier than the Egyptian?

9. Central to the instructions issued by Ptah-Hotep, a sage and advisor, was that pharaoh was to act in accordance with *ma'at*. What is *ma'at* and why was it so important to Ptah-Hotep? Do the cultures of all ancient civilization accept the existence of something like *ma'at*?

SAMPLE LECTURE 1: THE ORIGINS OF HYDRAULIC CIVILIZATIONS IN THE WEST

Lecture Objectives

1. To show how developments in the Neolithic Age prepared the foundation for the rise of Western civilizations

2. To examine similarities and differences between Mesopotamian and Egyptian development

3. To suggest that the primary civilizations explained the world through myth rather than science

THE NEOLITHIC REVOLUTION

Prehistory is divided into two periods: the Paleolithic or old Stone Age (two million years ago, and the Neolithic or new Stone Age (twelve thousand to five thousand years ago). The Paleolithic Age lasted from roughly two million years ago to the end of the last Ice Age, about twelve thousand years ago. Paleolithic man lived in a subsistence economy and a communal society. People lived in small bands or groups of families of fewer than one hundred souls. The evidence points to a division of labor based on gender and governed by patterns of food collection: males generally attended to hunting and scavenging while women went about gathering plants, seeds, and eggs. The survival of the group depended upon the work of both men and women. These were nomadic people who followed the migrations of animals and the seasonal growth of plants. Around thirty thousand years ago, spears and the bow and arrow became common and man's best friend, the dog, was domesticated. Around the same time, archeologists and anthropologists have discovered, Paleolithic society created a "cult of the dead." Intentionally burying the dead is a distinctly human activity, and it shows an awakening self-consciousness and group cohesion. Burial of the dead also suggests the beginning of symbolic thought.

At the end of the last Ice Age, around twelve thousand years ago, the Neolithic Revolution began. This revolution involved the shift from food-gathering to food-production. Quickly following this was the domestication of animals. Neolithic communities arose independently in several parts of the world at the same time—the Near East, India, Africa, North Asia, Southeast Asia, and Central and South America. This shift was slow to take place but radically altered human life. In various parts of the world human groups settled down in permanent villages but continued to practice hunting and gathering before they made the full transition to a Neolithic mode of production. These people lived in houses, and in this sense, these people were themselves a domesticated species. The point here is that humans domesticated themselves at the same time that they were domesticating plants and animals. But the pressure of population ultimately led to an increasing dependence on farming and a more efficient food-producing way of life. Human populations around the world independently domesticated and began cultivating a variety of plants, including wheat, barley, rye, keys, lentils, and flax in Southwest Asia; millet and soybeans in North China; rice and beans in Southeast Asia; maize or corn in Mesoamerica; and potatoes and beans in South America. The domestication of animals developed out of an intimate and long-standing human contact with wild species. Animals were valuable to humans in many ways:

- Meat contains more complex proteins than plants.
- Animals provide food on the move that keeps from spoiling until needed.
- Animals also produce valuable secondary products that were increasingly exploited.
- Cattle, sheep, and pigs are literally animal factories that produce more cattle, sheep, and pigs.
- Animal hides provide raw material for leather.
- Animals also provide traction and transportation.

As early man domesticated plants and animals, it suddenly became apparent that a surplus of food could be created. If a smaller number of humans was needed to produce the food necessary for existence, then this freed up people to pursue other tasks. So the shift to the Neolithic Age led to the creation of several new technologies, such as textiles and pottery. These new techniques produced a new mode of life. Neolithic peoples began to build permanent structures of wood, mudbrick, and stone. They twisted rope and developed a rudimentary form of metallurgy. Over time, populations expanded and the Neolithic economy spread rapidly. Five thousand years ago, thousands of agrarian villages dotted the ancient Near East, usually within a day's walk from one another. Regional crossroads and trading centers arose and by the late Neolithic Age, real towns had emerged. The Neolithic Revolution occurred without the input or assistance of any independent science—potters made pots because pots were needed. Most Neolithic peoples routinely observed the heavens and created astronomically aligned monuments that served as seasonal calendars. Stonehenge, on the Salisbury Plain in southwest England, is perhaps the most dramatic of such monuments. Neolithic societies never became complex kingdoms. They never build large cities or enclosed structures like palaces or temples. They had no need for writing to keep records and they never established a tradition of higher learning. Nor did they institutionalize science. All this only took place when Neolithic societies became civilizations, the second great transformation in human evolution.

THE URBAN REVOLUTION

Changes that began around five to six thousand years ago in the ancient Near East created the first, or primary, civilizations. These were civilizations of high population densities and centralized political and economic authority. The development of a complex and stratified society, monumental architecture, and the beginning of writing and learning were all hallmarks of these primary civilizations. A new mode of intensified agriculture provided the foundation for these primary civilizations. Simple gardening was superseded by field agriculture based on large-scale water management networks and irrigation canals. The Urban Revolution could sustain much larger populations, urban centers, armies, tax collectors, police, expanded trade, palaces and temples, a priestly class, and religious and educational institutions. In this instance the rise of civilization has been linked with a technology of large-scale hydraulic systems—irrigation and flood control require hydraulic engineering works and some level of communal action to build and maintain them. Some civilizations were environmentally restricted to areas in which intensified agriculture was possible or practical. Warfare became chronic and developed beyond raiding, toward outright conquest.

MESOPOTAMIAN CIVILIZATIONS

The earliest primary civilization in the West was Mesopotamia, the "land between the rivers." By 4000 B.C.E., great walled cities with populations between fifty thousand and two hundred thousand appeared between the Tigris and Euphrates Rivers. No one city-state dominated Mesopotamia. Instead, we find a series of city-states that rose and fell over the centuries. Sumer was one such culture, as was the Babylonia of Hammurabi. These were civilizations based on irrigation agriculture, which demanded centralized local authority and a complex bureaucracy to collect, store, and redistribute surpluses. Because agricultural surpluses were available, Mesopotamian cultures were also capable of building large temple complexes and pyramids known as ziggurats. The priests controlled the religious life of the community, the economy, land ownership, and the employment of workers, they also managed long-distance trade. By 3000 B.C.E., Mesopotamian civilization had made contact with other cultures of the Fertile Crescent (a term first coined by James Breasted in 1916).

The Sumerians inhabited southern Mesopotamia from 3000–2000 B.C.E. The origins of the Sumerians is unclear—what is clear is that Sumerian civilization dominated Mesopotamian law, religion, art, literature, and science for nearly seven centuries. One of the greatest achievements of Sumerian

civilization was their cuneiform ("wedge-shaped") system of writing. Using a reed stylus, they made wedge-shaped impressions on wet clay tablets that were then baked in the sun. Originally, Sumerian writing was pictographic and each figurerepresented a word identical in meaning to the object pictured. Over time, the characters were gradually simplified and their pictographic nature gave way to conventional signs that represented ideas. The Sumerians used writing primarily as a form of recordkeeping. The most common cuneiform tablets record transactions of daily life: tallies of cattle kept by herdsmen for their owners, production figures, lists of taxes, accounts, contracts, and other facets of organizational life in the community.

The city-state was Sumer's most important political entity. Each city-state consisted of an urban center and its surrounding farmland. The city-states were isolated from one another geographically, and so the independence of each city-state became a cultural norm with important consequences. For instance, it was held that each city-state was the estate of a particular god: Nannar (moon) was said to watch over the city-state of Ur; Uruk had An (sky); Sippar had Utu (sun); and Enki (earth) could be found at Eridu. Nippur, the earliest center of Sumerian religion, was dedicated to Enlil, god of wind (Enlil was supplanted by Marduk at Babylon). Located near the center of each city-state was a ziggurat with a temple at the top dedicated to the god or goddess who "owned" the city. Considerable wealth was poured into the construction of temples and the residences of priests and priestesses who attended to the needs of the gods. The priests also controlled all economic activities, since the economy was "redistributive." With its rather large pantheon of gods and goddesses animating all aspects of life, Sumerian religion was polytheistic in nature. Unlike humans, the gods and goddesses were divine and immortal. But they were not all-powerful since no one god had control over the entire universe. The relationship of human beings to the gods was based on subservience since, according to Sumerian myth, human beings were created to do the labor the gods were unwilling to do themselves. As a consequence, humans were insecure since they could never be sure of the gods' actions. The Sumerians also developed cultic arts to influence good powers (gods and goddesses), whose decisions could determine human destiny, and to ward off evil powers (demons).

The Sumerians were not the only people to inhabit Mesopotamia. By 2350 B.C.E., Semitic-speaking people united northern Mesopotamia with the Sumerian city-states and a new capital was set up at Akkad. The result was a centralized government under the authority of the king, his royal court, and the high class of priests. Sargon, whose name is taken to mean "the king is legitimate," carried out more than thirty battles against the Sumerian city-states and eventually, these city-states were incorporated into the Akkadian kingdom. The foundation of the Akkadian state was economic. Sargon and his royal court served as the focal point of all economic activity. Vast amounts of wealth were brought to the capital city and it became necessary to maintain a huge number of royal servants to help administer his kingdom.

THE CODE OF HAMMURABI

Mesopotamian men and women viewed themselves as subservient to the gods and believed humans were at the mercy of the gods' arbitrary decisions. To counter their insecurity, the Mesopotamians not only developed the arts of divination in order to understand the wishes of their gods, but they also relieved some anxiety by establishing codes that regulated their relationships with one another. The best-preserved Mesopotamian collection of law codes was that of Hammurabi (fl. eighteenth century B.C.E.). The Code of Hammurabi reveals a society of strict justice. Penalties for criminal offenses were severe and varied according to the wealth of the individual. According to the code, there were three social classes in Babylonia:

- an upper class of nobles (government officials, priests, and warriors)
- the class of freemen (merchants, artisans, professionals, and wealthy farmers)
- a lower class of slaves.

An offense against a member of the upper class was punished with more severity than the same offense against a member of a lower class. The principle of retaliation ("an eye for an eye, a tooth for a tooth") was fundamental. It was applied in cases where members of the upper class committed criminal offenses against their own social equals. But for offenses against members of the lower classes, a money payment was made instead.

Mesopotamian society, like any other society, had its share of crime. Burglary was common. If a person stole goods belonging to the temples, he was put to death, and so was the person who received the stolen goods. If the private property of an individual was stolen, the thief had to make a tenfold restitution. If he could not do so, he was put to death. An offender caught attempting to loot a burning house was to be thrown into that fire. Private individuals were often responsible for bringing charges before a court of law. To insure that accusations were not brought lightly, the accuser in cases of murder was responsible for proving his case against the defendant. If the accuser could not, he was put to death. Providing false testimony in a murder case meant the same fate. Hammurabi's code also took seriously the responsibilities of all public officials. The governor of an area and city officials were expected to catch burglars. If they failed to do so, public officials in the area where the crime took place had to replace the lost property. If murderers were not found, the officials had to pay a fine to the relatives of the murdered person. The law code also extended into the daily life of the ordinary citizen. Builders were held responsible for the buildings they constructed—if a house collapsed and caused the death of its owner, the builder was put to death.

The number of laws in Hammurabi's code dedicated to land and commerce reveal the importance of agriculture and trade in Babylonian society. Numerous laws dealt with questions of landholding, such as the establishment of conditions for renting farmland. Laws concerning land use and irrigation were especially strict. If a landowner or tenant failed to keep dikes in good repair, he was required to pay for the grain that was destroyed. If he could not pay he was sold into slavery and his goods sold, the proceeds of which were divided among the injured parties. The largest number of laws in the Code of Hammurabi were dedicated to marriage and family. Parents arranged marriages for their children. After marriage, the party signed a marriage contract. Without this contract, no one was considered legally married. While the husband provided a bridal payment, the woman's parents were responsible for a dowry to the husband. Dowries were carefully monitored and governed by regulations. A woman's place was at home and failure to fulfill her duties was grounds for divorce. If she was not able to bear children, her husband could divorce her but he had to repay the dowry. If his wife tried to leave the home in order to engage in business, her husband could divorce her and did not have to repay the dowry. Furthermore, if his wife was a "gadabout, . . . neglecting her house [and] humiliating her husband," she could be drowned.

Sexual relations were strictly regulated as well. Husbands, but not wives, were permitted sexual activity outside marriage. A wife caught committing adultery was pitched into the river. Incest was strictly forbidden. If a father committed incestuous relations with his daughter, he would be banished. Incest between a son and his mother resulted in both being burned. Fathers ruled their children as well as their wives. Obedience was expected: "If a son has struck his father, they shall cut off his hand." Although scholars have questioned the extent to which these laws were actually employed in Babylonian society, the Code of Hammurabi provides us an important glimpse into the values of Mesopotamian civilization.

EARLY EGYPTIAN CIVILIZATION

While the Sumerians, Babylonians, Akkadians, and other groups were busy creating the civilization of the Fertile Crescent, another civilization appeared in the West. Again, this civilization depended entirely upon geography and the management of water. It was the fertile valley of the Nile River that allowed Egyptian civilization to flourish over the course of many centuries. It is an area of the world in which much-needed natural resources were abundant. Furthermore, the climate of Egypt is very dry and almost changeless. Because of this static, changeless quality, the Egyptians obtained a sense of security from their environment. For centuries, ancient Egyptian civilization flourished in isolation from the rest of the ancient Near East.

Although Egypt was isolated, it was not unified. Geographically, it was divided between the Black Land and the Red Land, and politically, between Upper and Lower Egypt. Around 3100 B.C.E., various political factions struggled to gain control. Victory eventually fell to Menes (or Narmer) in Upper Egypt. The Egyptians considered the unification of Upper and Lower Egypt as the most important event in their history. Like Sargon, Menes ruled as a mediator between men and the gods. But Menes was also pharaoh—he was not only the mediator between men and the gods, but was himself divine. Pharaoh's rule was eternal and absolute—he ruled not just on behalf of the gods, but as a god himself. In assuming the position of king and chief priest, pharaoh shed his human qualities and assumed an unchanging, fixed, and divine position. This was the role that Menes assumed in 3100 B.C.E. The new state also derived authority and stability from the concept of *ma'at*, a quality or behavior which translates as truth, justice, order, and righteousness. *Ma'at* implied a divine force for harmony and stability that emanated from the beginning of time itself. Good rule by pharaoh signified the presence of *ma'at*.

Egyptian religion, like that of Mesopotamia, was polytheistic and each region had its own patron deity. Some of these local or regional gods gained notoriety throughout Egypt. For instance, the god Ptah gained power when the city of Memphis became the capital of Egypt. Later, the god Re of Heliopolis eclipsed that of Ptah. Finally, the god Amon rose to supremacy in Thebes in connection with the political authority of the Thebian pharaoh. As a rule, whenever a new capital was founded, a new supreme god was chosen. Egyptian gods were often represented as animals—falcons, vultures, cobras, dogs, cats, or crocodiles. For the Egyptians, because animals were non-human, they must have possessed religious significance. Other gods, such as Ptah and Amon, were given human representation, but the most important god, Re, was not represented at all.

The gods created the cosmos—they created order out of chaos. Egyptian religion inspired confidence and optimism in the external order and stability of the world. The gods guided the rhythms of life and death, and what really distinguished Egyptian religion from that of Mesopotamia was that any man or woman could share in the benefits of an afterlife. As one historian has put it: "death meant a continuation of one's life on earth, a continuation that, with the appropriate precautions of proper burial, prayer, and ritual, would include only the best parts of life on earth—nothing to fear, but on the other hand, nothing to want to hurry out of this world for." Religion was the unifying agent in ancient Egypt. Pharaoh indicated his concern for his people by worshipping the local deities in public ceremonies. The gods protected the living and guaranteed them an afterlife. The Egyptians believed they were living in a fixed, static, or unchanging universe in which life and death were part of a continuous, rhythmic cycle. Certain patterns came to be expected—grain had to be harvested, irrigation canals had to be repaired, and pyramids had to be built.

MONUMENTAL STRUCTURES

The first pyramids, built around 2900 B.C.E., were little more than mudbrick structures built over the burial pits of nobles. These structures protected the body from exposure and also provided a secure place for the personal belongings of the dead noble. By 2600 B.C.E. mudbrick structures were replaced by the familiar stone pyramid. The pyramids were completely inaccessible structures—once pharaoh was buried, hallways and passages were sealed and obliterated. In this way, the pyramids would stand eternal, unchanged, and fixed, as they stand today.

The pyramid symbolizes much of what we know about ancient Egypt. They reflect the centralization of the Egyptian government as well as rule by pharaoh. The great pyramids of Giza, built more than 4500 years ago, expressed pharaoh's immortality and divinity. The earliest built of the Giza pyramids is that of Khufu, better known as Cheops, the Greek name given to it by the Greek historian Herodotus, when he visited the pyramids around 480 B.C.E. Cheops covers thirteen acres and contains two million stone blocks, each weighing five thousand pounds. Its height originally stood at almost five hundred feet. One of the most compelling features of the pyramids, in addition to the architectural feat of just building them, was their mortuary art. Inside the pyramids was the royal burial chamber. The walls of the chamber were covered with hieroglyphics, which detailed the life of pharaoh. The emphasis of mortuary art was not death but life. We find art detailing people fishing and hunting. We also see people seated at banquets. Representations of food and wine were included as well. Jars of wine, grain, fruits and other foods were included, as well as boats, bows, arrows, and other objects from the real world. Slaves were often entombed as well. Pharaoh would need these things in the afterlife, since death was not final, but an extension of this worldly life. Like the seasons, man lives and dies. Death was nothing final but the beginning of yet another cycle. In the next life there would be birds, people, oceans, rivers, desert, food, and wine.

A MYTHOPOEIC WORLD VIEW

Religious beliefs gave the great river civilizations of Mesopotamia and Egypt their distinctive character. But this religion was not a religion of comfort or morality. Instead, these polytheistic religions were mythopoeic. The construction of myths was the first manner in which Western civilization attempted to explain life and the universe. Myths explained the creation of the universe as well as the role men and women would play in that universe. Nature, for these earliest river civilizations, was not an inanimate "it." Instead, nature, the world of nature, had a life, will, and vitality all its own. The mythmakers of the ancient Near East and of Egypt did not seek to rationally or logically explain nature. Although these civilizations certainly exercised their minds to build ziggurats and pyramids, irrigation canals and pottery wheels, cuneiforms and hieroglyphics, they did not advance to the creation of science. They did not deduce abstractions, nor did they make hypotheses or establish general laws of the nature world. These efforts—science and philosophy— were the product of another culture, located in another time and place: the Greeks.

SUGGESTED CLASSROOM FILMS

The Agricultural Revolution: Man as a Food Producer. 19 min. Color. 1982. McGraw-Hill. Explores the transition from hunting to farming.

Ancient Cultures of Mesopotamia. 75 min. Color. 1989. Insight Media. Three-part series includes: *The Sumerian Kingdom of Ur*; *Babylon: The Gate of the Gods*; and *Assurnasirpal: The Assyrian King.*

Ancient Egypt. 47 min. Color. 1997. Films for the Humanities and Sciences. Numerous interviews with Egyptologists as well as computer graphic recreations of pyramids, temples, and the sphinx.

Ancient Egypt: The Sun and the River. 58 min. Color. 1971. University Films Library Holder. Explores the art and architecture of Egyptian culture.

The Ancient Egyptian. 27 min. Color. 1967. Insight Media. Uses art and artifacts to explore religious beliefs and cultural values. Winner of the Blue Ribbon, American Film and Video Festival.

The Birth of Civilization: 6000 B.C.–2000 B.C. 26 min. Color. 1985. Insight Media. Traces the birth of civilization in the fertile valleys of the Near East and China.

Civilization and Writing. 23 min. Color. 1998. Insight Media. Explores the ancient river valley civilizations and traces the move from oral traditions to written literature.

Colliding Continents and the Age of Bronze. 55 min. Color. 1991. Insight Media. This BBC production explores the interaction between the use of bronze and the history of early humanity.

The Harvest of the Seasons. 52 min. Color. 1973. BBC-TV. The lifestyle of the Bakhtiari tribe of central Iran serves as an example of how nomads lived and waged war during the Neolithic Age. Part of Jacob Bronowski's *The Ascent of Man* series.

Human Prehistory and the First Civilizations. 36 segments, 30 min. each. Color. 2002. Insight Media. The latest scientific and archaeological research on the origins of human populations.

Hunters and Gatherers. 60 min. Color. 1989. Insight Media. A look at the arrival and dispersal of the first human beings in Australia.

Iraq: Cradle of Civilization. 60 min. Color. 1991. Insight Media. Michael Wood traces the growth of civilization along the banks of the Tigris and Euphrates Rivers. He looks at the growth of Ur, Nineveh, and Babylon and discusses the religions that arose in the region.

Life Under the Pharaohs. 21 min. Color. 1989. Insight Media. Uses ancient paintings to depict everyday life.

Mesopotamia: I Have Conquered the River. 59 min. Color. 2000. Insight Media. Profiles the Sumerian city-states, showing how they built a vibrant agricultural economy. Also discusses cuneiform writing, the Code of Hammurabi, and the *Epic of Gilgamesh.*

Mesopotamia: Return to Eden. 52 min. Color. 1995. Time-Life. Examines the roots of the world's major religions in the valleys of Mesopotamia's Fertile Crescent.

Out of the Ice. 55 min. Color. 1991. Insight Media. A BBC production that chronicles the story of humanity from the end of the last Ice Age to the first civilizations.

Sumer, Babylon, Assyria: The Wolves. 26 min. Color. 1991. Films for the Humanities. Uses collections of Near Eastern antiquities to explore the militarism of ancient civilizations.

CHAPTER 2

Gods and Empires in the Ancient Near East, 1700–500 B.C.E.

OUTLINE

I. Introduction
  A. Transformations in the ancient Near East
  B. New imperial powers
  C. The "international system"
  D. Iron and bronze
II. The Indo-European Migrations
  A. Language
    1. Sir William Jones discovers connection between Sanskrit, Latin, and Greek (1786)
    2. Shared features with Latin and Greek as well as Gothic and Old Persian
    3. Was there a Proto-Indo-European language spoken by a single population?
    4. Indo-European linguistic forms appear after 2000 B.C.E.
  B. The rise of Anatolia
    1. Natural resources
    2. The Assyrian presence
      a. Urban life (e.g., Cappadocia)
      b. Trade networks between Anatolia and Mesopotamia
      c. Carried Mesopotamian civilization into Anatolia and northern Syria
  C. Hittites and Kassites
    1. Indo-European speaking people
    2. Hittite rulers establish themselves in cities of central Anatolia
    3. Politically independent until 1700 B.C.E.
    4. Intensely militaristic culture
    5. Under Hattusilis I, Hittites extend power throughout Anatolian plateau
      a. Controlling overland trade routes
      b. Military conquest

6. Mursilis I (c. 1620–1590 B.C.E.)
      a. Sought to control Upper Euphrates
      b. Drove east to Babylon (1595 B.C.E.)
    7. The Kassites
      a. Unknown origins
      b. Brought peace and prosperity
  D. The Kingdom of Mitanni
    1. An Indo-European minority
    2. A warrior aristocracy
    3. United Upper Euphrates and northern Syria into a single kingdom
    4. Innovations
      a. Horse-drawn chariots
      b. Masters of horse training and cavalry tactics
    5. Collapsed in the face of Hittite aggression
III. Egypt in the Second Millennium B.C.E.
  A. Transformations
    1. Foreigners
    2. Middle Kingdom Egypt as anxious, uncertain place
    3. The Hyksos (1700 B.C.E.) invasion
      a. Legitimized rule in accordance with Egyptian precedents
      b. Retained their foreign material culture
      c. The Nubian kingdom
    4. Hyksos driven out, thus establishing the Eighteenth Dynasty
  B. The New Kingdom (1550–1075 B.C.E.)
    1. A radical departure in Egyptian history and culture
    2. Pharaonic rule in Dynasty 18
      a. New type of nobility—an aristocracy of military commanders

b. Wealth acquired through war

c. Thutmosis I (c. 1504–1491 B.C.E.)

    i. Strategy of defense through offense

    ii. Learned tactics from the Hyksos

3. Queen Hatshepsut and Thutmosis III

    a. Hatshepsut masked her femininity yet clearly the ruling force

    b. The "Valley of the Kings" (near ancient Thebes)

    c. Thutmosis begins his rule (c. 1458 B.C.E.)

        i. Military campaigns

        ii. Palestine and the Syrian coast

4. Amenhotep II (c. 1428–1397 B.C.E.)

    a. Undermining the strength of the Mitanni

    b. Unintended consequences: the Hittites and Assyrians

5. Amenhotep III (c. 1387–1350 B.C.E.)

    a. Effective administration

    b. Exploiting advantages already won

C. Religious change and challenge

1. New wealth

    a. Personal glorification of pharaoh

    b. Military aristocracy

    c. The temples

2. The temple of Amon (Thebes)

    a. Amon identified with the sun-god Ra

    b. An Egyptian national god

    c. The priests of Amon

3. The reign of Akhenaten (1352–1336 B.C.E.)

    a. Amenhotep IV inclined toward sun-god worship

    b. Replaced Ra with the Aten, the physical sun-disc

    c. From "Amon is pleased" to "He is effective for the Aten"

    d. Built capital between Memphis and Thebes (modern day el-Amarna)

    e. The Amarna period

        i. Monotheistic worship

        ii. The life-giving power of light

        iii. The affirmation of life

        iv. Queen Nefertiti

    f. Akhenaten as revolutionary intellectual or reactionary?

    g. Resistance to Akhenaten

4. King Tut (Tutakhaten/Tutankhamon)

IV. The International System of the Late Bronze Age

A. The age of superpowers

B. International diplomacy

1. A balance of power stabilized trade and diplomacy

2. The language of diplomatic rank

C. International trade

1. Flourishing seaborne trade

2. Trade routes as conduits for culture and cosmopolitanism

3. Treaty between Ramses II and the Hittites

    a. Geopolitical stability

    b. Furthered economic integration

D. Expansion and fragility

V. Aegean Civilization: Minoans and Mycenaeans

A. Heinrich Schliemann and the ancient Greeks

1. Homer and Troy

2. The citadel at Mycenae

B. Sir Arthur Evans and the great palace at Knossos

C. The Minoan thalassocracy

1. High degree of material and architectural sophistication (the Palace Age)

2. Redistributive economy

3. Knossos

4. Overseas trade

5. Powerful navy

6. The bull cult and human sacrifice

7. Written language: Linear A and Linear B

8. Contacts with the Mycenaeans

D. The Mycenaeans

1. Intermingling between various Greek and non-Greek-speaking groups

2. Mycenaean citadels

    a. Warrior culture

    b. Trade and piracy

    c. Centers of government

    d. Redistributive economy

3. Mycenaean imitation of Near Eastern examples

4. Warriors and mercenaries

5. Linear B tablets and economic and political rights

6. Greek gods

7. Mycenaean collapse

E. The Sea Peoples and the end of the Bronze Age

1. Waves of destruction—obscure origins

2. Disruption of northern trade networks

3. The Greek "Dark Age"

4. The survival of Egypt

5. Assyrian effects

6. New traditions and new cultural experiments

VI. The Small-Scale States of the Early Iron Age

A. Geopolitical changes

B. The Phoenicians
1. Roots lay in the ancient Near East
2. Independence of Phoenician cities
3. Aristocratic form of government
4. Egyptian connections and the papyrus trade
5. Textiles
6. Cities
   a. Planted Mediterranean trading colonies
   b. Established Carthage in modern Tunisia
   c. May have ventured as far as the Atlantic
C. Cultural influence
1. Greek trading partners
2. Near Eastern influences
3. The alphabet
D. The Philistines
1. Great national enemy of the Hebrews
2. Retention of a separate identity
3. Introduced grapevines and olive trees to the Levant
4. The Pentapolis (heavily fortified citadels)
   a. Gaza, Ashkelon, Ashdod, Ekron, and Gath
5. Virtually no written records
6. The Philistines and the Hebrews
E. The Hebrews
1. Origins: the Old Testament as historical resource
   a. God and his chosen people
   b. The covenant
   c. The creation and the flood
   d. The twelve tribes
2. Hebrews and Philistines
   a. Samuel and King Saul
   b. David and triumph over the Philistines
   c. King David
3. Consolidation of the Hebrew kingdom
   a. David strengthens his new kingdom (c. 1000 B.C.E.)
   b. Reduces Philistine influence
   c. Defeats the Moabites and Ammonites
   d. Builds Jerusalem as the political and religious capital
   e. The Ark of the Covenant and Jerusalem
   f. Reorganized priesthood of Yahweh
4. The reign of King Solomon (973–939 B.C.E.)
   a. The temple complex at Jerusalem
   b. Instituted oppressive taxation

c. Maintained a large standing army
d. Forced labor
5. The northern (Israel) and southern (Judah) kingdoms
VII. The Assyrian Empire
A. A Semitic-speaking people
B. The fight for existence
C. The middle Assyrian period (1362–859 B.C.E.)
1. Assuruballit I (1362-1327 B.C.E.)
   a. Extended power over northern Mesopotamia
2. Tukulti-Ninurta I (1243–1207 B.C.E.)
   a. Conqueror of the first order
   b. Sacked Babylon
3. Assurnasirpal II (883–859 B.C.E.)
   a. Revived Assyrian strength
   b. Founded the neo-Assyrian empire
D. The neo-Assyrian empire (859–627 B.C.E.)
1. Assyrian throne seized by Tiglath-Pileser III (744 B.C.E.)
   a. Conquered various western kingdoms
2. The dynasty of Sargon II (722–705 B.C.E.)
   a. The Sargonids
3. Government and administration
   a. An armed state
   b. King as hereditary monarch and earthly representative of the god Assur
   c. Divination and oracles
   d. Extensive bureaucracy
   e. Rigidly patriarchal
4. The Assyrian military-religious ethos
   a. Holy war and the exaction of tribute through terror
   b. The Assyrian army belonged to Assur
   c. The worship of Assur among conquered people
   d. Assyrian warfare
      i. Butchering and torturing enemies
      ii. Strategy and tactics
      iii. Heavily armed and armored shock troops
      iv. Archery and chariots
      v. Catapults and siege engines
E. The end of Assyria and its legacy
1. Sennacherib (704–681 B.C.E.)
   a. Rebuilt Nineveh
2. Assurbanipal (669–627 B.C.E.)
   a. Strong military presence
   b. Internal reforms
   c. The library at Nineveh
3. General hatred of the Assyrians

4. Nineveh captured and burned (612 B.C.E.)
5. The Chaldean Empire (612–539 B.C.E.)

VIII. The Persians
  A. The origins of the Persian empire
    1. Emerged from obscurity when Cyrus became ruler of all Persians
    2. Threw off the lordship of the Medes
    3. Lydian gold and silver
    4. Croesus launches a war against the Persians (546 B.C.E.)
    5. The annexation of Lydia to the Persian empire
    6. Cyrus invades Mesopotamia (539 B.C.E.)
  B. The consolidation of the Persian empire
    1. Cambyses—a worthy successor to Cyrus
    2. Darius I (521–486 B.C.E.)
      a. Consolidated military gains
      b. Improved state administration (*satraps*)
      c. Allowed various people to retain local institutions
      d. The erection of Persepolis
      e. The Royal Road (Susa to Sardis)
      f. Postal systems and spy networks
      g. Punishing Athens
      h. Marathon (490 B.C.E.)
  C. Zoroastrianism
    1. Zoroaster sought to purify traditional customs
      a. Eradicating polytheism, animal sacrifice, and magic
      b. There is one god—Ahura-Mazda ("the wise lord")
        i. Light, truth, and righteousness
        ii. The counter deity—Ahriman
      c. A personal religion
      d. Important to the conduct of Persian government
      e. Toleration
      f. The resurrection of the dead on judgment day

IX. The Development of Hebrew Monotheism
  A. From monolatry to monotheism
    1. A world conditioned by polytheism
    2. Monolatry—exclusive worship of one god without denying existence of others
    3. The Levites and the Yahweh cult
    4. Transcendent theology
    5. Ethical considerations and commandments
    6. Regional distinctions in the Yahweh cult
    7. The Assyrian threat
    8. Demands for an exclusive monotheism
    9. The prophets
      a. Religious and political figures

b. Only by worshiping Yahweh could the Hebrews combat Assyrian religious imperialism
      c. Amos and Hosea
      d. Isaiah and Jeremiah
      e. Ezekiel and the second Isaiah
      f. Doctrines
        i. Absolute monotheism
        ii. Yahweh is the god of righteousness
        iii. Yahweh demands ethical behavior
      g. Amos and the prophetic revolution
  B. Judaism takes shape
    1. Josiah, King of Judea (621–609 B.C.E.)
      a. A committed monotheist
      b. Used Jeremiah and other prophets at his court
      c. Purified cult practices
      d. Book of Deuteronomy discovered
    2. After Josiah
      a. Chaldeans under Nebuchadnezzar conquer Jerusalem
      b. The Babylonian captivity
      c. Ezekiel—salvation only through religious purity
      d. Jewish religious teachings as ethical obligations toward God

X. Conclusion
  A. The age of empires
  B. The international system
  C. New religions

GENERAL DISCUSSION QUESTIONS

1. How did entire nations such as the Hittites, Mitannians, Hurrians, and Assyrians quickly rise to power, then disappear from history? Or was their rise and fall more gradual, occurring over centuries?
2. During his lifetime, every pharaoh was Horus-Ra; at death he became Osiris. How did the evolution of Egyptian funeral customs demonstrate a "democratization of death"?
3. What was the religious revolution ordered by Akhenaten, and why did his efforts fail?
4. What political, economic, or even cultural forces might have made the late Bronze Age an "age of super-powers"? Can you identify any modern parallels? Are we justified in referring to an international system of the late Bronze Age?
5. What similarities or differences can you locate between the "palace citadels" of Mycenae and the civilizations of the ancient Near East?

6. Who were the Phoenicians? Why did they flourish during the Iron Age? What was their contribution to Western civilizations?

7. Were the Philistines as bad as their biblical reputation suggests? How does their case illustrate the risks of accepting historical information from biased sources?

8. The kingdom of Israel was small and lasted only a short time compared to other ancient states. Why has it attracted so much attention? How reliable is the main source, the Deuteronomic history of Israel found in the Jewish scriptures (the books of Judges, Kings, and Chronicles)?

9. How do legend and history blend together in the figure of King David? Why does the text say he was "more in keeping with early Greek than with Hebrew ideals"?

10. The text condemns the Assyrians for "terrible, brutal, long-lasting, and systematic victimization of their neighbors." Was the Assyrian Empire a terrorist state? What was the Assyrian military-religious ethos? How was it related to earlier Mesopotamian cultures?

11. What significance does Zoroastrianism, the Persian worship of Ahura-Mazda, have for Western civilizations? Which Christian and Jewish ideas suggest Zoroastrian influences?

DOCUMENT DISCUSSION QUESTIONS

Akhenaten, the Hebrews, and Monotheism

1. How does the "Hymn to the Aten" express monotheism? Why would a pharaoh, already acknowledged as divine, attempt a religious revolution? Why did he fail?

2. The praise of the greatness of God in Psalm 104 suggests an order in creation. How does this idea of order differ from the *ma'at* of the Egyptians? How does the monotheism of the Hebrews differ from that of Akhenaten? Why did polytheism emerge before monotheism?

The Mycenaeans and the Near East:

3. Why did the Hittite king Hattusilis III have such strong feelings about honor and respect? Why did he write his complaint letter to the king of Ahhiyawa?

4. Are certain standards of behavior expected of civilized nations? Which ancient states adhered to them and which did not? What sanctions or penalties could be imposed on them by the international system?

Two Accounts of Saul's Annointing

5. According to 1 Samuel 8:1–4, the sons of the prophet Samuel were dishonest judges, and the elders of Israel asked Samuel to appoint a king, "like [all] other nations have." Was this an expression of popular opinion? Or was it perhaps the view of a pro-monarchy party? Why were the Israelites unable to govern themselves and unwilling to rely on judges and prophets?

6. How does the brief biblical history of the three kings of united Israel present their personal strengths and weaknesses? How does it explain dangers to the state? Does that history show divine intervention?

7. The writers of Jewish scripture (priests and prophets) judged kings by their observance of the law, their zeal in fighting against competing religious cults, and their support of centralized worship at the temple in Jerusalem. How did this form of theocracy in ancient Israel compare to that in Egypt and Mesopotamia?

The Senjirli Stele of King Esarhaddon

8. Ancient inscriptions and chronicles often exaggerate when describing royal accomplishments. Can we separate Esarhaddon's actual accomplishments from his boastful propaganda? What function did this inscription serve?

9. The Assyrians have a reputation for arrogance and cruelty toward defeated enemies. What features of this text suggest that reputation may be well-deserved?

10. "I slew multitudes of his men," Esarhaddon boasted. Recall that "Saul slew his thousands, and David his ten thousands" (1 Samuel 29:5). Would it surprise you if the harsh Hebrew justice of "an eye for an eye, a tooth for a tooth" (Exodus 21:24; Leviticus 24:20; Deuteronomy 19:21) echoed Assyrian laws? What lasting influence did the Assyrians have on other cultures of the ancient Near East?

SAMPLE LECTURE 2: THE CENTRALITY OF RELIGION: NEW KINGDOM EGYPTIANS AND THE HEBREWS

Lecture Objectives

1. To analyze the presence of religion in the ancient world

2. To demonstrate the development of monotheism in New Kingdom Egypt and the Hebrews

THE EGYPTIAN PHARAOH

In Old Kingdom Egypt, royal power was absolute. The pharaoh (the term originally meant "great house" or "palace") governed his kingdom through his family and appointed officials. The lives of all Egyptians were carefully regulated while luxury accompanied the pharaoh in life and in death, as his people raised him to an exalted level. The Egyptians worked for pharaoh and obeyed him because he was a living god on whom the entire fabric of social life depended. No code of laws were needed since the pharaoh was the direct source of all law. In such a world, government was merely one aspect of religion and religion dominated Egyptian life.

The gods of Egypt came in many forms: animals, humans, and natural forces. Over time, Re, the sun god, came to assume a dominant place in Egyptian religion. The Egyptians had a very clear idea of the afterlife. They took great care to bury their dead and supplied the grave with things that the departed would need for a pleasant life after death. The pharaoh and some nobles had their bodies preserved in a process of mummification. Their tombs were decorated with paintings; food was provided at burial and after. Some tombs even included full-sized sailing vessels for the voyage to the beyond. At first, only pharaohs were thought to achieve eternal life; however, nobles were eventually included, and finally all Egyptians could hope for immortality.

The Egyptians also developed a system of writing. Although the idea may have come from Mesopotamia, their script was independent of the cuneiform. Egyptian writing began as pictographic and was later combined with sound signs to produce a difficult and complicated script that the Greeks called hieroglyphics ("sacred carvings"). Though much of what we have today is preserved on wall paintings and carvings, most of Egyptian writing was done with pen and ink on fine paper (papyrus). When Napoleon invaded Egypt in 1798, he brought with him a Commission of Science and Arts composed of more than one hundred scientists, engineers, and mathematicians. In 1799, the Commission discovered a basalt fragment on the west bank of the Nile at Rachid. The Egyptian hieroglyphics found on what came to be called the Rosetta Stone were eventually deciphered in 1822 by Jean François Champollion (1790–1832), a French scholar who had mastered Latin, Greek, Hebrew, Syriac, Ethiopic, Arabic, Persian, Sanskrit, and Coptic. The Rosetta Stone contains three inscriptions. The uppermost is written in hieroglyphic; the second in what is now called demotic, the common script of ancient Egypt; and the third in Greek. Champollion guessed that the three inscriptions contained the same text, and so he spent the next fourteen years (1808–1822) working from the Greek to the demotic and finally to the hieroglyphic, until he had deciphered the whole text. The Rosetta Stone is now on display at the British Museum in London.

MIDDLE AND NEW KINGDOM EGYPT

During the period of the Middle Kingdom (2050–1800 B.C.E.), the power of the pharaohs of the Old Kingdom waned as priests and nobles gained more independence and influence. The governors of the regions of Egypt (*nomes*) gained hereditary claim to their offices and subsequently their families acquired large estates. About 2200 B.C.E., the Old Kingdom collapsed and gave way to the decentralization of the First Intermediate Period (2200–2050 B.C.E.). Finally, the *nomarchs* of Thebes in Upper Egypt gained control of the country and established the Middle Kingdom. The rulers of the Twelfth Dynasty restored the power of the pharaoh over the whole of Egypt, although they could not control the *nomarchs*. They brought order and peace to Egypt and encouraged trade north toward Palestine and south toward Ethiopia. They moved the capital back to Memphis and gave prominence to Amon, a god who was identified with Re and eventually emerged as Amon-Re.

The Middle Kingdom disintegrated in the Thirteenth Dynasty with the resurgence of the power of the *nomarchs*. Around 1700 B.C.E. Egypt suffered an invasion by the Hyksos, who came from the east and conquered the Nile Delta. In 1575 B.C.E., a Thebian dynasty drove out the Hyksos and reunited the kingdom. In reaction to the humiliation of the Second Intermediate Period, the pharaohs of the Eighteenth Dynasty, most notably Thutmose III (1490–1436 B.C.E.), created a government based on a powerful army and an Egyptian empire extending far beyond the Nile Valley. One of the results of these imperialistic ventures was the growth in power of the priests of Amon and the threat it posed to the pharaoh. When young Amenhotep IV (1367–1350 B.C.E.) came to the throne he was apparently determined to resist the priesthood of Amon. Supported by his family, he ultimately made a clean break with the worship of Amon-Re. He moved his capital from Thebes to El Amarna, a city three hundred miles to the north. The pharaoh changed his name to Akhenaton ("it pleases Aton").

The new god was different from any that had come before him, for he was believed to be universal, not merely Egyptian. The universal claims for Aton led to religious intolerance of the worshipers of other gods. Temples were closed and the old priests were deprived of their posts and privileges. Only the pharaoh and his family worshiped Aton directly, the people worshiped the pharaoh. When Akhenaton died he was replaced by Tutankhamon (1347–1339 B.C.E.), the husband of Nefertiti, one of the daughters of Akhenaton. He restored Amon to the center of the Egyptian pantheon, abandoned El Amarna, and returned the capital to Thebes. His magnificent tomb remained intact until its discovery in 1922. The end of the El Amarna age restored power to the priests of Amon and to the military officers. Horemhab, a general, restored order and recovered much of the lost empire. He referred to Akhenaton as "the criminal of Akheton" and erased his name from the records.

EGYPTIAN RELIGION

Religious beliefs formed the basis of Egyptian art, medicine, astronomy, literature, and government. The great pyramids were burial tombs for the pharaohs, who were revered as gods on earth. Magical utterances pervaded medical practices since disease was attributed to the gods. Astronomy evolved to determine the correct time to perform religious rites and sacrifices. The earliest examples of literature dealt almost entirely with religious themes. The pharaoh was a sacrosanct monarch who served as the intermediary between the gods and humanity. Justice too, was conceived in religious terms, something bestowed upon man by the creator-god. From its earliest beginnings, Egyptian religious cults included animals. It is no accident that sheep, bulls, gazelles, and cats have been found carefully buried and preserved in their own graves. As time passed, the figures of Egyptian gods became human (anthropomorphism), although they often retained the animal's head or body.

Osiris, the Egyptian god who judged the dead, first emerged as a local deity of the Nile Delta in Lower Egypt. Isis was his wife and animal-headed Seth was his brother and rival. Seth killed Osiris. Isis persuaded the gods to bring him back to life, but thereafter he ruled below. Osiris was identified with the life-giving, fertilizing power of the Nile, and Isis with the fertile earth of Egypt. In the great temple cities such as Heliopolis ("city of the sun"), priests wrote down hierarchies of divinities. In the small communities of villages, all the forces of nature were deified and worshiped. One local god was part crocodile, part hippopotamus, and part lion.

Despite the ever-increasing number of deities that could be added to this hierarchy of deities, one thing is certain: Egyptian religion, unlike the religion of Mesopotamia, was centralized. In Sumer, the temple was the focus of political, economic and religious organization. By contrast, the function of an Egyptian temple was focused on religion. We are certain that ancient Egyptians were preoccupied with life after death. They believed that after death each human being would appear before Osiris and recount all the evil that one had committed during one's earthly existence. This was a negative confession and justification for admittance into the blessed afterlife. Osiris would then have the heart of the person weighed in order to determine the truth of their confession. The Egyptians believed not only in body and soul, but in *ka*, the indestructible vital principle of each person, which left the body at death but which could also return at other times.

HEBREW CIVILIZATION

Dwarfed by the great empires of the Sumerians, Akkadians, Babylonians, and Egyptians were the Hebrews. Of all the ancient hydraulic civilizations, it was the Hebrews who ex-

erted perhaps the greatest influence on the Western intellectual tradition. The Hebrews, a Semitic-speaking people, first appeared in Mesopotamia. Between 1900 and 1500 B.C.E., the Hebrews migrated from Mesopotamia to Canaan and then into Egypt. At this time, a tribe of Hebrews who claimed to be the descendants of Abraham began to call themselves Israelites ("soldiers of God"). The Hebrews were enslaved by the Egyptian pharaohs until 1250 B.C.E., when their leader, Moses, led them on an exodus out of Egypt to the Sinai peninsula. Moses persuaded his followers to become worshipers of Yahweh (or Jehovah). The Hebrews who wandered into the Sinai with Moses decided to return to Canaan. The move was not easy, and the Hebrews were faced with constant threats from the Philistines who occupied the coastal region. Twelve Hebrew tribes united first under Saul and then his successor, David.

By the tenth century, David and his son, Solomon, had created an Israelite kingdom. Economic progress was made as Israeli people began to trade with neighboring states. New cities were built and one in particular, Jerusalem, was built by David to honor God. In 586 B.C.E., the region of Judah was destroyed and several thousand Hebrews were deported to Babylon. The prophets Isaiah, Ezekiel, and Jeremiah declared that the Babylonian captivity was God's punishment. Despite this calamity, the Hebrews survived as people. In the fourth century, Alexander the Great conquered nearly all of the Near East and Palestine was annexed to Egypt. By the first and second centuries B.C.E., the Hebrews lost nearly all their independence under the Romans. But the Hebrews would never give up their faith or their religion.

The Hebrews were, as a people, committed to the worship of one god and his law as it was presented in the Old Testament, an oral history of the Jews written between 1250 and 150 B.C.E. There is only one god in the Old Testament. What separates the religious beliefs of the Hebrews from the belief systems of Egypt or Mesopotamia was clearly their monotheism. The Hebrews regarded God as fully sovereign: he ruled all and was subject to no laws himself. Unlike Near-Eastern gods, Jehovah was not created:

- God is eternal and the source of all creation in the universe.
- God created and governed the world and shaped the moral laws that govern humanity.
- God was transcendent: he was above nature and not part of nature.

In this sort of religion, there is no place for a sun god or moon god. Nature was demystified—it was no longer supernatural, but natural. That is, the Hebrews conceived of nature as an example of God's handiwork. This monotheism made possible a new awareness of the individual. In God, the Hebrews developed an awareness of the self or the "I" – the individual was self-conscious and aware of his own moral autonomy and worth. With this in mind, the Hebrews believed that man was a free agent and had the capacity to choose between good and evil. Men and women were to fulfill their morality by freely making the choice to do good or evil. God did not control mankind—rather, men had to have the freedom to choose. For the Hebrews, God was incapable of being represented in any form whatsoever. Because God was the center of all life, only he was worthy of worship. Therefore, the Hebrews would give no loyalty to kings or generals. To do so would have been to violate God's law to have "no other God but me." So, the Hebrews were morally free. For the Hebrews, to know God did not mean to understand him with the intellect or rationally prove his existence. To know God, one just had to be righteous, moral, loving, merciful, and just. One of the central religious principles of the Hebrew faith is that God had made a special agreement with his people: the Covenant. From the Book of Exodus we read "Now therefore, if ye will hearken unto My voice indeed, and keep My covenant, then ye shall be Mine own treasure from all peoples; for all the earth is Mine; and ye shall be unto Me a kingdom of priests and a holy nation." The Hebrews, then, were conscious of themselves as God's chosen people. Moses received the Ten Commandments—a code of moral "oughts." To violate the laws of God would have meant the Covenant was broken. This would have led to national disaster and the destruction of the Hebrew nation. Hebrew society had the moral obligation to make justice prevail. The poor, widows, children, and the sick were all protected by law and rich and poor were to be treated under the same laws, something unheard of in the Code of Hammurabi. The individual was clearly more important than his or her private property.

The Hebrews were perhaps the first culture of the ancient Western world to show any awareness of historical time. The events of their past were carefully celebrated. They also envisioned a great day in the future when God would establish peace on earth, prosperity, happiness, and brotherhood. Through history, God's presence was made known. History, then, had a purpose and meaning. And this kind of awareness would soon become part of the Western intellectual tradition itself.

SUGGESTED CLASSROOM FILMS

The Age of Minos. 38 min. B/W. 1969. BBC/Time-Life Films. Explores the legends of Zeus, Minos, and Theseus and the Minotaur.

The Age of Victory (Greece). 38 min. B/W. 1969. BBC/Time-Life Films. Discusses the revolt of Greece against Persian rule. Filmed on-site.

Ancient Egypt. 1997. 47 min. Color. Films for the Humanities and Sciences. Numerous interviews with Egyptologists as well as computer graphic recreations of pyramids, temples, and the sphinx.

Ancient Egypt: The Sun and the River. 58 min. Color. 1971. University Films Library Holder. Explores the art and architecture of Egyptian culture.

The Ancient Egyptian. 27 min. Color. 1967. Insight Media. Uses art and artifacts to explore religious beliefs and cultural values. Winner of the Blue Ribbon, American Film and Video Festival.

The Ancient Mediterranean: Conquest, Commerce, and Cultures. 27 min. Color. 2001. Films for the Humanities and Sciences. This program studies the unifying influence of the Mediterranean on the civilizations that developed upon its shores.

The Bible as Literature, Part 1: Saga and Story in the Old Testament; Part 2: History, Poetry, and Drama in the Old Testament. 26 min. each. Color. 1974. Encyclopaedia Britannica Educational Corporation. Examines the Bible from a literary perspective.

The Birth of Civilization, 6000 BC–2000 BC. 26 min. Color. 1985. Insight Media. Traces the birth of civilization in the fertile valleys of the Near East and China.

Civilization and Writing. 23 min. Color. 1998. Insight Media. Explores the ancient river-valley civilizations and traces the move from oral traditions to written literature.

Egypt: The Gift of the Nile. 29 min. Color. 1977. Centron Educational Films. Explores Egyptian history and the role of the Nile.

Greek Myths. 50 min. Color. 1971. Encyclopaedia Britannica Educational Corporation. Two-part series uses films of sculptures, animation, and re-enactments. *Myth as Fiction, History and Ritual* (1) and *Myth as Science, Religion and Drama* (2).

The Greeks. 200 min. Color. 1982. Films for the Humanities and Sciences. Four-part series covers the Mycenaean Age to the death of Alexander the Great. *The Greek Beginning*; *The Classical Age*; *Heroes and Men*; *The Minds of Men.*

Hymn to Aton. 15 min. Color. 1977. Phoenix. Examines the reign of Akhenaten and his attempts to introduce monotheism to Egypt.

The Legacy of Ancient Civilizations. 180 min. Color. 2000. Insight Media. Six-part program presents segments entitled *The Mycenaeans, Carthage and the Phoenicians, The Minoans, Ancient Arabia, Thera/Santorini,* and *Troy and Pergamum.*

Life Under the Pharaohs. 21 min. Color. 1989. Insight Media. Uses ancient paintings to depict everyday life.

Minoan Civilization. 53 min. Color. 1988. Insight Media. Explores the remains and reconstructions of Minoan civilization at Knossos and Phaistos on Crete, at Acrotiri on Santorini, and in museums.

Tut: The Boy King. 2 parts, each 26 min. Color. 1977. Films, Inc. Uses the treasure of his tomb to examine his reign.

Part II: The Greek and Roman Worlds

IDEAS FOR USING THE WESTERN CIVILIZATIONS DIGITAL HISTORY CENTER

The Map Exercises and Digital History Features at *www.wwnorton.com/wciv* offer a number of different ways to approach the significant contributions of Greece and Rome to the development of Western civilizations.

- Map Exercise 2: The Greek World (Chapters 3–4)
- Map Exercise 3: The Roman World (Chapters 5–6)
- Digital History Feature 2: Women and Mystery Cults (Chapters 3–6)
- Digital History Feature 3: Wine (Chapters 3–6)
- Digital History Feature 4: The Marketplace (Chapters 3–6)
- Digital History Feature 10: The Olympics—Past and Present (Chapter 3)

Map Exercise 2 can be used to highlight the development of Greece as a major naval power in the eastern Mediterranean and to suggest ways in which trade served as the major conduit of new ideas flowing into Athens from ancient western Asia. Map Exercise 3 shows how the Romans were able to construct the largest empire in the ancient world. Digital History Feature 2, "Women and Mystery Cults," can be used to illustrate the ways in which the Greek mind was fashioned from ideas from the Ancient Near East and Egypt. The mystery cults also played a prominent role in Roman history and in many ways paved the way for the eventual success of Christianity. Digital History Feature 3, "Wine," can be used in classroom discussions to demonstrate the importance of wine in trade, philosophical debate, and pagan ritual. By the late Roman period, wine had become a point at which pagan and Christian practices intersected, and so the history of winemaking can highlight the curious relationship between paganism and a religion that sought to stamp out that paganism. Use this Digital History Feature in conjunction with Digital History Feature 4, "The Marketplace," to show the importance of the market as a focal point for social intercourse as well as trade. In August 2004, Athens hosted the Games of the XXVIII Olympiad. Use Digital History Feature 10, "The Olympics—Past and Present," to show how the Olympic Games have evolved from their first appearance in 776 B.C.E.

CHAPTER 3 | The Greek Experiment

OUTLINE

I. Introduction
  A. The "image" of the ancient Greek world
  B. Near Eastern influences
  C. Western ideas/Western values
II. The Dark Age of Greece (1150–800 B.C.E.)
  A. The Dark Age
    1. Mycenaean decline
    2. Dorian Invasion
    3. Depopulation
    4. The Greeks and their gods
    5. The idea of hubris
  B. Homer and the heroic tradition
    1. The importance of renewed trade
    2. The *aristoi*—the best men
    3. The heroic ideal
    4. The *Iliad* and the *Odyssey*
      a. First "sung" as part of an oral tradition
      b. Finally written down around 800 B.C.E.
    5. Competition, status and the warrior-elite
    6. Hero cults
  C. Foreign contacts and the rise of the polis
    1. Phoenician influence
      a. alphabet
      b. seafaring
    2. Rapid population growth
    3. The *polis* (city-state)
      a. The *asty*—the urban community
      b. The *khora*—the land
      c. *Synoikismos*—bringing together of dwellings

III. Archaic Greece (800–480 B.C.E.)
  A. "Age of Experiment"—a new dynamism
  B. Colonization and Panhellenism
    1. Expansion of the Greek world (*Magna Graecia*)—new contacts and trade
    2. A new awareness of common culture and outlook—Hellenes
    3. Panhellenism
      a. Oracle of Delphi
      b. Games at Olympia (776 B.C.E.).
      c. Dating events by "olympiads"
  C. Hoplite warfare
    1. Common foot soldiers supporting aristocratic warriors
    2. Carried spears of short swords and the large round shield (hopla)
    3. The phalanx
    4. Formation of a "hoplite class"
      a. Every polis needed a hoplite force
      b. Ranks filled by farmers who could afford armor
      c. Wanted a share in the political decisions of the polis
  D. Aristocratic culture and the rise of tyranny
    1. Pursued wealth and power as well as a distinctive culture
    2. Office-holding and the symposium
    3. Homosexuality
    4. The aristocratic identity
    5. A new elite—problems
      a. Violence between aristocratic groups
      b. *Tyrannos*—someone who seized power and ruled outside traditional framework

      c. The tyrant had to satisfy the hoplites
      d. Important path from aristocracy to democracy
   E. Lyric poetry
      1. A new departure
      2. Hesiod (c. 700 B.C.E.)
         a. *Theogony* and *Works and Days*
      3. Archilochus of Paros (c. 680–640 B.C.E.)
      4. Sappho (c. 620–559 B.C.E.)
      5. The new expression of feelings

IV. The Archaic Polis in Action
   A. Athens
      1. Identity
      2. Agricultural economy
      3. Government
         a. Landed aristocracy
         b. Elected magistrates and the council of state
         c. Nine archons held executive power (civil, military, judicial and religious functions)
         d. Areopagus Council—elected the archons
      4. Political Change
         a. Debt slavery
         b. Political factions
         c. The failed coup of Kylon (632 B.C.E.)
         d. Drakon (621 B.C.E.)—"setting the laws"
            i. "draconian" punishments
         e. Solon (c. 640–c. 559 B.C.E.)
            i. Abolished debt slavery
            ii. Encouraged cash-crop farming and urban industries
            iii. Set up courts with citizen juries
            iv. Eligibility for political office based on property not birth
            v. The *boule* (steering committee)
            vi. The *ekklesia* (citizen assembly)
         f. Peisistratos (c. 600–527 B.C.E.)
            i. Established himself as tyrant (546 B.C.E.)
            ii. Public works projects
            iii. Strengthened the demos
         g. Cleisthenes (c. 570–c. 508 B.C.E.)
            i. Championed the cause of the demos (the people)
            ii. Reformed voting practices
            iii. Reorganized the population into ten tribes
            iv. Introduced ostracism

   B. Sparta
      1. The Peloponnesus
      2. Five villages combined (*synoikismos*) to become Sparta
      3. The conquest of Messenia
      4. The helots (slaves)
      5. The *Spartiate* (the "Equals")—professional soldier of the phalanx
      6. A society organized for war
      7. Early training of boys and girls
      8. The apella—the citizen assembly of *Spartiate* males over thirty years old
      9. The gerousia—council that proposed matters to the apella
     10. The krypteia—secret police
     11. Helots and *Spartiate*
         a. Helots outnumbered *Spartiate* ten to one
         b. The problem of revolts
         c. *Spartiate* could not engage in trade or farm their own land (distractions)
     12. Protectors of the "traditional constitutions" of Greece
     13. Demographic flaws
   C. Miletus
      1. Commercial, cultural and military power of Ionia (Asia Minor)
      2. Strong Hellenic identity shaped by Near Eastern influence
      3. Ionia and Lydia—cross-cultural exchange
      4. Ionians Hellenize interior of Asia Minor
      5. Strong trading interests (Black Sea and Egypt)
      6. Speculative thought—the "Milesian School"
         a. Pre-Socratic thought
         b. The cosmos, gods, and men
         c. Thales, Anaximander, and Anaximenes
         d. Theories of the cosmos and the problem of change
         e. From religious belief to philosophical speculation

V. The Persian Wars
   A. The Ionian Revolt (499–494 B.C.E.)
      1. Causes and origins (the account of Herodotus)
      2. Darius the Great—teaching Athens a lesson
   B. Marathon and its aftermath
      1. Athens is refused help from the Spartans
      2. Athenian victory (without Spartan help)
      3. Themistocles—building the Greek navy
   C. Xerxes' invasion
      1. Punish the Athenians—overland invasion

2. The Hellenic League (Athens, Sparta, Corinth, and other poleis)
3. Greek defeat at Thermopylae (480 B.C.E.)
4. Athens abandoned and burned by the Persians
5. Battle of Plataea and the end of the war

VI. The Golden Age of Classical Greece
   A. The Delian League
   B. Periclean Athens
      1. The strategos—general
      2. Anti-Spartan foreign policy
      3. Pushed reforms to make Athens more democratic
      4. Ostracism of Cimon
      5. Shifted power away from the Areopagus
      6. Public building—public confidence
   C. Literature and drama
      1. Aeschylus (525–456 B.C.E.)
      2. Sophocles (496–406 B.C.E.)
      3. Euripides (485–406 B.C.E.).
      4. Aristophanes (c. 448–382 B.C.E.)
      5. Herodotus (c. 485–425 B.C.E.)
      6. Thucydides (c. 460–c. 400 B.C.E.)
   C. Art and architecture
      1. Idealized beauty
      2. The dignity of the unadorned human form
      3. The Parthenon
   D. Women and men in the daily life of Athens
      1. Inequality of the sexes
      2. A male world
      3. Women in the shadows
         a. Rearing of children to supply the infantry
         b. A private space
         c. Marriage
         d. "Women's work"
   E. Slavery
      1. Athenian slavery widespread but small in scale
      2. Most families owned at least one or two slaves

VII. League Building and the Peloponnesian War
   A. Athenian control of the Delian League
   B. Animosities and jealousies—had Athens become a tyranny?
   C. The Peloponnesian War erupts
      1. Athens and Sparta
      2. A quick war?—a war of attrition
      3. Pericles' naval strategy
      4. Athenian plague
      5. Alcibiades
      6. Spartan victory
   D. The end of the war
      1. Lysander destroys the Athenian fleet (404 B.C.E.)

2. The Thirty Tyrants
3. Spartan success?
4. War brought demoralization and a questioning of former certainties
   E. The Pythagoreans and the Sophists
      1. Pythagoras—mathematics and musical theory
      2. The Sophists—"those who are wise"
      3. Protagoras—"man is the measure of all things"
      4. Socrates
         a. Questioning received truth—examine everything
         b. Socrates was wise because he knew nothing
         c. Examined ethics rather than the physical world
         d. The "philosopher of the marketplace"
      5. The life and thought of Socrates

VIII. Conclusion
   A. Image versus reality
   B. Freedom, competition, individual achievement, and human glory
   C. Primacy of the human intellect
   D. The Greeks and humanity
   E. *Paideia*

GENERAL DISCUSSION QUESTIONS

1. Can we draw a sharp distinction between the rational culture of classical Greece and the mystical or magical cultures that preceded it? How were Greek philosophy and religion influenced by their Near Eastern predecessors? Did the Greeks succeed in constructing a culture free of superstition?

2. The word *barbarian* appears in our text. It comes from the Greek *barbaros*, meaning "foreign, not Greek," or any person who could not speak proper Greek. Consider how it has been used as a generic term with negative connotations, not only by the ancients but also by writers of our own time.

3. What does our text mean by "The Greek Experiment"? In what sense did the Greeks use a scientific approach to politics and social problems?

4. What can epic poems such as the *Iliad* and *Odyssey* tell us about the Heroic Age? What are the specific characteristics of the "heroic ideal"? Can you locate that ideal in other historical periods?

5. Discuss the geographic and cultural reasons for the rise of the polis (pl. poleis).

6. How did the Greeks develop a unified culture—Hellenism—despite their political divisions and quarrels?

7. Why were the hoplites (soldiers) the cause of social and political change?

8. The comparison of Athens and Sparta is familiar, but perhaps too extreme. How was Miletus different from the other two, particularly in its ties to Near Eastern cultures?

9. Were the Persian Wars a victory for Greek civilization and democracy? Or were they the beginning of the end for the Greek ideal of freedom?

10. When Thucydides wrote about the Peloponnesian War between Athens and Sparta, he relied upon his memory, oral testimony, and public documents. He also admitted that he invented speeches when he did not know the exact words that were spoken. Was his writing fiction or history? Does it matter? Does our seeing it as fiction or as history affect our understanding of the Melian dialogue?

DOCUMENT DISCUSSION QUESTIONS

Greek Guest Friendship and Heroic Ideals

1. What is heroic about the meeting of Glaukos and Diomedes recounted in the *Iliad*? How do the participants identify themselves?

2. Does birth, in the sense of ancestry, make a difference in character? Are some families renowned for their military skills, honor, and virtue? Is there a natural aristocracy?

3. Instead of fighting one another, Glaukos and Diomedes resolve to be friends and "keep clear of each other's spears." Can soldiers on opposing sides be friends and continue to kill others? Does warfare create brotherhood, or "fraternity," among fighters? Can the spirit of fraternity be created among college students? Is it desirable, or not, in all contexts?

Thrasyboulos on How to be a Tyrant

4. Tyrants in Greece sometimes ruled by terror and other times by popular consent. Can you suggest positive aspects of tyrant-rule in the Greek states? Was Thrasyboulos simply a bad example, an unheroic character lacking in aristocratic virtue?

Two Views of Sophism

5. Socrates reportedly denied being a sophist and refused to teach the art of "making the weaker argument defeat the stronger"—a mark of sophism. In *The Clouds*, Aristophanes shows him teaching Right and Wrong how "to win any case at all." From your reading of the text, was Socrates really a sophist? What is the true meaning of "sophisticated"?

6. Rhetoric and the philosophy of persuasion became more important in classical Greece than in earlier cultures. How was this related to politics and government in the polis?

SAMPLE LECTURE 3: THE ANCIENT GREEKS FROM HOMER TO SOCRATES

Lecture Objectives

1. To investigate the heroic ideal as first expressed in Homer's *Iliad* and *Odyssey*
2. To situate the Classical Age of Greece within a historical context of continued warfare
3. To acknowledge the intellectual and cultural legacy of the Greeks of the Classical Age

HOMER AND THE HEROIC IDEAL

The ancient Greeks created the groundwork for Western society and the Western intellectual tradition that remains to this day. We take this foundation for granted, for the simple reason that the Greeks of the Classical Age seem to have discovered so many things which today matter a great deal. The first important society in the Greek world developed on the large island of Crete, just south of the Aegean Sea. The earliest inhabitants of Crete probably came from western Asia Minor before 3000 B.C.E. In 1900, English archeologist Arthur Evans (1851–1941) excavated Knossos, the greatest city of ancient Crete, and there discovered the remains of a magnificent palace which he named the Palace of Minos, after the mythical king of Crete (and so, Cretan civilization is also known as Minoan). The palace bureaucrats of Crete wrote in a script called Linear A, and although their language has not been fully deciphered, it is assumed that it was a member of the Indo-European family of languages, which includes Greek and Latin. With an estimated population of 250,000 people (40,000 in Knossos alone), the Minoans traded with the people of the Fertile Crescent. Their palaces became the centers of economic activity and political power. Although the Minoans were remarkable for their trade networks, architecture, and the arts, their civilization eventually declined and Minoan society was transformed by invaders from the Greek mainland.

How the Greeks settled on the Greek mainland is significant. Greece is a mountainous country, full of valleys, and is nearly surrounded by water. Their geography encouraged the Greeks to settle the land in independent political communities. These communities would soon come to be known as city-states. Each city-state, or polis, had its own political organization and thus was truly independent. The largest and most powerful of all the city-states in the period 1600–1100 B.C.E was that of Mycenae and this period of time is known as the Mycenaean Age. By the sixteenth century B.C.E., Mycenae was a wealthy, prosperous, and powerful state. Archeological discoveries of the area have uncovered swords, weapons, and the remains of well-fortified city walls, showing that this city-state was indeed a community of warriors. Each city-state in the Mycenaean period was independent and under the rule of its own king. The only time the city-states may have united was during the war with Troy in Asia Minor. By 1300 B.C.E., the Greek mainland was under attack by ships from Asia Minor, and by 1100 B.C.E., Mycenae was completely destroyed. This invasion is known as the Dorian Invasion.

Following the Dorian Invasion, Greece fell into its Dark Ages. For the most part, Greek culture began to go into decline—pottery became less elegant, burials were less ornate, and the building of large structures and public buildings came to an abrupt halt. However, this did not mark the end of Greek civilization. Some technological skills survived and the Greek language was preserved by those people who settled in areas unaffected by the Dorian Invasion. After 800 B.C.E., a new spirit of optimism appeared and became so intense that historians have called the period from 800–600 B.C.E. the Greek Renaissance. In literature, this is the age of the great epic poets. It is also the period of the first Olympic games, held in 776 B.C.E.

The best, though sometimes unreliable, source of Greek civilization in this period is Homer. We don't really know much about Homer. His place of birth is doubtful, although Smyrna, Rhodes, Colophon, Salamis, Chios, Argos, and Athens have all contended for the honor. His date of birth has been assumed to be as far back as 1200 B.C.E. but, based on the style of his two epic poems, 850–800 B.C.E. seems more likely. It has been said that Homer was blind, but even that is a matter of conjecture. And lastly, we are not even sure that Homer wrote those two classics of the Western literary canon, the *Iliad* and the *Odyssey*. The confusion arises from the fact that the world of Homer was a world of oral tradition and oral history. There is evidence to show that Homer's epics were really ballads and were chanted and altered for centuries until they were finally digested into the form we know today. In twenty-four books of dactylic hexameter verse, the *Iliad* narrates the events of the last year of the Trojan War, focusing on the withdrawal of Achilles from the contest and the disastrous effects of this act on the Greek campaign.

The Trojan War was fought between Greek invaders and the defenders of Troy, probably near the beginning of the twelfth century B.C.E.. Archeological evidence gathered in our own century shows that the war did indeed take place and was based on the struggle for control of important trade routes across the Hellespont, which were dominated by the city of Troy. About this war there grew a body of myth that was recounted by Homer in the *Iliad*, the *Odyssey*, and a number of now-lost epics. The characters we encounter are warriors through and through—not just soldiers, but aristocratic warriors who considered greatness in battle to be the highest virtue a man could have. This heroic virtue was composed of courage, bravery, and glory in battle and was necessary for a strong city-state in Greek civilization. The warrior fought bravely in service to his city-state. Virtue was what made man a good citizen, and good citizens made a great city-state. The world of Homer is a world of war, conflict, life, and death:

> At last the armies clashed at one strategic point,
> they slammed their shields together, pike scraped pike
> with the grappling strength of fighters armed in bronze
> and their round shields pounded, boss on welded boss,
> and the sound of struggle roared and rocked the earth.
> Screams of men and cries of triumph breaking in one breath,
> fighters killing, fighters killed, and the ground streamed blood.
> Wildly as two winter torrents raging down from the mountains,
> swirling into a valley, hurl their great waters together,
> flash floods from the wellsprings plunging down in a gorge
> and miles away in the hills a shepherd hears the thunder—
> so from the grinding armies broke the cries and crash of war.

In the Homeric world of war, men do not have rights, only duties. By serving the city-state with their virtuous behavior, they are also serving themselves. Indeed, there was nothing higher or more sublime in the Homeric world than virtue.

Homer's world is a closed and finite world. Completely unlike our own mechanical world, governed by mathematics and fixed physical laws, Homer's world is a living world—the earth, man, animals, and plants are all endowed with personality, emotion, and wills of their own. Even the gods and goddesses were endowed with these qualities. The gods could appear at any time and at any place. Although they had no permanent relations with the world of men and women, they were interested in their welfare and intervened in their affairs, as Homer's *Iliad* makes abundantly clear. In general, the gods were the guides and counselors of mortal men and women. Still, the gods and goddesses often deceived men. For Homer, the world was not governed by caprice, whim, or chance—what governed the world was "Moira" (fate, fortune, destiny). Fate was a system of regulations that controlled the unfolding of all life, all men and women, all things of the natural world, and all gods and goddesses. It was a fundamental law that maintained the world. It was Moira that gave men and women their place and function in Greek society. It was Moira that fixed the rhythm of human life—from childhood through youth to old age and finally death, it was Fate that regulated the personal growth of the individual. Even the gods had their destinies determined by Moira. Homer endowed the gods with personalities, and the gods differed from men in only their physical perfection and their immortality. In other words, gods and goddesses, like men and women, could be good, bad, honest, devious, jealous, vengeful, calm, sober, quick-witted, or dim. The gods assisted their favorite mortals and punished those who defied their will. Most gods were common to all Greeks, but each city-state also had their own patron deity. Gods and goddesses were worshipped in public. But there were also household gods—the gods of the hearth—specific to each family or clan. The general acceptance of these gods is a sign of a specific culture that arose during the Greek Renaissance, a culture we can identify as "Panhellenic."

THE PERSIAN INVASION OF GREECE

When we think of the ancient Greeks, it is usually the fifth century which commands our undivided attention. This is the age of the great historians Herodotus and Thucydides, great dramatists like Sophocles, Euripides, and Aeschylus, and the brilliant philosopher Socrates. The fifth century B.C.E. is also regarded as the age when the Greeks embraced their brilliant experiment in direct democracy. However, the fifth century was also an age of war and conflict.

By about 500 B.C.E. the Greek city-states had lost their kings (with the exception of Sparta) and had embraced a new form of government through councils of citizens. Almost immediately, however, these states were confronted by an invasion of the Persian Empire. King Darius (548–486 B.C.E.) had managed to build up the Persian Empire and now controlled Asia Minor, including Greek poleis on the west coast. In 499 B.C.E., some of the these poleis rebelled against the Persians in the Ionian Revolt. The Athenians lent their support, but the revolt ultimately collapsed in 493. Darius now proposed to invade Athens, and in 490 he sent his fleet across the Aegean and awaited news of victory.

The Persians landed at Marathon, a village just north of Athens. Commanded by Militiades, the Greek forces totaled only 10,000 men—the Persian force was perhaps 20,000–25,000 strong. The Greek forces charged, trapped the Persians, and won the battle. The remainder of the Persians attempted to attack Athens, but the Greek army rushed back and the Persians were forced to return to Asia Minor. The victory at Marathon was won by superior timing and discipline. Darius prepared a second invasion but died before his plans could be carried out. The task was taken up by Xerxes (c. 519–465 B.C.E.), who prepared a huge force that would attack by land and sea.

In 483 B.C.E. the Athenian statesman Themistocles (c. 523–c. 458 B.C.E.) persuaded his fellow Athenians to build a navy of one hundred *triremes*. He also oversaw the fortification of the harbor at Piraeus. Fearing destruction at the hands of the Persians, thirty poleis formed an alliance. Athens, Sparta, and Corinth were the most powerful members. In 480 B.C.E., Xerxes sent a force of 60,000 men and six hundred ships to Greece. Five thousand men took up their positions to defend the pass at Thermopylae. The Greeks held the pass, but eventually a traitorous Greek led a Persian force through the hills to the rear of the Greek forces, who were subsequently massacred. Meanwhile, the Greek navy tried to hold off the Persian ships at Artemisium. The Athenians eventually abandoned Athens ahead of the Persian army. The Persians marched across the Attic peninsula and burned Athens. Themistocles then sent a false message to Xerxes, telling him to strike at once. The Persians were taken in and sent their navy into the narrow strait between Athens and the island of Salamis. More than three hundred Greek ships rammed the Persians and heavily armed Greek soldiers boarded the ships. The Greek victory at Salamis was a decisive one. However, Persian forces remained in Greece. Their final expulsion came in 479 B.C.E. at the village of Plataea. By 479 B.C.E. the Greek forces had conquered the Persian army and navy.

After the Persian Wars, Athens emerged as the dominant political and economic force in the Greek world. The Athenian polis, buttressed by the strength of its Council of Five Hundred and Assembly of Citizens, managed to gain control of a confederation of city-states that gradually became the Athenian Empire. The Athenians not only had a political leadership based on the principles of direct democracy as set in motion by Cleisthenes, they also had wide trading and commercial interests in the Mediterranean world. There was a great sense of relief on the part of all Greeks that the Persians had been conquered. But there were some citizens who argued in the Assembly that a true Greek victory meant taking the war to Persia itself.

Dozens of Greek city-states joined together to form a permanent union for the war. Delegates met on the island of Delos in 478 B.C.E. and swore oaths of alliance. Right from the start, the Delian League was dominated by Athenian authority and leadership. Eventually, the Greeks liberated the cities of Asia Minor and by 450 B.C.E. the war with Persia came to an end. It was at this time that the power of Athens was being felt throughout the Greek world. And as the power of Athens reached new limits, its political influence began to be extended as well. The Athenians forced city-states to join the Delian League against their will. They refused to allow city-states to withdraw from the League. And other city-states they simply refused entry into the League. Athens stationed garrisons in other city-states to keep the peace and to make sure that Athens would receive their support, both politically and financially, by paying tribute to the League. By 454 B.C.E. Athenian domination of the Delian League was clear—the proof is that the League's treasury was moved from the temple of Apollo on the island of Delos to the temple of Athena at Athens. Payments to the Delian League now became payments to the treasury of Athens.

THE AGE OF PERICLES

Athens now enjoyed its greatest period of success. The period itself was dominated by the figure of Pericles and so the era has often been called the Age of Pericles. The Athenian statesman, Pericles (c. 490–429 B.C.E.), was born of a distinguished family, was carefully educated, and rapidly rose to the highest power as leader of the Athenian democracy. Although a member of the aristoi, Pericles offered many benefits to the common people of Athens, as a result, he earned their total support. Thucydides pointed out that "he controlled the masses, rather than letting them control him." The "Funeral Oration" of Pericles shows a man of forceful character. He was an outstanding orator and honest in his control of Athenian financial affairs. In the Assembly, Pericles argued convincingly that the affair with Persia was in the past. He decided to concentrate instead on Sparta, which he saw as a direct threat to the vitality of the Athenian Empire. From the 450s onward, Pericles rebuilt the city of Athens, a city ravaged by years of war with the Persians. He used the public money from the Delian League to build several masterpieces of fifth century Greek architecture, including the Parthenon and the Propylaea. Under Pericles, Athens became the city of Aeschylus, Socrates, and Phidias, the man in charge of all public buildings and statues. At this time Pericles also put down rebellions and sent his armies to colonize other areas of Asia Minor. While he was doing this, he was also trying to foster the intellectual improvement of the Athenian citizen by encouraging music and drama. Industry and commerce flourished. In 452–1 B.C.E. Pericles introduced pay for jurors and magistrates so that no one could be barred by poverty from service to the polis. But there were problems on the not-too-distant horizon.

THE PELOPONNESIAN WAR

These problems came to a head during the Peloponnesian Wars of 431–404 B.C.E. Sparta feared Athenian power—they believed that Athens had grown too quickly both in terms of population and military power. And Athens, of course, feared Sparta's isolationist position. What we have then, is a cold war turned hot. The Peloponnesian War was a catastrophe for Athens. The chief result of the war was that the Athenian Empire was divided, the subject states of the Delian League were liberated, direct democracy failed, and Pericles was ostracized. The Athenians also suffered a loss of nerve as their democracy gave way to the Reign of the Thirty Tyrants. The major result, however, was that the destruction of Athenian power made it possible for the Macedonian conquest of Greece. By mid-century there had been several clashes between Athens and Sparta and their respective allies. In 446 B.C.E. a treaty of non-aggression was signed that would be valid for thirty years (a form of détente, if you will). The peace did not last.

In 435 B.C.E. a quarrel developed between Corinth, an ally of Sparta, and Corcyra. In 433, Corcyra appealed to Athens to form an alliance. The Corinthians knew that such an alliance would make war inevitable. The combined naval power of Athens and Corcyra was the largest in Greece, and Sparta viewed such an alliance as a direct threat. The same year, the Athenians demanded that the town of Potidaea dismantle its defensive walls and banish its magistrates, a demand which further infuriated the Corinthians. Athens besieged the town. Fighting began in 431 B.C.E. Sparta wanted to break Athenian morale by attacking Attica annually, but the Athenians merely retreated behind their fortifications until the Spartan forces retired. Pericles refused to send the Athenian infantry to the field. Instead, he relied on raids on the Peloponnesus by sea. More damaging than any offensive by the Spartans was a plague that raged in Athens in 430. The following year, Pericles died. It was the Athenian campaign against Syracuse that eventually brought disaster. In 413 the Athenian navy lost a crucial battle. As they retreated, they were cut off and destroyed. Thucydides reported that "few out of many returned home." The war dragged on for another eight years. By 404 B.C.E. Sparta had "liberated" Greece and imposed an oligarchic regime (the Thirty Tyrants), which lasted until the following year. After the death of Pericles and the disorder of a century of warfare, the Greek city-states and direct democracy went into decline. This fragmentation and political disorder left the door open for political power to come from an entirely different area of Greece—Macedonia.

GREEK CULTURE IN THE CLASSICAL AGE

The brilliance of the classical Greek world rested on a blend of the old and the new. From the past came a profound religious belief in the just action of the gods and the attainment of virtue in the polis. Such a history helped develop a specific Greek "mind" in which the importance of the individual and a rationalistic spirit were paramount. The trade routes from the Aegean brought men and their ideas from everywhere to the great cultural center of Athens. Thanks to its economic initiative, the Athenian polis was quite wealthy, and Pericles generously distributed that wealth to the Athenian citizen in a variety of forms. For instance, the Athenian polis sponsored the production of dramas and required that wealthy citizens pay the expenses of production. At the beginning of every year, dramatists submitted their plays to the *archon*, or chief magistrate, who chose the dramas he considered best. On the appointed day, the Athenian public gathered at the theatre of Dionysus on the south slope of the Acropolis, paid their admission of two *obols*, and witnessed a series of plays. Judges drawn by lot awarded prizes to the poet (crown of ivy), the actor (an inscription on a state list in the *agora*) and to the *choregus* (a triumphal tablet).

The Athenian dramatists were the first artists in Western society to examine such basic questions as the rights of the individual, the demands of society upon the individual, and the nature of good and evil. Conflict, the basic stuff of life, is the constant element in Athenian drama.

Aeschylus (525–456 B.C.E.), the first of the great Athenian dramatists, was also the first to express the agony of the individual caught in conflict. In his trilogy of plays, *The Oresteia*, he deals with the themes of betrayal, murder, and reconciliation. Like Solon, Aeschylus believed that the world was governed by divine justice, which could not be violated with impunity. To act in accordance with the divine order meant caution and moderation. When men exhibited hubris (pride or arrogance), which led them to go beyond moderation, they had to be punished. Another common theme was that through suffering came knowledge.

Sophocles (496–406 B.C.E.) also dealt with personal and political matters. In his *Antigone*, he examined the relationship between the individual and the state by exploring conflict between the ties of kinship and the demands of the polis. Almost all of the plays of Sophocles stand for the precedence of divine law over human defects. In other words, human beings should do the will of the gods, even without fully understanding it, for the gods stand for justice and order. The characters in the tragedies of Sophocles resist all warnings and inescapably meet with disaster.

Euripides (c. 480–406 B.C.E.) also explored the theme of personal conflict within the polis and the depths of the individual. With Euripides, drama entered a new, more personal phase—the gods were far less important than human beings. Euripides viewed the human soul as a place where opposing forces struggle, where strong passions such as hatred and jealousy conflict with reason. The essence of Euripides' tragedy is the flawed character—men and women who bring disaster on themselves and their loved ones because their passions overwhelm their reason. It is the rationalist spirit of fifth-century Greek philosophic thought that permeates the tragedies of Euripides.

Aristophanes (c. 448–c. 380 B.C.E.) was an ardent lover of the city and a ruthless critic of cranks and quacks. He lampooned eminent generals, at times depicting them as little more than morons. He commented snidely on Pericles and poked fun at Socrates and Euripides. Even at the height of the Peloponnesian War, Aristophanes proclaimed that peace was preferable to war. Like Aeschylus, Sophocles, and Euripides, Aristophanes used his art to dramatize his ideas on the right conduct of the citizen and the value of the polis.

The experience of the Persian and Peloponnesian wars also helped develop the beginnings of historical writing. It is in the Classical Age, then, that we meet the father of history, Herodotus (c. 485–425 B.C.E.). Born at Halicarnassus in Asia Minor, Herodotus traveled widely before settling in the Athens, the intellectual center of the Greek world. In his book, *The History*, Herodotus chronicled the rise of the Persian Empire, the origins of both Athens and Sparta, and then described the laws and customs of the Egyptians. The scope of *The History* is awesome. Lacking newspapers, any sort of communications, or ease of travel, Herodotus wrote a history that covered all the major events of the ancient Near East, Egypt, and Greece.

The outbreak of the Peloponnesian War prompted Thucydides (c. 460–c. 400 B.C.E.) to write a history of its course in the belief that it would be the greatest war in Greek history. Thucydides saw the Peloponnesian War as highly destructive to Greek character. In his view, the fate of men and women was entirely in their own hands.

The ancient Greeks were clearly a people who warred and enslaved people. They often did not live up to their own ideals. However, their achievements in the areas of art, architecture, poetry, tragedy, science, mathematics, history, philosophy, and government were of the highest order and worthy of emulation by the Romans and others. Western thought begins with the Greeks, who first defined man as an individual with the capacity to use his reason. Underlying the Greek achievement was humanism. The Greeks expressed a belief in the worth, significance, and dignity of the individual. Man should develop his personality fully in the city-state, a development which would, in turn, create a sound city-state as well. The pursuit of excellence—*arete*—was paramount. Such an aspiration required effort, discipline, and intelligence. Man was master of himself.

SUGGESTED FEATURE FILMS

Aeschylus: The Oresteia (*Agamemnon*, 90 min.; *The Libation Bearers*, 70 min.; *The Furies*, 70 min.). Color. 1985. Films for the Humanities. The National Theatre of Great Britain production, directed by Peter Hall.

Antigone. 88 min. B/W. 1962. Fleetwood. Greek dialogue with English subtitles.

Euripides' Medea. 90 min. Color. 1982. Films for the Humanities. A Kennedy Center production with Zoe Caldwell as Medea. English text by Robinson Jeffers.

Helen of Troy. 118 min. Color. 1956. Warner Brothers. The *Iliad*'s story of the Trojan War, told from the Trojan viewpoint.

Oedipus the King. 105 min. Color. 1967. Alfredo Bini. Filmed in Morocco and set in modern times.

Orpheus and Eurydice: The Appia Staging. 91 min. Color. 1985. Films for the Humanities. Richard Beachame's re-creation of the opera as staged by Appia in 1912. With the University of Warwick Chamber Orchestra and Chorus.

Sophocles: The Theban Plays (*Oedipus the King, Oedipus at Colonus, Antigone*). 120 min. each. Color. 1987. Films for the Humanities. Films for the Humanities joined up with the BBC to produce these modern versions of classical Greek drama. Performers include John Gielgud, Claire Bloom, Anthony Quayle, and Juliet Stevenson.

Thucydides: The Peloponnesian Wars and *Plato: Alcibiades I*. 72 min. Color. 1991. Films for the Humanities. Seventeen British classical actors from the National Theatre and the Royal Shakespeare Company, including Ben Kingsley and Alex McCowen, enact the story. Set as a contemporary news program.

Troy. 163 min. Color. 2004. Warner Brothers. An adaptation of Homer's great epic, the film follows the assault on Troy by the united Greek forces.

SUGGESTED CLASSROOM FILMS

The Age of Victory (Greece). 38 min. B/W. 1969. BBC/Time-Life Films. Discusses the revolt of Greece against Persian rule. Filmed on site.

The Ancient Games. 28 min. Color. 1972. ABC. Modern athletes re-create the ancient Olympics in this documentary written and narrated by Erich Segal.

Ancient Greece. 47 min. Color. 1997. Films for the Humanities and Sciences. Beginning with Homer's account of the Trojan War, this program explores Greek ancient civilization.

The Ancient Mediterranean: Conquest, Commerce, and Cultures. 27 min. Color. 2001. Films for the Humanities and Sciences. This program studies the unifying influence of the Mediterranean on the civilizations that developed upon its shores.

Ancient Warriors: The Spartans. 26 min. Color. 1994. Films for the Humanities and Sciences. The program follows the training and education of a typical Spartan male from birth through the trials that would make him the most fearsome fighting machine of the ancient world.

The Ancient World: Greece, Part II. 29 min. Color. 1955. New York University. Examines the art and literature of Greece in the fifth century B.C.E., with narration drawn entirely from Greek authors.

Classical Comedy. 60 min. Color. 1976. Films for the Humanities. Performance of excerpts from Aristophanes' *Ecclesiazusai* and Plautius's *Miles Gloriosus.*

The Classical Ideal. 60 min. Color. 1989. Insight Media/ Annenberg CPB. A two-part series that traces the origins of humanism to ancient Greek art and culture and examines the classical aesthetic. It also explores the genius of Roman engineering and architecture.

Conversations with Ancient History. 60 min. Color. 1991. Insight Media. Classics scholar Edith Hamilton hosts a series of "conversations" with ancient figures.

Death of Socrates. 45 min. B/W. 1968. Time-Life Films. Modern-dress dramatization of Plato's account of Socrates' death.

Greek Thought. 2 parts, 30 min. each. 1989. Color. Insight Media. Dr. Eugen Weber's look at Greek art, science, and philosophy.

The Greeks: Crucible of Civilization. 160 min. Color. 1999. PBS. Three-part series about the ancient Greeks from the rise of democracy at Athens, the Persian Wars, and the Peloponnesian War. Includes *The Revolution, The Golden Age,* and *Empire of the Mind.*

The Greeks: In Search of Meaning. 26 min. Color. 1971. Learning Corporation of America. Dramatized conversations with Sophocles and performances from *Antigone* and *Lysistrata.*

It Started with the Greeks. 54 min. Color. 1986. BBC/RKO. Shows how the questioning and rational attitude of the classical Greeks is at the root of Western thought with its continuing exploration of new ideas. Part of James Burke series *The Day the Universe Changed.*

The Rise of Greek Tragedy: Oedipus the King. 45 min. Color. 1975. Films for the Humanities. Filmed in the theatre of Amphiaraion with the Athens Classical Theatre Company.

The Search for Ulysses. 53 min. Color. 1965. Carousel. Follows Ulysses' journey in the *Odyssey.*

The Temple of Apollo at Bassae. 16 min. Color. 1971. International Film Bureau. Features the temple built by the designer of the Parthenon.

The Trial of Socrates. 29 min. Color. 1971. Insight Media. A dramatization.

Troy: Battlefield of Myth and Truth. 30 min. Color. 2002. Films for the Humanities and Sciences. Traces the course of the modern search for Troy beginning with Schliemann's 1870 expedition; it reviews subsequent digs by other, and focuses on Korfmann's excavation, begun in 1988.

Women in Classical Greek Drama. 38 min. Color. 2003. Films for the Humanities and Sciences. In this program, the presentation of powerful women in *Medea, Antigone,* and *Lysistrata* is contrasted with the circumscribed role of women in Athenian society.

CHAPTER 4 | The Expansion of Greece

4. The "Companions"
5. Dynastic marriages
6. Expansion brought conflict with Athens
   a. Demosthenes (c. 383–322 B.C.E.)
      i. Saw Philip as an aggressor
7. Battle of Chaeronae (338 B.C.E.)
   a. League of Corinth
8. Assassination of Philip

B. The conquests and reign of Alexander (336–323 B.C.E.)
1. Visionary, genius, or butcher?
2. Further expansion
3. Battle of Gaugamela (331 B.C.E.)
4. Queen Roxane
5. The new empire
   a. New cities
   b. Mass marriages
   c. Breeding a new nobility
   d. Installs no administrative apparatus
6. Death of Alexander

V. The Hellenistic Kingdoms
A. Ptolemaic Egypt
1. Most durable kingdom
   a. Patronized science and the arts
2. Alexandria
3. Personal enrichment
B. Seleucid Asia
1. Near Eastern traditions
2. A Hellenized population
3. Planted new cities
C. Antigonid Macedon and Greece
1. Antigonus
   a. Keeping Ptolemaic Egypt and Seleucid Asia at war
2. Aetolian and Achaean Leagues

VI. The Growth of Trade and Urbanization
A. Long-distance trade
1. Spread east to Central Asia
2. Harbors improved
3. Encouragement of industry
4. Explosive population growth
B. Cities
1. Importation of Greek officials and soldiers
2. Alexandria
C. Wealth and poverty

VII. Hellenistic Culture: Philosophy and Religion
A. Stoicism
1. Founded by Zeno of Citium (324–270 B.C.E.)
2. Cosmos is ordered and rational
3. The individual is not the master of his own life
4. Submit to the universal order of things
5. Tranquility of mind
6. Duty and self-discipline
7. Duty of political participation
B. Epicureanism
1. Founded by Epicurus (c. 342–270 B.C.E.)
2. Democritus and atomism
3. There is no ultimate purpose of the universe
4. Highest good is pleasure
5. Serenity of the soul
6. No such thing as absolute justice
7. The wise man should abandon politics
C. Skepticism
1. Carneades (c. 213–129 B.C.E.)
   a. All knowledge is limited and relative
   b. No truth is certain
   c. Escape
D. Religion
1. A vehicle for escape
2. Mystery cults
   a. The quest for a personal and emotional religion
   b. The Orphic cult and Dionysus
   c. Mithraism
      i. Persian origins
      ii. Similarities to early Christianity

VIII. Hellenistic Culture: Literature and Art
A. Pastoral literature
1. The pastorals of Theocritus (c. 310–250 B.C.E.)
B. Prose
1. Polybius (c. 205–123 B.C.E.)
   a. Historical development proceeds in cycles
C. Architecture
1. The Lighthouse of Alexandria
2. The altar to Zeus at Pergamon
D. Sculpture
1. Extreme naturalism
2. Extravagance
   a. *Dying Gaul*
   b. *Winged Victory of Samothrace*
   c. *Laocoön*

IX. Science and Medicine
A. Origins
1. Mesopotamian and Egyptian science
2. Hellenistic rulers patronized scientific research
   a. Sole motive was prestige
B. Astronomy, mathematics, and geography
1. Aristarchus of Samos (310–230 B.C.E.)
2. Euclid (fl. fourth century B.C.E.)
3. Hipparchus (fl. 160–125 B.C.E.)
4. Eratosthenes (c. 276–194 B.C.E.)

C. Medicine
    1. Herophilus of Chalcedon
      (c. 335–c.280 B.C.E.)
D. Physics
    1. Archimedes of Syracuse
      (c. 287–212 B.C.E..)
X. The Transformation of the Polis
  A. From polis to cosmopolis
    1. From Hellene to Hellenistic
    2. The breakdown of traditional values
XI. Conclusion
  A. The Hellenistic Age as an age of transition
    between Greece and Rome
  B. Cosmopolitanism and modernity

GENERAL DISCUSSION QUESTIONS

1. The citizens of Greek city-states prided themselves on their independence, local patriotism, and political sophistication. They formed alliances, but in general, they failed to unite. Why were they unable to think in terms of a larger nation?

2. How can you explain social and economic inequality in the Greek polis? Was poverty, or even slavery, a "natural" condition of life, as Aristotle thought? What opportunities did the poor have to improve their lives?

3. How might it be argued that the Greek polis was destined for failure? Why has it been suggested that Athenian direct democracy was a "brilliant failure"?

4. Plato's doctrine of ideas, or "theory of forms," is an attempt to find absolute truth, certain knowledge, the Idea of the Good. How would this theory help us decide how to live our everyday lives?

5. Both Plato and Aristotle wrote about politics, but they came to different conclusions about how states are or should be organized. Compare and contrast their approaches to politics. In your opinion, which view is more practical?

6. How do Hellenistic philosophies, such as Epicureanism, Stoicism, and Skepticism, represent responses to the loss of individual and political control? The text states that "Hellenistic religion similarly tended to offer vehicles of escape from collective political commitments." But is escapism an appropriate function of religion?

7. Greeks of all classes turned to therapies such as Stoicism, Epicureanism, Cynicism, and mystery cults during the Hellenistic Age. What spiritual, political, and social forces perhaps made these therapies essential to their survival and well-being?

8. How do the achievements of Hellenistic artists and writers, architects and sculptors, and scientists and physicians reflect the tastes of the patrons of culture? Cite examples. Was or is official support of culture beneficial or harmful to society?

9. W. H. Auden once remarked that "Had Greek civilization never existed, we would never have become fully conscious, which is to say that we would never have become, for better or worse, fully human." What was it about Greek civilization that other generations have admired and attempted to emulate? What was the Greek contribution to the West and to the Western intellectual tradition?

10. It is clear that the Roman world would have been something entirely different had it not been for the Greek experiment. What specific contributions do you think the Greeks gave to the Roman world?

DOCUMENT DISCUSSION QUESTIONS

Two Views of Philip

1. Isocrates, in his advice to Philip, seems to have had in mind an ideal union of the Greek states and various imperfect copies. Why had previous attempts at national unity come to grief? How did Isocrates think Philip could succeed?

2. Philip II of Macedon had many other concerns besides unifying quarreling Greeks. How would unification have helped him to achieve his grand design? Was his campaign morally justified?

3. Rather than praising Philip for his leadership, Demosthenes denounced the Greeks for their failures. What specifically had they done and left undone?

4. Why did Demosthenes think that reciting the history of Philip's career would persuade his audience that the king of Macedon was untrustworthy? Didn't they know all about Philip? What does this speech suggest about political information and popular political participation in the Hellenistic polis ?

The Greek Influence on Israel

5. The Jews had disobeyed their religious leaders many times before they encountered Hellenistic culture. Why did Hebrew priests and prophets think the Greeks were so dangerous? What did they personally have to fear about "corruption"?

6. Why was the building of a gymnasium, or "Greek secondary school," in Jerusalem particularly symbolic and offensive to Jews? Could anyone have stopped

the project? By their insistence on maintaining separatism, were the Jews resisting or demanding special privileges from the rulers of the Hellenistic successor kingdoms?

Escape to the Countryside

7. Theocritus depicted the countryside as idyllic, but did his poetry have more fantasy in it than reality? Who is doing the farm labor while the well-fed urbanites frolic and pretend to be shepherds?

8. Is there any harm in fantasy literature? Is "producing pleasure" an appropriate function of literature? Should writers write and readers read for their own pleasure? You may want to set limits on what produces pleasure or who may enjoy it.

SAMPLE LECTURE 4: FROM POLIS TO COSMOPOLIS

Lecture Objectives

1. To explain the rise to prominence of Philip II and Alexander the Great

2. To suggest the tensions and conflicts implicit in the shift from the polis to the cosmopolis

3. To suggest that Hellenistic philosophies and mystery cults served as therapies for Greeks living in a dislocated and fragmented world

AFTER THE PELOPONNESIAN WAR

The Peloponnesian War ultimately signified the end of the city-state as a creative force and the Greek world degenerated into oligarchy. Spartan domination did not last very long. Full of arrogance and pride, Sparta found itself engaged in war after war. The three leading city-states of Athens, Sparta, and Thebes traded positions of influence and power, with two states sometimes joining against the other for protection. Although Athens was rebuilding itself and Sparta had been invaded by victorious Theban armies, the real center of Greek power in the first half of the fourth-century Greek world came from the Macedonian kingdom to the north, an area which the Attic Greeks regarded with disdain since it was inhabited by *barbaroi*.

PHILIP OF MACEDON

In 359 B.C.E., Philip II of Macedon (383–336 B.C.E.) came to the throne through a rather typical procedure—a round of family assassinations. Philip was an energetic and ambitious man—if anything motivated him besides greed, it was his awareness of just how divided and disordered the Greek

world had become. This disorder was a direct result of a century of warfare. With this in mind, Philip set out to conquer the Hellenic world. He accomplished this task by treachery, secrecy, speed, and dishonesty. He quieted his rivals, crushed rebellions, and made secret treaties that were broken almost as quickly as they were made. In 338, Philip announced that he would marry Cleopatra, the daughter of a wealthy Macedonian family—though he was already married to Olympias. Alexander was Philip's firstborn son and had the claim to the throne. But Philip confined Olympias on the grounds that she had committed adultery and encouraged rumors that Alexander was illegitimate. Philip then arranged for a wedding feast, which turned out to be an intense affair. Alexander entered the room, sat next Philip, and said, "When my mother gets married again I'll invite you to her wedding." Such a remark did nothing to improve anyone's temper.

Throughout the evening enormous quantities of wine were drunk. At last Attalus, the bride's uncle, arose, a bit unsteady, and proposed a toast. He called upon the gods for a legitimate successor to the Macedonia ingdom to be born. Infuriated, Alexander jumped to his feet and said, "Are you calling me a bastard?" He then threw his cup of wine in Attalus' face, who then did the same to Alexander. Philip stood, very drunk, and lunged forward with his sword drawn. His target was not Attalus, but Alexander. However, Philip missed, tripped over a footstool, and fell face-first on the floor. Alexander looked about him at his father's favorites and said, "That, gentlemen, is the man who's been preparing to cross from Europe into Asia, and he can't even make it from one couch to the next!" The night's events underscored the crucial question: who would succeed Philip?

By this time, Olympias had clearly sided with her son. The night before her wedding to Philip, Olympias had had a dream that her child would be a divine king. She had always taught him that he was not merely the next in line; she had taught him to think he was a king in his own right. There is little doubt that Alexander and Olympias wished Philip out of the way. The opportunity appeared in 336 B.C.E.

Philip arranged a massive festival to honor the marriage of Alexander's sister. With perfect timing, Philip's young wife, Cleopatra, had just given birth to a son. Meanwhile, Alexander had been all but isolated from his father's court. On the second day of the festivities, Philip was murdered by member of his own bodyguard. As the king entered the arena, a man drew a short, broad-bladed Celtic sword and thrust it into Philip's chest. Philip died immediately.

ALEXANDER THE GREAT

The throne fell to Philip's son, Alexander III (356–323 B.C.E.), or, as he is better known, Alexander the Great. When Alexander gained the throne he had just reached his twentieth birthday. Within fifteen months he had stamped out rebellions, marched into various Greek cities demanding submission, sent his armies as far north as the Danube

River, and destroyed the city of Thebes. In 334 B.C.E., and with 37,000 men under his command, he marched into Asia, still conquering lands for his empire. He added new lands to old and carefully consolidated his conquests by founding more than seventy Greek cities, many of which bear his name. By 327, Alexander's armies had moved as far east as India. His troops were exhausted and could go no further. We can only wonder how much more territory Alexander would have added to his empire had he had a fresh supply of troops. Regardless, his illustrious career as a leader and military strategist came to an end in 323, when he died from fever. He was 33 years old.

Alexander has been portrayed as an idealistic visionary and as an arrogant and ruthless conqueror. How did he view himself? He sought to imitate Achilles, the hero of Homer's *Iliad*. He claimed to be descended from Hercules, a Greek hero who was worshiped as a god. In Egyptian fashion, he called himself pharaoh. After victories against the Persians, he adopted features of their rule. He called himself the Great King. He urged his followers to bow down before him. He also married Roxane, a Persian captive, and arranged for more than ten thousand of his soldiers to do the same. He wore Persian clothes and used Persians as administrators. In doing so, Alexander was trying to fuse the cultures of East and West, of Asia Minor and Greece. This fusion, and all that it came to represent, is what historians mean by the expression Hellenization.

Alexander was loved by his loyal soldiers, but his fellow Macedonians often objected to him. More than one assassination attempt was made on his life. The cultural legacy of Alexander was that Hellenic art, drama, philosophy, architecture, literature, and language was diffused throughout the Near East. The cities he founded became the springboards for the diffusion of Hellenistic culture. Of the sixty to seventy thousand mercenaries he summoned from Greece, nearly forty thousand remained to inhabit these cities. His vision of empire no doubt appealed to the Romans, a people who would eventually inherit Alexander's empire and, as we shall see, quite a bit more. However, when Alexander died in 323, the Classical Age of Greece came to an abrupt end. Something very different was about to emerge.

FROM POLIS TO COSMOPOLIS

The immediate cause of the collapse of classical Greece was the experience of a century of warfare. The city-state could no longer supply a tolerable way of life. Intellectuals began to turn away from the principles of direct democracy and embrace the idea of the monarchy. For instance, Plato gave up on democracy in despair and insisted on a Philosopher-King, something he argued in his *Republic*. After all, the same democracy that had made Athens so great in the mid-fifth century had also killed his friend and teacher, Socrates. Furthermore, the transition from the Greece of Pericles to that of Alexander the Great involved something more than

just warfare. On a spiritual level, the fourth century witnessed a permanent change in the attitudes of all Greeks. What resulted was a new attitude toward life and its expectations—a new worldview. In the classical world of the polis, public and private lives were fused. Duty to the city-state was in itself virtuous. But in the Hellenistic world, public and private lives were made separate, and the individual's only duty was to himself. In art, sculpture, architecture, or philosophy—wherever we choose to look—we see more attention paid to individualism and introspection. Universal principles of truth—Plato's Ideas and Forms—were rejected in favor of individual traits. By the fourth century, Greek citizens became more interested in their private affairs than in the affairs of the polis. For example, in the fifth century, we find comedies in which the polis is criticized, parodied, and lampooned. But in the fourth century, the subject matter has turned to private and domestic life. In other words, whereas fifth-century comedies focused on the relationship between the citizen and city-state, fourth-century comedies made jokes about cooks, the price of fish, and incompetent doctors.

But the question remains: how do we account for the decline of the polis? Why did this brilliant experiment in direct democracy fail? In general, the democracy of the city-state was made for the amateur, not for the professional. The ideal of the polis was that it was the duty of every citizen to take a direct role in political, economic, religious, and social affairs. But perhaps this was just too much responsibility to place on the shoulders of the citizens. For instance, we have Socrates, the most noble Athenian. He spent his entire life trying to fathom the mysteries of life: what is virtue? What is justice? What is beauty? What is the best form of government? What is the good life? He didn't know the answer to these questions, but he tried to find out by asking as many people as many questions as possible. What Socrates found was that no Athenian citizen could give him a definition of any moral or intellectual virtue that would survive ten minutes of his questioning. The effect of such a discovery on the young men of Athens was profound. Faith in the polis was shattered, for how could the polis train its citizens to be virtuous if no one knew what it meant to be virtuous?

With this story of Socrates in mind, we turn to his most brilliant student, Plato. His *Republic*, his dialogue on the education required to fashion a new state, rejects both the polis and the idea of direct democracy. Just the fact that Plato was thinking in terms of an ideal state should tell you something—people don't think of ideal societies when times are good. Obviously, something was very wrong. Plato's solution was that the training of citizens in virtue should be left to those who understand the universal meaning of virtue, and in Plato's mind, that meant someone who had emerged from the cave of illusion and seen the light of reality—that is, a Philosopher-King. This is indeed a far cry from the ideal of direct democracy and the city-state as embraced by Solon, Cleisthenes, or Pericles.

The history of the Greek world following the death of

Alexander is one of warfare and strife as his generals struggled for control of Alexander's empire. By 275 B.C.E., Alexander's world had been divided into the three kingdoms:

- Macedonia—the Antigonids.
- Western Asia—the Seleucids.
- Egypt—Ptolemys.

The kingdom of Pergamum (southern Asia Minor) was soon added as the fourth Hellenistic monarchy. Hellenistic Greece was a predominately urban culture. The cities founded by Alexander were centers of government, trade, and culture. These were large cities by ancient standards. The Greeks brought their temples, theaters, and schools to other cities, thus exporting their culture. The library at Alexandria is said to have contained some half a million volumes. The upper classes in all four kingdomes began to copy the Greek spirit. They sent their children to Greek schools and the Greek language (*Koine*) became a common, almost international, language. What the breakdown of Alexander's empire had accomplished was nothing less than the Hellenization of the Mediterranean world. Cultures once foreign to the Hellenic world now became more Greek-like—they were Hellenized. One of the most important developments associated with this process of Hellenization, was the shift from the world of the polis to the new world of the cosmopolis. Such a shift was decisive in creating the Hellenistic world as a world of conflicting identities, and when identities are challenged or changed, intense internal conflicts are the result. We can identify this sense of conflict in the transition from classical to Hellenistic philosophy. Classical Greek philosophy, the philosophy of the Sophists and of Socrates in the fifth century, was concerned with the citizen's intimate relationship with the polis. You can see this clearly in the philosophies of Socrates, Plato, and Aristotle. Big questions, such as "what is the good life?", "what is the best form of government?", and "what is virtue?", loomed large in their thinking. When we enter the world of the Hellenistic philosopher, we encounter something very different. We must ask, why? The world of the polis had clearly given way to the world of the cosmopolis. And with that change from the smallness of the city-state to the immensity of the world-city, there were corresponding changes in the worldview. The city-state was no longer run by citizens. In the world-state, bureaucrats and officials took over the duties formerly given over to citizens. Citizens lost their sense of importance as they became subjects under the control of vast bureaucratic kingdoms, and as a result, they lost their identity.

Hellenistic Philosophy as Therapy

This tendency was reflected in philosophy, which turned to concern itself with the possibilities of survival in a world that had become much larger, less personal, and more complex. Philosophy, then, became less the love of wisdom than a therapy used to cope with a strange, fragmented world of disorder and isolation. As a result of this, there were two schools of thought—two therapies—that addressed themselves to an individualistic age. Citizens seemed less concerned about the nature of politics and their role in it. They became more concerned about their own lives and were searching for some kind of personal guidance. All this was reflected in Hellenistic thought as therapy.

Epicurus (341–270 B.C.E.) founded the school of Epicureanism at the end of the fourth century. He taught that:

- There was value in passivity and withdrawal from public life altogether.
- Individual happiness could be found anywhere.
- Politics deprived the citizen of his self-sufficiency and his freedom to choose.
- Wealth and power did little more than provoke anxiety.
- People should strive for inner peace and tranquility and live pleasurable lives while avoiding mental and physical pain.
- The wise person should withdraw from the world, study philosophy, and enjoy the companionship of a few close friends.

Epicurus adopted the atomic theory of Democritus, who taught that in a universe of colliding atoms there could be no room for divine activity. While he perhaps accepted the existence of the gods, he said it was pointless to worry about them. People could achieve happiness when their bodies were free from pain and their minds "released from worry and fear." Together with Aristotle, the motto of Epicurus could have been something like "nothing to excess."

The school of Stoicism was founded by Zeno (c. 336–c. 265 B.C.E.). Zeno was born at Citium, a small Phoenician-Greek city on Cyprus. His father was a merchant and, according to Diogenes Laertius (fl. second century C.E.), he brought Zeno many Socratic books when he was still a boy. At the age of twenty-two Zeno went to Athens, and in 300 B.C.E. he started his school, first called called the Stoics because he gave his lectures in the *Stoa Poikile* (Painted Colonnade), where he soon became a familiar part of Athenian intellectual life. Zeno taught that:

- A single, divine plan governs the universe.
- To find happiness, one must act in harmony with this divine plan.
- By cultivating a sense of duty and self-discipline, one can learn to accept their fate.
- All people belong to the single family of mankind.
- One should not withdraw from the world, but try to make something of the world.

The Stoics believed that the universe contained a principle of order, called the Divine Fire, God, or Divine Reason (*Logos*). This was the principle that formed the basis for reality—it permeated all things. Since reason was common to all, human beings were essentially brothers—it made no difference whether one were Greek, barbarian, free man, or slave, since all mankind were fellow citizens of a world community. By teaching that there was a single divine plan and that the world constituted a single society, Zeno gave perfect expression to the cosmopolitan nature of the post-Alexandrine world. Surrounded by a world of uncertainty, Stoicism promised individual happiness.

Both Epicureanism and Stoicism were therapies that reflected the change in man's social and political life during the Hellenistic Age. On the one hand, both therapies suggest a disenchantment with the overtly political world of Pericles or Thucydides, Athens or Sparta. So, they can be seen as direct reactions to the philosophy of both Plato and Aristotle. Given this, Hellenistic Greeks turned to personal philosophies—therapies—for comfort and, if you will, salvation. In the Hellenistic world, Stoicism became the point of view and therapy of choice for individuals who were still trying to bring order out of the chaos of Hellenistic life. The Epicureans appealed to those people who had resigned themselves to all the chaos and turned to the quest for pleasure and the avoidance of pain.

SKEPTICS AND CYNICS

Stoicism and Epicureanism were not the only two therapies available. The Skeptics simply denied that there was anything close to true knowledge. According to the fourth-century Skeptic Cratylus, since everything is changing, one cannot step once into the same river, because both that river and oneself are changing. Cratylus took his brand of skepticism to an alarming degree, arguing eventually that communication was impossible because since the speaker, listener and words were changing, whatever meaning might have been intended by the words would be altered by the time they were heard. He is therefore supposed to have refused to discuss anything and only to have wiggled his finger when someone spoke, to indicate that he had heard something but that it would be pointless to reply, since everything was changing. Whereas the Epicureans withdrew from the evils of the world, and the Stoics sought happiness by working in harmony with the *Logos*, the Skeptics held that one could achieve some kind of spiritual equilibrium only by accepting that none of the beliefs by which people lived were true or could bring happiness. Speculative thought did not bring happiness, either. For the most part, the Skeptics were suspicious of ideas and maintained no great love for intellectuals.

The Cynics rejected all material possessions and luxuries and lived simple lives totally divorced from the hustle and bustle of the Hellenistic world-city. The most famous of the Cynics was Diogenes the Dog (412–323 B.C.E.). Diogenes lived in a bathtub. He carried a lantern in daylight, proclaiming to all that he was looking for a "virtuous man." It is said that one day Alexander approached Diogenes, who was near death, and asked if there was anything that he could do for him. Diogenes is said to have replied, "Would you mind moving—you are blocking the sun." Plato described Diogenes as "Socrates gone mad." He called himself "citizen of the world," and when asked what the finest thing in the world might be, he replied, "Freedom of speech." Diogenes was disillusioned with what he saw as a corrupt society and hostile world, and he protested by advocating happiness through self-mastery of a spiritual freedom from all wants except the barest minimum.

Finally, there were the Neoplatonists, who combined Plato's ideas with the ancient religions that flourished in Asia Minor. The Neoplatonists used the "Allegory of the Cave" as their point of departure. They took the "Allegory" and "socialized" it by arguing that mankind can overcome this material world by mastering the sacred lore and special knowledge contained in the mystery cults.

THE MYSTERY CULTS

From Epicurean to Stoic, from Skeptic and Cynic to Neoplatonist, none of these therapies provided any sort of relief for the common person. After all, these therapies were specifically intended for citizens who were feeling the burdens of the cosmopolis upon their social, political, and economic life and who could study with Zeno or Diogenes or read the books of Epicurus or the Neoplatonists. The common person required something more practical, less demanding, and more helpful than what the philosophic therapists could offer. They found what they wanted in the mystery cults, cults that could explain their suffering in less complex terms. The most popular cults were those associated with a mother-goddess such as Ishtar (Sumer) or Isis (Egypt), or those that taught the coming of a savior such as Osiris or Mithra. These cults had many common characteristics:

- The savior would come to deliver man from the forces of darkness that had threatened to consume him.
- The mother-goddess cult taught that one should take comfort in the love that the mother figure offered and patiently await one's death, when one would be reunited with the mother-goddess.
- The savior cult invited one to worship a hero-god who would then offer protection from evil.
- Many of these cults believed in the resurrection of the body after death.

These cults were an amalgamation of Hebrew monotheism and Egyptian and Sumerian polytheism. We also should not forget that although faith in the Greek pantheon of gods and goddesses declined during the Hellenic age, its decline was felt most strongly among the citizenry and not the common people, who continued to maintain their traditional beliefs of gods and goddesses of the hearth. The mystery cults:

- Enforced certain dietary rules and required participation in various rites
- Were not exclusive

- Afforded a community of feeling and aspiration that took the place of the now defunct polis

When it first appeared in the Roman world, Christianity was identified by the Romans as merely another mystery cult. Only gradually did it dawn on the Romans that they were facing a completely new religious phenomenon. The mystery cults would contribute to the eventual Christianization of the Roman Empire—when Christianity did make its appearance, the mystery cults had already prepared the groundwork for its acceptance by the Roman people.

There was one distinct culture that knew the Greeks most intimately—the Romans. The Romans resembled the Greeks in many respects, but there was one fundamental difference: the Romans successfully created the kind of cosmopolitan world order—the empire—of which the Greeks had only dreamed.

SUGGESTED CLASSROOM FILMS

Alexander the Great: The Battle of Issus. 45 min. Color. n.d. Filmic Archives. Uses 3-D computer graphics to explore the terrain and tactics of this pivotal battle.

Ancient Greece. 47 min. Color. 1997. Films for the Humanities and Sciences. Beginning with Homer's account of the Trojan War, this program explores Greek ancient civilization.

The Ancient Mediterranean: Conquest, Commerce, and Cultures. 27 min. Color. 2001. Films for the Humanities and Sciences. This program studies the unifying influence of the Mediterranean on the civilizations that developed upon its shores.

The Ancient World: Greece, Part II. 29 min. Color. 1955. New York University. Examines the art and literature of Greece in the fifth century B.C.E. with narration drawn entirely from Greek authors.

Classical Comedy. 60 min. Color. 1976. Films for the Humanities. Performance of excerpts from Aristophanes' *Ecclesiazusai* and Plautius's *Miles Gloriosus.*

Classical Greek Philosophy. 51 min. Color. 2004. Films for the Humanities and Sciences. From the Milesian school to Socrates, Plato, and Aristotle, to the Skeptics, Epicureans, and Stoics.

The Classical Ideal. 60 min. Color. 1989. Insight Media/ Annenberg CPB. Two-part series traces the origins of humanism to ancient Greek art and culture and examines the classical aesthetic. It also explores the genius of Roman engineering and architecture.

Greek Thought. 2 parts, 30 min. each. Color. 1989. Insight Media. Dr. Eugen Weber's look at Greek art, science, and philosophy.

Heroes or History. 58 min. Color. 1978. Insight Media. From the *Crossroads of Civilization* series. Examines Alexander the Great's political and personal motives in his quest for power.

It Started with the Greeks. 54 min. Color. 1986. BBC/RKO. Shows how the questioning and rational attitude of the classical Greeks is at the root of Western thought, with its continuing exploration of new ideas. Part of the James Burke series, *Day the Universe Changed.*

Macedonia: The Land of a God. 2 parts, 90 min. each. Color. 1995. Insight Media. Explores the cultural history of Macedonia under Philip II and Alexander.

Plato's Apology: The Life and Teachings of Socrates. 29 min. Color. 1962. Encylopaedia Britannica Educational Corporation. Includes dramatization of selections from Plato.

Plato's Drinking Party. 40 min. B/W. 1969. Time-Life Films. Sets Plato's dialogue on love at a college reunion.

CHAPTER 5 | Roman Civilization

4. Slow shift to an aristocracy of wealth rather than birth
5. The equestrians
    a. Men who had wealth and influence but chose business over politics
    b. Some became equestrians but underwrote political careers of relatives
6. Was the Roman Republic democratic?

E. Culture, religion and morality
1. Limited education—fathers taught sons (sports, practical arts, military virtue)
2. Chief occupations—war and agriculture
3. Religion
    a. Roman gods—Greek gods
        i. Jupiter/Zeus, Neptune/Poseidon, Venus/Aphrodite
    b. Reverence of ancestors
    c. Household gods
    d. Religion tied up with political life
    e. The Roman priesthood
        i. Served as priests and politicians
4. Roman morality: patriotism, duty, masculine self-control, respect for authority
5. Primary duty to Rome and to family

IV. The Fateful Wars with Carthage
A. The Punic Wars
1. The First Punic War (264–241 B.C.E.)
    a. Roman fear of Carthaginian expansion
    b. Carthage cedes Sicily to Rome
    c. Rome seizes Corsica and Sardinia
2. The Second Punic War (218–202 B.C.E.)
    a. Carthaginian expansion in Spain
    b. Rome declares war
    c. Hannibal (247–182 B.C.E.)
    d. The victory of Scipio Africanus
    e. Carthage abandons all territory save Carthage
3. The Third Punic War (149–146 B.C.E.)
    a. "Carthage must be destroyed"
    b. Romans massacre Carthaginians

B. Territorial expansion
1. Increase in Roman territory (Sicily, North Africa, and Spain)
2. Policy of westward expansion
3. Greece and Macedon become Roman provinces (146 B.C.E.)

V. Society and Culture in the Late Republic
A. Transformations
1. New wealth poured into Rome
2. Increasing social and economic inequality
3. Small farmers left the land for the cities

B. Economic and Social Changes
1. Slavery
    a. Increase in slave population
    b. 200,000 Greek and Carthaginian slaves by end of second century B.C.E.
    c. Using slaves as agricultural laborers
2. No transition to industrialism
3. No incentive for technological initiative
4. Equestrians made contact with Eastern markets
    a. Operated mines, built roads, collected taxes, principal moneylenders

C. Family life and the status of women
1. Introduction of "free marriage"
2. New rules for divorce
3. Wives gained greater legal independence
4. Upper-class Romans adopted Greek customs
5. Latin and Greek language

D. Epicureanism and Stoicism
1. Lucretius (98–55 B.C.E.)
    a. *On the Nature of Things*
    b. Removing the fear of the supernatural
    c. Matter is a combination of atoms
    d. Everything is the product of mechanical evolution
    e. "Peace and a pure heart"
2. Stoicism
    a. Introduced around 140 B.C.E.
    b. Cicero (106–43 B.C.E.)
        i. "Father of Roman eloquence"
        ii. Tranquility of the mind is the highest good
        iii. Indifference to pain and sorrow
        iv. Bringing the best of Greek philosophy to Rome

E. Religion
1. Spread of Eastern mystery cults
2. A more emotional religion
3. Egyptian cult of Osiris (Serapis)
4. Great Mother (Egypt)
5. Mithraism (Persia)

VI. The Social Struggles of the Late Republic (146–30 B.C.E.)
A. Disorder, war, assassinations, and insurrections
B. Spartacus slave uprising (73–71 B.C.E.)
C. Tiberius Graachus (168–133 B.C.E.)
1. Proposed land grants to landless
2. Proposed law restricting size of estate to be owned by each citizen
3. The murder of Tiberius

D. Gaius Graachus (159–123 B.C.E.)
    1. Enacted laws for the less-privileged
    2. Stabilized price of grain in Rome
    3. Suggested full citizenship to Italian allies
    4. The murder of Gaius
E. The aristocratic reaction
    1. Marius (157–86 B.C.E.)
        a. Elected consul in 107 B.C.E., re-elected six times
        b. Abolished property qualification for the army
        c. Army became more loyal to him than to the Republic
    2. Sulla (138–78 B.C.E.)
        a. Appointed dictator (82 B.C.E.)
        b. Exterminated his opponents
        c. Extended the power of the Senate
F. Pompey (106–48 B.C.E.)
    1. Espoused cause of the people
    2. Elected consul by the Senate (52 B.C.E.)
G. Julius Caesar (c. 100–44 B.C.E.)
    1. The Rubicon
    2. Destroys the forces of Pompey at Pharselus (48 B.C.E.)
    3. Cleopatra and Egypt
    4. Dictator for ten years, then declares himself dictator for life (46 B.C.E.)
    5. Death of Caesar—Ides of March (44 B.C.E.)
    6. Treated the republic with contempt
    7. The Julian calendar
    8. Realized the importance of territory in northern Europe (Gaul, Britain)

VII. The Principate and Early Empire (27 B.C.E.–180 C.E.)
A. Octavian (64 B.C.E.–14 C.E.)
    1. Joined forces with Marc Antony and Marcus Ledipus
    2. Murder of Cicero
    3. Crushing the republican opposition
    4. Brutus and Cassius punished
    5. The Battle of Actium (31 B.C.E.)
B. The Augustan system of government
    1. Senate votes Octavian as emperor—calls him Augustus ("worthy of honor") (27 B.C.E.)
    2. Augustus rules as *princeps* ("*first citizen*")
    3. Republican institutions intact, but power resides with Augustus
    4. Controls the army, freely determines all government policy
    5. Achievements
        a. New coinage system
        b. Public services
        c. Abolished the "farming out" of the collection of taxes
        d. Defender of traditional values

    6. Augustus to Trajan
        a. Continued expansion
        b. Holds northern border at the Rhine and Danube
        c. The Roman Peace (*Pax Romana*)
        d. Tiberius (14–37) and Claudius (41–54)
        e. Nero (54–68) and Domitian (81–96)
        f. The "Five Good Emperors"
            i. Nerva (96–98)
            ii. Trajan (98–117)
            iii. Hadrian (117–138)
            iv. Antoninus Pious (136–171)
            v. Marcus Aurelius (161–180)
C. Romanization and assimilation
    1. *Pax Romana* was not universal
        a. Roman massacres in Britain and Judea
    2. Assimilating the residents of conquered territories
    3. The spread of Roman cultural forms (amphitheaters, baths, paved roads)
    4. Rights of citizenship
    5. Borders and frontiers

VIII. Culture and Life in the Period of the Principate
A. Exponents of Stoicism
    1. Seneca (4 B.C.E.–65 C.E.) and Epictetus (c. 60–120 C.E.)
        a. True happiness can be found by surrendering to the benevolent order of the cosmos
        b. Preached the ideal of virtue for virtue's sake
        c. Urged obedience to conscience
        d. The cosmos was divine—ruled by Providence
    2. Marcus Aurelius (121–180 C.E.)
        a. More fatalistic, less hopeful
        b. Immortality is not peace
        c. People should live nobly
        d. Resign yourself to suffering and pain with dignity
        e. "A man should be upright, not kept upright"
B. Literature
    1. The Golden Age—extolling the virtues of Rome
        a. Virgil (70–19 B.C.E.)—the *Ecologues* and the *Aeneid*
        b. Horace (65–8 B.C.E.)—the *Odes*
        c. Livy (59 B.C.E.–17 C.E.)—*History of Rome*
        d. Ovid (43 B.C.E.–17 C.E.)—the *Metamorphosis*

2. The Silver Age—self-conscious artifice
   a. Petronius (fl. first century C.E.)
   b. Apuleius (fl. second century C.E.)—*The Golden Ass*
   c. Juvenal (c. 55–140 C.E.)—the *Satires*
   d. Tacitus (c. 55–120 C.E.)—*Germania* and *Historiae*

C. Art and architecture
   1. Art imported from conquered territories
   2. The wealthy wanted art for their homes—as the demand increased, the Romans relied on copies
   3. Grand public architecture to delicate wall paintings
   4. The Pantheon and the Colosseum
   5. Engineering feats
      a. Roads and bridges
      b. Aqueducts
      c. Sewage systems

D. Aristocratic women under the Principate
   1. Important roles played by upper-class women
   2. Independent status from their husbands
   3. The very wealthy
      a. Could own property
      b. Invest in commercial ventures
      c. Could not hold public office
      d. Could act as priestesses and civic patrons
   4. Some were educated in the liberal arts
   5. Sexual freedom

E. Gladiatorial combats
   1. Most visible sign of Rome, yet the most distasteful
   2. The "Circus"
   3. Attended by commoners and aristocrats

F. New religions
   1. Deeper interest in salvationist religions
   2. Mithraism grew in numbers (favored by the Roman army)
   3. First Christians appear in Rome around 40 C.E.
   4. Emergence of emperor worship

G. Roman law
   1. Product of the Principate
   2. Wider field of jurisdiction
   3. Augustus appoints eminent jurists to deliver opinions on certain legal issues
   4. Three branches
      a. Civil law—the law of Rome and its citizens (both written and unwritten)
      b. Law of the peoples—early international law
      c. Natural law—a product of nature and of philosophy

H. The economy of Italy during the Principate
   1. Government stability
   2. Trade extended to all parts of the known world
   3. Manufacturing increased
   4. Prosperity not evenly distributed
      a. Led to labor shortages on the *latifundia*
      b. Many small farmers ended up tied to the great estates
      c. Unfavorable balance of trade
      d. Third century signs of collapse

IX. The Crisis of the Third Century (180–284)
A. Commodus (161–192)
   1. Both accommodated and terrified the Senate
   2. Few men of talent would work for him
   3. Alienated the army and the Senate
   4. Fought as a gladiator in the Colosseum
   5. Strangled by his wrestling coach

B. The Severan Dynasty
   1. Septimius Severus (145–211)
      a. Controlled the army
      b. Eliminated the rights of the Senate
      c. Ruled as a military dictator
      d. Cheapened Roman citizenship
   2. Imperial women keep the dynasty and empire together

C. The "barracks emperors"
   1. Twenty-six emperors between 235 and 284

D. The height of the third-century crisis
   1. Political chaos and civil wars
   2. Interruption of agriculture and trade
   3. Nearly confiscatory taxation of civilians
   4. Advance of Rome's external enemies: Germans, Persians, and Goths

E. Neoplatonism
   1. The third century produced an overwhelming sense of anxiety
   2. Plotinus (204–270)
      a. Everything that exists proceeds from the divine
      b. The stream of emanations
      c. Matter is despised as the symbol of evil and darkness
      d. Mysticism
         i. Through its union with matter, the human soul is separated from its divine source
         ii. Highest goal is the mystical reunion with the divine
      e. Asceticism

X. The Roman Rule in the West: A Balance Sheet
    A. Explaining the decline and fall of Rome
    B. Political failures
        1. Lack of a clear law of succession
        2. Civil war
        3. Lack of constitutional means for reform
        4. Violence
    C. Economic crisis
        1. Slavery and manpower shortage
        2. Little technological advance
        3. Wealth concentrated in the hands of few families
        4. Undermining of civic ideals
    D. Roman achievements
        1. A long-lasting empire
        2. Created systems of communication, trade, and travel
        3. The Roman economy
        4. The Roman political system
        5. Extending the franchise to outsiders
XI. Conclusion
    A. A standard of comparison: ancient and modern
    B. Architecture
    C. Roman law
    D. Sculpture
    E. The transmission of Greek civilization to the West
    F. The cultural inheritance

GENERAL DISCUSSION QUESTIONS

1. It has been said that the Romans managed to create a world that the Greeks had only dreamed about. What were the strengths of Roman civilization? How were the Romans able to conceive and sustain a civilization over a period of almost ten centuries?

2. Rome succeeded where previous conquerors failed. The Roman Empire lasted for five hundred years in the west, and nearly one thousand years more in the east. Why? Compare the Roman ways of empire-building with those of Alexander the Great, the Persians, the Assyrians, and other Near Eastern peoples.

3. The Romans had a reputation for practicality—in engineering, military science, law and order, agriculture, medicine, and natural science. Were the Romans any less philosophical, less spiritual, or less superstitious than the Greeks? How might it be argued that the Romans were natural Stoics?

4. Does every nation require a founding myth? Rome had the tales of Aeneas of Troy and the infant twins Romulus and Remus. Compare examples of other states that do and do not have a founding myth. How

seriously do we take such myths today? What is the purpose of a founding myth?

5. Can we understand Roman political history as a series of struggles between rich and poor factions, led or manipulated by cynical politicians and generals? Keep in mind that, when we confine motives to economic interests, it is hard to explain idealistic patriotism and self-sacrificing religious acts.

6. The *Struggle of the Orders* serves as an illustration of the technique the Romans used to reconcile conflicts. Why did the Romans use compromise and assimilation to solve their problems? How was this solution typically Roman? Can you think of other conflicts resolved by similar means?

7. The text discusses "the fateful wars with Carthage." In what sense were these wars fated to happen? Were they inevitable or coincidental? Since both Rome and Carthage were expanding states, were they bound to conflict in Spain, North Africa, and the western Mediterranean Sea?

8. The ancient Roman version of slavery differed from slavery in the American South before 1865, particularly in its ideas of identity, race, and authority. How could learned men such as Polybius be enslaved, and how could slaves become free? How did slavery in ancient times affect the economy?

9. How did Augustus Caesar consolidate his power at the beginning of the Roman Empire? Why have historians called his reign the Principate?

10. Edward Gibbon once remarked that "the decline of Rome was the natural and inevitable effect of immoderate greatness . . . as soon as time or accident had removed the artificial supports, the stupendous fabric yielded to the pressure of its own weight. The story of its ruin is simple and obvious: and instead of inquiring why the Roman Empire was destroyed we should rather be surprised that it has subsisted for so long." Comment.

11. Although Christianity stood opposed to everything the empire represented, it is clear that eventually the Roman world was Christianized. What was it about the Roman experience that might have made this possible?

DOCUMENT DISCUSSION QUESTIONS

The Rape of Lucretia

1. Livy believed that moral decline was responsible for the destruction of the Roman Republic. What historical and political functions did his anecdotes serve? Would

it make any difference to him and his readers if the stories were mythical rather than factual?

2. In Livy's history, Lucretia tries to resist her attacker, then realizes that she must yield to his superior force and survive the ordeal to preserve a remnant of her honor and tell others what happened. Why does she kill herself? Was there an alternative?

3. If the rape of Lucretia is a myth—a vivid portrayal of a deep truth, not a factual report of what happened—consider its symbolic significance. Lucretia's assailant, Sextus, was a playboy prince, son of King Tarquin the Proud. In response to the attack, Lucretia's father, Brutus, vowed vengeance not merely against Sextus but also against the tyrant king and his entire family. How was the Etruscan King Tarquin's reign equivalent to "rape" of the motherland of Rome, the "virtuous" country?

4. Brutus swore, "Never again will I let them or any other man be king in Rome!" Did the crime of Sextus justify abolishing the monarchy forever? Or was it just the last straw that broke the people's back?

The Influence of Greek Luxury

5. Why does Plutarch recount the life of Lucius Licinius Lucullus, who went from high commands in the army and offices in the state to a buffoon-like private life? What can we learn from this gossipy account?

6. Despite having left office, Lucullus had powerful friends, such as Sulla, Pompey, and Cato, which implied that he was still politically influential. How might his wealth and entertainments corrupt Roman politics just as much as military intervention did?

7. In the text excerpt, Plutarch, a biographer who wrote in Greek, doesn't explicitly criticize the Greeks for having introduced the Romans to luxury. Should we assign blame to the Hellenistic Age, in which oriental customs were spread from western Asia across the Mediterranean?

Two Views of Augustus' Rule

8. "The emperor Augustus was a master propagandist." The list of deeds that he thought most important begins with "the deified Augustus" recalling his campaigns as a young man seeking to liberate the republic, avenge the death of Julius Caesar, and remain true to accepted legal forms. Like traditional Roman heroes, Augustus repeatedly refuses honors and takes power only with great reluctance. Who would believe such inscriptions? Who was Augustus trying to impress?

9. Was Tacitus a moralist historian like Livy? Writing of events that occurred a century earlier, he had more freedom to comment on good and bad features of the emperor Augustus' character. What is his overall evaluation of Augustus?

A Scathing Critique of Roman Society

10. Why is good satire, like stand-up comedy, often aggressive, funny, outrageous, and vulgar? Juvenal was not a gentle comedian; he was an angry man who wanted to stir up his readers. For what causes was he fighting? Did Romans need to hear the unpleasant truths he presented?

11. Why did Juvenal repeatedly strike at the use and abuse of the human body—in this case, women's bodies? Was he a misogynist (woman-hater)? Were Roman women really like Maura and Tullia—drunk, lustful, scatological, contemptuous, "burning with the desire to get themselves laid"? As the text suggests, contrast Juvenal's portrayal of contemporary women with that of the virtuous Lucretia. What would you think if a report similar to Juvenal's appeared in your local campus newspaper?

SAMPLE LECTURE 5: ROME UNDER THE REPUBLIC

Lecture Objectives

1. To suggest the ways in which Rome became a republic

2. To look at the Roman spirit of compromise and assimilation

3. To examine how the Roman Revolution led to the death of the Republic and birth of the Empire

THE ROMAN REPUBLIC

In 509 B.C.E., after having expelled the Etruscans, the Romans constructed a form of political organization we call a republic. A series of documents were drawn up that together make up the Roman constitution, outlining the legal rights of citizens. The republic was not intended for the city-state. Instead, the Roman Republic was more like a confederation of states under the control of a representative, central authority. There were three major political components of the republic. Two magistrates or consuls served as the executive branch and had supreme civil and military authority. They held office for one year, then entered the Senate for life. Each consul could veto the action of the other. The consuls led the army, served as judges, and had religious duties. The Senate was a collection of citizens who served as the legislative branch of the government as well as an advisory body (*senatus* means "council of elders"). Members of the Senate were drawn from ex-consuls and other officers who served for life. The Assembly of Centuries (*comitia centuriata*), which conducted annual elections of consuls, was composed of all members of the army. In this Assembly, the wealthier citizen voted first and had a profound influence. Lastly, there was the Assembly of Tribes (*comitia tributa*), which contained all citizens. The Assembly approved and rejected laws and decided issues of war and peace. This is a mixed form of government. History—specifically Greek history—had shown the Romans that previous governments of the one, the few, or the many did not work. Instead, they mixed the three principal forms of government to create a republic. Their constitution was mixed as well: the executives served as monarchical element, the Senate as the aristocratic, and the Assembly as the democratic. Ideally, such a constitution would prevent any one man or group of men from seizing power on their own initiative. In other words, the republic was a government of checks and balances. What happened in practice was something decidedly different. The real locus of power in ancient Rome was the family. Alliances, marriages, divorces, adoptions, and assassinations could make or break a family's path to political power. The great families or clans (*gens*) grew so powerful that by 100 B.C.E. it was nearly impossible for a man to become a consul whose ancestors had not also been consuls.

THE STRUGGLE OF THE ORDERS

One of the most important developments during the early history of the Roman Republic was the "Struggle of the Orders." Between 500 and 300 B.C.E. the Roman citizenry was divided into two social groups—patricians and plebeians. The patricians were a small group of citizens (less than 10 percent of Rome's population) who were legally and socially superior to the majority of citizens. They had earned their position through wealth or the ownership of land. The patricians held a monopoly of social, political, and economic power. The plebeians were those citizens who lacked power, although their ranks included everyone from the landless peasant to the very wealthy individual who wanted to become a patrician. The "Struggle of the Orders"—a struggle between patricians and plebeians—developed over a legal issue. Only the patricians could belong to the Senate. The plebeians had the right to vote in the Assembly, but their votes were usually influenced by the patricians. And since the wealthier citizens of the Senate always voted first, they usually did so as an effective block against other groups. In 494 B.C.E., the plebeians threatened to leave Rome and set up their own independent state (*concilium plebis*). What the plebeians did was literally to create a state within a state. Their object was to acquire protection against the unjust and arbitrary acts of the Senate and consuls.

In typical Roman fashion, the Roman Senate compromised with the plebeians. In the end, the Roman constitution was modified to meet a few of the demands of the plebeians, but the patricians retained their measure of full control. What the plebeians gained was right to elect two representatives—the tribunes.

- They had absolute veto power.
- They could not be called to account for their actions.
- They could not be harmed in any way.
- The only actions a tribune could not veto were those of military commanders or dictators.

By 450 B.C.E. the plebeians had won another important concession—the Laws of the Twelve Tables, codes specifying civic matters, crimes, and the relations among citizens and family members. In 445 B.C.E., the plebeians also won the right to intermarry with the patricians (the *Lex Canuleia*). This was important for the simple reason that it allowed wealthy plebeians to become patricians themselves. In 367 B.C.E., the tribunes Gaius Licinius and Lucius Sextus passed the Licinian-Sextian laws which specified that:

- One consul every year must be a plebeian.
- The office of praetor should serve as assistant consul.
- A law would restrict the amount of land held by any citizen.

Finally, in 287 B.C.E., a law was passed that made the decisions of the Assembly of Tribes binding on the whole state without action by any other body (the *Lex Hortensia*). It seemed that for a time the plebeians had won all that they sought, and their struggles with the patricians were carried out with little bloodshed and a minimum of violence. The "Struggle of the Orders" did not lead to open civil war. The patricians needed the plebeians to defend Rome in times of war, and the plebeians needed the experience and leadership of the patricians.

COMPROMISE AND ASSIMILATION

The "Struggle of the Orders" provides a key to understanding the Roman world and the Roman mind. The key here is compromise and assimilation. Wealthy plebeians were assimilated into the patrician class. Through common sense and practicality, a compromise was reached that seemed to satisfy most citizens, regardless of which order they may have belonged to. This is a hallmark of Roman civilization. Compromises were reached in the interests of stability and peace. In this way, the Romans avoided outright civil war and at the same time provided all citizens with a tolerable way of life. A comparison with the Greeks may be necessary here. For the most part, the Greeks conducted politics in terms of principles and theory: what is the good life? What is virtue? They expended a great deal of energy trying to determine the best form of government for the polis. By the time they had perfected their direct democracy during the Periclean Age, the Greek world was entering a period of crisis. That crisis was the Peloponnesian War. And what followed that war was Philip II, Alexander the Great, and the replacement of the comfortable, virtuous life of the polis, with the much larger and more impersonal cosmopolis.

The Romans perhaps knew the Greeks best—after all, they inhabited the same Mediterranean world. But the Romans, always with an eye toward practicality, were not apt to make the same mistakes as had the Greeks. So, they mixed their government, bound the lives of its citizenry to a living constitution, and made compromises to insure the future life and growth of the republic. By the third century B.C.E., a new and larger class of patricians was created. These are the individuals who dominated the Senate because they held the highest positions of state and could pass their positions on to their descendants for posterity. It was also this nobility that controlled the state to the middle of the first century B.C.E. And although the plebeians gained the means to run the state as a democracy, they chose not to do so. Their political involvement was always based on the needs of defense rather than offense. The Romans also embarked on a path that would soon culminate in the establishment of the Roman Empire. Unlike the Greeks, who forced conquered lands into slavery or submission, the Romans took the conquered and made them partners. In other words, they assimilated them into the Roman cosmopolis. This was far more efficient and, at least in the short term, there were fewer problems. This policy of compromise and assimilation continually built up the strength of the Roman Republic.

The conquered communities were organized by various degrees of privilege and responsibility. For instance, some communities were granted full Roman citizenship; others were granted citizenship but could not vote in the Assembly. At a lower level, some states would simply receive Rome's support in the event of an invasion. This system of confederating states was far more successful than the Greek idea of domination and submission. The Greeks sought to demolish the social institutions of conquered lands and replace them with Greek institutions. Alexander left tens of thousands of his loyal soldiers in the areas that he conquered; he also exported the Greek language. The Romans accommodated the conquered people within their own political and administrative structure. All these people had to do was to pay taxes and serve Rome. In other words, the Romans gave these conquered people an "offer they couldn't refuse." They could maintain their history as long as they served Rome. And since most of these people were made Roman citizens, they too could feel themselves to be a part of this growing Roman world—and they could find the good life anywhere in the Roman world. Governing such a vast territory would become easier, the Romans understood, if everyone were made to feel as if they were a partner in the endeavor. The simply amazing thing is that the Romans pulled it off.

ROMAN IMPERIALISM

Rome was at war throughout most of the years of the Republic. The most famous of these wars were the Punic Wars with Carthage. The First Punic War (264–241 B.C.E.) began as a minor conflict over the presence of Carthaginian troops in the Sicilian town of Messana. The Messanians had invited the troops as protection but then decided to replace them with Roman troops. War broke out over control of Sicily. The Romans suffered heavy losses but eventually forced Carthage to abandon Sicily. The Second Punic War (218–201 B.C.E.) began in Spain. Rome protested to Carthage about its treatment of Saguntum, a town within the Carthaginian sphere of influence. As negotiations were underway, Hannibal (247–182 B.C.E.) seized Saguntum and made war inevitable. His nation had been humiliated at Sicily—this was his chance for revenge. In 218 B.C.E., he led an army from Spain, across the Alps, and into Italy, but could not arouse any of his allies to revolt. Roman tenacity eventually won out, although a great deal of farmland to the south was destroyed. The Third Punic War (149–146 B.C.E.) saw the capture and destruction of Carthage. Rome now controlled the province of Africa and almost all of Spain. At the same time, Rome was also fighting in Macedonia and in Asia Minor (205–148 B.C.E.) . The end result was the annexation of Greece and Asia Minor to the Roman world. Macedonia was officially made a province of the Republic, and thus the Romans brought an end to the independent political life of Greece. By 44 B.C.E., the Romans controlled all of Spain, Gaul, Italy, Greece, Asia Minor, and most of North Africa (80 percent of the coastal lands of the Mediterranean). The Roman Republic had to protect its people from outside invasion, and they did this by forming alliances with their neighbors. The constant warfare of the fourth and third centuries B.C.E. reinforced this need for common security and mutual defense. This was something the Greeks had not been able to accomplish primarily because of the predominance of Athens as the seat of government and the isolation of Sparta as a military power. The Romans had to administer their allies which was accomplished through provinces. Each province was assigned to a magistrate and it was his duty to administer government policy quickly and effectively.

THE ROMAN REVOLUTION

From 133 to 27 B.C.E., the Roman Republic was engaged in a constant succession of civil wars, making up what has come to be known as the Roman Revolution. The acquisition of empire did have disturbing effects on the social order and administrative structure of the Republic. The Punic and Macedonian Wars of the third and second centuries B.C.E. kept Roman soldiers away from Rome for years at a time. Many of these soldiers developed a greater loyalty to the land they were serving than to Rome. Others simply enjoyed the spoils and luxuries of conquered lands. Such a scenario also partially explains how a Roman strength became a Roman weakness. At the same time, the enormous wealth that Roman conquests attained became concentrated in the hands of the senatorial class. Peasants were driven off the land and into the cities. Most of the peasants were unemployed and lived by begging. Still others sold their votes to wealthy patricians, thus giving up one of the key features of their citizenship. By the middle of the second century, there was a threefold problem brewing in the Roman Republic:

- The senatorial class, growing in number and wealthier than ever before, wanted to maintain its political position.
- The urban masses were divorced from the land as well as from their citizenship and now were giving their political allegiance to any faction that would pay them.
- The army was disgusted by the senatorial class as well as by the greed and instability of the masses.

By 133 B.C.E., Roman politics had polarized around two factions in the Senate. On the one hand were the *Optimates* whose only interest lay with wealth and the senatorial class. Numerically small but politically powerful, the *Optimates* were by all accounts conservative—they were the defenders of the good old days, defenders of the status quo. On the other hand, there were the *Populares*, the champions of the depressed portion of the citizenry. The *Populares* demanded the redistribution of the land to the dispossessed peasants who were flooding into Rome, as well as a reform of the voting procedure. The struggle between these two factions came to civil war when the Senate resorted to the assassination of Tiberius Gracchus (168–133 B.C.E.). Tiberius had been elected Tribune in 133 B.C.E. He proposed a land bill to the Assembly of Tribes that would effectively divide the land and give it to the Roman citizenry. The bill limited the amount of land per individual to about 330 acres, and to this he added an allowance for each of two sons, bringing the total possible amount to 660 acres. The Senate would not pass his land bill, and so Tiberius went directly to the *concilium plebis*. As a result, Tiberius and three hundred of his followers were killed and their bodies thrown into the Tiber.

The program of Tiberius was taken up by his brother, Gaius Gracchus (159–121 B.C.E.). Elected tribune in 123 B.C.E., Gaius wanted to transform Rome into a democracy along Hellenic lines. In his attempt to place restraints on the power of the Senate, he had the near-total support of the public Assembly. He also won the support of the Assembly by legislating to keep the price of grain sold to citizens permanently low. Gaius built new storehouses, his road-building program kept the citizens at work, he revised the terms of military service, and he reorganized the collection of taxes. The Senate declared martial law. Riots broke out and three thousand of the *Populares*, along with Gaius, were killed. Gaius was beheaded and his body thrown into the Tiber.

These assassinations show the ugly realities behind Roman political life. When the selfishness of the Senate was revealed, they resorted to murder. Severe weaknesses in the senatorial system were brought into the light during a series of invasions of the Republic by Germanic tribes to the north of the Danube River. The armies sent by the Senate to dispel this threat were poorly organized, unwilling to fight, and corrupt. The situation was saved by Gaius Marius (c. 157–86 B.C.E.), a man who was politically well-connected. Marius managed to raise a professional army on his own. He eventually defeated the Germanic tribes and thus earned the support of the Roman army, which he then began to reform. He abolished the requirement that a solider must own property. He was elected consul seven times.

In 81 B.C.E., Gaius Marius and his army were overthrown by Sulla (c. 138–78 B.C.E.), a statesman and a general who had made his reputation in the Italian War of the 90s. In the 80s, civil war broke out in Rome among the factions of the Senate. One group rallied behind Sulla, and in 88 B.C.E. he invaded Rome. The following year, Sulla departed for a campaign against Mithridates, who ruled the kingdom of Pontus on the south coast of the Black Sea. While he was away, rival factions seized Rome. Returning in 82 B.C.E., Sulla once again occupied Rome. Hundreds of his opponents were killed and he had himself named dictator for life. Sulla used his power as dictator to refashion the Roman state by passing legislation forbidding the tribunes to pass a law without Senate approval. Sulla then restricted the term of governor of a province to one year—this prevented one commander from becoming a hero to his troops and leading a march on Rome. Sulla thus skillfully prevented the rise of another Sulla.

The careers of Gaius Marius and Sulla represent the path to political power in the last century of the Roman Republic. There were three stages that both men had followed. The first was to play off the senatorial fear of the masses as well as the resentment the masses harbored toward senatorial privilege. This was followed by the appearance of a soldier/hero who would again play one class off another. A personal army would then be created and the victor would march on Rome to bring peace and prosperity to the Roman people. This pattern was followed by Pompey in the 60s, Crassus in the 50s, and Julius Caesar in the 40s.

Mark Antony (c. 83–c. 30 B.C.E.) tried to embark on this same path in the 30s but was opposed by Octavian (63 B.C.E.–14 B.C.E.), Caesar's grandnephew. When Caesar's will was read, it was discovered that not Antony, but Octavian was the true heir to the throne. Rather than start yet another civil war, Antony, Octavian, and Lepidus formed the Second Triumverate. The Roman world was now divided between these rulers (Antony: eastern provinces; Octavian: western provinces; Lepidus: Sicily and North Africa). Octavian went on to present Antony as an enemy of Rome because of his alliance with Cleopatra in Egypt. He then made a solid alliance with the Senate and had Lepidus removed. By the time Octavian broke with Antony, the Roman people were tired. They had endured one hundred years of civil war. They wanted peace. They wanted to enjoy their world, not constantly defend it. At the decisive Battle of Actium (31 B.C.E.), the forces of Antony and Cleopatra were defeated. Both patricians and plebeians rallied behind Octavian, who soon took the name Augustus Caesar. With the rise of Augustus, the world of the Roman Republic came to an end.

SUGGESTED FEATURE FILMS

Barabbas. 134 min. Color. 1962. Columbia Pictures. Epic account of the thief Barabbas, who was spared crucifixion when the Jews chose Christ in his place.

Ben Hur. 217 min. Color. 1959. MGM. William Wyler's production of Lew Wallace's novel. Featuring Charlton Heston, along with three hundred sets, 365 speaking parts, and seventy-eight horses! Winner of eleven Academy Awards.

The Fall of the Roman Empire. 188 min. Color. 1964. Paramount Pictures. Epic film of Rome in the days of Marcus Aurelius and Commodus.

A Funny Thing Happened on the Way to the Forum. 99 min. Color. 1966. United Artists. Pseudolus (Zero Mostel) is the laziest slave in Rome, and his only wish is to purchase his freedom.

Gladiator. 155 min. Color. 2000. Universal Pictures. A dying Marcus Aurelius plans to name his loyal and brave General Maximus as his successor in order to restore the power of the Roman Senate. It's not specifically accurate, but the film is excellent for its images of the Roman world.

Julius Caesar. 121 min. B/W. 1953. MGM. This version of Shakespeare's play was selected by the National Board of Review as one of the Ten Best Films of 1953.

Life of Brian. 94 min. Color. 1979. Warner Brothers. Monty Python's satire of Biblical films and religious intolerance focuses on Brian, a Jew in Roman-occupied Judea. Brian joins an anti-Roman political organization, is mistaken for a prophet, and becomes a reluctant Messiah.

Quo Vadis. 171 min. Color. 1951. MGM. This production of Henry Sienkiewicz's novel highlights the physical brutality of the Roman world.

Satyricon (subtitled). 129. Color. 1970. United Artists. Fellini film loosely based on the book *Satyricon* by Gaius Petronius Arbiter, the "Arbiter of Elegance" in the court of Nero.

Spartacus. 198 min. Color. 1960 (1991 restored version). MCA/Universal Home Video. Stanley Kubrick film about a slave revolt against the Romans during the final century of the Roman Republic.

Terence: That Girl from Andros. 115 min. Color. Filmic Archives. This performance of *Andria* uses the earliest English verse translation (c. 1500).

SUGGESTED CLASSROOM FILMS

Ancient Rome. 47 min. Color. 1997. Films for the Humanities and Sciences. Scholars discuss Roman unification of Europe, Roman culture and institutions, the family structure, and the role of the army as a major force in Roman society and politics.

The Roman Empire in the First Century. 220 min. Color. 2001. PBS. Four-part series about the *Pax Romana*, from the rise of Augustus to the reign of Trajan. Includes *Order From Chaos*; *Years of Trial*; *Winds of Change*; and *Years of Eruption*.

The Classical Ideal. 60 min. Color. 1989. Insight Media/ Annenberg CPB. Two-part series traces the origins of humanism to ancient Greek art and culture and examines the classical aesthetic. It also explores the genius of Roman engineering and architecture.

Empire: The Romans. 200 min. Color. 2003. Films for the Humanities and Sciences. Four-part series brings together a wide range of scholars and experts to discuss the world of the people who made Rome what it was.

The End of the Ancient World. 26 min. Color. 1989. Insight Media. Covers the period from 100 to 600 C.E.

The Etruscans. 27 min. Color. 1982. Films for the Humanities. Uses tomb frescoes to explore Etruscan culture.

Four Views of Caesar. 22 min. B/W. 1964. BFA Educational Media. Interpretations by Caesar himself, Plutarch, Shakespeare, and Shaw.

I, Claudius. 13 parts. 58 min. each. Color. 1976. Filmic Archives. Derek Jacobi heads the cast of this now-classic dramatization of Robert Graves' unforgettable books.

Journey Through Ancient Pompeii. 31 min. Color. 1999. Films for the Humanities and Sciences. Program uses Pompeii's abundant archaeological evidence to re-create daily life at the time Mt. Vesuvius erupted in 79 C.E.

Julius Caesar: The Battle of Alesia. 45 min. Color. 1993. Filmic Archives. Uses 3-D computer graphics to explore the terrain and tactics of this pivotal battle.

Julius Caesar: The Forum Scene. 17 min. B/W. 1961. International Film Bureau. Act III, Scene II from Shakespeare's play.

The Rise of Rome, Fall of Rome. 4 parts. 30 min. each. Color. 1989. Insight Media. Traces the rise, decline, and fall of the Roman Empire.

The Romans: Life, Laughter, and Laws. 22 min. Color. 1971. Learning Corporation of America. Uses excerpts from Roman satire.

CHAPTER 6

Christianity and the Transformation of the Roman World

OUTLINE

I. Introduction
  A. Rome after 180 C.E.
  B. Transitions—ancient to medieval world: Late Antiquity
  C. The spread and triumph of Christianity
  D. "Barbarization"
  E. Cultural assimilation
II. The Reorganized Empire
  A. The reign of Diocletian (c. 236–305; emperor 284–305)
    1. Called himself *dominus* (lord)
    2. Persian-style ceremonial deference at court
    3. Took steps to define formal rules of imperial succession
    4. Divided his realm in half
      a. Diocletian took wealthier western half
      b. Maximian took the eastern half
    5. The Tetrarchy ("the rule of the four")
      a. Permitted a degree of decentralization
      b. Designed to end succession disputes
    6. Separated military from civilian chains of command
    7. Stabilized the currency and new system of taxation
    8. Ruled from Nicomedia (Asia Minor), retires at Split (Croatia) in 305
  B. The reign of Constantine (272–337; emperor 324–337)
    1. Followed Diocletian's footsteps
    2. Government
      a. Ruled by decree
      b. Extensive spy network
      c. Declared army service hereditary
      d. Bound farmers and craftsmen to their trade
    3. Moves the capital to Constantinople (324)
    4. Made imperial succession hereditary
      a. Brought Rome back to principle of dynastic monarchy
      b. Divided his realm among three sons
  C. From Constantine to Theodosius
    1. Constantinople as leading city
    2. Regionalism
    3. Growing gap between rich and poor
    4. Secessionist movements (Britain, Spain, Gaul, and Germany)
III. The Emergence and Triumph of Christianity
  A. How can we explain the appeal of early Christianity?
  B. The career of Jesus
    1. First-century sources
    2. Born in Judea
    3. Preaching, healing, and teaching
    4. Messianic entry (30 C.E.) into Jerusalem during Passover
    5. Arrest
      a. Pontius Pilate
      b. Crucifixion
      c. The Christ ("anointed one")
  C. Jesus and Second Temple Jerusalem
    1. The Dead Sea Scrolls
    2. Roman control of Judea was tenuous
    3. Zealots sought to expel the Romans by force

a. Destruction of the Jewish Temple
(66–70)

b. Destruction of Jerusalem (132–135)

D. Judaism, monotheism, and the Covenant

1. Interpreting the Covenant

a. The Torah—first five books of
Old Testament

b. Sadducees—hereditary temple
priesthood and aristocratic guardians

c. Pharisees—interpreters of religious
law

d. Essenes—radical, splinter group,
spiritual deliverance through
asceticism

E. Jesus as controversial figure

1. He was the Messiah promised by God
to deliver Israel

F. Reinterpretation of Jesus' role as messiah:
Greek theology

IV. The Growth of Christianity in the Hellenistic World

A. St.Paul (c. 10–c. 67)

1. Born at Tarsus (Asia Minor)

2. Converted to Christianity

3. Declared himself to be the apostle to
the Gentiles

4. Rejected Jewish law as irrelevant to
salvation

5. Making converts among Greek-speaking
Jewish communities

B. The appeal of Christianity

1. Communal aspect

2. Early organizational structure

3. Role of women

4. Appealed to broad range of social classes

5. Promise of salvation

C. Judaism and Christianity

1. Hostility

2. Understanding the Messiah

D. Christianity and the Roman Empire

1. Treated early appearance of Christianity
with indifference

2. Persecutions were intermittent and
short-lived

3. By 300, 1–5 percent of total Roman
population were perhaps Christians

4. Constantine's conversion—the Milvian
Bridge (312)

a. Made Christianity the favored
religion

5. Julian the Apostate—abandoned
Christianity and attempted to revive
Roman paganism

6. Theodosius the Great

a. Prohibits pagan worship

b. Makes Christianity the state religion

V. The New Contours of Fourth-Century Christianity

A. Doctrinal quarrels

1. Arians and Athanasians: the Trinity

B. The importance of orthodoxy

C. Christian theology and the classical tradition

D. Council of Nicea (325)

1. Arian heresy is condemned

2. Emperor presided over councils

E. The growth of ecclesiastical organization

1. Clergy and laity

2. Hierarchical organization

a. Distinctions of rank

b. The pope as bishop of Rome

c. The Petrine Succession

F. The spread of monasticism

1. Disillusionment

a. Asceticism as a substitute for
martyrdom

b. Response to increasing
worldliness

2. St.Benedict of Nursia (c. 480–c. 547)

a. The Latin or Benedictine Rule

i. Poverty, chastity, obedience,
labor and prayer

b. Absolute authority of the abbot

c. Missionary work

d. Dignity of human labor

G. Changing attitudes toward women, marriage,
and the body

1. Christianity favorable toward women

2. The denigration of women

3. Virginity as highest spiritual standard

4. The denigration of sexuality

VI. The Germanic Invasion and the Fall of the Western
Roman Empire

A. German-Roman relations

1. Roman attitudes: Germans are
barbarians

2. Shared common borders for centuries
(Rhine and Danube)

3. German tribes converted to Arian
Christianity

B. Battle of Andrianople (378)

C. Alaric sacks Rome (410)

D. Vandals move into Gaul and Spain (406/7)

E. Romulus Augustulus overthrown by
Odovacer (476)

F. The success and impact of the Germanic
invasions

1. Roman armies are depleted

2. Declining Roman population

3. Romans refused to defend themselves

4. Germans abandoned cities

VII. The Shaping of Western Christian Thought

A. The classical heritage and the church fathers

B. St. Jerome (c. 340–420)
   1. Translated the Bible into Latin (the Vulgate)
   2. Bible to be understood allegorically
C. St. Ambrose (c. 340–397)
   1. *On the Duties of Ministers*
   2. God helps some Christians and not others (the "gift of grace")
D. The life and thought of St. Augustine (354–430)
   1. The quest for Christianity
   2. Archbishop of Hippo (395)
   3. *Confessions*
      a. Predestination
      b. Doctrine of charity
   4. *On the City of God*
      a. Predestination
      b. City of Man—"live according to man"
      c. City of God—"live according to God"
      d. The Bible contains all wisdom
      e. A modified acceptance of classical thought
E. Boethius links classical and medieval thought (c. 480–524)
   1. The "last of the Romans"
   2. Wrote handbooks on the liberal arts
   3. Handbooks on arithmetic and music
   4. Aristotelian logic
   5. *Consolation of Philosophy*
      a. What is human happiness?
      b. The highest good is God
   6. Execution by Theodoric (524)
VIII. The Christianization of Classical Culture in the West
A. The challenge of classical ideas
B. Replacing paganism with Christianity
C. Winnowing out of classical texts
D. Neoplatonism
E. What is the relationship between classical thought and Christianity?
F. Cassiodorus (c. 490–c. 583)
   1. *History of the Goths*
   2. The *Institutes*
   3. Classical literature as primer for understanding the Bible
   4. Copying manuscripts
G. Preserving Christianity
IX. Eastern Rome and the Western Empire
A. Justinian's revival of the empire (482–565; emperor 527–565)
   1. Barbarian pressures
   2. The heir of imperil Rome
   3. Empress Theodora (c. 500–547)

B. The codification of Roman law
   1. *Code*
   2. *Novels*
   3. *Digest*
   4. *Corpus Juris Civilis*
C. Justinian's military conquests—the "Roman lake"
D. The impact of Justinian's reconquest on the western empire
   1. Devastation in northern and central Italy
   2. The Lombard invasion
   3. Visigoths in Spain
X. Conclusion
A. Late Antiquity
B. Vulgarization of learned culture
C. Christianization of the empire
D. Byzantium, Islam, and western Europe

GENERAL DISCUSSION QUESTIONS

1. The Roman Empire not only survived the terrible crises of the third century (180–284 C.E.) but, under Diocletian, it also regained lost territories, restored its economy and governmental institutions, and finished the century stronger than it had been at the beginning. Was the historian Edward Gibbon a bit hasty or premature in starting the decline in 180?. Why or why not? When exactly did decline begin?

2. The demise of Romulus Augustulus ("little Augustus") in 476 is usually taken as the end of the Roman Empire in the Wwest. Strange as it may sound, many Europeans, North Africans, Greeks, and other Roman subjects in the east did not even notice. Explain.

3. Why did the church fathers of the early Christian church believe that the classical heritage of learning was absolutely essential to their understanding and interpretation of Christianity? What specific problems were associated with the intellectual combination of the classical tradition of humanism with the Judeo-Christian tradition?

4. If the period known as Late Antiquity (284–610) is neither Roman nor medieval, then what was it? And why do many of its themes seem so familiar to us?

5. What role did early monasticism play in Late Antiquity? Why were the monks considered to be the heroes of Christian civilization?

6. It is remarkable that someone like St. Paul should remark that "there must also be heresies" within Christianity. What role did the existence of heresies play in the development of the early church? What was the relationship between heresy and the formation

of a systematic theology? Do all systems of belief also create their opposite? Cite some modern examples.

7. What aspects of Christianity had the strongest appeal to prospective members in the second, third, and fourth centuries? Did Christians intend to cause conflict and challenge Roman authority, or was that a coincidence? Did such challenges seriously threaten the social order?

8. The emergence of early Christianity was shaped by the Roman experience. But imagine that Jesus and a sect of Christians had appeared in the Hellenistic world of the fourth century B.C.E. How might Alexander have dealt with such a development?

9. In the first five centuries of its existence, Christianity was successful in converting large numbers of pagans. What forces were at work in the later Roman Empire and the period of Late Antiquity that contributed to the rise of Christianity? Why do you think the Roman Empire was Christianized?

DOCUMENT DISCUSSION QUESTIONS

Prosecuting Christians: The Letters of Pliny the Elder and the Emperor Trajan

1. Pliny and Trajan were friends, but Pliny was careful to get the emperor's approval of his legal procedures. He was unsure whether simply being a Christian was a crime, but he knew that lying about church membership constituted perjury and refusing to perform ritual honors to the emperor was equal to rebellion and treason, all crimes that should be punished. What does this say about official Roman ideas of honor, propriety, and justice?

2. During judicial examinations, subjects were routinely tortured to extort more information from them. Yet when Pliny tortured two deaconesses, he found only "absurd and excessive superstition." What did he conclude from this? What seemed the best way to fight this superstition?

3. Emperor Trajan and Governor Pliny rejected the use of anonymous denunciations as proof of punishable crimes because it did not accord with the enlightened spirit of the age. Would this policy affect the emperor's reputation? What were its likely effects in the general population?

Changing Attitudes Toward the Celibacy of Bishops

Note: The *Didascalia Apostolum*, or *Teachings of the Apostles*, was probably written by a bishop in Syria in the third century. The text suggests that the author was familiar with Jewish customs as well as with earlier Christian writings and the practice of medicine. Later, this book influenced church fathers and founders of monastic orders.

4. According to the two documents in the text, why should leaders of the Christian church possess a balance of worldly and spiritual qualities? Isn't good moral character enough? Why must the bishop be old ("not less than fifty years of age") and married once, at least?

5. Early Christians held mixed views on marriage. Some believed that Jesus would return in their lifetimes; if the world was coming to an end, they saw no need for marriage on earth or in heaven. The New Testament reports that Jesus attended a wedding and performed his first miracle, changing water into wine there, but Jesus and Paul also praised celibacy. Paul saw marriage as a moral compromise for weak individuals who could not remain celibate: "It is better to marry than to burn with lust." What is the *Didascalia*'s view of marriage?

6. Pope Damasus I (366–384) goes beyond Paul's reluctant tolerance of marriage to explicit condemnation of it, particularly for the clergy. He believes that marriage is inherently unclean because it involves sex, and "intercourse is defilement." Damasus is most upset over the idea of "carnal activity" among priests. Does the Christian faith require an absolute state of purity? Does the power of sacraments depend on the moral qualities of the priests who administer them?

Romanized Barbarians and Barbarianized Romans

7. What is the topic of the letter from Sidonius Apollinaris to Arbogastes?

8. Sidonius spent so much time on flattery, style, and witticisms that it is unclear whether he has anything significant to say. Consider these excerpts: "you are intimate with the barbarians but are innocent of barbarisms"; "Roman speech, if it still exists anywhere, has survived in you"; "the educated are no less superior to the unlettered than men are to beasts." Why would people write such polite but empty letters, and enjoy receiving them? Was the letter a form of aristocratic entertainment?

9. In his letter to Syagrius, Sidonius says that he is amazed that Syagrius has "quickly acquired a knowledge of the German tongue." He remembers that Syagrius had "a good schooling in liberal studies." How does that help Syagrius in his official duties? Why is it amusing to Sidonius that barbarians fear to make mistakes in their own language when they appear before Syagrius? Why does Sidonius advise him to continue reading and to maintain his knowledge of both Latin and German?

SAMPLE LECTURE 6: THE CHRISTIANIZATION OF THE ROMAN WORLD

Lecture Objectives

1. To suggest several reasons why the Roman world was eventually Christianized

2. To explain why the church fathers needed to understand the classical tradition of thought

3. To show that the history and development of the early church was inextricably connected to the Roman world in which it appeared

EARLY CHRISTIANITY AND THE ROMANS

Christian values stood directly opposed to the values of classical thought. The Greco-Roman tradition taught mankind to seek the good life in the present world, and for the Romans, that meant the empire. Christianity taught that earthly existence was merely a preparation for life after death. Life on earth was temporary, a stopping-off point before the journey into eternal life. The visible world was a world of exile; we are prisoners in Plato's Cave. Christianity first appeared in the Roman world as yet another mystery cult. For many mystery cults, salvation was to come from a person's association, through a mystical rite, with a hero who had conquered death. Jesus was one such hero. He claimed the faith of his followers because he had risen from the dead. Unlike other mystery cults, however, salvation for the Christian required more than rituals, mysteries, and sacraments. It required a moral life as well. Jesus was also an historical figure—he was a real man, not some mythical hero. We have little written evidence of the life and mission of Jesus apart from the Gospels, which were written by Christians who often shared information and wrote decades after Jesus' life. There are also no "original" manuscripts of the Gospels, only translated copies. There is virtually no mention of Jesus in Jewish or Roman documents, except for disputed passages in the writings of Flavius Josephus, a Hellenistic Jew who helped the Romans put down revolt.

From about 100 to 337, the church in the Roman Empire remained an illegal and persecuted sect. Still, the church succeeded in adding to its numbers. By the early fourth century, the Christian faith had penetrated much of the Mediterranean: it was the largest single religion within the empire. The reasons for this growth are diverse:

- Jewish communities were scattered throughout the empire.
- Christians moving from community to community could preach in Jewish synagogues.
- Christians also inherited the Old Testament of the Jews (written in Hebrew).
- By 300, the New Testament (written in Greek) was also complete.

- Christianity also held out the promise of man's ultimate salvation, that the meek shall inherit the earth.

Christian and Jew alike, however, were persecuted for their failure to follow the Roman civil religion. This religion asked for public loyalty to the state, to the genius of Rome, and to the traditional pantheon of Roman gods and goddesses. Christian and Jew refused to make this concession and so they became the objects of hatred and contempt among the pagan population. The number of persecutions was relatively small, but even the death of one person had wide significance, for this person became a martyr. This was an unintended consequence of Roman persecution. The martyrs became important because they had died holding true to their faith. The fact that many of them never cried out as they were about to die a horrible death must have impressed many in the audience. Their god must be a powerful one—their faith must be one without parallel. And so, the martyrs stood as supreme symbols of faith and integrity. In the historical context of mystery religions and paganism, early Christians stand out in their refusal to give homage to the emperors. Imperial test ceremonies had already been used by Pliny and, with wider persecution after 200, many Christians went into hiding or denial. Not everyone wanted martyrdom: some bribed officials to get false certificates stating that they had performed the test ceremony. The problem of wayward believers required strong church discipline. The Roman lawyer and bishop Cyprian of Carthage (c. 250) thought that rejoining the church after persecution had ended should not be easy for them.

CONSTANTINE I

The conversion of Constantine in the early fourth century was a political and psychological event. He tried to bring the Christian church into government affairs at Constantinople. This was a typically Roman notion: don't dominate, accommodate. By the 330s, for instance, Constantine extended complete freedom of worship to all Christians, he returned confiscated property, and he allowed the church to own property without paying taxes. He presided over the Council of Nicea in 325, received baptism on his deathbed in 337, and passed the Christian faith on to his successors. But even Constantine hedged his bets and supported pagan temples. His nephew, Julian "the Apostate," who was educated at Athens, attempted to reverse the course during his brief reign from 360–363, but he died fighting the Persians, and his pro-pagan edicts were revoked. Although Constantine made Christianity the favored religion of the Empire, it did not become an established or formal religion until 391, when emperor Theodosius (c. 346–395) outlawed heresy and closed all Roman pagan temples.

THEOLOGY

Christian intellectuals, or theologians, within the Roman Empire now quickly embarked on elaborating a systematic theology. In other words, they had to create a body of beliefs that all Christians would accept. They also developed a systematic government within the church. They believed themselves to be, as had the Jews before them, a community of people united by faith and discipline. This sense of unity became the foundation for two things: (1) a constitution of the church, which set down laws and determined authority; and (2) dogma—that is a collection of fixed opinions based on the authority of the church.

HERESIES

However, there were those people who developed their own sects within the church. The various heresies that appeared in the first three or four centuries after the birth of Christianity forced the church to define its theology even more rigidly. In a sense, dissent within the church led not to its dissolution, but to further strength and authority. In fact, Christianity would have become something quite different without heresies. As St. Paul said, "there must also be heresies." There were many heresies within the early church. Some heretics, such as the Gnostics, believed that:

- Mastery of special knowledge would assure man of salvation.
- Jesus was a real man for whom redeeming powers had come from above.
- Jesus was neither divine nor the son of God.
- There are two gods: one is knowable, the other is not.
- The universe is a prison—we are trapped inside our physical bodies.
- The only salvation is *gnosis* (inner, divine illumination).

There were Gnostic schools, sects, writings, teachers, myths, and churches. In general the Gnostic felt a homesickness for a lost paradise, knowable only through special knowledge. The significance of such heretical doctrines—and the Gnostics were only one among dozens of heretical sects—was that their appearance served to strengthen the church. The church was also strengthened when it defined its canon of sacred writings: the Old and New Testaments. The church also declared that the age of divine inspiration had come to an end, in order to quiet the claims of an ever-growing number of prophets.

GOVERNMENT

The most significant development was that of a formal government within the church. Bishops became church leaders and had authority over priests, who in turn presided over faithful followers. This political structure gave the Christians a stable form of government that no other mystery religion had ever enjoyed. Church government even rivaled that of the Roman state, at least until Christianity became the favored religion under Constantine. The number of bishops in the early church was never large, so bishops had authority over large areas of territory. And there were some cities, such as Rome and Alexandria, that claimed superior authority over all others. Eventually, the bishop of Rome became the head of the church and took the title "papa" (or "father") and would eventually call himself pope. By 300, then, the church had assumed all the characteristics that would be preserved down through the Middle Ages: a form of government, a theology, sacred books, rituals, martyrs, saints, and the faith of its believers.

THE CHURCH FATHERS

Throughout the fourth and fifth centuries, Christian thinkers were constantly trying to systematize theology. To do so, they were forced to use the learning and literature of the Greco-Roman tradition. They thought this tradition was full of lies and indecencies. What they learned or borrowed from classical culture were actually techniques. The first was the art of exegesis, a form of criticism in which an author undertook a line by line critique and interpretation of a written work. Exegetical studies became grand commentaries on the books of the Old and New Testaments. The second technique was the art of rhetoric—that is, the art of style, presentation, and composition. The significance of this cannot be overlooked, for it was through the church fathers that many of the texts of Greece and Rome were passed forward from generation to generation. In this way, the Judeo-Christian tradition became mixed with the Greco-Roman tradition. These texts—Plato, Zeno, Aristotle, Horace, Cicero, Homer, Virgil, and others—were preserved, copied, and passed on because the church fathers believed they would be useful in Christian theology as well as in Christian education.

The church fathers brought Christianity to all of educated Europe. This was accomplished because the Old Testament had been translated from Hebrew to Greek and the New Testament was written in Greek as well. These two texts existed prior to the church fathers of the fourth and fifth centuries, but their commentaries on these texts were of equal importance because they allowed Christianity to reach even more people. Using the language and techniques of Greek philosophy, Christian intellectuals changed Christianity from a simple ethical creed into a theoretical system. From this "Hellenization of Christianity," theology was born. Christ was depicted as the divine *Logos* (reason) in human form. Roman Stoicism was incorporated into the belief that all are equal and united in Christ.

ST. JEROME AND ST. AUGUSTINE

Christian theology became even more popular when the church father, St. Jerome (c. 342–420) translated the Old and New Testaments into Latin. Throughout his life, he remained an admirer of Cicero, Virgil, and Lucretius, and he defended the study of Latin literature by Christians. He lived for a while as a hermit in the desert near Antioch. He then visited Palestine and studied the Scriptures in Constantinople. Eventually, he became secretary to Pope Damasus and an advisor to a group of men and women drawn to the ascetic life. He later left Rome and established a monastery near Bethlehem. He wrote lives of the saints and promoted the spread of monasticism. But his Latin version of the Bible—known as the Vulgate or common version—was a major achievement, for Jerome's version of the Bible became the standard version down to the Protestant Reformation.

The most important of all church fathers was Augustine of Hippo, better known as St. Augustine (354–430). His father was a pagan; his mother, a Christian. Educated at Carthage in North Africa, he very quickly yielded to earthly temptation when he took a concubine; together, they had a son. It was at this time that Augustine was attracted to the heretical teachings of Mani (216–276), who believed that one God could not be responsible for both good and evil. In 387 and under the influence of men like St. Jerome, as well as his mother, he cast off his Manicheanism and became a Christian. In 399, Augustine was elected bishop of Hippo, one of the intellectual centers of North Africa. Augustine spent more than thirty years combating heresy and writing commentaries and interpretations of Christian theology. He wrote the first autobiography in western history, *The Confessions*. His most important work is *On the City of God*, a massive book written between 413 and 426.

City of God was written to show that it was God's plan that Rome would fall and that Christianity was the salvation of mankind. In other words, history had direction and meaning—the unfolding of God's grand plan. In *City of God*, Augustine brings together the sacred history of the Jewish people, the pagan history of the Greeks and Romans, and the Christian expectation of future salvation. He quotes Herodotus, Plato, Cicero, Seneca, Tacitus, Aristotle, and the Old and New Testaments, as well as the interpretations and commentaries of the church fathers. He taught that the City of Man (Rome) was evil and destined to decline and fall. Augustine saw this with his own eyes. In other words, he was not looking back into history, he was looking at his own experience. The City of God was invisible—it was otherworldly. The chosen—the true Christian—should recognize that earthly existence was little more than an illusion. There was a higher reality beyond Rome. It was only in the City of God that the chosen would find their final resting place. What Augustine accomplished was nothing less than a synthesis of Christianity and classical humanism. Of course, Augustine did not believe that Christ, by his death, had opened the door to heaven for every soul. Most of humanity remained condemned to eternal punishment—only a handful of souls had the gift of faith and the promise of heaven. People could not overcome their sins—moral and spiritual regeneration came only from God's grace, and it was God who determined who would be saved or damned. Although Augustine's influence was impressive, the church rejected his idea of predestination. Instead, the church emphasized that Christ had made possible the salva-tion of all. With Augustine, the human-centered outlook of classical humanism gave way to a God-centered world view.

EARLY MONASTICISM

Equally effective in the general diffusion of Christian ideas and Christianity in general was the monastic movement. Those Christians who joined monasteries were attempting to live a life of ascetic ideals. By denying oneself earthly or material pleasure, the monks became the heroes of Christian civilization because they were the visible examples of man's faith in God. The man who went off by himself to live and worship as a hermit found that he could not do it alone. What was needed was a community of worshipers, and so by the fifth century the idea of the monastery gained a powerful appeal in the West. In Ireland, entire clans and tribes adopted the monastic life. Irish monks traveled throughout the Continent, founding monasteries along the way. Of monasticism in general, however, it was St. Benedict (c. 480–c. 543) of Italy who brought order to the monastic movement.

Benedict drew up a rule for the monastic communities that was based on needs and functions. The constitution he developed endowed the abbot with full authority—he was elected for life and could not be replaced. Part of the Benedictine Rule was that all monks were to say prayers at regular intervals of the day and night. All monks were also required to labor—this gave labor the dignity the Romans had denied. Benedict established twelve small monastic communities during his lifetime, the most important located at Monte Cassino, near Naples. The monks influenced nearly every aspect of early medieval life. They managed large estates and set examples for good farming practice. They were also the most literate and learned people. They organized *scriptoria*, or writing offices, where they copied secular and religious manuscripts. European kings and princes recruited monks as officials, and nearly all administrative records of the period were written by monastic scribes. The monasteries were important because their communal organization allowed the monks to cope with the problems of the age while at the same time making them heroes of Christian civilization. They escaped from the disorder of their times, but not individually. Rather, These devout monks gathered together at monastic communities, such as Monte Cassino. Some would work in the fields, others in the bakeries, and still others would tend to the wine presses. But the ascetic temperament taught the monks to save and invest in the future. By denying themselves luxuries and by not consuming immediately all that they produced, the monks had considerable economic success.

Saving for the future made sense to the Benedictine monk. During the seventh and eighth centuries, the Celtic (Irish) and Benedictine monasteries played a vital role in the Christianization of the former Roman Empire. By the early ninth century, monasticism had ceased to be a vocation for the few. Instead, it became a highly influential way of life and was intertwined with large and wealthy houses that were involved in the daily life of the early medieval countryside. At the same time, the purpose of the monastic order was transformed. Their role essentially became a clerical one and they became a professional class of clerics who administered the welfare of society. To become a monk by the ninth century required professional competence and commitment—apparently gone was personal sanctity. The monastic ranks became filled not with those people interested in personal perfection, but with the children of aristocratic patrons, who believed they and their families would be closer to God if they built and maintained monasteries on their property. So the monks began to conceive of themselves as the "soldiers of Christ," striving to preserve the well-being of the clergy and faithful, the king, and his kingdom. By the eleventh and twelfth centuries, a series of great monastic reforms swept across Europe and new monastic orders, such as the Franciscans and Dominicans, did much to restore the original vigor and vitality of the early monastic movement. Monasticism was vital to the spread of Christianity in the early Middle Ages. But it was characteristic of these orders to fail to maintain their vitality and purpose. This was in large part due to the injection of aristocratic ideals.

SUGGESTED FEATURE FILMS

Agostino d'Ippona/Augustine of Hippo (subtitled). 121 min. Color. 1972. EMC. Roberto Rossellini's film about the life of St. Augustine of Hippo.

Barabbas. 134 min. Color. 1962. Columbia Pictures. Epic account of the thief Barabbas, who was spared crucifixion when the Jews chose Christ in his place.

Ben Hur. 217 min. Color. 1959. MGM. William Wyler's production of Lew Wallace's novel. Featuring Charlton Heston, along with three hundred sets, 365 speaking parts, and seventy-eight horses. Winner of eleven Academy Awards.

Constantino Il Grande/Constantine the Great (dubbed). 120 min. Color. 1961. Embassy Pictures Corporation. Film about Constantine's conversion and the battle at the Milvian Bridge.

The Fall of the Roman Empire. 188 min. Color. 1964. Paramount Pictures. Epic film of Rome in the days of Marcus Aurelius and Commodus.

The Gospel According to St. Matthew. 142 min. B/W. 1964. Acro/Lux. Directed by Italian novelist and poet Pier Paolo Pasolini and acted by nonprofessionals, with dialogue from the Gospel of Matthew.

Jesus of Nazareth. 300 min. Color. 1977. Independent Television Corp. A beautiful film, with Olivia Hussey as the Virgin Mary.

Life of Brian. 94 min. Color. 1979. Warner Brothers. Monty Python's satire of Biblical films and religious intolerance focuses on Brian, a Jew in Roman-occupied Judea. Brian joins an anti-Roman political organization, is mistaken for a prophet, and becomes a reluctant messiah.

The Robe. 135 min. Color. 1953. 20th Century Fox. Film about a Roman centurion who presides over Christ's crucifixion.

St. Patrick: The Irish Legend. 100 min. Color. 2001. Fox Family Channel. TV movie that outlines the life of St. Patrick.

SUGGESTED CLASSROOM FILMS

African Ascetics and Celtic Monks: Christianity in the Fifth and Sixth Centuries. 47 min. Color. 1999. Films for the Humanities and Sciences. Introduces St. Augustine and *The City of God* and.then tracks the spread of Christianity to Ireland. Part of the *Two Thousand Years: The History of Christianity* series.

Augustine. 53 min. Color. 1974. BBC/Time-Life Films. Malcolm Muggeridge narrates Augustine's life and achievements.

The Beginnings of Christianity. 25 min. Color. 1991. Insight Media. Examines the lives of Jesus and Paul and looks at the emergence of Christianity out of first-century Judaism.

The Birth of a New Religion: Christianity in the First and Second Centuries. 47 min. Color. 1999. Films for the Humanities and Sciences. Presents the life of Jesus against the backdrop of first-century Judea, inhabited by the Jews and occupied by the forces of the Roman Empire. Part of the *Two Thousand Years: The History of Christianity* series.

The Christian Empire. 45 min. Color. 1978. Contemporary Films. Traces the Christian Empire from Rome to Constantinople to Russia.

Christianity: The First Thousand Years, Part I—The Founding of a Faith. 50 min. Color. 1998. A&E Home Video. Ancient texts and modern scholars chronicle the first centuries of Christianity. Follows St. Paul, one of the most important early shapers of Christian belief. Shows how James, head of another branch of early Christianity, may have been related to Jesus.

Christianity: The First Thousand Years, Part II—Church and Empire. 50 min. Color. 1998. A&E Home Video. Looks at the scholarly controversy surrounding the conversion of Constantine, then examines the birth of the monastic movement and the shaping of the New Testament.

The Christians: A Peculiar People. (27 B.C.E.–300 C.E.). 39 min. Color. 1979. McGraw-Hill. This survey from the ministry of Jesus to the establishment of Christianity as a legal religion also includes a look at mystery religions.

The City of God. 52 min. Color. 1989. Films for the Humanities and Sciences. Discusses St. Augustine of Hippo as a symbol of medieval man, and his conception of the city of God is contrasted with the terrors of the City of Man.

Early Christianity and the Rise of the Church. 2 parts, 30 min. each. Color. 1989. Insight Media. Covers early history and beliefs.

The End of the Ancient World. 26 min. Color. 1989. Insight Media. Covers the period from 100 to 600 C.E.

The Rise of Rome, Fall of Rome. 4 parts, 30 min. each. Color. 1989. Insight Media. Traces the rise, decline, and fall of the Roman Empire.

The Romans: Life, Laughter, and Laws. 22 min. Color. 1971. Learning Corporation of America. Uses excerpts from Roman satire.

Part III: The Middle Ages

IDEAS FOR USING THE WESTERN CIVILIZATIONS DIGITAL HISTORY CENTER

The Map Exercises and Digital History Features at *www.wwnorton.com/wciv* focus attention on developments outside Europe in Byzantine and Islamic civilizations and then move to highlight the development of medieval trade and the renaissance of the twelfth century.

- Map Exercise 4: The Early Middle Ages (Chapter 7)
- Map Exercise 5: The Middle Ages, c. 1000–1300 (Chapters 8–9)
- Digital History Feature 4: The Marketplace (Chapters 7–9)
- Digital History Feature 6: Spices and the Spice Trade (Chapters 7–8)

Use Map Exercise 4 to illustrate developments outside Europe following the collapse of the Roman Empire. This exercise could be used to explain the rise and success of the Byzantine and Islamic worlds at the same time that Charlemagne and his successors were trying to forge a new European identity. Digital History Feature 4, "The Marketplace," allows students to gain an understanding of why the marketplace in the early medieval world was a force for trade with cultures outside Europe, as well as a forum for social discourse. You could also think in terms of a more long-term theme and connect the medieval marketplace with the rise of the spice trade discussed in Digital History Feature 6, "Spices and the Spice Trade." This would show students that trade routes are both local and global, a pattern that becomes more apparent toward the end of the medieval period. Map Exercise 5 contains a useful set of exercises that emphasize the routes of European crusaders and the period of European recovery associated with the renaissance of the twelfth century.

CHAPTER 7

Rome's Three Heirs: The Byzantine, Islamic, and Early Medieval Worlds

OUTLINE

I. Introduction
    A. The end of Late Antiquity
    B. Byzantium—Greek
        1. Greek-speaking
        2. Combined Roman imperial and bureaucratic traditions with intense pursuit of Christian faith
    C. Islam—Arabic
        1. The Roman ideal of expansion and cultural and religious assimilation
        2. Hellenistic philosophical and scientific interests
        3. Persian literary and artistic culture
    D. Western Europe—Latin
        1. Latin-speaking
        2. Germanic, Celtic, and Latin cultural influences
        3. Roman ideals of empire
II. The Byzantine Empire
    A. A successor to the Roman state
    B. Justinian and Heraclius
    C. Threats and challenges
        1. The Persians
            a. Theft of the relic of the original cross
            b. Heraclius routs the Persians (627)
        2. Islam
            a. By 650, Arabs had taken back most of the Byzantine territory that was formerly Persian
            b. Jerusalem in the hands of the Muslims
            c. Constantinople threatened (677)
            d. Pope Leo the Isaurian—defeats Arabs on land and at sea (717)
        3. Seljuk Turks
            a. Battle of Manzikert (1071)
            b. The fall of Byzantine civilization (1453)
    C. Sources of stability
        1. Why did Constantinople survive?
        2. Internal political history, the story of violence and palace revolts
        3. Efficient bureaucratic practices
            a. Education
            b. Religion
            c. Economic activity
            d. Entertainment
            e. The army and navy
            f . Sound economic base
            g. Role of Constantinople as trade emporium
            h. Stable gold and silver coinage
            i. Agriculture
    D. Byzantine religion
        1. Religious orthodoxy
        2. Emperors involved in intense religious debates
        3. The Iconoclastic Controversy
            a. The Iconoclasts prohibited the worship of icons—"graven images"
            b. Others argued that icons served as windows through which a glimpse of heaven might be granted
            c. Political and financial considerations
            d. The monasteries rallied behind the cause of images

e. Resolved in the ninth century—a return to the worship of icons

f. Consequences

    i. Much religious art destroyed as a result of the Controversy

    ii. Opened a serious breach between East and West

    iii. Led to renewed emphasis on Orthodox faith as key to political unity

    iv. Fear of heresy inhibited speculation

E. Byzantine culture

1. Preserved ancient Greek heritage

2. The role of Homer: a model, textbook, and guide to morality

3. Greek thought

    a. Revered Plato and Thucydides

    b. Aristotle regarded with less interest

    c. Neglected Greek scientific and mathematical tradition

    d. Preservation rather than innovation the hallmark of Byzantine classicism

4. Education extended to both men and women

    a. Princess Anna Comnena (1083–1148)

5. Art and architecture

    a. Church of Santa Sophia (Holy Wisdom)

        i. Symbol for the inward and spiritual character of Christianity

        ii. Exterior was plain, interior filled with mosaics, gold leaf, marble columns

        iii. Architectural uniqueness

F. Byzantium and the Western Christian world

1. Tense relations between East and West

2. Growing religious tensions

3. Sack of Constantinople by crusading armies (1204)

4. Legacy to the West

    a. Bulwark against Islam

    b. Preserved an independent and Christian West

    c. Preservation of classical literature

    d. Art and architecture

III. The Growth of Islam

A. The rise of Islam

1. Born in the desert of Arabia

2. Mecca and the Kabah (pilgrimage shrine)

    a. Quraish tribe—controlled the Kabah and the economic life of Mecca

3. Muhammad (c. 570–632)

    a. Early life

        i. Born at Mecca (Quraish family)

        ii. Orphaned early

        iii. Married the widow of a rich trader

    b. Religious experience (610)

        i. There is no god but Allah

        ii. Becomes an uncompromising monotheist

        iii. Called to be "the Prophet"

    c. Ignored by the Quraish of Mecca

    d. Leaves Mecca for Yathrib (Medina)—the Hijrah/Hegira (622)

        i. Organizes a religious community

        ii. Raids on Quraish caravans

    e. Enters Mecca (630)

B. The Religious teachings of Islam

1. Islam means "submission"

2. Allah—the Creator God Almighty

3. Muhammad as the last and greatest prophet

4. Men and women must surrender themselves to Allah

5. Practical steps for salvation and the Qur'an

6. Islam, Christianity, and Judaism

    a. Jesus was a prophet but was not the son of God

    b. Strict monotheism

    c. Old and New Testaments as divinely inspired

    d. Islam as a way of life—no sacraments or clergy

C. The Islamic conquests

1. Muhammad's death

2. Succeeded by his father-in-law, Abu-Bakr

    a. The *caliph* (deputy of the Prophet)

    b. Military campaign against those who followed Muhammad but would not follow Abu-Bakr

3. Umar

    a. Syria, Antioch, Damascus, and Jerusalem fall (636)

    b. Egypt falls (646)

    c. Persia subdued (651)

    d. Visogothic Spain (711)

4. Explanations

    a. Search for territory and booty

    b. Weakness of their neighbors

    c. Did not demand conversions

    d. Muslims preferable to old rulers

D. The Shiite-Sunni schism
   1. Shiites—followers of Ali (Muhammad's son-in-law)
   2. Sunnites—committed to the customs of the caliphate
E. Umayyads and Abbasids
   1. Westward-looking Umayyads
      a. Capital at Damascus
      b. A Byzantine successor state?
      c. Goal was to conquer Constantinople
   2. Eastward-looking Abbasids
      a. Rule stressed Persian elements rather than Byzantine
      b. New capital at Baghdad
      c. *The Arabian Nights*
      d. Harun al-Rashid (786–809)
      e. Ruled in Spain
      f. Library at Cordoba—400,000 volumes

IV. The Changing Islamic World
  A. Power declined (ninth and tenth centuries)
   1. Problems
      a. Impoverishment of economic base
      b. Tax revenues declined
      c. Unable to support civil service or mercenary army
   2. Major developments
      a. Growth of regionalism
      b. Religious division between Sunnis and Shiites, and among Shiites
      c. Egypt conquered by Shiite Fatimids (969)
   3. Umayyad Spain succumbs to Christian pressure by the ninth and tenth centuries
   4. Christian conquest of Spain complete by the mid-thirteenth century
   5. Internal ethnic tensions grew more divisive
  B. Muslim society and culture, 900–1250
   1. Cosmopolitan and dynamic society
   2. Geographic and social mobility
   3. At Baghdad and Cordoba, careers were open to those with talent
   4. Treatment of women
      a. Preserving male "honor"
      b. The Qur'an allowed a man four wives
      c. The harem
   5. Learned men
      a. *Ulama*—learned men who studied religion and religious law
      b. *Sufis*—religious mystics, stressed contemplation and ecstasy
  C. Muslim philosophy, science, and medicine
   1. The Greek philosophical tradition
   2. Arabic translations
   3. Reconciling Aristotelianism and Neoplatonism
   4. Reconciling Greek thought with Islamic theology
   5. Avicenna (980–1037)
   6. Al-Farabi (d. 950) and Al-Ghazzali (1058–1111)
      a. Difficulties in reconciling Aristotle, Neoplatonism, and Muslim theology
   7. Averroës (1126–1198)—"the Commentator"
      a. Turned his back on the mysticism of Avicenna and al-Ghazzali
      b. Subordinated theology to philosophy
   8. Science
      a. Astrology as applied science
      b. Astronomy
   9. Medicine
      a. Avicenna's Canon of Medicine
      b. Learned value of cauterization
      c. Diagnosed cancer of the stomach
      d. Organized and built hospitals
   10. Optics
   11. Alchemy and chemistry
   12. Developed decimal arithmetic based on place values
  D. Literature and art
   1. Umar Khayyam, the *Rubiyat* (c.1050–c.1123)
   2. Uninhibited lyric poetry
   3. Moses Maimonides (1135–1204), Misheh Torah
   4. Art
      a. Highly eclectic
      b. Byzantine and Persian influence
      c. Architectural elements—dome, column, and arch
      d. General prejudice against portraying human form in art
  E. Trade and industry
   1. Major trade routes
   2. Masters of the caravan routes
   3. Sea routes lost to the West (tenth and eleventh centuries)
   4. Important industries
      a. Baghdad: glassware, jewelry, pottery, silks
      b. Morocco and Spain: leather-working
      c. Toledo: swords
   5. Paper—brought about a revolution in record-keeping
  F. The impact of early Islamic civilization on Europe
   1. Economics

2. Technology
3. New vocabulary: traffic, alcohol, muslin, orange, lemon, sugar, musk
4. Greek philosophical and scientific knowledge
5. Preservation and interpretation of the works of Aristotle

V. Western Christian Civilization in the Early Middle Ages
  A. A transitional period
  B. Gregory of Tours (538–c.594)
  C. New attitudes
    1. A break with the Roman past
    2. Rather than continuation, a reconstruction
  D. Economic disintegration and political instability
    1. Causes
      a. Justinian's effort to reconquer the West
      b. Excessive Byzantine taxation of agricultural lands
      c. Islamic piracy
    2. Western Europe
      a. Urban life declined
      b. Land passed out of cultivation
      c. Too costly to maintain slaves
      d. Coinage system broke down
      e. Two-tier economy
        i. Gold and silver among the wealthy
        ii. The peasantry relied on barter
    3. Political instability
      a. Incessant wars between kings and lords
      b. Inability to regulate royal succession
      c. Rivalries
  E. Merovingian Gaul
    1. Survival of late Roman local administration
    2. Growth of monasteries
    3. Massive distribution of wealth
    4. Cultivating the rich, heavy soils of northern France
    5. Population growth
  F. Monasticism and conversion
    1. Rapid increase in new monastic houses (especially seventh century)
    2. Royal ties with monasteries
    3. Located in rural areas—Christianizing the countryside
    4. Women and the monastic life
    5. Conversion and missionary activity
      a. Pope Gregory I (c. 540–604)
      b. Roman Christianity brought to southeastern England

  G. The reign of Pope Gregory I
    1. Worked to prevent a breach with Constantinople
    2. Necessity of penance
    3. The concept of purgatory
    4. The Gregorian chant
    5. Asserted his authority over all Western bishops
    6. Encouraged the Benedictine rule in all monasteries

VI. The Rise of the Carolingians
  A. Pepin of Heristal and the "mayors of the palace" (d. 714)
  B. Charles "the Hammer" Martel (c. 688–741)
    1. The second founder (after Clovis) of the Frankish state
    2. The Battle of Tours (733/734)
    3. Developed alliances with English Benedictines in central Germany
  C. Pepin the Short (c. 715–768)
    1. Coronation
    2. Integration of the Frankish monarchy into the papal-Benedictine orbit
  D. The reign of Charlemagne (742–814, r. 768–814)
    1. United the Frankish Kingdom through armed expeditions
      a. Italy, Germany, and central Europe
      b. Forcing conversion to Christianity
    2. Counts and local administration
      a. The *comites* (followers)
      b. Administraion of justice
      c. Raising armies
      d. Courts, tolls, and taxation
      e. New coinage system
    3. New capital city at Aachen
  E. Christianity and kingship
    1. Leading a unified Christian society
    2. Kingship regarded as a divine office created by God to protect the church
    3. Religious reforms
      a. Appointed and deposed bishops
      b. Changed liturgy of Frankish church
      c. Reformed rules of worship
      d. Prohibited pagan observances
      e. The peasant tithe
    4. Spiritual responsibilities of kingship: the protector of the papacy
  F. The Carolingian renaissance
    1. The patron of poetry and learning
    2. The court as an intellectual center
    3. Classical learning
    4. Alcuin of York (c. 735–804)
      a. Correcting and copying texts
      b. Carolingian miniscule

G. Charlemagne and the revival of the western
  Roman Empire
  1. Charlemagne's coronation (Christmas
     Day, 800)
H. The collapse of the Carolingian empire
  1. Louis the Pious (d. 843)—the empire
     disintegrates
  2. Charles the Bald, Louis the German,
     and Lothair
  3. Civil wars
I. The legacy of the Carolingians
  1. The European political entity
  2. England become unified
     a. Alfred the Great (871–899)
     b. Reorganized the army, codified laws
     c. Cultural regeneration pattered on
        the Carolingian example
  3. The Saxon kings of Germany
     a. The Carolingian example
     b. Royal power based on conquest
        rather than trade and administration
     c. Otto I defeats Hungarians using
        Charlemagne's lance (955)
     d. Strengthening control of the church
  4. Catalunya
     a. Counts descended from
        Carolingian appointees
        continue to administer laws
  5. The growth of towns and cities
  6. Italian prosperity
  7. From Carolingians to Capetians
VII. Conclusion
  A. Western Europe and the East
  B. Urbanization
  C. Expanding borders
  D. Europe a society mobilized for war

GENERAL DISCUSSION QUESTIONS

1. Despite shifts in authority, ethnic composition, and
   religion from 400–600, Roman society in western
   Europe continued to exist. Discuss the features of
   Roman culture that were preserved and those that
   were lost.

2. Why did Byzantine emperors get involved in religious
   disputes? What were the consequences?

3. Who "saved" Europe from the Islamic forces that swept
   across the Near East, North Africa, the Mediterranean,
   and Central Asia in the seventh and eighth centuries?
   How was this done? What exactly was saved?

4. Can we see the Muslims as yet another group of foreign
   invaders of the Roman Empire, and their caliphates as

sub-Roman successor states? Compare and contrast
them with the northern European barbarians.

5. One great Islamic contribution to Western civilizations
   was the preservation of the literature, philosophy, medicine, and science of Greco-Roman antiquity. Why
   did the *faylasufs* (Islamic philosophers) keep, copy,
   study, and interpret these materials? How could they
   reconcile these pagan treasures with Islamic religion?

6. How did bishops and monasteries in the early Middle
   Ages acquire jurisdiction over nearby lands, villages,
   and towns? What did they do with their powers?

7. By what right did medieval European kings rule?
   How were they chosen? What problems arose in this
   system? How and why did the Franks succeed with a
   dynasty that lasted 250 years?

8. The monastery is sometimes seen as a retreat from
   worldly cares, but monks had economic, political,
   and social concerns. Besides offering regular worship
   services, what benefits did monasteries provide to
   surrounding communities?

9. How did Charlemagne build on the political base established by his father, Pepin? Does Charlemagne deserve
   to be called "the Great" or even "Saint"? (Your answer
   might have been different if you were a Saxon.)

10. Why did Charlemagne agree to be crowned emperor
    in Rome on Christmas Day, 800? Was that an astute
    political move on his part, or just an ornamental title?

11. How did the urban growth of the tenth and eleventh
    centuries affect Carolingian rulers? Did "city air"
    make the inhabitants free, or at least freer than the
    peasants?

12. The defense of their territories against foreign invaders
    was paramount in the minds of European rulers. They
    resisted Muslims and Byzantines, Norsemen and Vik-
    ings. But was this success worth the cost of militarizing
    Western European society?

DOCUMENT DISCUSSION QUESTIONS

Byzantine Classicism

1. The poetic prayer by an eleventh-century Byzantine
   scholar expresses a pious hope not only for Plato and
   Plutarch but also for the author, who wanted to hold
   onto both pagan classics and Christianity. From a
   Christian point of view, what problems arise from this
   position?

2. What would have to be changed in Plato's works (e.g.,
   The Republic) to make them acceptable to orthodox

Christians? Do the Platonic dialogues assist Christianity in any way? Would Christianity be something very different without Plato?

The Pact of Umar

3. Why did the Muslims tolerate other religions? If they believed all other religions were false, why didn't they stamp them out? Was early Christianity a religion of tolerance?

4. The Pact of Umar contains a long list of Christian promises to the ruler. What would have been the effect on the Christian community in the short or long term, if all these promises had been observed? Was it a good deal for them?

5. Although the natural tendency of minority religious communities may be toward extinction, Christians and Jews continued to exist in Muslim-dominated areas for centuries. Suggest practical reasons why this was so.

A Hebrew Poem in Praise of Wine, by Samuel the Nagid

6. Is this poem consistent with Jewish religious laws and traditions? Why or why not?

7. What does the career of Samuel the Nagid—poet, general, and lawyer—suggest about relations between Jewish and Muslim communities in medieval Spain?

Charlemagne on the Importance of Monks Studying Classical Literature

8. Compare the attitudes in this official letter by Charlemagne with the Byzantine prayer for Plato and Plutarch. According to his biographers, Charlemagne himself could barely read and could not write. Why did he think the study of pagan classics was necessary?

9. Charlemagne's letter suggests that good writing style is as important as content, and that bad style is an indication of "a more serious lack of wisdom." Do you agree or disagree? Should the teaching of good writing style be part of the Western Civilizations course?

10. According to Charlemagne's letter, before one can understand the Scriptures, solid grounding in classical literature is required. Problems in reading the "figures of speech, metaphors and the like" of the Scriptures could lead to grave errors in understanding. What did this mean in Charlemagne's time?

SAMPLE LECTURE 7: BYZANTINE, ISLAMIC, AND EARLY MEDIEVAL CIVILIZATION

Lecture Objectives

1. To show that Byzantine and Islamic civilizations flourished while the West was recovering from the fall of Rome

2. To demonstrate the importance of religion to the varied worlds of Late Antiquity

3. To suggest that with Charlemagne, the idea of Europe was born

BYZANTIUM

The period of history from roughly 500 to 1000 is called the early Middle Ages. It is oftentimes called Late Antiquity as well. It is important to understand that during the period of the early Middle Ages, Europe was born. This is a period of time in which a distinctive western European culture began to emerge. Whether we look to geography, government, religion, culture, or language, western Europe became a land distinct from both the Byzantine world and the Muslim world. The crucial feature of the early Middle Ages in the West was a unique blending of three distinct traditions: the Greco-Roman tradition, the Judeo-Christian tradition, and Germanic custom. As western Europe fell to the Germanic invasions, imperial power shifted to the Byzantine Empire. It was Constantine the Great who began the rebuilding of Byzantium in 324, renaming the city Constantinople and dedicating it in 330. Constantinople became the sole capital of the empire and remained so until the late eighth century.

JUSTINIAN

The greatest of all the Eastern emperors was Justinian (c. 482–565), who reigned for thirty-eight years between 527 and 565. Justinian was a reformer in the fashion of Augustus Caesar. It was Justinian's ambition to restore the empire of the East and West to all of its former glory. His greatest accomplishment toward this end was the revision and codification of Roman law. Justinian understood that a strong government could not exist without good laws. Although the Romans prided themselves on their written laws, several centuries of written laws had brought nothing but confusion. Justinian created a commission of sixteen men to bring order out of all the laws. These men worked for six years and studied more than two thousand texts. In 534, the commission produced the *Corpus Juris Civilis (Body of Civil Law)*, which became a standard legal work until the middle of the nineteenth century. As such, the *Corpus* is one of the most sophisticated legal systems ever produced and symbolized Justinian's efforts to create a reunited and well-governed empire. Justinian was clearly a man who was driven by his obsession. He was aided by his predecessors, who were able to fend off Germanic invasions, something the Western empire could not do until much later. Justinian was also aided by his wife, Theodora (c. 500–547), an actress and courtesan who was no less ambitious than her husband.

In 532, mob violence erupted in Constantinople. These riots were called the Nika Riots and grew from political unrest over the government's fiscal measures. Rival factions fought in the streets. Justinian wanted to leave the city during the riots, but two of his generals (Belisarius and Narses) and Theodora persuaded him to stay. Theodora took it upon herself to raise a personal army that eventually killed 35,000 people in a single day. In 533, Justinian sent his armies to North Africa to destroy the Vandal Kingdom. The same year his generals took Sicily and Rome. However, victory was only temporary. By 565, Roman Italy was invaded and overtaken by the Lombards. Back at Constantinople, Justinian tried to rebuild the city. He built aqueducts to supply the city with water and was responsible for the construction of at least twenty-five churches, the Hagia Sophia (Church of the Holy Wisdom) being the most well-known.

Religion as well as law served Justinian's efforts to centralize the imperial office. Since the fifth century, the patriarch of Constantinople had crowned emperors in Constantinople, a practice which reflected the close ties between secular and religious leaders. In 380, Christianity had been proclaimed the official religion of the eastern Empire. Orthodox Christianity was not, however, the only religion within the Empire with a significant number of followers. Others included:

- Arianism—the belief that Jesus was not of one substance with God
- Monophysitism—Jesus has one nature
- Iconoclasm—the attempt to abolish the use of icons and images in church services

At one time or another, each of these Christian heresies received imperial support. There were also a large number of Jews living in the Byzantine world. Under Roman law Jews had legal protection as long as they did not proselytize among Christians, build new synagogues, or attempt to enter public office. Whereas Justinian adopted a policy of voluntary Jewish conversion, the later emperors ordered all Jews to be baptized and granted tax breaks to those who voluntarily complied.

The Byzantine Empire's strength was in its more than 1500 cities. The largest city was Constantinople, the cultural crossroads of east and west, north and south. During the reign of Heraclius (610–641), the empire took a decidedly eastern, as opposed to Roman, direction. Heraclius spoke Greek, and his entire reign was preoccupied with resisting Persian and Islamic invasions. Islamic armies overran the empire after 632, directly attacking Constantinople for the first time in 677. Not until the reign of Leo III in the early eighth century were the Islamic armies defeated and most of Asia Minor retained by the Byzantines. Leo offended Western Christians when he forbade the use of images in Eastern churches and tried to enforce the ban in the West. This became a source of conflict to Western Christians, who had carefully nurtured the adoration of Jesus, Mary, and the saints in images and icons. The banning of images became a major expression of Eastern imperial involvement in church dogma and a practice that the Western church had always resisted. Throughout the period of the early Middle Ages, the Byzantine Empire provided an outstanding model of a civilized society and served as a protective barrier between western Europe and the Persian, Arab, and Turkish armies.

ISLAM

For centuries, Islam was both a threat and a source of new ideas to the Greek East and Latin West. Between the seventh and twelfth centuries, Islam became the center of a brilliant civilization and of a great scientific, philosophic, and artistic culture. Islam absorbed a great deal of Greek culture, which it managed to preserve for the Latin West. In the beginning the Muslims were both open and cautious. They borrowed and integrated elements of other cultures into their own. The new religion of Islam adopted elements of Christian, Jewish, and pagan religious beliefs and practices. The Muslims tolerated religious minorities within territories they had conquered, so long as these minorities recognized Islamic political rule, paid taxes, and did not proselytize among Muslims. Fundamental to Islam was its religion—this is true for the medieval West as well. The home of Islam is the Arabian Peninsula. The Peninsula is predominantly desert and the tribes who inhabited this area were nomadic. Politically, Islam was not a unified territory nor was there any centralized government.

MUHAMMAD

The great unifying agent in Islamic civilization was Muhammad (c. 570–632). Born at Mecca and raised by a family of modest means, Muhammad became an orphan at the age of six. Mecca was one of the most prosperous caravan cities but was still tied to the traditional social and religious life of the tribal world. Membership in the tribe was determined by blood descent. Each tribe worshiped its own gods in the form of objects from nature, but all Arabs worshiped one object in common: the Kaaba, a large black stone enshrined at Mecca. As a youth, Muhammad worked as a merchant's assistant and traveled the major trade routes. When he was twenty-five, he married the widow of a wealthy merchant and became a man of means. He also became a kind of social activist, critical of Meccan materialism, paganism, and the unjust treatment of the poor and needy. Muhammad worked hard at his career but he was plagued by doubts. He left

Mecca for the isolation of the desert, and in 610 he received his first revelation and began to preach. He believed his revelations came directly from God, who spoke to him through the angel Gabriel. These revelations grew into the Qur'an which his followers compiled between 650 and 651.

The basic message Muhammad received was a summons to all Arabs to submit to God's will. Islam means "submission to the will of God." There was little that was new in Muhammad's message. It had been uttered by a long line of Jewish prophets going back to Noah but now ending with Muhammad, the last of God's chosen prophets. The Qur'an also recognized Jesus Christ as a prophet but did not view him as God's equal and eternal son. Like Judaism, Islam was a monotheistic and theocratic religion, not a Trinitarian one like Christianity. The basic beliefs of Muhammad's religion are:

- God is good and omnipotent.
- God will judge all men on the last day.
- Men should thank God for making the world as it is.
- God expects men to be generous with their wealth.
- Muhammad was a prophet sent by God to teach men and warn them of the last judgment.

Many of these beliefs are similar to those of the Judeo-Christian tradition. Muhammad's religion grew as a result of the social and economic conditions of Mecca itself. For Muhammad, there were also five obligations which were essential to his faith:

- The profession of faith—there is no God but Allah and Muhammad was the last prophet
- Prayers had to be uttered five times daily
- The giving of alms, or charity
- Fasting
- The pilgrimage to Mecca

Muhammad believed that God had chosen him to be the last prophet. But despite the faith of his followers, Muhammad met with disappointment as he preached his religion at Mecca. Jews and Christians failed to convert. His faith was rejected by the authorities at Mecca who tried to quiet Muhammad, and so he left for the northern city of Medina in the year 622. The journey to Medina—the *hegira* (the breaking of former ties)—became the true foundation of the Islamic faith. The hegira also marks the beginning of the Islamic calendar. At Medina, Muhammad created an Islamic community. After settling in Medina, his followers began to attack the caravans on their way to and from Mecca. By 624 his army was powerful enough to conquer Mecca and make it the center of the new religion. Muhammad died in 632. He never claimed to be of divine origin, yet his followers saw no reason to separate religious and political authority. Muhammad never named a successor, and so after his death, some of his followers selected Abu Bakr, a wealthy merchant and Muhammad's father-in-law, as *caliph*, or temporal leader.

In the early seventh century, Muhammad took up the Arab custom of making raids against their enemies. The Qur'an called these raids the *jihad* (striving in the way of the Lord). The Byzantines and Persians were the first to feel the pressure of Arab raids. Beginning in 636, the Muslims defeated the Byzantine army, Syria, the entire Persian empire, Egypt, North Africa, and Spain. In 732, a Muslim army was defeated at the Battle of Tours, and Muslim expansion in Europe came to an abrupt halt. In the eight and ninth centuries Islamic civilization entered a golden age as Arabic, Byzantine, Persian, and Indian cultural traditions were integrated. Thanks to Muslim scholars, ancient Greek learning, acquired from their contact with Byzantine scholars, was kept alive and was eventually transferred to the West in the twelfth century and after. Muslim scholars preserved the heritage of Greek science and philosophy by adding their commentaries and glosses.

The Early Middle Ages in Europe

While Byzantine and Islamic civilization flourished between the sixth and ninth centuries the West had to remake itself. Our image of this period in Western history is one of darkness. People became more closely attached to the land because their very survival depended upon it. Serfdom (or manorialism) and feudalism held out the promise of security and protection. Although the majority of Europeans were busy reconstructing their lives, there were scholars who were desperately trying to keep learning alive. As you might expect, these were Christian scholars who retained a profound respect for the intellect of Greece and Rome. At the same time, they were devout Christians. They were trying to create a Christian culture that combined the Greco-Roman tradition with a faith in Christianity and support of the church.

Boethius

"The last of the Roman philosophers, and the first of the scholastic theologians," Boethius (c. 475–524) was a Roman statesman and philosopher descended from a prominent senatorial family. He studied philosophy, mathematics, and poetry at Plato's Academy (closed by Justinian in 529) and through his studies at Athens gained the knowledge that later enabled him to translate Greek philosophic writings into Latin. Soon after 500, he served the court of Theodoric (455–526), king of the Goths, who ruled Italy. In 510, Boethius was appointed consul and "Master of Offices." As consul, he attempted to check the oppressive behavior of his fellow officials, and in 522 he was arrested, condemned, and sent into exile to await execution. While awaiting execution, Boethius wrote a short book called *The Consolation of Philosophy*. In *The Consolation*, Boethius carried on a conversation with Philosophy, who appears as a woman. He reassured himself, in the tradition of Socrates and the Stoics, that "if then you are master of yourself, you will be in possession of that which you will never wish to lose, in which Fortune will never be able to take from you." This is classical humanism defined. Boethius exerted a major influence in Western intellectual life. Until the twelfth century, virtually all of what Europe knew about Aristotle came from Boethius. He even helped to diffuse Euclidean geometry to the Middle Ages. He wanted to unite faith and reason. But Boethius soon met a horrible fate. In 524, Theodoric confirmed his sentence and, after days of cruel torture, Boethius was bludgeoned to death. Like Boethius, Cassiodoris (c. 485–c. 580), Gregory of Tours (538–c. 5 94), and Isidore of Seville (c. 560–636) all helped to keep classical scholarship alive. There was something vital in this Greco-Roman tradition that had to be preserved.

THE KINGDOM OF THE FRANKS

It was during the early Middle Ages, roughly 500–1000, that a new form of government appeared. This government was Germanic in origin. Rome had built her government around an emperor and an elaborate and extensive administrative bureaucracy. The Germans had a different idea. What developed were individual kingdoms. Meanwhile, the church was controlled by members of the educated elite who provided the bureaucrats and administrative officials necessary to maintain religious authority. The Franks expanded their territory to the west, from Germany into Gaul (France). Although they remained tied to the traditions of their homeland, the further west they moved into Gaul, the less Germanized they became. The real impact of the Franks upon western Europe dates from the year 481, when the Frankish king Clovis (465–511) assumed the throne. He was an ambitious, able, and decidedly ruthless king who between 486 and 511 conquered provinces still ruled by Roman patricians. He also destroyed the kingdoms of the Alemanni, the Burgundians, and the Visogoths in Gaul. The most significant event of his career was his conversion to Christianity. Clovis compared himself to Constantine, and his loyal subjects followed suit and embraced Roman Christianity. Clovis turned his wars of aggression and conquest into holy wars. When Clovis died in 511, Gaul was the scene of numerous civil wars. The cause of these civil wars was the Frankish law of inheritance. The Frankish kingdom was regarded as a larger state that could be divided for purposes of administration. Such a scheme was fertile ground for conflict.

CHARLEMAGNE

It has been said that it was during the reign of Charlemagne (742–814) that the transition from classical to early medieval civilization was completed. His reign spans more than forty years and it was during this time that Europe was born. If anything characterized Charlemagne's rule, it was stability based on three elements: the Roman past, the Germanic way of life, and Christianity.

Frankish society was entirely rural and was composed of three classes or orders:

- the peasants—those who work
- the nobility—those who fight
- the clergy—those who pray

In general, life was brutal and harsh for the early medieval peasant. Even in the wealthiest parts of Europe, the story is one of poverty and hardship. Their diet was poor and many peasants died undernourished. Most were illiterate, although a few were devout Christians. The majority could not understand Latin. The nobility were better off. Their diet, although they had more food, was still not nutritional. They lived in larger houses than the peasants, but their castles were often just as cold as the peasant's small hut. Furthermore, most of nobility were illiterate and crude. They spent most of their time fighting. Their religious beliefs were, for the most part, similar to those of the peasants. At the upper level were the clergy. They were the most educated and perhaps the only people to truly understand Christianity, since they were the only people who had access to Scripture.

When Charlemagne took the throne in 771, he immediately implemented two policies. The first policy was one of expansion. Charlemagne's goal was to unite all Germanic people into one kingdom (*republica Christiana*). The second policy was religious: Charlemagne wanted to convert all of the Frankish kingdom to Christianity. As a result, Charlemagne's reign was marked by almost continual warfare. Because Charlemagne's armies were always fighting, he began to give his warriors land so they could support and equip themselves. With this in mind, Charlemagne was able to secure an army of warriors who were deeply devoted and loyal to him.

CHARLEMAGNE AND POPE LEO III

Toward the end of the year 800, Pope Leo III asked Charlemagne to come to Rome. On Christmas Day Charlemagne attended mass at St. Peter's. When he finished his prayers, Pope Leo prostrated himself before Charlemagne and then placed a crown upon his head. Pope Leo then said "life and victory to Charles Augustus, crowned by God, the great and peaceful emperor of the Romans." This was an extremely important act. Charlemagne became the first emperor in the West since the last Roman emperor was deposed in 476. Charlemagne's biographer, Einhard (c. 770–840), has recorded that Charlemagne was not very much interested in Pope Leo's offering. Charlemagne had no intention of being absorbed into the Roman church. From the point of view of Pope Leo, the coronation of Charlemagne signified the pope's claim to dispense the imperial crown. By gaining the imperial title, Charlemagne received no new lands. He never intended to make Rome the center of his empire. Charlemagne returned to France as emperor and began a most effective system of rule. He divided his kingdom into several hundred counties or administrative units. Along the borders of the kingdom, Charlemagne appointed military governors. To insure that this system worked effectively, Charlemagne sent out messengers (*missi domini*) to check on local affairs and report directly to him. There was no fixed capital, but Charlemagne spent most of his time at Aachen. Charlemagne standardized the minting of coins based on the silver standard and encouraged trade, especially in the North Sea. He also initiated trade between the Franks and the Muslims and made commercial pacts with the merchants of Venice who traded with both Byzantium and Islam.

THE REVIVAL OF LEARNING

The most durable of all Charlemagne's efforts was the revival of learning. This was especially so among the clergy, many of whom were barely literate. On the whole, the monks were not much better educated. Seventh- and eighth-century manuscripts were written in uppercase letters and without punctuation. There were many errors made in copying and handwriting was poor. There were, however, a few educated monks, as well as the beginnings of a few great libraries. But Charlemagne could not find one good copy of the Bible, nor a complete text of the Benedictine Rule. He had to send to Rome for them. Above all, Charlemagne wanted unity in the Frankish church. Although illiterate as a youth Charlemagne was devoted to new ideas and to learning. He studied Latin, Greek, rhetoric, logic, and astronomy. He was in northern Italy when he met the Anglo-Saxon scholar, Alcuin of York (c. 735–804). Charlemagne persuaded Alcuin to come to Aachen in order to design a curriculum for the palace school. Alcuin devised a course of study that was intended to train the clergy and the monks. Here we find the origins of the seven liberal arts:

- the *trivium*: grammar (how to write), rhetoric (how to speak), and logic (how to think)
- the *quadrivium*: geometry, arithmetic, astronomy, and music

All of this meant a classical and literary education. Students read Homer, Virgil, Horace, Ovid, Juvenal, Plato, and Cicero.

By the ninth century, most monasteries had writing rooms or *scriptoria* where manuscripts were copied and texts were studied with care. It was no longer merely a matter of copying texts. It was now first necessary to correct any mistakes that had been made over years of copying. Charlemagne instituted a standard writing style called the Carolingian minuscule, which included upper and lowercase letters. It should be obvious that this new script was much easier to read; in fact, it is the script we use today. Charlemagne also standardized medieval Latin. After all, much had changed in the Latin language over the past one thousand years. New words, phrases, and idioms had appeared over the centuries and these now had to be incorporated into the language. Charlemagne took account of all these changes and included them in a new scholarly language.

One of the most important consequences of the Carolingian Renaissance was that Charlemagne encouraged the spread of uniform religious practices as well as a uniform culture. Charlemagne set out to construct a *respublica Christiana*, a Christian republic. But despite the fact that Charlemagne unified his empire, elevated education, standardized coins, handwriting, and even scholarly Latin, his empire declined in strength within a generation or two following his death in the year 814. But, the death of Charlemagne was only one cause of the decline. There were renewed invasions from barbarian tribes. The Muslims invaded Sicily in 827 and 895 and disrupted trade between the Franks and Italy. The Vikings came from Denmark, Sweden, and Norway and invaded the Empire in the eighth and ninth centuries. The Danes attacked England and northern Gaul. The Swedes attacked areas in central and eastern Europe, and the Norwegians attacked England, Scotland, and Ireland and, by the tenth century, had found their way to Greenland. The third group of invaders were the Magyars, who came from modern-day Hungary. Their raids were so terrible that European peasants would burn their fields and destroy their villages rather than give them over. All these invasions came to an end by the tenth and eleventh centuries, perhaps because these tribes were converted to Christianity. It would be the complex institution known as feudalism that would offer true protection from these invasions, based as it was on security and mutual obligations.

SUGGESTED FEATURE FILMS

Alfred the Great. 122 min. Color. 1969. MGM. Aims for a realistic portrayal of Alfred's reign, with David Hemmings and Michael York.

Kampf um Rome/The Last Roman (dubbed). 92 min. B/W. 1968. Allied Artists Pictures. Film about a leader of the Roman nobility who travels to Byzantium and its leader Justinian to raise an army and march on the Goths.

The Message. 180 min. Color. 1976. Anchor Bay Entertainment. Film about the life of Muhammad.

Teodora Imperatice Di Bisanzio/Theodora Slave Empress (dubbed). 88 min. Color. 1954. I. F. E. Releasing Corporation. Story about a Roman courtesan and former slave girl who marries the Roman emperor Justinian and assumes the throne as Empress of Rome.

SUGGESTED CLASSROOM FILMS

The Birth of Europe. 39 min. Color. 1979. McGraw-Hill. The early Middle Ages, with the spread of Christianity as the focus.

The Byzantine Empire. 2 parts, 30 min. each. Color. 1989. Part I focuses on the forces that shaped the Byzantine Empire and enabled it to endure for over one thousand years. Part 2 looks at the role of religion in weakening the empire.

Byzantium and the Holy Roman Empire: Christianity in the Seventh and Eighth Centuries. 47 min. Color. 1999. Films for the Humanities and Sciences. Contrasts the ill health of the church with the spiritual and material vitality of Byzantium. Ends with Charlemagne's coronation by Pope Leo III in 800. Part of the *Two Thousand Years: The History of Christianity* series.

Byzantium: From Splendor to Ruin. 52 min. Color. 1989. Films for the Humanities and Sciences. Program about the flowering of Constantinople as a second Rome and its gradual decline and ultimate fall in 1453.

Charlemagne and the Holy Roman Empire. 52 min. Color. 1989. Films for the Humanities and Sciences. Program covering the life of Charlemagne, which counterpoints the glories of the Carolingian Renaissance with the everyday realities of hunger, plague, and violence.

The Christian Empire. 45 min. Color. 1978. Contemporary Films. Traces the Christian Empire from Rome to Constantinople to Russia.

Christianity: The First Thousand Years, Part IV—The Faith Conquers. 50 min. Color. 1998. A&E Home Video. Begins with Charlemagne's coronation in 800, which lifted Europe from the Dark Ages and established Christianity as the cornerstone of Western civilization.

Christians, Jews, and Moslems in Medieval Spain. 32 min. Color. 1989. Films for the Humanities and Sciences. The history of Spain from the time of the first landing, in 711, through the nearly 800-year-long war that ended in the expulsion of both Moors and Jews in 1492.

The Dark Ages and the Millennium: Christianity in the Ninth and Tenth Centuries. 47 min. Color. 1999. Films for the Humanities and Sciences. The chaos in Europe that broke out with the death of Charlemagne and the approach of the millennium. Part of the *Two Thousand Years: The History of Christianity* series.

Islam: Empire of Faith. 165 min. Color. 2001. PBS. Three-part series follows the history of Islam from Muhammad to the rise of the Ottoman Turks. Includes *The Messenger*; *The Awakening*; and *The Ottomans*.

Living Islam. 6 parts, 50 min. each. Color. 1993. Insight Media. This BBC series explores the history, practice, and politicization of Islam from its origins to the present.

Orient/Occident. 30 min. Color. 1982. Films for the Humanities. Examines Islam's impact on Western culture, and the West's impact on Islam. Part IV of the series, *The World of Islam*.

The Rise of Nations in Europe. 13 min. Color. 1978. Coronet. The origins of modern European nations are traced to the rise of the monarchies.

When the World Spoke Arabic: The Golden Age of Arab Civilization. 300 min. Color. 1999. Films for the Humanities and Sciences. Twelve-part series presents the history and the most significant cultural, scientific, and technical achievements of the Arab empire between the seventh and thirteenth centuries.

The Shadow of God on Earth. 58 min. Color. 1978. Insight Media. Explores both Muhammad's initial conquests and the nature of Islam today.

Spain: The Moorish Influence. 28 min. Color. 1990. Insight Media. Explores the role of the Moors in shaping Spanish culture. Received a "Highly Recommended" rating in the *Video Rating Guide*.

CHAPTER 8

The Expansion of Europe: Economy, Society, and Politics in the High Middle Ages, 1000–1300

OUTLINE

I. Introduction
   A. Europe in 1000
      1. Shifting balance of power
      2. A weakened Europe and the strength of Byzantine and Islamic civilization
      3. Viking, Hungarian, and Muslim attacks
   B. Europe in 1300
      1. Europe the dominant military, economic, and political power
      2. A Catholic European world
      3. Expansion of European commerce
      4. Urbanization
      5. Economic growth
      6. More powerful governments
      7. Social stratification
II. The First Agricultural Revolution
   A. Transformations
      1. Technological innovation
      2. Improved climate
      3. New crop-rotation system
      4. Investment in tools, livestock, and mills
   B. Technological advances
      1. Heavy-wheeled plow, horse collars, and harnesses
         a. Better aeration of the soil
         b. Saved labor
      2. Iron horseshoes, the tandem harness, and iron hand tools
      3. Mills
         a. After 1050, a craze in northern European water mills
         b. Windmills introduced in the 1170s

4. Results
   a. Greater security as Viking, Hungarian, and Muslim attacks decreased
   b. Growing confidence of entrepreneurial peasants and lords
   c. A new profit motive?
   d. Increased European population
   e. Efficient market for goods
C. Manorialism, serfdom, and agricultural productivity
   1. Changes in patterns of peasant settlement (England, northern Europe, and western Germany)
   2. The development of the manor
   3. Consolidation of individual peasant holdings
   4. The lord of the manor
      a. Dominant role
      b. Claimed largest share of peasants' production
      c. Strip farming
      d. The *demense* (private use)
      e. Peasant labor services
   5. The peasants
      a. Similar to slaves: worked without pay, paid humiliating fines
      b. Unlike slaves: their obligations were fixed by custom
D. New crop-rotation systems
   1. Three-field system of crop rotation
   2. Adaptable to wet, fertile soils of northern Europe
   3. Produced higher yields and was insurance against disaster

4. New types of food (for humans and horses)
5. Helped spread labor more evenly over the course of the year
E. Serfdom and the limits of manorialism
   1. Manorialism never predominant across Europe at any one time
   2. Mostly limited to England and parts of France and Germany
   3. Thirteenth-century breakdown
      a. Lords collect revenue in cash, avoiding the risks of the market
      b. Distinction between serf and free peasant slowly dissolves

III. The Growth of Towns and Cities
  A. Agricultural revolution served as foundation for a new commercial revolution
  B. Commerce
    1. By the twelfth century, trade controlled by Venetian, Pisan, and Genoese naval forces
    2. Created an expanding market for Eastern luxury goods
    3. Dominance of Italian trade networks (Constantinople, Alexandria, and the West)
    4. The Champagne fairs
      a. Flemish merchants sold cloth to Italians
      b. Italian merchants sold Eastern spices and silks to the Flemish
    5. Long-distance trade
      a. A risky enterprise
      b. Piracy
    6. Italian merchants develop new commercial methods
      a. Partnership contracts
      b. Double-entry bookkeeping
      c. New credit mechanisms
    7. Commerce and urbanization
  C. Towns
    1. Symbiotic relationship with the countryside
    2. Provided markets for manufactured goods
    3. Specialization in certain enterprises
      a. Paris and Bologna: university towns
      b. Venice, Genoa, Cologne, and London: long-distance trade
      c. Milan, Florence, Ghent, and Bruges: manufactures
    4. The guild system
      a. Male-dominated, professional associations of craftsmen—small, privately owned workshops

b. Preserving monopolies and limiting competition
c. The master craftsman
d. Apprentices and journeymen
e. The "masterpiece"
f. Controlled prices and wages
g. Formulated regulations governing methods of production and quality of goods
h. Social functions
i. Merchant guilds
    i. Monopolies in the local market
    ii. Controlled admission to citizenship
   5. Sanitation
   6. Fire
   7. Urban pride

IV. Byzantium, Islam, and the Crusades
  A. Abbasid decline
  B. Muslim pressure on the eastern borders of the empire
  C. The Byzantine Revival
    1. A changed position
    2. St. Cyril and St. Methodius convert Balkan Slavs to Orthodox Christianity
    3. A new written language—Old Church Slavonic (Cyrillic alphabet)
    4. Annexation of Greece, Bulgaria, and Serbia
    5. Military and commercial alliance with the western Rus
    6. Eastern conquests (930s and 970s)
      a. Greatly increased power of local noble families
      b. New centers of power outside Constantinople
      c. Tensions and rivalries
  D. The invasion of the Turks
    1. Venice, Pisa, and Genoa emerge as dominant traders in the eastern Mediterranean
    2. Growing power of Fatimid Egypt
    3. The Seljuk Turks moved into Asia Minor
      a. Battle of Manzikert (1071)
      b. The Turks now set to seize all of Anatolia
    3. Alexius Comnenus (1048–1118)
      a. Appeals to Pope Urban II for troops to repel the Turks
  E. The First Crusade
    1. Pope Urban's appeal
      a. Bring the Orthodox Church into communion with the papacy

b. Embarrass the German emperor, Henry IV
c. Achieving peace at home
d. Goal of Jerusalem
2. 1095: calls the First Crusade at Clermont
3. 100,000 men, women and children march to Constantinople
4. Motives
  a. Win new lands
  b. Prospect of adventure
  c. Religious—a mission from God
    i. Pilgrimage
    ii. Freed from punishment in purgatory
    ii. Plenary indulgences
5. Assaults against Jewish communities (Mainz, Worms, Speyer, and Cologne)
6. Byzantium seen as an obstacle to recovery of Jerusalem for Christianity
7. Crusaders capture Antioch and most of Syria (1098)
8. Crusaders take Jerusalem, slaughtering its inhabitants (1099)
9. Furthered the decline of Byzantine commerce

F. The later Crusades
1. Crusaders did not wish to interfere with trade routes
2. For the Muslims, the loss of Jerusalem was a religious affront
3. The Second Crusade
  a. Syrian principalities recaptured by the Muslims
  b. Christian warriors too internally divided to reverse any losses
  c. Muslim leader Saladin recaptures Jerusalem (1187)
4. The Third Crusade
  a. Frederick Barbarossa (c. 1123–1190)
  b. Philip Augustus (1165–1223)
  c. Richard the Lionhearted (1157–1199)
  d. A failed campaign
5. The Fourth Crusade
  a. Summoned by Innocent III
  b. A disaster for the crusading armies
    i. Civil war in Germany
    ii. War between England and France
    iii. Depleted ranks of crusading armies

G. The consequences of the Crusades
1. Disaster for Byzantium
2. Modest effect on the Islamic world

3. Trade between Islam and the West continued
4. The West learned new technologies of fortification
5. The Muslims learned about siege warfare
6. The crystallization of Christian and Islamic doctrines of the holy war against the infidel
7. Western Europe
  a. Difficult to assess
  b. Western expansionism
  c. Could not maintain colonies
  d. Greatest gains went to the republics of Venice and Genoa
  e. Cutting out the Islamic middle man
  f. The "crusading ideal"

V. Social Mobility and Social Inequality in High Medieval Europe
A. General observations
1. New commercial and professional elites
2. Wealthiest Europeans were merchants and bankers
3. Urban dwellers move to countryside—rural people moved to towns and cities
4. The emergence of schools—a growing professional class
5. Society became more fluid and more complex
6. Social advancement

B. Nobles and knights
1. A more highly stratified society
2. New families established as territorial lords
3. Knighthood
  a. A new social order of men of widely varying social rank
  b. A specialized warrior group associated with the nobility
  c. Increasing costs of knighthood
    i. More elaborate and expensive lifestyle
    ii. Needed an estate of at least 1200 acres

C. Chivalry and courtly love
1. Knightly code of values
2. A social ideology of values and identification
3. Knighthood and nobility
  a. An amalgamation of values and goals
4. Thirteenth-century chivalry—an ideology of a social class
  a. Dividing those who were of the nobility and those who were not
  b. The rules of battle

    5. Cult of courtly love
       a. Women as objects of male veneration
       b. Courtly love as refined love
       c. Noble women were courted, peasant women could be taken by force
    6. The literature of courtly love
       a. *The Song of Roland*
       b. Idealistic and artificial
    7. The hanging role of noble women

VI. Politics and Government
  A. Observations
    1. New forms of government and political life
  B. Urban government
    1. Nobility attracted to wealth of the cities
       a. Lent an aristocratic cast to political life of the towns
       b. A violent culture of honor and vendetta
    2. Informal government arrangements
       a. Special charters
       b. Self-government
       c. The "commune"
       d. Oligarchical control

VII. Feudalism and the Emergence of National Monarchies
  A. Observations
    1. Europe a continent of kingdoms
  B. The problem of feudalism
    1. Feudalism as a highly decentralized political system
    2. Varieties of interpretation
       a. Marxist historiography
       b. Social historians
       c. Legal historians
       d. Military historians
    3. Feudalism defined
       a. A political system in which public powers were exercised by private lords
       b. First took shape in tenth- and eleventh-century France
       c. Justified a hierarchical legal and political order
       d. Vocabulary
          i. Fief: a contract in which something of value was exchanged for service
          ii. Vassal: recipient of a fief
          iii. Homage: a solemn act in which a vassal becomes "the man" of his lord
       e. Personal relationships of service in return for land-holding

C. The Norman conquest of England
    1. 1066—feudalism first appears in England
    2. William the Conqueror (1027–1087)
       a. Rewarded his Norman followers with grants of English land
       b. Exercised a variety of public rights not derived from feudalism
       c. All landowners owed loyalty to the king—a centralized feudalism
       d. Represented a fusion of Carolingian public power with new feudal structures of power and landholding
D. Feudal monarchy in England
    1. The rise of administrative kingship
    2. Henry I (1068–1135)
       a. Created the clerks of the Exchequer
       b. Strengthened local administration
       c. Traveling circuit judges
E. The reign of Henry II (1133–1189)
    1. Already the ruler of Normandy, Anjou, Maine, and Aquitaine
    2. Orders juries of local men to report under oath every violation of the laws
    3. Origin of the grand jury
    4. System of "writs"
    5. Tried to reform operation of church courts
    6. Thomas Becket
       a. Archbishop of Canterbury
       b. The Constitutions of Clarendon (1164)
          i. Clerics convicted of serious crimes to be handed over to royal court for sentencing
       c. Becket objected
          i. Fled to France
          ii. Murdered upon his return to England
    7. Henry forced to surrender several of his claims (e.g., the right to sentence criminal clerics)
    8. Richard the Lionhearted (1157–1199)
F. The reign of King John and the Magna Carta
    1. Less-capable military leader
    2. Lost nearly all Angevin lands
    3. Devoted his reign to raising money to regain French lands
    4. Pressed feudal rights to their limit
       a. Fines the nobility
       b. Heavy taxation on the county
    5. Failed military expedition to France (1214)
    6. The magnates rebel
    7. Magna Carta (1215)
       a. The king must respect the traditional rights of his vassals

b. Taxation could not be raised by the crown without the consent of the barons

8. Parliament
   a. Emerged gradually after 1300
   b. A consultative body
   c. A political as well as financial and judicial body

G. Feudal monarchy in France
   1. Slow government centralization—faced greater problems
      a. Carolingian institutions had collapsed
   2. The Capetian Dynasty (987–1328)
   3. The reinvention of the French kingdom

H. The growth of royal power in France
   1. Louis VI, "the Fat" (1078–1137)
      a. Consolidated royal control over the Île-de-France by subduing "robber barons"
      b. Agriculture, trade, and intellectual life could flourish at Paris
   2. Louis VII (1137–1181)
   3. Philip Augustus (1165–1223)
      a. Undermined John's control over French territories
      b. John refused to submit to pressure
      c. A war of conquest
         i. Philip retained Angevin territories
      d. An effective system of local administration
         i. Superimposed new royal officials (*baillis*) over local government practice
         ii. The baillis had full judicial, administrative and military authority
   4. Louis IX, "Saint Louis" (1226–1270)
      a. Extended administrative pattern further
      b. The epitome of thirteenth-century kingship
   5. Philip IV, "the Fair" (1285–1314)
      a. Aggressive wars against Flanders and English territories in the southwest
      b. Sough to undermine papal control over the church in France
      c. The Estates General

I. England and France: comparisons and contrasts
   1. France the most powerful national monarchy in Europe
   2. England
      a. More unified
      b. One language
      c. Little internal division

3. France
   a. Regional separatism
4. Government
   a. England
      i. Administration built on local institutions
      ii. Local knights complete administrative work without pay
      iii. Appealed to formal consent from assemblies
   b. France
      i. A rich and larger country
      ii. Relied less on direct consent of the people
      iii. Faced with regional separatism

J. Germany
   1. General considerations
      a. Powerful Carolingian-style foundations
      b. Close alliance with the church
      c. Tradition of sacral kingship
   2. The conflict with the papacy
      a. Declining strength of the monarchy
      b. Conflict between regents for Henry IV and papal reformers
      c. Conflicts between the regents and the Saxon nobility
      d. Civil war (1073)
      e. Pope Gregory VIII convinced that the church should be separate from secular powers
      f. Henry refused
      g. The humiliation of Henry
         i. Abased himself before Gregory at Canossa
      h. Henry V
         i. Compromised with the papacy
         ii. German nobility won independence
   3. Frederick I, Barbarossa (1152–1190)
      a. Family of Staufen or Hohenstaufen ("high Staufen")
      b. Called his realm the Holy Roman Empire
         i. A universal empire blessed by God
      c. Tried to rule in cooperation with German princes
      d. Compromised with Lombard League and the papacy
      e. Imperial court at Mainz
      f. Died during the Third Crusade
      g. Succeeded by his son, Henry VI

4. Frederick II (1216–1250)
   a. Spoke Arabic, Latin, German, French, and Italian
   b. Patron of learning
   c. Supported territorial princes of Germany
   d. Enforced imperial rights in Italy
   e. With his death, German rule fell to several hundred German princes

K. Iberia
  1. Highly regionalized
  2. Successful reconquest of the Iberian peninsula from the Muslims
  3. Four major Christian kingdoms: Navarre, Portugal, the combined kindgdom of Aragon and Catalunya, and Castile

VIII. Conclusion
  A. By 1300, Europe's position had been transformed
  B. Economic foundations
  C. Political and military changes
  D. The national monarchies as middle ground between city-states and empires

GENERAL DISCUSSION QUESTIONS

1. What factors contributed to European economic growth between 1000 and 1300? Was this growth beneficial or harmful to the majority of the population?

2. In the High Middle Ages, what relationships do you see between economic growth and political power? And between economic growth and technological achievements?

3. If agriculture, tied to old ways, constituted the main medieval economy, where was there scope for innovation and invention? How would a change in crop-rotation systems immediately increase production? Why were Europeans slow to adopt such changes?

4. Was serfdom a successful economic system during the High Middle Ages? How was it justified, even though it was not fair to everyone?

5. Why did Pope Urban II issue the call for the First Crusade? Why did so many western Europeans join the cause? What evidence supports the idea that "the dominant motive for going on the First Crusade was religious"?

6. Later crusades were generally less glorious than the First Crusade. Why was this? What were the fundamental weaknesses in the idea of establishing a Latin Christian kingdom in Palestine, with Jerusalem as its capital?

7. Why, according to medieval writers, were some people born aristocrats and others born serfs? Did social inequality reflect a basic human inequality? Are some naturally stronger, better fighters, or more qualified to lead, while others must defer to them?

8. When warriors became courtiers, they had to learn the manners of chivalry. What was chivalry: a substitute for military activity, an ideology for the battlefield and the castle, an attempt by a parasitic caste to segregate and justify itself? How was chivalry associated with the status of nobility?

9. Is the term feudalism still useful as a historical concept, or has it become a misleading myth? What problems does it solve, and what others does it create?

10. In the period between 1066 (the Norman Conquest) and 1215 (Magna Carta), why did English kings try to restrict or supersede the feudal system? How successful were they?

11. Why did French kings face more obstacles to centralizing power than English kings? Why did they have greater success in expanding and enforcing their rule in the period between 987 and 1316 than the English did?

12. Between 1050 and 1250, Germany changed from being the strongest monarchy in western Europe to an elective empire with a weak central government. Why was the monarchical failure of medieval Germany "a problem of fundamental importance"?

DOCUMENT DISCUSSION QUESTIONS

Advice to the Byzantine Emperor, Eleventh Century

1. What does the author mean when he addresses the emperor as "a god on earth"?

2. If he is allowed to do as he wills, why should the emperor restrain his desires and arbitrary tendencies? What difference would it make for him to travel through the countries he rules?

3. What risks did traveling Byzantine emperors incur? Were they any greater or lesser than those faced by other rulers?

The Spurious Letter of Alexius Comnenus to Count Robert, Seeking His Aid Against the Turks

4. Why would you suspect this document's veracity even if it did not have "spurious" in the title?

5. Are charges of sexual misdeeds, whether true or false, the easiest way to discredit political opponents and followers of other religions, perhaps because it is hard to deny them? Why would the author stoop to such charges?

6. Why does the author present the oppression of Greek Christians as a primarily religious, rather than ethnic, problem?

7. The Byzantine emperor allegedly said, "I prefer to be subject to you, the Latins, rather than have Constantinople taken by the Turks. . . ." Was the Western crusaders' experience of Constantinople a pleasant one? Who would write about it in this fashion?

Preparing to Depart on Crusade

8. Feudal lords were allowed in some cases to level a tax on their lands, on both their own possessions and those of their vassals and peasants. How did Jean de Joinville take care of the people under his jurisdiction before leaving on a crusade?

9. How closely did the departing Joinville regulate his estates? As an educated but still rustic western European, what would he think about the lasting effects his departure would have on his estates?

10. What elements of the story strike you as practical? As magical? As both?

Frederick II Changes the Height of the Heavens

11. This story contains magical and practical elements as well as ridicule. Why was it considered exotic for the emperor to have scientific interests?

12. To discuss the previous question, you may have considered astrology a science, but if it is not, what would be the value of Frederick's test for the astrologer?

SAMPLE LECTURE 8: MEDIEVAL TECHNOLOGY AND SOCIAL CHANGE

Lecture Objectives

1. To illustrate how the agricultural revolution of the early Middle Ages set in motion profound social, economic, and political changes
2. To compare the technology of ancient Near Eastern hydraulic civilizations with medieval Europe
3. To show how medieval technology opened the door to the early modern European global expansion

Europe in 1000

After the fall of Rome, Europe was little more than thousands of rural settlements; it had very little literate culture. A patchwork of tribal societies existing under an essentially Neolithic economy brought together western Europe in the early Middle Ages, and repeated barbarian invasions after the

ninth century put at risk what social and institutional bonds there were. Security and protection were most important, and most people found existence to be little more than a quest for basic survival. Before the Renaissance of the twelfth century, the state of learning in Europe remained weak. It seemed as if Europe had entered a Dark Age. In the ancient Near East, the first hydraulic civilizations formed where centralized governments managed a basic agricultural economy. In Europe, rain fell in the spring and summer and no such governmental intervention was established or even required. Furthermore, urban civilization did not appear in the West until the eleventh and twelfth centuries, when Europe began its slow path to recovery. But once Europe found a way to intensify its agriculture, a very different civilization appeared. Its population grew to match that of India and China, and technologically, economically, and politically Europe became a major player on the world scene. Beginning in the fifteenth century, and based on its mastery of the technologies of firearms and shipping, the great powers of Europe began to set the foundations for large overseas empires. Western Europe also became the center of scientific learning and research. A series of interlocking technical innovations—an agricultural revolution, new military technology, and a dependence on wind and water for the generation of power—shaped the history of medieval Europe.

The Agricultural Revolution

The population of Europe rose thirty-eight percent between the years 600 and 1000. Land was put to many uses, not only to grow crops, but also to pasture dairy animals for food, cattle and horses for traction, and sheep for wool. The growth of cities also reduced the acreage available for agricultural production. Large forests provided timber for construction and shipbuilding. But there were problems. For instance, wood was used as the fuel in making iron, which consumed vast quantities of timber and placed a heavy strain on the land. By the ninth century, the people of Europe began to face the kind of ecological crisis that thousands of years earlier had forced Neolithic settlers of the Near Eastern river valleys to intensify their agriculture and make the transition to civilization. In Europe, agricultural intensification could not follow the ancient Near Eastern pattern of development. There, artificial irrigation provided a technological solution. But Europe was already irrigated by sufficient rainfall. The European farmer could increase his production only by plowing the heavy soils of areas that resisted the light Mediterranean scratch plow, which was basically little more than a stick.

Medieval Microchips

Mounted on wheels and armed with an iron cutter, the heavy plow tore up the soil at the root line and turned it over, forming a furrow and eliminated the need for cross-plowing. A second innovation involved the substitution of the horse, with its greater speed and endurance, for the ox as a draft animal. Europeans adapted the horse collar from the Chinese, who had started using it several centuries earlier. The device transferred the pressure points from the neck to the shoulders and therefore increased the horse's traction by four or five times. In combination with the iron horseshoe, a Roman invention, it resulted in a shift to horses from oxen as the principal draft animals.

Still another component of the Agricultural Revolution was the development of the three-field system of crop rotation. The two-field farming system typically involved farming one field while leaving another to rest. In the new three-field system that arose on the European plain, arable land was divided into three fields with plantings rotated over a three-year cycle. These new technologies produced a variety of social consequences:

- The deep plow made it possible to farm new lands, particularly the alluvial soils on the European plain, and this helps account for the northward shift of European agriculture in the Middle Ages.
- Because the heavy plow and its team of horses were expensive tools, and beyond the capacities of individual peasant farmers to own them, they brought collective ownership and patterns of communal agriculture.
- The solidification of the medieval village and the manorial system as the foundation of European society.

The three-field system of crop rotation produced important advantages. The spring crop of vegetables and oats significantly improved the lives of all Europeans. The three-field system also increased the productive capabilities of European agriculture by about fifty percent, thus creating enough food to feed the greater number of people now inhabiting cities. By 1300 the population of Europe had reached seventy-nine million from a low of twenty-six million in the year 600. Paris had increased in population by more than ten times, to 228,000 in 1300 and then to 280,000 in 1400. Together with urbanization and population growth came a great wave of cathedral building.

Agriculture was not the only activity in which technology contributed to the rise of medieval Europe. In military affairs, technological innovations produced some of the unique developments that characterized European feudalism and that began to account for Europe's eventual global dominance. One of the definitive figures of European feudalism, the armored knight mounted on the armored horse, was made possible by a key piece of technology—the stirrup. Prior to the eighth century the horse was used only to transport a warrior to the field of battle. He then dismounted and fought on foot. The stirrup, invented by the Chinese in the fifth century, stabilized the warrior on his horse and allowed for fighting on horseback without dismounting. This new technology matched easily with the manorial system brought about by the revolution in agriculture. The knight replaced the peasant-soldier

common in the early Middle Ages, and being a knight became a full-time job. The system resulted in truly feudal relations. The vassal knight placed his loyalty and his arms in the hands of a higher lord in exchange for part of the lord's domain, to be governed and taxed in the lord's name. This explains the decentralized character of European society in the Middle Ages. No strong central government, comparable to those of the earliest civilizations, was required to manage an agricultural economy that had no hydraulic foundation. The manorial system was well-adapted to the European ecology, and the knight-village relation became characteristic of European feudalism and the manorial system. The village now produced a surplus to support large numbers of knights, and those knights policed, taxed, and enforced justice at the local level. Because it was the feudal custom to pass land on to the firstborn son, the number of landless knights rose, and ultimately more knights populated Europe than could be accommodated. As a result, the first wave of European expansion erupted when Pope Urban II launched the First Crusade in 1096. Over the next two hundred years, European invaders encountered civilizations that were technologically their equal and culturally their superior. Faced with the material wealth of Byzantine and Islamic civilization, there was indeed little chance that the Europeans would prevail. And despite some victories, the Holy Crusades were little more than a bloodbath fought by Christian soldiers.

MEDIEVAL MACHINES

In the twelfth and thirteenth centuries Europe became the first great civilization not to be run primarily by human muscle power. The most outstanding example was the development of water-powered machines and their incorporation into the fabric of village life and European society. The waterwheel became widely used and powered a variety of other machines, including sawmills, flour mills, wine presses, and hammer mills. The need for water-driven mills may be attributed to a general lack of surplus labor and to the increased production generated by the Agricultural Revolution. That is, with more grain to grind, a widespread shift to water or wind powered machines was only to be expected. It is no coincidence that serfdom withered away in western Europe at the same time that labor-saving machines made their first appearance.

Medieval engineers mastered older kinds of mechanical gearing and linkage and invented new ones at the same time. European civilization was literally driven by powerful engines of wind and water, which tapped more energy than anywhere else in the world. The medieval world was fascinated with machines, and European civilization came to envision nature as a source of power to be exploited technologically for the benefit of humankind.

TECHNOLOGY AND SCIENCE

These technological innovations led to the transformation of European society and culture but owed little to theoretical science. If the twelfth century represents a period of translation, the thirteenth century represents a period of assimilation when European scholars began to absorb the scientific and philosophical traditions of antiquity. Much of this process amounted to attempts to reconcile a Christian world view with Aristotle. It was Thomas Aquinas who completed this process of assimilation. The elaboration and defense of Aristotle's works became a mission of the universities, and gave rise to a new philosophical school known as scholasticism. As Aristotelian teachings began to infiltrate the new European universities in the thirteenth century, faith and reason were harmonized. Certain points of Aristotle clearly contradicted Christian teaching. A series of intellectual battles between theologians and philosophers unfolded across the thirteenth century, culminating in the great condemnation of 1277. By freeing medieval thinkers from obedience to Aristotle, the condemnation liberated them to conceive of new alternatives in solving long-standing problems in Aristotle's natural philosophy. In this view, the Scientific Revolution did not begin with Copernicus in 1543, but perhaps 250 years earlier with the intellectual response to the condemnation of 1277.

In the fourteenth century, the major question facing scientific intellectuals no longer concerned simply uncovering new texts or assimilating Aristotle's natural philosophy to Scripture. Instead, the sciences built on the Aristotelian model and broke new ground. Scientific investigation, as a result, was broadened considerably. A new tradition of observational and mathematical astronomy arose in western Europe. There were groundbreaking calls for calendar reform. Serious and sustained research in astrology arose alongside medieval astronomy. Building on a strong Islamic tradition and propelled by the religious connotations associated with light, medieval investigators carried out research in optics.

FAMINE, PLAGUE, AND WAR

But a series of disruptions created havoc in large parts of Europe in the fourteenth century. The climate in Europe became cooler and wetter, disastrously affecting harvests and agricultural productivity. Unprecedented famines erupted across Europe in 1315 and 1317, and the resulting economic depression lasted well into the next century. The Black Death swept across Europe between 1347 and 1351, wiping out at least thirty-five percent of Europe's population. Thousands of European villages disappeared and outbreaks of the plague continued until the eighteenth century. Less dramatic was the removal of the papacy from Rome to Avignon, which broke the unity of Christendom and divided the allegiances of Christians. And the Hundred Years' War between England and France, which broke out in 1338, nearly devastated the heartland of France through the 1450s. Peasant revolts and threats of social unrest appeared as well. By the fourteenth century Europe had gained some but not all of the characteristics of early civilizations. Agriculture had been intensi-

fied, the population grew, urbanization took hold, building became more monumental, and higher learning had been institutionalized. But in this environment a centralized authority did not come into being. Only later, beginning in the sixteenth century, did centralized authority in the name of absolute monarchy come to play a role in European history. The historical dynamic that produced this innovation was a sweeping military revolution.

THE GUNPOWDER REVOLUTION

The technology of gunpowder passed into Europe from the Islamic world after the Crusades. By 1500, the manufacture of guns had become a universal technology. European military engineers actively developed the technologies of cannon-making and, with a superior gun design, soon surpassed their Asian counterparts, from whom they had initially learned the technology. Gunpowder and firearms began to play a decisive role on the battlefield of Europe and by the end of the fifteenth century, they had transformed warfare. The gunpowder revolution undermined the military roles of the feudal knight and the feudal lord and replaced them with expensive gunpowder armies and navies financed by central governments. War could only be financed by royal treasuries. The musket was introduced in the 1550s. Musketeers stood in long rows and fired volleys from standardized muskets. In the face of muskets and artillery, longbows, crossbows, cavalry, and the pike exercised smaller roles or vanished entirely from the scene of battle. Infantry, now carrying handguns, once again became a dominant arm on the field of battle. As a result, over the next two centuries the size of the standing armies of several European nations increased dramatically. By the time of Louis XIV, the French standing army stood at 400,000 soldiers.

TOWARD THE FUTURE

The military revolution shifted power from local authorities to centralized kingdoms and nation-states. This revolution also introduced competition between states and dynamic social mechanisms that relentlessly favored technological development. From the fifteenth century on, the creation of national armies and navies resulted in political centralization. Arsenals, shipyards, and fortresses were maintained as state-controlled public works. A major outcome of the military revolution, alongside political centralization, was a wave of European colonialism and the beginnings of European global conquest. A revolution in naval warfare formed the technological basis of this process. In part, this revolution in naval warfare entailed the creation of a new type of ship and new techniques of naval engagement. The global results of this new technological capability were stunning. The Portuguese made their first contacts along the west coast of Africa in 1443 and reached the Cape of Good Hope in 1488. Vasco de Gama's first voyage to the Indian Ocean by way of the Cape in 1497 involved four small ships, and Columbus sailed to the Indies in three small caravels. Cortez conquered Mexico in 1518 with a force of six hundred men, seventeen horses, and ten cannons. Later European voyages used larger and more heavily armed flotillas, which set the pattern for European colonialism for the next three hundred years.

SUGGESTED FEATURE FILMS

The 13th Warrior. 102 min. Color. 1999. Touchstone Pictures. An Arab accompanies a band of Vikings in a quest to destroy the Wendol. Loosely based on the Anglo-Saxon epic poem *Beowulf*.

Alexander Nevsky. 107 min. B/W. 1938. Mosfilm. Eisenstein's film about the thirteenth century army of Alexander Nevsky, who rallies the people to drive back an invasion by Teutonic knights.

Alfred the Great. 122 min. Color. 1969. MGM. In general, this is a realistic portrayal of Alfred's reign. With David Hemmings and Michael York.

Al-Massir/Destiny (subtitled). 135 min. Color. 1997. Cinema Village. The story of Averroes set in twelfth-century Al-Andalus.

Becket. 148 min. Color. 1964. Paramount Pictures. Based on the play by Jean Anouilh, the film explores the relationship between Thomas Becket (Richard Burton) and Henry II (Peter O'Toole).

Braveheart. 177 min. Color. 1995. 20th Century Fox. Mel Gibson's personal portrait of the thirteenth-century Scottish hero of independence, William Wallace. Film perhaps works best as a way to image medieval warfare.

The Crusades. 200 min. Color. 1995. A&E Television Network. Not really a feature film, but Terry Jones' four-part documentary offers up an irreverent look at the political, economic, and religious machinations behind the Crusades.

El Naser Salah el Dine/Saladin. 90 min. Color. 1963. Lotus Films. Saladin is presented as a prototype of Nasser in calling for Arab unity in order to expel the Western invaders.

The Lion in Winter. 135 min. Color. 1968. MGM/UA Home Entertainment. Henry II and Eleanor meet with their three surviving sons at Christmas to decide which of them should become the new king after Henry's death.

Lionheart. 104 min. Color. 1987. Warner Brothers. Story of a knight about to join King Richard's crusaders. Along the way, he encounters the Black Prince, who captures children and sells them as slaves to the Muslims.

Sorceress. 97 min. Color. 1987. Bleu Productions. A Dominican friar visits a thirteenth-century French village in search of heretics.

The Warlord. 123 min. Color. 1965. Universal Pictures. Film set in the eleventh century about a knight who

invokes the right (*ius primae noctis*) to sleep with another man's bride on their wedding night.

SUGGESTED CLASSROOM FILMS

Anglo-Saxon England. 22 min. Color. 1971. International Film Bureau. Uses aerial photographs, artifacts, and excavations to explore England from the end of Roman rule to 1066.

The Birth of Europe. 39 min. Color. 1979. McGraw-Hill. The early Middle Ages, with the spread of Christianity as the focus.

The Book of Kells. 21 min. Color. 1974. Ulster TV/Picture Films Corporation. With photographs of the manuscripts at Trinity College.

Byzantium: From Splendor to Ruin. 52 min. Color. 1989. Films for the Humanities and Sciences. Program about the flowering of Constantinople as a second Rome and its gradual decline and ultimate fall in 1453.

The Christian Empire. 45 min. Color. 1978. Contemporary Films. Traces the Christian empire from Rome to Constantinople to Russia.

Christians, Jews, and Moslems in Medieval Spain. 32 min. Color. 1989. Films for the Humanities and Sciences. The history of Spain from the time of the first landing, in 711, through the nearly 800-year-long war that ended in the expulsion of both Moors and Jews in 1492.

The Dark Ages and the Millennium: Christianity in the Ninth and Tenth Centuries. 47 min. Color. 1999. Films for the Humanities and Sciences. The chaos in Europe that broke out with the death of Charlemagne and the approach of the millennium. Part of the *Two Thousand Years: The History of Christianity* series.

Feast and Famine. 55 min. Color. 1991. Insight Media. This BBC production explores the agricultural underpinnings of medieval Europe.

The Feudal System. 52 min. Color. 1989. Films for the Humanities and Sciences. Illustrates life in a medieval village, including the role of the feudal lord and serf, the economy of the peasant community, and life on the landed estate.

The Jeweled City: The Cathedral of Chartres. 50 min. Color. 1995. Films for the Humanities and Sciences. Narrated tour of the cathedral, along with a historical portrait of the political and religious fervor surrounding its construction.

Islam: Empire of Faith. 165 min. Color. 2001. PBS. Three-part series follows the history of Islam from Muhammad to the rise of the Ottoman Turks. Includes *The Messenger*; *The Awakening*; and *The Ottomans*.

The Norman Conquest of England. 20 min. Color. 1971. Radim Films. Discusses the causes and consequences of the Norman conquest.

The Rise of Nations in Europe. 13 min. Color. 1978. Coronet. The origins of modern European nations are traced to the rise of the monarchies.

Spain: The Moorish Influence. 28 min. Color. 1990. Insight Media. Explores the role of the Moors in shaping Spanish culture. Received a "Highly Recommended" rating in the *Video Rating Guide*.

When the World Spoke Arabic: The Golden Age of Arab Civilization. 300 min. Color. 1999. Films for the Humanities and Sciences. Twelve-part series presents the history and the most significant cultural, scientific, and technical achievements of the Arab empire between the seventh and thirteenth centuries.

CHAPTER 9

The High Middle Ages: Religious and Intellectual Developments, 1000–1300

OUTLINE

I. Introduction
   A. A period of profound change
   B. Religion
      1. Emergence of the papacy as the dominant organizational force
      2. New monastic and religious orders
      3. Increased persecution of minority groups
   C. Revival of intellectual and cultural life
      1. The renaissance of the twelfth century
      2. A new reading public
      3. Education
II. The Reform of the Church
   A. Privatization of parishes and monasteries
   B. Incompetent popes and bishops
   C. Monastic reform, 900–1050
      1. Cluny (c. 910)
         a. A Benedictine house
         b. Placed under the protection of the papacy
         c. Reformed "daughter" monasteries
         d. A network of dependent Cluniac houses across Europe (sixty-seven by 1049)
         e. High spiritual standards and ordered liturgical life
         f. Cluniac influence strongest in France and Italy
      2. Other reforms
         a. German and English kings urge monastic reforms
         b. Guaranteed monasteries freedom from interference

c. Kings appointed bishops and abbots
      3. Monasticism as dominant spiritual model—mirrored the perfect harmony of heaven
         a. Monks as "angelic men"
         b. Monasteries housed the relics of the saints
         c. Attracted the laity—pilgrimages
   D. The papal reform movement
      1. Bishops rebuild and expand cathedral churches following the Cluniac example
      2. Cluniacs lobby for the reform of the entire church
      3. The attack upon simony (buying and selling of offices)
      4. German emperor Henry III deposed three nobles who claimed to be pope (1046)
         a. Appoints Leo IX as pope
         b. Promulgates decrees against simony, clerical marriage, and immorality
         c. Traveled through France, Italy, Germany, and Hungary disciplining clerics
         d. A new vision of the church as a hierarchical organization
      5. Reform popes were most successful when they had the support of secular rulers
      6. Pope Nicholas II issues decree on papal elections
         a. Right to select a pope rests with the College of Cardinals
         b. Opened a breach between the reform party in Rome and the German court

E. The Investiture Conflict
  1. Pope Gregory VII (1073–1085) supported by a Roman mob
     a. Well-known reformer
     b. His election violated the 1059 Electoral Decree
  2. Henry IV (German emperor) treats Gregory with deference
  3. For Gregory, pope and emperor are two eyes of a single, Christian body
  4. The major question: lay investiture
  5. Gregory's reforms
     a. Ending simony and clerical marriage
     b. Ensuring free elections to all church offices
     c. Prohibited clerics from accepting offices from laymen
  6. Henry refuses to submit to Gregory
     a. Traditional rights of the king
     b. Invests new archbishop in Milan
  7. Henry renounces obedience to Gregory
  8. Gregory excommunicates Henry
     a. Declares Henry no longer king of Germany
     b. Henry forced make a humiliating public submission to Gregory at Canossa (1077)
  9. The issue at stake
     a. Who was the supreme ruler, pope or emperor?
     b. The necessity of spiritual and temporal powers
  10. Consequences
     a. Lasting distinction between religion and politics
     b. Church and religious authority—state and political authority
     c. In essence, not a church-state conflict—by 1122, that is what it had become
     d. Concordat of Worms
        i. Resolved the papal-imperial conflict
        ii. Established the hierarchical order headed by the pope
F. The consolidation of the papal monarchy
  1. Investiture Conflict as papal victory
     a. Strengthened papacy's claim to jurisdictional supremacy over the clergy
     b. Resulted in greater popular interest in religious matters
  2. Growth of church government apparatus

  3. Development of church or canon law
     a. Gratian (fl. twelfth century)
        i. The *Decretum* or *The Concord of Discordant Canons*
     b. Cases in canon law courts increased
     c. The importance of legal expertise
G. The reign of Innocent III (1198–1216)
  1. Elected pope at thirty-seven
  2. Studied theology and canon law
  3. Goal was to unify Christendom under papal hegemony
     a. Never questioned the right of the king to rule in the secular sphere
     b. He would discipline kings whenever they sinned
  4. Founded the Papal States
  5. Engineered the triumph of Frederick II
  6. Fourth Lateran Council (1215)
H. Popes of the thirteenth century
  1. Popes after Innocent began to appear more like ordinary, acquisitive rulers
  2. Conflicts with Frederick
  3. Popes enhanced power of church government
     a. Asserted the right to name candidates for ecclesiastical positions
     b. Controlled curriculum at the University of Paris
     c. Political misuse of the institution of the Crusades (against Frederick)
     d. Loss of spiritual prestige
I. Decline of the papal monarchy
  1. Boniface VIII (1294–1303)
     a. The growth of national monarchies
     b. Disputes with English and French kings
        i. Clerical taxation
        ii. Papacy moves from Rome to Avignon (1316–1377)
  2. Balance of power shifted toward the state and away from the church
     a. Pious Christians looked to the state for campaigns of moral and spiritual improvement
III. The Outburst of Religious Vitality
  A. European religious revival
  B. Cistercians and Carthusians
     1. Founding of new orders
     2. Cistercians
        a. Followed the Benedictine Rule in a most austere manner
        b. Founded new monasteries away from civilization

        c. Shunned unnecessary church decoration

        d. Abandoned Cluniac stress on an elaborate liturgy

        e. Contemplation, prayer, manual labor

    3. Changing nature of religious belief and devotion

        a. Shift away from the cult of saints

        b. Emphasis on worship of Jesus and veneration of the Virgin Mary

        c. Veneration of relics replaced by concentration on the Eucharist

           i. Transubstantiation

          ii. The host elevated for all to see

         iii. The identification with Christ

C. The cult of the Virgin Mary

    1. Patron saint of the Cistercians

    2. Notre Dame ("Our Lady") cathedrals— Paris, Chartres, Rheims, and elsewhere

    3. Mary as intercessor with Jesus for human salvation

    4. Set a woman in an honored place in the Christian religion

D. Hildegard of Bingen (1098–1179)

    1. Religious visions, inspired by God

    2. Wrote Latin prose

    3. Composed religious songs

E. The challenge of popular heresy

    1. Difficult to control lay enthusiasm

    2. Had the church lost its idealistic goals?

    3. The "miraculous" powers of the priest

    4. The Cathars (Albigensians)

        a. Strongest in northern Italy and southern France

        b. Believed all matter was evil

        c. Holiness required extreme asceticism

        d. Dualistic religion

        e. Role of noblewomen in the spread of Catharism

    4. The Waldensians

        a. Originated by Peter Waldo at Lyons

        b. Imitated the life of Christ and the apostles

        c. Translated and studied the Gospels

        d. Dedicated themselves to poverty and preaching

        e. An alternative church?

    5. Innocent's reaction

        a. Crushing disobedience

        b. Supporting idealistic religious groups

        c. A crusade against the Albigensians

        d. The Inquisition (torture first used in 1252)

    6. Fourth Lateran Council (1215)

        a. Sacraments administered by the church would secure God's grace

        b. Emphasis on the Eucharist and penance

        c. Transubstantiation formally defined

F. Franciscans and Dominicans

    1. Imitated the life of Jesus while wandering the European countryside in small groups

    2. The Dominicans

        a. Founded by St. Dominic (1170–1221)

        b. Approved by Innocent (1216)

        c. Dedicated to fighting heresy

        d. The conversion of Jews and Muslims

        e. Preaching and public debate— intellectually oriented

        f. Heretics best controlled by legal procedure

    3. The Franciscans

        a. Founded by St. Francis of Assisi (1181–1226)

           i. Gave away all his property

          ii. Committed to an "emotional" religion

         iii. Imitated the life of Christ

         iv. Indifference toward doctrine, form or ceremony

          v. Revered the Eucharist

        b. Granted approval by Innocent (1209)

        c. Spread of the movement

        d. Specialized in revivalistic outdoor preaching

    4. Consequences

        a. Combated heresy

        b. Helped preach papal crusades

        c. Active missionary work

        d. Power by example

        e. Not completely successful in converting the heretic

G. Jews and Christians

    1. Church did little to condemn or contain anti-Semitism

    2. Popular Christian attitudes

        a. Jews were the agents of Satan

        b. The crucifixion of Christian children

    3. Thirteenth-century kings begin expelling Jews from their kingdoms

IV. The Medieval Intellectual Revival
  A. The growth of schools
    1. Antecedents—Charlemagne reorganized cathedral and monastic schools
    2. Twelfth-century monasteries abandon practice of educating outsiders
    3. Cathedral schools—main centers of European education
    4. Broadening of the curriculum (twelfth century)
    5. Growing demand for trained officials
      a. Knowledge of Latin grammar required
      b. Classical Roman authors
      c. Philosophy
    6. New schools
      a. Education for those not intended to join the clergy
      b. Children of the upper classes
      c. Future notaries, merchants, or estate officials
      d. Schools became independent of ecclesiastical control
      e. Nonreligious lines of inquiry
  B. The rise of universities
    1. Originally offered instruction beyond the cathedral school—advanced liberal arts
    2. Advanced liberal arts, law, medicine, and theology
    3. First university at Bologna—known for legal studies
    4. University of Paris —known for theological and philosophical studies
      a. Peter Abelard (1079–1142)
        i. Attracted students from across Europe
    5. "University" originally meant a corporation or guild of students or teachers
    6. University gradually came to mean an educational institution with a school of liberal arts
    7. Thirteenth-century schools: Oxford, Cambridge, Montpellier, Salamanca, and Naples
    8. Universities as student corporations
      a. Bologna
      b. Students hired and paid teachers
    9. Universities as teacher corporation
      a. Paris
        i. Arts, theology, law, and medicine
    10. Modern degree system—B.A., M.A., Ph.D.

      a. Emphasis on abstract analysis and disputation
    11. Student life
      a. Town and gown
      b. Study was intense
      c. The value of authority
      d. Rote memorization
      e. Public disputation
  C. The recovery of classical learning
    1. Greek and Arabic works given Latin translations
    2. Burst of translating activity centered in Spain and Italy
    3. Rediscovery of Aristotle, Euclid, Galen, and Ptolemy
    4. Building on past speculative thought
      a. Natural science
      b. Robert Grosseteste (c. 1168–1253)
        i. Translated all of Aristotle's *Ethics*
        ii. Theoretical advances in mathematics, astronomy, and optics
      c. Roger Bacon (c. 1214–1294)
        i. Further studies on optics
      d. Knowledge of nature more certain when based on sensory evidence
  D. Scholasticism
    1. A new worldview: highly systematic and respectful of authority
    2. The theory and practice of reconciling classical philosophy with Christian faith
    3. Peter Abelard (1079–1143)
      a. Taught at Paris
      b. The first intellectual?
      c. Adept at logic
      d. The seduction of Heloise (1118)
      e. *The Story of My Calamities*
      f. *Sic et Non* (*Yes and No*)
        i. Gathered 150 statements from the Church Fathers
        ii. Using careful study to arrive at truth
        iii. Abelard's method—Socratic questioning
        iv. Treated theology as a science, applying to it the laws of logic
        v. The harmony of reason and faith
  E. The triumph of scholasticism
    1. Peter Lombard (c. 1100–1164)
      a. *Book of Sentences*
      b. Raised theological questions in consequential order

c. Answered from both sides of
   the question
   2. The scholastic method
   3. Aristotle as "The Philosopher"
F. The writings of Saint Thomas Aquinas
   (1225–1274)
   1. Leading theologian at Paris
   2. Early Dominican education
   3. Faith could be defended by reason
   4. Nature complements grace
   5. Harmonized Greek philosophy with
      Christian theology
   6. *Summa Contra Gentiles* and *Summa
      Theologica*
   7. There are mysteries of faith that cannot
      be explained by reason
G. The pinnacle of Western medieval thought
   1. The receptivity to new ideas
   2. The authority of a text was not the sole
      judge in arguments
   3. Exalting the dignity of human nature as
      a divine creation
V. The Blossoming of Literature, Art, and Music
   A. The Goliards
      1. Wandering scholars
      2. Parodied the liturgy
      3. Rejection of Christian asceticism
   B. Vernacular literature
      1. *Song of Roland* (French)
      2. *Song of the Nibelungs* (German)
      3. *Poem of the Cid* (Spanish)
   C. Troubadours' poetry and courtly romances
      1. Sophisticated style
      2. Theme of courtly love
      3. Romances
         a. Long, narrative poems
         b. Written in the vernacular,
            Romance languages
         c. Chrétian de Troyes—wrote
            Arthurian romances
         d. Wolfram von Eschenbach,
            Parzival
         e. Gottfried von Strassburg, *Tristan*
      4. The *fabliaux* or verse fable
         a. Derived from Aesop
         b. Significant reflection of growing
            worldliness
   D. *The Divine Comedy*
      1. Dante Alighieri (1265–1321)
         a. Native of Florence
         b. Mastered religious, philosophical,
            and literary knowledge of his time
         c. Familiar with the Bible, the church
            fathers, Virgil, Cicero, and Boethius
         d. Expelled from Florence (1301)

   2. *The Divine Comedy*
      a. Narrative in Italian rhyming verse
      b Poet's journey through hell,
         purgatory, and heaven
      c. Virgil as the poet's guide
      d. Beatrice
      e. Stressed the priority of salvation
      f. Humans have free will
   E. Art and architecture
      1. The Romanesque
         a. Origins in tenth century
         b. Manifesting the majesty of God
            in stone
         c. Subordinated all architectural
            details to a uniform system
         d. Stability and permanence
      2. The Gothic
         a. Appeared in twelfth and thirteenth
            centuries
         b. Intricate building style
         c. Pointed arches, groined and ribbed
            vaults, flying buttresses
         d. Lighter and loftier construction
         e. Exterior ornamentation
         f. Stained-glass windows
         g. An "encyclopedia of medieval
            knowledge carved in stone"
   F. Drama and music
      1. Short religious plays held in church
         in Latin
      2. Supplanted by plays in the vernacular
      3. Outdoor performances (after 1200)
      4. Medieval polyphony (playing two or
         more harmonious melodies together)
VI. Conclusion
    A. The "renaissance of the twelfth century"
    B. Recovery and intensive study of classical texts
    C. New ideas, new attitudes

GENERAL DISCUSSION QUESTIONS

1. Contrast the impetus for monastic reforms in France
   and Italy with the reforms that took place in England
   and Germany. Why was it essential that medieval
   monasteries were in need of reform by the eleventh
   century?

2. What grave issues faced the church in the eleventh
   century? How widespread were papal abuses and
   corruption? Why and how did knowledge of papal
   abuses become public?

3. Why was the Investiture Contflict a victory for the
   papacy?

4. Why has Innocent III been called the most capable of all high medieval popes?

5. How do we account for the sudden increase of heresies in the twelfth century? What forces motivated the heretics?

6. Why was the twelfth century a century of promise for students who wished to pursue education outside the monastic or cathedral school?

7. How would you define scholasticism?

8. What role did vernacular literature play in the "renaissance of the twelfth century"?

DOCUMENT DISCUSSION QUESTIONS

A Miracle of Saint Faith

1. Why were medieval Europeans well-prepared to embrace a cult of relics? Is there any parallel in the modern age? What did medieval men and women hope to obtain from the veneration of relics?

2. What does the belief in the miraculous healing power of relics illustrate about medieval popular piety in general?

The Conversion of Peter Waldo

3. What drove a wealthy man like Peter Waldo to sacrifice his worldly life for the life of a heretic? Why would any medieval man or woman choose to become a heretic?

4. How does the conversion of Peter Waldo illustrate the kind of psychological tensions facing men and women in the High Middle Ages?

A Goliardic Parody of the Gospel of Mark, Satirizing the Papal Court

5. How seriously do you think medieval men and women considered the parodies of the Goliards? For what purpose did the Goliards choose parody over other forms of literature?

6. Do you think that the Goliards were a disruptive force in medieval society? Do they have any modern parallels?

SAMPLE LECTURE 9: RELIGIOUS AND INTELLECTUAL DEVELOPMENTS OF THE HIGH MIDDLE AGES

Lecture Objectives

1. To discuss the challenges faced by the church

2. To investigate the outburst of religious vitality during the High Middle Ages

3. To discuss how we account for the twelfth-century renaissance and to investigate its defining characteristics

ABELARD'S SEARCH FOR TRUTH

The life and career of the Paris theologian, Peter Abelard (1079–1142), illustrates many tendencies of twelfth-century intellectual life. Abelard was loved by his students but reviled by his peers: he asked too many questions, he wanted to know the truth, he was not satisfied with authority. In his popular book, *Sic et Non* (*Yes and No*), Abelard wrote:

> By collecting contrasting divergent opinions I hope to provoke young readers to push themselves to the limit in the search for truth, so that their wits may be sharpened by their investigation. It is by doubting that we come to investigate, and by investigating that we recognize the truth.

Doubt, investigation, truth—so many of these ideas seem particular to the modern frame of mind. Is it at all odd that these words were uttered more than eight hundred years ago, during the great Age of Faith?

THE CHURCH IN CONFLICT

The church, of course, regarded Abelard with a cautious eye. And rightly so, since the church was at this time confronted with a series of challenges to its hierarchical organization, its power, its authority, and its dogmas. The first hints of such challenges came from the monastic movement of the tenth and eleventh centuries:

- Monasteries had become the province of wealthy landlords and nobles
- The "privatization" of monasteries was a first step toward reform
- Bishops were helpless against the local powers of the nobility
- The Cluniac movement and daughter monasteries were directly protected by the papacy and strongest where the king's power was weakest (France and Italy)
- Cluny set high spiritual standards and revitalized the Benedictine Rule in its monasteries
- Monasticism provided the dominant spiritual model for the High Middle Ages

Meanwhile, the church initiated its own reform movement. The evidence for such a reform movement is clear: why else would Pope Leo IX issue decrees against simony, clerical marriage, and the general immorality of the clergy? One of the major issues facing the church pertained to the election of new popes: ought the power to nominate popes reside in the hands of secular rulers or in the College of Cardinals? The resolution of this question takes us to the heart of the papal reform movement of the eleventh and twelfth centuries, the "Investiture Conflict." Who had the right (or duty) to elect a pope? It seems that both popes and kings were violating Pope Nicholas II's Electoral Decree of 1059, which vested the cardinals with papal election rights. Pope Gregory spoke of the pope and emperor as "two eyes of a single, Christian body." Was there an alternative? Henry IV refused to accept the idea that the clergy could only be appointed by Rome; it threatened his Carolingian idea of kingship. We would tend to see the "Investiture Conflict" as a conflict between church and state and, although it did not begin that way, it ended with a partial resolution to that conflict with the Concordat of Worms (1122). It:

- brought an end to the Carolingian idea of "sacred kingship"
- established the independent jurisdictional authority of the church over secular rulers
- was a compromise, but one that rallied the clergy behind the pope

POPES INNOCENT AND BONIFACE

Innocent III (1198–1216) was the most capable and successful of the high medieval popes. He was trained in theology and canon law, and, unlike Gregory, he recognized the temporal power of kings and princes. Regarded as the founder of the Papal States, his goal was to unify all Christendom under papal authority:

- He disciplined kings when necessary; for example, Philip Augustus of France and King John of England.
- He consolidated papal territories in central Italy.
- He called a crusade against the Albigensians.
- He summoned the Fourth Lateran Council of 1215.

Thirteenth-century popes after Innocent enhanced their powers and centralized church government. They named candidates to church positions and controlled the curriculum at the University of Paris. Eventually, their actions brought them into a long political struggle, beginning with the crusade against Frederick II, and led to their demise as temporal powers. Boniface VIII (1294–1303) had to contend with the rise of new national monarchies, especially over secular issues like taxation. Eventually, he lost the support of the English and French clergy, was charged with heresy by Philip IV of France, and was arrested. The result was that, for the next seventy years, popes resided at Avignon and were regarded as pawns of French diplomacy.

AN AGE OF FAITH: RELIGIOUS VITALITY

As a partial result of papal reform and Pope Gregory's direct appeal to the laity to help discipline the clergy, the laity came to respect the clergy more. One manifestation of the new piety of the High Middle Ages was the popularity of the Cistercian movement. The Cistercian order had mass appeal:

- It provided full expression of "interiority" (self-examination) to better know God.

- It followed the Benedictine Rule in a pure manner.
- It shunned church decoration.
- It abandoned the Cluniac emphasis on an elaborate liturgy.
- Saint Bernard of Clairvaux (1090–1153) was a charismatic and influential leader.

The nature of religious belief and devotion was also changing. One piece of evidence for this was the popularity of the Cult of the Virgin Mary. Another example of changing beliefs was that the veneration of relics was replaced by reverence for the Eucharist:

- Theologians of the twelfth century had finally made the doctrine of transubstantiation workable, allowing the Eucharist to become a central feature of worship.
- The theology of the Eucharist enhanced the dignity of priests as mediators of God—a mixed blessing?
- The celebration of the Eucharist encouraged the faithful to meditate on Christ's suffering and imitate his life.

POPULAR HERESY

The church found it difficult to control religious enthusiasm, and some people wondered if it was the church that had lost its way. The people wanted something more; the church, so it seemed, promised them less. With more people congregating in cities—made possible by the rise of the university, the growth of trade, a lay literature, and the guild system—the moral laxity and indifference of the clergy was more visible and became the object of public scrutiny. The result was widespread popular heresy. A heretic was foremost a Christian, but a Christian who had lost his or her way and was in need of reform. Theologians argued that heretics ought to be converted; if that didn't work, they should be excommunicated or put to death. So why would anyone become a heretic?

- The wealthy found fewer positions in the church hierarchy.
- Monasteries had been somewhat "de-privatized."
- Women were excluded from church positions.
- Mysticism and spirituality had been unleashed.
- The quality and availability of learning prompted a new individualism; people began thinking for themselves; for example, the scholastic Peter Abelard.
- The poor had no way out of their suffering.

Although there were dozens of heretical movements, the two most prominent ones were the Waldensians and the Cathars (Albigensians). Confronted by a serious choice between wealth and spirituality, the Waldensian founder, Peter Waldo, gave up his wealth and began to preach to the people of Lyons. The Waldensians wished to imitate the life of Christ. They translated and studied the Gospels and dedicated themselves to preaching. The church considered them heretics when they refused to stop their unauthorized preaching. From then on, the Waldensians became more radical.

Far more dangerous than the Waldensians were the Cathars, or Albigensians. Strongest in northern Italy and southern France, they believed that all matter was evil, so they practiced extreme asceticism. Their heresy challenged the authority of a less zealous clergy and offered the people an outlet for intense spirituality. Faced with these challenges, as well as others, the church resorted to crusades and inquisitions, neither of which was successful in stopping heresy. The church's position on combating heresy was that of "peaceably if we may, forcibly if we must."

DOMINICANS AND FRANCISCANS

If torture and crusades were unsuccessful, perhaps conversion might be another alternative. So, from Spain came Saint Dominic (1170–1221) and the Dominican Order, whose policy of conversion involved intellectual argument with suspected heretics. By conducting public debate, the Dominicans hoped to convert the heretic, but not all people were so intellectually inclined.

From Italy came Saint Francis of Assisi (1182–1226), a wealthy man who gave up his riches to pursue a life dedicated to serving the poor. (Compare his "crisis of faith" to that of Waldo or even Muhammad and Luther.) Unlike the Dominicans, Saint Francis imitated the life of Christ and was indifferent to doctrine, form, and ceremony, with the exception of the Eucharistic sacrament.

The Dominicans and Franciscans added to their members and eventually received support from Rome. Although they did meet with some success, heresy continued to exist. The Dominicans and Franciscans can also be seen as an indictment of the church, for if the church had been doing its job correctly, there would have been no reason for these orders to exist. But exist they did, as evidence not only of something dreadfully wrong with the church but also of the intense religious piety of medieval men and women.

THE MEDIEVAL INTELLECTUAL REVIVAL

Historians have long recognized a renaissance of the twelfth century. Much of this period of rebirth was due to the spread of education and literacy, the rise of the medieval university, and the acquisition of classical thought and Muslim commentaries. Also, we must not forget that the spread of knowledge in the twelfth century never would have taken place had people not desired this knowledge. But why were people so eager learn?

- Economic revival attracted more people to urban areas and enabled more people to afford formal education.
- The growth of towns and cities necessitated the establishment of a greater number of schools.
- The emergence of strong government gave Europeans more freedom to devote themselves to basic education.
- Monasteries abandoned the practice of educating outsiders.
- Cathedral schools, supported by the papal monarchy, took over the role of training priests.

- The need for trained secular officials created a broadened curriculum.
- By the mid-twelfth century, the need for lawyers to litigate Church cases forced the quality of education to change.

THE UNIVERSITY

The university was not so much a place as a group of scholars. Accordingly, the word *university* originally meant a "corporation or guild," either of teachers or of students. Our modern degrees—B.A., M.A., and Ph.D.—all derive from the medieval university system. Of course, actual courses of study were quite different. Once a student entered the higher faculty, there were basically four areas of study: law, theology, medicine, and philosophy. Students came from all over Europe to attend universities at Paris, Oxford, or Bologna. The students, therefore, were usually strangers in a strange land and, as such, were critical of housing, tuition, and the level of scholarship of their instructors. Teachers were concerned about competition from other teachers. And, naturally, the church fretted over the implications of all this knowledge.

Bologna became known for its legal studies, and the majority of its students were adult males. Paris, on the other hand, specialized in philosophy and theology. No matter where students attended university, they comprised a separate and privileged community and, thus, were often the objects of scorn among the locals. Students also found university life itself difficult. Since there were no books, they had to copy manuscripts and memorize massive amounts of material. Education took the form of a disputation in which the student was forced to argue a particular opinion before an audience that might contain professors, doctors, lawyers, theologians, and perhaps even a prince.

CLASSICAL LEARNING

In the twelfth century, Europe had rediscovered its classical heritage. One legacy of the Crusades was that an enormous quantity of classical texts made their way back into Europe. Along with these texts came commentaries by Arabic philosophers and scientists such as Avicenna (980–1037) and Averroës (1126–1198). To be accessible to western Europeans, Greek and Arabic material needed to be translated, so what was needed was a common scholarly language, which became medieval Latin. Within this context, the primary worldview of the medieval intellectual, scholasticism, began to emerge. The following were features of Scholasticism:

- Its original meaning was the medieval method of teaching and learning.
- It was highly respectful of authority, especially Aristotle, who was known simply as "The Philosopher."
- It taught a compatibility between faith and reason.
- It reconciled classical thought with Christian faith.
- Two important scholastic thinkers were Peter Abelard and Peter Lombard.

No medieval scholastic was as important to the intellectual life of Europe as Saint Thomas Aquinas (1225–1274). As a Dominican monk, Aquinas was dedicated to the idea that faith could be defended by reason. What this signified was that the natural world might be understood by human reason, but that the highest truths could be obtained only through faith and revelation. He was responsible for producing a "Christian Matrix" of rigorous orderliness and extraordinary intellectual insights.

VERNACULAR LITERATURE

Although much of the revival of learning took place within the context of the university, vernacular language became popular as a means of literary expression in twelfth-century Europe:

- Goliardic verse was free-spirited and satirical; consider the Goliards as a twelfth-century Beat generation.
- Troubadours originated new verse styles and subjects—poetry as music, romantic love, and the idealization of women.
- Romances, so called because they were written in vernacular Romance languages, emphasized love and adventure tales, the most famous being Arthurian.
- Chrétien de Troyes, in contrast to the troubadours, elevated the ideal of love within marriage.
- Wolfram von Eschenbach, the author of *Parzival*, was the first Western writer since the Greeks to give full character development to his characters.
- The *fabliaux*, verse fables, were precursors to the style of realism that was later perfected by Boccaccio and Chaucer.
- *The Romance of the Rose* is another literary example of the increasingly earthly and jaded attitudes of the twelfth century.

While vernacular literature contributed to the growing worldliness of medieval Europe, perhaps the greatest work of medieval literature was Dante Alighieri's *Divine Comedy*. Writing in Italian verse, Dante (1265–1321) synthesized a wealth of knowledge and experience, including classical thought, the poems of the troubadours, the Holy Scriptures, and the everyday reality of Italy in the early fourteenth century. Although the point of the *Divine Comedy* is to direct the reader's attention to salvation, Dante stressed that the earth is for human benefit, thus "humanizing" Christianity. (Whereas humankind was Christianized in Late Antiquity, by the twelfth century, Christianity was becoming humanized.)

ART AND ARCHITECTURE

The ideals of the High Middle Ages also found expression in architectural changes. The earlier Romanesque style sought to demonstrate the majesty of God by subjugating all architectural details to a uniform and repetitive system. In a way, this focus on "system" parallels the theological work of Aquinas as well as Dante's grand scheme in the *Divine Com-*

edy. The Gothic style that followed was more intricate and sophisticated—note the text's comparison of Romanesque and Gothic styles to the epic and the romance, respectively (378). Thanks to its use of pointed arches, groined and ribbed vaults, and flying buttresses, the Gothic cathedral was brighter, sturdier, and loftier than its predecessor. It is for good reason that the Gothic cathedral has been described as an "encyclopedia of medieval knowledge carved in stone": its windows, sculptures, and basic existence represented expressions of daily life, religious glory, intellectual genius, and urban pride.

The intellectual developments that occurred in the High Middle Ages demonstrate that Europe had come to a period in its history when security and protection, although still important, were joined by an impetus for change. Medieval intellectual and cultural life was vibrant. The age pointed to the religious enthusiasm of the common person as much as it did the need for the church to reform itself from within. Finally, scholasticism offered a worldview that was specifically medieval and without which the future stages of human intellectual growth would have been far different.

SUGGESTED FEATURE FILMS

Alexander Nevsky. 112 min. B/W. 1938. Mosfilm. Eisenstein's depiction of the battle in 1242 between Russian peasants and Teutonic knights.

Becket. 148 min. Color. 1964. Paramount Pictures. Directed by Peter Glenville, and starring Peter O'Toole as Henry II and Richard Burton as Thomas Becket. An excellent film adaptation of Jean Anouilh's dramatization of the Becket affair.

Brother Sun, Sister Moon. 122 min. Color. 1972. Paramount. Franco Zeffirelli's dramatization of events in the life of Saint Francis of Assisi.

Die Nibelungen. 115 min. B/W. 1925. Decla-Bioscope. Silent. Fritz Lang's dramatization of the thirteenth-century verse epic.

El Cid. 160 min. Color. 1961. Miramax. Epic treatment of the Spanish hero, played by Charlton Heston.

Excalibur. 140 min. Color. 1981. Orion. John Boorman's version of *Le Morte d'Arthur.*

The Knights of the Teutonic Order. 180 min. Color. 1960. Studio Unit. Film of the fourteenth-century conflict between the Polish state and the Teutonic Knights. Useful for scenes of ordinary peasant life.

The Lion in Winter. 134 min. Color. 1964. MGM/UA Home Entertainment, Inc. Film by Anthony Harvey, starring Katherine Hepburn and Peter O'Toole, that depicts the scheming and intrigue between Henry II, Eleanor of Aquitaine, and their sons in 1183.

The Name of the Rose. 128 min. Color. 1986. Columbia/Tri-Star. Jean-Jacques Annaud directs and Sean Connery stars in this version of Umberto Eco's explanation of the medieval conflict between reason and faith.

Sorceress (Le Moine et la sorcière). 97 min. Color. 1987. European Classics Video. A Dominican friar visits a thirteenth-century French village in search of heretics.

Stealing Heaven. 108 min. Color. 1988. Amy International. Relates the passionate love affair between Peter Abelard and Heloise. Particularly good for its imagery of medieval intellectual life.

SUGGESTED CLASSROOM FILMS

The Circles of Light: The Divine Comedy. 50 min. Color. 1995. Films for the Humanities and Sciences. Dramatizations of scenes from Dante's *Divine Comedy* depicting courtly love, sexual love, and the love of God.

Cluny: A Light in the Night. 53 min. Color. 1995. Films for the Humanities and Sciences. Offers a look at the architecture and social impact of Cluny and the Cluniac movement.

Common Life in the Middle Ages. 2 parts, 30 min. each. 1989. Insight Media. A look at the consequences of the conflicts between church and secular rulers for ordinary people. Also looks at medieval cities and cathedrals.

The Crusades. 23 min. Color. 1989. Insight Media. Explores the three major crusades.

The Crusades: Saints and Sinners. 26 min. Color. 1970. Insight Media. A reenactment of the First Crusade.

The Disputation: A Theological Debate between Christians and Jews. 65 min. Color. 1986. Films for the Humanities. Re-creation of the Barcelona Disputation of 1263.

Early English Drama: The Second Shepherd's Play. 52 min. Color. 1975. Films for the Humanities. Traces the development of medieval theater through three reenactments: a tenth-century mystery play, the *Story of Abraham and Isaac*, and a fourteenth-century shepherd's play.

Everyman. 53 min. Color. 1981. Insight Media. A medieval morality play staged in period costume.

Faith and Fear. 39 min. Color. 1979. Insight Media. A look at religious responses to an uncertain world.

The Fall of Constantinople. 34 min. Color. 1970. Time-Life Films. Filmed on location.

The Fires of Faith: Dissidents and the Church. 50 min. Color. 1995. Films for the Humanities and Sciences. Discusses the rise of heresy, Saint Francis, the Cathars, and Innocent III.

The Flower of the Tales: The Burgundian Miniatures in the Royal Library of Belgium. 17 min. Color. 1975. International Film Bureau. Uses manuscript illustrations to describe medieval life.

Francis of Assisi. 12 parts, 30 min. each. Color. 2000. Films for the Humanities and Sciences. Concentrates on the life, teachings, and legacy of one of the most important saints of Christianity.

Medieval Women. 24 min. Color. 1989. Insight Media. Historian Joyce Salisbury leads this exploration of the lives of medieval women.

The Saint and the Scholar: Portrait of Abelard. 50 min. Color. 1995. Films for the Humanities and Sciences. Tells the story of the French theologian and scholar.

Thomas Aquinas: The Angelic Doctor. 12 parts, 30 min. each. Color. 2000. Films for the Humanities and Sciences. Traces the life, work, and development of his system of thought.

Triumph in Stone. Color. 1979. Alex McCowen narrates this study of Romanesque and Gothic architecture.

Part IV: From Medieval to Modern

IDEAS FOR USING THE WESTERN CIVILIZATIONS DIGITAL HISTORY CENTER

The following Map Exercises and Digital History Features at *www.wwnorton.com/wciv* concern the profound effects of the transition from the medieval world of famine, war, and plague to the world of the Renaissance, Reformation, and Age of Religious Wars.

- Map Exercise 6: Fourteenth and Fifteenth-Century Europe (Chapter 10)
- Map Exercise 7: Outside the West (Chapter 11)
- Map Exercise 8: Renaissance Europe (Chapter 12)
- Map Exercise 9: The Age of Religious Wars (Chapters 13–14)
- Digital History Feature 5: After the Black Death (Chapter 10)
- Digital History Feature 6: Spices and the Spice Trade (Chapters 11–12)

Map Exercise 6 will help students understand the speed at which the Black Death ravaged Europe in the middle of the fourteenth century. Use these exercises in conjunction with Digital History Feature 5, "After the Black Death," which gives graphic representation to the effects of the plague on popular consciousness and also highlights a series of peasant revolts that occurred in Europe in the mid-to-late fourteenth century. The Age of Exploration is detailed in Map Exercise 8. Use this alongside Digital History Feature 6, "Spices and the Spice Trade," which emphasizes the role spices have played throughout the history of Western civilization. Students will gain a greater understanding of the importance of spices, since spices have been used not only as flavor-enhancers for food, but also as currency, medicine, and forms of tribute or ransom. Map Exercise 9 will be useful in lecture and classroom discussion on the political effects of the Reformation. These exercises show just how a diversity of theological opinion could and did create the grounds for social conflicts, civil wars, and ultimately the Thirty Years' War.

CHAPTER 10 | The Later Middle Ages, 1300–1500

C. English Peasants' Revolt of 1381
  1. Rising economic expectations and political grievances
  2. Peasant standard of living increased due to decline in population
  3. Aristocrats sought to preserve their incomes
  4. Passed legislation to keep wages at pre-plague levels
  5. The head tax
  6. Peasants burned manor rolls and marched to London
  7. Richard II made promises to help—kept none of them
  8. The murder of Wat Tyler
  9. Effects
      a. The rebellion was a failure
      b. Frightened the English nobility
      c. Enforcement of wage controls on peasants came to an end
D. Urban rebellions
  1. Combination of social, political, and economic grievances
  2. Varied from city to city
  3. Brunswick (1374)
      a. One political alliance replaces another
  4. Lübeck (1408)
      a. A taxpayers' revolt
  5. The Ciompi Rebellion (1378)
      a. Wool-combers of Florence
          i. Unemployment and low wages
      b. Motivated by economic hardship and personal hatreds
      c. Radical reforms
          i. Tax relief and fuller representation
          ii. Political representation
      d. Failed after six weeks
  6. General observations
      a. Main catalyst was economic crisis
      b. Not specifically class revolts
      c. Political grievances
      d. Direct challenges to urban society
E. Aristocratic insecurities
  1. Rebellions posed a threat to their social status and privilege
  2. Gained most of their income from land
  3. Threatened also by rapid rise of merchants and financiers
  4. Set up cultural barriers to separate themselves from others
      a. Established sumptuary laws

b. New chivalric orders
    i. Knights of the Garter or the Golden Fleece
F. Emotional extremes
  1. Sorrow
      a. Shedding tears in abundance
  2. Obsession with mortality
  3. A "culture of death"
      a. The reality of death
      b. Putrefaction
      c. "Grinning Death"
IV. Trials for the Church and Hunger for the Divine
  A. The late medieval papacy
    1. Institutional crisis
    2. The Babylonian Captivity (1305–1378)
        a. Papacy located at Avignon
        b. Subservient to interests of French crown
    3. The Great Schism, 1378–1417
        a. Background
            i. All popes elected at Avignon were from southern France
            ii. Popes imposed new taxes on churches of France, England, Spain, and Germany
            iii. Avignon popes strengthened administrative control
            iv. Clergy and laity felt alienated by papal desires for wealth
            v. Clement VI (1342–1352)—notoriously corrupt and immoral
        b. Gregory returned to Rome in 1377, died the following year
        c. Roman people rioted, demanded the cardinals elect a Roman as pope
            i. Urban VI elected; quarrelled with the cardinals
            ii. Cardinals declared Urban's election void
        d. Clement VII retreated back to Avignon (1378)
            i. Recognized by France, Scotland, Castile, and Aragon
            ii. Rejected by the rest of Europe, who rallied behind Urban
        e. Some cardinals met at Pisa and deposed both popes (1409)
            i. Italian and French pope would not accept the council's decision
            ii. Now there were three popes

      f. Schism ends with the Council of
         Constance (1417)
           i. European ecclesiastical
             unity restored
           ii. Calls for a balanced,
             "conciliar" government
      g. Eventual papal victory over the
         conciliarists

B. Popular piety
   1. Growing dissatisfaction with the clergy:
      explanations
      a. Clergy demanded more from laity
      b. Increase in lay literacy
         i. Proliferation of schools and
           decline in cost of books
        ii. Religious primers
      c. Local priests were not living
         according to standards set by
         Jesus and his apostles
   2. Alternative routes to piety
      a. Repeated acts of external devotion
      b. Pilgrimages
      c. Obsession with reciting prayers
      d. Self-flagellation
   3. Mysticism
      a. Seeking union with God by
         "detachment," contemplation, or
         spiritual exercises
      b. Master Eckhart (c. 1260–1327)
         i. The inner spark
        ii. Renounced selfhood
        iii. Finding divinity within
        iv. Gave the laity the idea
           that the church was not
           necessary
      c. Heretics of the "Free Spirit"
      d. "Practical" mysticism
         i. Did not aim at full ecstatic
           union with God
      e. Thomas à Kempis (1379–1471)
         i. *The Imitation of Christ*
           (c. 1427)
        ii. Attractive to lay readers—
           widely translated
        iii. Urged readers to participate
           in one religious ceremony:
           the Eucharist
        iv. Emphasis on inward piety
   4. Lollards and Hussites
      a. John Wyclif (c. 1330–1384)
         i. Augustinian influences
        ii. Predestination
        iii. Most church officials were
           damned

        iv. Replace corrupt bishops and
           priests with men living
           according to apostolic
           standards
        v. Attacked the sacraments,
           including the Eucharist
        vi. The Lollards
        vii. Pious Christians should not
           trust the sacraments of a
           corrupt church
        viii. Instead, study the Bible
           (translated into the
           vernacular)
      b. Jan Hus (c. 1373–1415)
         i. Similar to the Lollards
        ii. Emphasized the Eucharist as
           central to Christian piety
        iii. Ultraquism—laity to receive
           the consecrated bread and
           wine at mass
        iv. Gained a mass following in
           Bohemia (aristocrats, artisans,
           and peasants)
        v. Concerns for social justice
        vi. Attended the Council of
           Constance (1415)
        vii. Tried for heresy and burned
           at the stake
        vi. Radical Hussites—the
           Taborites

V. Political Crisis and Recovery
  A. Major changes
   1. Incessant warfare
   2. Kings developed new powers to tax and
      control their subjects
   3. Armies became larger and military
      technology improved
   4. National monarchies became more
      aggressively expansionist
  B. Italy
   1. Time of troubles for papal states
   2. After 1417, popes ruled most of central
      Italy
   3. Venice—merchant oligarchy
   4. Milan—dynastic despotism
   5. Florence—a republic in name only,
      actually ruled by the Medici
   6. After 1400, Venice, Milan, and Florence
      expanded territorially
      a. Conquered almost all northern
         cities and towns except Genoa
   7. Kingdom of Naples
   8. Treaty of 1454 brought forty years of
      peace

C. Germany
1. Independent princes warred with weakened emperors or each other
2. Fragmentation of political authority
3. After 1450, some stronger princes began to rule more firmly
   a. Modeled on national monarchies of England and France
   b. Bavaria, Austria, and Brandenburg
D. France
1. The Hundred Years' War, 1337–1453
   a. Causes
      i. Problem of French territory held by English kings (Gascony and Aquitaine)
      ii. English woolen interests in Flanders
      iii. Succession dispute over the French crown
      iv. Valois dynasty replaced the Capets
   b. The war
      i. France the richest country in Europe with the largest population
      ii. English victories at Crécy (1346), Poitiers (1356), and Agincourt (1415)
      iii. The English longbow
      iv. The French were badly divided among themselves
   c. Joan of Arc (c. 1412–1431)
      i. Convinced Charles to let her raise an army
      ii. Brought Charles to Rheims
      iii. Captured in 1430, tried by the English for heresy
      iv. Burned at the stake in Burgundy (1431)
   d. War ends with capture of Bordeaux (1453)
   e. Results
      i. Powers of French crown strengthened
      ii. Valois kings collected national taxes and maintained a standing army
      iii. Monarchy strengthened under Louis XI and Louis XII
E. England
1. Hundred Years' War produced political instability
   a. In defeat, taxpayers held their kings (Edward III and Henry V) responsible
   b. Defeat undermined king's political and fiscal support at home
   c. Dangerous and incompetent kings
2. Henry VI (1422–1461)
   a. Insanity
   b. Provoked an aristocratic rebellion
   c. The Wars of the Roses
      i. York and Lancaster
      ii. Battle of Bosworth Field (1485)—Richard III killed
      iii. Origins of the Tudor dynasty
   d. Henry VIII (1509–1547)
3. Stability
   a. Local institutions continued to function
   b. Increasing importance of Parliament
   c. No challenges to the power of the English state
F. Spain
1. Ferdinand and Isabella
   a. Subdued their aristocracies
   b. Aragon and Castile retained their separate institutions
   c. Annexed Granada
   d. Expelled Spain's Jews
2. Influx of gold and silver from the New World
3. Spain as Europe's most powerful state in the sixteenth century
G. The triumph of national monarchies
1. Germany and Italy still politically divided
2. England and France
3. Spain
4. National monarchies as a sign of future developments
VI. Kievan Rus and the Rise of Muscovy
A. Observations
1. By 1500, Europe's leading Eastern empire
2. Swedish Vikings (the Rus), centered around Kiev
3. Maintained diplomatic and trading relations with western Europe and Byzantium
B. The Mongol invasions
1. Mongol conquest of eastern Slavic states
2. Overran Kiev
3. The Khanate of the Golden Horde (the "Tartar Yoke")
C. The rise of Muscovy
1. Moscow rose to power as a tribute-collecting center for the Khanate
2. Gradually became the dominant political power in northeastern Russia
3. Poor relations between Eastern Orthodoxy and Western Catholicism

D. The rivalry with Poland
  1. Poland a second-rate power
  2. Polish queen, Jadwiga, marries Jagiello (Lithuania) (1386)
  3. Doubled the size of Poland
  4. Lithuanian expansion increased after the union with Poland
  5. Battle of Tannenberg (1410)
E. Moscow and Byzantium
  1. Growing alienation between Moscow and western Europe
  2. Fall of Constantinople (1453)
  3. Tense religious relations between Moscow and Byzantium since 1054
    a. Split over wording of the Nicene Creed
    b. Moscow the center of anti-Roman ideology
  4. Russian ruler took title of tsar (caesar)
F. The reign of Ivan the Great (1462–1505)
  1. Transformed grand duchy of Moscow into an imperial power
  2. The "White Tsar"
  3. Annexed all independent principalities between Moscow and Poland-Lithuania
  4. Political autocracy and imperialism
    a. Built the Kremlin
    b. The "tsar of all the Russians"
VII. Thought, Literature, and Art
  A. Theology and philosophy
    1. A crisis of doubt
    2. Could man comprehend the supernatural?
      a. How to explain the plague?
    3. William of Ockham (c. 1285–1349)
      a. Denied that the existence of God could be demonstrated apart from scriptural revelation
      b. Emphasized God's freedom and absolute power
      c. Nominalism
        i. Only individual things are real
        ii. One thing cannot be understood by means of another
      d. Aided the development of empiricism—knowledge rests on experience alone
  B. Vernacular literature
    1. Trends
      a. Major trait was naturalism
      b. International tensions led people to identify themselves in national terms
      c. Continuing spread of lay education
      d. The emergence of a substantial reading public for vernacular literature
    2. Giovanni Boccaccio (1313–1375)
      a. *Decameron* (1348–1351)
        i. Collection of one hundred stories
        ii. Less interested in elegance, more in being entertaining
        iii. Describes what is, not what should be
    3. Geoffrey Chaucer (c. 1340–1400)
      a. *The Canterbury Tales*
        i. Written in verse, not prose
        ii. Recounted by people of all social classes
        iii. Each character tells a story that illustrates his or her world outlook
    4. Christine de Pisan (c. 1364–1431)
      a. A professional *literati*
      b. *The City of Ladies*
        i. A defense of the character, nature and capacities of women against male detractors
        ii. Written as an allegory
  C. Sculpture and painting
    1. Naturalism as the dominant trait
    2. Statues became more proportioned and realistic
    3. Realism extended to illuminated manuscripts and painting
    4. Frescoes
    5. Oil painting introduced in northern Europe (1400)
    6. Giotto (c. 1267–1337)
      a. Brought deep humanity to his images
      b. A naturalist
      c. The first to conceive of the painted space in three-dimensional terms
    7. Northern Europe
      a. Jan van Eyck (c. 1380–1441)
      b. Roger van der Weyden (c. 1400–1464)
      c. Hans Memling (c. 1430–1494)
VIII. Advances in Technology
  A. Gunpowder, the cannon, and the musket
  B. Eyeglasses, magnetic compass, navigational devices, and clocks
  C. Printed books and movable type
    1. Replacement of parchment by paper
    2. Growing market for less expensive editions

IX. Conclusion
   A. An attempt to understand the natural world
   B. The natural world operated according to its own laws, empirically verifiable
   C. Nature can be subdued
   D. An increasingly educated society

GENERAL DISCUSSION QUESTIONS

1. What environmental factors contributed to the growing economic depression of the fourteenth century?

2. Describe the psychological horror of the Black Death.

3. Why does it seem that the Jacquerie, the English Peasants' Revolt, and the Ciompi Rebellion were somehow destined to fail?

4. Do you think the Lollards and Hussites were trying to restore Christianity to its primitive state? Or were they trying to change it into something entirely different?

5. What were the causes of the Hundred Years' War?

6. What does the life and death of Joan of Arc illuminate about the Age of Faith in general? What motivated her to act in such an extraordinary fashion?

7. What forces were at work that helped to speed up the rise of national monarchies in fifteenth-century Europe?

8. In what ways was the development of medieval Russia so different from that of Europe?

9. How did the perfection of printing and the spread of books stimulate the growth of cultural nationalism?

DOCUMENT DISCUSSION QUESTIONS

Froissart on the English Peasant's Revolt, 1381

1. Would you consider Froissart's account of the English Peasants' Revolt to be trustworthy?

2. Why might Froissart have been more sympathetic to the uprising of the common people in England than he was to the French Jacquerie?

The Conciliarist Controversy

3. How might the conciliar movement be seen as a subtle challenge to the authority of the medieval papacy?

4. Why would a pope fear the decisions of a general council?

5. Why was it important to guarantee regular meetings of general church councils?

The Condemnation of Joan of Arc by the University of Paris, 1431

6. Why was Joan of Arc condemned for heresy?

7. Had Joan of Arc appeared outside of the context of the Hundred Years' War, do you think she would have still suffered as a convicted heretic?

8. In what ways does Joan of Arc highlight the major characteristics and preoccupations of the intensified popular piety of the late Middle Ages?

SAMPLE LECTURE 10: THE CALAMITOUS FOURTEENTH CENTURY: PLAGUE, WAR, AND UNCERTAINTY

Lecture Objectives

1. To discuss how medieval European men and women coped with the destruction wrought by the Black Death, peasant rebellions, and war

2. To investigate the nature of medieval piety in the fourteenth century; to discuss the primary characteristics of the Age of Faith

3. To outline the effect that the intellectual revival of the twelfth century had on the thought and culture of the fourteenth century

THE BLACK DEATH, 1347–1350

In September of 1348, Pope Clement VI issued an edict that referred to "this pestilence with which God is affecting the Christian people." By this date, the Black Death had ravaged large parts of the continent, including Italy, Spain, England, Switzerland, and Hungary. Florence would be one of the hardest hit of all European cities and, at Avignon, where Clement resided, it was recorded that four hundred souls lost their lives each day for a period of three months. Discoveries in the late nineteenth century (more than five hundred years after the fact) proved that the plague was caused by the bacillus, *Yersina pestis*, which was transferred to humans by flea or rat bites. But no one knew that in 1347; after all, medieval men and women had been sharing their lives with fleas and rats for centuries. They found another explanation: mankind had sinned, so God sent a plague to scourge mankind. People responded to the plague in a number of ways:

- Many people left the towns for the countryside, and those in the countryside fled from each other.
- People sought isolation, doctors refused patients, lawyers refused to hear wills, and the clergy refused to give the last rites.
- Some people simply ate, drank, and had a good time.

- Other people followed or participated in the processions of flagellants who tried to beat the devil out of their bodies, fighting anxiety with pain.

There was no way to escape the Black Death; it would just have to run its course, which it did by 1351, only to reappear in later centuries. Of course, if you survived the plague—always a possibility—you probably would have suffered a sense of collective guilt, asking yourself: "Why am I here? Why am I, a healthy twenty-year-old male, still alive?" or "Why am I, an unhealthy sixty-one-year-old woman, still alive?" And if the bubonic plague was God's punishment, then the committed sins must have been tremendous, which partially explains yet another resurgence of popular piety.

People also needed scapegoats, since damning God was not an alternative. So, despite the horror and futility of the Black Death, Europeans made the Jews the objects of their scorn. Christians blamed Jews for everything from poisoning the water supply to killing Christ. They were believed to be agents of the devil who ritually sacrificed Christian children. Not heretics but infidels, Jews were outsiders, the excluded. Perhaps 12,000 Jews were slaughtered as a result of the psychological terror of the Black Death. Whole Jewish populations disappeared or moved to new locations.

IN THE WAKE OF THE BLACK DEATH

Europe may have lost 35 percent of its population in four years, but, in the wake of the Black Death and the "dementia of despair" it produced, came economic change. Some of the effects were beneficial. Merchants accepted new business practices, such as double-entry bookkeeping, insurance, and "book transfers" (the medieval equivalent of the modern check). This was the period in which the Medici bankers of Florence rose to prominence.

On the other hand, the Black Death also created the conditions for rebellions among urban workers and peasants in the countryside. In the Jacquerie of 1358, French peasants responded to heavy taxation by burning castles and murdering their lords. Florentine wool-combers (the "Ciompi") rebelled against their masters in 1378 as a result of unemployment and low wages. And in England, in 1381, peasants revolted against aristocratic efforts to revert back to paying preplague wages and government attempts to collect a head tax to pay for the war with France. The peasants burned local records, sacked the homes of their exploiters, then marched into London and killed the lord chancellor and treasurer of England. The fifteen-year-old Richard II promised them support but kept none of his promises.

The main catalyst for these rebellions was economic. Each of them also had the same result: in no case were the workers' grievances resolved. Their aristocratic betters clung to older patterns of status and privilege, setting up cultural barriers against the other classes. Meanwhile, no one could escape the "culture of death" that had intruded upon their lives, nor could they escape the uncertainty of life.

THE LATE MEDIEVAL CHURCH

The medieval obsession with death—not surprising, given the state of fourteenth-century affairs—intensified religious enthusiasm. People looked to the church for answers. At the same time, the church was confronted with yet another series of challenges. During the Babylonian Captivity, the papacy was located at Avignon, where it served the interests of French diplomacy. There, by working out an efficient system of papal finance and by appointing more candidates to vacant church positions, the popes were more successful than ever in centralizing their power. They also became more corrupt and, as news of their lavish living got around, public pressure forced the popes to promise to return to Rome. Before they could do so, though, the Great Schism divided Europe over the issue of who was the true pope. The following are important points to know about the Great Schism:

- France, Scotland, Castile, and Aragon recognized the French Pope Clement VII as the true pope; the rest of Europe rallied behind the Italian pope Urban VI.
- After three decades of squabbling, the Council of Constance, in 1417, ended the schism and named Martin V as pope.
- The question of conciliar church government immediately followed.
- The Council of Constance decreed that a general council of prelates had more authority than the pope.
- In 1449, the Council of Basel dissolved and conciliarism was overturned by the papacy, who gained the support of European monarchs.

It is no surprise that the local clergy were losing prestige during this time. The greater financial demands of the pope meant that the clergy demanded more from the lay population. With the increase in general literacy, the laity could begin reading the Bible and popular religious texts. It became obvious to this literate population that the clergy were not living according to the standards set by Jesus Christ and the apostles. Two possible responses from lay people were to turn to anticlericalism or to demand reform of the church.

POPULAR PIETY

It seemed to more and more people that church rituals and clerical authority were not enough to satisfy the deep religiosity of the fourteenth century. People began to go on pilgrimages or join barefoot processions. Flagellation became the most dramatic form of religious ritual. If people found that the outward channels of expression were not enough to express their piety, then perhaps there was in inward road to godliness. Across Europe people began to turn to mysticism. The German Dominican Master Eckhart (c. 1260–1327) perhaps best represented this tendency. Features of Eckhart's mysticism included:

- the renunciation of selfhood or ego
- the idea that divinity is found within each individual
- the teaching that outward rituals were comparatively less important in reaching God than were the practices of detachment, contemplation, or other spiritual exercises

Eckhart provided an example to others. His message was taken up by Thomas à Kempis (1379–1471), whose *Imitation of Christ* enjoyed an immense lay readership because of its emphasis on inward piety while still going about one's daily affairs. The message of Eckhart and à Kempis fell on ready ears. The Christian people's adoption of biblical meditation and leading a simple, moral life served as an indictment of the church itself.

WYCLIF AND HUS

With the appearance of Wyclif and Hus we see tendencies that anticipate the Protestant Reformation of the sixteenth century. John Wyclif (c. 1330–1384) was an Augustinian to the core and believed that a certain number of humans were predestined for heaven. He thought that the predestined would naturally live moral lives, but he found that most members of the church did not. He and his followers, the Lollards, concluded that most church officials were damned. Wyclif and, after his death, his followers proposed these solutions:

- Secular rulers should take over ecclesiastical wealth and reform the church.
- Secular rulers would replace corrupt clergymen with men who would live an apostolic life.
- He attacked the sacrament of the Eucharist and other basic church institutions.
- The Lollards warned Christians not to trust their salvation to the sacraments of a corrupt church and, instead, to study the Bible in the vernacular.

Jan Hus (c. 1373–1415) studied at Oxford and was familiar with Wyclif's ideas. He too called for an end to ecclesiastical corruption but, unlike the Lollards, he emphasized the centrality of the Eucharist and insisted that the laity should also receive the consecrated bread and wine of the Mass. In 1415, Hus attended the Council of Constance to defend his views and, instead, was tried for heresy and burned at the stake. The Lollards and Hussites offered a direct assault on church hierarchy. The church did respond, but the damage had already been done. Wyclif and Hus—with their suggestions of predestination and reading the Bible in the vernacular, and their criticism of the clergy and questioning of the sacraments—had set the stage for Luther and Protestantism in the following century.

NATIONAL MONARCHIES AND THE HUNDRED YEARS' WAR

If the Black Death brought anxiety to the common person, the century following the plague was equally devastating for royal governments. Italy, for instance, contained a number of decentralized states, each with its own form of government: Venice embraced a merchant oligarchy, Milan was ruled by a dynastic despotism, Florence was supposedly a republic that was actually controlled by the wealthy. Fragmentation seems to characterize the fifteenth century, as feudal institutions could no longer provide any sort of stability. Despite this time of troubles, the national monarchies became stronger.

The major conflict of the age was clearly the Hundred Years' War (1337–1453) between France and England. The origins of this protracted conflict stretch back into the late thirteenth century, but we can identify a number of causes:

- The problem of French territory still held by English kings and the fact that the French wanted to expel the English made war inevitable.
- English economic interests in the Flanders woolen trade supported the frequent Flemish attempts to rebel against French rule.
- The dispute over the succession of the French crown involved the Valois dynasty and Edward III of England.

As the richest country in Europe, France should have had no problem defeating England. However, until the 1430s, the English had won most of the battles. At Crécy (1346), Poitiers (1356), and Agincourt (1415), the outnumbered English used a professional army and the longbow to defeat the French. In 1429, Joan of Arc captured the French imagination by announcing that she had been commissioned by God to drive the English out of France. The country rallied behind Joan, and her forces defeated the English in central France and brought Charles VII to Rheims, where he became king. Joan was eventually captured by the Burgundians and handed over to the English, who tried her for heresy and publicly burned her at the stake in 1431. By 1453, the English had been pushed off of the continent, with the exception of Calais, which they lost in 1558. Such a protracted struggle resulted in major changes in the French and English governments as well as long-term consequences for Europe in general:

- The war strengthened the powers of the French crown.
- French kings obtained the rights to collect national taxes and maintain a standing army.
- The war produced political instability in England.
- English taxpayers held Richard II and Henry VI responsible for military failure.
- The War of the Roses was provoked by an aristocratic rebellion against Henry VI.
- With the ascent of the Tudor dynasty in 1509, English royal power was restored.
- Parliament became increasingly important as a mediator between various political communities.

In general, the conflicts of the later Middle Ages put the existence of national monarchies to the test, but after 1450 they appeared to be stronger than ever. At the same time, Russia was also consolidating its power. But Russia was not like any Western nation-state; it was becoming an Eastern-style empire. There are four major reasons why Russia's history is quite different from that of either France or England:

- The conquest of eastern Slavic states by the Mongols in the thirteenth century had lasting effects on the whole of Russia for 150 years.
- The defeat of the Mongols by the duchy of Moscow unified much of Russia, but Moscow's hostility toward the Latin Christian tradition separated it from western Europe.
- As Poland grew in power, Moscow called upon national and religious sentiments to engage in war with its rival. Since Poland subscribed to Roman Catholicism, the already-existing religious animosity was exacerbated.
- Moscow saw itself as the divinely appointed successor to Byzantium after the fall of Constantinople to the Turks in 1453. This ideology further increased its alienation of western Europe.

Relations between Eastern and Western churches had been tense since 1054, when the two churches split the over the wording of the Nicene Creed. Eastern Orthodox Russians sympathized with the Byzantines after the Romans sacked Constantinople in 1204. After the Byzantines submitted to papal authority in 1438, hoping in vain to win military support against the Turkish onslaught, Moscow began to see itself as both a "second Jerusalem" and the "third Rome." It was at this time that the Russian ruler took the title of *tsar*, which means "caesar." Under a tsar like Ivan III (1462–1505), Russia moved toward political autocracy and imperialism, policies it would continue to embrace into the twentieth century.

THOUGHT AND LITERATURE

We would be inclined to think that the famines, plagues, and wars of the later Middle Ages would have led to a decline of intellectual thought and cultural experience. However, developments in theology, philosophy, literature, and the arts reveal quite a different story. In theology and philosophy, the major problem was a crisis of doubt about man's ability to comprehend the supernatural. Was it possible for mankind to know everything? Aquinas argued in the affirmative, that what reason could not explain, faith would. William of Ockham (c. 1285–1349), an English Franciscan, denied that the existence of God could be explained apart from scriptural revelation, and he argued God's freedom to do anything. He wanted truth, and he found it in a position known as nominalism. The formal logic he employed is evident in his argument that only individual things, not collectives, are real; therefore, one thing cannot be understood by means of another. Ockham's methodology became the most influential philosophical system of the late Middle Ages:

- It gained widespread adherence in medieval universities.
- Although questions such as, "How many angels can dance on the head of a pin?" seem absurd now, the underlying method of his reasoning had significant

effects on Western thought.
- Nominalism helped create the foundations for the modern scientific method.
- It encouraged empiricism, the belief that knowledge is derived from experience rather than abstract reason.

Ockham and the nominalists had clearly opened the door for the appearance of a natural science and natural philosophy we will encounter during the Scientific Revolution. Similarly, naturalism shows up in vernacular literature as the attempt to describe things as they really are. The reading public was growing in numbers. Impatient with philosophical and theological dispute, they instead sought entertainment.

The Italian Giovanni Boccaccio (1313–1375) was a master of vernacular prose fiction. His *Decameron*, set against the backdrop of the plague as it entered Florence in 1348, relates one hundred stories about love, sex, and adventure as told by ten aristocratic young ladies and men. Boccaccio wrote in a colloquial style and meant to be entertaining; again, the message was to portray men and women as they really are.

Geoffrey Chaucer (c. 1340–1400) wrote his own collection of stories, *The Canterbury Tales*. While Chaucer was also interested in portraying things as they really were, his tales are told from a variety of points of view—a knight, a miller, a university student (people of all social classes). Both Boccaccio and Chaucer were masters of literature for their wit, frankness, and profundity.

Christine de Pisan (c. 1364–c. 1430) was a professional writer who actually made her living through writing, mostly for her patron, King Charles VI of France. Her book, *The City of Ladies*, written for a larger audience, is an allegorical defense of the character and nature of women.

SCULPTURE AND PAINTING

In the sculpture and painting of the later Middle Ages we can also identify the dominant trait of naturalism, or realism, that we have seen in thought and literature. Artists continued to paint frescoes on walls, but in the thirteenth century, Italian artists began painting on wood and canvas. Around 1400, oil paints were introduced in northern Europe. Artists now had the freedom to produce smaller paintings, which could adorn altars as easily as they could the homes of the wealthy. Portraits began to appear in greater number as well. The most important painter of the period was perhaps the Florentine artist, Giotto (c. 1267–1337). He did not paint portraits but, rather, brought humanity to his religious images. He was the first to think of the painted space in full three-dimensional terms, "knocking a hole into the wall," so to speak. Giotto's influence eventually carried over into the great Italian renaissance in painting.

The later Middle Ages was clearly a creative and inventive age. Historians have pointed out that there was a persistent effort in the later Middle Ages to understand and control the natural world, qualities perhaps essential to the Scientific and Industrial Revolutions of the future. Nature was conceived of in accordance with its own laws, which could be verified by observation. This was an essential step toward a scientific worldview. The effects of the Black Death, famine, and war should have been enough to distract any culture from intellectual pursuits; however, if the later Middle Ages tell us anything, it is that medieval men and women were resilient, adaptive, and willing to try to understand the unknown.

SUGGESTED FEATURE FILMS

Chimes at Midnight. 119 min. B/W. 1966. Internacional Films Espanola/Alpine. Orson Welles stars in this film adaptation of *Henry IV, Part II.*

Henry V. 137 min. Color. 1944. Rank Distributors. Laurence Olivier's screen version of Shakespeare's work, which begins as a filmed play in a reconstruction of the Globe Theatre and gradually moves outward until the viewer finds himself in the midst of fifteenth-century war.

Henry V. 138 min. Color. 1989. Festival. Kenneth Branagh's brilliant rendition of Shakespeare's play.

Ivan the Terrible. Part One. 100 min. *Part Two.* 88 min. B/W. 1944–1946. Mosfilm. Eisenstein's celebrated depiction of the sixteenth-century tsar.

Messenger: The Story of Joan of Arc. 148 min. Color. 1999. Columbia Pictures. Film account of the conflict between Joan and her conscience.

The Passion of Joan of Arc. 85 min. B/W. 1928. M. J. Gourland. The silent-film classic based on actual transcripts of Joan's trial.

Richard III. 161 min. Color. 1956. London Films. Considered by many to be the best of Sir Laurence Olivier's film versions of Shakespeare's play.

The Seventh Seal. 95 min. B/W. 1957. Svensk Filmindustri. Ingmar Bergman's masterful allegory of man's quest for meaning, in which the crusading knight returns to plague-stricken Europe to battle Death in a game of chess. Excellent as much for its depiction of medieval realities as it is for Bergman's crisis of faith in the 1950s.

The Virgin Spring. 87 min. B/W. 1959. Svensk Filmindustri. Bergman's version of a fourteenth-century folktale.

A Walk with Love and Death. 90 min. Color. 1970. Twentieth Century Fox. Directed by John Huston, this film is about two people who fall in love during the Hundred Years' War and witness the brutal murder of a peasant.

SUGGESTED CLASSROOM FILMS

Al Andalus. 34 min. Color. 1975. University Films Library. Covers the intermingling of Spanish and Moorish cultures through the reign of Ferdinand and Isabella. Includes on-site photography.

Chaucer's England. 30 min. Color. 1969. Encyclopaedia Britannica Educational Corporation. Relates the background of the *Canterbury Tales* and dramatizes the "Pardoner's Tale" in its entirety.

Expansion of Europe: 1250–1500. 26 min. Color. 1985. Insight Media. Explores the internal devastation caused by the Black Death and the external expansion into East Asia and the New World.

Faith and Fear. 39 min. Color. 1979. Insight Media. A look at religious responses to an uncertain world.

From Every Shire's Ende: The World of Chaucer's Pilgrims. 38 min. Color. 1969. International Films Bureau. Recreates the trip to Canterbury with wood carvings, illuminated manuscripts, and films of other historic sites.

Giotto and the Pre-Renaissance. 47 min. Color. 1969. Universal Educational and Visual Arts. Highlights Giotto's artistic innovations.

The Late Middle Ages and the National Monarchies. 2 parts, 30 min. each. Color. 1989. Insight Media. Focuses on the economic and political changes of the fifteenth century.

Medieval England: The Peasants' Revolt. 31 min. Color. 1969. Learning Corporation of America. Reenactment of the English Peasants' Revolt of 1381.

Medieval Theatre: The Play of Abraham and Isaac. 26 min. Color. 1974. The Movie Show Company. Dramatization of a mystery play performance at an English estate in 1482.

The Mongols: Storm from the East. Part Two: World Conquerors. 50 min. Color. Films for the Humanities. Looks at the expansion of the Mongol empire into Russia and Europe.

Once Upon a Wall: The Great Age of Fresco. 18 min. Color. 1969. BFA Educational Media. The Metropolitan Museum of Art exhibit of Italian fresco paintings.

Queen Isabel and Her Spain. 32 min. Color. 1978. International Film Bureau. Covers Isabella's reign with special focus on the defeat of the Moors in Granada, the Spanish Inquisition and the expulsion of the Jews, and Columbus's expedition.

CHAPTER 11

Commerce, Conquest, and Colonization, 1300–1600

b. An enormous psychological shock to Europe

c. Minor economic impact

    i. Europe got most of its spices and silks through Venice

4. Effects

    a. Ottoman conquest did not force the Portuguese to establish new trade routes

    b. Ottoman attempts to control Egyptian grain trade

    c. Modest effects on Europe

    d. New wealth poured into Ottoman society

    e. Ottomans became a naval power in eastern Mediterranean and Black Sea

C. War, slavery and social advancement

1. Conquest created the need for a larger Ottoman army and administration

    a. Army and administration composed of slaves

2. Slaves were critical to Ottoman upper class

    a. Provided status

    b. Household servants and administrators

3. Slaves obtained through conquest and from the Ottoman Empire itself

4. Some people preferred to live as slaves than as poor peasants

5. Child slavery—helping to pay the child tax

6. Little social stigma associated with slavery

7. Muslims prohibited from enslaving other Muslims

    a. Elite positions in Ottoman government held by slaves

    b. Paradox—Muslims were excluded from social and political advancement

8. Power in the Ottoman Empire open to men of talent and ability

    a. Provided that they were slaves and not Muslims by birth

    b. Commerce and business also in the hands of non-Muslims

    c. Jews found a welcome refuge from the persecutions of medieval Europe

D. Religious controversy

1. Ottoman sultans were orthodox Sunni Muslims

    a. Supported religious and legal pronouncements of Islamic scholarly schools

2. Ottomans captured Medina and Mecca (1516)

3. Ottoman ruler adopted title of caliph (1538)

    a. Became legitimate successor to prophet Muhammad

4. Tolerant toward non-Muslims

5. Organized the major religious groups into legal units (the *millet*)

    a. Religious self-government

6. Protected and promoted Greek Orthodox patriarch of Constantinople

7. Principal religious conflicts were with Shi'ite Muslim dynasty in Persia

E. The Ottomans and Europe

1. Holy wars?

2. Western crusader army destroyed at Nicopolis (1396)

3. Besieged Vienna (sixteenth and seventeenth centuries)

4. Battle of Lepanto (1571)

    a. Victory for combined forces of Hapsburgs and Venice

    b. Battle did not put an end to Ottoman influence in the eastern Mediterranean

IV. Mediterranean Colonialism

A. Motives for westward expansion

1. African gold trade

2. Growth of European colonial empires in the western Mediterranean Sea

B. Silver shortages and the search for African gold

1. African gold trade was not new

2. Catalan and Genoese merchants traded woolen cloth for gold at Tunis

3. Gold needed because of a serious silver shortage

4. Balance-of-payments problem

    a. Too much silver flowing east in the spice trade

    b. Could not be replaced

    c. Gold as alternative for large transactions

C. Mediterranean empires: Catalunya, Venice, and Genoa

1. Catalunya

    a. Colonized Majorca, Ibiza, Minorca, Sicily, and Sardinia

    b. Expropriation and extermination of native population (usually Muslim)

    c. Economic concessions to attract settlers

    d. Reliance on slave labor

2. Venice

    a. Venetian colonization controlled by city's rulers

b. Concentrated in the eastern Mediterranean

c. Spices and silks

3. Genoa

    a. Focused on western Mediterranean

    b. Cloth, hides, grain, and timber

    c. More informal and family-based

    d. More closely integrated with native societies of North Africa, Spain, and the Black Sea

    e. Moved toward larger, fuller-bodied sailing ships

D. From the Mediterranean to the Atlantic

1. Italian merchants sailed through Straits of Gibraltar to the North Sea (c. 1270)

2. Canary Islands as "jumping-off point," especially for the Portuguese

E. The technology of ships and navigation

1. The Portuguese caravel

2. Changed to larger caravel with lateen sail

    a. Could sail against the wind

    b. Required smaller crews

3. Navigation

    a. Quadrants in use by 1450s

    b. Astrolabes

    c. Compasses

    d. Could not determine longitude until the eighteenth century

    e. Dead reckoning

    f. Maps and navigational charts (*rutters* and *routiers*)

    g. *Portolani*

F. Portugal, Africa, and the sea route to India

1. Chronology of Portuguese colonization

    a. Captured North African port of Ceuta (1415)

    b. Colonization of Madeira, the Canaries, and the Azores (1420s and 30s)

    c. Cape Verde Islands (1440s)

    d. Collection of gold and slaves for export to Portugal (1444)

    e. Exploration of the Gulf of Guinea (1470s)

    f. Portuguese reached the Congo River (1483)

    g. Bartholomeu Dias rounded Cape of Storms/Cape of Good Hope (1488)

    h. Vasco de Gama rounded the Cape and crossed the Indian Ocean to Calicutt (1497–98)

    i. Portuguese reach Malacca (1511)

    j. The Spice Islands and China (1515)

2. By 1500, Portuguese sailing ships sailed regularly to India

3. Built forts along the western Indian coastline

4. Total domination of the spice trade (1520s)

G. Artillery and empire

1. Increasing sophistication of artillery

2. Larger caravels—more effective artillery pieces could be mounted on them

3. Floating artillery platforms

4. Battle of Div (1509)

    a. Portuguese defeated Indian and Ottoman naval force

H. Prince Henry the Navigator (1394–1460)

1. His central place in European exploration has been debunked

2. Motives before 1480s

    a. Crusading ambitions against Muslims

    b. Establish direct links with sources of African gold production

    c. Desire to colonize Atlantic islands

    d. Slavery

    e. The myth of Prester John

3. Neither the architect nor visionary of Portuguese exploration

4. Main goal was to intercept trade in African gold at its source

I. Atlantic colonization and the growth of slavery

1. Major slave markets were in Muslim hands

2. Few early-fifteenth-century slaves were Africans

3. Most were European Christians (Poles, Ukrainians, Greeks and Bulgarians)

4. Mid-fifteenth-century Lisbon as major slave market for enslaved Africans

5. 150,000 African slaves imported into Europe by 1505

    a. Regarded as status symbols

    b. Slaves mostly used in sugar mills (Madeira and the Canaries)

V. Europe Encounters a New World

A. Spanish motives: sailing west to beat the Portuguese

1. Discovery of Azores and Canary Island

2. The Atlantic was dotted with islands all the way to China

B. The discovery of a New World

1. The Vikings in Newfoundland, Labrador, and perhaps New England (c. 1000)

C. Christopher Columbus (1451–1506)

1. Brought back no Asian spices and little gold

D. Amerigo Vespucci (1451–1512)

E. The disappointment of the New World
1. Spain could not hope to beat Portugal with this land mass between Europe and Asia
F. Vasco Núñez Balboa (1475–1517) viewed the Pacific Ocean (1513)
G. Magellan's crew circumnavigated the globe (1522)
H. The Spanish conquest of America
1. The New World perhaps had great stores of gold just waiting to be picked up
2. The *conquistador*
3. Hernando Cortés (1485–1547) subdued the Aztecs in Mexico (1519–1521)
4. Francisco Pizarro subdued the Incas in South America (1533)
I. The profits of empire in the New World
1. Cortés and Pizarro as plunderers
2. First gold deposits discovered in Hispaniola
   a. One million natives in 1492—five hundred in 1538
   b. Cattle ranching (Mexico)
   c. Sugar production (Caribbean)
      i. Imported African slaves
      ii. Sugar plantations fell into the hands of a few wealthy planters
3. Gold mining as the initial lure
4. Silver the most lucrative export
   a. The silver deposits of Potosí (Bolivia)
   b. Profits went directly to Spanish crown
   c. Slave labor
   d. New mining techniques
   e. Ten million ounces of silver per year arrived in Spain (1590s)
5. Effects of the influx of silver
   a. Exacerbated European inflation
   b. The Price Revolution
      i. Affected Spain most acutely
      ii. Spanish prices doubled twice between 1500 and 1600
      iii. Undermined the competitiveness of Spanish industries
      iv. Spanish economy collapsed (1620s and 30s)
   c. Less silver flowed into Europe but prices continued to rise
      i. Price of grain in 1650 was five to six times its level in 1500

ii. Social dislocation and misery
iii. Declining standard of living
VI. Conclusion
A. Colonization
B. Portugal and Spain
C. The rise of French, Dutch, and English empires

GENERAL DISCUSSION QUESTIONS

1. Who were the Mongols? What conditions led them to invade both the West and the East in the thirteenth century? How do we explain the expansionist policies of both the Mongols and the Ottoman Turks?

2. What difficulties did Portuguese and Spanish sailors face as they began their exploration of the ocean waters in the late fourteenth and fifteenth centuries? Why were the Portuguese the first European nation to seek a direct sea route from Europe to the Far East?

3. Why were Europeans so interested in spices? What was the ultimate importance of the spice trade?

4. Why did Spanish monarchs decide to finance the voyages of Columbus?

5. How did Portuguese and Spanish attempts to forge a maritime empire differ? Did each nation have clearly defined goals?

6. What effects did the massive infusion of New World silver have on the economy of early modern Europe? What was the Price Revolution?

7. Although the Portuguese and Spanish initiated the age of exploration, why did their maritime empires decline in the face of British, French, and Dutch competition?

DOCUMENT DISCUSSION QUESTIONS

Marco Polo's Description of Java

1. What effect did Marco Polo's *Travels* have on European images of the Far East?

2. Why did Marco Polo refer to various spices as "rich commodities"? Why were spices so highly valued by Europeans?

Ottoman Janissaries

3. What role did the janissary corps play in the Ottoman Empire?

4. What psychological effects might Europeans have experienced as the Ottomans moved into the Balkan peninsula in the mid to late fifteenth century?

5. Were the Ottoman incursions into the West a serious threat to the European balance of power?

The Legend of Prester John

6. How persuasive was the myth of Prester John? Would you consider such a myth important enough to serve as a primary motive for European exploration?

7. Why were fifteenth-century Europeans more prepared to accept the myth of Prester John than we might be today? In general, what is the power of myth in motivating human thought and action? Can you think of some contemporary examples?

Enslaved Native Laborers at Potosí

8. What was the human cost of the Potosí silver mine?

SAMPLE LECTURE 11:
AGE OF DISCOVERY, AGE OF CONQUEST

Lecture Objectives

1. To explain the practical and idealistic reasons that motivated Europeans to leave the world of the Mediterranean and venture out onto the oceans

2. To distinguish the differences between Portuguese and Spanish maritime ambitions

3. To compare the profits of European discovery and conquest with its costs

EUROPE ON THE MOVE

By the fourteenth century, European expansion on the continent had slowed down. At the same time, population growth was checked by plague and war. However, by the fifteenth century circumstances had changed so that Europe seemed to be on a steady path of recovery. Renewed confidence led Europeans to partake in exploration and colonization. The Portuguese and the Spanish led the way, creating maritime empires that dominated European trade for the next two centuries, only to be overcome by the British, French, and Dutch. Although it was the acquisition of spices from the Far East that motivated the first wave of European exploration, once gold deposits were found in Africa, the situation changed. The African slave trade became a lucrative business throughout the Mediterranean and, eventually, in the New World. As sugar plantations emerged in Portugal's Atlantic colonies, nearby Africans were enslaved to work them and,

later, exported to North and South America for the same purpose. The human costs of exploration were tremendous. Whole indigenous populations were destroyed by disease and enslavement as the European mania for gold and silver intensified in the fifteenth and sixteenth centuries.

NEW PLAYERS: THE MONGOLS AND OTTOMANS

It was during the fourteenth and fifteenth centuries that two new players entered the European scene: the Mongols and the Ottoman Turks. The Mongols were a nomadic people who inhabited the steppes of central Asia. In the thirteenth century, the various Mongol tribes were united and began their wholesale conquest of much of central Asia. By the late thirteenth century, the Mongol horde began moving west into southern Russia, Poland, Germany, and Hungary. Since they encouraged commercial contacts with traders, the Mongols acted as a middleman between Europe and the Far East. The Silk Road had been closed to the West until the unification of the Mongols opened valuable trade routes for merchants and Franciscan missionaries. Undoubtedly, the most famous of these merchants was Marco Polo (1254–1324). He spent twenty-three years in China and traveled to the Spice Islands, India, and Iran, leaving an account of his experiences in his *Travels*.

The importance of the Mongols and their expansion cannot be overlooked. They:

- served as an external threat to European confidence
- gave Europeans a view of a culture distant from the continent
- provided valuable information about spices and other luxury items
- fed the European thirst for the unknown
- stimulated the economic superiority of Genoa and Venice
- encouraged further European commercial and imperial expansion

From the late fourteenth century on, the Ottoman Turks had been trying to sack Constantinople. In 1453, Mehmet II (1432–1481) succeeded in taking the imperial city. Such an act had a tremendous psychological impact on all Europeans but little economic impact, for not much of the European trade actually passed through the Black Sea. The takeover of Constantinople had a greater effect on the Ottomans themselves:

- New wealth poured into Ottoman society
- Trade routes were redirected to feed the capital, which they renamed Istanbul
- The Ottomans became a naval power in the eastern Mediterranean and Black Seas
- Istanbul became the largest city in the world outside of China

The Ottomans were forced to staff the army and administration with slaves and, since their empire was in a period of growth, further conquests were required to contribute even more slaves to the bureaucracy, which required an even larger administration, which led to a vicious cycle:

- The Ottomans were also orthodox Sunni Muslims.
- They could not enslave other Muslims.
- Slaves staffed most of the higher positions in Ottoman government
- Muslims were excluded from social and political advancement in their own society.

In 1516, the Ottomans captured the cities of Medina and Mecca and, soon after, Jerusalem and Cairo. They practiced tolerance toward non-Muslim populations and gained the support of their Eastern Orthodox Christian subjects during sixteenth-century wars with the Latin Church; thus, their main religious conflicts were not with their own subjects but with the Persian Shi'ite Muslims, with whom they were constantly at war. Although the Ottoman Turks expanded into the Balkans, they were never a serious threat to European global dominance. Known throughout the nineteenth century as "the sick man of Europe," the Ottoman Empire collapsed in the wake of the First World War.

MEDITERRANEAN COLONIZATION

In the fifteenth century, European commercial ambitions moved to the western Mediterranean and the Atlantic world. The major impetus for such a move was the African gold trade and the European quest for colonial empire. As early as the late thirteenth century, Italian merchants had sailed west, out of the Mediterranean. Although their voyages did not bring back needed commodities in any form, these early expeditions did lead to the conquest of the Azores and the Canary Islands, which would later become stopping off points for Columbus and other explorers. These early sailors had a number of technological innovations at their disposal, including:

- new developments in the construction of larger caravels capable of sailing against the wind
- the increased use of astrolabes, which reckoned latitude by the height of the sun—more useful near the equator than quadrants, which calculated latitude in the Northern hemisphere by the height of the North Star above the horizon
- compasses, which were coming into widespread use
- the invention of marine chronometers, which finally made it possible to keep accurate time at sea and calculate longitude; new developments in maps and navigational charts, such as sailing guides to the Atlantic Ocean known as *portolani* and *rutters*

Of course, these sailors also had to deal with a number of problems: inaccurate maps, stormy seas, incompetent captains, fear of mythical dragons and monsters, and hostile natives. Conditions on board these ships were also far from comfortable, but the main problem was that none of them knew exactly where they were going.

PORTUGUESE EXPLORATION

The Portuguese were the first nation to ride the wave of Atlantic colonization. By 1488, Bartholomeu Dias had rounded the southern tip of Africa, which he named the "Cape of Storms;" the Portuguese king optimistically renamed it the Cape of Good Hope. A direct sea route now seemed secure between Europe and the Far Eastern spice trade. By 1500, the Portuguese were sailing regularly to India and beyond. But why did Europe need spices? There were practical and economic reasons for the European interest in spices:

- They enhanced the flavor of food and were used as preservatives.
- They were considered luxury items.
- Spices were useful for trade with other commodities.
- Spices had been known to give pleasure, restore health, and pay ransoms.
- Spices had been used as insect repellents, perfumes, cosmetics, antidotes for poisons, and as an aphrodisiac.

The Portuguese were fortunate, and their fortunes increased with the sophistication of artillery, a necessary ingredient of their military/commercial successes. The move from the caravel to the larger galleons was made not because they could carry more cargo, but because they could carry heavier artillery. It has often been noted that it was the guiding genius of Prince Henry the Navigator (1394–1460) that stimulated Portuguese exploration. Historians have now limited the effect of Prince Henry and point instead to the myth of Prester John, which may have had more to do with Portuguese inspiration than anything else. Prester John was a mythical Christian King who inhabited lands to the east and who would fight the Muslims, if only Europeans could find him.

The Portuguese did not manage to obtain the desired profits from the African gold trade; instead, they found profits in the slave trade. The port city of Lisbon emerged as a significant market for African slaves where, between 1440 and 1460, more than fifteen thousand Africans were sold as slaves. The Portuguese succeeded in colonizing Madeira, the Canary Islands, and the Azores, but found little use for slave labor there. They perhaps met their match when the Spanish decided to fund the voyages of Christopher Columbus.

SPANISH AMBITION

When Dias rounded the Cape of Good Hope, it seemed that Portugal would dominate the seas eastward to Asia. The only alternative, as their Spanish rivals saw it, was to sail west. King Ferdinand and Queen Isabella supported Christopher Columbus's expedition, mainly because the Portuguese discovery of the Canary Islands and the Azores reinforced the idea that the Atlantic Ocean was dotted with islands all the way to the Far East. North and South America were discovered only by accident; when Columbus reached the Bahamas and Hispaniola in 1492, he returned to Spain to report that he had reached Asia. Columbus, of course, found no Asian spices in the New World, but he did bring back enough gold to stimulate further transatlantic voyages. None of these voyages proved profitable and, although Columbus became something of a hero, the Spanish ambition for gold and silver went temporarily unfulfilled.

The New World, however, did contain great wealth. Between 1519 and 1521, the conquistador Hernando Cortés overthrew the Aztecs and carried off their wealth in gold. In 1533, Francisco Pizarro toppled the Inca Empire, carrying off its wealth. What is amazing is that both Cortés and Pizarro managed to subdue these indigenous populations with very few men and the simple advantage of artillery. It should be clear by now that Spanish ambition, unlike Portuguese, was dominated by the discovery of massive quantities of gold and silver. At the time, Europe had few gold and silver reserves, so this discovery and expropriation provided a boost to the European economy.

THE PROFITS OF EMPIRE

On the other side of the coin, the human costs of colonization and empire building were immense. Of the one million people who lived on Hispaniola in 1492, only five hundred survived to 1538. With the loss of so many workers, the gold mines of Hispaniola became impossible to operate, so the Spanish turned to sugar production and began to import African slaves to work the plantations, which were modeled after those that had been built on the Cape Verde Islands and St. Thomas. Although sugar production was important, it was mining—not only of gold but also of silver—that basically created the Spanish colonies of Central and South America. The Potosí deposits in Bolivia quickly became the most productive mining enterprise in the world. Of course, the profits of empire produced problems:

- The Spanish needed a steady supply of slaves to work the mines.
- The massive infusion of silver into the European economy exacerbated inflation.
- The renewed growth of the European population and a fixed supply of food also drove inflation.
- The Price Revolution dramatically affected European industry and standards of living.
- The Spanish economy ultimately collapsed with the moderation of the New World silver flow.
- Colonial and economic competition from the British, French, and Dutch increased.

The colonization and conquest of a world outside Europe led to many important changes. Most important, perhaps, was the movement of European economies away from the Italian centers of Venice and Genoa and toward the Atlantic. Venetian domination gradually withered away, as the Genoese moved into the world of banking and finance. The Age of Discovery and Conquest also managed to boost the confidence of Europe as a whole. It could be argued that a new spirit of adventure had permeated European society and, with the massive infusion of gold and silver into the European economy, Europeans found themselves confronted by the challenges of material wealth. What form would that wealth take? What problems—social, economic, religious, intellectual, and political—would all of that gold and silver produce? Is it likely that the "rebirth" of arts and letters in the fifteenth and sixteenth centuries would not have been possible had it not been for the intrepid explorers who set foot in a New World? The human costs of overseas conquests were both tragic and tremendous, but these conquests shaped the destiny of Europe as far forward as the twentieth century.

SUGGESTED FEATURE FILMS

1492: The Conquest of Paradise. 154 min. Color. 1992. Paramount. Ridley Scott's depiction of Columbus in the New World and the disastrous effects of the European discovery of the New World.

Aguirre, the Wrath of God. 95 min. Color. 1972. Werner Herzog, director. Set in 1560, the story centers on Pizarro's lieutenant.

Black Robe. 101 min. Color. 1991. Trimark/Samuel Goldwyn. A brutally honest examination of the impact of Christianity on Native American society.

The Mission. 126 min. Color. 1986. Warner Brothers. A Jesuit, portrayed by Robert DeNiro, goes into the wilderness of Paraguay to build a mission in the hope of converting the Indians.

The Royal Hunt of the Sun. 121 min. Color. 1969. Security Pictures. After capturing the Inca god-chief, Pizarro is torn between friendship and his desire for conquest.

Seven Cities of Gold. 103 min. Color. 1955. 20th Century Fox. Relates the story of Father Junipero Serra and the founding of the California missions.

SUGGESTED CLASSROOM FILMS

Age of Exploration and Expansion. 16 min. Color. 1970. Centron Films. Covers fifteenth and sixteenth centuries.

Archive of the New World. 18 min. Color. Films for the Humanities and Sciences. Short film showing original Spanish documents from the fifteenth-century age of exploration, including the papal bull of 1453, the Treaty of Tordesillas, and Cortés' letter to Charles V.

Civilisation: A Personal View by Kenneth Clark. No. 6. Protest and Communication. 52 min. Color. 1970.

BBC/Time-Life Films. Focuses on the Christian humanists, Luther, and Shakespeare.

Christopher Columbus: The Americas, 1492. Francesco Pizarro: The Incas, 1532. 30 min. each. Color. 1977. Time-Life Films. These docu-dramas from the *Ten Who Dared* series come with teachers' guides.

Columbus and the Age of Discovery. 7 parts, 58 min. each. Color. Films for the Humanities. A BBC/WGBH (Boston) production. Programs look not only at Columbus, but also at the political and economic context and consequences of his voyages.

Conquest of Souls. 45 min. Color. 1978. McGraw-Hill. Examines Catholic missionary efforts in the New World and in Protestant Europe.

Gold, God, and Glory. 48 min. Color. Films of the Humanities and Sciences. This film follows the recreation of the ship *Nina* and its 1492 tranatlantic voyage.

CHAPTER 12

The Civilization of the Renaissance, c. 1350–1550

          f. Best-educated upper class in Europe

    2. A greater sense of affinity with the classical past

        a. The omnipresence of the past—surrounded by the monuments of ancient Rome

        b. The attempt to establish a cultural identity independent from cholasticism

        c. Heightened antagonism between France and Italy

        d. Roman art as alternative to French Gothicism

    3. Italian wealth

        a. A wealthy Italy compared to the rest of Europe

        b. Italian writers and artists stayed at home rather than seeking employment abroad

        c. Urban pride and the concentration of per capita wealth

        d. Public urban support for culture

            i. Patronage of the aristocracy

            ii. Patronage of the papacy

B. The Italian Renaissance: literature and thought

    1. Francesco Petrarch (1304–1374)

        a. Deeply committed Christian

        b. Scholasticism was misguided

            i. Taught abstract speculation, not how to live virtuously

        c. The Christian writer must cultivate literary eloquence, inspire people to do good

            i. Models of eloquence to be found in Latin literature

            ii. Ethical wisdom

            iii. Wrote vernacular sonnets

        d. The ultimate ideal was contemplation and asceticism

    2. Civic humanism

        a. Leonardo Bruni (c. 1370–1444) and Leon Battitsa Alberti (1404–1472)

            i. Agreed with Petrarch on the need for eloquence and virtue

            ii. Also taught that man was equipped for action and usefulness to society and family

            iii. Refused to condemn material possessions

            iv. Human progress equivalent to man's mastery over nature

C. The emergence of textual scholarship

    1. The civic humanists went beyond Petrarch in their knowledge of classicism

        a. Aided by Byzantine scholars who migrated to Italy

        b. Italian scholars traveled to Constantinople looking for Greek texts

            i. Giovanni Aurispa brought 238 manuscript books to Italy (1423)

            ii. Translated into Latin sense for sense, rather than word for word

    2. Lorenzo Valla (1407–1457)

        a. Secretary in service to the king of Naples

        b. No allegiance to republican ideals

        c. Used an analysis of Greek and Latin texts to discredit old truths

        d. Proved the Donation of Constantine to be a medieval forgery

        e. Introduced the concept of anachronism into textual study

        f. *Notes on the New Testament*

            i. Elucidated the true meaning of Paul's letters

            ii. Believed they had been obscured by Jerome's translation

D. Renaissance Neoplatonism

    1. Blending the ideas of Plato, Plotinus, and ancient mysticism with Christianity

    2. Marsilio Ficino (1433–1499)

        a. Member of the Platonic Academy at Florence

        b. Translated Plato's works into Latin

        c. *Hermetica Corpus*

    3. Giovanni Pico della Mirandola (1463–1494)

        a. Also a member of the Academy

        b. Saw little worth in public affairs

        c. *Oration on the Dignity of Man*

            i. "Nothing more wonderful than man"

E. Niccolò Machiavelli (1469–1527)

    1. The man

        a. Reflected the instability of Renaissance Florence and Italy

        b. Became a prominent government official of the Florentine republic (1498)

            i. Went on diplomatic missions to other city-states

        c. Fascinated with the achievements of Cesare Borgia

        d. Deprived of his position (1512)

    2. The ideas

        a. Was he the amoral theorist of *realpolitik*?

        b. Was he an Italian patriot?

c. Was he a follower of Saint Augustine?

3. *The Discourses on Livy*
   a. Praises the ancient Roman republic as a model
   b. Constitutional government
   c. Equality among all citizens of a republic
   d. Subordination of religion to the needs of the state

4. *The Prince*
   a. A "handbook for tyrants" in the eyes of his critics

5. Machiavelli saw that only a ruthless prince could revitalize the spirit of independence

6. Dark vision of human nature

F. The ideal of the courtier
   1. Baldessare Castiglione (1478–1529)
      a. *The Book of the Courtier* (1528)
      b. A handbook of etiquette
      c. The Renaissance Man
         i. Multitalented, brave, witty, and courteous
   2. Helped spread the Italian ideal of civility
   3. Machiavelli, *Mandragola*
   4. Ludovico Ariosto (1474–1533)
      a. *Orlando Furioso*
      b. Lyric fantasy devoid of heroic idealism
      c. Written to make readers laugh
      d. Embodies the disillusionment of the late Renaissance
         i. Loss of hope and faith
         ii. Seeking consolation in pleasure and aesthetic delight

IV. The Italian Renaissance: Painting, Sculpture, and Architecture
   A. General tendencies
      1. Laws of linear perspective were discovered in the fifteenth century
      2. Experimented with the effects of light and shade (*chiaroscuro*)
      3. Careful studies of human anatomy
      4. Growth of lay patronage opened the door to nonreligious themes and subjects
      5. Delighting the intellect and the eye
      6. Oil does not dry quickly, allowing the painter to make changes
   B. Renaissance painting in Florence
      1. Masaccio (1401–1428)
         a. "Giotto reborn"
         b. Paintings imitated nature
         c. Employed perspective and *chiaroscuro*
      2. Sandro Botticelli (1445–1510)
         a. Classical and Christian subjects

b. *Allegory of Spring* and *Birth of Venus*
   i. Allegories compatible with Christian teachings
   ii. Ancient gods and goddesses represent various Christian virtues

3. Leonardo da Vinci (1452–1519)
   a. Personified the "Renaissance Man"
   b. Painter, architect, musician, mathematician, engineer, inventor, and artist
   c. Patronage of Lorenzo the Magnificent
   d. Worked slowly—difficulty finishing projects
   e. Left Florence for Milan and the Sforzas (1482–1499)
   f. A "camera eye" for what he painted
   g. The worship of nature and the essential divinity in all things
   h. *The Virgin of the Rocks*
      i. Passion for science, the universe as a well-ordered place
   i. *The Last Supper*
      i. A study of psychological reactions
   j. *Mona Lisa* and *Ginevra de Benci*

4. The Venetian School
   a. Giovanni Bellini (c. 1430–1516)
   b. Giorgione (1478–1510)
   c. Titian (c. 1490–1576)
   d. Characteristics
      i. Their art reflected the luxurious life of Venice
      ii. Their aim was to appeal to the senses, not the mind
      iii. A mirror of the tastes of wealthy merchants

5. Painting in Rome
   a. Raphael (1483–1520)
      i. Native of Urbino
      ii. Portrayals of man as temperate, wise, and dignified
      iii. Influenced by Leonardo
      iv. *Disputà* and the *School of Athens*
   b. Michelangelo (1475–1564)
      i. An idealist, embraced Neoplatonism
      ii. Painter, sculptor, architect, and poet
      iii. The centrality of the male figure—powerful and magnificent

iv. The Sistine Chapel paintings (1508–1512)

v. *God Dividing the Light from Darkness, The Creation of Adam, The Flood*

vi. Commitment to classical aesthetic principles of art (harmony, solidity, dignified restraint)

vii. *The Last Judgment* (1536)

6. Sculpture

   a. Donatello (c. 1386–1466)

      i. *David*—the first free-standing nude since antiquity

   b. Michelangelo

      i. Sculpture allowed the artist to imitate God in recreating human forms

      ii. Subordinated naturalism to the force of imagination

      iii. *David* (1501) as expression of Florentine civic ideals

      iv. *Moses* (c. 1515)—anatomical distortion and emotional intensity

      v. *Descent from the Cross* (unfinished)

7. Architecture

   a. New building style was a composite of elements from antiquity and medieval Europe

   b. Italian Romanesque as model

   c. Cruciform floor plan

   d. Geometrical proportions

   e. St.Peter's Basilica (Rome)

   f. Andrea Palladio (1508–1580)

V. The Waning of the Italian Renaissance

  A. Causes of decline, c. 1550

    1. War

      a. French invasion of 1494 and incessant warfare

      b. French inroads on northern Italy by Charles VIII

         i. Duchy of Milan and Kingdom of Naples

         ii. Aroused the suspicions of the Spanish

      c. Louis XII invaded a second time (1499–1529)

      d. Rome sacked by the Holy Roman emperor, Charles V (1527)

    2. The waning of Italian prosperity

      a. Gradual shift of trade from the Mediterranean to the Atlantic

      b. Warfare contributed to economic decline

3. The Counter-Reformation

   a. The Inquisition (1542) and Index of Forbidden Books (1564)

   b. Censorship

      i. The death of Giordano Bruno

      ii. The trial of Galileo

VI. The Renaissance in the North

  A. Observations

    1. Italian merchants were familiar figures at northern courts

    2. Students from all over Europe attended Italian universities

    3. Northern European intellectual life dominated by universities

      a. Paris, Oxford, Charles University (Prague)

      b. Focus was on logic and Christian theology

      c. Little room for study of classical literature

    4. More secular, urban-oriented educational tradition in Italy

    5. Northern rulers less interested in patronizing artists and intellectuals

  B. Christian humanism and the northern Renaissance

    1. Northern Christian humanists looked for ethical guidelines in the Christian past

    2. They sought wisdom from the Christian ancients

      a. New Testament

      b. The church fathers

    3. Northern artists inspired by Italian example to learn classical techniques

  C. Desiderius Erasmus (c. 1469–1536)

    1. "The prince of the Christian humanists"

    2. Born near Rotterdam but was a citizen of the world

    3. Devoured the classics and the teachings of the church fathers

    4. Attended University of Paris

      a. Rebelled against Parisian scholasticism

    5. Made his living by teaching and writing

    6. Traveled to England, Germany, Italy, and the Netherlands

    7. A Latin prose stylist

      a. Verbal effects, puns, and irony

    8. Promoted the "philosophy of Christ"

      a. All society is corrupt, go back to the Gospels

    9. *The Praise of Folly* (1509)

      a. Sarcasm and parody of everything, including himself

10. *Colloquies* (1518)
    a. Examined contemporary religious practices
11. *Handbook of the Christian Knight* (1503)
    a. Urged the laity to pursue lives of inward piety
12. *Complaint of Peace* (1517)
    a. Christian pacifism
13. Textual criticism
    a. New versions of Jerome, Augustine, and Ambrose
    b. The New Testament (1516)
       i. Greek and Latin translations

D. Sir Thomas More (1478–1535)
   1. Lord Chancellor of England (1529)
   2. Imprisoned for not taking an oath naming Henry VIII as head of the Church of England (1534)
      a. Thrown into the Tower of London and executed
      b. Martyrdom
   3. *Utopia*
      a. An Erasmian critique of contemporary society
      b. An indictment against unearned wealth, persecution, punishment, and the slaughter of war
      c. No private property or war

E. Ulrich von Hutten (1488–1523)
   1. German disciple of Erasmus
   2. Dedicated to German cultural nationalism
   3. Collaborated with Crotus Rubianus
      a. Wrote *Letters of Obscure Men* (1515)
      b. A satire on Scholasticism

F. The decline of Christian humanism
   1. John Colet (c. 1467–1519)
   2. Jacques Lefèvre d'Étaples (c. 1455–1536)
   3. Cardinal Francisco Ximénez de Cisneros (1436–1517)
   4. Juan Luís Vives (1492–1540)
   5. Thrown into disarray by the Protestant Reformation
   6. Devastating critiques of clerical corruption and religious ceremonialism
   7. Caught between Catholicism and Lutheranism

G. Literature, art, and music in the northern Renaissaance
   1. Pierre de Ronsard (c. 1524–1585) and Joachim du Bellay (c. 1522–1560)— wrote Petrarchan sonnets
   2. Sir Philip Sidney (1554–1586) and Edmund Spenser (c. 1552–1599)

3. François Rabelais (c. 1494–1553)
   a. Began his career in the clergy
   b. Studied medicine, became a physician in Lyons
   c. *Gargantua and Pantagruel*
      i. Satirized religious ceremonialism, scholasticism, superstitions, and bigotry
      ii. Written in French
      iii. Glorified the human and the natural
      iv. The "abbey of Thélème"— "do what thou wouldst."

H. Architecture
   1. French châteaux
   2. Combined elements of French Gothic with classical horizontality
   3. The Louvre, Paris (1546)

I. Painting
   1. Albrecht Dürer (1471–1528)
      a. Mastered Italian techniques of proportion and perspective
      b. The details of nature
      c. Erasmus the hero
   2. Hans Holbein the Younger (1497–1543)
      a. The portraits of Sir Thomas More and Erasmus
      b. Capturing the essence of human individuality

J. Music
   1. Humanistic efforts to recover and imitate classical musical forms
   2. New expressiveness: coloration and emotional quality
   3. New musical instruments: lute, viol, violin, and harpsichord
   4. New musical forms: madrigal, motets, opera
   5. Less distinction between sacred and profane music
   6. The *Ars Nova* (New Art)
      a. Flourished in Italy and France
      b. Francesco Landini (c. 1325–1397)
      c. Guillaume de Machaut (c. 1300–1377)
      d. Secular music
      e. Also adapted for ecclesiastical motets
   7. Franco-Flemish compositions
      a. Roland de Lassus (1532–1594)
      b. Giovanni Pierluigi da Palestrina (c. 1525–1594)
      c. Choral music written for Catholic church services
   8. England
      a. William Byrd (1543–1623)

GENERAL DISCUSSION QUESTIONS

1. For what reasons do historians no longer argue that the Renaissance served as a decisive break between the medieval and modern world? Why did the Renaissance originate in northern Italian city-states in the fourteenth century?

2. What did Renaissance scholars hope to learn from the classical past? If the word *renaissance* means "rebirth," what exactly was reborn? What were the general characteristics of Renaissance humanism?

3. Why is Machiavelli usually considered to be the "father of modern political thought"? Why was Machiavelli more interested in "what is" rather than "what ought to be"? What is Machiavelli's view of human nature?

4. What is a "Renaissance Man"?

5. Why was Florence the Renaissance city *par excellence*?

6. Why did northern European intellectuals embrace Christian humanism?

7. How does François Rabelais's attitude of "do what thou wouldst" differ from Desiderius Erasmus's worldview?

8. Compare and contrast Italian civic humanism with northern Christian humanism.

DOCUMENT DISCUSSION QUESTIONS

The Humanists' Educational Program

1. Why did the Italian Renaissance produce such a strong spirit of civic humanism?

2. Do you think that Socrates' and Cicero's perceptions of "virtue" were identical to those of Vergerius and Bruni? Were Renaissance virtues and classical virtues one and the same thing?

3. Why did humanists such as Leonardo Bruni consider the study of history essential to a full education?

Some Renaissance Attitudes Toward Women

4. For what reasons did Leon Batista Alberti argue that his wife should have no access to his books or records?

5. Would you expect Renaissance attitudes toward women to have been more liberal and more modern? Did Alberti's comments refer to Italian society as a whole, or merely a small segment of it?

Machiavelli's Italian Patriotism

6. Why did Machiavelli argue that Italy needed the type of prince he had outlined in his book, *The Prince*?

7. According to Machiavelli, what was wrong with the Italy of his own day?

8. Did Machiavelli espouse the cause of Italian nationalism or the banner of a strong prince like Lorenzo de Medici? Or were his visions of patriotism and leadership concurrent?

SAMPLE LECTURE 12: "LIKE A GOLDEN AGE": THE RENAISSANCE AND MODERN MAN

Lecture Objectives

1. To present humanist values and discuss why Renaissance thinkers revered the past

2. To compare the Italian Renaissance with the northern Renaissance

3. To consider whether the Renaissance represented a sharp break with the medieval past

"LIKE A GOLDEN AGE"

In 1492, the Italian philosopher Marsilio Ficino, in a letter to his friend, Paul of Middleburg, wrote:

> . . . if then we are to call any age golden, it is beyond doubt that age which brings forth golden talents in different places. That such as true of this our age . . . [no one] will hardly doubt. For this century, like a golden age, has restored to light the liberal arts, which were almost extinct. . . . And all this in Florence.

Ficino's words seem to capture much of the essence of the historical Renaissance. The key phrase "like a golden age" highlights the significance of history to Renaissance scholars. Ficino knew that his own age—the age of late-fifteenth-century Florence—was quite unlike any age that had preceded it. Of course, the age that had directly preceded Ficino's appeared as a "dark age," an age in which intellect, the arts, and sciences had succumbed to medieval numbness. By contrast, the Classical Age was an age of light, and from that light Renaissance scholars such as Ficino would fashion a new humanism that has come to signify the essence of the Italian Renaissance. The word *renaissance* means "rebirth." But rebirth of what? And, perhaps even more important, rebirth for whom?

Although Renaissance thinkers did not discover historical consciousness, they were keen students of history, so it was natural for them to look for ideals in the past that would give them identity in the present and hope for the future. Their view of the preceding centuries as a "dark age" may have blinded subsequent generations of human thought to the contributions of the medieval world, but it gave Renaissance historians two new metaphors with which to work: darkness and light. This leads us to a major historical question: was the Renaissance more modern than medieval? Many historians have argued that modern man was born during the Renaissance. If so, what is modern man?

ORIGINS OF THE RENAISSANCE

Although we can certainly find medieval antecedents to a shift in the Western intellectual tradition, the Renaissance originated as a European cultural movement of the fourteenth and fifteenth centuries. The Renaissance made its first appearance in Italy for a number of reasons:

- Italy was the most advanced urban society in the later Middle Ages.
- Italian aristocrats lived in urban centers, rather than the countryside, and so were more deeply involved in urban public affairs.
- Aristocrats and the upper bourgeoisie engaged in banking or mercantile enterprises, rather than living off of the land.
- Greater demands for education arose to meet the needs of the growing merchant class and interest in urban politics.
- Italy had a greater sense of continuity with the classical past, having constant reminders of it in Roman architecture and literature.
- Italians were intent on recapturing their classical heritage to better establish their own identity apart from France and its scholasticism.
- Late-medieval Italian economy was more prosperous, compared to the rest of Europe, than it had ever been before.
- The wealth of the city-states, combined with urban pride and competition, encouraged aristocratic and private patronage of the arts.

And the list could be extended even further.

CIVIC HUMANISM: THE RENAISSANCE IN ITALY

The earliest signs of the emergence of something like a renaissance can perhaps be understood through the work of Petrarch (1304–1374). A deeply committed Christian, Petrarch believed that the medieval tradition of scholasticism was misguided because it taught abstract speculation instead of concrete ways to attain salvation:

> Living, I despise what melancholy fate
> has brought us wretches in these evil years.
> Long before my birth time smiled and may again,

> for once there was, and yet will be, more joyful days.
> But in this middle age time's dregs
> sweep around us, and we beneath a heavy
> load of vice. Genius, virtue, glory now
> have gone, leaving chance and sloth to rule.
> Shameful vision this! We must awake or die!

Petrarch wanted to cultivate a literary eloquence—and, indeed, eloquence became one of the hallmarks of Renaissance humanism—that would inspire people to do good. For Petrarch, the best examples of eloquence could be found in the texts of the classical world.

Many ancient texts had made their way back into Europe, and scholars began a long process of translation, which took them to the study of classical Greek and Latin. Because they wanted to preserve the original meaning rather than verbatim transcriptions of classical works, there was a new attention to language and grammar. Such emphasis on classical literature could mean, on the one hand, literary eloquence and, on the other, textual criticism, such as that of Lorenzo Valla (1405–1457). But perhaps the greatest contribution of the ancient world to the Renaissance was Neoplatonism—a blending of the ideas of Plato, Plotinus, mysticism, and Christianity. The Renaissance movement might have needed an alternative to Aristotelian logic chopping, and Plato was the answer.

One of the more original thinkers of the Italian Renaissance was the Florentine Niccolo Machiavelli (1469–1527). Most of his fame rests on the publication of a small handbook of political advice, *The Prince*, which is seen by his critics as an endorsement of tyranny. Contrasted with his lesser-known *Discourses on Livy*, in which he praises the ancient Roman Republic as a model government, Machiavelli emerges as a controversial and complex thinker. Along with his understanding of classical history and experience in Florentine politics, Machiavelli was a keen observer of human nature. He argued that it is more important to describe the way human nature really is rather than what it ought to be. Thus, he wrote *The Prince* not as a blueprint for a future society but for the prince of his own day. From his understanding of Roman history and his hopes for a free republic, Machiavelli came to embrace the virtues of civic humanism.

His contemporary, Baldessare Castiglione (1478–1529), was less interested in the mechanics of politics and more interested in the way man ought to act. With Castiglione's *Book of the Courtier*, we are in the world of the "Renaissance man," a gentleman who is multitalented, brave, witty, and learned. Extremely popular throughout Europe, Castiglione's book had great influence in spreading the ideals of civility to court society, which resulted in increased patronage of the arts.

THE ARTS

We know so much about the Renaissance mostly from its most tangible manifestations: art. Few have read Machiavelli, but everyone knows the *Mona Lisa*. In Florence, Renaissance painting assumed the following characteristics:

- The laws of linear perspective were developed and used to impart a three-dimensional sense in the two-dimensional nature of painting.
- Artists experimented with the effects of light and shadow (*chiaroscuro*).
- Human anatomy, human form, and the natural world were closely studied.
- Nonreligious themes and subjects were open to artists through lay patronage.
- Paintings were made to delight the eye as well as the intellect.
- The introduction of oils in place of fresco pigments allowed artists to develop advanced techniques.

The greatest of the Florentine artists was Leonardo da Vinci (1452–1519). A true Renaissance Man, he was a skilled painter, architect, musician, mathematician, engineer, and scientist. He sought to obtain the most accurate imitation of nature possible. But Renaissance art took many forms: alongside paintings of the luxurious life of the city are Botticelli's *Birth of Venus* and da Vinci's *The Last Supper*. In the work of Michelangelo (1475–1564), we see an idealist who embraced Neoplatonism, making him very different from da Vinci. He was committed to classical aesthetic principles of art: harmony, solidity, and restraint. His sculpture of *David* was a shining example of what he believed was the sculptor's ability to imitate God in recreating the human form.

The Renaissance Man was an artist whether he was a painter, sculptor, or political theorist. After all, Machiavelli had succeeded in "painting" the duties of a late-fifteenth-century Florentine prince just as well as Michelango had executed his *David*. Individual creativity came to express all that was best in Italian humanism, reinforced as it was by models provided by the ancient world.

CHRISTIAN HUMANISM: THE RENAISSANCE IN NORTHERN EUROPE

The Italian Renaissance flourished until the middle of the sixteenth century. By that time the Protestant Reformation had swept across the Holy Roman empire to present Rome with its gravest challenge. Meanwhile, European trade had shifted from the Mediterranean to the Atlantic and beyond. Just as the Renaissance was waning in Italy, it took on a new shape in northern Europe, what we usually call "Christian humanism." How was the northern Renaissance different?

- The North lacked a tradition of urban intellectuals.
- Northern universities did not supply a desirable environment for humanist learning.
- Italian ideals were combined with preexisting northern traditions, especially in the Christian humanist movement.

- Northern Renaissance thinkers and artists sought wisdom from the early Christian fathers and traditions rather than from classical antiquity.

Like the Italian civic humanists, the Christian humanists of the North also abandoned scholasticism for its attention to Aristotelian logic, believing that it had nothing to do with the practical conduct of life. They looked for that practical guidance to come from the Bible rather than from the ancients, although Erasmus could write, "Saint Socrates, pray for me."

Desiderius Erasmus of Rotterdam (c. 1469–1536) was the greatest of the Christian humanists. He was known across Europe and was himself cosmopolitan in outlook. Well-versed in the literature of the ancients, Erasmus was able to use irony and satire to his advantage. But beneath his irony and wit, best understood by reading his *Praise of Folly* (1509), was a serious message: man had somehow strayed from God, society and the clergy had become morally lax, and faith must return to its apostolic origins. In 1516, he also brought out a new version of the New Testament, with the best Greek translations published along with his own Latin translation. It was a translation that would fall into the hands of Martin Luther, with profound ramifications.

NORTHERN LITERATURE AND ART

Christian humanism began to fade with the Protestant Reformation started by Luther in 1517, as most Christian humanists were caught in the middle between Lutheranism and Catholicism. But the northern Renaissance continued on, even though the age produced a measure of uncertainty

One French author who dwelled on this uncertainty was François Rabelais (c. 1494–1553). Similar to Erasmus in that he also began his career in the clergy and went on to write humorous satire, Rabelais was perhaps more worldly and more interested in the foibles of man than in preaching morality. Running beneath the rollicking humour in his *Gargantua and Pantagruel* is Rabelais' theme: glorification of what is natural and human. "Do what thou wouldst" became his guiding motif.

One of the problems historians face when investigating the Renaissance is that there is no unifying Renaissance position on anything. There are philosophies but no single philosophy. If we can locate a secular tendency in the civic humanism of Machiavelli or Valla, we can identify the opposite in the Christian humanism of Sir Thomas More (1478–1535) or Erasmus. At best, the Renaissance represents a stage in human history when the quest for identity assumed a new prominence. The medieval world had found its comfort in a matrix of Christianity as interpreted by the church and as embraced by the common people. With the infusion of gold and silver from the age of discovery, the growth of cities and trade, the multiplication of universities, and the end to devastating plagues and famines, Europe seemed to find itself in a period of recovery. The Renaissance certainly did take place but only for a select few, and humanists of all flavors did create a new identity for themselves, but what of the rest of Europe?

SUGGESTED FEATURE FILMS

The Agony and the Ecstasy. 140 min. Color. 1965. 20th Century Fox. Based on Irving Stone's novel about Michelangelo.

Andrei Rublev. 181 min. Color. 1966. Mosfilm. Russian re-creation of the life of a fifteenth-century painter.

Henry VIII and His Six Wives. 125 min. Color. 1972. EMI. Inspired by the six-part BBC series.

A Man for All Seasons. 120 min. Color. 1966. Columbia. Academy Award-winning film adaptation of Robert Bolt's play about Sir Thomas More and his conflict with Henry VIII.

A Man for All Seasons. Color. 1988. Turner Home Entertainment. Made-for-TV version that is perhaps truer to Bolt's original play. Directed by and starring Charlton Heston.

Prince of Foxes. 107 min. B/W. 1949. 20th Century Fox. Lavish production about the life of Cesare Borgia.

Rembrandt. 85 min. B/W. 1936. London Films. Dramatization of the last years of Rembrandt's life, with Charles Laughton.

Romeo and Juliet. 152 min. Color. 1968. Paramount. Franco Zeffirelli set his beautiful version of Shakespeare's play in Renaissance Italy.

SUGGESTED CLASSROOM FILMS

Civilisation: A Personal View by Kenneth Clark. No. 4. Man: The Measure of All Things. Color. 1970. BBC/Time-Life Films. Presents the early fifteenth century as the period when modern man emerges. Focuses on the courts of Ferrara, Mantua, and Urbino. *No. 5. The Hero as Artist.* Focuses on Renaissance art. *No. 6. Protest and Communication.* Focuses on the Christian humanists, Luther, and Shakespeare.

François I. 22 min. Color. Films for the Humanities. A biography of the patron of the Renaissance in France.

Galileo, the Challenge of Reason. 26 min. Color. 1969. Learning Corporation of America. Centers on Galileo's conflict with the Church.

I, Leonardo da Vinci. 52 min. Color. 1965. McGraw-Hill. Uses his journals and writings.

Michelangelo: The Last Giant. 68 min. Color. 1967. McGraw-Hill. Focuses on Michelangelo's art and Renaissance politics.

Michelangelo: The Medici Chapel. 22 min. Color. 1964. West. Includes Michelangelo's sonnets read as commentary.

Paracelsus. 30 min. B/W. 1965. Indiana University. Uses Paracelsus to illustrate the Renaissance spirit of inquiry.

The Power of the Past: Florence with Bill Moyers. 90 min. Color. 1990. PBS documentary with much excellent footage of Florence.

Renaissance Art and Music. 54 min. Color. 1984. Insight Media. Examines the interactions of artistic production and humanist philosophy.

CHAPTER 13 | Reformations of Religion

OUTLINE

I. Introduction
  A. General considerations—Europe in 1500
    1. Population growth, an expanding economy, and increased urbanization
    2. National monarchies created in England, France, Spain, and Poland
    3. Resumption of commercial and colonial expansion
    4. Suppression of heresy
    5. Popular devotion had increased
II. The Lutheran Upheaval
  A. Explaining the success of Martin Luther (1483–1546)
    1. Peasants hoped Lutheranism would free them from the exactions of their lords
    2. Towns and princes were trying to consolidate their political independence
    3. Nationalist demands for liberation from foreign popes
    4. From reforming the church to a frontal assault on the church
  B. Luther's quest for religious certainty
    1. Luther and his father
    2. Sent to the University of Erfurt to study law
    3. 1505: Luther enters an Augustinian monastery
    4. 1513: Conversion experience—the quest for spiritual peace
    5. The problem of the justice of God
      a. How could God issue commands man could not obey?
      b. Eternal damnation as punishment

6. The "tower experience"
  a. Meditated upon the Psalms ("deliver me in thy justice")
  b. God's power lay in his mercy to save sinful mortals through faith
7. Paul's Letter to the Romans (1:17)— "the just shall live by faith"
8. God's justice does not depend on "good works" and religious ceremonies
9. Humans are saved by grace alone ("justification by faith alone")
10. Piety and charity as visible signs of the faithful
11. Salvation and the church
  a. The church (sacraments) and the believer (piety and charity) could affect salvation
  b. The church "quantified" the process of salvation
  c. The "Treasury of Merits"
  d. The indulgence
    i. Remission of the penitential obligations imposed by priests
    ii. Indulgences earned by demanding spiritual exercises (eleventh and twelfth centuries)
    iii. Indulgences granted with a monetary payment
12. Indulgences seen by many as just another form of simony (selling grace in return for cash)
13. "Here I stand; God help me, I can do no other."

C. The Reformation begins
  1. Albert of Hohenzolern
     a. Debt and simony
     b. The bargain with Pope Leo X
        i. Granted Albert an indulgence
        ii. Half the money went to build St. Peter's Basilica at Rome
        iii. Half the money went to Albert
  2. Johann Tetzel
     a. Hawked indulgences in northern Germany with Fugger support
     b. Sold indulgences as "tickets to heaven"
  3. October 31, 1517: Luther's *Ninety-Five Theses*
     a. Written in Latin, intended for academic dispute
     b. Translated and published in German
     c. 1519: public disputation in Leipzig
        i. Luther maintained that the pope and all clerics were merely fallible men
        ii. The highest authority for an individual's conscience was the truth of Scripture
  4. Pope Leo charged Luther with heresy
  5. Luther's pamphlets of 1520—general ideas
     a. Justification by faith alone
     b. The primacy of Scripture
        i. The literal meaning of Scripture takes precedence over church traditions
     c. The "priesthood of all believers"
        i. All Christian believers are spiritually equal before God
  6. General consequences
     a. Good works do not lead to salvation
        i. Fasts, pilgrimages, and the veneration of relics were valueless
     b. The dissolution of all monasteries and convents
     c. Proposed substituting German for Latin in church services
     d. Reduced the number of sacraments from seven to two (baptism and the eucharist)
     e. Denied that the Mass was a repetition of Christ's sacrifice on the cross
     f. Proposed the abolition of the entire ecclesiastical hierarchy of popes and bishops

D. The break with Rome
  1. The role of the printing press in spreading Luther's message
  2. Luther's defiance touched off a national religious revolt against the papacy
     a. Popes bribed the cardinals to gain the papacy
     b. Moral corruption
     c. Popes waged war to gain territory
  3. There were no agreements (concordats) between pope and German emperor
  4. Princes complained that taxes were too high
  5. Many German princes sided with Luther as a way to attack Roman influence and corruption

E. The Diet of Worms (1521)
  1. Luther handed over to Elector Frederick the Wise for punishment as a heretic
  2. Frederick convened a Diet (formal assembly) to give Luther a "fair hearing"
  3. Initiative lay with presiding officer, Charles V (Holy Roman emperor)
     a. Would not tolerate attacks on the church or the emperor
  4. Luther kidnapped by Frederick and brought to the castle of the Wartburg
  5. Edict of Worms declared Luther an outlaw (never enforced)

F. The German princes and the Lutheran Reformation
  1. The new religion prevailed in areas where princes formally established Lutheranism
  2. Rulers sought to control appointments to church offices and restrict flow of money to Rome
     a. 1487: Innocent VIII consented to the establishment of the Spanish Inquisition
     b. 1516: Concordat of Bologna—French king to choose bishops and abbots
  3. The consolidation of the authority of the German princes
  4. Free cities adopted Lutheranism in order to establish supreme governing authority
  5. Luther and temporal authority
     a. 1523: *On Temporal Authority*—God must be obeyed in all things
     b. 1525: *Against the Thievish, Murderous Hordes of Peasants*

III. The Spread of Protestantism
  A. German Imperial Diet (1529) originated the term "Protestant"

B. The Reformation in Switzerland
 1. The independence of prosperous Swiss cities
 2. Ulrich Zwingli (1484–1531)
    a. Theologically moderate form of Lutheranism
    b. Catholic theology and practice conflicted with the Gospels
    c. Condemned religious images and hierarchical authority
    d. The Eucharist was a reminder of Christ's sacrifice, not the real presence of Christ's body (Luther)
       i. Prevented Lutherans and Zwinglians from joining forces in a united front
 3. Anabaptism
    a. Radical Protestant sect
    b. Convinced that baptism was effective only if administered to willing adults
    c. Men and women are not born into any church
    d. Feared by both Catholics and Protestants
    e. Münster (1534)
       i. Sectarianism and millenarianism
       ii. The New Jerusalem
       iii. John of Leyden
       iv. Obligatory religious practices, private property abolished, polygamy permitted
    f. Anabaptists persecuted across Europe
       i. Menno Simons (c. 1496–1561) and the Mennonite sect
 4. John Calvin's reformed theology
    a. John Calvin (1509–1564)
       i. Born near Paris, studied law, became a humanist
       ii. *Institutes of the Christian Religion*
       iii. The omnipotence of God
       iv. Man is sinful by nature
       v. Predestination and the elect
       vi. An active life of piety and morality
    b. Calvin and church government
       i. Rejected popery outright
       ii. Eliminated all traces of hierarchy
       iii. Congregational election of ministers and assemblies of ministers and electors
       iv. "Four bare walls and a sermon"
 5. Calvinism in Geneva
    a. Calvin began preaching in 1536, expelled in 1538, returned in 1541
    b. Calvinist theocracy
    c. The Consistory—twelve lay elders, ten to twenty pastors
    d. The supervision of morality
    e. Spread of Calvinism
       i. John Knox (c. 1513–1572)—brought Calvinism to Scotland (Presbyterians)
       ii. The Dutch Reformed Church
       iii. French Huguenots
       iv. English Puritans

IV. The Domestication of the Reformation, 1525–1560
   A. Protestantism and the family (Germany and Switzerland)
      1. Protestant attacks on monasticism and clerical celibacy
         a. Resented immunity of monastic houses from taxation
      2. Guilds and town governments also interested in increasing control by town elites
      3. Reinforced individual craftsmen's control over their households
      4. Family as a "school of godliness"
      5. New religious ideals for women
         a. The married and obedient Protestant "goodwife"
         b. Resolving the tension between piety and sexuality
         c. Reinforcement of male and female roles
      6. Shut down convents
         a. Property handed over to the town
   B. Protestantism and control over marriage
      1. Increased parental control over children
      2. Parents wanted the power to prevent unsuitable matches
      3. Luther declares marriage to be a secular matter only

V. The English Reformation
   A. Henry VIII (r. 1509–1547) and the break with Rome
      1. 1527: Henry sought a divorce from Catherine of Aragon in order to marry Anne Boleyn
      2. Appealed to Rome for an annulment of his marriage
         a. If the pope agreed, doubt would be cast on the validity of all papal dispensations

b. It would also provoke the wrath of Charles V, Catherine's nephew

3. 1531: Henry declared himself to be "protestor and supreme head" of the church in England

4. 1534: the Act of Supremacy

5. Consequences

    a. Pilgrimages and relics were prohibited

    b. English church remained Catholic in organization, doctrine, ritual, and language

    c. 1539: the Six Articles of the faith

B. Edward VI (r.1547–1553)

1. Came to the throne at nine years of age

2. Altered ceremonies of the English church

    a. Priests were permitted to marry

    b. English was substituted for Latin

    c. The veneration of images was abolished

    d. New articles of faith were drawn up repudiating all sacraments except baptism and communion

    e. Justification by faith alone

C. Mary Tudor (r. 1553–1558) and the restoration of Catholicism

1. Reversed Edward's religious policies

2. Many were burned at the stake for refusing to give up Protestantism

3. Asked Parliament to vote a return to papal allegiance

4. "Bloody Mary"

D. The Elizabethan religious settlement

1. Elizabeth I (r. 1558–1603)

    a. Daughter of Henry and Anne Boleyn

2. The new Act of Supremacy (1559)

    a. Repealed Mary's Catholic legislation

    b. Prohibited foreign powers from exercising authority within England

    c. Declared herself "supreme governor" of the English church

    d. Retained some Catholic vestiges

3. 1562: the Thirty-Nine Articles of Faith

4. Protestantism and English nationalism: God has chosen England for greatness

VI. Catholicism Transformed

A. The Catholic Reformation

1. First phase (c. 1490s)

    a. A movement for moral and institutional reform within the religious orders

        i. Papacy showed little interest in this

    b. Influence of northern humanists (Erasmus and More)

        i. Encouraged the laity to lead lives of simple but sincere religious piety

2. Second phase (c. 1530s)

    a. More aggressive phase of reform

    b. New style of papal leadership

        i. Excessive holiness

        ii. Accomplished administrators

        iii. Reorganized papal finances

3. Third phase: the Council of Trent (1545–1563)

    a. Reaffirmed Catholic doctrine

        i. Good works declared necessary for salvation

        ii. The seven sacraments

        iii. Papal supremacy

    b. Bishops and priests were forbidden to hold more than one spiritual office

    c. Establishment of theological seminaries

    d. Established the Index of Forbidden Books (1564)

4. St. Ignatius Loyola (1491–1556)

    a. Spanish noble wounded in battle (1521) became a "spiritual solider of Christ"

    b. Ecstatic visions

    c. *The Spiritual Exercises*

        i. Practical advice on how to master the will

        ii. A program of meditations on sin and the life of Christ

    d. The Society of Jesus (Jesuits) founded at Paris in 1534

        i. Formally constituted as a holy order by Pope Paul III (1540)

        ii. A company of soldiers sworn to defend the faith

        iii. Eloquence, persuasion, and instruction

        iv. The suppression of individuality

        v. Proselytized Christians and non-Christians alike

        vi. Established schools

        vii. Became an international movement

5. Counter-Reformation Christianity

    a. Defended and revitalized the faith

    b. Spread literacy and intense concern for acts of charity

    c. New importance given to religious women

   i. St. Teresa of Avila
    (1515–1582)
   ii. The Ursulines and the
    Sisters of Charity
VII. Conclusion: The Heritage of the Protestant
 Reformation
  A. The Reformation and the Renaissance
   1. Christian humanist influences
    a. Exposed abuses
    b. Close textual study of the Bible
   2. Luther and Erasmus
    a. Erasmus had no sympathy with
     Lutheran principles
    b. Most humanists believed in free
     will and that human nature was
     somehow good
  B. Consequences
   1. Increasing power of Europe's sovereign
    states
   2. The growth of German cultural
    nationalism
   3. Protestantism and the role of women

GENERAL DISCUSSION QUESTIONS

1. Why did the Reformation occur in the sixteenth century? Could it have occurred earlier? What specifically caused the Reformation?

2. According to Martin Luther, why was the doctrine of good works insufficient to secure human salvation? What were the ramifications of Luther's acceptance of the doctrine of "justification by faith alone"?

3. How do you account for the relatively quick success of Lutheranism in Germany and Scandinavia? Why did German princes, who had nothing to fear in terms of their authority, suddenly side with Luther?

4. How did the theology of Martin Luther and John Calvin differ?

5. What is meant by the expression the "domestication of the Reformation"?

6. Why was the Council of Trent one of the most important general councils in the history of the Church?

7. How did the church attempt to combat Protestantism?

DOCUMENT DISCUSSION QUESTIONS

Humanism, Nationalism, and the German Universities

1. Why does Conrad Celtis urge his reader to emulate "the ancient nobility of Rome"? Why was ancient Rome so appealing?

2. Are humanism and nationalism in any way compatible with one another?

Luther on Celibacy and Women

3. Why did Luther believe that the monastic demands for celibacy were impossible to meet? How important an issue was celibacy in the context of sixteenth-century religious conflicts?

The Six Articles

4. If he leaned more toward Catholicism, then why did Henry VIII allow his son to be raised a Protestant? What does this tell us about the Reformation in England?

Obedience as a Jesuit Hallmark

5. Did total obedience to the Church contradict the aspirations of Renaissance humanism?

6. What role did the Jesuits play in the Catholic Reformation? Did the establishment of the Jesuit Order somehow serve as a general indictment of the church itself?

SAMPLE LECTURE 13: THE PROTESTANT REFORMATION: NEW CHOICES

Lecture Objectives

1. To establish who Martin Luther was and why he and the Lutheran revolt were able to gather so much support in such a short period of time

2. To compare the differences between the faith of Martin Luther and that of John Calvin

3. To discuss the ways in which the church reformed itself in the wake of the Protestant Reformation

NEW RELIGIOUS CHOICES

There is little doubt that the Protestant Reformation produced fundamental changes in European society. By the beginning of the sixteenth century, many people in Europe were more than aware that the church was in need of reform. The Lollards and Hussites, two prominent heretical groups of the previous century, had already offered their criticism of the clergy and church hierarchy:

- The clergy had become indifferent in their administration of the sacraments
- Bishops held more than one office
- Popes seemed to live more like princes than mediators between man and God
- Clerical moral corruption and laxity seemed to be commonplace

As people crowded into cities and printing presses were able to make use of a literate audience, more people became aware of church abuses at all levels. Such awareness called for two primary responses: anticlericalism or reform. The Reformation was a revolutionary event in that it forced all European men and women to make fundamental choices in their faith:

- How should they find God?
- From where does salvation come?
- Can humans be saved by doing good works, or is faith alone enough justification for eternal life?

In the context of the age of religious wars from the late sixteenth century on, a person's choice could mean life or death, so it was hard to imagine in 1517 that the religious dominance of the church at Rome could be so fundamentally shattered. But in that year, one man obsessed with life, death, and salvation was forced to take a stand.

THE FAITH OF MARTIN LUTHER

The Protestant Reformation was dominated by the figure of Martin Luther (1483–1546), the son of a copper miner from Thuringia, Germany. As a young man Luther studied law, theology, and philosophy, and, like most university scholars of the period, he was unimpressed with the scholasticism of the schools. He was not taken with humanism either. Instead, as a young man Luther was plagued by doubts about life, death, and the justice of God. Thirsting for a religion that would provide comfort to him in his quest for faith, he joined an Augustinian monastery, where he was able to cleanse his soul but not his doubts. While serving as a scholar of biblical theology at the University of Wittenberg, Luther had his famous "tower experience." He enhanced his sudden insight by further meditations on God's mercy, which led him to his central doctrine of "justification by faith alone": the belief that salvation has nothing to do with human actions but with the gift of God's grace alone, which was bestowed upon those who were predestined for salvation—the faithful. Faith came first, and good deeds naturally followed. This was a faith of deep, inward intensity that did not rely on the sacraments, the clergy, the trappings of church office, nor even the papacy. Luther had no intention of disrupting the church in any way, but in 1517, something happened that would change the course of European history.

THE LUTHERAN REVOLT

On October 31, 1517, Luther circulated a list of ninety-five theses to his Wittenberg colleagues, all of which pertained to the church's sale of indulgences. Although indulgences had been used by the papacy for centuries as a way of obtaining funds to build churches, by the early part of the sixteenth century they were being sold indiscriminately, even to save the souls of those who were already dead. The business of buying and selling indulgences particularly bothered Luther because he believed salvation to be a matter of faith, not money. Although he didn't mean for his theses to be read by a wide audience, someone translated them from Latin into German and published them across the land. Also, in response to Pope Leo X's charge of heresy in 1520, Luther defiantly published more pamphlets defending his ideas. His three main premises, as follows, were to become the backbone of the new Lutheran religion:

1. The highest authority is the truth of Scripture

2. The theory of "justification by faith"

3. His "priesthood of all believers," which meant that the faithful embodied the true spiritual congregation, rather than a society of ordained priests

The elucidation of Luther's premises had significant consequences for the church. Luther did away with the practices of fasting, relics, and pilgrimages, since they had no inherent value for salvation. He recognized only the sacraments of baptism and the Eucharist; however, without faith, even these were irrelevant to salvation. To make the meaning of Mass clear to all, he proposed substituting German for Latin in church services. And, to emphasize the priesthood of all believers, he insisted that priests be called simply "ministers" or "pastors."

THE BREAK WITH ROME: LUTHERANISM IN GERMANY

One basic question we must raise is, why was Germany so receptive to the message that Luther delivered? Luther's message would have spread much more slowly had it not been for the printing press, but it would have fallen on deaf ears had the people not been prepared for what he had to say in the first place. Historians agree that Germany was ripe for a religious revolt because of these factors:

- The papacy continued to demand money and gave nothing in return.
- The scandals of Pope Alexander VI didn't help the church's image.
- Germans were not represented in the College of Cardinals and, so, had no influence in Rome's papal affairs.
- By 1500, Germans had been exposed to enough church criticism to believe that the church needed to be reformed.
- German humanists played an anticlerical role with their satirical propaganda.
- The belated growth of German universities provided an intellectual center for revolt.
- Luther himself incited Germans with the phenomenal success of his 1520 *To the Christian Nobility of the German Nation*, in which he openly criticized the papacy, stating that the "reign of Antichrist could not be worse."

Frederick the Wise saved Luther from almost certain condemnation and death at the Diet of Worms in 1521. Luther stayed in hiding for a year but emerged victorious in 1522 to find that his university cohorts had put all of his ecclesiastical changes into practice. Several German princes rapidly converted to Lutheranism, and their territories followed suit. Why did German princes establish Lutheranism in their territories and thereby guarantee its success? In general, political and economic considerations played a greater role than personal piety in their cases. By adopting Lutheranism, princes could guarantee that the political and religious boundaries of their territories would coincide. They could also exploit monastic wealth, which Luther encouraged them to do, recognizing that he would need political authorities on his side.

THE ENGLISH SITUATION

Although Luther's ideas had their greatest influence in Germany, Lutheranism also became the state religion of Denmark, Norway, and Sweden. Outside of those areas, Lutheranism didn't achieve the same popularity; it did, however, spread in different forms and the word "Protestant" came to mean any non-Catholic, non-Eastern Orthodox Christian. When Henry VIII (r. 1509–47) broke with Rome, he had the support of most of his subjects. But the reason why the Reformation came to England when it did has very little to do with Rome, or perhaps even Luther. Thanks to his inability to produce a male heir with Catherine of Aragon, Henry VIII needed a divorce. Since the pope would not issue a dispensation, Henry made his own break with the church and induced Parliament, in 1534, to pronounce him the head of the Church of England. This did not yet make England a Protestant country. It was under Henry's son, Edward VI, who reigned from 1547 to 1553, that Protestantism gained new ground. Since Henry was only nine years old when he was crowned king, his government's religious policies fell into the hands of Thomas Cranmer, archbishop of Canterbury, and the dukes of Somerset and Northumberland—all of whom were Protestants. The Church of England was then drastically changed:

- Priests were permitted to marry.
- English was substituted for Latin.
- The veneration of icons was abolished.
- All sacraments were repudiated, save baptism and the Eucharist.
- New articles of faith emphasized Luther's justification by faith alone.

When Mary I (r. 1553–58) assumed the throne, she immediately attempted to return England to Catholicism by restoring the celebration of the Mass. But many leading families had become wealthy from the dissolution of monastic lands and were not that enamored of Mary's policy. She also made the mistake of ordering the execution of Cranmer as well as a few hundred Protestants. The question of whether England would be Catholic or Protestant was settled in favor of the latter by Elizabeth I's rule (1558–1603). By a new Act of Supremacy in 1559, she repealed all of Mary's Catholic legislation and became the "supreme governor" of the English church—Christ alone was head of the church.

LUTHER AND CALVIN

John Calvin and Martin Luther were contemporaries of one another, but Calvin (1509–1564) was of a different generation and a different education. Born and educated in France, Calvin spent his youth studying law, theology, and Greek art, as well as Hebrew, Greek, and Latin. We could almost call him a humanist. In the early 1520s, Calvin moved to the Swiss city of Basel and wrote the first version of the *Institutes of the Christian Religion*, the work that was to become the most authoritative statement of basic Protestant beliefs. Calvinism was a rigorous theology with the following precepts:

- God is omnipotent.
- The universe is dependent upon the will of God alone.
- All humans are sinners by nature.
- The Lord has predestined some for salvation, the rest for damnation.
- Humans cannot alter their fate.
- God will plant the desire to live rightly in the "elect," but moral conduct is a only a sign of one's preordained fate.
- Good Christians should act as though they are the sole instruments of God, always living an active life of morality.

Some of this sounds like Luther and some does not. For Luther, man must endure the tribulations of life on earth; for Calvin, man must labor for the sake of God. Calvinism was also more firmly rooted in the Old Testament and stricter on its adherents than was Lutheranism. Also, Luther accepted that hierarchy was necessary within his church, whereas Calvin rejected all ecclesiastical hierarchy, arguing instead for the congregational election of ministers and assemblies of ministers and laymen. He also insisted on the barest simplicity in church services: "four bare walls and a sermon." Like Lutheranism, though, Calvinism spread beyond its point of origin in Geneva. John Knox (1505–1572) brought Calvinism to Scotland, where it became known as Presbyterianism. Calvinists formed a majority in Holland, where they founded the Dutch Reformed Church, and a large minority in France, where they were known as Huguenots. The Puritans in England were Calvinists who eventually fled to the North American colonies.

CATHOLIC REFORMATION/COUNTER-REFORMATION

Although the Catholic Church was clearly threatened by Luther and Calvin, as early as the late fifteenth century it had also embraced its own movement toward reform. This was largely due to the influence of Christian humanism and carried on without the assistance of the papacy. By the 1530s, however, it became clear to the church that a more vigorous approach to reform was needed to defend itself. The popes of the mid-sixteenth century created a new style of papal leadership based on living morally correct lives, something they ought to have been doing all along. They reorganized papal finances and filled posts with bishops who led ascetic lives. These papal activities culminated in Pope Paul III's Council of Trent, which met between 1545 and 1563. As one of the most important councils in the history of the church, it reaffirmed all the Catholic doctrines that were challenged by Protestants:

- Good works were upheld as necessary for salvation.
- The sacraments were affirmed as an indispensable means for salvation.
- Transubstantiation, apostolic succession of priests, celibacy for the clergy, and the belief in purgatory and the saints were all confirmed as essential Catholic elements.
- Papal supremacy over the clergy and all church councils was maintained.
- The doctrine of indulgences was upheld.

The Council did provide for the elimination of abuses: bishops and priests were forbidden to hold more than one office. To help stop the further growth of Protestantism, the church also instituted the Index of Prohibited Books in 1564 and the Inquisition was called into action.

In addition to papal reform activities, the Society of Jesus (Jesuits) was founded by the Spanish nobleman Ignatius Loyola (1491–1556) and quickly became another way in which the Church sought to win back converts from Protestantism. The Jesuits were mainly in the business of proselytizing through missionary work, sometimes risking their lives, sometimes succeeding in spreading Catholicism or regaining territory that was lost to Protestantism. They were also responsible for building schools and colleges throughout Europe, since they believed that Catholicism depended on literacy and education.

TOWARD THE SEVENTEENTH CENTURY

While the Renaissance did not cause the Protestant Reformation to unfold, it is clear that Christian humanism played an important role in creating an atmosphere of religious questioning. The northern humanists were critical of church corruption, but their real effect was in the area of textual criticism of the Bible: a line of "communication" runs from Valla through Erasmus to Luther and Calvin. Of course, Erasmus had nothing but contempt for Luther's principles, particularly on the issue of free will versus predestination. The humanists saw human nature as primarily good; the Lutherans and Calvinists, as substantially evil. Whereas the humanists favored toleration, Luther and especially Calvin emphasized conformity and obedience. The Reformation gave Europeans a new religious alternative: they either revived their faith in the church or broke with the church to embrace one of the many shades of Protestantism. The choices one made in terms of faith could have drastic consequences as we shall see when we investigate the Age of Religious Wars.

SUGGESTED FEATURE FILMS

Luther. 113 min. Color. 2003. R. S. Entertainment, Inc. Eric Till's film begins with Luther as an Augustinian monk and follows his struggle to reconcile his faith with church corruption and hypocrisy.

Luther. 110 min. Color. 1973. American Film Theatre. Excellent character study of Martin Luther, based on the play by John Osborne.

A Man for All Seasons. 120 min. Color. 1966. Columbia. Academy Award-winning film adaptation of Robert Bolt's play about Sir Thomas More and his conflict with Henry VIII.

A Man for All Seasons. Color. 1988. Turner Home Entertainment. Made-for-TV version that is perhaps truer to Bolt's original play. Directed by and starring Charlton Heston.

SUGGESTED CLASSROOM FILMS

Civilisation: A Personal View by Kenneth Clark. No. 6. Protest and Communication. 52 min. Color. 1970. BBC/Time-Life Films. Focuses on the Christian humanists, Luther, and Shakespeare.

Conquest of Souls. 45 min. Color. 1978. McGraw-Hill. Examines Catholic missionary efforts in the New World and in Protestant Europe.

Pilgrims and Puritans: The Struggle for Religious Freedom in England (1517–1692). 22 min. Color. 1997. Films for the Humanities and Sciences. Focuses on the origins of Puritanism and daily life at New Plymouth.

Reformation: Age of Revolt. 24 min. Color. 1973. Encyclopaedia Britannica Educational Corporation. Portrays the sixteenth century as an era of revolt, with Luther as the detonator.

Reformation Overview. 2 parts. 180 min. total. Color. 1995. Films for the Humanities and Sciences. Traces the history of the Protestant Reformation and profiles the ideas of Wyclif, Hus, Luther, Zwingli, Calvin, and others. Highly recommended.

The Reformation and the Rise of the Middle Class. 2 parts. 30 min. each. Color. 1989. Insight Media. Explores the relationship among the centralization of political power, the Protestant Reformation, and the emergence of urbanized middle classes.

CHAPTER 14

Religious Wars and State Building, 1540–1660

6. Henry IV (r. 1589–1610)
   a. Initiated the Bourbon dynasty
   b. 1598: the Edict of Nantes
      i. Catholicism established as the official religion
      ii. Huguenots allowed to worship, attend universities, and serve as public officials
   c. Divided France into religious "spheres of influence"
C. The revolt of the Netherlands (1566–1609)
   1. Southern Netherlands—grew prosperous from trade and manufacture
   2. 1560: Charles V ceded all territories to his son, Philip
   3. Philip II (r. 1556–1598)
      a. Used the Netherlands as a source of income to pursue Spanish affairs
      b. French Calvinists spread to Antwerp, converting others along the way
   4. William the Silent
      a. Leader of the Catholic nobility
      b. Appealed to Philip to allow toleration for Calvinists
   5. Radical Protestant mobs ransacked Catholic churches
   6. Philip dispatched an army under the duke of Alva
      a. The Council of Blood (reign of terror)
   7. The 1609 truce
      a. Implicit recognition of the northern Dutch Republic
D. England and the defeat of the Spanish Armada (1618–1648)
   1. Sources of antagonism
      a. The English under Elizabeth
      b. English economic interests opposed to Spanish interests
      c. England determined to resist any Spanish attempt to block England's trade with the Low Countries
      d. Naval contests in the Atlantic
   2. The "Invincible Armada"
   3. English naval victory—Spanish defeat
      a. Protestant enthusiasm
      b. "Good Queen Bess"
      c. The Elizabethan Age
E. The Thirty Years' War (1618–1648)
   1. Began as a war between Catholics and Protestants
   2. Ended as an international struggle transcending religion

3. Causes
   a. Religious conflict
   b. Ferdinand (Catholic Habsburg) elected king of Protestant Bohemia
   c. Protestantism suppressed in Bohemia
4. Gustavus Adolphus (1594–1632)
   a. Lutheran king of Sweden
   b. Marched into Germany (1630), championed the Protestants
   c. Earned the support of Catholic princes
      i. Wished to see religious balance restored
      ii. Did not want to submit to Ferdinand II
   d. Subsidized by France
   e. 1632: Adolphus killed in battle
5. 1635–1648: war pits France and Sweden against Austria and Spain
6. The Peace of Westphalia (1648)
   a. Marked the emergence of France as a predominant continental power
   b. The Germans and Austrian Habsburgs as greatest losers
IV. Divergent Paths: Spain, France, and England, 1600–1660
   A. The decline of Spain
      1. By 1600, the Spanish empire was the mightiest European and global power
      2. Primary weakness was economy
         a. Lacked agricultural and mineral resources
         b. Needed to develop industries and a balanced trading pattern
         c. The nobility lived in splendor and dedicated itself to military exploits
         d. Huge military expenditure
      3. The question of Castile
         a. A dominant power after taking over Portugal (1580)
         b. The revolt in Catalunya (1640)
         c. Italian revolts
      4. Spain abandoned its ambition of dominating Europe
   B. The growing power of France
      1. Adding territories (Languedoc, Dauphiné, Provence, Burgundy, and Brittany)
      2. Henry IV set out to restore the prosperity of France
         a. Manual for proper farming technique
         b. Rebuilt roads, bridges, and canals
         c. Constructed royal factories
         d. The exploration of Canada

3. Cardinal Richelieu (1585–1642)
   a. Major goals
      i. Enhance central power at home
      ii. Expand French influence across Europe
   b. 1629: deprived Huguenots of all political and military rights
   c. Abolished the semi-autonomy of Burgundy, Dauphiné, and Provence
   d. Introduced a new system of local government by the "intendants"
4. The Fronde (1648–1653)
   a. A reaction against French governmental centralization
   b. "The slingshot tumults" (Fronde)
   c. Louis XIV, Anne of Austria, and Cardinal Mazarin
   d. Popular and aristocratic resentments reached boiling point
   e. Aristocrats joined commoners against the corruption and mismanagement of Mazarin
   f. Louis implemented new taxation
   g. The absolutism of Louis XIV
C. The English civil war
1. General causes
   a. Constitutional hostilities
   b. Religious animosities
   c. Power struggles between competing aristocratic factions at court
   d. Outdated fiscal system
   e. Rebellion in Ireland
   f. Widespread crop failures
2. The origins of the English civil war
   a. James I (r. 1603–1625)
      i. A Scottish king disliked by the English
      ii. The prerogatives of kingship
      iii. Raised taxes without parliamentary approval
   b. The Puritans
   c. James planted eight thousand Scottish Calvinists in Ulster
   d. Charles I (r. 1625–1649)
      i. Launched a new war with Spain
      ii. Further financial problems
      iii. Married the Catholic daughter of Louis XIII of France
      iv. With William Laud, began to favor anti-Calvinist elements in the English church
      v. 1640: a Scottish army marched into England demanding the withdrawal of Charles's religious reforms
   e. Charles summoned Parliament
   f. 1628: Parliament forced Charles to accept the Petition of Right
      i. Declared all taxes not voted by Parliament to be illegal
      ii. Condemned quartering of soldiers in private homes
      iii. Prohibited arbitrary imprisonment and martial law in times of peace
   g. Charles ruled without Parliament
   h. 1642: Charles tried to arrest five leaders in the House of Commons
      i. Charles raised his own army
      ii. Parliament voted itself taxation to fight Charles and his army
3. Civil war and Commonwealth
   a. King's supporters ("Cavaliers")
      i. Aristocrats and large landowners
      ii. Loyal to the Church of England
   b. Parliamentary supporters ("Roundheads")
      i. Small landholders, tradesmen, and artisans
      ii. Most were Puritans
   c. Quarrel within the parliamentary party
      i. Most were ready to restore Charles as a limited monarch
      ii. A radical minority of Puritans ("Independents") distrusted Charles
      iii. Insisted on religious tolerance
      iv. Oliver Cromwell (1599–1658)
   d. Charles renewed the war (1648) but was forced to surrender
   e. The Rump Parliament
   f. Charles beheaded (January 30, 1649)
   g. The Commonwealth (Republic)
      i. 1653: Cromwell marched troops into Parliament
      ii. The Protectorate—thinly-disguised autocracy
      iv. The *Instrument of Government*
      v. Cromwell as lord protector
4. The restoration of the monarchy
   a. The Puritans had been discredited
   b. Charles II (r. 1660–1685)
      i. Agreed to respect Parliament
      ii. Agreed to observe the Petition of Right

iii. Agreed to summon
Parliament every three years

V. The Problem of Doubt and the Quest for Certainty
  A. From certainty to doubt
    1. The New World
    2. The destruction of religious uniformity
    3. Political allegiances were threatened
    4. The search for new foundations
  B. Witchcraft accusations and the power of the state
    1. The mortal threat of witchcraft
    2. 1494: Pope Innocent VIII ordered papal inquisitors to detect and eliminate witchcraft
    3. Torture increased the number of accused witches who confessed to alleged crimes
    4. Witchcraft trials were European phenomena—not confined to Catholic countries
    5. Fear of witchcraft most intense where secular and religious powers were close
    6. 1660 and after: witchcraft accusations died down
    7. Conclusions
      a. Witch mania reflected the fears Europeans held about the devil
      b. Reflected the growing conviction that only the state had the power to protect people
  C. The search for authority
    1. Michel de Montaigne (1533–1592)
      a. A searching skepticism
      b. The *Essays* (*essai*—trial, experiment)
        i. *Que sais je?* (what do I know?)—very little for certain
        ii. What is true to one nation may be false to another
        iii. Moderation—no government or religion is really perfect; no belief is worth fighting for
      c. Helped combat fanaticism and religious intolerance
    2. Jean Bodin (1530–1596)
      a. Looked to resolve the disorder of his own day
      b. *Six Books of the Commonwealth* (1576)
        i. Absolute governmental sovereignty
        ii. Once a state is constituted it should brook no opposition
        iii. Nation-states can in no way be limited governments
        iv. Resistance to the state leads to anarchy

3. Thomas Hobbes (1588–1679)
    a. The doctrine of political absolutism
    b. *Leviathan* (1651)
      i. Any form of government that protects subject and property might act as sovereign
      ii. The state exists to rule over atomistic individuals
      iii. Pessimistic view of human nature
      iv. The sovereign can tyrannize as he likes
    c. A new science of politics
      i. Political obligation grounded in empirical observation, not tradition or divine right
4. Blaise Pascal (1623–1662)
    a. Began as a mathematician and scientific rationalist
    b. Abandoned science as a result of a conversion experience
    c. Became a Jansenist (puritanical faction within Catholicism)
    d. *Pensées* (*Thoughts*)
      i. Faith alone can show the way to salvation
      ii. Terror, anguish, and awe in the face of evil and eternity

VI. Literature and the Arts
  A. Miguel de Cervantes (1547–1616)
    1. *Don Quixote*
    2. The knight-errant (Quixote) and the practical man (Sancho Panza)
    3. Human nature—idealism and realism
  B. Elizabethan and Jacobean drama
    1. Christopher Marlowe (1564–1593)
      a. *Tamburlaine* and *Doctor Faustus*
      b. Larger-than-life heroes
      c. His heroes meet unhappy ends because there are limits to human striving
    2. Ben Jonson (c. 1572–1637)
      a. Wrote corrosive comedies exposing human vice and foibles
      b. *Volpone*
        i. Shows people behaving like deceitful and lustful animals
      c. *Alchemist*
        i. An attack on quackery and gullibility
    3. William Shakespeare (1564–1616)
      a. His reputation as an author
        i. Forty plays, 150 sonnets, and two long narrative poems
      b. The gift of expression and profound analysis of human character

c. First period
- i. The world is orderly and just
- ii. *Romeo and Juliet*, *A Midsummer Night's Dream*, *Twelfth Night*, *As You Like It*, and *Much Ado About Nothing*

d. Second period
- i. Bitterness, pathos, and the search for the meaning of existence
- ii. *Hamlet*, *Measure for Measure*, *All's Well That Ends Well*, *Macbeth*, and *King Lear*

e. Third period
- i. The spirit of reconciliation and peace
- ii. *The Tempest*

4. John Milton (1608–1674)
- a. Wrote the official defense of Charles I's beheading
- b. Justified Puritan positions in contemporary affairs
- c. Loved the Greek and Roman classics (*Lycidas*)
- d. *Paradise Lost*
  - i. Epic poem based on Genesis
  - ii. The creation and the fall of man
  - iii. Created the character of Satan

C. Mannerism
1. Italian and Spanish painting, 1540–1600
- a. Fascinated the viewer with special effects

2. A blending of two styles
- a. Raphael
  - i. Pontormo (1494–1557) and Bronzino (1503–1572)
  - ii. Bordering on the bizarre and surreal
- b. Michelangelo
  - i. Tintoretto (1518–1594)— large canvases devoted to religious subjects
  - ii. El Greco (c. 1541–1614)—a deeply mystical Catholic art

D. Baroque art and architecture
1. A school of painting, sculpture, and architecture
- a. Retained the dramatic and irregular
- b. Avoided the bizarre
- c. Aimed to instill a sense of the affirmative
- d. Originated in Rome
- e. Expressed the ideals of the Counter-Reformation papacy and the Jesuits

2. Gianlorenzo Bernini (1598–1680)
- a. Architect and sculptor
- b. Combined classical elements to express aggressive relentlessness and great power
- c. Experimented with church facades built "in depth"
- d. Incited response rather than passive observation

3. Diego Velázquez (1599–1660)
- a. Southern-European Baroque
- b. Court painter in Madrid
- c. More-restrained thoughtfulness
- d. *The Maids of Honor*

E. Dutch painting in the "golden age"
1. The greatness and wretchedness of man
2. Peter Brueghel (c. 1525–1569)
- a. Portrayed the busy life of the peasantry
- b. *Peasant Wedding*, *Peasant Wedding Dance*, and *Harvesters*
- c. Appalled by the intolerance he witnessed during Calvinist riots and Spanish repression in the Netherlands
- d. *The Blind Leading the Blind*
- e. *Massacre of the Innocents*

3. Peter Paul Rubens (1577–1640)
- a. Painted thousands of canvases glorifying resurgent Catholicism
- b. Reveled in the sumptuous extravagance of the Baroque
- c. *The Horrors of War*

4. Rembrandt van Rijn (1606–1669)
- a. Lived in staunchly-Calvinist Holland
- b. An active portrait painter who knew how to flatter his subjects
- c. A life of personal tragedy
- d. *Aristotle Contemplating the Bust of Homer* and *The Polish Rider*

VII. Conclusion
A. Undermined confidence in traditional social, religious, and political structures
B. Skepticism and the search for meaning
C. The new power of the state

GENERAL DISCUSSION QUESTIONS

1. Was it inevitable that the Protestant Reformation would also sow the seeds of a series of devastating religious wars?

2. How did the Price Revolution add to the turbulence of the period 1540–1660?

3. Why did most European states try rigorously to repress all minority religious opinion? What did these states fear?

4. How did the Thirty Years' War begin as a religious war in Germany and end as an international struggle? In the aftermath of the Peace of Westphalia, who were the greatest winners and losers?

5. Why does the expression "Age of Doubt, Age of Uncertainty" describe the intellectual climate of seventeenth-century Europe?

6. Why did an outbreak of witchcraft mania occur during the seventeenth century?

7. How did the age of religious wars affect the development of political theory in the early modern period?

8. What is the connection between Baroque art and the Counter-Reformation?

DOCUMENT DISCUSSION QUESTIONS

The Destructiveness of the Thirty Years' War

1. Defend the statement that the Thirty Years' War was the first modern war, and the Peace of Westphalia was the first modern peace.

2. Why was the Thirty Years' War the scene of such devastating carnage? Did the motivation of the combatants determine the nature of this devastation?

Cardinal Richelieu on the Common People of France

3. According to Cardinal Richelieu, what does the state need to fear from an educated populace?

4. What theory of the state can be adduced from Richelieu's *Political Testament*?

Montaigne on Skepticism and Faith

5. How does Montaigne reconcile the seemingly contradictory nature of skepticism and faith? How can one be skeptical and maintain faith?

Democracy and the English Civil War

6. What issues did the English civil war raise regarding the rights of freeborn Englishmen? What are the natural rights of man? What are civil rights?

7. For what reasons was Charles I brought to trial and ultimately beheaded? Was Charles truly the "martyr of the people"?

SAMPLE LECTURE 14: THE AGE OF RELIGIOUS WARS, 1540–1660

Lecture Objectives

1. To examine why Europe's religious divisions intensified into war and to look at the political ramifications of the conflicts

2. To explore the uniqueness of the forms of government developed by France and Britain

3. To analyze why this period has been described as one of doubt and uncertainty and to look at how this doubt and uncertainty were reflected in Western thought and literature

RELIGIOUS DIVISION: RELIGIOUS WARS

Although Luther never intended to obliterate the leadership of the Roman Catholic Church, the Reformation, which he set in motion, intensified the religious divisions of Europe. Protestants and Catholics fought with devastating results. Meanwhile, Protestantism splintered into numerous sects. The age also produced anxiety and tension, despite the fact that the scientific revolution would forever change our understanding of the universe, humanity, and society. Human reason was embraced by the scientific revolutionaries as much as it would later be by the *philosophes* of the eighteenth century. The French mathematician and philosopher Blaise Pascal (1623–1662) was a skilled observer of human consciousness, and in the late seventeenth century, while most scholars were overjoyed with the prospects of human reason, Pascal cast his net of doubt over Europe:

> If there is a God, he is infinitely beyond our comprehension, since, being indivisible and without limits, he bears no relation to us. We are therefore incapable of knowing either what he is or whether he is. That being so, who would dare to attempt an answer to the question? Certainly not we, who bear no relation to him.

Such a statement ran counter to many of the tendencies of the age, in which religious war, civil war, and the quest for political stability dominated Europe.

THE PRICE REVOLUTION

The general turbulence of the era was overshadowed by massive inflation, which was produced by the influx of silver and gold into the European economy. Grain prices quadrupled in some areas, while the cost of living in other areas doubled. Between 1450 and 1600, the population of Europe almost doubled, jumping from 50 to 90 million. Because food prices were driven to artificial heights by increased demand, entrepreneurs, merchants, and landlords profited, while laborers stood to lose the most since their wages ordinarily rose more slowly than prices. By 1600, prices stabilized and population growth slowed, as did the flow of silver from South

America. The Price Revolution took place within the context of religious rivalries—neither Protestant nor Catholic could tolerate the existence of the other. Meanwhile, nations attempted to impose religious uniformity by quieting religious minorities. Furthermore, political instability plagued most European nations. One result of this instability was civil war. Although the conflicts of the period were sometimes generated by economics or politics, religious conflict served as the main motive for war in this century.

GERMANY

Religious wars in Germany began when Charles V attempted to establish Catholic unity in Germany through a military campaign to defeat Lutheran princes. This effort met with failure:

- Catholic princes feared that Charles would suppress their independence.
- Catholic support for Charles was weak.
- Some Catholic princes joined forces with Protestant princes.

A settlement was reached at the Peace of Augsburg (1555), which rested on the principle of *cuius regio, eius religio* (as the ruler, so the religion). Thus Lutheranism would be the sole religion in Lutheran territories, and Catholicism would be the sole religion in Catholic territories. The agreement reached at Augsburg excluded Calvinists, thus ensuring that German Calvinists would remain an opposition group.

FRANCE

The wars of religion in France took a much different shape. By the 1560s, Calvinists represented between 10 and 20 percent of France's population. Many aristocratic women converted to the French Calvinist group, the Huguenots, and converted their husbands, who maintained large armies, as well. When the king died in 1562, a conflict developed between the Calvinist Condé and the Catholic duke of Guise over control of the regency. Because both Protestants and Catholics argued that France could only have one king, one faith, and one law, this political struggle became a religious one. In 1572, the Protestant leader Henry of Navarre was supposed to marry the Catholic sister of the king to make a religious truce. Catherine de Medici intervened and led a faction to kill the Huguenot leaders just before the wedding in the St. Bartholomew's Day Massacre (August 24). More than three thousand Protestants were slaughtered in the streets of Paris by Catholic mobs. The civil war came to an end in 1589, when Henry of Navarre assumed the throne as Henry IV (1589–1610). Although he wished to placate the Catholic majority, in 1598 he offered limited religious toleration to Huguenots in the Edict of Nantes, which

- Recognized Catholicism as the official religion of the state

- Guaranteed Catholics the right to practice the religion everywhere
- Allowed Huguenot nobles to hold services privately in their castles; other Huguenots could worship at specified places
- Guaranteed Huguenots the right to serve in public office and to enter universities and hospitals

The Edict of Nantes was not intended to provide absolute religious toleration. The idea was to create one France with two faiths—a state within a state.

REVOLT IN THE NETHERLANDS

Catholics and Protestants fought one another in the Netherlands, a country ruled by the Habsburgs. The Netherlands had become a wealthy nation, and Antwerp was the commercial center of northern Europe. The rule of Charles V was also popular because he was born in Belgium. Before Charles died in 1558, he gave his territories outside the Holy Roman Empire to his son Philip II (1556–1598). Born in Spain, Philip fought as a Spaniard and made Spain his home. The Netherlands were necessary to him as a source of income, although they contained a large number of Huguenots, who made converts wherever they went, something Catholic Philip could not tolerate. Philip went on to raise an army to wipe out Protestantism forever. His forces arrested 12,000 Protestants, convicted 9,000 of them, and executed 1,000. William the Silent, a wealthy nobleman, converted to Protestantism and sought the help of Protestants in France, Germany, and England. His combined forces seized the northern territories, and the Spanish crown agreed to a truce in 1609. Thus the northern Dutch Republic won independence. Spain would also meet defeat at the hands of the English navy in the defeat of the Spanish Armada in 1588.

THE THIRTY YEARS' WAR

In 1618, a major religious war broke out in Germany. As Spain and France became engaged in the conflict, the war quickly assumed an international dimension. The causes of the Thirty Years' War highlight the characteristics of the age of religious wars:

- Religious conflict between Protestant and Catholic
- The election of the Catholic Ferdinand as king of Protestant Bohemi
- The suppression of Protestantism by Ferdinand

Protestant forces were joined by the Lutheran king of Sweden, Gustavus Adolphus (1595–1632), who championed the Protestant cause in 1630. He was also supported by several German Catholic princes, who preferred to see a return to the status quo rather than surrender anything to Ferdinand. The war ended in 1648, and Germany suffered a terrible loss of life and territory. The Peace of Westphalia brought the war to a close:

- It marked the emergence of France as a continental power.
- It marked the decline of Spain as a power.
- The greatest losses were those of the Austrian Habsburgs.
- Germany remained hopelessly divided and would not be united until the late nineteenth century.

DECLINE OF SPAIN AND GROWTH OF FRANCE

By 1660, France had become the most powerful country in Europe, a position formerly held by Spain. The reasons for Spain's decline were primarily economic:

- Spain lacked agricultural and mineral resources.
- Spain needed to develop industries to compete with England and France.
- Spanish nobility prized chivalry over business.
- Spanish nobles used American silver to buy goods from Europe and live in splendor.
- Gold and silver left the country as soon as it arrived.

The French did not have such difficulties, perhaps due to France's greater wealth and prestige. By 1600, France set out to restore its prosperity. One point worth mentioning is that France could feed itself, unlike Spain. Henry IV also supported the construction of royal factories to produce luxury items and silk, linen, and woolen cloth. Under Cardinal Richelieu (1585–1642), power was centralized at home, and French influence expanded across Europe. In 1629, Huguenots lost all political and military rights. Richelieu also imposed royal taxation via *intendants*. But all was not well in France. The French people reacted to centralization with a series of revolts between 1648 and 1653 known collectively as the Fronde. In the Fronde, aristocratic leaders and commoners of all ranks joined in revolt against the alleged corruption and mismanagement of the state. The Fronde came to an end only because the aristocratic leaders could rarely agree with one another. The new king, Louis XIV, was only a child at the time, but remembered the Fronde until he died.

THE ENGLISH CIVIL WAR

Perhaps the greatest challenge to established governments came during the English civil war of the mid-sixteenth century. Henry VIII and Elizabeth had brought the church under royal control, and although Parliament met regularly, its independence had been weakened. Conflict flared under James I (1603–1625), who insisted that his rule was based on divine right. He also antagonized his subjects by raising taxes without the consent of Parliament and interfering with the freedom of business. He was most disliked by the Puritan sect. English Protestants profited under James I's mismanagement. Charles I (1625–1649) was also at odds with Parliament, which refused to grant money for his war with France. As a result, Charles forced his subjects to give him

loans. Parliament pushed the Petition of Right on Charles in 1628. The Petition of Right

- Declared illegal any taxes not voted by Parliament
- Condemned the quartering of soldiers
- Prohibited arbitrary imprisonment and martial law in times of peace

Charles reacted to the Petition by ruling without Parliament from 1629 to 1640. The storm finally broke in Presbyterian Scotland, where Charles had introduced church government. This resulted in a rebellion by the Scots and a civil war in England. The war was a religious and political conflict: on one side were aristocrats and landowners loyal to the Church of England (Cavaliers), and on the other were the commoners, tradesmen, and manufacturers, most of whom were Puritans (Roundheads). The Independents, a rival radical minority of Puritans led by Oliver Cromwell (1599–1658), also took part. On January 30, 1649, Charles I was beheaded for breaking the social contract with his people, and England became a Commonwealth. Real power remained with Cromwell, the Lord Protector for life. But by 1660, the English people had had enough of Calvinist austerity and so restored a Stuart king, Charles II (1660–1685), to the throne.

DOUBT AND CERTAINTY

Added to the many problems of the age was an outbreak of witchcraft hysteria: many regarded magic as a moral threat. Witchcraft trials were held in all European countries, Catholic and Protestant alike, and were strongest where secular and religious power formed a close relationship. Intellectuals meanwhile sought certainty and authority. Michel de Montaigne (1533–1592), a wealthy French nobleman, remained skeptical of certain knowledge. In his *Essays* he combined a wealth of classical knowledge with contemporary experience in order to answer the question: What do I know? The French political theorist Jean Bodin (1530–1596), troubled by the St. Bartholomew's Day Massacre, argued that the maintenance of order is the duty of the state. In England, Thomas Hobbes (1588–1679) advocated unrestrained state power at all times. Although it would be easy to say that he argued such a case because of the English civil war, he based his arguments on his pessimistic view of human nature. Pascal, terrified by the prospect of evil and eternity, still held out for the existence of God.

LITERATURE AND THE ARTS

If the age of religious wars produced a great deal of anxiety and tension, it also produced great literature and equally great art. For instance, we have Cervantes' (1547–1616) *Don Quixote*, a novel that pits idealism and realism against one another. In England, Christopher Marlowe (1564–1593) and Ben Jonson (1572–1637) wrote Elizabethan dramas. And of course there was William Shakespeare (1564–1616), the master of expression and wit and a keen observer of human nature in all its wonder. The ironies of human nature, so well portrayed by Shakespeare, found tangible expression in Mannerist painting, a mostly Italian style that borrowed as much from Raphael as it did from Michelangelo and created many special effects.

In southern Europe, the Baroque style appeared in painting, sculpture, and architecture; it:

- Focused on the dramatic and the irregular
- Aimed to instill a sense of the affirmative (necessary in an age of doubt)
- Came to the service of the Counter-Reformation church
- Was represented by Bernini and Velázquez

In northern Europe, Dutch painting entered its golden age, creating art that portrayed both the greatness and the wretchedness of humanity (Brueghel, *Peasant Wedding*; Rubens, *Horrors of War*; and Rembrandt, *The Polish Rider* and *Aristotle Contemplating the Bust of Homer*).

The period from 1540 to 1660 was certainly traumatic for most Europeans. The Christian faith and the worldview of medieval Europe had been challenged by the Protestant Reformation, and as Protestantism spread across the Continent, so did civil and foreign wars. Anxiety, tension, terror, and horror may perhaps best describe the age. But intellectual activity also emerged in politics, art, and science. All of this helped shape the Europe of the early modern period. New forms of government were beginning to appear—absolutism and limited monarchy—as well as the new worldview of science.

SUGGESTED FEATURE FILMS

Cromwell. 141 min. Color. 1970. Columbia. Richard Harris as Cromwell and Alec Guinness as Charles I.

Day of Wrath. 105 min. B/W. 1943. Palladium Films. Carl Dreyer's look at witch hunting and religious persecution in a seventeenth-century Danish community.

Don Quixote. 105 min. Color. 1957. Lenfilm. A Soviet version of Cervantes' masterpiece.

Elizabeth. 124 min. Color. 1998. 20th Century Fox. The reign of Elizabeth I of England and her difficult task of learning what is necessary to be a monarch.

Mary of Scotland. 123 min. B/W. 1936. RKO. John Ford's depiction of the life of Elizabeth's rival. With Katharine Hepburn.

Queen Margot. 144 min. Color. 1994. Buena Vista Home Video. Unforgettable portrayal of Maguerite of Valois's arranged marriage to Henri of Navarre and of the subsequent Huguenot massacre. Controversial in its deliberate use of Holocaust imagery.

SUGGESTED CLASSROOM FILMS

Babel: Brueghel and the Follies of Men. 18 min. Color. 1970. Contemporary Films. With commentary drawn from contemporary proverbs.

Brueghel's People. 19 min. Color. 1974. International Film Bureau. An examination of sixteenth-century Flanders.

The Civil War in England 1645–1649. 37 min. Color. Films for the Humanities and Sciences. Examines the English civil war as a model for subsequent revolutions.

Civilisation: A Personal View by Kenneth Clark, No. 7: Grandeur and Obedience. 52 min. Color. 1970. BBC/Time-Life Films. The Baroque in art and religious literature.

El Greco. 30 min. Color. 1970. Graphic Curriculum. Uses both dramatization and photography to tell the story of the painter's life and work.

Oliver Cromwell. 31 min. Color. 1999. Films for the Humanities and Sciences. Raises the question of whether Cromwell was a hero, villain, or both.

The Puritan Revolution: Cromwell and the Rise of Parliamentary Democracy. 33 min. Color. 1972. Learning Corporation of America. Edited version of the feature film, *Cromwell*.

Rubens. 27 min. Color. 1974. International Film Bureau. Contrasts Rubens as a court painter with Rubens after 1630.

Seven Ages of Fashion: The Stuarts. 26 min. Color. 1992. Films for the Humanities and Sciences. Part of a series that explores changes in fashion as a means of opening up cultural history.

'Tis Pity She's a Whore: The First Women on the London Stage. 26 min. Color. 1994. Films for the Humanities and Sciences. Explores the lives and careers of Moll Davis and Nell Gwynn as a means of looking at attitudes toward gender and sexuality in the seventeenth century.

Part V: Early Modern Europe

IDEAS FOR USING THE WESTERN CIVILIZATIONS DIGITAL HISTORY CENTER

The Map Exercise and Digital History Features at *www.wwnorton.com/wciv* will enable you to explain the general economic, political, and intellectual changes of seventeenth-century Europe.

- Map Exercise 10: Europe in the Seventeenth Century (Chapter 15)
- Digital History Feature 6: Spices and the Spice Trade (Chapter 15)
- Digital History Feature 7: Astrology, Astronomy, and Galileo (Chapters 16–17)

Use Map Exercise 10 to generate classroom discussion about the growth of absolute monarchy in the seventeenth century. These exercises are also useful as ways to suggest how empire-building was as much a preoccupation of Louis XIV in France as it was of Peter the Great in Russia. Trade on a global scale continued throughout the seventeenth century as British and Dutch commercial interests took the lead away from the overseas empires of Spain and Portugal. The Digital History Feature "Spices and the Spice Trade" will help students understand the importance of spices to the European economy and how the spice trade was a preoccupation of British and Dutch shipping. The seventeenth century was the age of many things, but it was the Scientific Revolution that gave the period its intellectual flavor. Use the Digital History Feature "Astrology, Astronomy, and Galileo" to show that modern science was as much a product of the revolutionary genius of men like Copernicus, Kepler, Galileo, Descartes, and Newton as it was of the scientific heritage of the medieval past. This Digital History Feature also demonstrates that astrology, alchemy, and astronomy were mutually supporting sciences.

CHAPTER 15 | Absolutism and Empire, 1660–1789

OUTLINE

I. Introduction
   A. Absolutism defined
      1. A political theory that encouraged rulers to claim complete sovereignty within their territories
      2. Sometimes defined by "divine right"
   B. Age of absolutism as an age of empire
      1. Colonial rivalries
   C. The rise of limited monarchies and republics
   D. Russian autocracy
II. The Appeal and Justification of Absolutism
   A. Absolutism promised stability, prosperity, and order
   B. Louis XIV (r. 1643–1715)
      1. Squabbles among the nobility meant he had to rule assertively
   C. Absolutist control
      1. Command of the state's army
      2. Control over the legal system
      3. Right to collect and spend the state's financial resources
      4. The need to create an efficient centralized bureaucracy
      5. Weakening privileged "special interests"
   D. Obstacles
      1. Legally-privileged estates of the nobility and clergy
      2. The political authority of semi-autonomous regions
      3. Interference of parliaments, diets, and estates general

   E. Religion
      1. France, Spain, and Austria: attempts to "nationalize" the church and clergy
      2. Consolidating authority over the church into the hands of the monarchy
   F. The nobility
      1. Important opponents of royal absolutism
      2. Louis XIV: deprived the nobility of power but increased their social prestige (Versailles)
      3. Peter the Great (r. 1689–1725): forced his nobles into lifelong government service
      4. Catherine II (r. 1762–1796): nobility surrendered administrative and political power into the empress's hands
      5. Prussia: the army was staffed by nobles
      6. Joseph II (r. 1765–1790): denied the nobility tax exemption and blurred the distinction between noble and commoner
III. Alternatives to Absolutism
   A. Limited monarchy: the case of England
      1. Parliament as longest-surviving representative institution
   B. The reign of Charles II (r. 1660–1685)
      1. General observations
         a. Initially welcomed by most English men and women
         b. Declared limited toleration for Protestant dissenters
         c. Promised to observe Magna Carta and the Petition of Right
         d. Admired all things French

2. 1670s: open admiration of the kingship of Louis XIV
   a. New party labels
      i. Tories—Charles's supporters
      ii. Whigs—Charles's opponents
      iii. Both parties feared a return to the civil war of 1640 as well as royal absolutism
3. Religion
   a. Charles was sympathetic to Roman Catholicism
   b. Suspended civil penalties against Catholics and Dissenters
      i. Ignored Parliament
      ii. Led to a series of Whig electoral victories (1679–1681)
   c. The Exclusion Crisis: Whigs attempted to keep Charles's brother, James, from obtaining the throne
   d. Charles governed without relying on Parliament for money
   e. Executed several Whigs
C. King James II (r. 1685–1688)
   1. A zealous Catholic convert
   2. Alienated his Tory supporters
   3. June 1688: ordered the clergy to read his decree of religious toleration
      a. The trial of the bishops
   4. Crisis of succession and the birth of the "warming-pan baby"
   5. Whigs and Tories invited Mary Stuart and her husband, William of Orange, to invade England and preserve Protestantism
D. The Glorious Revolution of 1688
   1. A bloodless coup
   2. James fled the country, William and Mary claimed the throne
   3. The Bill of Rights (1689)
      a. Passed by Parliament
      b. Reaffirmed trial by jury, *habeas corpus*, and the right to petition Parliament
   4. Act of Toleration (1689)
      a. Granted dissenters the right to worship freely, but they could not hold political office
   5. The Act of Succession (1701)
      a. Ordained that every future English monarch must be a member of the Church of England
   6. Act of Union (1707) between England and Scotland
   7. Why "glorious"?
      a. No bloodshed

b. Established England as a mixed monarchy governed by "the King in Parliament"
   c. Protestants saw 1688 as another sign of God's special favor to England
8. The reality
   a. 1688 consolidated the position of large property-holders
   b. A restoration of the status quo on behalf of wealth
E. John Locke (1632–1704) and the contract theory of government
   1. *Two Treatises of Government* (1690)
      a. The state of nature
         i. Absolute freedom and equality
         ii. No government
         iii. The only law is the law of nature
         iv. The individual enforces his own natural right to life, liberty, and property
      b. Civil society
         i. The inconveniences of nature outweigh its advantages
         ii. Humans establish a civil society based on absolute equality
         iii. Set up a government to arbitrate all disputes
         iv. All powers not surrendered to the government were reserved for the people themselves
         v. Governmental authority is contractual and conditional
      c. Absolutism
         i. Condemned by Locke
         ii. Government is instituted to protect life, liberty, and property
   2. Influence
      a. American and French Revolutions
      b. Supporters of William and Mary saw Locke as defender of their "conservative" revolution
IV. The Absolutism of Louis XIV
   A. The façade that was Louis
   B. Performing royalty at Versailles
      1. A stage upon which Louis mesmerized the nobility into obedience
      2. Daily rituals and demonstrations of royalty
      3. Royal "choreography"
      4. Nobles were required to live at Versailles for part of the year

a. Raised their prestige

b. Louis could keep an eye on them

5. Louis as hard-working and conscientious

6. Personal responsibility for the well-being of all his subjects

C. Administration and centralization

1. For Louis, royal power meant domestic tranquility

2. Conciliated the upper bourgeoisie by making them royal administrators

    a. Intendants: administered the 36 *generalités* into which France was divided

        i. Unconnected with local elites

        ii. Held office at the king's pleasure (his men)

3. Taxation

    a. Collection of taxes necessary to maintain a large standing army (very expensive)

    b. The *taille* (land tax), *capitation* (head tax), and the *gabelle* (salt tax)

    c. Other indirect taxes on wine, tobacco, and other goods

4. Regional opposition

    a. Reduced but not curtailed

    b. Members of any *parlement* (law court) that did not enforce his laws were exiled

    c. Never called the Estates-General (last convoked in 1614)

D. Louis XIV's religious policies

1. Louis was determined to impose religious unity on France (God would favor him)

2. Outside Roman Catholicism

    a. Quietists—Catholics who preached personal mysticism

        i. Dispensed with the church as intermediary

        ii. Suspect in the eyes of Louis

    b. Jansenists—held to the Augustinian notion of predestination

        i. Persecuted by Louis

    c. Jesuits—earned the support of Louis

    d. Huguenots—French Calvinists

        i. Hated by Louis

        ii. Protestant churches were destroyed

        iii. Protestants banned from many professions (medicine and printing)

3. 1685: Louis revokes the Edict of Nantes

    a. Protestant clerics were exiled

    b. Laymen were sent to the galleys as slaves

    c. Children were forcibly baptized as Catholics

    d. Two hundred thousand Protestants flee to England, Holland, Germany, and America

E. Jean Baptiste Colbert (1619–1683) and royal finance

1. Colbert as finance minister, 1664–1683

2. Tightened the process of tax collection

    a. Eliminated tax farming

    b. 1664—25 percent of taxes collected ended up in the treasury; by 1683, 80 percent

3. Sold public offices

4. Allowed guilds to purchase the right to enforce trade regulations

5. Controlled and regulated foreign trade

    a. Imposed tariffs on foreign goods imported to France

    b. Used state money to promote domestic manufactures

6. Improved France's roads, bridges, and waterways

7. His policies foundered because of the wars of Louis XIV

F. The wars of Louis XIV to 1697

1. For Louis, glory at home was to be achieved by military victories abroad

2. Objectives

    a. Lessen any threat to France by the Habsburg powers (Spain, Spanish Netherlands, and the Holy Roman empire)

    b. Promote the dynastic interests of his own family

3. 1667/68: attacked the Spanish Netherlands

4. 1672: attacked Holland and William of Orange

    a. Treaty of Nijmegen (1678/79)

5. Captured Strasbourg (1681), Luxembourg (1684), and Cologne (1688)

    b. Pushed across the Rhine and burned the middle Rhineland

6. William of Orange organized the League of Augsburg

    a. Holland, England, Spain, Sweden, Bavaria, Saxony, the Rhine Palatinate, and Austrian Habsburgs

    b. The Nine Years' War (1689–1697)

        i. Fought mostly in the Low Countries

        ii. 1697: Peace of Ryswick

        iii. Louis returned most territory except Strasbourg and parts of Alsace

iv. Treaty recognized William of Orange as king of England

G. The War of the Spanish Succession

1. Preserving a "balance of power"
   a. Designed to prevent any one country from assuming too much power
   b. An operative principle of foreign policy until 1914
   c. England, United Provinces, Prussia, and Austria as the main proponents
   d. Louis sought a French claim to the throne of Spain
      i. Controlling the Spanish empire in the New World, Italy, the Netherlands, and the Philippines

2. Who would succeed to the Spanish throne?
   a. Louis married eldest daughter of Philip IV of Spain
   b. Philip's youngest daughter married Leopold I of Austria
   c. Charles II left his possessions to Louis XIV's grandson, Philip of Anjou (the will was secret)
      i. Philip was to renounce his claim to the French throne
      ii. Keeping the Spanish empire intact
   d. Charles II dies, Philip V (r. 1700–1746) proclaimed the king of Spain
   e. Louis XIV rushed his troops into the Spanish Netherlands

3. War
   a. England, the United Provinces, Austria, and Prussia against France, Bavaria, and Spain
   b. French defeat at Blenheim (1704)
   c. English navy captureD Gibraltar and Minorca
   d. 1709: France on the verge of defeat

H. The Treaty of Utrecht

1. Terms were reasonably fair to all sides
   a. Philip V remained on the throne of Spain and retained his colonial empire
   b. Louis agreed that France and Spain would never unite under the same ruler
   c. Austria gained territories in the Spanish Netherlands and Italy
   d. The Dutch were guaranteed protection of their borders from French invasion

e. Great Britain as greatest winner
   i. Kept Gibraltar and Minorca
   ii. Obtained large chunks of French territory in the New World
   iii. Extracted from Spain the right to transport and sell African slaves in Spanish America

2. Reshaping the balance of power
   a. By 1713, Spain's collapse was complete
   b. Gradual decline of Dutch power
   c. Balance gradually shifted to Britain's favor
   d. The British navy would rule the imperial and commercial world of the eighteenth century

V. The Remaking of Central and Eastern Europe

A. The Habsburg empire

1. 1683: Ottoman Turks assaulted Vienna, then their power in southeastern Europe declined

2. Austria reconquered most of Hungary from the Ottomans (1699)
   a. Controlled all of Hungary, Transylvania, and Serbia (1718)
   b. Acquired Silesia from Poland (1722)
   c. Hungary as buffer state
   d. Vienna emerged as cultural capital of Europe

3. Austrian Habsburgs retained title as Holy Roman emperors
   a. Real power lay in Austria, Bohemia, Moravia, Galicia, and Hungary
      i. Geographically contiguous but divided by ethnicity, religion, and language
   b. Bohemia and Moravia
      i. Habsburgs forced peasants to provide labor service for their lords
      ii. Reduced political independence of traditional legislative estates
   c. Administered Hungary through the army and imposed Catholic religious uniformity

4. Maria Theresa (r. 1740–1780) and Joseph II (r. 1765–1790)
   a. Pioneered "enlightened absolutism"
   b. Centralized administration in Vienna
   c. Increased taxation to create a large standing army
   d. Tightened control over the church

e. Statewide system of education, relaxed censorship, abolished serfdom, liberal criminal code

B. The rise of Brandenburg-Prussia
  1. Prussia a composite state
      a. Two main holdings: Brandenburg and duchy of East Prussia
      b. Dominant military power in central Europe
  2. Foundations
      a. Frederick William the "Great Elector" (r. 1640–1688)
          i. Diplomatic triumphs
          ii. Built a huge standing army
          iii. Granted Junkers (powerful nobles) the right to enserf peasants
          iv. Junkers staffed the army, immune from taxation
          v. Junkers surrendered management of the state to a centralized bureaucracy
  3. Frederick I (r. 1688–1713)
      a. Developed the cultural life of Berlin
  4. Frederick William I (r. 1713–1740)
      a. Returned to policies of the "Great Elector"
      b. Built a first-rate army ("the sergeant king")
      c. The Potsdam Giants
      d. Increased taxes and shunned expensive luxuries of the court
  5. Frederick the Great (r. 1740–1786)
      a. Prussia as a major power
      b. Mobilized the army and occupied Silesia
      c. Gained the support of the Junkers for his policies
      d. An "enlightened absolutist"
          i. Social reforms
          ii. Prohibited torture and bribing of judges
          iii. System of elementary education
          iv. Encouraged toleration of Christians
          v. Fostered scientific forestry and cultivation of new crops

VI. Autocracy in Russia
  A. Peter the Great (1672–1725)
      1. Mercurial personality
      2. Policies were decisive in making Russia a great European power
  B. The early years of Peter's reign
      1. The Romanov dynasty
      2. The time of troubles
      3. Stenka Razin rebellion (1667–1671)
          a. Supported by oppressed serfs and non-Russian tribes in the lower Volga
      4. Tsar Alexis I (r. 1654–1676)
      5. Peter comes to the throne as a young boy
          a. Political dissension and court intrigue
          b. Overthrew regency of Sophia (1689)
          c. Traveled to Holland and England to study shipbuilding and recruit skilled workers
      6. The *Streltsy* rebellion
          a. Peter crushed the rebellion with savagery
  C. The transformation of the tsarist state
      1. Western influences
          a. Peter published a book of manners
          b. Encouraged polite conversation between the sexes
          c. Russian nobility sent their children to European schools
      2. Peter's goal
          a. Make Russia a real military power
          b. New taxation system (1724)
          c. Table of Ranks (1722)
              i. Insisted that all nobles work themselves up from lower landlord class to highest military class
              ii. Reversed the traditional hierarchy of Russian nobility
          d. Peter as absolute master of his empire
              i. Russian peasants legally the property of their masters (1649)
              ii. By 1750, half were serfs, the other half lived on lands owned by Peter
              iii. State peasants could be conscripted, work in factories, or be forced to work on public projects
              iv. The Duma was replaced by nine administrators
          e. Religion
              i. Peter took direct control over the Russian Orthodox church
          f. Noble status depended upon service to the government
  D. Peter's foreign policy
      1. Goal was to secure warm-water ports on the Black and Baltic Seas

2. Began a war with Sweden (1700–1721)
   a. Secured the Gulf of Finland
   b. Began building St. Petersburg
   c. Peace of Nystad (1721)
      i. Realignment of power in eastern Europe
      ii. Gulf of Finland, Livonia, and Estonia passed to Russia
3. The cost of war
   a. Direct taxation increased five hundred percent
   b. Aroused resentment among the Russian nobility
4. Peter dies (1725) with no heir to the throne

E. Catherine the Great (r. 1762–1796) and the partition of Poland
1. Came to the throne after Tsar Peter III was deposed and executed in a palace coup
2. The image of the enlightened Catherine
3. Determined not to lose the support of the nobility
4. Summoned a commission to codify Russian law (1767)
5. The Pugachev Rebellion (1773–1775)
   a. Forced Catherine to centralize her government
   b. Tightened aristocratic control over the peasantry
6. War and diplomacy
   a. War with the Ottoman Turks
      i. Russia won the northern Black Sea and secured the independence of Crimea
   b. Russian gains alarmed Austria
   c. The Partition of Poland (1772)
   d. The Partition of Poland (1795)

VII. Commerce and Consumption
A. Economic growth in eighteenth-century Europe
1. Balance of power was shifting to the west (Britain and France)
2. New intensive agriculture in Britain and Holland
   a. Produced more food per acre
   b. New crops (maize and potatoes)
3. Urbanization
   a. By 1800, two hundred cities with a population over ten thousand
   b. Most of these cities were concentrated in northern and western Europe
   c. Extraordinary growth of the very largest cities
4. Developments in trade and industry
   a. Entrepreneurs and the "putting-out" system (protoindustrialization)
      i. Employment during slack agricultural season
      ii. Avoided expensive guild restrictions
      iii. Reduced levels of capital investment
   b. Cities as manufacturing centers
      i. The growth of workshops
      ii. New inventions and the role of technological innovation
      iii. Machines and labor-saving devices
   c. Obstacles to innovation
      i. Machines put people out of work
      ii. Governments blocked widespread use of machines
      iii. Mercantilist protection of commercial and financial backers
   d. Europe's insatiable appetite for goods
B. A world of goods
1. A mass market for consumer goods (especially northwestern Europe)
2. Houses of ordinary people filled with luxuries (sugar, teas, books, toys, china, razors)
3. Demand outstripped supply
4. Encouraged the provision of services
5. Golden age of the small shopkeeper

VIII. Colonization and Trade in the Seventeenth Century
A. The age of empires
B. Spanish colonialism
1. Established colonial governments in Peru and Mexico
2. Government allowed only Spanish merchants to trade with American colonies
3. All colonial exports had to pass through Seville (later Cadiz)
4. Dominated by mining (silver)
5. Promoted farming in Central and South America
6. Spanish success prompted other countries to grab a share of the treasure
C. English colonialism
1. American colonies offered no significant mineral wealth
2. Profits obtained through agricultural settlements
   a. Jamestown, Virginia (1607)
3. Plymouth, Massachusetts (1620)
   a. Escaping religious persecution
   b. No attempts made to Christianize Native Americans

4. English settlements were privately organized
5. Navigation Acts (1651 and 1660)
   a. All exports from English colonies to England must be carried by English ships
6. Sugar and tobacco
7. Sir Walter Raleigh (1552–1618)

D. French colonialism
1. Colbert regarded overseas expansion as part of state economic policy
2. Encouraged sugar trade in the West Indies
3. French fur traders occupied the interior of North America
   a. Preached Christianity to Native Americans

E. Dutch colonialism
1. By the 1670s, the Dutch maintained the most prosperous commercial empire
2. Followed the "fort and factory" model of the Portuguese
3. Dutch East India Company (founded 1602)
   a. Controlled spice trade in Sumatra, Borneo, and the Moluccas
4. Secured an exclusive right to trade with Japan
5. Maintained military and trading outposts in China and India
6. The Dutch as the primary financiers of seventeenth-century Europe
   a. The joint-stock company
      i. Raised cash by selling shares in their enterprise to investors

F. Contrasting patterns of colonial settlement
1. Important differences in settlement patterns
2. Spain and Central and South America
   a. Small number of Spaniards conquered complex, large populations
   b. Did not attempt to replace their culture
   c. Focus was on controlling native labor for maximum profit
   d. Collecting tribute and Catholic conversions
   e. High degree of intermarriage
   f. Complex system of racial and social castes
3. France
   a. Colonies established as direct crown enterprises
   b. Military outposts and trading centers
   c. Fur trade and fishing—relied on cooperative relationships
   d. Intermarriage was common

4. England
   a. Colonies established as joint-stock companies or proprietary colonies
   b. Planned settlements and plantations
      i. Replicating English life
   c. Primarily agricultural communities
   d. No need to control large native labor force
   e. Their goal was exclusive control of native lands
   f. Expulsion and massacre of native populations
   g. Rare incidence of intermarriage
   h. Rigid racial divisions

G. Colonial rivalries
1. Spain and Portugal declined in importance
2. Eighteenth-century British merchants dominated world trade routes

IX. Colonialism and Empire
A. The triangular trade in sugar and slaves
1. Sugar and slaves dominated eighteenth-century colonial trade
2. British naval superiority
   a. British ship sails from New England to Africa to exchange rum for slaves
   b. African slaves sent to sugar colonies and are traded for molasses
   c. Molasses brought to New England where it was made into rum
3. Seventy-five to ninety thousand African slaves brought to the New World yearly
4. Eighteenth-century slave trade was open to private entrepreneurs
5. The middle passage

B. The commercial rivalry between Britain and France
1. Value of colonial commerce increased in the eighteenh century
2. Tied together the interests of governments and merchants
3. British dominance in commerce and finance

C. War and empire in the eighteenth-century world
1. War of the Austrian Succession spread beyond the frontiers of Europe
2. Continued colonial conflicts
3. The Seven Years' War (1756–1763)
   a. Ended in stalemate
   b. Indian mercenaries employed by the East India Company eliminated French competitors
   c. The British captured Louisbourg and Quebec
   d. The Treaty of Paris (1763)
      i. France surrendered Canada and India to the British

D. The American Revolution
   1. To pay for the cost of war, Britain increased taxes in the American colonies
   2. Colonists complained they had no representatives in Parliament—taxation without consent
   3. George III—vacillation and force
   4. The Boston Tea Party (1773)
   5. The Continental Congress at Philadelphia (1774)
   6. Lexington and Concord (April 1775)
   7. Independence (July 4, 1776)
   8. France sides with the colonists (1778)
   9. British surrender at Yorktown, Virginia (1781)
X. Conclusion
   A. American War of Independence as final military conflict between Britain and France
   B. Britain remained most important trading partner with American colonies
   C. European population increased
   D. European prosperity unevenly distributed
   E. Gradual political changes

GENERAL DISCUSSION QUESTIONS

1. What were the aims of an absolute monarch? What is the connection between royal absolutism and mercantilism?

2. Why did Louis XIV force his nobility to "perform" at Versailles?

3. How did the absolutism of Louis XIV differ from that of his eastern European counterparts?

4. What obstacles did the Austro-Hungarian Empire face as it attempted to become an absolutist state?

5. Why did Peter the Great wish to modernize Russia on the Western model?

6. How had the absolutism of the seventeenth century changed the nature and scope of diplomacy and warfare?

7. Describe the shifting balance of power in eighteenth-century Europe.

8. What is capitalism? Have private enterprise, competition, and the quest for profit always existed? What is mercantilism? What relationship is there between mercantilism and capitalism?

9. Compare French, English, Spanish, and Dutch patterns of colonial settlement. What are the major similarities and differences?

10. Why did Great Britain assume the lead in the triangular trade in sugar and slaves?

DOCUMENT DISCUSSION QUESTIONS

Absolutism and Patriarchy

1. Why did some political theorists argue the necessity of absolutism based on the model of the father? Was there an alternative to this model?

2. What would John Locke find so objectionable about the political theory of Robert Filmer? How would Filmer have answered Locke?

Mercantilism and War

3. Could Colbert's economic policies have been used more wisely by Louis XIV? Can mercantilist policies be implemented without resorting to warfare? Is war a necessary component of mercantilism?

The American Declaration of Independence

4. In what way was the Declaration of Independence a document that could have been drafted by John Locke? Could the Declaration have been written in the seventeenth rather than the eighteenth century?

5. What is meant by the expression, "life, liberty, and the pursuit of happiness"?

SAMPLE LECTURE 15: ABSOLUTISM AND EMPIRE IN THE *ANCIEN RÉGIME*

Lecture Objectives:

1. To present the shape of absolute monarchy taken by Louis XIV

2. To explain why England adopted a limited, constitutional monarchy

3. To detail the defining characteristics of the commercial revolution of the eighteenth century

4. To explain how colonization led to the creation of empire

Toward Absolutism

Historians frequently use the expression *ancien régime* to describe the political and social realities of eighteenth-century Europe. The fact that the expression is French should tell us something. Eighteenth-century France was an international power whose form of government—royal absolutism—became the model for governments across Europe. Of course, the English form of government—limited or constitutional monarchy—was quite different, as was the autocratic government of Russia. Louis XIV, the Sun King, has always been regarded as the epitome of the absolute monarch, and perhaps rightly so. However, Louis XIV made profound errors of judgment that ultimately led to the French Revolution. Absolutism was a political theory and practice that encouraged rulers to claim complete sovereignty over their subjects. While some monarchs claimed to rule by the divine right theory of kingship, for the most part absolutism was the notion that the realm was the particular property of the monarch. Such a theory was founded on the idea that it was the duty of all subjects to obey authority. In many respects, this idea came as a partial solution to the disorders of the century of religious wars. Absolutism implied total command of the army, the legal system, and the collection of taxes. Such a state also required an efficient and centralized bureaucracy, which Louis XIV succeeded in building at Versailles. There were obstacles, however:

- The clergy and nobility, by their very existence, stood in opposition to the king.
- Semi-autonomous regions presented another problem.
- Parliaments, Diets, and Estates-General also served as opposing forces.

THE MODEL: LOUIS XIV AT VERSAILLES

When we think of an absolute monarch, we think of Louis XIV (1643–1715). Hyacinthe Rigaud's portrait illustrates how Louis thought of himself as the consummate absolute monarch. His reign was filled with the theater of court; his palace at Versailles was intended as a showplace for his nobility. Of course, Versailles also allowed Louis to keep his eyes on the quarrelsome nobles. Louis understood his role in absolutist terms. He was to:

- control the nobility
- concentrate royal power in order to produce domestic tranquility
- placate the upper bourgeoisie by bringing them into the administration.
- appoint intendants
- collect taxes to finance a large standing army
- increase power through conquest and display and crush local revolts

Because Louis considered the realm to be his personal property, he also sought to impose religious unity on all the subjects. At the time, France was faced with heterodoxy in religious opinion:

- Quietists preached personal mysticism.
- Jansenists accepted predestination.
- Huguenots were French Calvinists.

Louis sought to do away with them all—he destroyed their churches and schools, and their families were forced to convert to Catholicism. After he revoked the Edict of Nantes (1685), more than two hundred thousand fled the country. With Jean Baptiste Colbert (1619–1683) as his finance minister, Louis tightened tax collection and eliminated "tax farming." He also continued the practice of buying and selling public offices, which would eventually lead to a bloated and inefficient bureaucracy. Mercantilists to the core, Louis and Colbert discouraged the import of foreign goods and used state money to promote the growth of French industry. Louis overextended himself by leading a series of expensive foreign wars. His aggressive foreign policy led France to near bankruptcy: in 1788, Louis XVI was forced to convoke the Estates-General in order to raise funds to pay off the war debt of Louis XIV.

CENTRAL AND EASTERN EUROPE

The situation in Central and Eastern Europe was somewhat different from that in France. Here we have three major players—the Holy Roman empire, Brandenburg-Prussia, and the Austro-Hungarian empire—all trying to copy or outdo Louis XIV. The Thirty Years' War (1618–1648) devastated the Holy Roman empire, giving substance to Voltaire's quip that it was "neither holy, nor Roman, nor an empire." Power was now in the hands of more than three hundred princes, bishops, and magistrates within a totally fragmented region. These local rulers attempted to establish themselves as absolute monarchs on the model supplied by Louis XIV. They attempted to maintain their absolute power with standing armies and local tariffs. The Great Elector, Frederick William (1640–1688), tried to enforce a foreign policy that would establish effective sovereignty over the fragmented territories under his control. Besides creating a large standing army, he also instituted an effective system of taxation. In addition, he

- bargained with the Junkers
- forced the Junkers to give away their right to oppose a permanent tax system
- forced the Junkers to give up the management of their lands to the state
- used Junkers in the army to maintain order and turned the peasants into serfs

The Habsburgs had similar problems in creating a cohesive state out of four distinct regions complicated by ethnic and linguistic diversity. Added to these complications were the inroads the Ottoman Turks made in Hungary. Overall, absolute monarchy in central and eastern Europe was at best limited.

THE CASE OF RUSSIAN AUTOCRACY

The situation in Russia was unique. Russia at first seemed more Eastern in its orientation than Western. Tsar Peter I (1689–1725) brought Russia into direct communication with the European world with his quest to create an autocracy for Russia. His achievements were many:

- recruited skilled workers from Holland
- attempted to westernize Russia and "civilize" the nobility
- considered himself above the law (autocrat of all the Russias)

- created a large standing army based on universal conscription
- fostered the growth of the iron and munitions industries
- replaced the Duma with a senate without power
- created a new bureaucracy of *boyars* (noble servants)

As we might expect, Peter's foreign policy was imperialist. He wanted Russia to have an outlet onto the Baltic Sea, and he went to war with Sweden. Peter also took a lesson from Louis XIV, when he moved the Russian capital from Moscow to the newly-built city of St. Petersburg.

ENGLAND AND CONSTITUTIONAL MONARCHY

With the restoration of Charles II (1660–1685), England tried to overcome the difficulties that had plagued the nation during the civil war. Charles granted limited religious toleration for Protestants and promised to observe the Magna Carta and the Petition of Right. But Charles also admired all things French, which would eventually cause him problems. It was during the reign of Charles that new party labels made their appearance: the Tories were those who supported Charles, while those in opposition were called Whigs.

Despite granting toleration for Protestants, Charles remained sympathetic to Roman Catholicism. Following his death in 1685, the throne fell into the hands of his brother James II (1685–1688), a Catholic convert. He alienated the Tories in the Church of England by dismissing them in favor of Roman Catholics. In 1688, his second wife gave birth to a son, which led to a crisis of succession. It was at this time that the opposition, led by both Whigs and Tories, took the initiative and asked William of Orange (of the United Provinces) to invade England in order to restore religious and political freedom.

- James fled the country.
- A Bill of Rights was passed in 1689, reaffirming civil liberties.
- The monarchy was now subject to the laws of the land.
- The Act of Toleration (1689) granted Protestants who were not members of the Catholic Church the right to worship.
- The Act of Succession was passed.
- Parliament required that all English monarchs be members of the Church of England.
- No king or queen could govern without parliament.

The Glorious Revolution, although it seemed to grant civil liberties to all freeborn Englishmen, actually consolidated the position of wealthy property-holders.

The Revolution, bloodless as it was, reflected the turn away from absolutism by political theorists like Hobbes, Bodin, Filmer, and Bossuet. The political theory of limited monarchy was taken up by John Locke (*Two Treatises of Government*, 1690) in order to justify the Revolution itself. For Locke, all government authority was contractual and conditional. Society had the right to dissolve government and create a new one only if government abused the authority granted to it by its people. Locke was no democrat, and so his political theory was also intended to justify the interests of the wealthy.

DIPLOMACY AND WARFARE

The eighteenth century managed to reach a kind of balance of power through both diplomacy and warfare. Religion was no longer the issue at stake; instead, territorial expansion and political power were major concerns. This required that nations create large, professional, standing armies. For example, in 1661 the French army totaled twenty thousand men. A little more than thirty years later, it had risen to four hundred thousand men. In order to induce men to enlist, promotions and small pensions were offered.

Louis XIV realized he needed to stabilize his government and improve commerce, and the only way he knew how to accomplish these aims was through war. In 1686, Holland, Austria, Sweden, and several German allies formed the League of Augsburg in order to counteract an expansionist France. In this regard, the League attempted to maintain a European balance of power. Louis invaded the Palatinate (1688), which prompted England and Spain to join the League.

Meanwhile, Spain had its own problems of dynastic succession. Charles II had no direct heirs, so European monarchs became obsessed with the question of who would succeed to the Spanish Habsburg throne. Such a question involved Spain and its overseas empire, so the issue was extremely complicated. The War of the Spanish Succession was a professional war that tested the strength of the armies of Europe to the fullest. Because the war was international in scope, it involved complicated measures of diplomacy, which were negotiated in the Treaty of Utrecht (1713):

- There were no major winners or losers.
- France and Spain would never be united.
- Austria gained territory in the Netherlands and Italy.
- The English retained Gibraltar.

ECONOMY AND SOCIETY

In the seventeenth and eighteenth centuries, the economy of Europe was transformed. Part of this transformation was due to the creation of overseas empires by the Spanish and Portuguese and later by the British, French, and Dutch. European governments were forced to adjust to the growth of empire, and the economic theory known as mercantilism came to dominate government policy. European society developed quite slowly, since the medieval idea of order and hierarchy was still prominent. European society was one of orders, in which everyone from the wealthiest landlord to the lowliest peasant knew his or her place. It would not be until the Industrial Revolution of the late eighteenth century that a society based on a hierarchy of orders would give way to new social relations based on class. For most Europeans, existence meant subsistence, and this meant a constant battle against the environment. Famine was common, and local parish records tell us that population at the local level rose or fell with a good or bad harvest. Throughout the seventeenth and eighteenth centuries, the growth of population was determined by warfare, famine, and disease. After 1750, the population began to increase. The causes of this shift are complicated and heavily debated:

- decreasing infant mortality
- tendency toward earlier marriage
- gradual decline in the death rate
- gradual increase in the food supply
- new agricultural methods and crops

The growth in population brought new problems as the land was forced to yield more; as a result, many peasants moved from the country to the city, which created even more problems. Urbanization proceeded along with population growth, although the rates at which cities grew varied from region to region. What was unusual was the way cities were distributed across the continent—more of them appeared in the north and west than elsewhere (reports of 250 percent growth between 1600 and 1750 were not unusual). Large cities grew up around the administrative capitals of Europe.

AGRICULTURE AND AGRICULTURAL PRODUCTION

The early modern period witnessed important changes in European agriculture. Peasants were slow to adapt to new methods of production, but nonetheless late-eighteenth-century innovations in agriculture changed the shape of the European economy. The medieval farmer had used the open-field system of farming, in which land was divided into long strips. This system was inefficient, but did spread the risk for the individual peasant in times of bad harvest. It also prevented experimentation with new agricultural methods. Landlords in England suggested that by enclosing the fields, the land could be made to yield greater profits. Some landlords opted to raise sheep, since it was not labor-intensive and the profits were high. Other landlords scientifically investigated soil and fertilizers and introduced new crops, such as clover, alfalfa, and turnips; these provided winter food for animals, thereby making for better livestock. More livestock meant more manure, allowing farmers to stop leaving the land fallow. The possibilities for higher yield were enormous. Peasants gained the least, since their customary right to use the land had now been abolished, and they became landless laborers. Enclosure seemed to work best in England, with its system of absolute property rights, and less well in France, where peasants were better able to resist landlords.

RURAL MANUFACTURING

The putting-out system was used by entrepreneurs to bypass the artisanal and guild restrictions of the city and to meet the demand of new markets created as Europe spread its empires around the globe. Raw wool would be "put out" to one group of rural workers for carding (cleaning); then it would be picked up by the merchants, who passed the cleaned wool to rural weavers. The cloth was then taken to other workers who bleached and dyed the cloth, and it was finally sold to a wholesaler or other customer. From the standpoint of the laborer, there were practical advantages to such a system:

- They could regulate the pace of their own labor.
- They could work from home.
- They could earn extra income.
- Cottage labor ordinarily involved the entire family.
- Working at home was preferable to working in a shop in a town or city.

Although later critics of industrialization would somewhat idealize the putting-out system, it still did not relieve the boredom of peasant life. Nor was the system as efficient as entrepreneurs would have liked. Part of the problem was that Europe lacked a system of transportation. This would begin to change by the late eighteenth century. Not only would canals, rivers, and roads aid in the distribution of goods, but new labor-saving machinery also meant that a greater quantity of a particular commodity could be produced with less human labor.

THE COMMERCIAL REVOLUTION

Overseas empires, the lust for profit, improvements in agricultural productivity, the putting-out system, and the rise of investments all produced what historians have called the commercial revolution. Commerce and industry were founded on the assumptions of capitalism and mercantilism. We must look at these two forms of economic organization carefully. Capitalism has its roots in the early modern period:

- It is a system of production in which wealth is invested for profit.
- It calls for private enterprise, competition, and profit.
- It mandates a wage system as a method of payment.
- It encourages commercial expansion on a national and international scale.
- It is designed to reward individual effort.

Mercantilism, on the other hand, emphasized direct intervention of government in the economic organization of a nation. Its origins were medieval, in that it assumed that subjects should work at whatever task had been assigned to them by their rulers. Mercantilism:

- enhanced the prosperity of the state and increased political authority
- reflected the expansion of state power
- allowed for the State's power to depend on actual wealth
- led to the establishment of overseas colonies

- encouraged government to optimize industrial production
- had as a general goal the reduction of the volume of trade among a country's rivals

The commercial revolution facilitated the growth of international trade. Antwerp, Amsterdam, and London became centers of trade. None of this commercial expansion would have been possible had not investors found capital available for them to use. This was based on the gradual increase of agricultural prices. All this promoted the rise of banking, especially that of the Medici (Florence) and the Fuggers (Augsburg). Larger units of business organization were required, as were partnerships that spread the risk of investment (such as the joint-stock company and chartered companies). In other words, the commercial revolution of the seventeenth and eighteenth centuries called new financial institutions into existence. Of course, there were problems with these systems:

- the Price Revolution
- businessmen's too-rapid extension of their enterprises
- bankers' too-ready extension of credit
- speculative greed
- the South Sea Bubble (1720)

NEW WORLDS FOR OLD

The commercial revolution took place on the high seas as well as in Europe. The Spanish established colonial governments in Peru and Mexico and controlled them from Madrid; all imports and exports had to pass through Seville. The English obtained great profits from their colonies in the Caribbean and North America, mostly through the export of sugar and tobacco. A series of Navigation Acts were passed in the mid-seventeenth century stipulating that all exports from English colonies to England must be carried by English ships. The French considered overseas expansion integral to state economic policy and organized sugar colonies in the West Indies. The Dutch created perhaps the most successful commercial empire in the early modern period. They:

- formed the East India Company (1602)
- monopolized trade in the Spice Islands (Sumatra, Borneo, and the Moluccas)
- drove out the Portuguese
- created a monopoly in pepper, cinnamon, nutmeg, mace, and cloves
- obtained exclusive trading rights with Japan and established outposts in India and China

Of course, the creation of these overseas empires also created colonial rivalries among nations competing for trade and gain. Because their economy was stagnating, the Spanish lost much of their hold on overseas trade. Domestic squabbles and warfare did nothing to alleviate this situation. Portugal fared no better. The English, however, sought every

means at their disposal to win an empire. International trade became dominated by the demand for West Indian sugar and African slaves. The British eventually led the way in the triangular trade in sugar and slaves, six million of whom were transported in the eighteenth century alone:

- Slave traders exchanged North American rum for African slaves.
- Slaves were forced to work at sugar plantations in the West Indies.
- Slaves were then traded for molasses.
- Molasses was shipped to New England.

The human costs of the slave trade were immense, although it was only at the end of the eighteenth century that critics urged its abolition. Britain abolished slavery in the colonies in 1833, France in 1793.

PATTERNS OF COLONIAL SETTLEMENT

Throughout the seventeenth and eighteenth centuries, the major empire-builders of Europe circumnavigated the globe in search of new markets and new trading partners. Early Spanish successes prompted other nations to grab a share of the treasure that seemed to be everywhere just waiting to be exploited. But there were important differences in patterns of colonial settlemen. A small number of Spaniards conquered and controlled complex and large populations of Central and South America. The Spanish did not attempt to replace native culture with their own because their focus was on controlling native labor for maximum profit. They collected tribute and created a highly complex system of racial and social caste. Intermarriage among the Spanish and native populations was high. In its North American and Caribbean colonies, the French also practiced intermarriage because the goals of French trade relied on a cooperative relationship with natives. English colonialism provides perhaps the greatest contrast to either the Spanish or French model. The English established colonies as joint-stock companies or as proprietary colonies. These were planned settlements and plantations that were intended to replicate English social life. Because there was no need to control a large native labor force, the English sought exclusive control of native populations. As a result, the incidence of intermarriage was rare.

WAR AND EMPIRE

By the eighteenth century, the major players in the quest for empire were the British, French, and Dutch, although by the end of the century, the British had clearly built the largest empire. Empire-building had its problems, and one by-product was that commercial rivalries often resulted in warfare. The War of the Austrian Succession spread beyond the frontiers of Europe while the Seven Years' War (1756–1763) ended in a stalemate. The British captured Quebec and Louisbourg, and with the Treaty of Paris, France surrendered Canada and

India to the British. Finally, the American Revolution signified that the British had lost control of the American colonies.

THE LEGACY

Most historians assume that absolutism met its death in 1789 as the French revolutionaries swept away the last remnants of the *ancien régime*. But perhaps the idea and practice of royal absolutism had already declined. Louis XIV was not only an absolute monarch, but perhaps the last absolute monarch. There was no European king whose power advanced beyond that of Louis, nor did any attempt to acquire such power. Louis provided not only the model, but the lesson. It is more probable that the events of the eighteenth century—especially in terms of warfare and diplomacy—made it almost impossible for a monarch to reign absolutely. Louis XVI tried to imitate the Sun King and unleashed a revolution that took his life (although it created another monarch in Napoleon). The commercial and industrial revolutions of the eighteenth century fundamentally changed not only the economy, but society and politics as well. Europe was not at peace during the eighteenth century, but wars of religion no longer dominated European or international events as they had a century earlier. By 1800, the nobility and clergy continued to play a role in European society, but their power and influence had been curbed by the rise and fall of absolute monarchy. The middle classes advanced in terms of numbers and influence—any government that hoped to rule effectively could not afford to recognize this class of enterprising men and women.

SUGGESTED FEATURE FILMS

Barry Lyndon. 187 min. Color. 1975. Warner. Stanley Kubrick's masterful production of Thackeray's novel about an eighteenth-century rogue.

The Count of Monte Cristo. 131 min. Color. 2002. Buena Vista Pictures. Recent film adaptation of Dumas' novel of betrayal.

Cromwell. 145 min. Color. 1970. Columbia Pictures. Lengthy and somewhat historically inaccurate film nonetheless provides a glimpse into the turmoil that was the English civil war.

The Madness of King George. 103 min. Color. 1994. Goldwyn. With a screenplay by Alan Bennett, this film explores the clash between madness and sanity, modernity and tradition, in the late-eighteenth-century world of George III.

Moll Flanders. 169 min. Color. 1996. MGM. Film version of the Defoe novel. See also David Attwood's four-part made-for-TV version (1996, WGBH), *The Fortune and Misfortunes of Moll Flanders*.

Mutiny on the Bounty. 135 min. B/W. 1935. MGM. With Charles Laughton and Clark Gable.

Mutiny on the Bounty. 185 min. Color. 1962. MGM. With Marlon Brando. Tale of an ill-fated eighteenth-century commercial venture.

Restoration. 117 min. Color. 1995. Miramax. An aspiring young doctor finds himself in the service of Charles II and saves the life of someone close to the king.

Rob Roy. 139 min. Color. 1995. United Artists. Set around 1715, a depiction of Scottish hero Rob Roy MacGregor's revolt.

Tempest. 125 min. Color. 1959. Paramount. Film account of the Pugachev peasant uprising in the Russia of Catherine the Great.

Tom Jones. 129 min. Color. 1963. Universal. A delightful version of Fielding's novel. With Albert Finney and Susannah York.

Vatel. 100 min. Color. 2000. Miramax. Focuses on the three days when the Prince de Condé hosted Louis XIV and his court at a chateau in Chantilly.

SUGGESTED CLASSROOM FILMS

Absolutism and the Social Contract. 2 parts, 30 min. each. 1989. Insight Media. Looks at the development of political absolutism and the theories of Grotius, Locke, and Hobbes.

The Age of Charles II. 50 min. Color. 1994. Films for the Humanities and Sciences. Covers both Charles's life and times, with special focus on intellectual and artistic developments.

The Battle of Culloden. 72 min. B/W. 1964. BBC/Time-Life Films. Recreation of the 1746 battle between Bonnie Prince Charlie and the British army.

John Locke. 52 min. Color. 1994. Films for the Humanities and Sciences. Uses dramatized conversations to explore the character and ideas of John Locke.

The London of William Hogarth. 27 min. B/W. 1957. International Film Bureau. Looks at eighteenth-century London through Hogarth's engravings.

Peter the Great. 51 min. Color. 1996. Films for the Humanities and Sciences. An exploration into Peter's contradictions and character.

Seven Ages of Fashion: The Stuarts. 26 min. Color. 1992. Films for the Humanities. Part of a series that explores changes in fashion as a form of cultural history.

'Tis Pity She's a Whore: The First Women on the London Stage. 26 min. Color. 1994. Films for the Humanities. Explores the lives and careers of Moll Davis and Nell Gwynn to look at attitudes toward gender and sexuality in the seventeenth century.

CHAPTER 16

The Scientific Revolution

OUTLINE

I. Introduction
  A. Transformations
    1. Heliocentricity
    2. The new physics
    3. A new method of enquiry
    4. Natural philosophy as science—a new form of knowledge
  B. Reason
    1. Reform government
    2. Reorder society
    3. Purify religion
II. The Intellectual Roots of the Scientific Revolution
  A. The evolution of medieval science
    1. Christian Neoplatonism and Aristotelianism
      a. Thomas Aquinas
      b. God created a world capable of being understood by human reason
      c. Faith as the certain and complete road to God
      d. Reason as a divine attribute spurring mankind to salvation
      e. Encouraged rational argument and investigation
  B. Fourteenth-century developments
    1. The Nominalists
      a. Nature was distinct from God the Creator
      b. Only revelation and faith could reveal God's truth
      c. Freed the investigation of the natural world from theology

      d. Opened the way for a mechanistic or materialist worldview
    2. The Renaissance
      a. Humanists placed low value on science
      b. Neoplatonist influence
      c. Led the search for ideal and perfect structures
      d. Works of Archimedes were republished in 1543
      e. The universe as machine
      f. Developing amalgamation between artisans and intellectuals
      g. Mechanical engineering
      h. Investigation of the laws of perspective and optics
      i. Alchemy and astrology
II. A Revolution in Astronomy
  A. Medieval science
    1. Common-sense observations
    2. Aristotle and Ptolemy
      a. Explanations of the whole universe
      b. The orderliness of the cosmos
      c. The fundamental elements
      d. The problem of retrograde motion
  B. The Copernican revolution
    1. The old Roman calendar out of alignment with movement of heavenly bodies
      a. Especially significant for identifying the correct date of moveable feasts like Easter
    2. Nicholas Copernicus (1473–1543)
      a. Careful mathematician and faithful Christian

b. The Ptolemaic system had become too messy

c. The sun was not a fixed planet orbiting the stationary earth

d. The earth moved through the heavens

e. Believed he had restored a pure understanding of God's plan but troubled by implications

f. New ideas based on mathematics, not observation

    i. Assumed orbits were perfect circles

g. *On the Revolutions of the Heavenly Spheres* (1543)

C. Tycho's system and Kepler's laws

1. Tycho Brahe (1546–1601)

    a. High-ranking Danish nobleman

    b. Observed a completely new star

    c. Observed the movement of the whole heavens

    d. Built a giant laboratory

    e. Planets orbited the sun, which orbited the stationary earth

    f. Avoided the theological implications of the Copernican system

    g. Became court astronomer to the Holy Roman emperor

2. Johannes Kepler (1571–1630)

    a. Was Tycho's assistant

    b. Combined Copernicus's observations with mysticism, astrology, and mathematics

    c. Nature was created according to mathematical laws

    d. Musical harmonies

    f. The three laws of planetary motion

III. New Heavens, New Earth, and Worldly Politics: Galileo Galilei (1564–1642)

A. Galileo and the new role of natural philosophy

1. Transformed Copernicanism into a larger debate about the role of natural philosophy

2. The earth moved

3. Religion and science

B. Life and career

1. Successful mathematician and astronomer at Padua

2. The problem of motion

3. The theory of inertia

4. Small, practical experimentation

C. The telescope

1. Built his own telescope in 1610

2. Observed sun spots, craters on the moon, the moons of Jupiter, the phases of Venus

3. *The Starry Messenger* (1610)

4. Gained the favor of the Medici of Florence

D. Conflict with the church

1. Cardinal Robert Bellarmine (1542–1621)

    a. Skilled mathematician and Jesuit

    b. Cautioned Galileo for going too far

2. *Letter to the Grand Duchess Christina di Medici* (1615)

3. Galileo a sincere Catholic and Copernican

4. Natural philosophers and theologians were partners in a search for truth

5. Cardinal Maffeo Barberini—patron and friend of Galileo

6. Copernicus's *De Revolutionibus* placed on Index of Prohibited Books in 1616

7. *A Dialogue Between the Two World Systems* (1632)

    a. Thorough case for Copernicus "protected" in the form of a dialogue

    b. Galileo charged with attacking the authority of the church

8. Galileo brought to trial

    a. Charged with heresy

    b. Recanted his beliefs

    c. Placed under house arrest for life

9. *The Two New Sciences* (1638)

E. Galileo's legacy

1. Combination of mathematics and practical experimentation produced a new physics

2. His trial made the coexistence of reason and faith impossible

3. The "new philosophy" moves out of Italy to northern Europe

IV. Methods for a New Philosophy: Bacon and Descartes

A. The need for a scientific method

B. Bacon and Descartes

1. A new age of profound changes and great opportunities for discovery

2. The "ancients" and "moderns"

C. Sir Francis Bacon (1561–1626)

1. Lord Chancellor of England

2. *Novum Organum* (*New Instrument*, 1620)

3. Natural sciences cannot advance until the errors of the past had been cast off

4. Knowledge of the ancients no longer the best guide to truth

5. The "progressive stages of certainty"— the empirical approach

6. The inductive method
    a. Combining evidence from observations to make a general conclusion
    b. The goal was "useful knowledge"
    c. Cooperation between researchers
    d. Carefully recorded experiments
    e. "Solomon's House"—a knowledge factory

D. René Descartes (1596–1650)
    1. The importance of questioning established knowledge
    2. The value of an idea is its usefulness
    3. *Discourse on Method* (1637)
        a. Systematic doubt
        b. The process of thought proved his own existence
        c. *Cogito ergo sum* (I think, therefore I am)
    4. The deductive method
        a. Reasoning from a set of first principles
        b. Organized his logic on mathematical lines
        c. Mathematics as a tool for natural philosophers
    5. Toward a purely mechanistic view of the world
    6. All of creation, except man, existed solely in terms of physical laws
    7. Man as machine

V. The Power of Method and the Force of Curiosity: Seventeenth-Century Experimenters
    A. The Cartesians
        1. Turned toward mathematics and philosophical theory
        2. Christian Huygens (1629–1695)
            a. Combined mathematics with experiments in order to understand orbital motion
        3. Blaise Pascal (1623–1662)
            a. Applied mathematical skills to theology
        4. Baruch Spinoza (1632–1677)
            a. Applied geometry to ethics
            b. Believed he had gone beyond Descartes
    B. The Baconians
        1. Began with more practical work and experimentation in the laboratory
        2. Sought empirical laws based on observed evidence
        3. William Harvey (1578–1657)
            a. Dissected live animals
            b. Observed the circulation of the blood
    4. Robert Boyle (1627–1691)
        a. Boyle's Law
    5. Robert Hooke (1635–1703)
        a. Observed cellular structure of plants
        b. The microscope
            i. New evidence of God's existence

C. Science, societies, and the state
    1. The Royal Society
        a. Established by Boyle and Hooke in 1660
        b. The combination of collective research and discovery
        c. Offered scientific support for the restoration of royal power
        d. The *Transactions* (1666)—reaching scholars in England and on the Continent
        e. The work of science as a collective enterprise
        f. Crossing national and philosophical boundaries
    2. Women and science
        a. Margaret Cavendish (1623–1673)
            i. *Philosophical Letters, Observations upon Experimental Philosophy* (1666)
            ii. *Grounds of Natural Philosophy* (1668)
        b. Maria Winkelmann (1670–1720)
            i. Discovered a comet
            ii. Refused admission to Berlin Academy of Science
        c. Maria Sibylla Merian (1647–1717)
            i. Entomology
            ii. *Metamorphosis of the Insects of Surinam*

D. "And all was light:" Isaac Newton (1642–1727)
    1. Newton the man
        a. An unattractive personality
        b. Secretive, obsessive, vindictive, and petty
        c. Studied at Trinity College, Cambridge
        d. Worked alone—no close friends
        e. A secret Antitrinitarian
    2. Newton the scientist
        a. Extraordinary mathematician (mostly at Cambridge)
        b. Respected observation
        c. Dismantled larger problems into their individual components

d. Work on optics brought him out of obscurity and to the attention of the Royal Society (1672)

e. Argued with Hooke over who could claim to be the best scientist

f. Studied alchemy and theology

3. Work on physics

a. Refined Galileo's theory of inertia

b. A descriptive answer to the problem of motion

c. A single, clear, mathematical description of forces at work in the natural world

d. Universal gravitation—a single law for understanding motion

e. The *Principia Mathematica* (*Mathematical Principles of Natural Philosophy*, 1687)

   i. Geometric proof of the forces of nature

   ii. The evidence of observation and experience

   iii. The practicality of the Newtonian achievement

4. The legacy

a. An orderly and comprehensible picture of the heavens and the earth

b. Gave humanity greater power over the environment

c. An English national hero

d. Alexander Pope wrote epitaph (1727)

e. "I frame no hypotheses"

   i. Vain to seek a scientific explanation for God's handiwork

5. Natural philosophy and religion

a. Even by 1800, no clear break between the two

b. Most scientific enterprise moved outside the university

c. The Royal Society and its Continental imitators

d. New scientific methods meant more difficult problems in the physical sciences could be investigated

VI. Conclusion

A. Science fully compatible with faith

B. From a science of nature to a science of man and society

GENERAL DISCUSSION QUESTIONS

1. What are the medieval intellectual foundations of the Scientific Revolution? Why could Newton admit that none of his work would have been possible unless he had "stood on the shoulders of giants"?

2. Why did some sciences progress faster than others? Why were some countries more receptive to scientific progress than others?

3. Why was mathematics so important to scientific progress in the seventeenth century? How did mathematics displace other methods of reasoning and proof?

4. Why did Francis Bacon and his followers emphasize careful observation of nature?

5. Explain how both Bacon and Descartes arrived at their scientific method. In what ways was the Cartesian method different from that of Bacon?

6. Why was Galileo brought to trial by the authorities at Rome? What was the outcome of that trial?

7. In what ways was the Roman Catholic Church under attack by the revolution in science? Why did the church feel so threatened by the "New Science"?

8. His achievements in optics, mathematics, and universal gravitation aside, why was Isaac Newton such an important figure in the development of modern science? What was the Newtonian achievement?

DOCUMENT DISCUSSION QUESTIONS

Galileo on Nature, Scripture, and Truth

1. Why did Galileo need to defend his views in a letter to Christina de Medici?

2. For Galileo, what is the relationship between God, man, and nature?

Newton on the Purposes of Experimental Philosophy

3. Why did Isaac Newton declare that "hypotheses, whether metaphysical or physical, whether of occult qualities or mechanical, have no place in experimental philosophy."

SAMPLE LECTURE 16: THE SCIENTIFIC REVOLUTION

Lecture Objectives

1. To explain how modern science was built upon medieval foundations of thought

2. To show that the essence of the Scientific Revolution was a transformation in human knowledge

3. To highlight the Newtonian achievement in the Enlightenment

A REVOLUTION IN HUMAN THOUGHT

The Scientific Revolution of the sixteenth and seventeenth centuries signified a profound transformation in the orientation of Western intellectual thought. It was a revolution in ideas about the natural world and how that world functions. Because the revolution was largely about ideas, it was also an epistemological revolution that transformed the foundations of human knowledge. From Copernicus's theory of heliocentricity to Newton's universal laws of gravitation, science, or what was then called natural philosophy, offered a new understanding of the universe. Whereas medieval science saw nature as something miraculous, the scientific revolutionaries of the sixteenth and seventeenth centuries sought to explain and understand the inner workings of these miracles. Recognition was not the same thing as understanding. With this in mind, the scientific revolutionaries set about to discover new knowledge about the natural world, knowledge that could be verified by empirical observation and mathematical proof. Certainty was the goal in this endeavor. Although we speak of a revolution in science, this revolution would not have been at all possible had it not been for centuries of previous scientific inquiry. Even Isaac Newton was careful to say that "if I have seen further it is because I have stood on the shoulders of giants." Although ancient astronomers and scientists had established the foundations of science, it would fall upon the shoulders of men like Copernicus, Galileo, and Newton to set in motion a revolution in scientific thinking, a revolution whose legacy is with us today.

THE MEDIEVAL ORIGINS OF THE NEW SCIENCE

When medieval scientists thought about the world of nature, it was a world shaped and conditioned by miracles, forever new and forever renewed. The "stuff" of the material world, what we call matter, was composed of four fundamental elements: earth, air, fire, and water. Each element, it was argued, was said to follow its own nature. Because air and fire were light, their true nature was to move upward. Likewise, because earth and water were coarse and heavy, their tendency was to move downward. The movement of these four elements was what kept the universe intact.

Medieval scientists believed that the Earth was a stationary celestial body about which the other heavenly bodies (moon, planets, sun, comets, and stars) rotated. Medieval science postulated that each heavenly body occupied space on its own celestial sphere since the sphere was a perfect shape that had neither beginning nor end. An Earth-centered universe (geocentrism) was first suggested by Claudius Ptolemy (c. 85–c. 165), a Roman astronomer and geographer of Greek descent. Carrying out his celestial observations from Alexandria in Egypt between 127 and 141, Ptolemy's

explanation of the cosmos was relatively simple. But over time, human observations of the heavens suggested that some bodies seemed to move in one direction, stop, reverse direction, stop again, and then continue on in their original path. This retrograde motion is easily explained today since observation now considers the movement of the observer relative to the movement of the heavenly body. But since geocentricity stipulated that the Earth did not move, scientists after Ptolemy added epicycle after epicycle to explain retrograde motion. So, although geocentrism originally provided a simple explanation for the movement of the heavens, by the sixteenth century this simple system had become far too complicated.

THE RENAISSANCE

One question that has plagued historians of modern science is why the Scientific Revolution took place when it did. We have already seen how the simplicity of the Ptolemaic system had become more complicated thanks to centuries of observation. In the fourteenth century, the nominalist philosophers, such as William of Ockham (1285–1347), suggested that nature was distinct from God the creator. This was indeed an important step toward a new understanding of nature. Since the nominalists believed that only revelation and faith could reveal God's truth, the investigation of the natural world was freed from theology. What the nominalists achieved was a step toward a mechanistic or material worldview—the world as machine—that is, a worldview based on the careful observation of phenomena.

Although the majority of Renaissance scholars placed little value on science, the Renaissance nonetheless served as a fertile breeding ground for the New Science. A strong Neoplatonist influence led to the search for ideal and perfect structures. At the same time, humanists turned away from Aristotle. The Renaissance helped scientists to see the universe as a machine; mechanical engineering was improved, as was the association between artisans and intellectuals. Artists began to investigate the laws of perspective and optics at the same time that alchemy and astrology continued to suggest ways of understanding nature without appealing to either revelation or faith.

THE COPERNICAN REVOLUTION

An original and fundamental challenge to the Ptolemaic system came in 1543 with the publication of *De revolutionibus orbium coelestium* by Nicolas Copernicus (1473–1543), a Polish astronomer. Copernicus studied Latin, mathematics, astronomy, geography, and philosophy at the university at Kracow. While his mathematics courses introduced him to Aristotle and Ptolemy's view of the universe, these courses were also important because they enabled students to understand the calendar and calculate the dates of holy days. Especially significant was the need to identify the correct date for moveable feasts such as Easter. A major part of the astronomy that he learned was actually astrology. Copernicus was also familiar with Euclid's *Elements*, the *Alfonsine Tables* (planetary theory and eclipses), and the *Tables of Directions* of Regiomantanus. Copernicus also spent a number of years at the university at Bologna, where he studied law, Greek, mathematics, and astronomy, and at Padua, where he studied medicine. Copernicus was clearly something of a Renaissance man. In his *Little Commentary* of 1514, Copernicus set down several general axioms regarding his astronomical observations:

- The earth is not the center of the universe.
- The center of the universe is near the sun.
- The distance from the earth to the sun is imperceptible compared with the distance from the earth to the stars.
- The rotation of the earth accounts for the apparent daily rotation of the stars.
- The apparent annual cycle of movements of the sun is caused by the earth revolving around it.
- The apparent retrograde motion of the planets is caused by the motion of the earth, from which one observes.

There, in a nutshell, were the foundations of heliocentricity, which were to become central to his argument in *De revolutionibus*. Copernicus knew he had stumbled onto a more pure understanding of God's plan, but he was troubled by its implications. For this reason, he delayed the publication of this work until after his death in 1543. Although the notion of heliocentricity was not new—Aristarchus of Samos (310–230 B.C.E.) had already proposed such an idea—what was new and significant was that Copernicus based his theory on mathematics and not observation. He also assumed, for instance, that the orbits of the planets were defined by perfect circles.

The Copernican system was taken up by the Danish astronomer, Tycho Brahe (1546–1601) and by the Swabian astronomer Johannes Kepler (1571–1630). Brahe was not completely convinced by heliocentricity and he could not abandon Aristotelian physics either. For Brahe, heavy bodies fell to their natural place, the earth, which was the center of the universe. But the Copernican system had a number of advantages, some technical, and others based on harmony. Tycho's system combined the best of both worlds. He kept the earth in the center of the universe and the moon and sun revolved about the earth, and the shell of the fixed stars was centered on the earth. The other planets revolved about the sun. Brahe also understood that advancements in astronomy would only come with improved instrumentation, and so he designed and built his own instruments. A contemporary of Brahe, Kepler was a profoundly religious man who believed that it was man's Christian duty to understand the works of God, and that since man was made in the image of God, he was capable of understanding the universe, a universe created according to a mathematical plan. Kepler is known primarily for discovering the three laws of planetary motion:

- The orbits of the planets about the sun are elliptical. (Law of Ellipses)
- An imaginary line drawn from the center of the sun to the center of the planet will sweep out equal areas in equal intervals of time. (Law of Equal Areas)
- The ratio of the squares of the periods of any two planets is equal to the ratio of the cubes of their average distances from the sun. (Law of Harmonies)

Kepler's three laws were situated within the framework of a heliocentric universe and so it seemed the paths of the planets were mapped forever. All that remained would be to see these three laws as part of a single law which held each planet in its orbit about the sun. This, of course, would have to wait for the genius of Isaac Newton. But what was needed before Newton could go to work was a more practical and elaborate understanding of the mechanics of motion.

GALILEO—NEW HEAVENS AND NEW EARTH

It was left to Galileo Galilei (1564–1642) to transform Copernicanism from a theory about astronomy into a larger and more fundamental debate about the role of natural philosophy in revealing the mysteries of the natural world. For instance, Galileo offered evidence that the earth indeed moved, a suggestion that flew in the face of Aristotle and the church. Although his ideas were seen as a challenge to the authority of the church, what Galileo intended was to redefine the relationship between reason and faith. Born in Florence, Galileo's education was broad and included mathematics as well as medicine. He was obsessed with the problem of motion, particularly the motion of objects on a moving earth. Rejecting Aristotle's theory of inertia, Galileo proposed instead that only a change in motion required a cause. In other words, objects either stayed in motion or were at rest.

Galileo combined mathematic prowess with the observation of moving bodies. Around 1610 he learned that someone in Holland had fastened a ground lens at opposite ends of a brass tube. Galileo procured his own telescope and immediately trained his sight on the heavens above. Looking through his telescope, he discovered:

- craters on the moon, sun spots, and the rings of Saturn
- the phases of Venus
- that the Earth's moon was not a source of light but rather of reflected light
- the moons of Jupiter

Galileo published his findings in *The Starry Messenger* (1611) and then went to Rome. It was there that his ideas first came into conflict with the church. Cardinal Robert Bellarmine (1542–1621), who was himself a skilled mathematician, cautioned Galileo that he had gone too far. Galileo responded with his *Letter to the Grand Duchess Christina di Medici* (1615). In this *Letter*, Galileo argued that he was a sincere member of the church but that he was also dedicated to Copernicanism. Natural philosophers and theologians,

Galileo suggested, were partners in the search for truth. Bellarmine eventually ordered that Galileo not teach or preach Copernican theory, nor could he write about it. In 1616, the *De Revolutionibus* was placed on the Index of Forbidden Books. Galileo abided by this injunction but in 1632 published his *Dialogue Between the Two World Systems*. It was important that Galileo cast his ideas in the form of a dialogue. After all, the words in a dialogue were just that, words. But it was obvious where Galileo's sympathies lay. He was eventually brought to trial for heresy. On June 22, 1633, Galileo recanted all of his beliefs before the judges of the Inquisition:

> Wishing to remove from the minds of your Eminences and of every true Christian this vehement suspicion justly cast upon me, with sincere heart and unfeigned faith I do abjure, damn, and detest the said errors and heresies, and generally each and every other error, heresy and sect contrary to the Holy Church; and I do swear for the future that I shall never again speak or assert, orally or in writing, such things as might bring me under similar suspicion.

The life and career Galileo was significant for a number of reasons:

- He combined mathematics and practical experimentation and created a new physics.
- His trial made the coexistence of reason and faith nearly impossible.
- His trial also meant that the New Science was forced to move away from Italy and move north to places like England, France, and the Low Countries.

THE SEARCH FOR A METHOD: BACON AND DESCARTES

Following the trial of Galileo, the New Science moved north. While scientists continued to investigate the heavens, several important thinkers began to devote their attention to the principles and goals of the New Science. Natural philosophy was undergoing a process of rethinking as they considered such questions as:

- What proved a theory correct?
- How should science function?
- What answers to questions about the natural world are most satisfying?
- What method is best to determine those answers?

There was a need for a new scientific method. Sir Francis Bacon (1561–1626), Lord Chancellor of England under James I, was clearly not a scientist. But in his work, the *Novum Organum* (the *New Instrument*, 1620), Bacon argued that the natural sciences could not advance until the errors of the past had been cast off. Just because the ancients had been intelligent men did not imply that their "truths" were eternal. Instead, Bacon argued that the best approach to the study of natural philosophy was the empirical approach. It was a method based on observation and experience, but more im-

portant, on what he called the "progressive stages of certainty." This method is called the inductive method and contains the following characteristics:

- a combination of evidence from observations to make a general conclusion
- the goal of "useful knowledge"
- cooperation between researchers
- carefully recorded experiments
- "Solomon's House"—a knowledge "factory"

The Baconian method was based on questioning established opinion. Nothing should be taken for granted. Instead, observation of phenomena, the careful collection of information, and the framing of a general theory based on experimentation would reveal the greatest amount of useful knowledge. And since, according to Bacon, "knowledge is power," the more observation and experimentation, the greater the chance of man's improving his lot here on earth.

Often called the father of modern philosophy, René Descartes (1596–1650) would have agreed with Bacon on a few points. Both thinkers, for instance, believed that the knowledge of the ancients was no longer the best guide to the truth. Likewise, Bacon and Descartes would have agreed that the true value of an idea was its usefulness. But there all similarities end. Descartes' method was worked out in his *Discourse on Method* of 1637. In that philosophical work, Descartes used systematic doubt to prove his own existence. Indeed, the intellectual act of "doubting away" all knowledge proved to Descartes that the only thing he knew for certain was that he was doubting, and because he doubted, he existed. Or, as Descartes put it, *cogito ergo sum* (I think, therefore I am). Descartes's method was extremely influential on the Continent but less so in the England of Bacon and John Locke (1632–1704). However, Descartes managed to secure the role of mathematics as a tool for all natural philosophers because he organized his logic on mathematical principles. All of creation, with the exception of man himself, existed solely in terms of physical laws. In the last analysis, Descartes's philosophy led to a mechanistic view of the world—man was a machine.

THE GENIUS OF ISAAC NEWTON

In his biography of Isaac Newton, the eminent historian of science, Richard Westfall, wrote that:

> The end result of my study of Newton has served to convince me that with him there is no measure. He has become for me wholly other, one of the tiny handful of supreme geniuses who have shaped the categories of the human intellect, a man not finally reducible to the criteria by which we comprehend our fellow beings.

Isaac Newton (1642–1727) grabs our attention for a number of reasons. First, he was genius who was respected by his contemporaries, although he was a secretive man who made little attempt to befriend anyone. Second, his discovery and analysis of the universal laws of gravitation seemed to be the crowning achievement of the Scientific Revolution. What Copernicus had set in motion, Newton synthesized into a system that had an unprecedented impact on the thought of the Enlightenment and after. Upon his death in 1727, the British poet Alexander Pope, who was then working on a translation of Homer, wrote a couplet which more or less defines Newton's position in the western intellectual tradition. Pope wrote:

> Nature and Nature's laws lay hid in night:
> God said, "Let Newton be!" and all was light.

As a man, Newton was quite unlike most of the other scientific revolutionaries. For one thing, he spent the majority of his time as a student and professor at Trinity College, Cambridge, where he held the Lucasian Chair in mathematics. It was at Cambridge that Newton worked out the calculus that would allow him to explain the universal laws of gravitation. His was an unattractive personality. He was secretive, obsessive, vindictive, and petty. He worked alone and in short bursts of activity and was always hesitant to publish his findings.

As a scientist, Newton was an extraordinary mathematician who respected observation. His own scientific method required the dismantling of larger problems into their individual components. It was his work on optics, the science of light, that brought him out of obscurity and into the limelight of the English scientific community. In 1672, he was elected a member of the Royal Society, where he became embroiled in an argument with Robert Hooke (1635–1703) over which man could claim to be the best scientist. Newton also studied theology and alchemy (Newton had the largest collection of alchemical books in all of Europe). Newton devoted equal amounts of time to his investigations of optics, physics, theology, and alchemy. No one field occupied more attention than any other. In the end, however, it was his physics that attracted the most amount of attention from his contemporaries and those who came after him. Newton refined Galileo's theory of inertia and came up with a descriptive answer to the problem of motion. What Newton was after was a clear, mathematical description of the those forces at work in the natural world. In 1687, Newton published his greatest work, the *Philosophiae naturalis principia mathematica*. The title of this work, written in Latin, was important, for what Newton had done was describe nothing less than the mathematical principles of natural philosophy—in other words, the mathematical principles of science itself. The *Principia* is a work of awesome power in that Newton offered geometric proof of the forces of nature based on the evidence of observation and experience.

THE NEWTONIAN ACHIEVEMENT

Newton's gift to the eighteenth century was an orderly and comprehensible picture of the heavens and the earth. But not every thinker of the eighteenth century could claim to be a scientist. If this is so, then how could Newton come to symbolize so much to so many. If Newton could use human reason to unlock the mysteries of universal gravitation—a singular law that explained the physical world—then it seemed a short step indeed to use human reason to unlock the mysteries of man and society. It was no accident, then, that the social sciences of geography, anthropology, economics, political science, and sociology made their appearance after Newton. Newton gave humanity greater power over the environment. If man was a product of his environment, an environment that could be understood by the social sciences, then it was possible that man could be changed by changing his environment. Such a belief was predicated on the notion that man, like the physical world, was uniform in his nature.

SUGGESTED FEATURE FILMS

Galileo. 145 min. Color. 1975. American Film Theater. Josephs Losey's film adaptation of Bertolt Brecht's play about the seventeenth-century Italian astronomer who helped lay the foundation for modern science.
Galileo: On the Shoulders of Giants. 57 min. Color. 1998. Devine Entertainment Corporation. Made-for-television film starring Michael Moriarty as Galileo.

SUGGESTED CLASSROOM FILMS

The Ascent of Man: The Starry Messenger. 52 min. Color. 1994. Historian of science Jacob Bronowski treats the major conflict between the Scientific Revolution and religious dogma, as in the trial of Galileo.
Galileo's "Dialogue." 53 min. Color. 1997. Discovery University Production. This program examines Galileo's controversial *Dialogue* and the tumultuous events surrounding Galileo's scientific achievements.
Science Revises the Heavens. 55 min. Color. 1986. Insight Media. James Burke discusses scientific developments from Copernicus to Newton.
Scientific Imagination in the Renaissance. 55 min. Color. 1986. Insight Media. From the series *The Day the Universe Changed*.

CHAPTER 17 | The Enlightenment

OUTLINE

I. Introduction
   A. The Calas Case and Voltaire (1762)
      1. Intolerance and ignorance
      2. Fanaticism and infamy
   B. Enlightenment concerns
      1. The danger of unchecked and arbitrary authority
      2. The value of religious toleration
      3. The importance of law, reason, and human dignity
II. The Foundations of the Enlightenment
   A. An eighteenth-century phenomenon
   B. Basic characteristics
      1. The power of human reason
      2. Self-confidence
      3. Newtonian methods had wide application
      4. "Dare to know!" (Kant)
      5. Reason needed autonomy and freedom
      6. The "Holy Trinity": Bacon, Newton, and Locke
         a. Locke's Essay *Concerning Human Understanding* (1690)
            i. Education and environment
            ii. Sense perception and the *tabula rasa*
            iii. The goodness and perfectibility of humanity
            iv. Moral improvement and social progress
      7. The organization of knowledge
         a. The scientific method
         b. Collected evidence on the rise and fall of nations
         c. Compared government constitutions

8. The "cultural project" of the Enlightenment
   a. Practical, applied knowledge
   b. Spreading knowledge and free public discussion
   c. "To change the common way of thinking" (Diderot)
   d. Writing for a larger audience
   e. Academies sponsored essay contests
   f. The expansion of literacy
   g. The first "public sphere"
9. Criticism and satire
   a. Irreverence toward custom and tradition
   b. Belief in human perfectibility and progress
   c. The relationship between nature and culture
III. The World of the Philosophes
   A. The *philosophe*
      1. A free thinker unhampered by the constraints of religion or dogma in any form
   B. Voltaire (born François Marie Arouet, 1694–1778)
      a. The personification of the Enlightenment
      b. Life
         i. Educated by Jesuits
         ii. Spent time in the Bastille for libel
         iii. Temporary exile in England
         iv. Great admirer and popularizer of all things English (especially Newton and Locke)

c. *Philosophical Letters* (1734)
   i. Religious and political liberties of the British
   ii. British open-mindedness and empiricism
   iii. Admiration for English culture and politics and respect for scientists
   iv. Religious toleration
   v. Observations on England as criticisms of France
d. *Écrasez l'infâme*—"crush infamy" (all forms of repression, fanaticism, and bigotry)
   i. Loathed religious bigotry
   ii. Did not oppose religion— sought to rescue morality from narrow dogma
   iii. Common sense and simplicity
   iv. Contacts with Frederick of Prussia and Catherine the Great

B. Baron de Montesquieu (1689–1755)
   1. Life
      a. Born of a noble family, inherited an estate
      b. Served as magistrate in the parlement of Bordeaux
      c. A cautious jurist
      d. *The Persian Letters* (1721)
         i. Series of letters between two Persian visitors to France
         ii. Likened French absolutism to Persian despotism
         iii. Thinly-veiled criticism of France
   2. *The Spirit of the Laws* (1748)
      a. A work in comparative historical sociology
      b. Newtonian in its empirical approach
      c. How do structures and institutions shape laws?
      d. Different forms of government— what spirit characterized them?
         i. Republic—virtue
         ii. Monarchy—honor
         iii. Despotism—fear
      e. Spelled out the dangerous drift toward despotism in France
      f. Admired the British system of separate and balanced powers
      g. Checks and balances

C. Diderot and the *Encyclopedia*
   1. A vast compendium of human knowledge
   2. Grandest statement of the philosophes' goals

   3. Scientific analysis applied to human reason—happiness and progress
   4. Guided by Denis Diderot (1713–1784) and Jean d'Alembert (1717–1783)
   5. Seventeen large volumes of text, eleven volumes of illustrations (1751–1772)
      a. Purpose was to change the general way of thinking
      b. Demonstrated how the application of science could promote progress
      c. Heavy circulation despite the high price
      d. Government revoked permission to publish for trying to "propagate materialism" (1759)

IV. Internationalization of Enlightenment Themes
   A. The "party of humanity"
      1. French books widely distributed and read
      2. Cosmopolitan movement of ideas
   B. Enlightenment themes: humanitarianism and tolerance
      1. Cesare Beccaria (1738–1794)
         a. *On Crimes and Punishments* (1764)
            i. General themes: arbitrary power, reason, and human dignity
            ii. Attacked the view that punishment represented society's vengeance on the criminal
            iii. Legitimate rationale for punishment was to maintain social order, prevent other crimes
            iv. Opposed torture and the death penalty
      2. Religious toleration
         a. End religious warfare and the persecution of heretics and religious minorities
         b. Few philosophes were atheists (materialists)
         c. Most were deists—God as "divine clockmaker"
         d. Most philosophes viewed Judaism and Islam as backward
         e. Gotthold Lessing (1729–1781)
            i. Treated Jews sympathetically
            ii. *Nathan the Wise* (1779)
            iii. Three great monotheistic religions are three versions of the same truth
         f. Moses Mendelssohn (1729–1786)
            i. Took up the question of Jewish identity
            ii. *On the Religious Authority of Judaism* (1783)

iii. Defended Jewish communities against anti-Semitic policies

C. Economics, government, and administration
1. Rising states and empires made economic issues important
2. The French physiocrats
   a. Mercantilist policies were misguided
   b. Real wealth came from land and agricultural production; advocated a simplified tax system
   c. *Laissez-faire*—wealth and goods to circulate without government interference
3. Adam Smith (1723–1790)
   a. *Inquiry Into the Nature and Causes of the Wealth of Nations* (1776)
      i. Disagreed with the centrality of agriculture
      ii. Central issue was the productivity of human labor
      iii. Mercantile restrictions did not create real economic health
      iv. The "invisible hand" of the marketplace
      v. Rational individuals should pursue their interests rationally
      vi. The stages of economic growth
      vii. Following the "obvious and simple system of natural liberty"

V. Empire and Enlightenment
A. The economics of empire and the profitability of colonies
1. New world of natural humanity and simplicity
2. The slave trade and humanitarianism, individual rights and natural law
B. Abbé Guillaume Thomas Francois Raynal
1. *Philosophical History . . . of Europeans in the Two Indies* (1770)
   a. A total history of colonization, natural history, exploration and commerce
   b. Industry and trade brought improvement and progress
   c. Condemned the Spanish in Mexico and Peru, the Portuguese in Brazil, the English in North America
   d. A good government required checks and balances
   e. The problem? Europeans in the New World had unlimited power

C. Slavery and the Atlantic world
1. Atlantic slave trade hit its peak in the eighteenth century
2. For Raynal and Diderot, slavery defied natural law and natural freedom
3. A condemnation of slavery in a metaphorical sense
4. Slavery as a violation of self-government
5. Few philosophes advocated the total abolition of slavery
D. Exploration and the Pacific world
1. Mapping the Pacific and scientific missions
2. Louis-Anne de Bougainville (1729–1811)
   a. Sent by the French government to the South Pacific in 1767
   b. Looked for a new route to China and new spices
   c. Described Tahiti
3. Captain James Cook (1728–1779)
   a. Two trips to the South Pacific
   b. Charted coasts of New Zealand, New Holland, New Hebrides, and Hawaii
   c. Explored the Antarctic continent, the Bering Sea, and the Arctic Ocean
4. Travel accounts of these voyages read by a large audience eager for such information
E. The impact of the scientific missions
1. The eighteenth century fascinated by stories of new cultures
2. Diderot, *Supplément au Voyage de Bougainville* (1772)
   a. Tahitians as original human beings
   b. Humanity in its natural state
   c. Uninhibited sexuality and freedom from religious dogma
   d. Simplicity versus overcivilized Europeans
3. Alexander von Humboldt (1769–1859)
   a. Spent five years in Spanish America
   b. *Personal Narratives of Travels* (1814–1819)
   c. Toward Darwin and evolutionary change
VI. Nature, Gender, and Enlightenment Radicalism: Rousseau and Wollstonecraft
A. How revolutionary was the Enlightenment?
B. The world of Jean-Jacques Rousseau (1712–1778)
1. General observations
2. Quarreled with and contradicted other philosophes

3. Attacked privilege and believed in the goodness of humanity
4. Introduced the notion of sensibility (the "cult of feeling")
5. The first to speak of popular sovereignty and democracy
6 The most utopian of the philosophes

C. *The Social Contract* (1762)
1. "Man was born free, and everywhere he is in chains"
2. The origins of government
3. The legitimacy of government
4. Social inequality and private property
5. Legitimate authority arises from the people alone
   a. Sovereignty should not be divided among different branches of the government
   b. Exercising sovereignty transformed the nation
   c. The national community would be united by the "general will"
      i. Citizens bound by mutual obligation rather than coercive laws
      ii. Citizens' common interests represented in the whole

D. *Émile* (1762)
1. Story of a boy educated in the "school of nature"
2. Children should not be forced to reason early in life
3. The aim was moral autonomy and good citizenship
4. Women useful as mothers and wives only
5. "Natural" is better, simpler, uncorrupted

E. *Julie, ou la nouvelle Heloise* (1761)
1. Seventy editions in thirty years
2. Domestic and maternal virtues
3. Humans ruled by their hearts as much as their heads
4. Middle class and aristocratic sensibility: spontaneous feelings
5. The Enlightenment and gender
   a. Education as key to social progress—education for all?
   b. Were men and women different?
   c. Were gender differences natural, or socially created?

F. The world of Mary Wollstonecraft (1759–1797)
1. Rousseau's sharpest critic
2. *A Vindication of the Rights of Women* (1792)
   a. Republican ideas
   b. Spoke against inequality and artificial distinctions of rank, birth, or wealth
   c. Society ought to seek "the perfection of our nature and capability of happiness"
   d. Women had the same innate capacity for reason and self-government as men
   e. Virtue the same thing for men and women
   f. Relations between the sexes ought to be based on equality
3. The family
   a. The legal inequalities of marriage law
   b. Women taught to be dependent and seductive in order to win husbands
   c. Education has to promote liberty and self-reliance
   d. The common humanity of men and women
   e. The natural division of labor between men and women
   f. Hinted that women might have political rights

VII. The Enlightenment and Eighteenth-Century Culture
A. The book trade
1. The expansion of printing and print culture
2. An international and clandestine book trade
3. Growth of daily newspapers
4. British press was relatively free of restrictions
5. Censorship only made books more expensive
6. "Philosophical books"—subversive literature of all kinds
7. The eighteenth-century literary underground

B. High culture, new elites, and the "public sphere"
1. Networks of readers and new forms of sociability and discussion
2. Elite or high culture was small but cosmopolitan
3. Joined together members of the nobility and wealthy members of the middle classes
4. "Learned societies"
   a. American Philosophical Society (Philadelphia)
   b. Select Society of Edinburgh
   c. Organized intellectual life outside universities

d. Provided libraries, meeting places for discussion, published journals

5. Elites also met in academies
   a. Royal Society of London
   b. French Academy of Literature
   c. Berlin Royal Academy
   d. Fostered a sense of common purpose and seriousness

C. Salons
   1. Organized by well-connected and learned aristocratic women
   2. Brought together men and women of letters with members of the aristocracy
   3. Located in all major cities
   4. Other societies
      a. Masonic Lodges
      b. Secret societies with elaborate rituals
      c. Egalitarian
      d. Pledged themselves to rational thought in all human affairs
   5. Coffeehouses
      e. Aided the circulation of new ideas

D. The public sphere and public opinion
   1. The ability to think and criticize freely
   2. Effect on politics—moving politics beyond the court

E. Middle-class culture and reading
   1. Shopkeepers, small merchants, lawyers, and professionals—a different reading public
   2. Bought and borrowed books
   3. Targeted middle-class women
   4. Popularized Enlightenment treatises on education and the mind
   5. Popularity of the novel
      a. Samuel Richardson (1689–1761)—*Pamela* and *Clarissa*
      b. Daniel Defoe (1660–1731)—*Moll Flanders* and *Robinson Crusoe*
      c. Henry Fielding (1707–1754)—*Tom Jones*
      d. Fanny Burney (1752–1840)—*Evelina*
      e. Ann Radcliffe (1764–1823)—*The Romance of the Forest*
      f. Maria Edgeworth (1767–1849)—*Castle Rackrent*
      g. Jane Austen (1775–1817)—*Pride and Prejudice* and *Emma*

F. Popular culture: urban and rural
   1. Literacy
      a. Varied by gender, class, and location
      b. Greater literacy in northern Europe
      c. Ran high in towns and cities

2. Broadsides, woodcuts, prints, drawings, cartoons
3. The availability of new reading material
4. The "blue books"—inexpensive, small paperbacks
   a. Traditional popular literature
   b. Short catechisms
   c. Tales of miracles
   d. The lives of saints
5. Networks of sociability
   a. Guild organizations offered discussion and companionship
   b. Street theater and singers
   c. Market days and village festivals
   d. Oral and literate cultures overlapped
6. The philosophes and popular culture
   a. The Enlightenment was an urban phenomenon
   b. Looked at popular culture with distrust and ignorance

G. Eighteenth-century music
   1. The last phase of the Baroque
   2. Bach and Handel
      a. Johann Sebastian Bach (1685–1750)
         i. Remained a German provincial his entire life
         ii. A church musician at Leipzig
         iii. Supplied music for Sunday and holiday services
         iv. An ardent Protestant, unaffected by the the secularism of the Enlightenment
      b. George Frederick Handel (1685–1759)
         i. Public-pleasing cosmopolitan
         ii. Established himself in London
         iii. The oratorio—musical drama to be performed in concert
         iv. *The Messiah*
   3. Hayden and Mozart
      a. The classical style
      b. Imitating classical principles of order, clarity, and symmetry
      c. The string quartet and the symphony
      d. Wolfgang Amadeus Mozart (1756–1791)
         i. Began composing at age four, a keyboard virtuoso at six
         ii. Wrote his first symphony at age nine
         iii. Attracted attention across Europe
         iv. Freemasonry
         v. Died relatively poor

vi. *The Marriage of Figaro,*
Don Giovanni, and *The*
Magic Flute

e. Joseph Haydn (1732–1809)

i. Spent his life with a wealthy
Austro-Hungarian family

ii. Moved to London—
"commercial market for
culture"

iii. The father of the symphony

4. Opera

a. A seventeenth-century creation

i. Claudio Monteverdi
(1567–1643)

ii. Combined music with theater

b. Christoph Willibald von Gluck
(1714–1787)

i. Came to Paris from Austria

ii. The musical tutor of Marie
Antoinette

iii. Simplified arias, emphasized
dramatic action

iv. High entertainment for the
French court

5. Aristocratic and court patronage

6. Pierre Augustin de Beaumarchais
(1732–1799)

a. Author of *The Marriage of Figaro*

b. Satirized the French nobility

VIII. Conclusion

A. Science as a form of knowledge

B. Raising problems to public awareness

C. The language of the Enlightenment

GENERAL DISCUSSION QUESTIONS

1. Why was the "Holy Trinity" of Francis Bacon, Isaac Newton, and John Locke so important to the eighteenth-century philosophes? What ideas did they lend to the Enlightenment?

2. In his essay *What Is Enlightenment?*, argued that "there are only a few who have pursued a firm path and have succeeded in escaping from immaturity by their own cultivation of the mind." What are the implications of such a statement?

3. Consider the twenty-eight-volume *Encyclopedia*, a compendium of human knowledge. In what ways did Diderot and the other philosophes think that this enterprise would "change the general way of thinking"? What exactly needed to be changed?

4. How did the discovery and exploration of new worlds inspire the philosophes?

5. Voltaire once wrote, "If there were only one religion in England there would be danger of despotism, if there were two they would cut each other's throats, but there are thirty, and they live in peace and happiness." In what ways was Voltaire's passion for England little more than an attack upon the *ancien régime* in France?

6. Why did deism seem to be the only "rational" religion for the philosophes?

7. What characteristics did the majority of philosophes share that might have made them a "party of humanity"? For what purpose did they utilize reason and criticism?

8. In what ways was Kant's *Sapere Aude!* the motto of the Enlightenment? What conditions were required for this age of light to become so widespread?

9. Do you find that the ideas and aspirations of the philosophes have something in common with the modern world? If so, where do the worlds of the Enlightenment and our own world cross paths?

DOCUMENT DISCUSSION QUESTIONS

The Impact of the New World on Enlightenment Thinkers

1. Why was the discovery of America of such profound significance for eighteenth-century Europe?

2. Why was Raynal so concerned with man's conduct and happiness?

Slavery and the Enlightenment

3. What arguments against slavery does the *Encyclopedia* article present? Do you agree with the claim that slavery is legally impossible because no one can sell his or her natural rights? What are natural rights?

4. The enslavement of conquered peoples was historically an ancient and well-established custom, approved by civil and religious authorities. Even some philosophes such as Thomas Jefferson were slave owners. How did some Enlightenment philosophes use universal ideas of freedom to argue against custom in regard to slavery and other questions?

Rousseau's Social Contract

5. How can one join a political association and yet remain free?

6. If sovereignty is a contract, how long does it last? Can anyone refuse to accept it? Or ignore it?

Rousseau and His Readers

7. How could Rousseau assert that women were unsuited to study the sciences? What evidence did he produce? What arguments might persuade his contemporary readers?

8. According to Rousseau, what would women gain from the "study of men, and the attainment of agreeable accomplishments"?

9. Mary Wollstonecraft thought Rousseau's views on women were "nonsense." Why?

SAMPLE LECTURE 17: THE AGE OF ENLIGHTENMENT

Lecture Objectives

1. To explore the foundations of Enlightenment thinking in general

2. To show how the philosophes used reason as a starting point for the general reform of society

3. To show how Enlightenment ideas help us to understand the modern age

THE FOUNDATIONS OF THE ENLIGHTENMENT

The Enlightenment was a cultural and intellectual movement of the eighteenth century. Cosmopolitan in outlook, the Enlightenment spread its ideas throughout Europe, Russia, Great Britain, and the United States. In this respect it was also a transatlantic happening. The philosophes would have felt themselves at home in London, Edinburgh, Paris, Berlin, and St. Petersburg just easily as they would have in Boston, New York, or Philadelphia. Thanks to Isaac Newton, human reason was capable of explaining the natural world. But Newton's ideas had wide application to man and society. If Newton could explain the cosmos using reason, then it seemed possible—indeed, even essential—that the most advanced thinkers of the eighteenth century would use reason to explain the mysterious workings of society. But reason needed autonomy and freedom to embark on such a path. In general, the philosophes shared a faith in the power of human reason. The medieval synthesis, based as it was on a matrix of Christianity, had broken down over the past several centuries. Under attack by Renaissance humanists, Luther and the Reformation, and the discoveries of the New Science, medieval Christianity was no longer capable of explaining humanity. The philosophes had to break free from centuries of what they identified as intolerance, bigotry, prejudice, enthusiasm, and fanaticism in order to recreate themselves, in order to make their own history, guided by reason.

In many respects, the Enlightenment of the eighteenth century highlights an age obsessed with creating its own unique identity. However, unlike the Renaissance humanists who went back to the classical world to find virtues worthy of emulation in the present, the philosophes made the conscious decision to create themselves according to the principles of human reason alone. And it would be the principles of human reason as expressed by the "Holy Trinity" of Bacon, Newton, and Locke. This is the meaning of Voltaire's battle cry, "*Écrasez l'infâme!*"—"wipe out the infamous!" Sweep away anything that did not conform to human reason. This quest for identity is also illustrated by the fact that the philosophes called their own age an age of enlightenment. Historians use that label to define the age, but they did not themselves create the label. The philosophes did, and this should tell us a great deal about what the philosophes thought about themselves

Although the philosophes rarely agreed with one another on every question, they were united in combating whatever did not conform to reason. Using reason and its twin, criticism, the philosophes believed in the improvement of human knowledge, happiness, and morality. Humanity, then, was capable of much more if only one had the courage to use one's own reason. Or, as Immanuel Kant put it in his essay, *What is Enlightenment?* (1784), "*Sapere Aude!*" Dare to Know!" The philosophes were indeed an eclectic lot but together they comprised a "party of humanity." The general characteristics of the Enlightenment were:

- faith in the power of reason
- self-confidence
- belief that reason needed autonomy and freedom
- determination that all knowledge should be organized
- spread of knowledge through unfettered public discussion
- ireverence toward custom and tradition
- belief in progress and human perfectibility
- belief in the uniformity of human nature
- belief that society can and must be reformed

The foundations of this set of opinions were fashioned by Bacon, Locke, and Newton. Bacon laid the groundwork for the new scientific method and Newton showed that humanity was capable of unlocking the mysteries of the universe. John Locke gave the eighteenth century his political theory and theory of human knowledge based on experience alone.

THE PHILOSOPHES

The thinker who personified the Enlightenment was François Marie Arouet, better known as Voltaire (1694–1778). Voltaire was educated by the Jesuits and as a young man spent time in the Bastille for libel. After his release he exiled himself to England, where he became a great admirer and popularizer of all things British. It was thanks to Voltaire that Newton's ideas became popular among thinkers who were not themselves versed in the sciences or in mathematics. In his *Philosophical Letters* (1734), Voltaire celebrated the open-mindedness, empiricism, and religious and political liberties of the British. Only in England, Voltaire added, could one find true religious toleration. Of course, Voltaire's observations on the British served as a condemnation of the *ancien régime* in France. Voltaire loathed religious bigotry and fanaticism. He did not, however, oppose religion. Instead, he sought to rescue morality from its narrow dogmatic confines. His goal was to bring reason to bear on everything. He was a man of common sense and simplicity. What Erasmus was to the sixteenth century, Voltaire was to the eighteenth century.

Baron de Montesquieu (1689–1755) was born of a noble family and served as a magistrate in the *Parlement* of Bordeaux. His earliest work was *The Persian Letters*, published in 1721. In a series of letters between two Persian visitors to France, Montesquieu presented a thinly-veiled criticism of France by suggesting that French absolutism was similar to Persian despotism. Montesquieu's major work was *The Spirit of the Laws*. A work in comparative historical sociology, Montesquieu asked how structures and institutions shape laws. He characterized three different forms of government, each defined by a specific quality:

* republic (virtue)
* monarchy (honor)
* despotism (fear)

Like Voltaire, Montesquieu admired the British system of separate and balanced powers with its use of checks and balances to control any drift toward despotism. Of course, like *The Persian Letters*, Montesquieu's *Spirit of the Laws* was critical of the *ancien régime* in France.

One of the greatest philosophical enterprises of the eighteenth century was the multivolume *Encyclopedia*, edited by Denis Diderot (1713–1784). Diderot's plan was to create a vast compendium of human knowledge that would at the same time give the grandest statement of the goals of the philosophes. Diderot understood that a scientific analysis of human reason would also lead to the general happiness and progress of humanity. With the able assistance of the mathematician Jean d'Alembert (1717–1783), the *Encyclopedia* was published over a period of twenty years (1751–1772) and resulted in seventeen large volumes of text with an additional eleven volumes of illustrations. The *Encyclopedia*:

* attempted to change the general way of thinking
* demonstrated how the application of science would promote progress
* enjoyed widespread circulation despite its enormous cost
* was eventually discontinued by the French government for trying to "propagate materialism"

The inclusion of illustrations is important to recognize. The illustrations give graphic representation to all the arts then available: weaving, cannon-making, spinning, coal mining, rope-making, etc. In other words, Diderot was trying to spread human knowledge by revealing the secrets of each and every trade. Articles were written by numerous philosophes, some of whom remained anonymous.

GENERAL THEMES

The Enlightenment was certainly an international movement. French books were widely distributed and read by a middle- and upper-class culture on both sides of the Atlantic. Humanitarianism was one such theme that was illustrated by the work of the Italian philosophe, Cesare Beccaria (1738–1794). In his book *On Crimes and Punishments* (1764), Beccaria attacked the prevailing view that punishment represented the vengeance of society upon the criminal. Beccaria argued that the legitimate rationale for punishment was to maintain order and prevent other crimes. He opposed torture and the death penalty. One of the key features of the Enlightenment hinged upon the issue of religious toleration. The philosophes desired an end to religious warfare and the persecution of heretics and religious minorities. Very few of the philosophes were atheists (also called materialists). Most of them, like Voltaire, Tom Paine, or Thomas Jefferson, were deists who saw God as the "divine clockmaker." It was God who created the world, but it was left to man to explain that world. However, most philosophes also viewed Judaism and Islam as backward religions. Two philosophes, Gotthold Lessing (1729–1781) and Moses Mendelssohn (1729–1786), treated Jews sympathetically.

The rising states and empires of the eighteenth century made economic issues increasingly important. The French physiocrats were perhaps the first to argue that mercantilist policies were misguided. The physiocrats:

* argued that real material wealth comes from the land (agriculture)
* advocated a simplified tax system
* suggested that wealth and goods ought to circulate freely without government interference
* helped create the notion of *laissez-faire*

Although he was a professor of moral philosophy at Edinburgh, Adam Smith (1723–1790) took the ideas of the physiocrats and wrote the classic statement of laissez-faire. Smith's *Inquiry Into the Nature and Causes of the Wealth of Nations* (1776), a massive work of economic history, illustrated the passing of mercantilism and its replacement by "liberal" economics. The general conclusions of the *Wealth of Nations* were:

* The central issue of the economy was the productivity of human labor.
* Mercantile restrictions did not create economic health.
* The "invisible hand" of the marketplace ought to guide economic activity.
* Rational individuals ought to be allowed to pursue their interests rationally.
* There are specific stages of economic growth.

COLONIZATION AND EMPIRE

Of course, the acquisition of empire in the eighteenth century forced the philosophes to think above and beyond economics. In the new world of the Pacific, North and South America, Australia, and elsewhere, the philosophes' attention was drawn to the natural humanity and simplicity of native peoples. The slave trade from Africa to the Caribbean and North American colonies also forced them to consider the issues of the individual rights of man as well as natural law. Abbé Raynal (1713–1796) wrote a philosophical history of European colonization in the Indies (1770). Raynal:

- looked at natural history, exploration, and commerce
- condemned the Spanish in Mexico and Peru
- criticized the Portuguese in Brazil and the British in North America
- suggested that a good government required checks and balances

Raynal concluded by arguing that the major problem of colonization was that Europeans had unlimited power in the New World. As the slave trade hit its peak in the mid-eighteenth century, Raynal and Diderot criticized slavery because it defied natural law and natural freedom. Slavery was seen as a violation of self-government, although few philosophes went so far as to suggest the total abolition of slavery.

The eighteenth century was generally fascinated by accounts of the Pacific islands that began to filter back into Europe by mid-century. Louis-Antoine de Bougainville (1729–1811) was sent to the South Pacific by the French government and described Tahiti. Captain Cook (1728–1779) explored the coasts of New Zealand, New Hebrides, and Hawaii as well as the Arctic and Antarctic Oceans. Diderot used these voyages of discovery in his *Supplément au Voyage de Bougainville* (1772), a short work that:

- depicted the Tahitians as "original" human beings
- described humanity in its natural state
- celebrated the Tahitian's uninhibited sexuality and freedom from religious dogma

Diderot concluded the *Supplément* by contrasting the simplicity and moral goodness of the Tahitians with the problems experienced by overcivilized Europeans. In many respects, the vogue in travel literature also offered the philosophes a vehicle with which to criticize contemporary European society.

HOW REVOLUTIONARY WAS THE ENLIGHTENMENT?

Historians have long pondered the relationship between the ideas of the philosophes and the tumultuous years of the French Revolution. There is perhaps no direct causal relationship between the two, but historians agree that the philosophes created a "climate of opinion" which created a general dislike for "things as they were" (the *ancien régime*).

No philosophe advocated revolution, since tumult and violence were anathema to their program of reform. However, there were clearly some radical ideas that emanated from the Enlightenment.

Jean-Jacques Rousseau (1712–1778) was perhaps the most utopian of all philosophes. He quarreled with and contradicted other philosophes—he was an outsider looking in. He attacked privilege and believed that the natural goodness of humanity had been corrupted by society. In one of the most important works of modern political theory, *The Social Contract* (1762), he wrote, "Man was born free, and everywhere he is in chains." In *The Social Contract*, Rousseau:

- outlined the origins of civil society and government
- explained the legitimacy of government
- criticized social inequality and private property
- argued that sovereignty should not be divided among different branches of government
- concluded that the nation ought to be united by the "general will"
- suggested that citizens ought to be bound by mutual obligation and not coercive laws

In his book on education, *Émile, ou l'education* (1762), Rousseau argued that children should not be forced to reason early in life. The aim of all education was moral autonomy and good citizenship. For Rousseau, what was natural was preferable because it was simpler and uncorrupted by human institutions. Rousseau's ideas on gender issues were discussed in his immensely popular novel, *Julie, ou al Héloïse* (1761), which went through seventy editions in thirty years. There Rousseau suggested that humans are ruled by the hearts as much as their minds. Rousseau introduced the notion of sensibility and the "cult of feeling" in the *Émile* and *Julie*, themes that would be taken up by the Romantics in their criticism of the Enlightenment. Rousseau also helped create the issue of gender for the eighteenth century:

- If education was the key to progress, did this mean education for men and women?
- Were men and women different?
- Did men and women have identical natural rights?
- Were gender differences natural or socially created?

Rousseau's sharpest critic was Mary Wollstonecraft (1759–1797), a British republican writer, wife of the philosophical anarchist, William Godwin, and mother of Mary Shelley. Her circle of friends included Joseph Priestly and Richard Price as well as numerous radical publishers in London. Her *Vindication of the Rights of Man* (1791) served as the first response to Edmund Burke's *Reflections on the Revolution in France*. The following year Wollstonecraft spoke against inequality and the artificial distinctions of rank, birth, or wealth in *A Vindication of the Rights of Women*. She wrote that society ought to seek "the perfection of our nature and capability of happiness." Her radical republicanism also led her to argue that women had the same innate capacity for reason and self-government as men and that virtue (the republican ideal) meant the same thing to both men and women. Finally, the relations between the sexes ought to be based on equality. Wollstonecraft criticized the family:

- The family illustrated the legal inequalities of marriage law.
- Women were taught to be dependent and seductive in order to win husbands.
- A proper education should promote liberty and self-reliance.

Although Wollstonecraft was consistently ridiculed in the popular press, she did suggest the common humanity of men and women and that both men and women had natural rights, both of which were advanced ideas for the age.

EIGHTEENTH-CENTURY CULTURE AND THE ENLIGHTENMENT

The program of the philosophes can only be understood if it is recognized that there was a growing reading public eager for its ideas. Printing and print culture had expanded, as had an international and clandestine book trade. At the same time, the number of daily newspapers had increased. The British press was relatively free of restraints, while the French censored books, thus making them more expensive. By the mid-eighteenth century there existed subversive ("philosophical") literature of all kinds in a sort of literary underground.

More readers led to new forms of sociability and discussion, especially among the new elite culture, which was small but cosmopolitan in outlook. This elite or high culture also joined together members of the nobility and the wealthiest members of the middle classes. Learned societies such as the American Philosophical Society of Philadelphia also organized intellectual life outside the university. (The majority of philosophes were not associated with the universities—Adam Smith and Immanuel Kant were two exceptions.) These societies provided libraries and meeting places for discussion, and many published their own journals. Organized by wealthy aristocratic women and located in all major cities, the eighteenth-century salon brought together the philosophes with their upper-class audience. Coffeehouses also aided in the circulation of new ideas. Meanwhile, Masonic lodges and other secret societies pledged themselves to rational thought in all human affairs. What all this discussion signified was the ability of more and more people to think and criticize freely. In the political world, this meant that politics moved beyond the court and into the public sphere.

A different reading public developed within a middle-class culture of shopkeepers, small merchants, lawyers, and other professionals. This group:

- bought and borrowed books
- opularized Enlightenment treatises on education
- also helped increase the popularity of the novel

In other words, the novels of Defoe, Fielding, Richardson, Edgeworth, and Austen were made popular by a middle-class audience eager for the empirical approach and style of the novel. The rise of the novel is then consistent with the growth of the middle classes in Britain, Europe, and the United States.

Urban and rural popular culture varied by gender, class, and location. Broadsides, woodcuts, prints, drawings, cartoons, and "blue books" were all available to the urban and rural working classes. Guild organizations offered discussion and companionship, and market days and village festivals continued to be occasions in which oral and literate cultures overlapped. The philosophes pretty much overlooked this segment of the population, since they looked at the popular classes with distrust and ignorance. In the end, it seemed that for the majority of philosophes the general enlightenment of humanity needed to begin at the top of society, not the bottom.

SUGGESTED FEATURE FILMS

Barry Lyndon. 187 min. Color. 1975. Warner. Stanley Kubrick's masterful production of Thackeray's novel about an eighteenth-century rogue.

Dangerous Liaisons. 119 min. Color. 1988. Lorimar Film Entertainment. Film set in France in the 1760s about a scheming widow, her lover, and a bet regarding the corruption of a recently married woman. See also Milos Forman's *Valmont* (1989).

The Madness of King George. 103 min. Color. 1994. Goldwyn. With a screenplay by Alan Bennett, this film explores the clash between madness and sanity, modernity and tradition, in the late-eighteenth-century world of George III.

Mutiny on the Bounty. 135 min. B/W. 1935. MGM. With Charles Laughton and Clark Gable.

Mutiny on the Bounty. 185 min. Color. 1962. MGM. With Marlon Brando. Tale of an ill-fated eighteenth-century commercial venture.

La Religieuse (The Nun). 135 min. Color. 1966. Altura Films International. Based on a novel by Denis Diderot about a young woman forced against her will to take vows as a nun.

Sense and Sensibility. Approx. 2 hours. Color. 1995. Columbia. Emma Thompson wrote and starred in this brilliant dramatization of Jane Austen's novel.

Tom Jones. 129 min. Color. 1963. Universal. A delightful version of Fielding's novel. With Albert Finney and Susannah York.

Voltaire. 72 min. B/W. 1933. Warner. With George Arliss as the philosophe.

SUGGESTED CLASSROOM FILMS

The Christians: Politeness and Enthusiasm (1689–1791). 45 min. Color. 1978. McGraw-Hill. Compares and contrasts the Church of England of the eighteenth century with the revivalist faith of Methodism.

Civilisation: A Personal View by Kenneth Clark. No. 9— The Pursuit of Happiness. 52 min. Color. 1970. BBC/Time-Life Films. Eighteenth-century music and architecture.

Moliere: The Misanthrope. 49 min. Color. 1975. Films for the Humanities and Sciences. A dramatization.

The Enlightenment. 2 parts, 30 min. each. Color. 1989. Insight Media. Focuses on the unlikely alliances between the philosophes and the absolutist rulers.

The Enlightenment and the Age of Louis XIV. 30 min. Color. 1985. Insight Media. Interprets the Enlightenment as a clash between the old ideas of hierarchy and new ideas of liberty, equality, and fraternity.

Part VI: The French and Industrial Revolutions and Their Consequences

IDEAS FOR USING THE WESTERN CIVILIZATIONS DIGITAL HISTORY CENTER

The Map Exercises and Digital History Features at *www.wwnorton.com/wciv* can be used to examine the social, political, and economic effects of the French and Industrial Revolutions during the nineteenth century.

- Map Exercise 11: Europe in the Eighteenth Century (Chapter 18)
- Map Exercise 12: The French Revolution and Napoleon (Chapter 18)
- Map Exercise 13: The Industrial Revolution (Chapter 19)
- Map Exercise 14: Revolution and Nationalism in the Nineteenth Century (Chapters 20–21)
- Map Exercise 15: Nineteenth-Century America (Chapters 20-21)
- Digital History Feature 8: Revolutionary Paris (Chapter 18)
- Digital History Feature 9: Nationalism and Music (Chapter 21)

Use Map Exercise 11 in your lecture and classroom discussions to demonstrate why eighteenth-century wars no longer revolved around religious issues, and also how the Seven Years' War was a global war that had drastic results for France and Great Britain. Map Exercise 12 highlights the ways in which the French revolutionaries and Napoleon rationalized and streamlined the administration of the French nation. The speed at which Great Britain and Europe industrialized in the first half of the nineteenth century is suggested in Map Exercise 13. Use Map Exercise 14 to investigate the growth and development of nationalist ideologies in central and eastern Europe. These exercises will also help you show students just how explosive ethnic and linguistic diversity could become, especially in an age of nationalism. The Digital History Feature "Music and Nationalism" could be used at this point to illustrate the ways in which the nationalist spirit of central Europe found an outlet in "poetic symphonies" that exalted the people and their common heritage. The Digital History Feature "Revolutionary Paris" looks at the city of Paris from the standpoint of four specific moments of its history: 1789, 1830, 1848, and 1968. You can use this feature as a way to discuss the mob in European history, or perhaps the ways in which an urban environment seems to be the breeding ground for revolutionary activity. Looking at the city of Paris over a period of two hundred years also reveals something about revolutions in general. Use Map Exercises 14 and 15 to draw attention to the nationalist endeavor in both the United States and Europe in the nineteenth century. You could also compare the efforts to unify Germany and Italy with the problems facing the United States during this period.

CHAPTER 18 | The French Revolution

3. The peasantry
   a. Owed obligations to landlord, church, and state
   b. Direct and indirect taxation a heavy burden
   c. The *corvée*
4. Finances
   a. Inefficient tax system
   b. Taxation tied to social status and varied from region to region
   c. Paying off the debts of Louis XIV
5. Administration
   a. Louis XVI was anxious to serve as an enlightened monarch
      i. His efforts at reform undermined his own authority
   b. Turgot and Necker as finance ministers
   c. Marie Antoinette and the dispensation of patronage among her friends
   d. Tensions between the central governments and the provincial parlements slowed reform
      i. Parlements defend nobility's exemption from paying taxes to pay for the Seven Years' War
D. General conclusions on the eve of the Revolution
   a. Louis XVI was a weak monarch
   b. Chaotic financial situation
   c. Severe social tensions
IV. The Destruction of the Old Regime
   A. Moderate stage, June 1789–August 1792
   B. Fiscal crisis
      1. Calonne and Brienne proposed new taxes, a stamp duty, and direct tax on agricultural produce
      2. Louis summons the Assembly of Notables (last called in 1626)
      3. Aristocrats used the financial emergency to extract constitutional reforms
      4. Insisted that any new tax scheme be approved by the Estates-General
   C. The Estates-General
      1. Summoned by Louis in summer, 1788 (first time since 1614)
      2. The three estates elected delegates
         a. Delegates draw up the *cahiers et doléances* (list of grievances)
         b. Delegates of the Third Estate represented the outlook of the elite
            i. 25 percent lawyers, 43 percent government officials

ii. Strong sense of common grievance and common purpose
3. Areas of disagreement
   a. Should the estates vote by estate or by individual?
   b. Abbé Sieyès, *What is the Third Estate?* (1789)
   c. Third Estate agreed the Estate delegates should sit together and vote as individuals
      i. Also insisted the Third Estate have as many delegates as the First and Second Estates combined
4. "Doubling the Third"
   a. Louis opposed, then changed his position (December 1788)
5. June 17, 1789: the delegates of the Third Estate declared themselves to be the National Assembly
6. June 20, 1789: the Oath of the Tennis Court
7. June 27, 1789: Louis ordered all delegates to join the National Assembly
D. The first stages of the French Revolution
   1. Popular revolts
      a. Public attention to the events in Paris was high
      b. Price of bread soared
      c. Rumors circulated that Louis was about to stage a coup d'état
      d. Parisian workers (*sans-culottes*) organized a militia of volunteers
   2. July 14, 1789: the fall of the Bastille
      a. Bastille as symbol of royal authority
      b. Its fall as symbol of the people's role in revolutionary change
   3. The Great Fear
      a. Rumors that the king's armies were on their way
      b. Peasants attacked and burned manor houses
      c. Destroyed manor records
   4. The October Days
      a. Brought on by economic crisis
      b. Demanded Louis return to Paris
      c. Parisian women marched to Versailles (October 5) and demanded to be heard
      d. The National Guard led Louis back to Paris
   5. August 4, 1789: National Assembly abolished all forms of privilege

a. Church tithe, the *corvée*, hunting privileges, tax exemptions, and monopolies

b. Obliterated the remnants of feudalism

E. The National Assembly and the liberal revolution

1. The Declaration of the Rights of Man and Citizen

   a. Written in August, issued in September

   b. Declared natural rights

      i. Private property

      ii. Liberty, security, and resistance to oppression

   c. Declared freedom of speech, religious toleration, and liberty of the press to be inviolable

   d. Equality before the law

2. Man and citizen

   a. "Passive citizen": guaranteed rights under law

   b. "Active citizens": paid taxes, could vote and hold office

      i. Represented about half of all male citizens

      ii. They could only vote for "electors"

3. National Assembly

   a. Full civil rights to Protestants and Jews

   b. Abolished serfdom and banned slavery in France

4. The rights of women

   a. Wollstonecraft, *A Vindication of the Rights of Women* (1792)

   b. Olympe de Gouges, *Declaration of the Rights of Women and Citizen* (1791)

      i. Women have the same rights as men

5. Women and the Revolution

   a. General participation in the Revolution

      i. Joined clubs, demonstrations, and debates

      ii. Women as citizens

6. Religion and the Revolution

   a. The most divisive issue

   b. National Assembly confiscated church property (November 1789)

   c. Used this property as collateral for the issue of *assignats* (revolutionary currency)

d. The Civil Constitution of the Clergy (July 1791)

   i. Bishops and clergy subject to the laws of the state

   ii. Salaries to be paid from public treasury

e. Church reforms polarized France

   i. Many resented the privileged position of the church

   ii. Parish church an institution of great local importance

7. Other reforms of the National Assembly

   a. Sold off church lands

   b. Abolished guilds

   c. Restructured local governments

   d. France was divided into eighty-three equal departments

   e. The defense of liberty and freedom from ancient privilege

V. A New Stage: Popular Revolution

A. The Radical Revolution, August 1792– July 1794

1. From moderate leaders to radical republicans

2. Why did the Revolution become radical?

   a. The politicization of the common people, especially in cities

      i. Newspapers

      ii. Political clubs

      iii. Greater political awareness heightened by fluctuations in prices

      iv. Demands for cheaper bread

      v. Demands for government to do something about inflation

   b. Lack of effective national leadership

      i. Louis XVI remained a weak and vacillating monarch

      ii. Forced to accept the Civil Constitution of the Clergy

      iii. Louis urged on by Marie Antoinette, sister of Leopold II of Austria

      iv. June 20, 1791: the Flight to Varennes

      v. Louis now a "prisoner" of the Revolution

   c. War

      i. All Europeans took a side in the conflict

      ii. Political societies formed outside France proclaimed their allegiance to the Revolution

B. The counterrevolution
  1. The *emigrés* stirred up counterrevolutionary sentiment
  2. Edmund Burke (1729–1797), *Reflections on the Revolution in France* (1790)
      a. Attacked the revolution as a crime against the social order
      b. The French had turned their back on history
      c. Men and women had no natural rights
      d. Aroused sympathy for the counterrevolutionary cause
  3. Thomas Paine (1737–1809), *The Rights of Man* (1791–92)
      a. Written in response to Burke's *Reflections*
      b. Political liberalism
  4. Outside France
      a. Austria and Prussia declared support for French monarchy (August 1791)
      b. April 20, 1792: the National Assembly declared war on Austria and Prussia
  5. National Assembly expected the war to bolster public opinion behind the Revolution
  6. Radicals hoped the war would expose "traitors"
  7. August 1792: Austria and Prussia close to capturing Paris
  8. August 10, 1792: Parisians attacked the king's palace
C. The Jacobins
  1. More egalitarian leaders of the Third Estate
  2. Membership extended throughout France
  3. Jacobins proclaimed themselves the voice of the people and the nation
  4. The National Convention (September 1792)
  5. The September Massacres
      a. Patriotic Paris mobs convened revolutionary tribunal to try traitors
      b. Over a thousand killed in one week
  5. The end of the French monarchy
      a. France declared a republic (September 21, 1792)
      b. Louis placed on trial (December 1792)
      c. Louis executed (January 23, 1793)
  6. The National Convention and domestic reforms
      a. Abolition of slavery in French colonies
      b. Repeal of primogeniture
      c. Confiscated property of enemies of the Revolution
      d. Set maximum prices for grain
      e. The revolutionary calendar
  7. Small armies of sans-culottes attacked hoarders and profiteers
  8. Military reforms
      a. France faced Britain, Holland, Spain, and Austria (February 1793)
      b. French revolutionary armies
      c. The revolutionary government drafted all men capable of bearing arms (August 1793)
      d. French military successes
          i. Low Countries, Rhineland, Switzerland, parts of Spain, and Savoy
D. The Reign of Terror
  1. Convention delayed adoption of constitution with male suffrage (1793)
  2. The Committee of Public Safety (CPS)
      a. The Twelve
  3. New radical leaders
      a. Jean-Paul Marat (1743–1793)
          i. Did not admire Great Britain
          ii. Opposed moderates
          iii. Edited *The Friend of the People*
          iv. Killed by Charlotte Corday, a royalist (summer 1793)
      b. Georges-Jacques Danton (1759–1794)
          i. Popular political leader
          ii. Member of the CPS
          iii. Wearied of the Terror
          iv. Sent to the guillotine (April 1794)
      c. Maximilien Robespierre (1758–1794)
          i. Trained as a lawyer
          ii. Became president of the National Convention
          iii. Member of the CPS
          iv. Enlarged the Terror
  4. Committee faced sabotage from the political left and right
          i. Need for absolute control
          ii. The "Mountain" allies with Parisian artisans
          iii. Rebellions: Lyons, Bordeaux, and Marseilles
          iv. CPS rounds up suspects in the countryside

      v. September 1793–July 1794: executions as high as twenty-five to thirty thousand

      vi. Five hundred thousand incarcerated between March 1793 and August 1794

E. The legacy of the second French Revolution

  1. The sans-culottes

    a. Workers' trousers replaced breeches

    b. The red cap of liberty

    c. Citizen and citizeness

    d. Festivals

  2. Second revolution reversed trend toward decentralization

    a. Replaced local officials with "deputies on mission"

    b. Closed down women's political clubs

  3. The erosion of traditional institutions

    a. Church, guild, and parish

    b. Replaced with patriotic organizations

  4. Mobilization for revolution

  5. Counterrevolutionary groups were also popular movements

VI. From the Terror to Bonaparte: The Directory

A. The Ninth of Thermidor (July 27, 1794)

  1. Robespierre kicked out of the Convention

  2. Guillotined the following day (along with twenty-one other "conspirators")

B. After Thermidor

  1. Jacobins driven into hiding

  2. Law of maximum prices repealed

  3. National Convention adopted new conservative constitution (1795)

    a. Suffrage for all adult males who could read and write

    b. Indirect elections

      i. Citizens voted for electors, who chose the legislative body

      ii. Wealthy citizens held authority

    c. Constitution included a bill of rights

C. The Directory

  1. Five men chosen by the legislative body

  2. Could not stabilize the government

  3. Faced discontent on the radical left and conservative right

    a. On the left

      i. Stopped radical movements to abolish private property

      ii. Graachus Babeuf

    b. On the right

      i. Elections in March 1797 returned a large number of constitutional monarchists

  4. Could not control developments

  5. Called Napoleon Bonaparte to their assistance

  6. Napoleon Bonaparte (1769–1821)

    a. Recaptured Toulon from the British (1793)

    b. Made brigadier general at age twenty-four

    c. Delivered the "whiff of grapeshot" that saved the Convention (1795)

    d. Victories in the Italian campaign

    e. Attempted to defeat Britain by attacking British forces in Egypt and the Near East

    f. French fleet defeated by Nelson at Abukir Bay (1798)

    g. Napoleon declared a "temporary consul" (18 Brumaire, November 9, 1799)

D. The Haitian Revolution

  1. The Caribbean sugar trade and slavery

  2. Delegation from St. Domingue asked to be seated by the Assembly

  3. The Assembly refused

  4. Mulatto rebellion in St. Domingue (August 1791)

  5. Slave rebellion—British and Spanish invaded

  6. The success of the rebellion

    a. France made free men of color citizens

  7. Toussaint-Louverture (c. 1743–1803)

    a. Victorious over French planters, the British, and the Spanish

    b. Set up a constitution (1801)

      i. Slavery abolished

      ii. Reorganized the military

      iii. Christianity established as state religion

  8. Napoleon sends twenty thousand troops to bring the island under control (January 1802)

  9. Toussaint captured and brought to France (died in 1803)

  10. The war became a French nightmare, the army collapsed (December 1803)

  11. Haiti declared its independence (1804)

VII. Napoleon and Imperial France

A. Did Napoleon consolidate or repudiate the Revolution?

B. Consolidating authority, 1799–1804
 1. Napoleon rose from obscurity to become the savior of France
 2. Was able to master his plans in every detail
 3. Assumed title of First Consul and governed in the name of the Republic (1799)
 4. New constitution
  a. Universal male suffrage
  b. Two legislative bodies
  c. The plebiscite—put questions directly to popular vote
   i. Bypassed politicians and legislative bodies
 5. Asked the legislature to proclaim him consul for life (1802)
 6. The reorganization of the state
  a. Abolition of privileges
  b. "Careers open to talent"
  c. Generally fair system of taxation
   i. Halted the inflationary spiral
  d. Replaced local elected officials with centrally appointed prefects and subprefects
C. Law, education, and a new elite
 1. The Napoleonic Code (1804)
  a. Uniformity and individualism
  b. Abolition of all feudal privileges
  c. Property rights
  d. Paternal authority and the subordination of women and children
  e. Equality before the law
  f. Outlawed arbitrary arrest and imprisonment
 2. Rationalized the educational system
  a. Established *lycées* (high schools) to train civil servants
  b. Brought military and technical schools under state control
  c. Founded a national university to supervise the entire system
 3. Benefited the new elites (businessmen, bankers, and merchants)
D. Other issues
 1. Made allies without regard to their political past or affiliations
 2. Readmitted the *emigrés*
 3. The Concordat of 1801
  a. Ended hostility between France and the church
  b. Pope had the right to depose bishops and discipline the clergy
  c. Church lands expropriated by the Revolution would not return to the church

 4. Married the ambitious Josephine de Beauharnais
 5. Napoleon crowns himself Napoleon I at Notre Dame (December 1801)
E. In Europe as in France: Napoleonic wars of expansion
 1. Collapse of the First Coalition— Austria, Prussia, Britain (1795), revived in 1798
 2. Russia and Austria withdrew (1801)
 3. The new empire
  a. Series of small republics from Austria's empire and old German kingdoms
  b. France's revolutionary "gift" of independence to all European patriots
  c. Military buffers and system of client states
  d. The Confederation of the Rhine
 4. Napoleon introduced his reforms throughout the new empire
  a. Eliminated manorial and church courts
  b. Careers open to talent
  c. Equality before the law
  d. Created a vast bureaucratic networks
  e. All government emanated from Paris and Napoleon
 5. The new empire as a mixed blessing
  a. In some areas of Europe, Napoleon was regarded as the great liberator
  b. In other areas, the local lord and priest had been replaced by the French tax collector
VIII. The Return to War and Napoleon's Defeat, 1806–1815
 A. The Continental System
  1. Blockade of British goods from the continent (1806)
  2. Napoleon's first serious mistake
   a. British developed trade with South America
   b. Europe divided into economic camps
 B. Napoleon's ambition
  1. Remaking Europe as new Roman Empire, ruled from Paris
  2. Republican Roman ideals—art, architecture, clothing
  3. Made his brothers and sisters monarchs of newly created kingdoms
  4. Divorced Josephine (1809), married Marie Louise, daughter of Francis I (Habsburg)

C. Continuing war
   1. France against Russia, Prussia, Austria, Sweden, and Britain
   2. Napoleon on the battlefield
      a. Personally led his men
      b. Shock attacks
      c. The *Grande Armee*
      d. Battle of Austerlitz (December 1805)
      e. Prussian army humiliated at Jena (1806)
   3. French defeat at Trafalgar (1805)
   4. The invasion of Spain (1808)
      a. Invasion aimed at conquest of Portugal
      b. Napoleon installed his brother on the Spanish throne
      c. Guerilla warfare
   5. The Russian campaign (1812)
      a. Ended in disaster
      b. Russians drew the French further into Russia
      c. Napoleon ordered his troops to retreat (October 19, 1812)
      d. The Russian winter
   6. Renewed attacks by Prussia, Russia, Austria, Sweden, and Britain
      a. Wars of liberation
      b. The Battle of Nations (October 1813)
      c. Tsar Alexander I and Frederick William III enter Paris (March 31, 1814)
   7. Napoleon's abdication
      a. Exile at Elba
   8. The Bourbon Restoration of Louis XVIII (brother of Louis XVI)
   9. The Last One Hundred Days
      a. The Battle of Waterloo (June 15–18, 1815)
      b. Exile on St. Helena
IX. Conclusion
   A. The French Revolution and popular movements
   B. Liberty, equality, and nation
   C. Europe polarized

GENERAL DISCUSSION QUESTIONS

1. In what ways does the French Revolution signify the onset of the modern world? What is the legacy of the Revolution?

2. What were the causes of the French Revolution? Why did a revolution occur in France—one of Europe's strongest nations—and not elsewhere in Europe?

[handwritten: 1— How does French Reval. compare to Brittish and what kind of american?]

3. Who were the leaders of the moderate stage of the Revolution? How did leadership change after it passed into the hands of the Jacobins?

4. What role did the French people play in the course of the Revolution? In what ways did they contribute to the radicalism of the Revolution after August 1792?

5. Why was Louis XVI placed on trial and eventually executed in January 1793?

6. Why did the Jacobins under Robespierre and the Committee of Public Safety institute a Reign of Terror? What does the Terror tell you about revolutions in general?

7. Comment on the following: Napoleon embraced the ideas of the Revolution at the same time that he perverted them. In what ways did the Revolution "make" Napoleon?

8. Was Napoleon mistaken in thinking that efficiency in government was more important than popular representation or political participation?

9. What is the connection between the French Revolution and nineteenth-century ideologies like liberalism, conservatism, socialism, communism, and nationalism?

10. Comment on the following statement by François Furet: "In 1789, the French had created a Republic, under the name of a monarchy. Ten years later, they created a monarchy, under the name of a Republic."

DOCUMENT DISCUSSION QUESTIONS

What Is the Third Estate?

1. Why did Abbé Sieyès, a successful member of the First Estate, side with the Third Estate? Upon what basis did he justify his position?

2. Do you feel that Sieyès was trying to incite a revolution?

3. Sieyès offered his criticism in the form of a pamphlet. If Sieyès were alive today, how would he have broadcast his message?

Declaration of the Rights of Man

4. How could a group of deputies elected to advise Louis XVI on constitutional reforms proclaim themselves a National Assembly? Why was the creation of the National Assembly a truly revolutionary act?

5. In what ways was the *Declaration of the Rights of Man* a moral document? What is it about the style or tone of the *Declaration* that identifies is as a peculiarly eighteenth-century document?

Olympe de Gouges, Declaration of the Rights of Women

6. Why did Gouges write that men were "blocked by science and degenerate, in the century of enlightenment and wisdom"? Were male revolutionaries somehow different from other men? How are revolutionaries "made"?

Debating the Revolution: Edmund Burke and Thomas Paine

7. What sort of liberties does Burke have in mind when he suggests that they are "an entailed inheritance derived to us from our forefathers"?

8. Why does Burke argue that the "good things" of civilization are based upon the "spirit of a gentleman" and the "spirit of religion"?

9. Paine mentions a change in the meaning of "revolutions." What was this change? Can you cite more recent examples of both kinds of revolutions?

SAMPLE LECTURE 18: THE FRENCH REVOLUTION, 1789–1799

Lecture Objectives

1. To grasp the social origins of the French Revolution

2. To understand the narrative chronology of the Revolution

3. To understand the differences between the aims of the "men of 1789" and the aims of the radical stage of the Revolution

Overture: The End of the *Ancien Régime*

The French Revolution seemed to many observers to have realized the lofty ideals of the Enlightenment. Liberty had triumphed over tyranny. New institutions were created on the foundations of human reason and justice alone and not on authority or blind faith. For the revolutionary generation, it seemed as if the natural, inalienable rights of man had become an instant reality. So 1789 stands as a pivotal year—a watershed. The revolutionaries believed that the future would be one of moral and intellectual improvement. This optimism could only have been possible in an age whose spokesmen proudly proclaimed it to be an age of enlightenment. The enthusiasm with which this dawn of a New Jerusalem was announced was often colored with religious zeal. And so, on November 4, 1789, the Protestant minister Richard Price (1723–1791) addressed a crowd of fifty members of the Society for the Commemoration of the Revolution in Great Britain. "What an eventful period this is!" said Price.

Be encouraged, all ye friends of freedom, and writers in its defense! The times are auspicious. Your labours have not been in vain. Behold kingdoms, admonished by you, starting from sleep, breaking their fetters, and claiming justice from their oppressors! Behold, the light you have struck out, after setting America free, reflected to France, and there kindled into a blaze that lays despotism in ashes, and warms and illuminates EUROPE!

The language is certainly inflammatory. The message is passionate and quite clear. "Tremble all ye oppressors of the world!" (It was Price's *Discourse* that prompted Burke to write his *Reflections on the Revolution in France* in 1790.)

The Social Origins of the French Revolution

In general, the central cause of the Revolution must be located in the rigid social structure of eighteenth-century France. French society was divided into three estates or orders. The First Estate consisted of the clergy (those who pray) and the Second Estate the nobility (those who fight). Together, these two estates accounted for approximately five hundred thousand individuals. At the bottom of this hierarchy was the vast Third Estate (those who work) of about 25 million people. This structure was based on custom and on inequalities sanctioned by law. The clergy was itself divided into the lower and upper clergy. Members of the lower clergy were usually humble, poorly paid, and overworked village priests. They resented the wealth and arrogance of the upper clergy, men who regarded their office as a way of securing larger incomes and the property. Most of the upper clergy sold their offices to subordinates, kept the revenue, and lived in Paris or at Versailles. Like the clergy, the nobility was a privileged estate and held the highest positions in the army and government. As an order, they were virtually exempt from paying taxes of any kind. They collected rent from a peasant population who lived on their land and paid a number of indirect dues:

- the labor obligation, or *corveé*
- dues on salt, cloth, bread, wine
- dues on the use of mills, granaries, presses, and ovens

The nobility were also involved in banking, finance, shipping, insurance, and manufacturing and were also the leading patrons of the arts. They often opened their homes and salons to the likes of Voltaire, Gibbon, Diderot, Franklin, and Rousseau. The Nobility of the Sword carried the most prestige and served the king at Versailles. The Nobility of the Robe had been created by monarchs who needed money, so it seemed logical to offer positions to those men who were willing to pay. Some of the lesser nobility were partial to the philosophes (liberal nobles). They wished an end to royal absolutism but not necessarily an end to the monarchy (their example was Britain's limited monarchy).

The Third Estate was composed of the bourgeoisie, the peasantry, and urban artisans. The bourgeoisie had wealth—

in some cases, enormous wealth. But wealth in the *ancien régime* did not mean status or privilege. The bourgeoisie were influenced by the nobility and tried to imitate them by becoming landowners themselves. They were upwardly mobile but were frustrated by the nobility. By 1789, the bourgeoisie had numerous grievances they wanted addressed:

- Church, army, and government positions ought to be open to men of talent.
- Only a written constitution would limit the king's prerogative.
- Fair trials and religious toleration were necessary.
- There should be vast administrative reforms.

About 21 million souls made up the French peasantry. Although their standard of living was perhaps better than that of other European peasants, French peasants continued to live in poverty. Most did not own their land but rented it from either wealthier peasants or the nobility. They tried to supplement their income by hiring themselves out as day laborers, textile workers, or manual laborers. The peasants paid taxes to the king, taxes to the church, and taxes and dues to the lord of the manor, as well as numerous indirect taxes. In the later 1780s, taxes and rent increased and peasants continued to use antiquated methods of agriculture. The price of bread soared and prices continued to rise at a faster rate than wages. To make matters worse, there was the poor harvest of 1788–89. Urban workers and artisans also lived in poverty, a poverty made more grinding by 1789 since wages had increased 22 percent while the cost of living had increased 62 percent.

OTHER CAUSES

The social origins acted as a breeding ground for the grievances and passions the Revolution would unleash. It is now time to turn to more administrative issues. Eighteenth-century France was, in theory, an absolute monarchy. But by the time Louis XVI assumed the throne in 1774, the situation had changed. France had no Parliament on the British model. It did have an Estates-General, which was a semi-representative institution composed of representatives from the Three Estates. By 1750, the bureaucracy had become large, corrupt, and inefficient. Furthermore, France had no single, unified system of law. Each of the thirteen regions into which France was divided determined its own laws, based on the rule of local judges and the legal elites of the Parlement who:

- tried cases for murder, theft, forgery, sedition, and libel
- served as public censors
- fixed the price of bread
- were hated by everyone, including the king

Of course, the king had his loyal lackeys. The intendants were even more hated than the Parlement. Created to help curb the power of the nobility, the intendants were adept at

the arbitrary arrest and taxation of the peasantry. In financial matters, by 1789 France was bankrupt and still paying off the war debt of Louis XIV. The United States owed money to France for its support during the Revolutionary War. Furthermore, a number of social groups and institutions did not pay taxes at all and the monarchy continued to tax those people with the least means to pay—the peasantry.

Most historians agree that there is no direct causal relationship between the ideas of the philosophes and the outbreak of the French Revolution. Few philosophes, if any, advocated revolution—violence and tumult were contrary to reason. But because the philosophes attacked the *ancien régime*, their ideas helped to produce a "revolutionary mentality." The philosophes knew that reason could effect changes in morality, knowledge, and human happiness. Voltaire had few problems with monarchy—all he required was an enlightened monarch. And for all his talk about representative governments, social contracts, and the "general will," Rousseau perhaps had more to do with nascent totalitarianism than he did with democracy. The point is this: the eighteenth century had no prophet of revolution. The prophets of revolution (like Marx and Lenin) were made by the French Revolution.

The American Revolution of the 1770s and the formation of a republic in the 1780s served as a profound example to all European observers. Hundreds of books, pamphlets, sermons, and addresses analyzed and criticized the American rebellion. American independence fired the imagination of aristocrats who were unsure of their status and gave the hope of greater equality to the common man. The American example served as a great lesson—tyranny could be challenged and new governments could be conceived. As one historian has written:

> Whether fantastically idealized or seen in a factual way, whether as mirage or as reality, America made Europe seem unsatisfactory to many people of the middle and lower classes and to those of the upper classes who wished them well. It made a good many Europeans feel sorry for themselves, and induced a kind of spiritual flight from the Old Regime.

THE MODERATE STAGE: 1789–1792

Because of the mounting financial crisis, Louis XVI called for a meeting of the Estates General in July 1788. After electing deputies, the full body was to meet in June of the following year. For the next twelve months the deputies of each estate drew up the *cahiers de doléances* (list of grievances). Among the lists drawn up by the Third Estates were the following concerns:

- loyalty to Louis and the church
- the sanctity of private property
- trial by jury and careers open to men of talent
- a written constitution and an elected Assembly

Hopes were high among the French people. As yet, no one was talking about revolution. The Estates-General met at

Versailles (May 5, 1789) and immediately stalemated over voting procedure. The nobility argued that the Estates meet separately and vote as individual bodies. The Third Estate proposed that all deputies of the Estates meet as one body and vote by head. This is important since the Third Estate was composed of solidly middle-class deputies whose total number exceeded that of the First and Second Estates combined. Since the Third Estate had the support of liberal priests and nobles, they were almost assured a majority. The Third Estate invited the other estates to join them on June 10, 1789, but the stalemate continued. On June 17, the Third Estate began the Revolution by declaring itself a National Assembly. Days later, locked out of their meeting hall, the Third Estate moved to a tennis court and took a solemn oath (Oath of the Tennis Court) containing the following statements of purpose:

- "To bring about the regeneration of public order"
- "To maintain the true principles of monarchy"
- That "the National Assembly exists wherever its members are gathered"
- "Decrees that all members of this assembly . . . take a solemn oath never to separate"
- "To reassemble whenever circumstances require, until the constitution of the realm is established"

Louis responded on June 23 by ordering the National Assembly to disband. The Third Estate refused to yield. On June 27, Louis then ordered the clergy and nobility to join the Third Estate, a plan that backfired. The Third Estate would not compromise, and neither would the clergy or nobility. Instead, the nobility joined with Louis against the National Assembly and Louis ordered the army to station itself at Paris and Versailles.

By the beginning of July, Paris had reached a high level of tension. The price of bread was soaring and there was a growing fear of an aristocratic plot against the National Assembly. On July 14, about nine hundred Parisians, mostly women, stormed the Bastille looking for weapons and gunpowder. Ninety-eight were killed and seventy-three wounded. Although the Bastille contained no weapons, its destruction served as a great symbol of the Revolution itself. It seemed that there was no turning back. Something very different took place in the countryside. The peasants believed that if Louis only knew their plight then he would take care of them. But by July, they were restless. As the price of bread continued to soar and its supply decrease, the peasants:

- began to attack food convoys on their way to Paris
- refused to pay taxes, tithes, and manorial dues
- began to burn down the houses of their landlords
- destroyed the records of their obligations to their lords

The peasants turned violent because of a rumor that the aristocrats had organized an army. The Great Fear led the peasants to take arms against an imaginary foe. The Great Fear worked to the advantage of the Parisian revolutionaries

and provided the National Assembly the opportunity to force the aristocrats to surrender their special (feudal) privileges by the decrees of August 4, 1789 (ratified August 11). On the night of August 4 several members of the National Assembly also drew drafted the *Declaration of the Rights of Man and the Citizen* (formally adopted by the National Assembly on August 26). The *Declaration* outlined man's natural rights and rallied the country to the support of the National Assembly. The *Declaration* specified that:

- Men are born free and remain free and equal in rights.
- The aim of every political association is the preservation of . . . liberty, property, security, and resistance to oppression.
- Liberty consists in the power to do anything that does not injure others.
- Law is the expression of the general will.
- The law ought only to establish penalties that are strict and obviously necessary.
- Every man is presumed innocent until he has been pronounced guilty.
- No one should be disturbed on account of his opinions, even religious ones.
- The free communication of ideas and opinions is one of the most precious of the rights of man.

Barely three hundred words long, the *Declaration* appeared all over France and was translated into every major European language; it became the gospel of the new French order. Louis did not accept the decrees of August 4 nor the *Declaration*. However, during the October Days several hundred Parisian men and women marched to Versailles to protest their lack of bread to Louis and the National Assembly. twenty thousand Paris guards joined the mob at Versailles, and Louis had no choice but to promise bread and return to Paris along with the National Assembly.

On June 20, 1791, Louis did something which earned him the general distrust of his subjects. He had planned to raise an army with the help of Leopold II, the brother of Marie Antoinette. Leopold promised Louis an army if Louis could reach Montmédy and mobilize a French force. On the night of June 20, Louis and his family, dressed in disguise, left Paris. They were eventually stopped on a bridge at Varennes and by morning were met by ten thousand peasants. On June 22 representatives of the National Assembly arrived on the scene, escorted by the National Guardsmen, and three days later Louis was back in Paris and a prisoner of the Revolution. Between the October Days of 1789 and September 1791, the National Assembly consolidated reforms meant to dismantle the *ancien régime*.

- The special privileges of the nobility were abolished through the legalization of equality (August 4, 1789).
- *Declaration of the Rights of Man and the Citizen* (August 4, 1789) was drafted.
- The Civil Constitution of the Clergy was adopted (1790).

- A new constitution specified a limited monarchy and equality before the law (1791).
- France was divided into eighty-three administrative units.
- A standardized system of courts was introduced.
- The sale of judicial offices was abolished.
- Citizen-filled juries were introduced and torture was abolished.
- A uniform system of weights and measures was adopted.
- Guild restrictions were abolished.
- Customs on goods transported within the country were eliminated.

There was a sizable faction within the National Assembly that claimed the Revolution to be at an end. But revolutions are unpredictable. By 1792 the Revolution turned more violent. There are two reasons why this is so. First, there was a strong counterrevolutionary movement, loyal to church and king, led by the clergy and nobility and supported by the peasantry. Second, the social and political discontent of the urban classes propelled the Revolution in radical directions. These were the sans-culottes, small shopkeepers, artisans, and wage-earners. As one historian has written: "The sans-culottes saw that a privilege of wealth was taking the place of a privilege of birth. They foresaw that the bourgeoisie would succeed the fallen aristocracy as the ruling class."

The Radical Stage: August 1792–1795

Inflamed by their poverty and hatred of wealth, the sans-culottes demanded that it was the duty of government to guarantee to right to existence, a policy that ran counter to the National Assembly. The sans-culottes demanded that the revolutionary government increase wages, fix prices, end food shortages, and deal with counterrevolutionaries. They also wanted laws to prevent extremes of poverty and wealth. They favored a democratic republic in which the voice of the common man could be heard. Like Thomas Paine (1737–1809), they wanted a government that governed least. On August 10, 1792, enraged Parisian men and women attacked the king's palace. This *journee* marks the radicalization of the Revolution. Louis and the royal family fled to the Tuileries and were placed under house arrest. By September, Paris was in turmoil. Fearing counterrevolution, the sans-culottes destroyed prisons believed to hold conspirators, street fights broke out, and barricades were set up in various quarters of the city. The Revolution had to keep moving forward. On September 21–22, 1792, the monarchy was abolished and a republic declared (Day One of the Year One in the revolutionary calendar). In December 1793, Louis XVI was placed on trial and on January 21, 1793, he was executed by guillotine. The National Assembly, now known as the National Convention, faced enormous problems:

- The value of *assignats* (paper currency) had fallen by 50 percent.

- There was price inflation and continued food shortages.
- Various peasant rebellions continued to erupt.
- France was at war with Austria and Prussia, and war was pending with Holland, Spain, and Great Britain.

Meanwhile, revolutionary leadership grew more radical. Up to June 1793, the moderate Girondins, who favored a decentralized government, dominated the National Convention. In June, the Girondins were replaced by the Jacobins, a far more radical group. Although both groups were liberal and bourgeois, the Jacobins:

- desired a centralized government with Paris as the national capital
- sought temporary government control of the economy
- won the support of the sans-culottes
- were tightly organized and well-disciplined
- were convinced that the success of the Revolution was in their hands

On June 22, 1793, eighty thousand armed sans-culottes surrounded the National Convention and demanded and secured the immediate arrest of twenty-nine Girondins. The Jacobins now controlled the Convention and the nation. But with power came more pressing problems—civil war was everywhere, economic distress continued, the sans-culottes had to be satisfied, there was the threat of foreign invasion, and the ports were blockaded. The Committee of Public Safety (CPS) assumed leadership in April 1793. It organized the nation's defenses, arrested and tried counterrevolutionaries, and imposed its authority across the nation. The Committee was dominated by Robespierre (1758–1794), a middle-class lawyer and disciple of Rousseau. He knew that a "republic of virtue" was impossible unless foreign and civil wars came to an end. To preserve the Republic, the CPS instituted the Reign of Terror, which set out to crush all opposition. About seventeen thousand people died as a result of the Terror—the choice instrument was the guillotine. Over one hundred thousand people were detained as suspects. Robespierre and the CPS resorted to the Terror because they wished to create a temporary dictatorship to save the Republic (a Roman idea). By the summer of 1794 there seemed to be less of a need for the Terror, and so on July 27, 1794 (ninth of *Thermidor*), Robespierre was arrested. He was guillotined the following day. The sans-culottes did not step in to rescue him.

The Revolution Continued? 1795–1799

Following the death of Robespierre, the Jacobin republic was dismantled and leadership passed into the hands of a five-man Directory (1795). The new legislature sat in two chambers: the Council of 500 and the Ancients (or Senate). The Directory tried to preserve the Revolution of 1789—they opposed the restoration of the *ancien régime* as well as popular democracy. They refused to leave the door open for either the excessive radicalism of the Jacobins or the spontaneity of the sans-culottes. The Directory muddled on until

1799. By this time the French Revolution was over and the French tried to get back to business as usual. Radicalism had been effectively thwarted as well. But France was still at war with the rest of Europe. Because of the war, leadership began to pass into the hands of generals. One of these generals seized control of the government on November 10, 1799 (eighteenth of *Brumaire*). And on December 2, 1804, this general, Napoleon Bonaparte, declared himself emperor of the French—a new Augustus Caesar. This has led one French historian to write that "in 1789, the French had created a Republic, under the name of a monarchy. Ten years later, they created a monarchy, under the name of a Republic."

What did the Revolution accomplish? First, the Revolution weakened the political influence and leadership of the aristocracy. The aristocrats lost their privileges based on birth because from this point on, privilege was to be based on property and wealth. But the sans-culottes quickly realized, one evil simply replaced another. Second, because careers were open to talent, the bourgeoisie had access to the highest positions in the state. Third, the Revolution transformed the dynastic state of the *ancien régime* into the modern state (natural, liberal, secular, and rational). The state was no longer the private property of the king. Instead, the state belonged to the people. The individual, formerly a subject in the old order, was now a citizen, with specific rights as well as duties. Lastly, the Revolution managed to give practical application to the ideas of the philosophes—equality before the law, trial by jury, the freedom of religion, speech, and the press. In the nineteenth century, all these ideas led to the quickening pace of reform, which was accelerated by the Industrial Revolution. While the French Revolution politicized the sans-culottes, the Industrial Revolution industrialized them.

SUGGESTED FEATURE FILMS

Danton (subtitled). 136 min. Color. 1983. Triumph Releasing Corporation, Inc. The film begins in November of 1793, with Danton (Gérard Depardieu) returning to Paris upon learning that the Committee of Public Safety has instituted the Terror.

Jefferson in Paris. 139 min. Color. 1995. Touchstone Pictures. James Ivory's account of Thomas Jefferson's (Nick Nolte) period as U.S. ambassador in Paris in the five years leading up to the French Revolution

La Marseillaise (in French). 130 min. B/W. 1938. World. A newsreel like film about early part of the French Revolution, directed by Jean Renoir.

Napoléon. 235 min. B/W. 1981. Images Film Archive. Restored version of the 1927 film about Napoleon's life, from his days as a schoolboy, his flight from Corsica, through the French Revolution, and the Terror, culminating in his invasion of Italy in 1797.

La Nuit de Varennes (subtitled). 135 min. Color. 1983. Triumph Releasing Corporation, Inc. The film imagines a group of travelers on the same road as Louis XVI as he flees France. The travelers include Thomas Paine (Harvey Keitel), Casanova, Restif de La Bretonne, and one of the queen's ladies-in-waiting.

La Révolution Française (in French). 360 min. Color. 1989. Les Films Ariane. Hard-to-locate epic of the French Revolution, from the calling of the Estates-General to the guillotining of Robespierre.

Waterloo. 123 min. Color. 1970. Paramount Pictures. Film about Europe's shock to find that Napoleon (Rod Steiger) has escaped and has caused the French Army to defect from the king back to him.

SUGGESTED CLASSROOM FILMS

The Age of Revolution (1776–1848). 26 min. Color. 1989. Insight Media. Looks at the spread of revolutionary ideas and politics.

The Battle of Austerlitz: 1805. 30 min. Color. 1990. Films for the Humanities and Sciences. A study of the battle of the three emperors.

The Battle of Waterloo: 1815. 30 min. Color. 1990. Films for the Humanities and Sciences. Looks not only at the battle but also at the political and military context.

The Death of the Old Regime and *The French Revolution*. 2 parts, 30 min each. Color. 1989. Insight Media. An examination of the French and American revolutions and the spread of revolutionary ideas throughout Europe.

The French Revolution: The Terror. 29 min. Color. 1971. Learning Corporation of America. Focuses on the role of Robespierre.

The Hundred Days: Napoleon from Elba to Waterloo. 53 min. Color. 1969. Time-Life. Filmed on-site.

Napoleon: The End of a Dictator; the Making of a Dictator. 27 min. each. Color. 1970. 1971. Learning Corporation of America. From the *Western Civilization: Majesty and Madness* series.

Napoleon Bonaparte. 12 min. Color. 1988. Films for the Humanities and Sciences. Napoleon as military strategist and empire-builder.

CHAPTER 19

The Industrial Revolution and Nineteenth-Century Society

OUTLINE

I. Introduction
   A. An industrial revolution
      1. From agriculture and craft to large-scale manufacturing
      2. Capital-intensive enterprises
      3. Urbanization
   B. New forms of energy
      1. Led to unprecedented economic growth
      2. Altered the balance of humanity
   C. Mechanization
      1. Gains in productivity
      2. Shifted the basis of the economy
      3. New livelihoods
      4. Did not dispense with human toil—the intensification of human labor
      5. New social classes and new social tensions
   D. "Industry"—from industriousness to an economic system
   E. Partial causes
      1. New territories
      2. Economic expansion
      3. Expanding networks of trade and finance
      4. New markets for goods and sources for raw materials
      5. Population growth
   F. Regional variations
II. The Industrial Revolution in Britain, 1760–1850
   A. Why England?
      1. Natural, economic, and cultural resources
      2. Small and secure island
      3. Empire
      4. Ample supply of coal, rivers, and a developed canal system
      5. The commercialization of agriculture
         a. New techniques and crops, changes in property-holding
         b. Enclosure
         c. Yielded more food for a growing population
         d. Concentration of property in fewer hands
      6. Growing supply of available capital
         a. Well-developed banking and credit institutions
         b. London as leading center for international trade
      7. Investment and entrepreneurship
         a. Pursuit of wealth seen as a worthy goal
         b. The British as a commercial people
      8. Domestic and foreign markets
         a. The British were voracious consumers
         b. A well-integrated domestic market
         c. No system of internal tolls and tariffs
         d. A constantly improving transportation system
      9. Favorable political climate
         a. Foreign policy responded to commercial needs of the nation
      10. Production for export rose 80 percent between 1750 and 1770
      11. The British merchant marine and navy
   B. Innovation in the textile industries
      1. The British prohibited the import of East Indian cottons

2. Textile manufacturers imported raw cotton from India and the American south
3. Revolutionary breakthroughs
   a. John Kay—the flying shuttle (1733)
   b. John Hargreaves—the spinning jenny (1764)
   c. Richard Arkwright—the water frame (1769)
   d. Samuel Crompton—the spinning mule (1799)
   e. Eli Whitney—the cotton gin (1793)
4. Textile machines
   a. First machines inexpensive enough to be used by spinners in their homes
   b. As machines grew in size, they were located in mills and factories
   c. By 1780, British cotton textiles flooded the world market
5. A revolution in clothing
   a. Cotton was light, durable, and washable
   b. Large domestic and foreign market for cotton cloth
6. The tyranny of the new industries
7. Factory working conditions and the factory acts

C. Coal and iron
1. Technological changes
   a. Coke smelting, rolling, and puddling
   b. Substitution of coal for wood
   c. Thomas Newcomen—fashioned an engine to pump water from mines in 1711
   d. James Watt and Matthew Boulton—the steam engine
      i. 289 engines in use by 1800

D. The coming of railways
1. George Stephenson and the Stockton to Darlington line (1825)
2. Railway construction as enterprise
   a. Risky but profitable
   b. Global opportunities—building the infrastructure of nations
3. The "navvies"
4. Toil and technology
5. Steam and speed as a new way of life

III. The Industrial Revolution on the Continent
A. A different model of industrialization
B. Reasons for the delay
1. Lack of raw materials, especially coal
2. Poor national systems of transportation
3. Little readily-accessible capital

4. Tenacity of the small peasant leaseholder
5. The French Revolution and Napoleonic Wars

C. Economic climate changes after 1815
1. Population growth (parts of France, Belgium, Rhineland, Saxony, Silesia, and Bohemia)
2. New railway construction
3. Older methods of putting-out persisted alongside factory work
4. Governments played a major role in subsidizing industry
   a. Subsidies to private companies (railroads and mining)
   b. Incentives for and laws favorable to industrialization
   c. Limited-liability laws
5. Mobilizing capital
   a. Joint-stock investment banks
      i. *Société Générale* (Belgium, 1830s)
      ii. *Creditanstalt* (Austria, 1850s)
      iii. *Crédit Mobilier* (1850s)
6. Promoting invention and technological development
   a. State-established educational systems

D. Industrialization after 1850
1. Individual British factories remained small but output was tremendous
   a. Iron industry the largest in the world
2. Continental changes
   a. Mostly in transport, commerce, and government policy
   b. Free trade and the removal of trade barriers
   c. Guild controls relaxed or abolished
   d. Communications
      i. Transatlantic cable (1865)
      ii. Telephone (1876)
   e. New chemical processes, dyestuffs, and pharmaceuticals
   f. New sources of energy—electricity and oil
   g. Internal combustion engine (Carl Benz and Gottlieb Daimler, 1880s)
   h. Eastern Europe
      i. Developed into concentrated, commercialized agriculture
      ii. The persistence of serfdom
3. The industrial core
   a. Great Britain, France, Germany, Italy, Netherlands, and Switzerland

4. The industrial periphery
    a. Russia, Spain, Bulgaria, Greece, Hungary, Romania, and Serbia
E. Industry and empire
    1. European nations begin to control the national debts of other countries
    2. Where trade agreements could not be made, force prevailed
    3. New networks of trade and interdependence
    4. The world economy divided
        a. Producers of manufactured goods (Europe)
        b. Suppliers of raw materials and buyers of finish goods (everyone else)
    5. Toward a global economy
VI. The Social Consequences of Industrialization
    A. Population
        1. Europe. 205 million (1800), 274 million (1850), 414 million (1900), 480 million (1914)
        2. Explanations
            a. Fatal diseases became less virulent
            b. Edward Jenner and smallpox vaccination (1796)
            c. Improved sanitation
            d. Governments became more concerned with improving the lives of their people
            e. Less-expensive foods of high nutritional value
            f. Rising fertility
                i. Men and women married earlier
                ii. Rural manufacture allowed couples to marry and set up households
                iii. More people married
    B. Life on the land: the peasantry
        1. Rural poverty
            a. Harsh conditions of the countryside
            b. Millions of tiny farms produced a bare subsistence
            c. Rising population put pressure on the land
            d. Unpredictability of weather and the harvest
        2. Great Famine of 1845–1849
            a. Potato blight
                i. No alternative food source
            b. At least one million Irish died of starvation

c. Forced 1.5 million people to leave Ireland for good
        3. The role of the state
            a. Became more sympathetic to commercialized agriculture
            b. Encouraged the elimination of small farms and the creation of larger farms
        4. Serfdom
            a. land owners and serfs had little incentive to improve farming or land management
            b. Serfdom made it difficult to buy and sell land freely
            c. An obstacle to the commercialization and consolidation of agriculture
        5. Industrialization in the countryside
            a. Improved communication networks
            b. Government intervention in the countryside
            c. Centralized bureaucracies
                i. Made it easier to collect taxes and conscript soldiers from peasant families
        6. Rural violence
            a. Captain Swing, southern England (1820s)
            b. Insurrections against landlords, taxes, and laws curtailing customary rights
            c. Russian serf uprisings as a result of bad harvests and exploitation
            d. Governments seemed incapable of dealing with rural discontent
    C. The urban landscape
        1. Growth of cities
        2. Urbanization moved from northwest Europe to the southeast
        3. London's population grew from 676,000 (1750) to 2.3 million (1850), Paris from 560,000 to 1.3 million
        4. Overcrowding and poor sanitation
        5. Construction of housing lagged well behind population growth
        6. Governments passed some legislation to rid cities of slums
    D. Industry and environment in the nineteenth century
        1. Air pollution
        2. Water pollution
        3. Fertile breeding grounds for cholera, typhus, and tuberculosis

E. Sex in the city
    1. Prostitution
        a. Seen as one of the dangers and corruptions of urban life
    2. The problems of the cities posed dangers that were not just social but political
    3. Social surveys and studies
    4. Critics of the urban scene
        a. Victor Hugo (1802–1885)
        b. Charles Dickens (1812–1870)
        c. Honoré de Balzac (1799–1850)

VII. The Middle Classes
  A. Balzac as observer
    1. The French and Industrial Revolutions had replaced one aristocracy with another
        a. From rank, status, and privilege to wealth and social class
  B. Who were the middle classes?
    1. Not a homogenous group in terms in income or occupation
    2. Upward mobility impossible without education
        a. Easier in Britain than on the continent
    3. The examination system
    4. "Getting ahead"
        a. Intelligence, pluck (luck), and hard work
        b. Samuel Smiles, *Self-Help* (1859)
    5. Respectability
        a. A code of behavior
        b. Financial independence
        c. Providing for family
        d. Avoiding gambling and debt
        e. Merit and character
        f. Hard work
        g. Live modestly and soberly
    6. Aspirations and codes not social realities
  C. Private life and middle-class identity
    1. The family
    2. A well-governed household served as an antidote to the confusion of the business world
  D. Gender and the cult of domesticity
    1. The respectable home
        a. Rituals, hierarchies, and distinctions
    2. The "separate sphere"
        a. Women were supposed to live in subordination to men
        b. Boys educated in secondary schools, girls educated at home
        c. The idea of legal inequality between men and women
    3. Middle-class identity—neither aristocratic nor working-class values

    4. The "angel in the house"
        a. Middle-class women to be free from unrelenting toil
        b. The moral education of children
    5. The "cult of domesticity"
        a. Central to middle-class Victorian thinking about women
        b. The reassessment of femininity
        c. Keeping the household functioning smoothly and harmoniously
        d. The servant as the mark of middle-class status
    6. Outside the home
        a. Few options to earn a living
        b. Voluntary societies and campaigns for social reform
        c. Protestantism and charity
        d. Florence Nightingale (1820–1910)
    7. Queen Victoria (r. 1837–1901)
        a. Reflected contemporary feminine virtues of moral probity and dutiful domesticity
        b. Successful queen because she embodied middle-class virtues
  E. "Passionlessness": gender and sexuality
    1. Victorian sexuality usually seen as synonymous with anxiety, prudishness, and ignorance
    2. Beliefs about sexuality came from convictions about "separate spheres"
    3. Scientists taught that specific characteristics were inherent to each sex
        a. Men and woman had different roles
        b. Auguste Comte and "biological philosophy"
    4. Women's moral superiority embodied in their "passionlessness"
    5. Absence of reliable contraceptives
  F. Middle-class life in public
    1. Houses and furnishings as symbols of material prosperity
        a. Solidly built and heavily decorated
        b. Homes were built to last
        c. Rooms crowded with furniture, art, carpets, and wall hangings
    2. Suburban life
        a. Moved to the west side of cities
        b. Lived away from the city but managed the affairs of their city
    3. Leisure

VIII. Working-Class Life
  A. General observations
    1. Working classes divided into several subgroups

a. Based on skill, wages, gender, and workplace
2. Some movement from unskilled to skilled (required children with education)
3. Movement from skilled to unskilled due to technological change
4. Housing was unhealthy and unregulated
5. The daily round of life for the working-class wife

B. Working-class women in the industrial landscape
  1. Problems observed
    a. Promiscuous mixing in workshops
    b. Children left unattended
    c. Industrial accidents
    d. Women laboring alongside men
  2. Women's work not new— industrialization made it more visible
  3. Women workers were paid less and were less troublesome
    a. Most began to work at age ten or eleven
    b. They put their children out to wet nurses or brought them to the mills
  4. Gender division of labor
    a. Most women labored at home or in small workshops ("sweatshops")
    b. Domestic service
      i. Less visible
      ii. Low wages
      iii. Coercive sexual relationships
  5. Working class sexuality
    a. Different from middle-class counterpart
    b. Increase in illegitimate births
    c. Weaker family ties
    d. The collapse of the family?

C. A life apart: class consciousness
  1. The factory created common experiences and difficulties
    a. Denied skilled laborers pride in their crafts
    b. Guild protections abolished
    c. Decline of apprenticeship
  2. The factory
    a. Long hours under dirty and dangerous conditions
    b. The imposition of new routines and discipline
      i. The factory whistle
      ii. The pace of the machine
      iii. The division of labor into specialized steps
      iv. Machinery as the new tyrant

3. Working-class vulnerability
  a. Unemployment, sickness, accidents, and family problems
  b. The varying price of food
  c. Seasonal unemployment
  d. Markets for manufactured goods were small and unstable
  e. Cyclical economic depressions
  f. Severe agricultural depressions
4. Working-class survival
  a. Families worked several small jobs
  b. Pawned possessions
  c. Joined self-help societies and fraternal associations
  d. Early socialist movement
5. Social segregation of the city
  a. Implied that working people lived a life apart from others
  b. Class differences embedded in experience and beliefs

IX. Conclusion
  A. The Industrial Revolution as major turning point in the history of the world
  B. The global balance of power
  C. Technology as progress
  D. The new wealth and the new poverty
  E. Social identities and class consciousness

GENERAL DISCUSSION QUESTIONS

1. Why did the Industrial Revolution take place in Britain first? What conditions existed in Britain that did not exist elsewhere?

2. Was the Industrial Revolution inevitable? Was it a spontaneous or a planned event? What were the alternatives to industrialization?

3. Did the free-enterprise system and the "invisible hand" of the marketplace correct abuses and improve conditions, or was government intervention required?

4. Why was railway building one of the keys to the industrialization of Europe and North America? How did the construction of railways require new sources of capital as well as new types of management?

5. What social effects did industrialization have on both the peasantry and urban workers?

6. Describe the code of respectability as it existed among the middle classes of nineteenth-century Britain and Europe. Was such a code a reality or an ideal?

7. Did the Industrial Revolution change a general understanding of gender in the nineteenth century? In what ways did women become more visible?

8. How did the factory system create class consciousness among factory workers?

DOCUMENT DISCUSSION QUESTIONS

The Factory System, Science, and Morality

1. According to Andrew Ure, why was industrialization good for Britain. How can the blessings of "physico-mechanical science" lead to the improvement of humanity?

2. Why does Ure argue that the urban factory worker is far better off than his non-factory counterpart?

3. What criticism did Engels level at Ure and other optimists on industrialization? Why did Engels think conditions for workers were getting worse instead of better?

4. Was Engels right about "the process whereby machine-continually supersedes hand-labour"? Or did the abundant supply of low-wage labor in many countries reduce the incentive to replace people with machines?

Thomas Malthus on Population and Poverty

5. In what ways was the Enlightenment vision of nature so vastly different from that of Malthus? According to Malthus, is humanity capable of progress of any kind?

6. How did early-nineteenth-century society and government deal with the existence of poverty? What attitudes animated the way the poor were treated during the Industrial Revolution? Where did poverty come from?

The Irish Famine: Interpretations and Responses

7. Would you agree with Trevelyan that dealing with "social evil" was beyond the function of government? What actions could or should governments take in times of famine?

8. In what ways did new economic doctrines, changing assumptions about society, and a shift in the relationship between religion and government affect British government officials?

Marriage, Sexuality, and the Facts of Life

9. The French doctor believed that an increasing population was a sign of a healthy state. Sex was lawful within marriage for procreation, he argued, and artificial birth control interfered with nature. How and why does he describe the birth control methods as "conjugal frauds"?

10. What happened to a "very amorous" couple that practiced birth control? Why did the doctor think excessive sexual indulgence led to physical and mental deterioration?

11. What was the cause of Mrs. Pettigrew's death? Did calling Dr. Warren make any difference in the outcome? Given the technologies and treatments available in 1830, does it sound as if doctors could have saved her life?

SAMPLE LECTURE 19: THE INDUSTRIAL REVOLUTION: WHY BRITAIN?

Lecture Objectives

1. To situate the Industrial Revolution within its intellectual and cultural context

2. To suggest various reasons why this revolution occurred in Britain first

3. To demonstrate how the Industrial Revolution contributed to the nineteenth-century faith in human progress

THE AGE OF REVOLUTIONS

The Industrial Revolution of the late eighteenth and early nineteenth centuries was revolutionary because it altered the productive capacities of Great Britain, Europe, and the United States. But the revolution was something more than just new machines, smoke-belching factories, increased productivity, and a higher standard of living. It was a revolution that transformed British, European, and American society down to their very roots. Everyone was touched in one way or another—peasant and noble, parent and child, artisan and captain of industry. The Industrial Revolution serves as a key to the origins of modern Western society. As one historian of English society has observed, "the Industrial Revolution was no mere sequence of changes in industrial techniques and production, but a social revolution with social causes as well as profound social effects." The Industrial Revolution can be said to have made the European working class. It made the European middle class as well. In the wake of the revolution, new social relationships appeared. People no longer treated each other as people, but as commodities that could be bought and sold on the open market. This commodification of man is what bothered Karl Marx. As he sat at his desk in the British Library, Marx discovered that the solution to the dehumanizing effects of what he called "machino-facture" was to transcend the profit motive by social revolution.

There is no denying the fact that the Industrial Revolution began in Britain sometime after the middle of the eighteenth century. Britain was the first industrial nation, the first nation to execute "the takeoff into self-sustained growth." And by 1850, Britain had become an economic titan. Its goal was to supply two-thirds of the globe with cotton spun, dyed, and woven in the industrial centers of northern England. Britain proudly proclaimed itself to be the "Workshop of the World," a position that country held until the end of the nineteenth century, when Germany, Japan, and the United States overtook it. More than the greatest gains of the Renaissance, the Reformation, the Scientific Revolution or the Enlightenment, the Industrial Revolution implied that man now had not only the opportunity and the knowledge but the physical means to completely subdue nature. No other revolution in modern times can be said to have accomplished so much in so little time.

The Industrial Revolution attempted to effect man's mastery over nature. This was an old vision. In the seventeenth century, the English statesman and "father of modern science," Francis Bacon, believed that natural philosophy (what we call science) could be applied to the solution of practical problems—thus, the idea of modern technology was born. For Bacon, the problem was this: how could man enjoy perfect freedom if he had to constantly labor to supply the necessities of existence? Bacon's answer was clear—machines. These laborsaving devices would liberate mankind, they would save labor that then could be utilized elsewhere. The vision was all-important. It was optimistic and progressive. Man was going somewhere, his life had direction. This vision is part of the general attitude known as the idea of progress, which holds that the history of human society is a history of progress, forever forward, forever upward. This attitude was implicit throughout the Enlightenment and was made reality during the French and Industrial Revolutions.

With relatively few exceptions, the philosophes of the eighteenth century embraced this idea of man's progress with intensity. Human happiness, improved morality, and the increase in knowledge were now within man's reach. This was indeed the message, the vision, of Adam Smith, Denis Diderot, Voltaire, Thomas Jefferson, and Ben Franklin. The American and French Revolutions, building on ideas of the Enlightenment, swept away tyranny, fanaticism, superstition, and oppressive and despotic governments. "Sapere Aude!" exclaimed Kant—"Dare to know!" Man could not only understand man and society, man could now change society for the better. These were all glorious and noble visions of the future prospect of mankind. By the end of the eighteenth century, these ideas became tangible. Engines and machines, the glorious products of science, began to revolutionize the idea of progress itself. If a simple machine could do the work of twenty men in a quarter of the time formerly required, then could the New Jerusalem be far behind? But while the Industrial Revolution brought its blessings, there was also much misery. Revolutions, political or otherwise, are always mixed blessings. If technophiles thank the Industrial Revolution for giving us fluoride, internal combustion engines, and laser-guided radial arm saws, critics also damn it for the effect it has had on social relationships. As the mid-nineteenth century Scottish critic Thomas Carlyle held,

one legacy of the Industrial Revolution is the legacy of the "cash nexus," where the only connection between men is the one of money, profit, and gain.

THE ORIGINS OF THE INDUSTRIAL REVOLUTION IN BRITAIN

The origins of the Industrial Revolution are complex and varied and, like the French Revolution, historians still debate its origins, developments, and end results. This debate has raged among historians since at least 1884, when Arnold Toynbee, an English historian and social reformer, published the short book, *Lectures on the Industrial Revolution in England*. Toynbee, after all, was in a fairly good position to assess the revolution in industry: by the 1880s, Britain had endured more than a century of industrialization. Still, like any revolution, the Industrial Revolution left us with many questions. Was the revolution in industry simply an issue of new machinery or mechanical innovation? Did young boys and girls work and live shoulder-to-shoulder for more than twelve hours a day? Was industrial capitalism nothing more than a clever system devised by clever capitalists to exploit the labor of ignorant workers? Was the revolution in industry the product of conscious planning or did it appear spontaneously?

In the end, what the Industrial Revolution accomplished was nothing less than a structural change in the economic organization of British and European society. What made it revolutionary was a profound shift from a traditional, premodern, agrarian society to that of an industrial economy based on capitalist methods, principles, and practices. In general, the spread of industry across Great Britain was sporadic. In other words, not every region of Britain was industrialized at the same time. In some areas, the factory system spread quickly, in others not at all. Such a development also applies to the steam engine—one would think that once steam engines made their appearance, each and every factory would have one. But this was clearly not the case. The spread of industry, or machinery, or steam power, or the factory system itself, was erratic. The reason that we assume industrialization was a quick process is that we live in an age of rising expectations—we expect change to occur rapidly and almost without our direction.

Historians now agree that beginning in the seventeenth century and continuing throughout the eighteenth century, Britain witnessed an agricultural revolution. British (and Dutch) farmers were:

- the most productive farmers of the century
- continually adopting new methods of farming and experimenting with new types of vegetables and grains
- eager to obtain information about manures and other fertilizers
- beginning to treat farming as a science
- perhaps more enterprising than their European counterparts

British society was far more open than French. The British farmer could move about his locale or the country to sell his goods while the French farmer was bound by direct and indirect taxes, tariffs, or other kinds of restrictions. In 1700, 80 percent of the British population earned its income from the land. A century later, that figure had dropped to 40 percent. The result of these developments was a period of high productivity and low food prices. And this, in turn, meant that the typical English family did not have to spend almost everything it earned on bread (as was the case in France before 1789), and instead could purchase manufactured goods.

There are other assets that helped make Britain the "first industrial nation:"

- Britain had an effective central bank and well-developed credit market.
- The British government allowed the domestic economy to function with few restrictions.
- The government also encouraged both technological change and a free market.
- Britain had a labor surplus which meant there was an adequate labor supply to work in factories.
- Britain experienced an agricultural revolution.

Britain's agricultural revolution came as a result of increased attention to fertilizers, the adoption of new crops and farming technologies, and the enclosure movement. In the early eighteenth century, Jethro Tull invented a mechanical seeder that allowed seeds to be planted in orderly rows, and Charles "Turnip" Townshend stressed the value of turnips and other field crops in a rotation system of planting rather than letting the land lay fallow. Finally, Thomas William Coke suggested the utilization of field grasses and new fertilizers as well as greater attention to estate management. In order for these "high farmers" to make the most efficient use of the land, they had to manage the fields as they saw fit. This was, of course, impossible under the three-field system that had dominated European agriculture for centuries. Since farmers, small and large, held their property in long strips, they had to follow the same rules of cultivation. The local parish or village determined what ought to be planted. In the end, the open-field system of crop rotation was an obstacle to increased agricultural productivity. The solution was to enclose the land, and this meant enclosing entire villages. Landlords knew that the peasants would not give up their land voluntarily, so they petitioned Parliament. The first enclosure act was passed in 1710 but was not enforced until the 1750s. In the ten years between 1750 and 1760, more than one hundred and fifty acts were passed and between 1800 and 1810, Parliament passed more than nine hundred acts of enclosure. While enclosure ultimately contributed to an increased agricultural surplus, necessary to feed a population that doubled over the course of the eighteenth century, it also brought disaster to the countryside. Peasant farmers were dispossessed of their land and were now forced to find work in the factories which began springing up in towns and cities. Britain faced increasing pressure to produce more manufactured goods due to the eighteenth century population explosion. And the most important industry, in the rise of Britain as an industrial nation, was cotton textiles.

COTTONOPOLIS

No other industry can be said to have advanced so far so quickly. Although the putting-out system was fairly well-developed across the Continent, it was fully developed in Britain. A merchant would deliver raw cotton to a household. The cotton would be cleaned and then spun into yarn (thread). The merchant would return, pick up the yarn, and drop off more raw cotton. The merchant would then take the spun yarn to another household where it was woven into cloth. The system worked fairly well except under the growing pressure of demand. There was a constant shortage of thread, so the industry began to focus on ways to improve the spinning of cotton. The first solution to this bottleneck appeared around 1765, when James Hargreaves, a carpenter by trade, invented his cotton-spinning jenny. At almost the same time, Richard Arkwright invented another kind of spinning device, the water frame. Thanks to these two innovations, ten times as much cotton yarn was manufactured in 1790 than had been possible just twenty years earlier. Hargreaves's jenny was simple, inexpensive, and hand-operated. The jenny had between six and twenty-four spindles mounted on a sliding carriage. The spinner (almost always a woman) moved the carriage back and forth with one hand and turned a wheel to supply power with the other. Of course, now that one bottleneck had been relieved, another appeared—the weaver (usually a man) could no longer keep up with the supply of yarn. Arkwright's water frame was based on a different principle. It acquired a capacity of several hundred spindles and demanded more power. The water frame also required large, specialized mills employing hundreds of workers. The first consequence of these developments was that cotton goods became much cheaper and were bought by all social classes. After all, cotton is the miracle fiber—it is easy to clean, spin, weave, and dye, and it's comfortable to wear.

Although the spinning jenny and water frame managed to increase the productive capacity of the cotton industry, the real breakthrough came with developments in steam power. Developed in Britain by Thomas Savery (1698) and Thomas Newcomen (1705), these early steam engines were used to pump water from coal mines. In the 1760s, James Watt, a Scottish engineer, created an engine that could pump water three times as quickly as the Newcomen engine. In 1782, Watt developed a rotary engine that could turn a shaft and drive machinery to power the machines to spin and weave cotton cloth. Because Watt's engine was fired by coal and not water, spinning factories could be located virtually anywhere.

OTHER EXPLANATIONS

Aided by revolutions in agriculture, transportation, communications, and technology, Britain was able to become the "first industrial nation." This is a fact that historians have long recognized. Although the Industrial Revolution was clearly an unplanned and spontaneous event, it never would have happened had there not been men who wanted such a thing to occur. There must have been entrepreneurs who saw opportunities not only for advances in technology, but also the profits those advances might create. Which brings us to one very crucial cultural attribute—the English, like the Dutch of the same period, were a very commercial people. They saw little problem with making money, or with taking their surplus and reinvesting it. Whether this attribute has something to do with their "Protestant work ethic," as Max Weber put it, or with a specific English trait is debatable, but the fact remains that English entrepreneurs had a much wider scope of activities than did their Continental counterparts at the same time. This commercial spirit also meant that the British were voracious consumers of manufactured items. Their domestic market was well-integrated and there was no system of internal tolls and tariffs, a feature that plagued industrial development on the continent. The fact that Britain was a small and somewhat isolated island helped as well. There were no language barriers and its culture was more homogenous. The British government produced a favorable climate for manufacturing since its foreign policy responded to the commercial needs of the nation. Thanks in large part to the British merchant marine and navy, production for export rose 80 percent between 1750 and 1770. Britain was also blessed with natural resources such as coal and rivers. And the well-developed canal system aided in the transport of raw materials around the country. Lastly, we must grasp the significant contribution of the Protestant Dissenters who, because of their beliefs, were denied certain civil and political rights. Many of them were trying to make their mark, and the only way possible to do so was to go into manufacturing. Some of the most impressive of the eighteenth century captains of industry were themselves Dissenters.

The Industrial Revolution marked a major turning point in world history, and it seemed to all that progress was now part of human existence itself. Humanity was moving forward and would continue to do so. Not everyone enjoyed the fruits of technological innovation, nor should we forget that laborers—men, women, and children—were now expected to heed factory discipline and the factory whistle. Task work was replaced by time work. The Revolution also made it implicitly known that technology held the keys to future progress, a notion that is perhaps still with us today.

SUGGESTED FEATURE FILMS

Great Expectations. 118 min. B/W. 1946. Universal Pictures. David Lean directed this Dickens classic, which is excellent for the way in which it depicts the atmosphere of nineteenth-century London.

Hard Times. 100 min. Color. 1994. PBS. Masterpiece Theatre's adaptation of Dickens' novel about the life of a victorian family, set in a grim, dark place in the north of England called Coketown.

Middlemarch. 90 min. Color. 1994. BBC in association with WGBH. Masterpiece Theatre's six-part adaptation of the George Eliot novel set against the background of the Industrial Revolution.

Modern Times. 87 min. B/W. 1936. United Artists. Although this Charlie Chaplin masterpiece is about the twentieth century, it remains a solid introduction to the dehumanizing effects of industry. Timeless.

SUGGESTED CLASSROOM FILMS

Adam Smith and the Wealth of Nations. 28 min. Color. 1975. Insight Media. The life, career, and ideas of Scottish economist and philosopher Adam Smith.

The Ascent of Man: The Drive for Power. 52 min. Color. 1974. Time-Life Films. Jacob Bronowski explores the eighteenth-century economic revolution.

Coal, Blood, and Iron: Industrialization. 55 min. Color. 1991. Insight Media. Examines the technological and social transformations centering on the use of coal as fuel.

The Industrial Revolution. 20 min. each. Color. 1992. Films for the Humanities and Sciences. This series explores the Industrial Revolution in Britain through the approach of case studies: I. *Working Lives*; II. *Evolving Transportation Systems*; III. *The Railway Age*; IV. *Harnessing Steam*; V. *The Growth of Towns and Cities*.

The Industrial Revolution. 44 min. Color. 1995. Insight Media. Two-part series that traces the Industrial Revolution from its origins through its momentous growth in the eighteenth and nineteenth centuries.

The Industrial Revolution and the Industrial World: Part One. 30 min. Color. 1989. Insight Media. Looks not only at changes in industry but also the related changes in commerce, agriculture, and communications.

Material World. 30 min. Color. 2003. Films for the Humanities and Sciences. Shows how England's insatiable appetite for tea, cotton, and china fueled that country's industrial revolution. Part of the *What the Industrial Revolution Did for Us* series.

CHAPTER 20 | From Restoration to Revolution, 1815–1848

d. Established a ruler's legitimacy based on international treaties and not divine right
B. Revolt against Restoration
   1. Secret organization: the Carbonari
      a. Vowed to oppose the government in Vienna
      b. Spread through southern Europe and France in the 1820s
      c. Aims
         i. Some called for a constitution
         ii. Others sang the praises of Bonaparte
   2. Naples and the Piedmont
      a. Opposition turned to revolt
      b. Restored monarchs abandoned their promises
   3. Metternich summoned Austrian, Prussian, and Russian representatives
      a. The Troppau memorandum (1820)
         i. Declared they would aid each other in suppressing revolution
         ii. France and Britain declined to sign
C. Revolution in Latin America
   1. The unsteady foundations of colonial rule
   2. Argentina declared independence in 1816
   3. The liberation of Chile and Peru
   4. Simon de Bolivar (1783–1830)
      a. Led uprisings from Venezuela across to Bolivia
   5. Political revolts unleashed conflict and civil war
      a. Some elites sought liberation from Spain
      b. Radicals wanted land reforms and an end to slavery
      c. The repression of radical movements
   6. Metternich and the conservative response—no revolutions in Latin America
   7. The United States
      a. The Monroe Doctrine (1823)
         i. Warned Europe that intervention in the New World was an unfriendly act
   8. Britain
      a. Recognized South American republics
      b. New trading partner
   9. Brazil declared independence in 1822
D. Russia: the Decembrists
   1. Death of Tsar Alexander I (1825)
   2. The Decembrists

a. Most came from noble families or were members of elite regiments
b. Saw Russia as the liberator of Europe
c. Russia needed reform
   i. Serfdom contradicted the promise of liberation
   ii. Curbing the tsar's power
d. No political program
   i. Ranged from constitutional monarchs to Jacobin republicans
   ii. Wanted Constantine to assume the throne and guarantee a constitution
   3. Nicholas I (1796–1855, r. 1825–1855)
      a. Crushed the Decembrist revolt
      b. The Third Section (secret police force)
         i. The culture of fear and suspicion
   4. Signs of change
      a. The bureaucracy became more centralized and efficient
      b. Less dependence on the nobility for political support
      c. The codification of the legal system (1832)
      d. Landowners reorganized their estates
E. Southeastern Europe: Balkans (Greece and Serbia)
   1. Local movements in Greece and Serbia began to demand autonomy
   2. Greek war for independence (1821–1827)
      a. European sympathy and European identity
      b. Christians cast the rebellion as a war between Christianity and Islam
         i. A crusade for liberty
         ii. A crusade to preserve the classical heritage (Philhellenism)
      c. Delacroix, Massacre at Chios (1824)
      d. Celebrating Greeks and demonizing Turks
      e. British, French, and Russian troops went in against the Turks in 1827
      f. The London Protocols (1829–1830)
         i. Established Greek independence from the Ottoman Empire
   3. Serbia
      a. Europe sided with the Serbs against the Ottomans

b. Serbian semi-independence
 i. An Orthodox Christian principality under Ottoman rule
4. Results
 a. European opportunism
 b. Greece and Serbia did not break close ties with the Ottomans
III. Taking Sides: New Ideologies in Politics
 A. Principles of conservatism
  1. The concept of legitimacy as a general antirevolutionary policy
  2. The monarchy was a guarantee of political stability
   a. The nobility as the rightful leaders of the nation
  3. Change must be slow, incremental, and managed
  4. Edmund Burke (1729–1797)
   a. *Reflections on the Revolution in France* (1790)
   b. Opposed all talk of natural rights (too abstract)
   c. The dangers of human reason
   d. Deference to experience, tradition, and history
  5. Joseph de Maistre (1753–1821) and Louis-Gabriel-Ambroise Bonald (1754–1840)
   a. Defended absolute monarchy
   b. The Catholic Church
  6. The monarchy, aristocracy, and church as mainstays of the social and political order
  7. The revival of religion
   a. Expressed a popular reaction against revolution
   b. Emphasis on order, discipline, and tradition
 B. Liberalism
  1. The commitment to individual liberties and rights
  2. Most important function of government was to protect these rights
   a. Justice, knowledge, and progress
  3. Components
   a. Equality before the law
   b. Government rests on the consent of the governed
   c. Laissez-faire economic principles
  4. The roots of liberalism
   a. John Locke
   b. American and French Revolutions
   c. Inalienable rights
    i. Freedom from arbitrary authority, imprisonment, and censorship
    ii. Freedom of the press
    iii. The right to assemble
   d. Written constitutions
  5. Advocated direct representation in government (for property-owners)
  6. Economic liberalism
   a. Adam Smith (1723–1790), *The Wealth of Nations* (1776)
    i. Attacked mercantilism in the name of free markets
    ii. The economy should be based on a "system of natural liberty"
   b. Political economy
    i. Identified basic economic laws (supply and demand, balance of trade)
   c. David Ricardo (1772–1823)
    i. Laws of wages and rents
   d. Economic activity ought to be unconstrained
    i. Labor contracted freely
    ii. Property unencumbered by feudal restrictions
    iii. Goods to circulate freely
    iv. An end to government-granted monopolies
   e. The government should preserve order and protect property
  7. Liberty and freedom
   a. In lands occupied by foreign powers, liberty meant freedom from foreign rule
   b. Central and southeastern Europe
    i. The elimination of feudal privilege
    ii. More rights for local parliaments
   c. Great Britain
    i. Expanding the franchise
    ii. Laissez-faire economics and free trade
    iii. Creating a limited and efficient government
   d. Jeremy Bentham (1748–1832)
    i. *The Principles of Morals and Legislation* (1789)
    ii. Human interests are not naturally harmonious
    iii. Utilitarianism—"the greatest happiness of the greatest number"
 C. Radicalism, republicanism, and early socialism
  1. Republicans
   a. Demanded constitutions and governments by the people

b. An expanded franchise and democratic participation in politics

2. Socialism
   a. Raising the "social question" as an urgent political matter
   b. Socialism as a response to rapid industrialization
      i. The intensification of labor, miseries of the working classes, and social class
      ii. Competition, individualism, and private property

3. Robert Owen (1771–1858)
   a. Built a model workshop at New Lanark (Scotland)
   b. The principles of cooperation not profitability
   c. Organized good housing, sanitation, free schooling, social security

4. Charles Fourier (1772–1837)
   a. The abolition of the wage system
   b. The division of labor based on natural inclinations
   c. Complete equality of the sexes

5. Louis Blanc (1811–1882)
   a. Campaigned for universal male suffrage
   b. Giving working men control of the state
   c. "Associations of producers"

6. Pierre-Joseph Proudhon (1809–1865)
   a. What is property?—"Property is theft"

D. Karl Marx (1818–1883) and socialism
   1. Influenced by Hegel's philosophy
   2. Studied philosophy but became a journalist
      a. The *Rheinische Zeitung* (1842–1843)
      b. Marx exiled to Paris, then Brussels, then London
   3. Partnership with Friedrich Engels (1820–1895)
      a. Experience in the Manchester textile factories
      b. *The Condition of the Working Classes in England* (1844)
   4. In 1847, Marx and Engels joined the League of the Just (later renamed the Communist League)
   5. *The Communist Manifesto* (1848)
      a. History and conflict
         i. Master and slave
         ii. Lord and serf
         iii. Bourgeois and proletariat
      b. Capitalism would "dig its own grave"

c. With the collapse of capitalism, the workers would seize the state
   d. Communism
   e. Dialectical materialism

E. Citizenship and community: nationalism
   1. Nation, from the Latin *nasci* (to be born)
   2. The French Revolution defined "nation" to mean the people, or the sovereign people
   3. Celebrating a new political community, not a territory or ethnicity
   4. Nationalism in the early nineteenth century
      a. Nation symbolized legal equality, constitutional government, and an end to feudal privilege
      b. Nationalism as a threat to the local power of aristocratic elites
   5. Nationalism and the liberals
      a. Associated with political transformations
      b. The awakening of the common people
      c. But nationalism could undermine liberalism as well
         i. Nationalism might require the sacrifice of some freedoms
   6. National identity developed and changed historically
   7. Nationalism and the state
      a. Developing national feelings
      b. Linking citizens to the state
      c. Educational systems taught a national language
      d. "Inventing" a national heritage

IV. Cultural Revolt: Romanticism
   A. General observations
      1. A diverse intellectual and cultural movement
      2. A reaction against the Classicism of the eighteenth century
      3. Instead of reason and discipline, Romanticism embraced emotion, freedom, and imagination
      4. The individual, individuality, and the subjective experience
      5. Intuition, emotion, and feelings as the guides to truth
   B. British Romantic poetry
      1. William Wordsworth (1770–1850) and Samuel Taylor Coleridge (1772–1834)
         a. *Lyrical Ballads*
         b. Compassion and feeling bind all men together
         c. Nature as humanity's most trusted teacher

2. William Blake (1757–1827)
   a. Individual imagination and the poetic vision
   b. Fierce critic of industrial society
   c. The imagination could awaken human sensibilities
3. George Gordon, Lord Byron (1788–1824)
   a. Poetry was the "lava of imagination"
   b. An aristocrat who rebelled against conformity and inhibition
   c. His Romanticism was inseparable from his liberal politics
4. Percy Bysshe Shelley (1792–1822)
   a. *Prometheus Unbound* (1820)
   b. Defined romantic heroism and the cult of individual audacity

C. Women writers, gender, and Romanticism
   1. Mary Godwin Shelley (1797–1851)
      a. Daughter of William Godwin and Mary Wollstonecraft
      b. Fascination with contemporary scientific developments
      c. *Frankenstein, or, the Modern Prometheus* (1818)
         i. A twisted creation myth
         ii. Individual genius gone wrong
   2. George Sand (1804–1876)
      a. Defying convention
      b. Rebellion against middle-class moral values
   3. Madame de Staël (1766–1817)
      a. Popularized German Romanticism in France
      b. *De l'Allemagne* (*Germany*, 1810)
      c. Suggested that men could be emotional and that men and women shared a common human nature

D. Romantic painting
   1. Britain
      a. John Constable (1776–1837)
         i. "It is the soul that sees"
         ii. Emphasized the artist's individual technique
      b. J. M. W. Turner (1775–1851)
         i. Intensely subjective, personal, and imaginative
         ii. Experimented with brush strokes and color
   2. France
      a. Eugene Delacroix (1798–1863)
   3. New ways of visualizing the world
   4. Pointed to early-twentieth-century modernism

E. Romantic politics: liberty, history, and nation
   1. Victor Hugo (1802–1885)
      a. Dealt sympathetically with the experience of the common people

   b. *Nôtre Dame de Paris* (1831) and *Les Misérables* (1862)
   2. François de Chataubriand (1768–1848)
      a. *The Genius of Christianity* (1802)
      b. Religious experiences of the national past are woven into the present
      c. Accent on religious emotion, feeling, and subjectivity
   3. The Romantic uniqueness of cultures
      a. Johann von Herder (1744–1803)
         i. *Ideas for a Philosophy of Human History* (1784–1791)
         ii. Civilization arises out of the *Volk* (common people), not elites
         iii. The *Volkgeist*—spirit or genius of the people
   4. Brothers Grimm
      a. *Grimm's Fairy Tales* (1812–1815)
      b. Collected German folktales
   5. Friedrich Schiller (1759–1805) and *Wilhelm Tell* (1804)
      a. A rallying cry fir German national consciousness
   6. Sir Walter Scott (1771–1832)
   7. Adam Mickiewicz (1798–1855), *Pan Tadeusz* (1834)

F. Orientalism
   1. Napoleon's invasion of Egypt (1798)
      a. Brought back the Rosetta stone
      b. Establishment of the Egyptian Institute
      c. *The Description of Egypt* (23 volumes, 1809–1823)
   2. Defined Europe by looked at the Orient
   3. A fascination with ethnography and new regions
   4. Looking for the roots of Christianity
   5. Fascination with medieval history and religion (especially the Crusades)
   6. The "oriental renaissance"

G. Goethe and Beethoven
   1. Johann Wolfgang von Goethe (1749–1832)
      a. *The Sorrows of Young Werther* (1774)
         i. Yearnings and restless love
      b. Backed away from the excesses of Romanticism
      c. *Faust* (1790)
         i. Faust sells his soul to the devil in return for eternal youth and universal knowledge
   2. Ludwig van Beethoven (1770–1827)
      a. A Classicist and Romantic

b. Glorification of nature and individuality

c. The poetry of instrumental music

d. Raised music as an art form at the center of the Romantic movement

3. Goethe and Beethoven as transitional figures

V. Reform and Revolution

A. The 1830 Revolution in France

1. Louis XVIII succeeded by Charles X (1757–1836, r. 1824–1830)

a. Determined to reverse the legacies of the Revolution and Napoleon

b. Appeased the ultraroyalists by compensating nobility whose land had been confiscated during the Revolution

c. Restored the Catholic Church to its traditional place

d. Provoked widespread discontent

2. Charles called new elections, then tried to overthrow the parliamentary regime

3. The July Ordinances (1830)

a. Dissolved the newly elected chamber before it had even met

b. Imposed strict censorship of the press

c. Further restricted suffrage to exclude all non-nobles

d. Called for new elections

4. Revolution

a. Paris took to the streets for three days of battles

b. The abdication of Charles

5. Louis Philippe (1773–1850, r. 1830–1848)

a. Promoted as a constitutional monarch

b. The July Monarchy

i. Doubled the number of eligible voters

ii. Voting remained a privilege

6. Major winners—the propertied classes

B. Belgium and Poland in 1830

1. Congress of Vienna joined Belgium to Holland

a. Never popular in Belgium

2. News of the July Revolution catalyzed Belgian opposition

3. Brussels rebelled and the great powers guaranteed Belgian neutrality (in force until 1914)

4. Poland

a. Not an independent state—under Russian governance

b. Had its own parliament, a constitution, and guarantees of basic liberties

c. Ignored by Russian-imposed head of state, Constantine

d. Moved toward revolt in 1830

e. Drove Constantine out

f. By 1831, Russian forces retook Warsaw

g. Poland placed under Russian military rule

C. Reform in Great Britain

1. The end of the Napoleonic wars

a. Agricultural depression, low wages, unemployment, and bad harvests

b. Social unrest

2. Peterloo (1819)

3. Parliament passed the Six Acts (1819)

a. Outlawed "seditious and blasphemous" literature

b. Increased stamp tax

c. Restricted the right of public meeting

4. Tory reforms

a. Some toleration for Catholics and Dissenters

b. Refused to reform political representation in the House of Commons

5. Liberal reforms

a. Whigs, industrial middle classes, and radical artisans demand reform

b. The desire to enfranchise responsible citizens

6. Reform Bill of 1832

a. Eliminated "rotten" boroughs

b. Reallocated 143 parliamentary seats from the rural south to the industrial north

c. Expanded the franchise

d. The political strength of landed aristocratic interests remained

7. The repeal of the Corn Laws (1846)

a. Corn Laws protected British landlords from foreign competition

b. Kept the price of bread artificially high

c. The Anti–Corn Law League

i. Held large meetings throughout northern England

ii. Lobbied members in Parliament

iii. Persuaded Prime Minister Peel to repeal the Corn Laws

D. British radicalism and the Chartist Movement

1. The Six Points of the People's Charter

a. Universal white male suffrage

b. The secret ballot

c. Abolition of property qualification for membership in the Commons

d. Annual parliamentary elections

e. Payment of salaries to members of the Commons

f. Equal electoral districts

2. With deteriorating economic conditions, Chartism spread in the 1840s

3. Chartists disagreed about tactics and goals

    a. William Lovett

      i. Self-improvement

      ii. Education of artisans was the answer

    b. Feargus O'Connor

      i. Appealed to the impoverished and desperate class of workers

      ii. Attacked industrialization

    c. Bronterre O'Brien

      i. Openly admired Robespierre

4. Opposition to the Chartists

5. Chartists presented petitions to Parliament in 1839 and 1842—both rejected

6. April 1848: Chartists planned a major demonstration and show of force in London

    a. Twenty-five thousand workers marched to Parliament with a petition of 6 million signatures demanding the Six Points

    b. The failure of Chartism

E. The Hungry Forties and the Revolutions of 1848

1. The poor harvests of the early 1840s

2. Food prices doubled

3. Bread riots

4. Cyclical industrial slowdowns and unemployment

F. The French Revolution of 1848

1. July Monarchy under Charles X seemed little different from that of Louis XVIII

2. Political crises

    a. Republican disillusionment

    b. Republican societies proliferate

    c. Rebellions in Lyons and Paris

3. The banquet of February 22, 1848

    a. The French government banned the meeting

    b. The revolution began

    c. Louis Philippe abdicates

4. Provisional government

    a. A combination of liberals, republicans, and socialists

    b. A new constitution based on universal male suffrage

    c. Tensions between middle-class republicans and socialists

5. The National Workshops

    a. A program of public works in and around Paris

    b. Planned to support twelve thousand workers

    c. Unemployment reached 65 percent

    d. Workers streamed in to join the Workshop

      i. 66,000 (April), 120,000 (June)

6. Popular politics

    a. Provisional government lifted restrictions on freedom of speech and political activity

    b. Women's clubs and newspapers appeared

7. The end of the National Workshops

    a. French assembly decided the Workshops were a financial drain

      i. May—closed the Workshops to future enrollment

      ii. June 21—the government ended the program

8. The June Days (June 23–26): Parisian workers barricade the streets

9. Repression

    a. Three thousand killed, twelve thousand arrested

10. The government of Louis Napoleon Bonaparte (1808–1873)

    a. Spent most of his life in exile

    b. Used his position to consolidate his power

    c. Permitted Catholics to regain control of the schools

    d. Banned meetings, workers' associations

    e. Asked the people to grant him the power to draw up a new constitution (1851)

11. The Second Empire of Napoleon III (1852–1870)

12. Significance of the 1848 Revolution in France

    a. Its dynamics would be repeated elsewhere

    b. The pivotal role of the middle classes

    c. Many saw the June Days as naked class struggle

      i. Shattered many liberal aspirations

    d. Middle-class and working-class politics were more sharply differentiated

VI. Conclusion
  A. The partial success of the Congress of Vienna
  B. The Revolution of 1848 as the opening act of a larger drama

GENERAL DISCUSSION QUESTIONS

1. What were the goals and principles of the Congress of Vienna? How did delegates from the great powers respond to the grievances of their people? How successful were they in creating a European system to deal with these problems?

2. In what ways did the revolutionary years in Europe between 1789 and 1830 lead to revolutions in Latin America? How were Latin American revolutions different from the European variety?

3. What are the general characteristics of socialism as it appeared in the works and careers of Owen, Fourier, Blanc, and Proudhon? How was early-nineteenth-century socialism a product of both the French and Industrial Revolutions?

4. Describe the relationship between conservatism, liberalism, socialism, and nationalism in early-nineteenth-century Europe. What was the inspiration for these various ideologies? Did they emerge from a similar or different historical context?

5. Karl Marx was quite specific when he argued that "capitalism would dig its own grave." How did Marx arrive at this conclusion? In other words, what had Marx learned by studying the history of human society?

6. If eighteenth-century Classical art stressed reason, discipline, and harmony, what were the contrasting qualities of nineteenth-century Romanticism? How was it possible for some great artists such as Johann Wolfgang von Goethe and Ludwig van Beethoven to belong to both movements?

7. Popular revolts had taken place in Europe for centuries, though most of them failed when the authorities used heavily armed professional soldiers to put down unruly peasants. How did the French Revolution of 1789 mark a change in power relations, inspiring fear in rulers and hope among revolutionaries in other areas? Was there a natural "right of revolution"?

8. By the 1840s there was an upsurge of radicalism in Britain, but the British did not have a revolution. How was the "People's Charter" movement a polite expression of a desire for democracy and social justice? Had many of the Chartists learned the rules of the game of reform?

10. How was Great Britain able to avoid revolution in 1789, 1830, and 1848?

11. What were the causes of the French Revolution of 1848? Was there unfinished business from 1789, 1799, and 1830? Did history repeat itself, as Karl Marx said, "the first time as tragedy, the second as farce"?

DOCUMENT DISCUSSION QUESTIONS

Popular Unrest in Paris

1. Paid spies and informers had an interest in dramatizing their information, yet here the general tone of popular complaints is unmistakable. Did Parisian workers make the same complaints in 1828 as in 1789? Were working people more vocal in 1789, 1828, or 1848?

2. Why was the Restoration so unpopular with the French people? Was the mystique of monarchy lost or missing? What had happened to that mystique between 1789 and 1815?

3. Despite rising public discontent, there was no political revolution in France in 1828. There was, however, a partially successful revolution in July 1830. Why did it result in a monarchy instead of a republic? How did the leadership of old conspirators make a difference in the plotting, execution, and outcome of the revolt?

Women and the Anti–Corn Law League

4. The Corn Laws of 1815 sought to reduce food imports and maintain high prices. Wealthy farmers benefited; the truly poor, the working class, and wage-paying manufacturers were disadvantaged. Consider the Anti–Corn Law League as a case study in political interest groups and explain the economic and non-economic interests that held the group together.

5. What objections were raised to the role of women as political agitators? Recall that while Victoria was queen, women were not allowed to vote in Britain, and they were allowed to vote in only a few states in the United States. Try to reconstruct the conservative author's reasoning.

6. The Anti–Corn Law League obtained repeal of the Corn Laws in 1846. How? Who supported the repeal and why? Compare and contrast the success of repeal with the failure of the Chartist movement, which represented different interests.

Two Views of the June Days, France, 1848

7. On what grounds did Marx call one revolution "beautiful" and the other "ugly" and "repulsive"? Should a

reporter make aesthetic judgments and embellish the facts? Marx had a private axe to grind: he saw the revolution of 1848 as quite different from earlier revolts and revolutions. How and why was it different?

8. Tocqueville, a liberal nobleman who studied prison reform and wrote *Democracy in America*, was puzzled by the French Revolution of 1848. He called it "the greatest and strangest that had ever taken place in our history," because of the massive participation and coordination despite a lack of leaders. Do revolutions have to be led, or can they break out spontaneously? Do good leaders follow the public's wishes, or do they lead the public toward their chosen goal?

9. Tocqueville raised the "social question" as a cause of the 1848 revolts, which he considered more significant than struggles for political control. Why? Consider that the poor are easily distracted from political goals, but often reminded of their own poverty. Thus they favor redistribution of wealth and offices, a more radical social change than replacing the nation's political leaders. Robespierre, Saint-Just, and the Jacobins had debated these topics in 1794. How were the issues different in 1848?

SAMPLE LECTURE 20: AN AGE OF IDEOLOGIES, 1780–1850

Lecture Objectives

1. To bring attention to the number of ideologies that flourished in the early nineteenth century
2. To examine Romanticism, conservatism, liberalism, and nationalism as by-products of the French Revolution

THE FRENCH REVOLUTION AND THE RISE OF IDEOLOGIES

The nineteenth century in Europe has been given many descriptive labels. For instance, the impact of the Industrial Revolution was great enough and revolutionary enough to touch almost every European subject. The century could also be called an Age of Progress, or an Age of Improvement, or even the Victorian Age. But the nineteenth century has also been considered as an Age of Ideology—better yet, an Age of Ideologies. Darwinism, Marxism, and Freudianism are all products of the long nineteenth century. So too were realism, naturalism, socialism, anarchism, communism, nihilism, and positivism. The flowering of all these "isms," these grand systems of thought, belief, and action, were products of the Enlightenment and the French Revolution. It was the latter revolution that really forced people to make a decision, to choose a side, to voice or elaborate their own opinions. The revolutionary spirit of the last quarter of the eighteenth century forced people to make political decisions, economic decisions, and religious decisions, and as various people voiced similar opinions, ideologies were

born. By 1815 the Napoleonic Wars had come to an end. The "concert of Europe" was fashioned at the peace settlement at Vienna. European rulers were determined to prevent the appearance of future Robespierres and Napoleons. They were equally concerned about the common people. These rulers defended their prerogative to rule and attacked the liberal ideas of the later eighteenth century. Conservatism was born to protect tradition and custom from the onslaught of change, reform, or outright rebellion. Conservatism as an ideology was a product of the French Revolution itself. But the forces unleashed by that Revolution also produced the enemy of conservatism. The ideology of liberalism, in its political or economic guise, aimed to secure the liberty and equality proclaimed by the men of 1789. So the French Revolution unleashed two powerful forces—conservatism and liberalism. Meanwhile, nationalism emerged as a form of liberation for subject peoples and for the unity of nations that had weathered the storms of Napoleon's Grand Empire. Ideologies came in many shapes—political, economic, and religious. Some were cultural in nature and exceedingly difficult to define.

ROMANTICISM

The Romantic movement was so complex and varied that historians have never reached a clear consensus as to what it exactly meant or even did not mean. Among the ranks of the Romantics we find liberals and conservatives and revolutionaries and reactionaries. Some began their lives as Catholics, became revolutionaries, and died conservatives. Some were preoccupied with God, others were atheists to the core. Between 1780 and 1850, most of Europe's cultural life was dominated and defined by this complex movement in art, literature, music, philosophy, and even the writing of history itself. In Britain we have the poetry of Blake, Wordsworth, Coleridge, Keats, Shelley, and Byron. In France, the novels of Victor Hugo. Germany had the historian Herder, the Grimm brothers, Goethe, and Schiller. In music, we have Beethoven, Berlioz, Chopin, Schubert, and at the end of the nineteenth century, Richard Wagner.

The essential message of the Romantics was that the imagination of the individual should determine the form and content of all art. And the key virtues were creativity and genius. Such an intellectual attitude ran counter to the rationalism of the Enlightenment. The philosophes attacked the church because it blocked human reason—the Romantics attacked the Enlightenment because it blocked the emotions and creativity. As Wordsworth reminded us in *The Tables Turned* (1798):

> Books! 'tis a dull and endless strife:
> Come, hear the woodland linnet,
> How sweet his music! on my life,
> There's more of wisdom in it.

Or, as William Hazlitt once remarked, "for the better part of my life all I did was think." William Godwin, the philosophical anarchist whose soul depended on human reason, could opine after the death of his wife Mary Wollstonecraft, "What shall I do when I have read all the books?" Christianity had formed the matrix within which medieval man situated himself. The Enlightenment replaced the Christian matrix with the mechanical matrix of Newtonian natural philosophy. For the Romantics, the result was the demotion of the individual. Imagination, sensitivity, feeling, spontaneity, and freedom were stifled by reason, choked to death. Man must liberate himself from these chains. Like Rousseau, the Romantics yearned to discover human freedom. Habits, values, rules, and standards imposed by civilization had to be abandoned. Or as Rousseau put it in *The Social Contract* (1762), "Man is born free and everywhere he is in chains." The philosophes embraced the uniformity of human nature—the Romantics saw diversity and uniqueness. And if individuals are unique so too are nations. So the Romantics asked that we discover ourselves, express ourselves—play our own music, write our own poetry, paint our own personal visions, live, love, and suffer in our own ways. Whereas the motto of the Enlightenment was "Dare to know!" the battle cry of the Romantics was perhaps "Dare to be!" The Romantics were rebels, and they knew it.

They were also passionate about their subjectivity. Again we turn to Rousseau. In the introduction to his *Confessions*, he wrote:

> I am commencing an undertaking, hitherto without precedent and which will never find an imitator. I desire to set before my fellows the likeness of a man in all the truth of nature, and that man myself. Myself alone! I know the feelings of my heart, and I know men. I am not made like any of those I have seen. I venture to believe that I am not made like any of those who are in existence. If I am not better, at least I am different.

For the Romantics, poetry revealed the highest truth. Poetry could do what rational analysis and geometric calculation could not. Poetry could speak to the heart, clarify life's mysteries, and bring out the imagination of the soul. "O for a life of sensations rather than of thoughts," said John Keats. "Bathe in the waters of life," said William Blake. The Romantics gave European culture an antidote to the excessive rationality of the eighteenth-century philosophes. Intensely subjective and introspective, the Romantics discovered the soul behind the mind. Perhaps it was Shelley who best captured the spirit of the age in *Prometheus Unbound* (1820):

> The joy, the triumph, the delight, the madness!
> The boundless, overflowing, bursting of gladness,
> The vaporous exultation not to be confined!
> Ha! Ha! The animation of delight
> Which wraps me, like an atmosphere of light,
> And bears me as a cloud is borne by its own wind.

THE CONSERVATIVE REACTION

For the rulers of Europe in 1815, the French Revolution was a great evil that had inflicted the greatest wound upon Europe. The execution of Louis XVI in January 1793 was an act of anarchy. So too was the confiscation of church property, Robespierre's Reign of Terror, and the rise and fall of Napoleon Bonaparte. These rulers were disgusted by the Revolution, disgusted by its violence, war, terror, and cruelty. For conservative rulers and political thinkers, the natural rights of man, the inherent goodness of man, and the idea of progress were perverse ideas created by the greatest of murderers—the Jacobins. This general characteristic was given an ideological formulation by the Irish-born statesman and parliamentary orator Edmund Burke. In 1790 Burke published his *Reflections on the Revolution in France* in order to caution Britain about the dangers of revolution. Burke's more specific target was a November 1789 sermon delivered by the Protestant Dissenter Richard Price in London. It was Price who inflamed his audience with statements like "tremble all ye oppressors of the world." Burke knew that the French Revolution would turn violent and eventually lead to a military dictatorship. He feared a similar upheaval in Britain. For Burke, the Jacobins were fanatics, armed with abstract ideas divorced from tradition and history. The Jacobins, like the philosophes, all agreed that man could transform his environment and so transform human nature. This notion was central to the idea of progress as it had been working out over the course of the century. But Burke saw progress as nothing more than an arrogance of attitude. Appeals to the future cannot be made without appeals to the past, and according to Burke, the revolutionaries not only abandoned the past, they had destroyed it. The philosophes knew no limitation to the use of human reason. The conservatives did—man could not be trusted to make intelligent decisions, least of all the common people (or "swinish multitude," as Burke called them). For the conservative, man was not inherently good, and so society created laws and customs to keep evil in check. If these laws and customs broke down anarchy would prevail, and this is precisely how Burke saw the Revolution. Since monarchy, aristocracy, and the church had stood for centuries past, they should stand in the future as well. Touch nothing, venerate ancient traditions, and do not destroy history, seemed to be Burke's message. Unlike the eighteenth-century philosophes, conservatives like Burke did not see society as a complex mechanism that obeyed natural laws. Instead, society was compared to an organism—destroy vital organs, as the French revolutionaries had done, and the entire edifice of society would collapse. Whereas the philosophes attempted to elevate the individual over the state, conservatives believed that the state was more important than the individual. According to Burke, there were no natural rights of man. The only rights were those given to man by virtue of being French, German, or British.

LIBERALISM

The years after 1815 saw a spectacular rise of the European middle class. The rise of this class to prominence was part of a trend that had been growing throughout the eighteenth century. The middle classes consisted of ambitious men—bankers, merchants, manufacturers, and other professionals. As a class they resented the stranglehold that the landed nobility held on political power and social prestige, and so they wanted to eliminate all restrictions on the unlimited pursuit of material gain and profit. Early-nineteenth-century liberals were children of the Enlightenment:

- They wanted to alter the status quo.
- They wanted a piece of the action.
- They wanted to carry out the promises and ideals of the philosophes.
- They wanted to pursue many of the liberal ideals of the French Revolution.

While conservatives like Burke extolled the virtues of the state, liberals focused on individual liberties and freedom. They believed that the value of an individual was not based on birth but on the talent and merit of the individual. Liberals had confidence in man—confidence in his inherent goodness and his capacity to control his own destiny. The early-nineteenth-century liberal was the direct heir to the program of the Enlightenment:

- liberty of opinion
- freedom of conscience
- religious toleration
- life, liberty, and the pursuit of happiness

Montesquieu and Voltaire had already looked to Britain for an example, and the American Revolution gave expression to Locke's notion of the natural rights of man. The United States Constitution demonstrated that the people could choose their own form of government while the Bill of Rights protected the person and property of the individual. The French National Assembly of 1789 implemented the liberal idea of equality under the law, while the Declaration of the Rights of Man and Citizen guaranteed the inalienable rights of man. The primary concern of all nineteenth-century liberals was the protection and enhancement of individual liberty. If the individual were simply left alone, he could make his own decisions, based on universal moral principles, and respect the rights of others. Such opinion was once again grounded in the eighteenth century:

- Man is rational; man is good.
- Leave man alone and he will rationally act with goodness.
- If everyone acted in this way, harmony would be the result.

This had all been argued by Adam Smith in *The Wealth of Nations.* The conclusion was perhaps quite simple—the government that governs best is the one that governs least, a theme taken up by Thomas Paine in his *Rights of Man*, a book written to refute Burke's *Reflections.* The great question that confronted the liberal was the relationship between the individual and the state. Liberals demanded written constitutions:

- to protect the individual from the arbitrary authority of kings

- to grant freedoms of speech, the press, and religion
- to prevent arbitrary arrest
- to protect private property

Liberalism also meant that the economy ought to follow its own natural laws. Since people are self-interested beings, they work harder and achieve more when they receive the benefits of their work. Man's passion to competition spurred economic activity and insured the production of more commodities for the lowest possible price. This, in the end, would benefit the well-being of an entire nation. The state should block neither individual liberty nor free enterprise. All the state should do is maintain domestic order and tranquility. Liberals clearly believed that individuals were their own masters.

NATIONALISM

Nationalism may be defined as a conscious bond between a group of people who share several things in common—language, religion, region, culture, and history. The nationalist believed that the highest duty and devotion should be directed toward the state, or at least toward some higher goal. Such a notion became implicit in the French Revolution. After all, the revolutionaries were trying to determine a new identity for the French nation. Nationalism is a religion. It provides the individual with an intense sense of community and belonging and with a cause worthy enough to die for. Since Christianity's influence was waning throughout the eighteenth century, nationalism became a predominant spiritual force across Europe, but especially in central and eastern Europe. Nationalism provided new beliefs, martyrs, and holy days that stimulated reverence. It gave people identity, community, and brotherhood. Nationalism also supplied the people with a mission—the improvement of the nation is always in the interest of the nation and its people. This ideology appears full-blown during the days of the French Revolution:

- The French created their own nation.
- An arbitrary monarch had been dethroned.
- The state now invoked the will of the people.
- The French no longer viewed themselves as noble or bourgeois, or as Breton or Norman, but as citizens of the French nation.

By 1793, the Jacobins had created a national army who fought not for gain or individual glory, but for the love and glory of France. The Romantic movement also aided in the development of a nationalist ethos, especially in Germany. By examining the German language, culture, myths, and fol tales, Romantic thinkers instilled a sense of national pride. The discovery of such a *Volkgeist* (soul of the people) meant that cultures were unique and creative entities. Each nation expressed its cultural genius in language, literature, and folk traditions. All Europeans were not the same. Nationalism was a product of the heart, not the excessive rationalism of the philosophe. But after the French Revolution, nationalist passions were aroused. By the end of the nineteenth century, nationalism included a few other ideas unknown a century earlier—the irrational and mythic quality of nationalism intensified. Nationalism would now provoke racial and ethnic hatred toward other nationalities.

SUGGESTED FEATURE FILMS

Goya (subtitled). 107 min. Color. 1999. Sony Pictures Classics. Tells the story of Francisco Goya's last years, spent in voluntary exile in Bordeaux as a liberal protesting the oppressive rule of Ferdinand VII.

Haunted Summer. 88 min. Color. 1986. Cannon Films. Ivan Passer film about the summer of 1816, when Mary Shelley wrote *Frankenstein* in the company of Byron, Shelley, and Mary's stepsister Claire Godwin.

Immortal Beloved. 120 min. Color. 1994. Columbia Pictures. Film dealing with the life and death of the legendary Ludwig van Beethoven (Gary Oldman).

Les Enfants du siècle (subtitled). 105 min. Color. 1995. Empire Pictures. True tale of the tumultuous love affair between novelist George Sand and poet Alfred de Musset.

Many of Jane Austen's novels have made it to the big screen or television. For instance, see: *Pride and Prejudice* (1995); *Sense and Sensibility* (1995); *Persuasion* (1995); *Emma* (1996); and *Mansfield Park* (1999).

SUGGESTED CLASSROOM FILMS

Age of Reason/Age of Passion. 130 min. Color. 1994. Kultur Video. European art and artists from the mid-eighteenth-century through the Romantics. Part of Sister Wendy's *Art of the Western World* series.

Breaking the Trade: The Abolition of Slavery in the British Empire. 30 min. Color. 2001. Films for the Humanities and Sciences. The story of the three men largely responsible for slavery's abolition: William Wilberforce, Granville Sharp, and Thomas Clarkson.

Early Victorian London: 1837–1870. 20 min. Color. n.d. Films for the Humanities and Sciences. Good survey of the city and the period. Part of the *London: The Making of a City* series.

Famine to Freedom: The Great Irish Journey. 52 min. Color. 2003. Films for the Humanities and Sciences. Film about the catastrophic Irish potato famine. Provides an account of the mass exodus through which America ultimately gained so much.

The Luddites. 50 min. Color. n.d. Films for the Humanities and Sciences. Docudrama examining the Luddite disturbances in England in 1812, when new machines were introduced into the wool industry.

Karl Marx and Marxism. 52 min. Color. 1983. Films for the Humanities and Sciences. Looks at Marx the man and discusses the roots of his philosophy, as well as the outcome of Marxism in the former Soviet Union.

Master Poets Collection IV: The Glorious Romantics. 140 min. Color. 1995. Monterey Home Video/PBS. Readings from the poems of Byron, Keats, and Shelley.

CHAPTER 21

What Is a Nation? Territories, States, and Citizens, 1848–1871

        iii. Crushed revolt of Silesian
            weavers
        iv. Openly opposed
            constitutionalism
        v. Shaken by violence, the
            Kaiser finally capitulated

C. The Frankfurt Assembly and German
   nationhood
   1. Most delegates represented the
      professional classes
   2. Most were moderate liberals
   3. Desired a constitution for a liberal,
      unified Germany
      a. Problems
         i. No resources, no sovereign
           power, and no single legal
           code
   4. The nationalist question
      a. The "Great German" position and
        "Small Germany"
      b. The Assembly accepted the "Small
        Germany" solution
         i. Left out all lands of the
           Habsburgs
        ii. In April 1849 offered the
           crown to Frederick Wilhelm
           IV, who refused it
      c. Kaiser wanted the crown and
        larger state on his terms alone
      d. The delegates left the Assembly
        disillusioned
         i. Perhaps liberal and
           nationalist goals were
           incompatible
        ii. Many delegates fled to the
           United States
      e. Popular revolution
         i. Peasants ransacked tax
           offices and burned castles
        ii. Workers smashed machines
        iii. Formation of citizen militias
        iv. Newspapers and political
           clubs

D. Peoples against empire: The Habsburg lands
   1. Ethnic and language groups
      a. Germans, Czechs, Magyars, Poles,
        Slovaks, Serbs, and Italians
   2. Nationalist sentiment strongest among
      Polish aristocrats
      a. Habsburgs played Polish serfs
        against Polish lords
   3. Hungarian nationalist claims advanced
      by the small Magyar aristocracy
      a. Lajos Kossuth (1802–1894)
         i. Member of the lower nobility

        ii. Published transcripts of
           parliamentary debates
        iii. Campaigned for independence
           and a separate Hungarian
           parliament
        iv. Wanted to bring politics to
           the people (staged political
           "banquets")
   4. Pan-Slavism
      a. Russians, Poles, Ukrainians, Czechs,
        Slovaks, Slovenes, Croats, Serbs,
        Macedonians, and Bulgarians
      b. Desire for a union of Slavic-speaking
        people
      c. Resented oppressive Russian rule

E. 1848 in Austria and Hungary: springtime of
   peoples and autumn of empire
   1. Kossuth stepped up his campaigns
      against the Metternich system of
      Habsburg autocracy and control
      a. Demanded representative institutions
      b. Autonomy for the Hungarian
        Magyar nation
   2. Vienna: popular movement of students
      and artisans
      a. Demanded political and social
        reforms
      b. Built barricades and attacked the
        imperial palace
      c. Central Committee of Citizens
      d. Metternich fled to Britain
      e. Government concessions
         i. Male suffrage and single
           house of representatives
        ii. Withdrew troops from Vienna
        iii. Worked toward the abolition
           of serfdom
        iv. Yielded to Czech demands
           in Bohemia
      f. Italian liberals and nationalists
        attacked empire's territories in
        Naples and Venice
   3. The paradox of nationalism
      a. No cultural or ethnic majority
        could declare its independence
        without prompting rebellion
        elsewhere
   4. Student- and worker-led insurrection in
      Prague (May 1848)
      a. Austrian troops sent to restore
        order
      b. Slav congress disbands
   5. The March Laws
      a. Hungarian parliament abolished
        serfdom and noble privilege

b. Established freedom of the press and of religion

c. Changed suffrage requirements, enfranchised small-property holders

d. Provoked opposition from Croats, Serbs, and Romanians within Hungary

6. Austrian government appointed anti-Magyar Josip Jelasic as governor of Croatia

7. Kossuth severed all ties between Hungary and Austria

8. Franz Joseph asked Nicholas I of Russia for military support

9. The Hungarian revolt was crushed (August 1849)

10. Liberal government capitulated on October 31, 1849

    a. Reestablished censorship

    b. Disbanded the National Guard and student organizations

    c. Twenty-five revolutionary leaders went to the firing squad

    d. Kossuth exiled himself to Turkey

F. 1848 and the early stages of Italian unification

1. A patchwork of small states

    a. Piedmont-Sardinia, the Papal States, and the Kingdom of the Two Sicilies

    b. Lombard and Venetia controlled by Austria

    c. Tuscany, Parma, and Modena ruled by the Habsburgs

2. Giuseppi Mazzini (1805–1872)

    a. Former member of the Carbonari

    b. Founded the Young Italy Society (1831)

      i. Anti-Austrian

      ii. Favored constitutional reforms

      iii. Dedicated to Italian unification

    c. Mission was to bring democracy to the world

    d. Invaded Sardinia—Mazzini driven to exile in England

3. The liberal impulse

    a. Many shared Mazzini's commitment but not his methods

    b. Hoped for a merger of existing governments into a constitutional monarchy

4. 1848 raised hopes for political and social change and Italian unification

    a. The *risorgimento*—Italian resurgence

III. Building the Nation-State

A. Nationalism after 1848

1. States and governments took the initiative

2. Alarmed by revolutionary ferment

3. Promoting economic development and social and political reform

B. France under Napoleon III

1. Believed in personal rule and a centralized state

    a. Control of finances, the army, and foreign affairs

    b. An elected Assembly had no real power

    c. Aimed to put the countryside under the rule of the modern state

    d. Undermined traditional elites, fashioned a new relationship with the people

2. Economic changes

    a. Took steps to develop the economy

    b. Faith in the ability of industrial expansion to bring prosperity and national glory

    c. Passed new limited-liability laws

    d. Signed a free-trade agreement with England (1860)

    e. Founded the *Crédit Mobilier*

    f. Reluctantly permitted trade unions and the legalization of strikes

3. Paris and Napoleon III

    a. Massive rebuilding of the medieval infrastructure

    b. Financed by the *Crédit Mobilier*

    c. Erected 34,000 new buildings

    d. New water pipes and sewer lines

    e. Wholesale renovation did not benefit everyone

4. Aggressive foreign policy

C. Victorian England and the Second Reform Bill (1867)

1. British government faced demands to extend the franchise beyond the middle classes

2. Industrial expansion had created a "labor aristocracy" of skilled workers

    a. Building, engineering, and textile industries

    b. Favored collective self-help through cooperative societies and trade unions

      i. Collected funds against old age and unemployment

    c. Education as a tool for advancement

3. The need to vote

a. Championed by middle-class reformers
   i. Responsible members of society deserved the vote and direct representation
4. The Dissenters
   a. Denied civil and political rights
   b. Could not attend Oxford or Cambridge
   c. Resented paying taxes to the Church of England
5. Campaign for a new reform bill
   a. Working-class leaders joined middle-class dissidents
   b. Backed by Benjamin Disraeli (1804–1881)
      i. Political life would be improved by including the "aristocrats of labor"
6. Great Reform Bill (1867)
   a. Doubled the franchise
      i. Men who paid poor rates or rent of £10 per year in urban areas
      ii. Rural tenants paying rent of £12 or more
   b. Large northern cities gained representation
7. The bill was silent on women
   a. Mobilized a women's suffrage movement
   b. John Stuart Mill (1806–1873)
      i. *On Liberty* (1859)
      ii. *The Subjection of Women* (1869)
      iii. Women should be considered on the same plane as men
      iv. Women's freedom as a measure of social progress
8. 1867 Reform Bill as the high point of British liberalism
D. Italian unification: Cavour and Garibaldi
  1. Two visions of Italian statehood
   a. Giuseppi Garibaldi (1807–1882)
      i. Achieving national unification through a popular movement
   b. A constitutional monarchy as favored by moderate nationalists
      ii. Economic and political reforms without democracy
      iii. Pinned their hopes on Charles Albert, king of Piedmont-Sardinia
   c. Victor Emmanuel II (1849–1861)

2. Count Camillo Benso di Cavour (1810–1861)
   a. Pursued pragmatic reforms guided by the state
   b. Promoted economic expansion and a modern transportation infrastructure
   c. Reformed the currency
3. Cavour and Italy
   a. Relied on diplomacy
   b. Cultivated an alliance with France in order to drive the Austrians from Italy
   c. War with Austria (1859)
   d. Piedmont-Sardinia annexed Lombardy
   e. Joined by Tuscany, Parma, and Modena
   f. The southern states
      i. Francis II (1859–1860) faced a peasant revolt in the Two Sicilies
      ii. Garibaldi landed in Sicily (1860)
      iii. "The Thousand" gained widespread support for unification
      iv. Garibaldi took Sicily in the name of King Victor Emmanuel
      v. Garibaldi marched on Rome
4. Garibaldi and Cavour
   a. Cavour worried that Garibaldi would bring French or Austrian intervention
   b. Cavour preferred that unification take place quickly, without domestic turmoil
   c. The king ordered Garibaldi to cede military authority
5. Final gains
   a. Venetia remained in Austrian hands until 1866
   b. Italian soldiers occupied Rome in September 1870
   c. Rome became the capital of a united Italian kingdom in July 1871
   d. Law of Papal Guarantees defined and limited the pope's status
   e. "We have made Italy, now we must make Italians"
   f. Widening gap between industrial north and rural south
E. The unification of Germany: Realpolitik
  1. Realpolitik as the watchword of the 1850s and 60s

2. Frederick William of Prussia
    a. Granted a Prussian constitution
    b. Established a bicameral parliament
    c. Modified electoral system to reinforce hierarchies of wealth and power
        i. Divided voters into three classes based on the amount of taxes they paid
        ii. A large landowner or industrialist had 100 times the voting power of a common working man
3. Growth of the Prussian middle class
    a. Active liberal intelligentsia
    b. Liberal civil service
4. Liberalism and Frederick William IV (1840–1861)
    a. King wanted to expand the standing army and take military matters out of parliamentary control
    b. Opponents saw the king perhaps creating a personal army
    c. William named Bismarck minister-president of Prussia (1862)
5. Otto von Bismarck (1815–1898)
    a. Prussian Junker and defender of the monarchy
    b. Opposed liberalism and nationalism
    c. Believed that some sort of union was inevitable and that Prussia ought to take the initiative
    d. Bismarck and the opposition
        i. Defied parliamentary opposition
        ii. Dissolved parliament over the levy of taxes
6. Bismarck and foreign policy
    a. Played the "nationalist card" to pre-empt his liberal opponents
    b. Believed that the German Confederation was no longer useful
    c. The dispute over Schleswig-Holstein
    d. The Seven Weeks' War
        i. Austria gave up Schleswig-Holstein and surrendered Venetia to the Italians
        ii. Austria agreed to dissolve the Confederation
    e. Bismarck created the Northern German Confederation
    f. Prussian victories weakened liberal opposition
7. The Franco-Prussian War (1870–1871)
    a. A conflict with France would aid German nationalism in Bavaria,

Württemberg, and other southern states
    b. Skillful propagandist—played off public opinion
    c. German states rallied to Prussia's side
    d. No European powers came to the aid of France
    e. The Prussian army
    f. Napoleon III captured at Sedan
8. The German empire was proclaimed in the Hall of Mirrors at Versailles on January 18, 1871
9. A "revolution from above"
F. The state and nationality: centrifugal forces in the Austrian empire
    1. The Habsburgs abolished serfdom but made few other reforms
    2. The Hungarians were essentially reconquered
    3. Administrative reforms
        a. New and more-uniform legal system
        b. Rationalized taxation
        c. Imposed a single-language policy favoring German
    4. Ethnic relations
        a. Grew more tense
        b. The "nationalities" protested the powerlessness of their Diets, military repression, and cultural disenfranchisement
    5. Francis Joseph (1848–1916, emperor of Austria)
        a. Agreed to the new federal structure
    6. The Dual Monarchy (Austria-Hungary)
        a. Common system of taxation, common army, made foreign and military policy together
        b. Internal and constitutional affairs were separated
        c. *Ausgleich* (Settlement) allowed Hungarians their own constitution and capital (Buda and Pest)
    7. No national unification in Habsburg lands
IV. Nation- and State-Building in Russia, the United States, and Canada
    A. Territory, the state, and serfdom: Russia
        1. Abolition of serfdom as part of a project to rebuild Russia as a modern state
        2. "Slavophiles"
            a. Preserving Russia's distinctive features
            b. Idealized traditional Russian culture
            c. Rejected Western secularism, commercialism, and bourgeois culture

3. "Westernizers"
    a. Russia should adopt European science, technology, and education
    b. Liberalism and individual rights
4. The Emancipation Decree of 1861
    a. Massive in scope, limited in change
    b. Granted legal rights to 22 million serfs
    c. Gave former serfs title to a portion of the land
    d. Required the state to compensate landowners
    e. Newly liberated serfs had to pay installments for their land
    f. Law granted land to the peasant commune (*mir*), not individual serfs
5. Expansion
    a. Russia pressed east and south
    b. Invaded and conquered independent Islamic kingdoms along the Silk Road
    c. Founded Siberian city of Vladivostok in 1860
    d. In most cases, Russia did not assimilate the populations of new territories

B. Territory, the nation-state, and slavery: the United States
    1. The Jeffersonian Revolution
        a. Combined democratic aspirations with national expansion
        b. Thomas Jefferson (1801–1809)
        c. The Bill of Rights
        d. The separation of powers
        e. An aristocracy of "virtue and talent"
        f. Opposed national religion and special privilege
        g. The independence of the yeoman farmer
    2. Territorial expansion—the Louisiana Purchase (1803)
        a. Added millions of acres of prime cotton land
        b. Extended the empire of slavery
    3. Andrew Jackson (1829–1837)
        a. Transformed Jeffersonian liberalism
        b. Campaigned to extend the suffrage to all white males
        c. All officeholders should be elected and not appointed
        d. Frequent rotation of men in power
    4. Manifest Destiny—"to overspread the continent"
        a. Brought Oregon and Washington into the Union
        b. Arizona, Texas, New Mexico, Utah, Nevada, and California brought in during war with Mexico
        c. Northern "free labor" ideology
        d. Southern plantation slavery
    5. The question of slavery
        a. An unavoidable question
        b. The new states—free or slave?
    6. The Civil War
        a. The abolition of slavery
        b. Established preeminence of the national government over states' rights
        c. Fourteenth Amendment: all Americans are citizens of the United States
        d. Established "due process"—defined by the national, not state, government
        e. Expansion of the economy

C. Territorial expansion: Canada
    1. Treaty of Paris (1763) passed "New France" into British hands
    2. Strained relations between French-speaking people of Quebec and British settlers
    3. The drive west—vast wheat and timber resources
    4. Demands for greater Canadian autonomy
    5. Canadian independence (1867)
        a. State remained a dominion within the British Commonwealth
        b. Economic expansion and settlement

D. Eastern questions and international relations: the Crimean War, 1854–56
    1. The Eastern Question
    2. Ottoman empire lost its grip on provinces in southeastern Europe
    3. Strategic interest, systems of alliances, and the balance of power in Europe
    4. The Crimean War
        a. Russia invaded Ottoman territories of Moldavia and Walachia
        b. Austria garrisoned its troops
        c. Russia turned on the Turks
        d. Provoked French and British fears of Russian expansion
        e. A short but gruesome war
        f. "The Charge of the Light Brigade"
    5. Importance of the war
        a. Peace settlement was a setback for Russia
        b. Romania becomes an independent nation
        c. Embarrassed French prestige

d. Innovations in warfare
  i. Rifled muskets, underwater mines, and trench warfare
  ii. Railroads and telegraphs
e. Correspondents and photojournalists—a "public" war
f. Florence Nightingale (1820–1910)

E. Realism: "democracy in art"
  1. A strict rejection of artistic conventions
  2. The movement toward honest, objective, authentic representations of the world
  3. Focus on the material world
    a. A debt to nineteenth-century science
  4. Émile Zola (1840–1902)
    a. An exact, scientific presentation of society
    b. Profound sympathy with the common person and a desire for social justice
    c. Confronted the social problems of working-class life
  5. The critique of contemporary society
    a. Dominated by bourgeois hypocrisy and an unjust social system
    b. Artists and writers call for "democracy in art"
    c. The lower classes have a right to literacy and artistic representation
  6. Russian writers joined realism with philosophical themes
    a. Ivan Turgenev (1818–1883)
      i. *Fathers and Sons* (1862)
      ii. Condemned existing social order
      iii. Provided inspiration to young Russian intellectuals
    b. Feodor Dostoevsky (1821–1881)
      i. The psychology of anguished minds
    c. Leo Tolstoy (1828–1910)
      i. *War and Peace* (1863–1869)
      ii. The fate of individuals caught up in the powerful movement of history

V. Conclusion
  A. 1850–1870 as decades of intense nation-building
  B. Unifications of Italy and Germany
  C. The rise of the United States
  D. Nationalism as an erratic and malleable force

GENERAL DISCUSSION QUESTIONS

1. "1848 was the turning point at which modern history failed to turn." Consider this statement in light of the nationalist revolts, Mexican-American War, Seneca Falls Convention, and California gold rush. What is the relationship between these events and revolution, liberalism, and nation-building?

2. The ideas of creating a new nation and establishing self-government for a group of people who live together and call themselves a nation are both appealing and troubling. Why? The American nation is largely composed of descendants of immigrants who fled other countries. Should people in Europe have the right to found new nations, instead of emigrating?

3. Ethnic and linguistic differences divided nationalities in the Austrian empire. Shared culture, economic interests, and government brought them together, not always happily. However, cultural revival often preceded or accompanied political activism, as we see with the Czechs, Italians, Germans, and Poles. Discuss the uses and abuses of culture that can occur with nation-building.

4. Why was the unification of Germany important to all Europeans as well as to the Germans? Why didn't the Germans achieve unification during the revolts of 1848–1849? What was lacking?

5. Otto von Bismarck was the architect of German unification in the 1860s and 1870s. Although Bismarck led Prussia's aggressive assertion of German superiority, he sought to preserve peace in Europe after 1871. Why? What is your assessment of his achievements?

6. Compare the German and Italian unification movements from 1850 to 1870. Note the different styles of leadership, negotiation, and military action used to achieve the national goal.

7. How did nationalism serve the needs of statesmen and bureaucrats rather than those of the general population, especially as more people were allowed to vote and hold public office? Was that sort of nationalism real or invented?

8. How did Thomas Jefferson combine democratic aspirations with national expansion? Was this a revolutionary combination? In what ways did Andrew Jackson transform Jeffersonian liberalism?

9. Why did realism—a movement toward honest, objective, authentic representations of the world—become so popular among writers after the 1850s? What was the specific role of "democracy in art"? Does the function or role of art change with time?

DOCUMENT DISCUSSION QUESTIONS

Frederick William IV Refuses the "Throne from the Gutter"

1. As the hereditary ruler of Prussia, Frederick William IV was a logical choice for emperor (kaiser) of the united Germany. However, the king of Prussia believed he ruled by divine right. He did not want to rule all Germany because of an unruly bunch of revolutionaries and professors at the Frankfurt Assembly of 1849, even if other German princes approved. What was his rationale?

2. Bismarck said, "The great questions of the day . . . will be settled by blood and iron." When the Prussian army defeated the Austrians at Königgrätz in 1866, Bismarck told his wife he was forced "to pour some water into their wine" to rein in the officers' enthusiasm for further conquests. What methods to achieve German unification were available in the mid-nineteenth century? Why was Bismarck careful not to offend the three other major powers (Russia, Prussia, and France), each of whom had ambitions of their own?

Building the Italian Nation: Three Views

3. Mazzini was a visionary with ideas about Italian unification and the regeneration of Italian glory, as sanctioned by God. "Why should not a new Rome arise . . . to create a third and still vaster Unity?" he wrote. Yet given the Italians' geographic diversity and political discord, why *should* a new Rome arise? What factors made Italian unification more likely to succeed in the late nineteenth century? How did industrialization, improved transport, communication, education, and financial infrastructure contribute to the effort?

4. The Political Creed of 1858 provided rational arguments in favor of Italian unification as a necessary counterweight to Austrian influence in northern Italy. Pro-unification forces wanted to allow Italians to identify with their society, show their pride, and enjoy political liberty. How and why did they argue that only a unified Italian state offered true freedom?

5. Cavour was a much-admired diplomat: Petruccelli della Gattina ranked Cavour third among European statesmen, behind Lord Palmerston and Napoleon. Why did he gain this reputation?

6. Does Garibaldi deserve credit for raising the necessary armed force and using it effectively? Why and why not?

The Abolition of Serfdom in Russia

7. In France in 1789 and Russia in 1861, peasants heard the news about their new freedom and celebrated; they did not stop to consider compensating the former owners, although the new laws required compensation. How should this classic conflict between human rights and property rights be resolved?

8. In Russia, there were complaints about the nobility's response to emancipation: reapportionment of land, as in the enclosure movement in England, is always controversial. Why? What forms did their protests take?

SAMPLE LECTURE 21: THE REVOLUTION OF 1848 IN FRANCE

Lecture Objectives

1. To establish the context in which the 1848 Revolution in France took place

2. To survey some of the causes of the Revolution of 1848

3. To look at the policies of Napoleon III

THE HISTORICAL CONTEXT

The Congress of Vienna opened in September 1814 and continued, with interruptions, until June 1815. Four major victors over Napoleon were represented along with the French envoy: from Austria came Emperor Francis II and Prince Klemens von Metternich; the British brought Lord Castlereagh and the Duke of Wellington; from Prussia, King Frederick William III and Karl von Hardenberg; Tsar Alexander I represented Russia; and the restored Bourbon king of France, Louis XVIII, was represented by Charles-Maurice de Talleyrand, a former bishop, co-conspirator, and foreign minister of Napoleon. The goals of the Congress were reactionary and nationalistic to the core:

- to break up the Napoleonic empire, and prevent its revival
- to acquire territory all over Europe: peace had a price

Each country had more specific aims, as well. The Austrian Metternich feared revolution and sought to construct a balance of powers. The French Revolution had crushed the *ancien régime*, but in its place came Napoleon and the Grand Empire. This was not to be repeated. The British desired peace on the Continent and freedom of trade. The Napoleonic Wars also caused social unrest at home as returning soldiers and sailors were often thrown into casual work and joined the ranks of the unemployed. The dislocation of trade had to be solved if Britain was to have any hope of maintaining their world empire and dominance of global trade. For the state of Prussia, the sole motive was to gain territory across Germany, especially the Rhineland and Saxony. The Russians sought to annex all of Poland as well as some buffer states. At the same time, Tsar Alexander wanted a "Holy Alliance" of Christian rulers. And then came France. The best it could hope for was the best deal that Talleyrand could get. The restoration attempted to bring back old rulers and regimes, as if the French Revolution had never happened. Pretending didn't help much; it was impossible to return to the status quo of 1789. After all, the *ancien régime* had been obliterated and replaced with Napoleon's armies and administrators.

The Congress of Vienna resulted in a Concert of Europe. A system of alliances was set up to keep the peace. Metternich and those like him rejected liberalism, nationalism, democracy, and human rights. These had all been objects of the French Revolution. Castlereagh told the British Parliament, "The Congress of Vienna was not assembled for the discussion of moral principles, but for great practical purposes, to establish effective provisions for general security." Thus the Bourbons were restored in Spain, Naples, and France. In 1824, the dying Louis XVIII said to his childless brother Charles X, "After you, Charles, it's over." (*Après toi, Charles, c'est fini.*) Revolts were suppressed by foreign troops. Metternich's era was one of good times for the bourgeoisie, and Romanticism and sentimentality flourished. Middle-class coziness, family virtues, self-satisfaction, and solidity were hallmarks of the age. Theater, art, dancing, and music were popular bourgeois interests. Beethoven, Schubert, Chopin, and Liszt were composing too. The authorities thought nonpolitical entertainments were harmless and so let them spread. The emperor of Austria exercised a repressive rule with no freedom of speech or of the press. Police used spies and informers, and liberal thinkers were intimidated. The old order persisted in rural areas. Industrialization was slow to arrive in central and eastern Europe and in the large agricultural areas of Austria, Prussia, and Russia. Many peasants were still tied to the land as serfs. Nobles had wealth, status, and privileges and enjoyed idleness; landowners had assemblies to protect their interests and tax exemptions. Aristocrats engaged in official service and absentee ownership.

But all was not as peaceful as it might have seemed. Nationalist revolts broke out in Greece in 1823 and in Belgium seven years later. Latin American nations also witnessed vast independence movements. Europeans wondered if they should intervene. Meanwhile, the American Monroe Doctrine argued against intervention by Europe in the New World and was enforced by the British Royal Navy. This hands-off stance fostered free trade. Then, a social revolt shook France in July 1830. Agitators protested the unpopularity of the Bourbon government. Once again, the old plotters Talleyrand, Lafayette, and Thiers took leadership positions. The people were hostile to the monarchy, high bread prices, unemployment, and government repression, which lead to fighting in the streets of Paris. But this was not a repeat of 1789. The revolution was quickly hijacked by Louis-Philippe of Orléans, a former revolutionary nobleman with a bourgeois sensibility, a successful business owner, and a family man. He became the new king. History has stamped the July Monarchy with the motto "Enrich yourselves!" It was a government by the rich and for the rich: voting and officeholding were controlled by a tiny minority. Vivid illustrations from this period can be seen in Daumier's caricatures and the novels of Balzac and Stendhal. The passion for gain was reflected in the growth of industry, railways, and colonies. The many disorders of the July Monarchy met ferocious repression.

THE REVOLUTION OF 1848 IN FRANCE

In 1848 Europe was once again shaken by popular revolutions. Only Great Britain and Russia remained untouched as the common people built barricades in the streets of Paris, Berlin, and Vienna, and European governments toppled. It seemed that the grand liberal and nationalist dreams of the French Revolution had become the battlecry of a new generation of radicals and revolutionaries who were intent on making a new Europe. Perhaps it was time that yet another *ancien régime* should fall. But despite all the talk and revolutionary activity about liberal and democratic constitutions or profound social reforms, the revolutions of 1848 ultimately failed.

The 1840s were difficult years across Europe. The Irish potato famine, a Polish revolution in Austria, and a civil war in Switzerland all contributed to the tense atmosphere. As in 1789, revolution came first to France. The government of Louis-Philippe and François Guizot served as a model of inactivity. It was also a government of the wealthy that refused to sanction any talk of electoral reform. On the night of February 22, 1848, the citizens of Paris set up barricades in the streets and two days later, Louis-Philippe abdicated the throne. The people of Paris took matters into their own hands and issued a proclamation of a provisional government headed by an executive committee. The provisional government:

- pledged itself to guarantee the means of the working man's subsistence by labor and to guarantee labor to all citizens
- recognized that working men ought to enter into associations among themselves in order to enjoy the advantage of their labor
- ordered the immediate establishment of national workshops

And in words strikingly familiar to the liberal ethos of the Revolution of 1789, the provisional government made it clear that:

> The unity of the nation (formed henceforth of all the classes of citizens who compose it); the government of the nation by itself; liberty, equality, and fraternity, for fundamental principles, and 'the people' for our emblem and watchword: these constitute the democratic government which France owes to itself, and which our efforts shall secure for it.

The provisional government then had the task of creating a constitution for the second French Republic. This constitution would be a truly democratic one in which the voices of the common people could be heard. As a result of such aspirations, the vote was given to all adult males. Furthermore, the French went on to abolish slavery in the colonies and established the ten-hour workday for Paris.

There were problems, however. As soon as the provisional government had written a new constitution, there was a split between moderate reformers who saw the increased franchise as a concession to the people and the radical reformers, many of whom were committed to socialism. Louis Blanc, the leading socialist in the new coalition government, proposed a radical demand for national workshops organized by trade into producers and cooperatives. The idea was quite simple—put people to work. The national workshops were organized to help those people who were unemployed and intended to support no more than twelve thousand workers. But by April 1848, the workshops were flooded by 66,000 workers, and by June the number had risen to 120,000. The events of the first half of 1848 duplicated the heady atmosphere of 1789. The government relaxed censorship and new political journals made their appearance, as did hundreds of republican societies in which both men and women were involved. For the moderate middle-class reformers it seemed that the people were once again taking things into their own hands, and so they began to worry about future insurrection. By late spring it became clear that the national workshops had become a drain on French finances. At the same time members of the assembly worried that the workshops might indeed become threats to social order. So at the end of May, the provisional government closed the national workshops to new enrollment and sent all members between eighteen and twenty-five to the army. Finally, on June 21, the government ended the program outright. The result was bloody conflict as laborers, journeymen, the unemployed, and socialists once again set up barricades in the streets of Paris. For four days (June 23–26) the people of Paris defended themselves against an armed force recruited from those willing to repress the aspirations of the Parisian working classes. Three thousand revolutionaries were killed and another twelve thousand were arrested. The French government was forced to act and in the wake of the "June Days," the assembly arranged for the election of a strong president who would restore order to the country: Louis Napoleon Bonaparte, the nephew of Napoleon. For Karl Marx, the "fraternal illusions" of the events of February 1848 were shattered by the June Days. He wrote that:

> The June revolution is the ugly revolution, the repulsive revolution, because things have taken the place of phrases, because the republic uncovered the head of the monster itself, by striking off the crown that shielded and concealed it. . . . None of the numerous revolutions of the French bourgeoisie since 1789 was an attack on order, for they allowed the rule of the class, they allowed the slavery of the workers, they allowed the bourgeois

order to endure, however often the political form of this rule and of this slavery changed. June has attacked this order. Woe to June!

Because of the French revolution of 1830, Louis Napoleon had spent most of his life in exile. In the spring of 1848 he decided it was safe to return to France from England. Conservatives saw him as a protector of private property and social order. But Louis was never satisfied with just being the president of France and so it was not long after his election as president that he used his power to obtain even more. He gained the support of French Catholics by restoring to the pope the temporal power he had lost during 1848. For the workers and middle classes he introduced some social welfare programs. However, the most drastic change came with his effort to quiet radicalism in France. Louis Napoleon:

- banned meetings and associations of workers
- proclaimed a temporary dictatorship in 1851
- arranged for a plebiscite to draft a new constitution
- made the president an actual dictator and established the Second Empire in 1852
- assumed the title of Napoleon III

CONSEQUENCES: FRANCE UNDER NAPOLEON III

Louis Napoleon believed in personal rule and set about to create a centralized state in which he could control finances, the army, and foreign affairs. Although there was an elected Assembly, it had no real power. Traditional elites were undermined as Louis fashioned a new relationship with the people. The economic changes were dramatic, and Louis went on to take steps to further develop the economy. He had faith in the ability of industrial expansion to bring prosperity and national glory. France passed new limited-liability laws, signed a free-trade agreement with England (1860), the *Crédit Mobilier* was founded, and Louis reluctantly permitted trade unions and the legalization of strikes. The city of Paris was rebuilt since much of it had been under fire since the days of 1848 and the barricades. More than 34,000 buildings were erected and new sewer and water lines were added. In terms of politics and the political discourse of the people, the revolutionary year of 1848 as well as the rise of Napoleon III, meant that the politics of middle- and working-class people became more sharply differentiated. Despite the romantic imagery of Delacroix's *Liberty Leading the People*, the revolution of 1848 in France failed. Middle-class, moderately liberal reformers needed the support of the working classes of Paris, but the relationship went both ways. But if the history of revolutions tell us anything, it is that a dynamic situation results from the cataclysmic overthrow of the established order.

SUGGESTED FEATURE FILMS

The Charge of the Light Brigade. 141 min. Color. 1968. United Artists. Tony Richardson directed this film version of the tragedy and glory of the Crimean War. Based in part on Cecil Woodham Smith's *The Reason Why*.

Cousin Bette. 108 min. Color. 1998. 20th Century Fox. Film adaptation of Balzac's novel set in Paris on the eve of the 1848 revolution.

Immortal Beloved. 121 min. Color. 1994 Columbia/Tri-Star. Unforgettable, although sometimes inaccurate, account of Beethoven's life; includes a poignant dramatization of the first performance of the Ninth Symphony.

The Leopard. 125 min. Color. 1963. 20th Century Fox. Based on the Giuseppe de Lampedusa novel about a nineteenth-century noble Sicilian family.

The Life of Émile Zola. 116 min. B/W. 1937. Warner Brothers. Traces the career of the French novelist (played by Paul Muni), including Zola's involvement in the Dreyfus Affair (note that the anti-Semitism surrounding the affair is not fully developed).

SUGGESTED CLASSROOM FILMS

An Age of Revolutions. 23 min. Color. 1996. Films for the Humanities and Sciences. Examines Europe in the age of the dual revolution up to the publication of Marx and Engels' *Communist Manifesto*.

Between Empire and Nation. 53 min. Color. 1993. Films for the Humanities and Sciences. An examination of the revolutions of 1848 and the conflict between liberal and conservative ideas of the Habsburg rulers, and the inevitable results of this conflict.

Bismarck: Germany from Blood and Iron. 30 min. Color. Learning Corporation of America. Uses Bismarck's words to describe the process of German unification.

The Creation of Italy. 30 min. Color. n.d. Films for the Humanities and Sciences. Traces the development of Italian unification and focuses on the Battle of Solferino in 1859.

Crime and Punishment. 51 min. Color. 1999. Films for the Humanities and Sciences. Donald Sutherland narrates this examination of evil's intellectual appeal and its moral repercussions as portrayed in Dostoevsky's novel.

Gustave Courbet: The Place of Death. 32 min. Color. n.d. Films for the Humanities and Sciences. The shift toward realism is analyzed from the standpoint of Courbet's *A Burial at Ornans* (1851).

European Thought and Culture in the Nineteenth Century. 24 parts, 30 min each. Color. 2002. Insight Media. Examines the birth of nationalism, capitalism, socialism, liberalism, and feminism, using examples from the work and writings of Marx, Darwin, Nietzsche, de Staël, and George Sand.

Karl Marx and Marxism. 52 min. Color. 1983. Films for the Humanities and Sciences. Looks at Marx the man and Marx the philosopher, and the failed Soviet Union.

Karl Marx: The Massive Dissent. 57 min. Color. 1977. Films, Inc. A look at Marx and other socialist thinkers.

The Making of the German Nation: Part One—The Struggle for Unity. 20 min. Color. 1983. Insight Media. Covers the Congress of Vienna, Bismarck, and the Franco-Prussian War.

The Paris Commune. 32 min. Color. n.d. Films for the Humanities and Sciences. Looks at the conditions that gave rise to the Commune, the Communards, and the brutal manner in which Commune was abolished.

The Unification of Germany. 33 min. Color. 1989. Insight Media. Covers the period from 1815 through 1871.

The Unification of Italy. 30 min. Color. 1989. Insight Media. A look at both the process and the players.

Part VII: The West at the World's Center

IDEAS FOR USING THE WESTERN CIVILIZATIONS DIGITAL HISTORY CENTER

Late-nineteenth-century colonialism and the new imperialism, the second industrial revolution, and the First and Second World Wars are the various subjects of the Map Exercises and Digital History Features at *www.wwnorton.com/wciv*.

- Map Exercise 16: *Fin de Siècle* Europe (Chapters 22–23)
- Map Exercise 17: War and Revolution (Chapter 24)
- Map Exercise 18: Europe at War (Chapters 25–26)
- Digital History Feature 10: The Olympics—Past and Present (Chapters 22–23)
- Digital History Feature 12: War and Technology (Chapters 22 and 26)

Use Map Exercise 16 to identify the areas in which European nations were extending their colonial reach throughout the nineteenth century. These exercises will be useful in classroom discussions of the new imperialism and will also show how trade facilitated territorial gains on a global scale among the great powers. Map Exercises 17 and 18 are useful adjuncts to any discussion of twentieth-century world wars, since they supply a narrative of developments leading up to war as well as the progress of the wars themselves. The Digital History Feature "The Olympics—Past and Present" is a useful tool in examining how politics influenced sport in this age of war. This is especially evident in the important 1936 Olympic Games, held in Berlin and overseen by Adolf Hitler. Digital History Feature 12, "War and Technology," offers a comparative perspective of several landmark battles of the past two centuries. The Battle of Rorke's Drift (1879) can be used to show what happens when an outnumbered Western colonial power, armed with Western technology, went to war against native Zulus. The Battle of Stalingrad (1942–1943) showed the world that Hitler's armies were not invincible and that spirit could overcome superior technology and numbers. This Feature also includes episodes from the Vietnam War and the war in Iraq, and can be used to discuss the nature of twentieth-century warfare from the vantage point of weapons, technology, and the men and women who fight.

CHAPTER 22 | Imperialism and Colonialism (1870–1914)

b. Lenin (1870–1924), *Imperialism: The Highest Stage of Capitalism* (1917)
   i. Imperialism as an essential stage in the development of capitalism
   ii. The internal contradictions of capitalism produced imperialism
   iii. The overthrow of capitalism would check imperialism
c. London as the banker of the world
d. Demand for raw materials made colonization a necessary investment
2. Strategic and nationalist motives
   a. International rivalries fueled the belief that national interests were at stake
   b. The French supported imperialism as a means of restoring national honor
   c. The British worried about German and French industrialization and losing world markets
   d. The link between imperialism and nation-building
3. The cultural dimension
   a. David Livingston (1813–1873) and putting an end to the African slave trade
   b. Rudyard Kipling (1865–1936) and the "white man's burden"
   c. Civilizing the barbaric and heathens
4. Imperial policy
   a. Less a matter of long-range planning
   b. More a matter of quick responses to improvised situations
III. Imperialism in South Asia
   A. India and the British empire
      1. The "Jewel of the British Crown"
      2. The British East India Company
         a. Had its own military divided into European and Indian divisions
         b. Held the right to collect taxes on land from Indian peasants
         c. Held legal monopolies over trade in all goods (the most lucrative was opium)
         d. Constituted a military and repressive government
         e. Offered economic privileges to those who allied themselves with the British against others

3. British policy divided
   a. One group wanted to westernize India
   b. Another thought it safer and more practical to defer to local culture
B. The Sepoy Rebellion (1857–1858)
   1. Uprising began near Delhi
   2. Social, economic, and political grievances
   3. Indian peasants attacked law courts and burned tax rolls
   4. A protest against debt and corruption
   5. Hindu and Muslim leaders denounced Christian missionaries
   6. The British response
      a. Systematic campaign of repression
      b. Rebel-supported towns and villages were destroyed
      c. Defeat of the rebellion fired the imagination of the British public
C. After the mutiny: reorganizing the Indian empire
   1. New strategies of British rule
   2. East India Company was abolished
   3. British raj governed directly
   4. Military reorganization
   5. Queen Victoria as empress of India
   6. Reform of the civil service
   7. Missionary activity subdued
D. India and Britain
   1. India as Britain's largest export market
   2. India provided Britain with highly trained engineers and bureaucrats
   3. 1.2 million Indian troops fought with the British in World War I
   4. British indirect rule sought to create an Indian elite to serve British interests
   5. Large social group of British-educated Indian civil servants and businessmen
      a. Provided the leadership for an Indian nationalist movement
IV. Imperialism in China
   A. Europe and China
      1. Forcing trade agreements
      2. Set up treaty ports
      3. Established outposts of missionary activity
      4. British aimed to improving terms of the China trade
   B. The opium trade
      1. A direct link between Britain, British India, and China
      2. Opium one of the few products Europeans could sell in China

3. Northeast India as richest opium-growing area
4. A "narco-military empire"
5. Opium production was labor-intensive
6. A triangular trade
   a. East India Company sold opium to British, Dutch, and Chinese shippers
   b. Opium sent to southeast Asia and China
   c. Silver paid for opium was used to buy Chinese goods for the European market
7. China banned opium imports (1830s)
8. A collision course with British opium traders

C. The Opium Wars (1830–1842)
   1. The first Opium War
      a. Drugs not the main focus
      b. The issue was sovereignty and economic status
      c. European rights to trade
   2. Treaty of Nanking (1843)
      a. British trading privileges
      b. Hong Kong
   3. The second Opium War
      a. Britain granted further rights
   4. Other countries demand similar rights and economic opportunities
      a. French, German, and Russian mining rights
      b. Begin manufacturing with Chinese labor
   5. The United States and the "open door"
   6. Sino-Japanese War (1894–1895)
      a. Forced China to concede trading privileges
      b. The independence of Korea
   7. The Taiping Rebellion (1850–1864)
      a. Radical Christian rebels challenged the authority of the emperor
      b. China's agricultural heartland was devastated

D. The Boxer Rebellion (1900)
   1. The Boxers
      a. Secret society of men trained in martial arts
      b. Antiforeign and antimissionary
      c. Attacked foreign engineers, destroyed railway lines, and marched on Beijing
   2. The European response
      a. Great powers drew together

      b. Repression of the Boxers
   3. The rebellion highlighted the vulnerability of European imperial power

E. The new imperialism in 1900
   1. Asia is partitioned
   2. Japan alone retains its independence
   3. British: India, Burma, Malaya, Australia, and New Zealand
   4. Dutch: Indonesia
   4. French: Indochina
   5. Problems
      a. Struggle between great powers exacerbated nationalist feelings
      b. The destabilizing effects of the new imperialism

F. Russian imperialism
   1. Policy of annexation
   2. Southern colonization
      a. Georgia (1801)
      b. Bessarabia, Turkestan, and Armenia
      c. Brought Russia and Britain close to war, especially over Afghanistan
   3. The "Great Game"
   4. Toward the East
      a. The Russo-Japanese War (1905)
         i. Russian naval forces were humiliated
         ii. United States brokered the peace treaty

V. The French Empire and the Civilizing Mission
   A. The French in Algeria
      1. Algeria as a settler state
         a. Utopian socialist communities
         b. Exiled revolutionaries of 1848
         c. Winegrowers
         d. Not all settlers were French
      2. Under the Third Republic (1870), Algeria was made a department of France
         a. Gave French settlers full rights of republican citizenship
         b. Consolidated privileges
         c. Disenfranchised indigenous populations
         d. Differentiated "good" Berbers and "bad" Arabs
      3. After 1870: the "civilizing mission"
         a. Reinforcing the purpose of the French republic and French prestige
         b. Jules Ferry (1832–1893), argued for expansion into Indochina
         c. French acquisitions
            i. Tunisia (1881)

  ii. Northern and central
   Vietnam (1883)
  iii. Laos and Cambodia (1893)
 d. Federation of French West Africa
  (1893)
   i. Rationalizing the economic
    exploitation of the area
   ii. "Enhancing the value" of
    the region
   iii. Public programs served
    French interests only

VI. The "Scramble for Africa" and the Congo
 A. The Congo Free State
  1. The 1870s
   a. A new drive into central Africa—
    the fertile valleys of the Congo
    River
   b. European colonizers under the
    Belgian king, Leopold II
    (1835–1909, r. 1865–1909)
   c. Herbert M. Stanley and his
    "scientific journals"
   d. International Association for the
    Exploration and Civilization of the
    Congo (1876)
     i. Signed treaties with local
      elites
     ii. Opened the Congo to
      commercial exploitation
      (palm oil, rubber, diamonds)
   e. Other colonizers reacted
    (especially Portugal)
   f. The Treaty of Berlin (1884)
     i. Chaired by Otto von
      Bismarck (1815–1898)
     ii. Established ground rules for
      a new phase of European
      expansion
     iii. Britain, France, and Germany
      joined forces to settle the
      issue
     iv. The Congo would be open
      to free trade and commerce
   g. The Congo Free State
     i. Actually run by Leopold's
      private company
     ii. Slave trade to be suppressed
      in favor of free labor
     iii. The Congo becomes a
      Belgian colony (1908)
 B. The partition of Africa
  1. Colonial powers increase their holdings
   in Africa (1880s)
  2. Germany
   a. Bismarck was a reluctant colonizer

   b. Seized strategic locations
    (Cameroon and Tanzania)
  3. France
   a. Aimed to move eastward across
    the continent
  4. Britain
   a. Southern and eastern Africa
   b. Cecil Rhodes (1853–1902)
    i. Made a fortune from South
     African diamond mines
     (DeBeers)
    ii. Prime minister of Cape
     Colony (1890)
    iii. Personal goal was to build
     an African empire founded
     on diamonds
    iv. Carved out territories in
     Zambia, Zimbabwe, Malawi,
     nd Botswana
   c. The "Cape-to-Cairo" railway
   d. Making Britain self-sufficient

VII. Imperial Culture
 A. Images of empire
  1. Images of empire were everywhere
  2. Advertising
  3. Museums displayed the products of
   empire
  4. Music halls and imperial songs
 B. Empire and identity
  1. The "civilizing mission" of the French
  2. Bringing progress to other lands
  3. Women and empire
 C. Theories of race
  1. Arthur de Gobineau (1816–1882)
   a. *The Inequality of the Races*
    (1853–1855)
   b. Race as the master key to
    understanding the world's problems
   c. The racial question overshadowed
    all others
   d. Slavery proved the racial
    inferiority of the slave
  2. Houston Stewart Chamberlain
   (1855–1927)
   a. Making racial theory more scientific
   b. Tied racial theories to Darwinism
    and Herbert Spencer
   c. Races change (evolve) over time
  3. Francis Galton (1822–1911)
   a. Eugenics: the science of
    improving the racial qualities
   b. Selective breeding
  4. Karl Pearson (1857–1936)
   a. Systematic study of intelligence
    and genius

5. The rhetoric of progress, the civilizing mission, and race
   a. Provided a rationale for imperial conquest
D. Critics
   1. Hobson and Lenin criticized imperialism as an act of greed and antidemocratic arrogance
   2. Joseph Conrad argued that imperialism signified deep problems
   3. The Pan-African Congress (1900)
      a. The problem of the twentieth century is the problem of race
E. Colonial cultures
   1. Growth of Bombay, Calcutta, and Shanghai
   2. Colonialism created new hybrid cultures
   3. Annexed areas as laboratories for creating orderly and disciplined societies
   4. Worry over preserving national traditions and identity
      a. Should education be westernized?
      b. Fraternization with indigenous peoples might undermine European power
      c. Sexual relations
   5. Compromises about "acceptability"
VIII. Crisis of Empire at the Turn of the Twentieth Century
   A. Europe in 1900
      1. Crisis
      2. Sharp tensions between Western nations
      3. The expansion of European economic and military commitments to territories overseas
   B. Fashoda (1898)
      1. Britain and France faced one another for dominance of Africa
   C. Ethiopia
      1. Italy developed a small empire along the shores of the Red Sea (1880s–1890s)
         a. Annexed Eritrea and parts of Somalia
      2. An expedition sent to conquer Ethiopia (1896)
      3. The Ethiopians killed six thousand Italians at Adowa
   D. South Africa: the Boer War
      1. Afrikaners (Boers)—Dutch and Swiss settlers who had arrived in the early nineteenth century
      2. Troubled relationship with the British in South Africa
      3. Afrikaners set up two free states: Transvaal and the Orange Free State
      4. Afrikaners and British went to war (1899)

5. British army was completely unprepared for war
6. British government refused to compromise
   a. The British eventually seized Pretoria
7. A guerilla war dragged on for three years
8. British used concentration camps where Afrikaner citizens were rounded up
9. The Union of South Africa—British and Boers shared power
   E. U.S. imperialism
      1. Spanish-American War (1898)
         a. A "splendid little war"
      2. The annexation of Puerto Rico and protectorate of Cuba
      3. The Panama Canal (1903)
IX. Conclusion
   A. Rapid extension of formal European control
   B. The West as a self-consciously imperial culture

GENERAL DISCUSSION QUESTIONS

1. What drives the imperialist impulse? Why would Europeans leave their homes and families, risk illness and misadventure, and encounter peoples and cultures completely foreign to their own?

2. What were some significant distinctions between the European powers involved in late-nineteenth-century imperialism? Did some countries build their empires too soon (before industrialization) and others start too late (after the most desirable territories were already taken by competitors)? Which imperialists had better or worse than average records on human rights in their colonies? Why?

3. What happened when subjects of older empires came into contact with those of newer ones? Consider the interactions of Britain and Russia with Iran and Afghanistan, or of France and Britain with Ottoman Turkey.

4. In the eighteenth century, a large share of European trade with Asia was handled by privately owned but semi-official firms like the British and Dutch East India Companies. Why was this arrangement, which supposedly saved the taxpayers money, later found to be impractical?

5. How did Europeans profit from the opium trade in China? Did the British have the right to trade freely in any commodity? Did the Chinese have the right to ban opium imports, outlaw the use of opium, and fight the drug traffickers? What was the outcome?

6. While French imperialists wanted to make profits, they said they were fulfilling their "civilizing mission" by

giving natives French culture and technological progress. Were French administration, education, cuisine, engineering, public works, railways, and sanitation superior to Asian and African ways? Was imperialism a free and fair exchange of primitive independence and native ways for French rule and modern civilization?

7. Possession of an empire affected the metropole as well as the colonies. The French, Dutch, and British enthusiasm for art, literature, and music with colonial themes is an example. Efforts to liberate women and abolish slavery, debates about race and nationality, and regulation of interracial relationships and personal identity had important consequences. Discuss, with examples.

8. Consider the causes of the new imperialism. Although economic causes have been considered to be the most important, what other explanations have historians suggested that might account for the appearance of the new imperialism at the end of the nineteenth century?

9. Was there a single pattern of imperialism? How did European imperialism in Africa differ from Asia?

10. What were the immediate consequences of European imperialism? Did imperialism in any way shape the contours of the twentieth century?

DOCUMENT DISCUSSION QUESTIONS

Lord Curzon on the Importance of India and Indians to the British Empire

1. George Nathaniel Curzon served as viceroy of India and foreign minister. Curzon also had extensive knowledge of Afghanistan and Persia. Drawing on his expertise, what did he think was the greatest value of India to the British empire?

2. How did British adventurers and merchants get rich in India, a country regarded as poor today? Was India rich or poor in Curzon's time? How have recent economic, demographic, and political developments changed the situation?

3. When Indian soldiers and laborers were assigned to other parts of the empire, they did not always return to India after completing their tour of duty. What potential social and political problems did this create? Did imperialism have other unintended effects? How might you measure them?

Atrocities in the Congo

4. Unlike other European colonies, the Congo was not at first ruled by administrators reporting to a government. Between 1885 and 1908, the Independent State was the personal possession of Leopold II of Belgium. Foreign visitors such as George Washington Williams and Joseph Conrad were horrified at the treatment of the natives there. What went wrong in the mission of scientific exploration and civilization?

5. Williams saw that Leopold's agents exploited the natives while spending nothing on native education or industrialization. Though the slave trade was abolished, the Congolese became slave laborers for the king. Leopold acknowledged that abuses had been committed by native soldiers still attached to barbaric ways, but said "it was most salutary to teach the natives that all must work." Was there a problem of cross-cultural incomprehension here? Or was the problem simply greed?

6. During the Industrial Revolution, European workers were exploited; they lived in poor conditions and were denied education and political rights. Yet the natives of the Congo suffered much worse treatment. Why? Did Leopold and his agents regard the Congolese as less than fully human? George Washington Williams, an African American, addressed Leopold politely and did not mention the race factor. Why not?

Rudyard Kipling and His Critics

7. Kipling's poem "The White Man's Burden" has been widely read, analyzed, attacked, and praised. What does it mean? What were Kipling's intentions? How does the poem show his belief in Victorian colonial ideals?

8. Kipling's immediate goal in writing "The White Man's Burden" was to influence American public opinion during the Spanish-American War (1899), but he also wanted to celebrate the moral and religious values of European imperialism in general. In his view, imperialists were motivated by a lofty mission more than by economic gain or territorial greed. They sacrificed the comforts of home and suffered hardships abroad because they felt a missionary duty to bring Christianity and Western civilization to peoples in other parts of the world. What were the benefits they brought? Were they worth fighting for? How did Africans and Asians respond to them?

9. The racism characteristic of imperialists in Kipling's day appears in phrases such as "your new-caught sullen peoples, / Half devil and half child." In other writings he praised the bravery of native soldiers ("Ballad of East and West") and recounted folk stories of India (*The Jungle Book*). Did Kipling think Africans and Asians could become civilized? Did he suggest they would be grateful? How would God regard the imperialists' efforts, in Kipling's view?

10. What reasons did Webb give for disagreeing with Kipling? Why did he think imperial talk was "almost sickening"? Did Europeans really suffer in their colonial posts? In Kipling's British India, with a well-established civil service, Webb thought not. Why did he mention the opium trade and the salt tax?

SAMPLE LECTURE 22: CAUSES OF THE NEW IMPERIALISM

Lecture Objectives

1. To show how the second industrial revolution helped make the new imperialism possible

2. To suggest several causes of the new imperialism

IMPERIALISM AND THE NINETEENTH CENTURY

From the perspective of the last quarter of the nineteenth century, there is little doubt that Europe had experienced vast and dramatic political, economic, social, and cultural change since the eighteenth century. The Industrial Revolution, although it began first in Great Britain, eventually spread to the continent and the United States. The result of this was nothing less than a structural change in the economy of Europe. On a cultural or psychological level, the revolution in industry was tangible proof that Europe was now on a path of continued progress. The Crystal Palace Exhibition, held in London in 1851, served as an example of this heady faith in human progress. Although more than forty nations were invited to the Exhibition, it quickly became a showpiece of British innovation and technological might. The British would eventually lose their lead in industry and manufacturing. By the end of the nineteenth century Germany, Japan, and the United States had all caught up and surpassed the industrial output of Britain. It wasn't so much that British industry failed, as it was that other nations simply industrialized more quickly. The British tended to rely on what worked in the past, while other nations managed to accomplish in twenty-five years what took Britain a century or more. The notion that progress was indeed without limit began to permeate European and American culture. While Britain industrialized, Europe was confronted by yet another revolution. Beginning in 1789, the French experienced a political revolution that not only cashiered a king for breaking the social contract with his people, but also brought Napoleon to the throne. France went to war with Britain and the rest of Europe until 1815, when the Congress of Vienna worked out the Concert of Europe. While European monarchs sought to prevent another revolution, the language of the French Revolution entered into popular discourse—words like conservative, liberal, revolutionary, reactionary, socialist, nationalist, and radical became central to the political discourse of the nineteenth-century radical and reform impulses. And this was true of reformers and radicals of either the middle or working classes of Europe. These people were also aware that they were living in a special age of progress and change. The convulsions of revolution were felt throughout the nineteenth century, and the year 1848 saw almost all European nations in the throes of popular revolution, none of which were ultimately successful. By the last quarter of the nineteenth century, Germany and Italy were unified. The United States had suffered four years of bloody civil war. The British had granted the right to vote to nearly all adult males.

THE SECOND INDUSTRIAL REVOLUTION

Europe was also experiencing a second industrial revolution. This revolution was unlike the first in many ways. The second industrial revolution featured the development of two new and revolutionary industries—electricity and chemicals. From these industries came the internal combustion engine, the telegraph and telephone, science-based chemicals, and the beginning of communication technologies. Although there were continuities between the first and second revolutions, there was also one main difference: the decisive importance of scientific knowledge in guiding technological development after 1870. To be sure, technological innovation continued to make its appearance on the shop floor, but by the end of the century, the modern corporation was born and industrial research and design became a specific department within the corporation itself. Tinkers were slowly replaced by university-trained engineers. Eventually this development forced a shift toward more scientific knowledge, and the center of gravity tended more toward Germany and United States, where the main developments in chemicals, electricity, and communications took place.

The second industrial revolution created the foundation for the modern corporation. Factories were larger and more complicated to manage. The railroad industry made vertical and horizontal integration almost necessary and required vast amounts of capital. Managers on the shop floor also began to pay more attention to their labor force in an effort to increase production. Machines had already accomplished this, and in a way, the first Industrial Revolution had solved the problem of getting people to produce. By the end of the nineteenth century, the problem was how to get people to produce more quickly and with greater efficiency. Since efficiency entailed an understanding of the relationship between the input and output of a machine, it seemed almost natural that managers turned to measuring human labor in the same way—work itself was considered to be an object of scientific scrutiny. The experiments of Frederick Winslow Taylor at Midvale Steel in the 1870s and 1880s created a school of management thought called scientific management. While Taylorism was slow to catch on in British and European factories, more managers became convinced that increased productivity would result from the efficiencies created by rationalized production involving both machines and their human counterparts.

Connected to this was yet another problem—consumption. The captains of industry had solved the problem of getting people to produce and to produce more efficiently. Advertising made more people aware of new manufactured goods. Machines, the scientific study of labor, and the rationalization of the productive process pushed Europe toward mass society—a society defined by uniformity and consensus. Such a development created the notion that all civilizations ought to somehow become more alike. It is in such a context that European nations embarked on a path of colonizing the globe. Culture and language, as well as the fruits of industry and manufacturing, would be exported abroad.

THE NEW IMPERIALISM

The quest for empire is indeed an old one. In the ancient Near East the Akkadians, Assyrians, and Persians built mighty empires based on trade and military conquest. The empire of Alexander the Great exported language, custom, and trade all the way to the Indus River. However, of all the ancient empires, none exercised the imagination of European nations throughout the centuries as did Rome. But the Roman world ultimately collapsed. Throughout the eighteenth and nineteenth centuries, the British managed to build an empire that was truly global in scope. Trade and political power were the essence of this empire. But in the last three decades of the nineteenth century, the British found that they were not alone. France, Germany, Belgium, and Russia were busy extending their territories. And wherever Europeans went, they built docks and warehouses, built new companies, and made massive investments. New markets were tapped for raw materials. Spices and slaves no longer dominated foreign trade. The new electrical and chemical industries required rubber and petroleum, neither of which was to be found in Europe. By the end of the century, Britain, France, Germany, the Netherlands, Russia, and the United States had colonized about one quarter of the world as the quest for empire reached from China to Turkey and from South America to Southeast Asia. But it was trade in raw materials or manufactured goods alone that drove this new imperialism. The project was vast and expansive and involved administrators, educators, and engineers. Culture and language were exported as Europeans began to look at themselves as part of a vast "civilizing mission." But European colonization was met with resistance and rebellion during the nineteenth century, and so Europeans were obliged to develop new strategies. The result was what historians call the "new imperialism."

EXPLANATIONS

Historians have long pondered why the new imperialism appeared at the end of the nineteenth century. In 1902, the British economist John Arthur Hobson published *Imperialism*, an important book that traced the origins of the "scramble for Africa" to the interests of a relatively small group of wealthy financiers. Although the British people subsidized colonization throughout the century and the press whipped up the public's jingoism, it was international capitalism that lay behind the new imperialism. Hobson admitted that "so long as England held a virtual monopoly of the world markets for certain important classes of manufactured goods, Imperialism was unnecessary." But during the 1870s it became apparent that Britain was competing in an international economy with Germany, the United States, and Belgium, and that "their competition made it more and more difficult to dispose of the full surplus of our manufactures at a profit." So it was only natural that Britain had to find new markets for its manufactured goods, and that meant "hitherto undeveloped countries, chiefly in the tropics, where vast populations lived capable of growing economic needs which our manufacturers and merchants could supply." For Hobson, international investors were joined by manufacturers involved in colonial trade, the military, and the armaments industry. Lenin agreed with Hobson—the motives of the new imperialism were clearly economic. But because competition had lowered domestic profits, capitalists could only enlarge their markets at home by raising wages. Of course, this would have decreased profits. So for Lenin, the new imperialism was produced by the "internal contradictions of capitalism" itself. Lenin offered this critique in his book, *Imperialism: The Highest Stage of Capitalism* (1917). For most Western nations, the late nineteenth century witnessed a high demand for raw materials that made colonies a necessity—imperialism almost seemed a natural consequence. However, there are limits to this economic explanation. In general, colonial markets offered fewer benefits to European manufacturers. Most colonies were too poor to meet the needs of European manufacturers.

The new imperialism may also have been a response by European governments that were intent on controlling the government and economies of their colonies. In other words, it may be that national interests were at stake. Proponents of imperialism argued that colonies illustrated a nation's military and economic strength. The French adopted imperialist policies as a way of restoring national honor lost during the Franco-Prussian War. The British were alarmed at the prospect of German industrial growth and were concerned that they might lose both old and new markets to them. Meanwhile, the newly unified Germany wanted its own stake in the world, and imperialism seemed to offer a way for them to become one of the great powers. Although Bismarck considered colonialism to be a distraction, by the end of the century he had fallen from power and Germany joined France and England in the race for empire.

The past two centuries had shown Europe the benefits of progress made by civilization itself. It now became clear that civilization and the values it represented could be exported into the noncivilized colonies of the world. It then became Europe's mission to civilize the uncivilized. This cultural dimension to the new imperialism was represented by Rudyard Kipling's comment about the "white man's burden." For

Kipling and others, colonization was necessary because it was a duty consistent with a superior civilization. In general, most Europeans were caught up in the late-nineteenth-century quest for empire. Just the same, resistance and rebellion accompanied the imperialist drive. And while imperialism did bring profits to the great powers of Europe, it also engendered a sense of crisis that swept across Europe at the turn of the century. In many ways, this crisis would find some kind of reconciliation, or at least some kind of release, during the Great War of 1914–1919. The war required the resources of empire for victory. Although imperialism gave a new sense of confidence to Europeans in the midst of a psychological crisis, it also produced further conflict as decolonization accelerated in the twentieth century.

SUGGESTED FEATURE FILMS

Anna and the King. 148 min. Color. 1999. 20th Century Fox. Story of an English schoolteacher who came to Siam in the 1860s to teach the children of King Mongkut.

Breaker Morant. 107 min. Color. 1980. New World Pictures. Three Australian lieutenants are on trial for shooting Boer prisoners during the Boer War.

Fitzcarraldo. 158 min. Color. 1982. New World Pictures. An opera lover wants to build an opera in the jungle, but first he must make a fortune in the rubber business.

The Four Feathers. 131 min. Color. 2002. Miramax Films. Film adaptation of A. E. W. Mason's 1902 novel about a British officer who resigns his post right before his regiment ships out to battle the Sudanese in 1898.

Heart of Darkness. 100 min. Color. 1994. Turner Pictures. Nicholas Roeg's version of the classic Joseph Conrad novel about greed and insanity in an African colony.

Khartoum. 134 min. Color. 1966. United Artists. Charlton Heston and Lawrence Olivier star in this account of General Gordon's unsuccessful Sudanese campaign against the Mahdi in the 1880s.

Lagaan: Once Upon a Time in India. 224 min. Color. 2001. Sony Pictures Classics. Excellent Indian film about British imperialism and a village uniting to resist the land tax.

The Man Who Would be King. 129 min. Color. 1975. Columbia Pictures. Rudyard Kipling story of two ex-soldiers in British India who travel to Kafiristan in order to become kings in their own right.

Noirs et blancs en couleur/Black and White in Color (subtitled). 90 min. Color. 1976. Allied Artists Picture Corporation. French colonists in Africa learn that they are at war with the Germans, seven months after warfare had broken out.

Queimada/Burn! (dubbed). 112 min. Color. 1970. United Artists. A look at economic imperialism on a fictitious nineteenth-century Caribbean island. With Marlon Brando.

Rhodes. 455 min. Color. 1996. BBC/WGBH. Eight-part series tells the story of Cecil Rhodes, the nineenth-century British businessman who founded Rhodesia (now Zimbabwe).

Zulu. 138 min. Color. 1964. MGM/UA Home Entertainment. Film version of the battle of Rorke's Drift (1879) during the Anglo-Zulu war.

Zulu Dawn. 115 min. Color. 1979. American Cinema. A dramatization of the Battle of Isandlwana during the Anglo-Zulu war of 1879.

SUGGESTED CLASSROOM FILMS

The Colonial Idea. 56 min. Color. 1977. BBC/Films, Inc. A study of imperialism from the Crusades through the twentieth century.

The End of Empires. 49 min. Color. 1995. Films for the Humanities and Sciences. This program looks at the end of European imperialism and colonial rule in Asia and Africa.

Europe, the Mighty Continent: Day of Empire Has Arrived. 52 min. Color. 1976. Time-Life Films. Colonial and artistic unrest at the turn of the century.

Europe, the Mighty Continent: Hey-Day Fever. 52 min. Color. 1976. Time-Life Films. The glory of Europe in 1900.

Maharajas: Imperialism by Conspiracy. 25 min. Color. 1974. Centron Educational Films. History of the interrelationship between the Indian princes and the British raj.

The Scramble for Africa. 37 min. Color. 1986. Insight Media. Examines the link between European nationalism and the colonization of Africa.

The Triumph of the West. 13 parts, 50 min. each. Color. 1987. Insight Media. BBC series featuring British historian John Roberts in a discussion of the interactions between Western and non-Western cultures.

The West and the Wider World. 26 min. Color. 1985. Insight Media. A broad survey, extending from Magellan to the scramble for Africa.

CHAPTER 23

Modern Industry and Mass Politics, 1870–1914

OUTLINE

I. Introduction
   A. Marinetti and futurism
      1. A radical renewal of civilization through "courage, audacity, and revolt"
      2. The beauty of speed
      3. The heroic violence of warfare
   B. A radically new world
      1. Second industrial revolution
      2. Mass consumption
      3. New demands in the political arena
      4. Socialist mobilization of industrial workers
      5. White suffragists demanded the franchise
   C. The challenge of the twentieth century
II. New Technologies and Global Transformations
   A. New technologies
      1. Steel
         a. Between the 1850s and 1870s, the cost of producing steel decreased
         b. Three innovations: Bessemer, the Sieman brothers, and Pierre Martin
         c. Steel industry dominated by Germany and the United States
      2. Electricity
         a. Volta invented the chemical battery in 1800
         b. Faraday discovered electromagnetic induction and the electromagnetic generator in 1866
         c. By the 1880s, alternators and transformers produce high-voltage alternating current
         d. Edison invented the incandescent-filament lamp in 1879

      3. Chemicals
         a. Efficient production of alkali and sulfuric acid
            i. Transformed manufacture of paper, soaps, textiles, and fertilizer
         b. British led the way in soaps and cleaners and in mass marketing
         c. German production focused on industrial uses—synthetic dyes and refining petroleum
      4. The liquid-fuel internal combustion engine
      5. By 1914, most navies had converted from coal to oil
      6. Discovery of oil fields in Russia, Borneo, Persia, and Texas
      7. Discovering the potential for worldwide industrialization
   B. Changes in scope and scale
      1. Technological changes created changes in scope and scale of industry
      2. Technology as cause and consequence of the race toward a bigger, faster, cheaper, and more efficient world
      3. The rise of heavy industry and mass marketing
      4. National mass cultures
         a. Watched as Europe divided the globe
         b. Feats of engineering mastery
         c. The ideals of modern European industry
      5. Changes
         a. Population grew constantly
         b. Food shortages declined

c. Populations less susceptible to illness, lower infant mortality

d. Advances in medicine, nutrition, and personal hygiene

e. Improved housing and sanitation

6. Consumption

    a. Consumption as a center of economic activity and theory

    b. The appearance of the department store

    c. Modern advertising

    d. Credit payments

7. New patterns of consumption were decidedly urban

C. The rise of the corporation

1. Economic growth and demands of mass consumption spurred the reorganization of capitalist institutions

2. The modern corporation appeared

    a. Limited-liability laws

        i. Stockholders would only lose their share value in the event of bankruptcy

        ii. Middle classes now considered corporate investment promising

3. Size and control

    a. Larger corporations became necessary for survival

    b. Control shifted from the family to distant bankers and financiers

    c. An ethos of impersonal finance capital

    d. Demand for technical expertise

        i. Undercut traditional forms of family management

        ii. University trained engineers

    e. The white collar class: middle-level salaried managers, neither owners nor laborers

4. Consolidation would protect industries from cyclical fluctuations and unbridled competition

5. Vertical integration

    a. Industries controlled every step of production

        i. From acquisition of raw materials to distribution of finished goods

        ii. Andrew Carnegie's steel company in Pittsburgh

6. Horizontal integration

    a. Organized into cartels

    b. Companies in the same industry would band together

        i. Fixing prices and controlling competition

        ii. Coal, oil, and steel were particularly well-adapted

        iii. Rockefeller's Standard Oil

7. Dominant trend was increased cooperation between government and industry

8. Appearance of businessmen and financiers as officers of state

D. International economics

1. Search for markets, goods, and influence fueled imperial expansion

2. Trade barriers arose to protect home markets

    a. All nations except Britain raised tariffs

3. An interlocking, worldwide system of manufacturing, trade, and finance

4. Near-universal adoption of the gold standard

5. Most European countries imported more than they exported

    a. Relied on "invisible" exports: shipping, insurance, and banking

    b. London as money market of the world

6. Mass manufacturing and commodity production changed patterns of consumption and production

III. Labor Politics, Mass Movements

A. Changes in the European working class

1. In general, workers resented corporate power

2. The "new unionism"

    a. Labor unions evolved into mass, centralized, national organizations

    b. Organization across whole industries

    c. Brought unskilled workers into the ranks

    d. Gave labor power to negotiate wages and conditions of work

    e. provided the framework for the socialist mass party

3. Changes in national political structure

    a. Opened the political process to new participants

    b. Efforts to expand the franchise (1860s–1870s)

    c. New constituencies of working-class men

    d. Labor's struggle with capital cast on a national scale

e. Socialist organizations abandoned their insurrectionary radicalism and opted for reform
4. Karl Marx
  a. Published first volume of *Das Kapital* in 1867)
    i. Attacked capitalism in terms of political economy
    ii. A systematic analysis of production
  b. The Marxist appeal
    i. Provided a crucial foundation for building a democratic mass politics
    ii. Made powerful claims for gender equality
    iii. The promise of a better future
5. The workers' movement
  a. The First International (1864–1876)
  b. Some followed Marx
  c. Others followed the Russian anarchist, Mikhail Bakunin (1814–1876)
B. The spread of socialist parties—and alternatives
1. Marxist socialism spread to social democratic parties in Germany, Belgium, France, Austria, and Russia
  a. Disciplined, politicized workers' organizations
  b. Aimed at seizing control of the state for revolutionary change
2. The model of all socialist parties was the German Social Democratic Party (SPD, founded 1875)
  a. Strove for political change within Germany's parliamentary system
  b. Eventually adopted an explicitly Marxist platform
3. Before World War I, the Social Democrats were the best-organized workers' party in the world: explanations
  a. Rapid and extension industrialization
  b. Large urban working class
  c. A new parliamentary constitution
  d. A national government hostile to organized labor
  e. No tradition of liberal reform
4. Britain
  a. Labour Party (1901)
  b. Remained moderate and committed to incremental reform
5. Anarchism
  a. Opposed to centrally organized economics and politics
  b. Advocated small-scale, localized democracy

c. Similar foundations as Marxism, but different approaches to change
d. Conspiratorial vanguard violence
e. The assassination of Tsar Alexander II (1881)
f. Peter Kropotkin (1842–1921) and Bakunin: "exemplary terror" could spark popular revolt
6. Syndicalism
  a. Popular among agricultural laborers in France, Italy, and Spain
  b. Demanded that workers share ownership and control of the means of production
  c. The capitalist state must be replaced by workers' syndicates or trade associations
  d. Called for mass forms of direct action
  e. The general strike and industrial sabotage
  f. Georges Sorel (1847–1922) and the general strike
C. The limits of success
1. Socialist parties never gained full worker support
  a. Some workers retained loyalty to liberal traditions or religious affiliation
  b. Others were excluded
  c. What constituted the working class?
2. German revisionism
  a. Eduard Bernstein (1850–1932) called for a shift to moderate reform
3. German radicals
  a. Rosa Luxembourg (1870–1919) called for mass strikes, hoping to ignite a proletarian revolution
4. Conflict over strategy and tactics reached its climax in the years before World War I
IV. Demanding Equality: Suffrage and the Women's Movement
A. Women's rights
1. By 1884, Germany, France, and Britain had enfranchised most men
2. Women relegated to status as second-class citizens
3. Women pressed their interests through independent organizations and forms of direct action
B. Women's organizations
1. General German Women's Association
  a. Pressed for educational and legal reforms

2. Votes became the symbol for women's ability to attain full personhood
3. Middle-class women founded clubs, published journals, organized petitions

C. British women's suffrage campaigns
  1. Exploded in violence
  2. Millicent Fawcett (1847–1929)
    a. National Union of Women's Suffrage Societies (1897)
      i. Composed of sixteen different organizations
      ii. Her movement lacked political and economic clout
  3. Emmeline Pankhurst (1858–1928)
    a. Founded the Women's Social and Political Union (1903)
    b. Adopted tactics of militancy and civil disobedience
      i. Women chained themselves to the visitor's gallery in the House of Commons
      ii. Slashed paintings in museums
      iii. Disrupted political meetings
      iv. Burned the homes of politicians
    c. The British government countered this violence with repression
  4. Six-hour riot between suffragists and police in 1910
  5. The martyrdom of Emily Wilding Davison (1913)

D. Redefining womanhood
  1. Campaign for women's suffrage helped redefine Victorian gender roles
  2. The increasing visibility of women
  3. Middle-class women and work
    a. Worked as social workers and clerks, nurses and teachers
    b. British women established their own colleges at Oxford and Cambridge in the 1870s and 1880s
  4. Women, politics, and reform
    a. Poor relief, prison reform, temperance movements, abolition of slavery, education
  5. The "new woman"
    a. Demanded education and a job
    b. Claimed the right to be physically and intellectually active
    c. The new woman as image
      i. Few women actually for the image created by artists and journalists
    d. Opposition
      i. Never exclusively male opposition

      ii. Mrs. Humphrey Ward— women in politics would sap the strength of the empire
      iii. Christian commentators criticized suffragists for moral decay
      iv. Others argued that feminism would dissolve the family

V. Liberalism and its Discontents: National Politics at the Turn of the Century
  A. Late-nineteenth-century liberalism
    1. Middle-class liberals found themselves on the defensive after 1870
    2. Mass politics upset the balance between middle-class interests and traditional elites
    3. Trade unions, socialists, and feminists all challenged Europe's governing class
    4. The government's response was a mixture of conciliation and repression
    5. What was required was a distinctly modern form of mass politics
  B. France: the embattled republic
    1. Franco-Prussian War (1870) as humiliating defeat for France
    2. Government of the Second Empire collapsed
    3. The Third Republic
      a. A new constitution (1875)
        i. Triumph of democratic and parliamentary principles
      b. Class conflict
    4. The Paris Commune (1871)
      a. Pitted the nation against the radical city of Paris
      b. Paris refused to surrender to the Germans
      c. Paris proclaimed itself to be the true government of France
      d. Government sends troops to Paris in March 1871
      e. Barricades and street fighting
      f. 25,000 were executed, killed in fighting, or consumed in fires
  C. The Dreyfus Affair and anti-Semitism as politics
    1. French anti-Semitism: a new form of radical right-wing politics (nationalist, antiparliamentary, and antiliberal)
    2. Édouard Drumont (1844–1917)
      a. Successful anti-Semitic journalist
      b. Attributed all of France's problems to a Jewish conspiracy
      c. Merged three strands of anti-Semitism
        i. Christian anti-Semitism (Jews as Christ killers)

      ii. Economic anti-Semitism
         (Rothschild as representative
         of all Jews)

      iii. Racial thinking (Jews as an
         inferior race)

   d. An ideology of hatred

      i. Jews in the army subverted
         national purpose

      ii. Mass culture corrupted
         French culture

      iii. Jews and wealth

   e. *La Libre Parole* (*Free Speech*, 1892),
     the Anti-Semitic League, and
     Jewish France (1886)

3. The Dreyfus Affair (1894)

   a. Dreyfus convicted of selling
     military secrets to Germany

   b. Sent to Devil's Island

   c. The verdict was questioned and
     documents proven to be forgeries
     (1896)

   d. Émile Zola (1840–1902) backed
     Dreyfus

      i. Blasted the French estab-
         lishment in *J'accuse* (*I
         Accuse*)

   e. Dreyfus eventually freed in 1899
     and cleared of all guilt in 1906

   f. Consequences

      i. Separation of church and
         state in France

      ii. Republicans saw church
         army as hostile toward the
         republic

4. The Third Republic

   a. Showed that the radical right
     and anti-Semitism were plainly
     political forces

D. Zionism: Theodor Herzl (1860–1904)

1. Considered the Dreyfus Affair to be an
   expression of a fundamental problem

   a. Jews might never be assimilated
     into European culture

2. Endorsed Zionism—building a separate
   Jewish homeland outside Europe

3. Zionism as a modern nationalist
   movement

4. *The State of the Jews* (1896)

5. Convened the first Zionist Congress in
   Switzerland in 1897

E. Germany's search for imperial unity

1. Bismarck united Germany under the
   banner of Prussian conservatism
   (1864–1871)

   a. Sought to create the centralizing
     institutions of a modern state

   b. Safeguarding the privileges of
     Germany's national interests

   c. The conservative upper house
     (Bundesrat) and the democratic
     lower house (Reichstag)

   d. Executive power rested solely with
     William I (1797–1888, r. 1861–
     1888), king and kaiser (emperor)

   e. Cabinet ministers answered only
     to the kaiser

2. Three problems

   a. Divide between Catholics and
     Protestants

   b. Growing Social Democratic party

   c. Divisive economic interests of
     agriculture and industry

3. *Kulturkampf* (cultural struggle)

   a. Bismarck unleashed an
     anti-Catholic campaign

   b. Apealed to sectarian tensions
     over public education and ccivil
     marriages

   c. Passed laws that imprisoned
     priests for political sermons

   d. Banned Jesuits from Prussia

   e. The campaign backfired

      i. Catholic Center party won
         seats in the Reichstag in 1874

      ii. Bismarck negotiated an
         alliance with the Catholic
         Center

4. The new coalition

   a. Agricultural and industrial interests
     as well as socially conservative
     Catholics

5. Social Democrats as the new enemies of
   the empire

   b. Bismarck passed antisocialist laws
     in 1878

   c. Expelled socialists from major cities

6. Social welfare

   a. Workers guaranteed sickness and
     accident insurance

   b. Rigorous factory inspection

   c. Limited working hours for women
     and children

   d. Old-age pensions

7. Social welfare legislation did not win
   the loyalty of workers

8. William II (1859–1941, r. 1888–1918)

   a. Suspended antisocialist legislation
     in 1890 and legalized the SPD

F. Britain: from moderation to militance

1. The Second Reform Bill (1867)

2. Liberal and Conservative political
   parties

3. New laws
    a. Legality of trade unions
    b. Rebuilding large urban areas
    c. Elementary education for all
       children
    d. Male Dissenters can attend Oxford
       or Cambridge
    e. 75 percent of adult males
       enfranchised by 1894
4. Benjamin Disraeli (1804–1881)—
   Conservative and William Gladstone
   (1809–1898)—Liberal
    a. Both offered moderate programs
       that appealed to a widening
       electorate
5. The moderate working class
    a. The Independent Labour Party
       (1901)
6. 1906 welfare legislation
7. David Lloyd George (1863–1945) and
   the People's Budget of 1909
    a. Progressive income and inheritance
       taxes
8. Problems
    a. Liberal parliamentary framework
       began to show signs of collapse
    b. Nationwide strikes of coal and
       railway workers
    c. Irish radical nationalists began to
       favor armed revolution
    d. Sinn Fein and the Irish Republican
       Brotherhood
    e. Home Rule tabled (1913)

G. Russia: the road to revolution
    1. Internal conflicts and an autocratic
       political system
    2. Threatened by Western industrialization
       and Western political doctrines
    3. Russian industrialization (1880s–1890s)
        a. State-directed industrial
           development
        b. Serfs emancipated in 1861
        c. No independent middle class
           capable of raising capital
        d. Heightened social tensions
        e. Workers left their villages
           temporarily to work, and then
           returned for planting and harvest
    4. The legal system
        a. No recognition of trade unions or
           employers' associations
        b. Outdated banking and finance
           laws
    5. Alexander II (1818–1888, r. 1855–1881)
        a. The "Tsar Liberator"
        b. Tightened restrictions

c. Set up *zemstvos*, provincial land
   and county assemblies (1804)
d. Curtailed the rights of *zemstvos*,
   censorship of the press
e. Assassinated by a radical
6. Alexander III (1845–1894, r. 1881–1894)
    a. Steered the country toward the right
    b. Stern repression
        i. Curtailed power of the
           zemstvos
       ii. Increased authority of the
           secret police
7. Nicholas II (1868–1918, r. 1894–1917)
    a. Continued these "counterreforms"
    b. Advocated Russification to extend
       the language, religion, and culture
       of Greater Russia
    c. Pogroms and open anti-Semitism
8. The Populists
    a. Russia to modernize on its own
       terms, not those of the West
    b. Based on the ancient village
       commune (mir)
    c. Mostly middle class, students,
       and women
    d. Overthrowing the tsar through
       anarchy and insurrection
    e. Dedicated their lives to the people
    f. Read Marx's *Capital* and
       emphasized peasant socialism
9. Russian Marxism
    a. Organized as the Social
       Democratic party
        i. Concentrated on urban
           workers
       ii. Russian autocracy would
           give way to capitalism
      iii. Capitalism would give way
           to a classless society
10. Social Democratic party split (1903)
    a. Bolsheviks (majority group)
        i. Called for a central party
           organization of active
           revolutionaries
       ii. Rapid industrialization
           meant they did not have to
           follow Marx
    b. Mensheviks (minority group)
        i. Gradualist approach
       ii. Reluctant to depart from
           Marxist orthodoxy
    c. Lenin
        i. Leader of the Bolsheviks
           while in exile
       ii. Coordinated socialist
           movement

iii. Russia was ripe for revolution

iv. *What Is to Be Done?* (1902)

H. The first Russian Revolution (1905)

1. Causes
   a. The Russo-Japanese War
   b. Rapid industrialization had transformed Rusia unevenly
   c. Low grain prices resulted in peasant uprisings
   d. Student radicalism
   e. Russian inefficiency
   f. Radical workers organized strikes and demonstrations

2. Bloody Sunday (January 22, 1905)
   a. 200,000 workers led by Father Gapon demonstrated at the Winter Palace
   b. Guard troops killed 130 and wounded several hundred

3. The protest grew
   a. Merchants closed stores
   b. Factory owners shut down factories
   c. Lawyers refused to hear cases
   d. The autocracy had lost control

4. Nicholas II issued the October Manifesto
   a. Guaranteed individual liberties
   b. Moderately liberal franchise for the election of a Duma
   c. Genuine legislative veto powers for the Duma

5. Nicholas failed to see that fundamental change was needed
   a. 1905–1907: Nicholas revoked most of the promises made in October
   b. Deprived the Duma of its principal powers

6. Peter Stolypin (1862–1911) and the Stolypin Reforms (1906–1911)
   a. Agrarian reforms for the sale of five million acres of royal land to peasants
   b. Granted peasants permission to withdraw for the mir
   c. Canceled peasant property debts
   d. Legalized trade unions
   e. Established sickness and accident insurance

7. Russian agriculture remained suspended between emerging capitalism and the peasant commune

I. Nationalism and imperial politics: the Balkans

1. Rising nationalism divides the disintegrating Ottoman Empire

2. The Turks ceded territories to rival European powers, especially Russia and Austria

3. The Ottoman Empire as "the sick man of Europe"

4. Uprisings in Bosnia, Herzegovina, and Bulgaria (1875–1876)
   a. Reports of atrocities against Christians
   b. Led to the Russo-Turkish War (1877–1878)
   c. The Treaty of San Stefano
      i. Terminated the conflict
      ii. Forced the Turkish sultan to surrender all of his European territory
   d. The great powers intervened

5. The Treaty of Berlin (1878)
   a. Bessarabia to Russia, Thessaly to Greece
   b. Bosnia and Herzegovina under Austrian control
   c. Montenegro, Serbia, and Romania become independent states

6. The independent kingdom of Bulgaria (1908)

7. Austria annexed Bosnia and Herzegovina

8. Turkish nationalism
   a. Turks had grown impatient with weakness of the sultan
   b. The Young Turks
      i. Forced the sultan to establish a constitutional government in 1908
      ii. Mohammed V (1909–1918) came to the throne
      iii. "Ottomanize" all imperial subjects
      iv. Tried to bring Christian and Muslim communities under more centralized control
      v. Spreading Turkish culture

VI. Science and the Soul of the Modern Age

A. Darwin's revolutionary theory

1. Organic evolution by natural selection transformed the conception of nature itself

2. An unsettling new picture of human biology, behavior, and society

3. Jean Lamarck (1744–1829)
   a. Behavioral changes could alter physical characteristics within a single generation
   b. New traits could be passed on to offspring

4. Charles Darwin (1809–1882)
   a. *The Origin of Species* (1859)
      i. Five years aboard H. M. S. *Beagle*

ii. Observed manifold variations
of animal life

b. Theorized that variations within a
population made certain individuals
better adapted for survival

i. Drew on the population
theories of Thomas Malthus
(1766–1834)

ii. Malthusian competition led
to adaptation and ultimately
survival

c. Darwin used natural selection to
explain the origin of new species

d. Applied to plant and animal species
as well as to man

e. *The Descent of Man* (1871)

i. The human race had evolved
from an apelike ancestor

B. Darwinian theory and religion

1. Darwinian theory challenged deeply
held religious beliefs

2. Sparked a debate on the existence of God

3. For Darwin, the world was not governed
by order, harmony, and divine will but
by random chance and struggle

4. Thomas Henry Huxley (1825–1895)

a. Argued against Christians appalled
by the implications of Darwinism

b. Called himself an agnostic

c. Opposed to all dogma

d. Follow reason as far as it can
take you

C. The rise of the social sciences

1. Influence of Darwinism on sociology,
psychology, anthropology, and economics

2. New ways of quantifying and interpreting
human experience

3. Social Darwinism

a. Herbert Spencer (1820–1903)

i. Applied individual competition to classes, races, and
nations

ii. Coined the expression
"survival of the fittest"

iii. Condemned all forms of
collectivism—the individual
who "fit" was all-important

b. Popularized notions of social
Darwinism were easy to
comprehend

i. Integrated into popular
vocabulary

ii. Justified the natural order
of rich and poor

iii. Nationalists used social
Darwinism to rationalize

imperialism and warfare

iv. Also used to justify racial
hierarchy and white superiority

D. Early psychology: Pavlov and Freud

1. The irrational and animalistic side of
human nature

2. Ivan Pavlov (1849–1936)

a. "Classical conditioning"

b. A random stimulus can produce a
physical reflex reaction

c. Behaviorism

i. Eschewed mind and
consciousness

ii. Focused on physiological
responses to the environment

3. Sigmund Freud (1856–1936)

a. Behavior largely motivated by
unconscious and irrational forces

b. Unconscious drives and desires
conflict with the rational and
moral conscience

c. The psyche

i. Id: undisciplined desires for
pleasure and gratification

ii. Superego: the conscience
(conditioned by morality
and culture)

iii. Ego: area where the conflict
between id and superego is
worked out

4. An objective (scientific) understanding
of human behavior

5. Anxiety over the value and limits of
human reason

E. Friedrich Nietzsche (1844–1900) and the
attack on tradition

1. Middle-class culture dominated by
illusions and self-deceptions

2. Rejected rational argumentation

3. Bourgeois faith in science, progress, and
democracy as a futile search for truth

4. Ridiculed Judeo-Christian morality for
instilling a repressive conformity

5. Themes of personal liberation

F. Religion and its critics

1. The Roman Catholic Church on the
defensive

2. Pope Pius IX issued the Syllabus of
Errors in 1864

a. Condemned materialism, free
thought, and religious relativism

b. Convoked a church council (first one
since the late sixteenth century)

c. Doctrine of papal infallibility

d. Denounced by the governments of
several Catholic countries

3. Pope Leo XIII
   a. Brought a more accommodating climate to the church
   b. Acknowledged that there is good and evil in modern civilization
   c. Added a scientific staff to the Vatican, opened archives and observatories
4. Protestants
   a. Little in the way of doctrine to help them defend their faith
   b. Pragmatism (Charles Peirce and William James)
      i. Truth was whatever produced useful, practical results
      ii. If belief in God provided mental peace, then that belief was true
G. New readers and the popular press
   1. Facilitated the spread of new ideas
   2. Rising literacy rates and new forms of printed mass culture
   3. Journalism
      a. Emphasis on the sensational
      b. Advertising
      c. "Yellow" journalism—entertainment, sensationalism, and the news
H. The first moderns: innovations in art
   1. Modernism
      a. Questioning the moral and cultural values of liberal, middle-class society
      b. Characteristics
         i. Self-conscious sense of rupture from history and tradition
         ii. Rejection of established values
         iii. Insistence on an expressive and experimental freedom
      c. A new understanding of the relationship between art and society
   2. Wassily Kandinsky (1866–1944)
      a. Devotee of occult mysticism
      b. The role of the visionary artist
      c. From soulless materialism to the psychic-spiritual life
I. The revolt on canvas
   1. Modernism defined itself in opposition to the past
   2. A rejection of mainstream academic art
      a. Against the "shackles of verisimilitude" (Gauguin)

3. Artists begin to turn their backs on the visual world
4. New focus on the subjective, psychologically-oriented forms of self-expression
5. French Impressionism
   a. Attempted to objectively record natural phenomena
   b. Captured the transitory play of light on surfaces
   c. The legacies of Claude Monet (1840–1926) and Pierre-Auguste Renoir (1841–1919)
      i. Paved the way for younger artists to experiment more freely
      ii. Impressionist artists organized their own independent exhibitions
6. Post-Impressionism
   a. Paul Cézanne (1839–1906)
      i. Reducing natural forms to geometric equivalents
      ii. Emphasis on subjective arrangement of color and form
      iii. Art as a vehicle for an artist's self-expression
   b. Paul Gauguin (1848–1903) and Vincent van Gogh (1853–1890)
      i. Explored art's expressive potential with greater emotion and subjectivity
7. German Expressionism
   a. Emil Nolde (1867–1956)
      i. Disillusionment with modern society
   b. James Ensor (1860–1949)
      i. The corruption of artistic culture
   c. Painters turned to acidic tones, violent figural distortions, and crude depictions of sexuality
8. Edvard Munch (1863–1944) and Egon Schiele (1890–1918)
9. Henri Matisse (1869–1954) and Pablo Picasso (1869–1954)
10. Cubists, vorticists, and futurists
    a. Embraced a hard, angular aesthetic of the machine age
    b. The uncertainty of the future
VII. Conclusion
   A. Progress and the forces of change
   B. Decline and the forces of change

GENERAL DISCUSSION QUESTIONS

1. Make a list of the various characteristics of the first and second industrial revolutions. In what ways were these revolutions in industry vastly different?

2. Who, besides Karl Marx and Friedrich Engels, would speak up for the cause of the oppressed working classes of Europe? What qualities and qualifications did these leaders have to lead the communist movement?

3. What is socialism and how does it differ from communism or capitalism? What were some specific ideas for reforming society proposed by socialists and communists in the nineteenth century? How many of these ideas have been adopted today?

4. How did late-nineteenth-century women claim greater rights and wider participation in the public sphere? When women failed to get the vote in Britain in 1900, what happened to the women's suffrage movement?

5. If mass participation requires a learning process, how politically sophisticated were the French people between 1870 and 1914? How strong was their political support for the Third Republic, compared to their patriotic commitment to France?

6. Between 1870 and 1914, Germany and Russia had governments that were minimally democratic or participatory and were resistant to change or even reactionary. How was Bismarck able to achieve many of his goals, including progressive social legislation? By contrast, how and why was the tsarist government hampered in its efforts to modernize Russia as industrialization began?

7. How was Charles Darwin's theory of biological evolution influenced by the social and philosophical ideas of the Enlightenment? Why has Darwin's theory of evolution been so influential far beyond the field of evolutionary biology?

8. How are social Darwinism and the social sciences related? Both capitalists and communists found social Darwinism useful in economics and sociology. Likewise, it appealed to those who cherished the idea of the triumph of Western civilization and those who regarded all societies as equally adaptive to conditions in the environment. How can this be?

9. It has been said that Sigmund Freud was a child of the Enlightenment, in that he recognized reason and science as a means to understand the world. What did it mean for Freud to formulate an objective understanding of irrational behavior? Why is Freud so significant today? Are we all Freudians in one way or another?

10. Friedrich Nietzsche has been categorized as a thinker whose ideas resound with liberation. What forces implicit in nineteenth-century European culture caused Nietzsche to condemn society, culture, and morality? What did Nietzsche mean when he said "Gods, too, decompose. God is dead. God remains dead. And we have killed him."

DOCUMENT DISCUSSION QUESTIONS

The Dangers of Consumer Culture

1. The industrial revolution of the early nineteenth century was faced with the challenge of production. In what ways was the problem of the late nineteenth century that of consumption? What obstacles did merchants face when faced with the problem of getting people to produce?

2. Why does Zola say that the department store "was all regulated and organized with the remorselessness of a machine"? What were the problems of a consumer culture as indicated by Zola? Is there anything inherently wrong with a consumer culture?

Anti-Semitism in Late Nineteenth-Century France

3. Why did European Jews gain more legal and political rights over the course of the nineteenth century? What rights were gained?

4. Drumont argued that prior to 1789 Jews had little influence in France, but by cleverly using the rights they gained in the Revolution, they conquered France. Was anti-Semitism correlated with the real economic power of the Jews? Or was it a projection of the anti-Semites' fears that Jews were more manipulative and clever than themselves?

5. In what ways does Drumont's book, *Jewish France* (1885), serve as a founding document of new forms of anti-Semitism?

Lenin's View of a Revolutionary Party

6. In *What Is to Be Done?* Lenin more or less set down the rules for the revolutionary vanguard. How much of this text can be directly related to the French Revolution? That is, what debt did revolutionaries like Lenin owe to the men and women of 1789?

7. Lenin demands the formation of vanguard fighters. Discuss the characteristics of these fighters. What does it mean to be a revolutionary? Were dedicated

professional revolutionaries the only people who could seize power?

8. In the absence of free speech, free press, and free elections, how could professional revolutionaries represent the will of the people? How can the revolutionaries develop their political consciousness?

Darwin and His Readers

9. Why did people think the natural world was governed by laws? Was this a religious belief or a scientific fact? How did Charles Darwin both resemble and differ from his eighteenth-century predecessors in arriving at evolutionary thought?

10. Is it fair to say that what Newton was to the seventeenth and eighteenth centuries, Darwin was to the nineteenth? What had Darwin done? Why was the theory of evolution so revolutionary? What are the social consequences of natural selection?

11. How does Osterroth's autobiography suggest that reading books can change minds? How did he become aware of class differences in forms of knowledge? Do people need a *Weltanschauung* or worldview? What is your worldview? How do you make sense of the world?

SAMPLE LECTURE 23: THE SHAPE OF THINGS TO COME: DARWIN'S REVOLUTION IN EVOLUTION

Lecture Objectives

1. To place the ideas of Charles Darwin in historical and scientific context

2. To explain the basic principles of natural selection

3. To tentatively suggest the implications of Darwinism for nineteenth- and twentieth-century culture

NINETEENTH-CENTURY SCIENTIFIC DEVELOPMENTS

One of the hallmarks of nineteenth-century thought was the growing tendency among thinkers to value science and its effect on the possibilities for human progress. Of course, this was the age of the Industrial Revolution, in which science was beginning to serve the needs of industry in a more direct way. Keep in mind, however, that not every technological advance was made at the hands of a scientist, nor was it made by a university-trained engineer. If the history of the early Industrial Revolution tells us anything, it is that oftentimes innovation came by trial and error on the shop floor. It was only during the second industrial revolution, after the 1870s, that technological innovation was removed from the shop floor and brought into the corporate laboratory, where results

could be obtained more efficiently and rationally. The nineteenth century itself made enormous advances in science. For instance:

- John Dalton formulated atomic theory (1808).
- Michael Faraday discovered the principle of electromagnetic induction (1831).
- Hermann von Helmholtz formulated the laws of the conservation of energy (1847).
- Gregor Mendeleev constructed the periodic table of elements (1869).
- Louis Pasteur developed the germ theory of disease (1860s–1870s).
- Heinrich Hertz discovered electromagnetic waves (1887).

There is little doubt that one of the most important scientific advances came in the biological sciences with Charles Darwin's theory of evolution. What Copernicus had done for astronomy, and what Newton had done for physics, Darwin would do for biology. Furthermore, whereas the scientific revolution of Copernicus and Newton fundamentally changed our notion of space, Darwin's evolutionary theory profoundly altered our sense of time. During the eighteenth century almost all people believed in the biblical account of creation—that is, that God created a perfect universe including the variety of species of plants and animals. The world was a perfect world—perfect, fixed, and unchanging. All this, it was commonly assumed, occurred 6000 years ago. In 1658, Bishop James Ussher, Archbishop of Armagh, Primate of All Ireland, and Vice-Chancellor of Trinity College in Dublin, established the first day of creation as Sunday, October 23, 4004 B.C.E., using the arguments set forth in Old Testament. Ussher also calculated that Adam and Eve were driven from Paradise on Monday, November 10, 4004, and that the ark touched down on Mt. Ararat on May 5, 1491 B.C.E., "on a Wednesday." This knowledge was incorporated into an authorized version of the Bible printed in 1701 and came to be regarded as truth. In 1833, the Scottish geologist Charles Lyell demonstrated that the planet had evolved over many stages and so was much older than popularly assumed. And as early as 1794, Erasmus Darwin, the grandfather of Charles Darwin, had already argued that the world was millions of years old before humans, plants, and animals made their first appearance.

DARWIN'S EARLY LIFE AND INFLUENCES

Charles Darwin (1809–1882) was gentleman born into a privileged Victorian family. His father and grandfather were respected members of the community, and his cousins were Wedgwood china makers (Darwin married Emma Wedgwood in 1839, a marriage that would produce ten children). The young Darwin was interested in specimen-collecting and chemistry, especially the study of animals, plants, and rocks. He had little success as a medical student at Edinburgh. At

Cambridge Darwin studied divinity. He had conventional religious beliefs, a mediocre academic record, and an active social life. He graduated in 1831 with few prospects and thought about becoming a clergyman. He read the accounts of Humboldt's travels to South America and did geological fieldwork. Then he received an opportunity to travel on the H. M. S. *Beagle*, a Royal Navy survey ship, as the ship's naturalist. The job also introduced him to Captain Robert FitzRoy, a Tory aristocrat. Darwin was "an acute observer of nature, a meticulous narrator of detail, and of a mildly speculative mind." His duties on the H. M. S. *Beagle* were to observe and collect specimens, to take careful notes, and to classify data. Darwin kept a journal of his five-year voyage (1831–1836). The *Beagle* visited South America, Tierra del Fuego, the Galapagos Islands, Tahiti, South Africa, South America (again), and then went back to England. His journal shows his careful observations and the questions in Darwin's mind. Why had God created so many species? How did they get to their present locations? Was there one creation in the Garden of Eden, or many? The problems he identified were those of classification and order.

Among Darwin's many influences were his own grandfather, Erasmus Darwin, a physician and a member of the Lunar Society of Birmingham. Another major influence was the *Essay on the Principle of Population* (1797), in which Robert Malthus argued that population expands geometrically while the food supply expands arithmetically. Population will inevitably outrun the food supply and human misery will result, unless positive checks (war, plague, or famine) or moral restraint are applied. Life is competition for survival, according to Malthus. Another thinker who affected Darwin was the geologist Charles Lyell. In his *Principles of Geology* (1830–1833), Lyell asked whether changes in the earth's surface are caused by catastrophic events or by orderly and continuing change. Lyell argued for continuing processes. He was not a radical antireligious thinker and did not deny the biblical flood story. He only rejected its uniqueness. He suggested that layers of sediment in the landscape were a map of change over time. Darwin joined in the debates prompted by the ideas of Malthus and Lyell, raising more questions. Are species permanent, or can they change? Is there a movement of species? His observations of finches in the Galapagos Islands forced him to wonder whether visible differences in species show a map of differences over time and many generations. An essential point of Darwin's theory of evolution is that environmental conditions give rise to different plants and animals over time. But how?

THE ORIGIN OF SPECIES

Darwin's early notions, developed in 1835 on the *Beagle*, were refined in later years through his studies of animal breeding and varieties. His theory was clear by the late 1850s. But Darwin was reluctant to publish until he found out that others, like Alfred Wallace, were working on the same area. Darwin at last published his work in *On the Origin of Species by Means of Natural Selection, or the Preservation of Favoured Races in the Struggle for Life*, in 1859, a 500-page essay and bestseller in Britain and America. A mainstay of Darwin's theory of evolution is that species change by mutation and variation, not by acquiring characteristics. This process is natural selection, which is distributed by migration. Jean-Baptiste Lamarck (1744–1829) had already argued that individuals acquire characteristics and transmit them to their descendants. Darwin was attracted to this idea, but in his formulation, random mutations occur all the time—individuals who have advantageous mutations survive and propagate, while others die out. (Darwin did not know about genetics, then studied by his contemporary, the Austrian monk Gregor Mendel, who published his *Experiments in Plant Hybridization* in 1866.) Darwin described mutations as spontaneous changes, both good and bad. Why do giraffes have long necks, for example? Long necks are more advantageous for survival, so long-necked mutants survive and have descendants. Darwin called this "survival of the fit," in which the fittest, best-adapted organisms survive, and others become extinct. Species become better and better adapted to their environment. This is natural selection. Human beings are included in evolution, too. Thomas H. Huxley argued this in *Man's Place in Nature* (1863), as did Darwin in *The Descent of Man, and Selection in Relation to Sex* (1871) and *The Expression of Emotions in Man and Animals* (1872). This was a very controversial point.

THE IMPACT OF DARWINISM

Favorable reviews, pirate editions, and strong sales followed the publication of *The Origin of Species*. Huxley responded with enthusiasm, since here was another opportunity to attack religion. "This nineteenth century, the dawn of modern science . . . extinguished theologians," like snakes strangled by Hercules, he wrote. Science was Cinderella, the kitchen maid who was in the end more useful than her ugly stepsisters, Theology and Philosophy. Churchmen condemned Darwin's work because it contradicted biblical stories of creation and changed the principles of faith. Cruel competition and the struggle for survival seemed simply immoral or amoral. Could people still believe in God? Yes, Darwin thought, because God used evolution to produce human beings. The end (people) justifies the means (evolution). Huxley was a skeptic or agnostic. Huxley debated Bishop Wilberforce, known as "Soapy Sam," who slyly asked if Darwin was descended from monkeys on his father's side or his mother's side. Darwin argued for common ancestry of monkeys and human beings and praised the noble virtues of apes. He'd rather be descended from them than from Wilberforce, he joked.

Many Christians did accept Darwin's ideas. Creationism (especially scientific creationism) is a twentieth-century reaction among fundamentalist Protestants. In 1996, Pope John

Paul II stated that "evolution is more than a theory" and approved it for the Roman Catholic Church. Social Darwinism found support across the political spectrum, from right to left. Proponents included Thomas H. Huxley, Herbert Spencer, Andrew Carnegie, J. P. Morgan, Karl Marx, and Friedrich Engels, who praised Marx as "the Darwin of sociology." Was social Darwinism suited to both socialism and free enterprise? Industrialism and engineering were quickly linked to physics and biology. Freedom, progress, and necessity were tied together. "Nature is a little cruel, that she may be very kind," wrote Spencer. Darwin's theory changed biological and social thought, providing scientific support for ideas of struggle for survival and the triumph of some and destruction of others. But if "survival of the fittest" means that the best-adapted organisms survive in nature and society, it does not mean that they are always morally better or even remotely desirable.

SUGGESTED FEATURE FILMS

1900. 245 min. Color. 1976. Paramount Pictures. Bertolucci epic focuses on the rise of fascism and the peasants' eventual reaction by supporting communism.

Angels and Insects. 116 min. Color. 1995. Samuel Goldwyn Company. A perceptive and often hilarious look at the impact of evolutionary ideas on British culture.

The Battleship Potemkin. 66 min. B/W. 1925. Goskino. Eisenstein's classic silent film about the historical events surrounding the riot on the battleship *Potemkin* in 1905. The most famous scenes of the film come with the slaughter of helpless citizens by the Cossacks on the Odessa steps leading to the harbor.

The Elephant Man. 124 min. B/W. 1980. Paramount Pictures. David Lynch film about John Merrick, a nineteenth-century Englishman afflicted with a disfiguring congenital disease. Excellent for the images of late-nineteenth-century London.

Freud. 139 min. B/W. 1962. Universal International Pictures. John Huston directed Montgomery Clift in this film about Freud's life in the early 1890s.

The Life of Émile Zola. 116 min. B/W. 1937. Warner Brothers. Traces the career of the French novelist (played by Paul Muni), including Zola's involvement in the Dreyfus Affair (note that the anti-Semitism surrounding the affair is not fully developed).

Lust for Life. 122 min. Color. 1956. MGM. Directed by Vincent Minnelli and starring Kirk Douglas. Looks at both van Gogh's work and the changing art world.

Rosa Luxembourg (subtitled). 122. Color. 1986. New Yorker Films. Swedish film about Rosa's stay in a German prison during World War I where she writes and gives strength to the small Spartacus League she founded to oppose the war.

Stachka (Strike). 82 min. B/W. 1925. Goskino. Eisenstein silent film about restlessness and strike-planning among factory workers in tsarist Russia.

Wilde. 118 min. Color. 1997. Dove International. Brian Gilbert's film about Oscar Wilde—genius, poet, and playwright.

SUGGESTED CLASSROOM FILMS

The Christians: The Roots of Disbelief (1848–1962). 42 min. Color. 1978. McGraw-Hill/ the effect of nationalism, Victorianism, and Darwinism on Christianity.

Charles Darwin. 23 min. Color. 1973. Extension Media Center. Uses excerpts from *The Journal of the Voyage of the* Beagle to describe Darwin's achievement.

Darwin's Revolution. 52 min. Color. 1986. Insight Media. James Burke hosts this examination of Darwin's ideas and the social ideologies built upon them.

Evolution by Natural Selection. 48 min. Color. 1997. Insight Media. Program describes how Darwin developed his evolutionary theory and defines natural selection, kin selection, and sexual selection.

Karl Marx and Marxism. 52 min. Color. 1983. Films for the Humanities and Sciences. Covers the biography of Marx, the development of his ideas, and the efforts to embody his ideas in the political world.

The Paris Commune. 30 min. Color. 1990. Films for the Humanities and Sciences. Looks at both the context and consequences of the Commune.

A Third Testament: Tolstoy. 53 min. Color. 1974. BBC/ Time-Life Films. Malcolm Muggeridge on location in Russia.

CHAPTER 24 | The First World War

b. August 4: Britain reluctantly
entered the war against Germany

7. August 7, 1914: Montenegrins joined
the Serbs against Austria

8. July: the Japanese declared war on
Germany

9. August: Turkey allied itself with
Germany

10. A "tragedy of miscalculation"
a. Little diplomatic communication
b. Austrian mismanagement
c. The lure of the first strike

III. The Marne and its Consequences
A. General observations
1. War as national glory and spiritual
renewal
2. War put centuries of progress at risk
3. Bankers and financiers were most
opposed to war—financial chaos
would result
4. For the young there was the excitement
of enlistment
5. "Over by Christmas"
a. A short, limited, and decisive war
b. Size and bigger armies
c. Speed and quick offensives

B. The Schlieffen Plan
1. Designed to suit Germany's efficient
but small army
2. Attack France first, neutralize the
Western Front, then attack Russia
3. Problems
a. The plan overestimated physical
and logistical capabilities
b. The speed of movement was too
much for the troops
c. Supply lines could not keep up
d. The resistance of the Belgian army
e. Frequent changes made to the plan
i. Troops sent to the Eastern
Front
ii. Attacked Paris from the
northeast instead of the
southwest

C. The Battle of the Marne
1. Joffre led the Germans into a trap
2. British and French counteroffensives
3. German retreat
4. The "race to the sea"
5. The Western Front
a. The Great Powers dug in
b. Trench warfare
6. The importance of the Marne
a. Changed Europe's expectation
of war
b. The war would now be long,
costly, and deadly

c. Russian intervention pulled
Germany away from the Western
Front

IV. Stalemate, 1915
A. The search for new partners
1. Ottomans joined Germany and Austria
in 1914
2. Italy joined the Allies in May 1915
3. Bulgaria joined the Central Powers
in 1915
4. Major effect was to expand the war
geographically

B. Gallipoli and naval warfare
1. Turkish intervention
a. Threatened Russia's supply lines
b. Endangered British control of the
Suez Canal
2. Churchill argued for a naval offensive in
the Dardanelles
3. Gallipoli landing (April 25, 1915)
a. Incompetent naval leadership
b. Lacked adequate planning, supply
lines, and maps
c. Fought for seven months and then
the British withdrew
d. Major Allied defeat
i. 200,000 casualties
ii. Gallipoli did not shift the
focus away from the Western
Front

C. A war of attrition
1. The nature of modern war
2. The total mobilization of resources
3. The Allies imposed a naval blockade
on Germany
4. Germany responded with submarine
warfare
a. Germans sank the *Lusitania*
(May 7, 1915)
i. Almost 1200 killed
ii. Provoked the animosity of
the United States
5. The blockade stained Germany's
national economy

D. Trench warfare
1. War as a "matter of holes and ditches"
2. 25,000 miles of trenches from
Switzerland to the North Sea
a. Attack, support, and reserve
trenches
b. German trenches as permanent
defensive positions, comfortable
amenities
c. British and French trenches
designed as offensive positions
i. Poorly constructed
ii. Cold, wet, dirt, lice, and rats

3. "Wastage"
    a. Seven thousand British soldiers killed daily
4. New weapons
    a. Artillery, machine guns, and barbed wire
    b. Exploding bullets and liquid fire
    c. Poison gas
        i. First used by the Germans at the second battle of Ypres (April 1915)
        ii. Physically devastating and psychologically disturbing
        iii. Gas took more lives but did not alter the stalemate

V. Slaughter in the Trenches: The Great Battles, 1916–1917
  A. General observations
    1. Bloodiest battles occurred during 1916–1917
    2. Hundreds of thousands of casualties with little territorial gain
    3. War as carnage
    4. Military planners refused to alter traditional offensive strategies
    5. The "cult of the offensive"
    6. Little protection against new weapons
    7. Poor communication between command and the front line
    8. Firepower outpaced mobility
  B. Verdun (February 1916)
    1. Little strategic importance
    2. Verdun as symbol of French strength
    3. Germany's goal was to break French morale
    4. The battle
        a. Germans fired one million shells on the first day
        b. Ten-month struggle
        c. Offensive and counteroffensive
    5. By June, 400,000 French and German soldiers were killed
    6. The advantage fell to the French, but there was no clear victor
  C. The Somme (June–November 1916)
    1. Britain on the offensive
        a. 1400 guns delivered three million shells in five days
        b. The ideas was to destroy the German trenches
    2. German trenches withstood the attack
    3. Brutal fighting
        a. Hand-to-hand combat
        b. 20,000 British killed on the first day
        c. By November, 1.1 million British, German, and French soldiers were dead

4. Neither side won—"The War had won"
D. Other battles
  1. Nivelle Offensive (April–May 1917)
  2. Third Battle of Ypres (July–October 1917)
    a. 500,000 casualties
  3. Introduction of tanks had little effect
  4. Airplanes used for reconnaissance only
  5. Further stalemate on the Eastern Front
  6. The war at sea was indecisive

VI. War of Empires
  A. Europe's colonies provided soldiers and material support
  B. Britain
    1. Canada, Australia, New Zealand, India, and South Africa
    2. Fought on the Western Front, Mesopotamia, and Egypt
    3. 800,000 causalities
    4. Colonies as theaters for armed engagement
        a. Allies pushed the Turks out of Egypt in 1916
        b. Lawrence of Arabia
        c. British encourage Arab nationalism
        d. Balfour Declaration and European Zionism
        e. War drew Europe into the Middle East
  C. The Irish revolt
    1. British vulnerability
    2. Sinn Fein ("Ourselves Alone")
        a. Formed in 1900 for Irish independence
    3. Home Rule Bill passed Parliament (1912)
    4. "Irish question" tabled with outbreak of war
    5. The Easter Revolt (1916)
        a. Dublin
        b. Plan to smuggle German arms failed
        c. Revolt as military disaster
        d. The British executed the rebels in public
    6. New Home Rule Bill (1920)
    7. Dominion status granted to Catholic Ireland in 1921
    8. Civil war
    9. Irish Free State established (1937)
    10. Irish Republic (1945)

VII. The Home Front
  A. The costs of war: money and manpower
  B. Mobilizing the home front
    1. Single goal of military victory
    2. "Total war"
    3. Civilians were essential to the war economy
        a. Produced munitions
        b. Purchased war bonds

c. Tax hikes, inflation, and material
privation (rationing)

C. Shift from industrial to munitions production

  1. Increased state control of production
and distribution

  2. Germany and the Hindenburg Plan

D. Women in the war

  1. Women as symbols of change

  2. Massive numbers entered the munitions
industry

  3. Women entered clerical and service
sectors

  4. New opportunities

    a. Breaking down restrictions

    b. A new freedom

    c. Vera Brittain, *Testament of Youth*

    d. The "new woman"

      i. Symbol of freedom and
a disconcerting cultural
transformation

  5. Long-term changes

    a. Women sent home after the war

      i. Giving jobs to veterans

    b. Governments pass "natalist" policies

      i. Encouraging women to
marry and raise children

    c. Birth control

    d. Universal suffrage: Britain (1918),
United States (1919), France (1945)

E. Mobilizing resources

  1. Mobilizing men and money

  2. Conscription

    a. Before 1914, military service seen
as a duty, not an option

    b. France called up 8 million men
(two-thirds of the population of
men age eighteen to forty)

    c. British introduced conscription
in 1916

  3. Propaganda

    a. Important in recruitment

    b. German *Kultur*

    c. Films, posters, postcards,
newspapers

      i. The absolute necessity of
total victory

  4. Financing the war

    a. Military spending rose to half a
nation's budget

    b. Allies borrowed from Britain, who
borrowed from the United States

    c. Germany printed its own money

      i. Dramatic rise in inflation

      ii. Prices rose 400 percent

F. The strains of war, 1917

  1. Declining morale of the troops

    a. Troops saw their commanders'
strategies as futile

    b. Rise in number of mutinies

    c. Self-mutilation

    d. War neuroses

  2. On the home front

    a. Shortages of basic supplies
(clothing, food, and fuel)

    b. Price of bread and potatoes
soared

  3. From restraint to direct control

    a. Governments issued ration cards

    b. Government regulation of working
hours and wages

    c. Political dissent, violence, and
large-scale riots

    d. Industrial strikes

  4. Governments pushed to their limits

VIII. The Russian Revolution

A. Disillusionment with Nicholas II as general

B. World War I and the February Revolution

  1. Russia was unable to sustain the
political strains of extended warfare

  2. After 1905, Nicholas was severely
unpopular

  3. Corruption in the royal court

  4. Nicholas insisted on personally
commanding his army

    a. Alexandra and Rasputin

  5. Poland and most of the Baltics fell to
the Germans

    a. One million Russian casualties

  6. Russian army was poorly trained and
undersupplied

  7. Domestic discontent

    a. Nicholas faced liberal opposition
from the Duma

    b. Soldiers were unwilling to fight

    c. Militant labor movement and a
rebellious urban population

  8. February 23, 1917: International
Women's Day (Petrograd)

    a. Women marched demanding food,
fuel, and political reform

    b. Within a few days, a mass strike
of 300,000 people

    c. Nicholas sent in the police and
military

    d. 60,000 troops stationed in
Petrograd sided with the revolt

    e. Nicholas abdicated on March 2,
1917

9. New centers of power
    a. Provisional government (mostly middle-class leaders in the Duma)
        i. Wanted to establish a democratic system under constitutional rule
        ii. Set up an election for a constituent assembly
        iii. Granted some civil liberties
    b. The Petrograd Soviet
        i. Organized by Leon Trotsky after the 1905 Revolution
        ii. Claimed to be the legitimate power
        iii. Pressed for social reform and the redistribution of land
        iv. Desired a negotiated settlement with Germany and Austria
C. The Bolsheviks and the October Revolution
    1. Leadership of the Russian Social Democrats split over revolutionary strategy (1903)
        a. Bolsheviks ("members of the majority")
            i. Favored a centralized party of active revolutionaries
            ii. Revolution would lead to a socialist regime
        b. Mensheviks ("members of the minority")
            i. Move toward socialism gradually
            ii. Supported "bourgeois" or liberal reform
    2. Mensheviks gained control of the party
    3. Lenin (1870–1924)
        a. Life
            i. Born into the middle class
            ii. Expelled from the university for radical activity
            iii. His brother was executed for his part in a plot to assassinate Alexander III
            iv. Spent three years in Siberian exile
        b. Lenin and socialism
            i. Russian capitalism made socialism possible
            ii. Organizing the new class of industrial workers
            iii. Revolutionary zeal and Western Marxism

4. February–October 1917
    a. Bolshevik demands
        i. An immediate end to the war
        ii. Improvement in working conditions
        iii. Redistribution of aristocratic lands to the peasantry
    b. General Kornilov tried to restore order to Petrograd
    c. Lenin called for "Peace, Land, and Bread, Now" and "All Power to the Soviets"
    d. Bolsheviks won support from workers, soldiers, and peasants
5. October 1917
    a. Trotsky attacked the Provisional Government (October 24–25)
    b. Lenin announced that "all power has passed to the Soviets" (October 25)
    c. Provisional government flees the Winter Palace
    d. A quick and bloodless revolution
6. The Bolsheviks in power
    a. Moved against all political opposition
    b. Expelled parties who disagreed with the Bolsheviks
    c. Dispersed the Constituent Assembly
    d. The one-party dictatorship
    e. Peasant soldiers returned home
    d. The redistribution of land, the nationalization of banks, and workers' control of factories
7. The Bolsheviks and the war
    a. Negotiated a separate treaty with Germany at Brest-Litovsk (March 1918)
    b. Russia surrendered the Ukraine, Georgia, Finland, Polish territories, and the Baltic states
    c. Led to civil war
8. Not so much a crisis of government, but an absence of government
9. John Reed and "the ten days that shook he world"
    a. The Allies: the revolution allowed Germany to win the war on the Eastern Front
    b. Conservatives: feared a wave of revolution sweeping away other regimes
    c. Socialists: startled to see a regime gain control so quickly in such a backward country

IX. The Road to German Defeat, 1918
  A. With Russia out of the war, Germany concentrated its efforts on the Western Front
  B. The Allies feared Germany would win the war before the United States entered the war (April 1917)
  C. Major German assault (March 21, 1917) brought the Germans within fifty miles of Paris
  D. Allied counteroffensive (July and August)
    1. New tanks and the "creeping barrage"
    2. American troops
    3. Allies' material advantage overcame the Germans
    4. The German army was pushed into Belgium
    5. The dismantling of the Central Powers
    6. Germany fought alone
  E. Germany surrendered on November 3, 1918
    1. On the verge of civil war
    2. Bavarian republic (November 8)
    3. Kaiser Wilhelm abdicated
    4. The war officially came to an end on November 11, 1918
  F. The United States as a world power
    1. A fast and efficient wartime bureaucracy
    2. 300,000 soldiers shipped "over there" per month
    3. Food and supplies
    4. American intervention prompted by unrestricted warfare by German U-boats
    5. The Zimmerman telegram
    6. Woodrow Wilson
      a. Making the world safe for democracy
      b. Banish autocracy and militarism
      c. Establishing a league of nations
      d. Maintaining the international balance of power
  G. The peace settlement
    1. Negotiations held at Paris in 1919 and 1920
    2. Five separate treaties, one with each defeated nation
    3. Controlled by the Big Four
      a. Wilson (United States), Lloyd George (Britain), Clemenceau (France), and Orlando (Italy)
    4. Wilson's Fourteen Points
      a. An end to secret diplomacy
      b. Freedom of the seas
      c. The removal of international tariffs
      d. Reduction of national armaments
      e. "Self-determination of peoples"
      f. A League of Nations

    5. German reparations
      a. The desire to punish Germany
      b. Forced to surrender huge territories
      c. Forbidden to build an air force
      d. The "war-guilt" clause (Article 231)
        i. Reparations of $33 billion
    6. Treaties and the Central Powers
      a. Europe carved up without regard to language or ethnic divisions
      b. Led to challenges to stability in the 1930s
      c. The end of the Ottoman empire
      d. Little was done about reforming colonial rule
    7. Modern Turkey
      a. Mustafa Kemel Attaturk (r. 1923–1938)
    8. The Covenant of the League of Nations
      a. Never achieved its idealistic aims
      b. Japan would not join unless it could keep German concessions in China
      c. France demanded the exclusion of Germany and Russia
      d. United States Congress refused to approve U.S. membership

X. Conclusion
  A. Nine million dead
  B. The "lost generation"
  C. Global political and social discontent
  D. Economic consequences: Europe displaced as the center of the world economy
  E. The rise of the United States and Japan
  F. Disillusionment and the decline of liberal democracy

GENERAL DISCUSSION QUESTIONS

1. Why was the European war of 1914–1918 called the Great War and the "war to end all wars"? What made this war so great or different compared to wars of the past?

2. In what ways was the assassination of Archduke Ferdinand and his consort at Sarajevo on June 28, 1914, only the spark that ignited the Great War? What tensions had been building up in Europe well before 1914 that made war almost inevitable? Could the Great War have been avoided?

3. What was the general experience of warfare before 1914? How can it be argued that the governments of Europe were ill-prepared to fight this war?

4. How did the Great War affect women's working lives and perceptions of women's role in society? How did governments respond to these changes, and how successful were the official responses?

5. What country had the best strategic plan for war in 1914? How was this plan put into practice? What were the immediate, mid-term, and long-term results?

6. Why could the general staffs of the major armies not understand the Christmas truce of 1914? What does the Christmas truce tell us about the ordinary soldier and their generals and statesmen?

7. Was victory on the front merely a question of using existing resources and time, or were changes in leadership and vast new reserves of manpower needed to win? Either way, how would each side obtain and control those resources?

8. Compare the narration of events of the French and Russian Revolutions. What major similarities and differences can you uncover? In what ways were the Jacobins and Bolsheviks alike? Would the Russian Revolution have occurred in the way it did if the French Revolution had never taken place?

9. To what extent did the poor training of the Russian military during the Great War make the October Revolution likely and possible? Did the Revolution bring about the end of the war more quickly? Did it influence the discussions at Versailles?

10. How did the Great War make obsolete the idea of progress that had animated European society and culture for the past two centuries? Why is the "age of anxiety" perhaps an ideal label to describe the postwar cultural and intellectual climate?

DOCUMENT DISCUSSION QUESTIONS

Toward World War I: Diplomacy in the Summer of 1914

1. Why did a world war break out in 1914 and not earlier? With tensions and conflicts of all kinds manifest in the years leading up to war, why did the great powers exercise restraint until 1914?

2. Why did events in the Balkans serve as the touchstone for the Great War? Were tensions in that area of Europe new, or had they been slowly reaching the boiling point since the nineteenth century?

3. Emperor Franz Joseph's letter to Kaiser Wilhelm II tells of the Austrian investigation into the assassination of Archduke Franz Ferdinand. What did Franz

Joseph seek from his German ally? What did the emperors understand by the phrase, "if Serbia . . . is put out of action as a factor of political power in the Balkans"? Even if proof were at hand, would the Germans support a war against Serb-sponsored terrorism?

4. Could the Serbians have accepted the Austrian ultimatum without total loss of face and sacrifice of their independence? While British and Russian foreign ministers may have been shocked by the demands on Serbia, others thought the Austrians were justified, and that Britain would act similarly if threatened by terrorism. If, as Leo von Bilinsky said, "The Serb understands only force," why didn't Austria declare war without an ultimatum?

One Woman's War

5. Keeping up morale on the home front was a serious issue for the countries at war. Besides demands for able workers to replace men in uniform and care for the casualties, Britain had to deal with labor disputes and an uprising in Ireland. France faced inflation and mutinies that were kept secret. Germany and Russia suffered from severe shortages of munitions, supplies, and food. Yet these problems also provided women with opportunities to serve. What were the resulting social and political effects?

6. How did Vera Brittain explain women's responses to conflicting personal and national claims during wartime? Was there "a loss of innocence" among women at home as well as among men at the front?

Toward the October Revolution: Lenin to the Bolsheviks

7. Lenin was surprised by the sudden collapse of the tsarist regime in the February Revolution of 1917. He was in exile in Switzerland, but he soon made a deal with the Germans to return to Russia and destabilize the provisional Russian government. Why did he think the Bolsheviks could seize power? What were the key elements of his strategy for winning the necessary popular support?

8. Convinced he was right, Lenin returned to St. Petersburg in disguise and personally presented his arguments for an armed takeover to the Bolshevik Central Committee. What did he mean by saying that "it would be naïve to wait for a 'formal' majority on the side of the Bolsheviks; no revolution ever waits for *this*"?

9. How much of the success of the Bolshevik revolution in October 1917 was attributable to Lenin's aggressive

leadership? To Trotsky's organization of the Red Guards workers' militia? To the weakness of Kerensky's provisional government, and its commitment to continue fighting the war?

SAMPLE LECTURE 24: THE GREAT WAR AND THE AGE OF ANXIETY

Lecture Objectives

1. To understand the complicated causes of the Great War

2. To show how the Great War served as a watershed in the history of the modern world

3. To show how the Great War led to the death of the idea of progress and the creation of a "lost generation"

THE CAUSES OF THE GREAT WAR

The first and most immediate cause of the Great War was the assassination of Archduke Franz Ferdinand, the heir to the Austro-Hungarian throne, and his wife, Countess Sophie, at Sarajevo on June 28, 1914. The assassin was Gavrilo Princep, a nineteen-year-old Serbian student and member of the Black Hand Secret Society. The main objective of the Black Hand was the creation, by means of violence, of a Greater Serbia. What underlay this isolated act of one man (there had been other assassins but they either missed their opportunity or their weapons—pistols and bombs—did not function properly) were the social, political, and economic tensions that were raging in the Austro-Hungarian empire. The secret treaties and alliances made between the great powers (Britain, France, Germany, Russia, the Ottoman empire, and Austria-Hungary) had broken down and a scenario was created for a war involving all of Europe, Russia, and ultimately the United States. A rigid and inflexible system of nineteenth-century alliances, engineered between statesmen and the royal courts of Europe but masterminded for the most part by Bismarck, could no longer sustain peace and stability. This Bismarckian system could no longer control the European balance of power that had been worked out since the Congress of Vienna almost a century earlier. The assassination, then, merely highlighted what would have perhaps happened anyway. Russia and France insisted on being treated as equals, as they had been in Bismarck's time. (Bismarck was forced to resign in 1890 because his policies had become unpopular.) The system of alliances was tested several times before 1914:

- Russo-Japanese War (1904–1905)
- First and Second Morocco Crisis (1905–1906 and 1911)
- Bosnian Annexation Crisis (1908)
- Haldane Mission (1912)
- First and Second Balkan War (1912–1913 and 1913)

The second cause, one that is tied to the first, turned upon the issue of the Balkan states. Countries such as Serbia, Bosnia,

Bulgaria, Romania, and Greece had been struggling to establish their national identity throughout the nineteenth century. This identity could only be established by forming alliances with the great powers themselves. These small Balkan nations played upon the competing claims of the great powers, and as Germany, Italy, Britain, and France partitioned the African continent into spheres of influence, they also attempted to establish such spheres in Europe, a notion that was certainly played out during the Cold War following World War II. Tied to these first two explanations was the fact that by 1914, the alliance system was steadily breaking down. As A. J. P. Taylor once remarked, it wasn't the alliance system itself that caused World War I, but the breakdown of this system. The dam was ready to burst and, once again, it was the assassination of the heir to the Austro-Hungarian throne that served as the impetus toward world war.

The fourth cause was certainly one of the most important— the massive mobilization of men, weapons, and ammunition. Thanks to the second industrial revolution, not only had production increased and labor been made more efficient, but new weapons of war had been developed—huge guns, huge battleships (*Dreadnought*), barrage balloons, machine guns, airplanes, and poison gas. It seems that between 1890 and 1914, a military development in one country was quickly matched by a similar development in other countries. By 1914, the German and French armies had doubled in size since 1870, and the British claimed that their navy must be equal in size to the two largest European fleets. This was enough of an indication that Europe had mobilized and would continue to mobilize their forces for the duration of the war. This arms race had significant effects on both the economy and social conditions of all the belligerent forces. And then there was the new imperialism itself. Tied as it was to nineteenth-century nationalism, this meant that European nations wanted to establish:

- their borders on the continent
- their dominance as world economic powers
- their control of hitherto uncontrolled lands around the globe

The significance of these imperialist endeavors of the last quarter of the nineteenth century was that they prepared the world for war by producing a belligerent spirit among the great powers. Lastly, although few Europeans wanted to go to war, when hostilities did break out in August 1914, the majority of people looked to war with joy and anticipation. It was believed that it would be a quick war, over no later than Christmas 1914. The strains and stresses of late-nineteenth-century economic and imperial competition and progress had prepared people to welcome open conflict and the excitement of war provided many people with feelings of unity and common purpose. The Anglo-French fought for the preservation of what they called "civilization" while the Germans stood for *Kultur*, the foundation and spirit of German culture, rooted in the *Volk* of the soil.

THE CONSEQUENCES OF THE GREAT WAR

There are a number of important consequences surrounding the Great War. For most people, the war gave them a sense of a "before and after." No one could really look at their own historical time without referencing it to events of the war itself. In this sense, we could also say that the war altered the sense of time itself, a theme that the artists and writers of modernism would take up in their own work. Time no longer seemed linear. Now it was broken up, fragmented, disjointed, out of balance. On a more tangible level, the war left more than nine million dead, many of them noncombatants. The French suffered a massive loss of their male population and the French countryside lay in ruins. On the home front, the war meant increased wages for war work, increased membership in trade unions, and the increased mobility and visibility of women in industry. Many of these changes would come to an abrupt stop at the war's end. Women probably suffered the most as they left factories and vacated positions now taken up by men. However, they did carry with them the respect and humility that came from supporting their nation in a most direct and influential way.

The desire to punish Germany after the war was manifest in the provisions of the Treaty of Versailles. Germany was forced to surrender huge blocks of territory, was forbidden to build an air force, its general staff was dissolved, and its standing army was reduced in size. Overshadowing these provisions were the stipulations of the Treaty's Article 231. By accepting these provisions, Germany was also forced to accept the "war guilt clause" and pay reparations totaling $33 billion, a figure so enormous that it would take decades to make the final payment. The whole issue of reparations brought Germany's economic stability to its knees as unemployment soon hit 70 percent. Galloping inflation made the German Deutschmark practically worthless. The Great War also served as the salvation for Hitler. The end of the war gave him his platform from which to criticize Weimer and rally his audience to his message of *Lebensraum* and German racial supremacy. In the 1920s and 1930s, Hitler and the Nazi party made the German humiliation at Versailles the touchstone of a campaign to create a thousand-year *Reich*.

The Great War also meant the displacement of the European great powers by the United States as the world's creditor nation. The Ottoman empire, long the "sick man of Europe," was dismantled. Meanwhile, David Lloyd George, Vittorio Orlando, Georges Clemenceau, and Woodrow Wilson met at Versailles, and under the provisions of five distinct treaties, carved up Europe without regard for linguistic or ethnic division—ensuring that certain areas of the continent would remain hot spots, especially in the Balkans. Wilson's Fourteen Point Plan provided for:

- an end to secret diplomacy
- the freedom of the seas
- the removal of international tariffs
- a reduction of national armaments
- "self-determination of peoples"
- a League of Nations

A Covenant of the League of Nations was drawn up but it did not achieve its idealistic aims. Japan would not join unless it could keep German concessions in China, France demanded the exclusion of Germany and Russia, and the United States Congress refused to approve U.S. membership. The war created the seeds of the fascist regimes of the interwar period, regimes that seemed to spring up across central and eastern Europe, with the exception of Czechoslovakia. The war also hastened revolution in Russia. One can only wonder what shape Russia would have taken had World War I not taken place. Lastly, in the cultural or intellectual realm, the war led many people to postulate the bankruptcy of European culture itself. The Great War created the "Lost Generation" of the 1920s. The ideas of Nietzsche and Freud assumed greater prominence as artists, writers, and philosophers had come to grips with a world gone mad.

MODERNISM

At the same time that Nietzsche and Freud broke away from the Enlightenment tradition that specified the natural goodness of man, artists and writers rebelled against traditional forms of artistic and literary expression. Their work created a great cultural revolution that we call modernism. Modernism can be characterized by the heightened awareness of the self. For the modernist artist or writer, intellect had become a barrier to creativity and the expression of human emotion. Human reason, rather than man's liberator, had now been fashioned as man's captor. The modernist artists abandoned all artistic traditions and literary conventions and began to experiment with new modes of expression. They destroyed history in order to create their own. Writers such as Thomas Mann, Marcel Proust, D. H. Lawrence, James Joyce, and Franz Kafka explored the inner, psychic life of the individual. Their novels, plays, and poems dealt with the theme of modern men and women—men and women who rejected the values of their own age. Their intense introspection forced them to come to grips with their anxiety caused by a society-imposed guilt, their awakened sexuality, their cravings for self-destruction, and in general, their overwhelming feelings of isolation, drift, meaninglessness, and alienation. For the modernist, there was no one reality. Reality was personal—it was individual and subjective. As a general rule, modernism was less concerned with reality than with how the artist or writer could transform reality. In this way, the artist made reality his own. Whereas the middle-class, industrial society of the nineteenth century valued reason, industry, thrift, organization, faith, and values, the modernists were fascinated by the bizarre, the mysterious, the surreal, the primitive, and the formless. In a word, the modernists fashioned a world shaped by the irrational. In this way, the modernist artist and writer reflected the concerns of someone like Nietzsche or Freud.

A similar motif can be found in music. Around the turn of the century, composers began to experiment with atonality, dissonance, and primitive rhythms. When Igor Stravinsky's ballet *The Rites of Spring* (1913), was first performed in Paris, the audience rioted. The work had broken with all past conventions. It was too much to bear—too much innovation, too quickly. And, of course, the most tangible evidence of modernism is in the world of art. The impressionists, centered in Paris, broke with a tradition stretching back centuries. As one of them wrote: "Don't proceed according to rules and principles but paint what you observe and feel." Impressionist painters like Pierre Auguste Renoir, Claude Monet, Édouard Manet, Edgar Degas, and Pablo Picasso, tried to capture movement, color, and light as it appeared to the mind at one specific moment. It is, in other words, the representation of a brief moment in time and space as perceived by the artist. By 1900, artists attempted to penetrate the deep recesses of the unconscious mind. The unconscious was the true source of creativity, and so these artists tried to portray their own minds in their art. In a way, they tried to visually represent what could not yet be given verbal expression. Cubists, like Picasso and Georges Braque, attempted to show the interplay between a one-dimensional canvas and the three-dimensional world of reality. The modernists rejected the view that the world was a rational and orderly place. It was an era of new possibilities as well as completely new problems. Modernism is part of the same European experience that produced Nietzsche and Freud. They did not "make" modernism. But they were keen observers of their own age and each, in their own way, served as physicians of Western civilization. Their diagnosis was not good. As Nietzsche wrote in 1884:

> Disintegration characterizes this time, and thus uncertainty nothing stands firmly on its feet or on a hard faith in itself; one lives for tomorrow as the day after tomorrow is dubious. Everything on our way is slippery and dangerous, and the ice that still supports us has become thin: all of us feel the warm, uncanny breath of the thawing wind: where we still walk, soon no one will be able to walk.

THE OLD LIE: *DULCE ET DECORUM EST, PRO PATRIA MORI.*

It was William Tecumseh Sherman who remarked, in 1879, that "war is at best barbarism. . . . Its glory is all moonshine. It is only those who have neither fired a shot nor heard the shrieks and groans of the wounded who cry aloud for blood, more vengeance, more desolation. War is hell." But it was the British poet Siegfried Sassoon who added, "war is hell and those who initiate it are criminals." This was the final verdict of the Great War, especially among the Anglo-French— "The old lie: *Dulce et decorum est, pro patria mori*." The initial "vision of honor and glory to country" faded quickly and was replaced by sorrow, pity, and cruelty. For the British war poets the whole affair ended in bitterness. People felt betrayed by those men who were running the war. The horrors of the trench—rotting horseflesh, mud, poor food, weapons that would not fire, poison gas, and the sheer terror of wait-

ing for death—these were the images and experiences of the Great War. It was the Big Lie. There was no tangible enemy, except the one the popular press could fashion. The soldier looked across the parapet and saw himself. This partially explains the Christmas truce. A bond was created between the soldiers who fought the war, a bond the general staff could neither understand nor accept. No, the war was insanity, irrationality, and the triumph of unreason in a world that was taught that reason was the way to the good life. Soon the soldiers began to despise the people back home. They had no idea what the war was like. They knitted socks and sang patriotic songs. They were the "little fat men," as George Orwell was to call them, men who made decisions carried out by wooden-headed generals. The soldiers were drawn closer to one another by the common bond of experience. They were closer in spirit to the enemy than to those they left behind. "The immediate reaction of the poets who fought in the war was cynicism," wrote Stephen Spender in *The Struggle of the Modern* (1963):

> The war dramatized for them the contrast between the still-idealistic young, living and dying on the unalteringly horrible stage-set of the Western front, with the complacency of the old at home, the staff officers behind the lines. In England there was violent anti-German feeling; but for the poet-soldiers the men in the trenches on both sides seemed united in pacific feelings and hatred of those at home who had sent them out to kill each other.

There's no doubt about it: war was horror, terror, and futility. The romance of war had been taken out of warfare forever. nineteenth-century ideals of warfare—Napoleonic ideals— were no match for the new weapons of destruction that the second industrial revolution had helped to make a reality. Technology was supposed to be the servant of mankind— liberation would result from more technology. What World War I showed was how quickly new technology could be put to use. In the end, it was the European idea of progress that became the victim of improved technology. The rules of warfare had changed, and with this change the twentieth century plunged into what one historian has called "the age of total war."

Immediately following the end of the war, one of France's literary giants called attention to the very clear fact that a crisis had now overtaken the European mind in the twentieth century. Paul Valéry brooded on both the greatness and decline of Europe in his essay *The Crisis of the Mind* (1919). Of the greatness of Europe, Valéry had no doubt. Europe was "the elect portion of the terrestrial globe, the pearl of the sphere, the brain of a vast body." Europe's superiority, according to Valéry, rested on a combination of various qualities— imagination and rigorous logic, skepticism and mysticism, and above all, curiosity. "Everything came to Europe," he wrote, "and everything came from it. Or almost everything—until recently." The Great War had made Valéry ponder the utter fragility of civilizations—that of Europe, as well as Babylon, Nineveh, and Persepolis. Europe's decline had begun, as Valéry saw it, long before the outbreak of world war. By 1914, Europe had perhaps reached the limits of modernism, which was characterized, above all, by disorder in the mind. By disorder Valéry meant the lack of any fixed system of reference for living and thinking. This lack he ascribed to "the free coexistence, in all her cultivated minds, of the most dissimilar ideas, the most contradictory principles of life and learning. This is characteristic of a modern epoch." The decline also owed much to politics, which had never been Europe's strong suit. The export of European knowledge and applied science had enabled others to upset the inequality on which Europe's predominance was based.

For these and other reasons, Europe ultimately succumbed to anxiety and anguish. The military crisis that was World War I might have ended, but the economic crisis remained, as did, above all, the crisis of the mind. Thus, Valéry and his contemporaries announced the beginning of a new "age of anxiety" in European history. Despite his pessimism, Valéry would have been the first to say that Europe's greatness persisted through most of his lifetime. He died in 1945. It is true that twentieth-century Europe lived, to a large extent, on the accumulated intellectual capital of past centuries. But along with European greatness came decline and anxiety, as Valéry suggested. Not outsiders but Europeans themselves invented the expression *age of anxiety* (W. H. Auden) to describe their own age. "Today," said the Protestant theologian-philosopher Paul Tillich at mid-century, "it has become almost a truism to call our time an age of anxiety." The special form of anxiety that Tillich identified was the "anxiety of meaninglessness." He traced it to the modern world's loss of a spiritual center. Suffering is the result of living without purpose or faith. The knowledge that man was alone caused anxiety because the responsibility for making whatever values there were came entirely from man. The death of God, announced first perhaps by Friedrich Nietzsche in the last quarter of the nineteenth century, was not the only observed cause of anxiety. Also cited were the death of man and the death of Europe—in fact, the death of all the great modern idols: man, reason, science, progress, and history. The external events of a world at war obviously had a great deal to do with the fall of these idols, and so with anxiety as well. In a time of total doubt, men escaped from freedom to authority that promised meaning and imposed answers.

SUGGESTED FEATURE FILMS

All Quiet on the Western Front. 131 min. B/W. 1930. Universal Pictures. Excellent adaptation of Remarque's novel about German schoolboys who enlist in World War I and discover tragedy, anger, and confusion. See also TV miniseries by CBS (1979) and the BBC (1994).

Battleship Potemkin. 75 min. (Sound version: 60 min.) B/W. 1925. Goskino. Eisenstein's study of the 1903 Odessa Mutiny. Judged in 1948 and again in 1958 to be the best film ever made.

The Childhood of Maxim Gorky. 101 min. B/W. 1938. Soyuz det film. *Out in the World.* 98 min. 1939. *My Universities.* 104 min. 1940. Film biographies of the Russian writer Maxim Gorky.

Hell's Angels. 127 min. B/W. 1930. The Caddo Company. Two brothers attending Oxford enlist with the Royal Air Force when World War I breaks out.

Gallipoli. 110 min. Color. 1981. Paramount. Peter Weir's story of young Australians who join the ANZACS and are sent to the fight the Turks at Gallipoli.

Grand Illusion. 114 min. B/W. 1937. World Pictures Corporation. Jean Renoir's meditation on World War I and the collapse of the old order of European civilization.

J'accuse (subtitled). 104 min. B/W. 1939. Arthur Mayer and Joseph Burstyn, Inc. Abel Gance's chilling film about the horrors of war.

Lawrence of Arabia. 216 min. Color. 1962. Columbia Pictures. David Lean's epic "desert classic" about T. E. Lawrence, a British officer who united the desert tribes of Arabia against the Turks during World War I.

Paths of Glory. 87 min. B/W. 1957. United Artists. Stanley Kubrick's film of the Humphrey Cobb novel about the futility and irony of war.

Regeneration. 105 min. Color. 1997. BBC. World War I soldiers are sent to an asylum for emotional troubles where they meet the British war poets, Wilfred Owen and Siegfried Sassoon.

SUGGESTED CLASSROOM FILMS

1914–1919: Shell Shock. 45 min. Color. 1999. Films for the Humanities and Social Sciences. Peter Jennings of ABC News narrates this analysis of U.S. involvement in the Great War and discusses the psychological toll of this war.

Churchill and British History, 1874–1918. 29 min. B/W. 1974. Centron Educational Films. Still and newsreel films are used to outline the world that shaped Churchill.

The Decline of Czarism. 30 min. Color. 1986. Insight Media. Covers the decline of the Romanov dynasty.

Europe, the Mighty Continent: The Drums Begin to Roll. 52 min. Color. 1976. Time-Life Films. Examines the preparations for war between 1904 and 1914.

Europe, the Mighty Continent: A World to Win. 52 min. Color. 1976. Time-Life Films. Intellectual, political, and social ferment in prewar Europe.

The Social Classes—1900: A World to Win. 52 min. Color. 1990. Insight Media. Examines the intellectual and political turmoil that marked Europe at the turn of the century.

Stalin and Russian History, 1879–1927. 29 min. B/W. 1974. Centron Films. Biography of Stalin from his seminary days through Lenin's death. Includes films of the industrialization of Russia.

CHAPTER 25 | Turmoil Between the Wars

c. Produced enough grain to feed the country
7. Failure
    a. Peasants refused to participate in markets to benefit urban areas
    b. Kept excess grain for themselves
    c. Cities experienced grain shortages

D. Stalin and the "Revolution From Above"
1. Stalin the man
    a. Born in Georgia as Iosip Jughashvili (1879–1953)
    b. Exiled to Siberia for revolutionary activity
    c. Lenin's death (1924: Stalin or Trotsky)
2. Stalin the strategist
    a. Isolate all opposition
    b. Used the left to isolate the right, used the right to isolation the left
    c. By 1929, Trotsky and Bukharin were removed from positions of power
    d. Abandoned NEP
    e. Increases tempo of industrialization
3. Forced industrialization and the total collectivization of agriculture

E. Collectivization
1. Local party and police officials forced peasants to join collective farms
2. Peasant resistance: 1,600 large-scale rebellions between 1929 and 1933
3. Peasants slaughtered livestock rather than turn it over to farms
4. The "liquidation of the kulaks as a class"
5. The famine (1932–1933)
    a. The human cost was 3–5 million lives
    b. The Bolsheviks retained grain reserves in other parts of the country
    c. Grain reserves sold overseas for currency and stockpiled in the event of war

F. The Five-Year Plans
1. Campaign of forced industrialization
2. First Five-Year Plan (1928–1932)
    a. Most stunning period of economic growth
    b. Industrial output increased 50 percent in five years
    c. Built new industries in new cities
        i. Magnitogorsk
    d. Urban population more than doubled (26 to 56 million) between 1924 and 1939

3. The human cost
    a. Large-scale projects carried out with prison labor
    b. The Gulag system
        i. By 1940, 3.6 million people were incarcerated by the regime
4. Structural problems
    a. The command economy: production levels planned from Moscow in advance
    b. Heavy industry favored over light industry
    c. Emphasis on quantity over quality
5. Cultural and economic changes
    a. Soviet cities
    b. Women entered the workforce
    c. The conservative shift
        i. Divorce was difficult to obtain
        ii. Abortion made illegal except in emergency situations
        iii. Homosexuality declared a criminal offense

G. The Great Terror (1937–1938)
1. One million dead—1.5 million to the Gulag
2. The elimination of Stalin's enemies, real or imagined
3. Mass repression of internal enemies from the top to the very bottom
4. Purged the old Bolsheviks
5. Staged show trials
6. Industrial managers, intellectuals, and the military
7. Targeted ethnic groups (Poles, Ukrainians, Lithuanians, Latvians, and Koreans)
8. Stalin and total control
9. Social advances
    a. Illiteracy reduced
    b. Higher education made available to more people
    c. Government assistance for working mothers
    d. Free hospitalization

III. The Emergence of Fascism in Italy
A. In the aftermath of war
1. A democracy in distress
2. 700,000 dead, $15 billion debt
3. Territorial disputes
    a. Militant nationalists seized Fiume
4. Problems
    a. Split between the industrial north and agrarian south

b. Conflict over land, wages, and local power

c. Government corruption and indecision

d. Inflation, unemployment, and strikes

e. Demands for radical reform

B. The rise of Mussolini (1883–1945)

1. Editor of *Avantia* (leading socialist daily)

   a. Lost editorship when he urged Italy to side with the Allies during World War I

2. Founded *Il Poplo d'Italia*

3. The *Fasci*

   a. Organized to drum up support for the war

   b. Attracted young, idealist, fanatical nationalists

4. The Fascist platform (1919): universal suffrage, the eight-hour day, and tax on inheritance

5. Fascist support

   a. Gained respect of middle classes and landowners

   b. Repressed radical movements of workers and peasants

   c. Attacked socialists

   d. Fifty thousand fascist militia marched on Rome on October 28, 1922

     i. The black shirts

     ii. Victor Emmanuel III invited Mussolini to form a cabinet

C. Italy under Mussolini

1. One-party dictatorship

   a. Statism—"nothing above, outside, or against the state"

   b. Nationalism—the "highest form of society"

   c. Militarism—the "ennoblement" of man in war

2. Changed the electoral laws

3. Abolished cabinet system

4. Mussolini assumed role of prime minister and party leader (Il Duce)

5. Repression and censorship

6. Ending class conflict

   a. A managed economy

   b. A corporate state

7. Granted independence to papal residence in the Vatican City

8. Roman Catholicism established as the state religion

9. Maintaining the status quo and "making the trains run on time"

IV. Weimar Germany

A. November 9, 1918: Revolution

1. Bloodless overthrow of the imperial government

2. Social Democratic Party (SPD) announced a new German republic

3. The kaiser abdicated

4. Socialists wanted democratic reforms within existing imperial bureaucracy

B. Problems

1. Elections not held until January 1919

2. Communists and independent socialists staged armed uprisings in Berlin

3. Social Democrats tried to crush the uprisings

   a. The martyrdom of Rosa Luxemburg and Karl Liebknecht

C. The *Freikorps*

1. Former army officers fighting Bolsheviks, Poles, and communists

2. Called themselves Spartacists

3. Fiercely right-wing anti-Marxist, anti-Semitic, and antiliberal

D. The Weimar coalition

1. Socialists, Catholic centrists, and liberal democrats

2. Parliamentary liberalism

   a. Pluralistic framework

   b. Universal suffrage for men and women

   c. Bill of rights

E. The failure of Weimar

1. Social, political, and economic crisis

2. The humiliation of World War I

   a. Germany "stabbed in the back" by socialists and Jews

   b. What was needed was authoritarian leadership

3. Versailles and reparations

   a. $33 billion debt

   b. The Dawes Plan (1924), a new schedule of payments

4. The government continued to print money

   a. By October 1923, a pound of potatoes cost 40 million marks

   b. Middle-class employees, farmers, and workers hit hardest by inflation

5. Economic recovery (1925)

   a. Scaled-down reparation payments

   b. Government sponsored building projects

   c. Large infusion of capital from the United States

6. Further problems
    a. United States stock market crash
    b. Unemployment
    c. Production dropped by 44 percent
    d. Peasants staged mass demonstrations
    e. Government cut welfare benefits
    f. Left the door open for the opponents of Weimar

V. Hitler and the National Socialists
    A. Adolf Hitler (1889–1945)
        1. Born in Austria, aspired to be an artist
        2. Spent his youth as a tramp in Vienna
            a. Learned his anti-Semitism, anti-Marxism, and pan-Slavism
        3. The outbreak of World War I as his liberation
        4. After the war, he joined the German Workers' Party
            a. 1920: became the National Socialist Workers' Party (Nazi)
            b. Refused to accept the November (1918) Resolution
    B. Hitler and the Nazis
        1. November 1923: Munich putsch
            a. Hitler imprisoned
            b. Dictated *Mein Kampf*
        2. Portrayed himself as the savior of the German people
        3. Nazi elections
            a. 1924: Nazis polled 6.6 percent of the vote
            b. 1928: Politics polarized between left and right
                i. The impossibility of a coalition
                ii. People abandoned traditional political parties
        3. Joseph Goebbels and propaganda
        4. Nazi supporters
            a. Small-property holders and rural middle classes
            b. Elitist civil servants
        5. 1930 election
            a. Nazis won 107 of 577 seats in the Reichstag
            b. No party gained a majority
            c. Nazis claimed no coalition government not headed by Hitler
    C. Hitler as chancellor
        1. January 1933: Hindenberg appointed Hitler chancellor
        2. February 27, 1933: Reichstag set on fire by Dutch anarchist
            a. Hitler suspended civil rights

3. March 5, 1933: New elections
    a. Hitler granted unlimited power for four years
    b. Hitler proclaimed the Third Reich
D. Nazi Germany
    1. A one-party state
        a. *Gauleiters*—regional directors of the nation
        b. Propaganda
    2. Opposition
        a. Storm troopers (SA)—used to maintain party discipline
        b. June 30, 1934: Night of the Long Knives
    3. *Schutzstaffel* (SS)
        a. Most-dreaded arm of Nazi terror
        b. Organized by Heinrich Himmler
        c. Fighting political and racial enemies
    4. Support
        a. Played off fears of communism
        b. Spoke a language of national pride
        c. Hitler as the symbol of a strong, revitalized Germany (the Führer cult)
            i. Charismatic leader
            ii. Gave people what they wanted
        d. The recovery of German national glory
    5. National recovery
        a. Sealed Germany off from the rest of the world
        b. Unemployment dropped from 6 million to 200,000
        c. Outlawed trade unions and strikes, froze wages
        d. Organized workers into the National Labor Front
        e. Popular organizations cut across class lines
            i. The Hitler Youth
            ii. The National Labor Service
E. Nazi racism
    1. Nazi racism inherited from nineteenth-century opinions
    2. Anti-Semitism
        a. Joined by nationalist anti-Jewish theory
        b. The Jew as outsider
            i. Dreyfus Affair
            ii. A wave of late-nineteenth-century pogroms
        c. An "international Jewish conspiracy"

3. April 1933: New racial laws excluded Jews from public office
4. 1935 Nuremberg Decrees
   a. Deprived Jews of citizenship (determined by bloodline)
5. November 1938: *Kristallnacht* (Night of Broken Glass)

F. National socialism and fascism
  1. Both arose in the interwar period as responses to war and revolution
  2. Intensely nationalistic
  3. Opposed parliamentary government and democracy
  4. Favored mass-based authoritarian regimes

VI. The Great Depression in the Democracies
  A. Western democracies
    1. France
      a. Continued to fear Germany
      b. Policy of deflation
      c. Class conflict and labor troubles
    2. Britain
      a. Policy of deflation
      b. Reduction in wages and decline in the standard of living
      c. The Labour Party (1924 and 1929)
      d. Increasing trade union militancy
    3. United States
      a. Bastion of conservatism
      b. Presidents and the Supreme Court
  B. The origins of the Great Depression
    1. Causes
      a. Instability of national currencies
      b. Interdependence of national economies
      c. Widespread drop in industrial productivity
      d. Restrictions of free trade
    2. October 1929: Collapse of the New York Stock Exchange
      a. United States as world's creditor nation
      b. Immediate and disastrous consequences for European economy
      c. Banking houses closed, manufacturers laid off entire workforces
    3. Government response
      a. Britain
        i. Abandoned gold standard and free trade
        ii. Cautious relief efforts
      b. France
        i. The Popular Front under Léon Blum

        ii. Nationalized munitions industry
        iii. Forty-hour week
        iv. Fixed the price and regulated the distribution of grain
      c. United States
        i. The New Deal and FDR
        ii. Recovery without destroying capitalism
        iii. Managing the economy and public-works projects
        iv. John Maynard Keynes

VII. Interwar Culture: Artists and Intellectuals
  A. The rejection of tradition and the experiment with new forms of expression
  B. Interwar intellectuals
    1. Disillusionment with war and the failure of victory
    2. Frustration, cynicism, and disenchantment
    3. Ernest Hemingway (1899–1961): *The Sun Also Rises* (1926), the "lost generation"
    4. T. S. Eliot (1888–1965): *The Waste Land* (1922), life is a living death
    5. William Butler Yeats (1865–1939): deplored the superficiality of modern life
    6. Bertolt Brecht (1898–1956): the pointlessness of war, high culture, and middle-class values
    7. James Joyce (1882–1941): *Ulysses* (1922), "stream of consciousness"
    8. The politicization of literature
  C. Interwar artists
    1. Developments paralleled those in literature
    2. The dominance of the avant-garde
      a. Subjective experience
      b. Multiplicity of meanings
      c. Personal expression
      d. The rejection of traditional forms and values
      e. Pushing the boundaries of aesthetics
    3. Expressionism—paintings need not have subjects at all
      a. Wassily Kandinsky (1866–1944)
        i. His "improvisations" meant nothing
      b. George Grosz (1893–1959)
        i. Attacked the greed and decadence of postwar Europe
    4. The Dadaists
      a. Marcel Duchamp (1887–1968), Max Ernst (1891–1976), and Hans Arp (1886–1966)
      b. Rejected all forms of artistic conventions

c. Haphazard "fabrications"

d. Meaningful and playful works or expressions of the unconscious mind?

5. Surrealism
   a. Giorgio de Chirico (1888–1978) and Salvador Dali (1904–1989)
   b. The interior of the mind
   c. Political undertones

6. Art for a mass audience
   a. Diego Rivera (1886–1957) and José Clemente Orozco (1883–1949)
   b. Thomas Hart Benton (1889–1975) and Reginald Marsh (1898–1954)
   c. Depicting social conditions of the modern world
   d. The hopes and struggles of ordinary people

7. Architecture
   a. Functionalism
      i. Otto Wagner (1841–1918) and Le Corbusier (1887–1965)
      ii. Louis Sullivan (1856–1924) and Frank Lloyd Wright (1867–1959)
      iii. "Form ever follows function" (Sullivan)
      iv. Ornamentation to reflect an age of science and machines
   b. Walter Gropius (1883–1969) and Bauhaus
      i. An international style

D. Interwar scientific developments
   1. Albert Einstein (1879–1955)
      a. Revolutionized modern physics
      b. Challenged our beliefs about the universe
      c. New ways of thinking about space, matter, time, and gravity
      d. Time, the fourth dimension
      e. The theory of relativity
   2. James Chadwick (1891–1974)
      a. Discovery of the neutron (1932)
   3. Otto Hahn (1879–1968) and Fritz Strassman (1902–1980)
      a. Split atoms of uranium (1939)
      b. Chain reaction
   4. Werner Heisenberg (1901–1976) and the uncertainty principle (1927)
   5. Relativity and uncertainty as metaphors for the ambiguity of modern life

E. Mass culture and its possibilities
   1. Explosive rise of mass media—media for the masses

a. Mass politics as a fact of life

b. Cut across class lines, ethnicity, and nationality

c. Democratic and authoritarian possibilities

2. The radio
   a. Europe: broadcasting rights owned by the government
   b. United States: broadcasting managed by corporations
   c. National soapbox for politicians
      i. FDR's fireside chats
      ii. Nazi propaganda
   d. The new ritual of political life—communication and persuasion

3. Advertising
   a. Visual images replaced older ads
   b. Efficient communication, streamlined and standardized
   c. Drew on modern psychology

4. Film
   a. France and Italy had strong film industries
   b. 1927: Sound added to films
   c. United States gained the competitive edge in Europe
      i. Size of home market
      ii. Huge investments in equipment and distribution
      iii. The Hollywood "star system"
   d. Germany had the best-equipped studios in Europe
      i. Universum Film AG
      ii. Fritz Murnau (1888–1931): *Der letzte mann* (1924)
      iii. Fritz Lang (1890–1976): *Metropolis* (1926) and *M* (1931)
   e. The "Americanization" of culture
      i. A threat to European culture?
      ii. Introduced Europe to new ways of life
   f. Stalin and socialist realism
   g. Mussolini and classical kitsch
   h. Hitler despised modern art as decadent

5. The Nazis and propaganda
   a. Used film as a means of indoctrination and control
   b. "Spectacular politics"
      i. Glorifying the Reich
   c. Leni Riefenstahl (1902–2003): *Triumph of the Will* (1934)

d. Tried to limit influence of
American popular culture
   i. Dance and jazz
e. Anti-Semitic films
   i. *The Eternal Jew* (1940) and
   Jew Sus (1940)
VIII. Conclusion
   A. The strains of World War I
   B. The Great Depression
   C. International tensions

GENERAL DISCUSSION QUESTIONS

1. What was the political situation in Russia for the first five years after the Bolsheviks seized power? Why did the Communists have to fight a civil war against the Whites? What were the effects of armed intervention by the United States?

2. In 1917, Lenin favored a system of state capitalism in the short term, but the civil war forced a different policy. How did this period resemble Robespierre's Reign of Terror? What were the characteristics of the Russian policy of war communism?

3. How did Stalinist collectivization and the Five-Year Plans relate to Stalin's "revolution from above"? Why did Stalin find it necessary to implement the Great Terror of 1937–1938?

4. What were the essential points of Italian fascism? How did Mussolini seize power in 1922 and rule for twenty years? What is the legacy of Italian fascism?

5. How and why did National Socialism emerge as an important political force in Weimar Germany? What political and economic pressures on the republic opened the door for the Nazi seizure of power in January 1933?

6. How were Nazi racist ideas formed from earlier philosophies? Why was there such enthusiasm for "scientific" racism and anti-Semitism among the conservative German right?

7. Beyond the Wall Street crash of 1929, what were the causes of the Great Depression? Why would problems in the New York market affect banks, businesses, and employment in Germany, Austria, and elsewhere across Europe?

8. Hitler biographer Ian Kershaw has written that "the Nazi road to the *Final Solution to the Jewish Problem* was built by hate, but was paved with indifference." What arguments can you draw up to support such a statement?

9. Looking back on the twentieth century it will perhaps become common to consider Mussolini, Hitler, and Stalin together. Why? What did these three men have in common that will make us consider them as one? Do they represent a modern Napoleon? Or Charlemagne? Or Alexander the Great?

10. What intellectual, cultural, political, or even economic forces might have contributed to the idea that the interwar years ought to be called the "Age of Anxiety"?

DOCUMENT DISCUSSION QUESTIONS

Stalin's Industrialization of the Soviet Union

1. How was Stalin able to mobilize the industrial capacity of the Soviet Union? That is, how was Stalin able to motivate workers to do in ten years what European countries had done in a decidedly longer period of time?

2. Stalin suggested that "Bolsheviks must master technique. It is time Bolsheviks themselves became experts." Just what must the Bolsheviks become expert in?

3. Was it at all possible for anyone living in the Soviet Union in the 1930s to lead a normal life when all around them was the Great Terror?

Nazi Propaganda

4. How did Goebbels use metaphors of illness and health, growth and decay? Do the metaphors suggest what the Nazis would try to do to cure the ills of Germany if they took power?

5. How could intelligent Germans believe that Jews were responsible for all German miseries? What happened when Goebbels and Hitler repeatedly sounded this theme? Could anyone doubt or argue against it?

6. The Nazi campaign pamphlet of 1932 targeted German farmers. How did the pamphlet play on their fears of market manipulation by American big business and Bolshevik demands for collectivization and seizure of private land? How did the Nazis identify themselves with Christianity and traditional values, sincerely or not?

Cinema: Fritz Lang on the Future of the Feature Film in Germany, 1926

7. Why does Lang suggest that his own time is in search of "new forms of expression"? Do artists always search for new forms, or might this be a specifically twentieth-century phenomena?

8. What did Lang mean by calling "the rediscovery of the human face" and "visual empathy" gifts of film? Did television, video, and electronic media have comparable effects on how we see the world and other beings in it?

9. In general, how would you describe the prospects for media technology: in the positive terms Lang used about German films in 1926, or in more guarded terms, aware of the propaganda films Goebbels and Hitler made in the 1930s?

SAMPLE LECTURE 25: STALIN AND HITLER IN THE DECADE BEFORE WAR

Lecture Objectives

1. To examine the conditions under which Stalin implemented his "revolution from above"

2. To understand the rise of Hitler and the Nazis Party in the 1930s

3. To examine the appearance of fascist and totalitarian regimes in the interwar years

AN AGE OF ANXIETY: FASCISM AND TOTALITARIANISM

The Age of Anxiety was an age in which modern fascism and totalitarianism made their appearance. By 1939, liberal democracies in Britain, France, Scandinavia, and Switzerland were realities. But elsewhere across Europe, various kinds of dictators reared their ugly heads. Dictatorship seemed to be the wave of the future. It also seemed to be the wave of the present. This is what bothered such writers as Koestler, Huxley, Capek, and Orwell. It was a nightmare world in which human individuality was subsumed under the might of totalitarian collectivism. Totalitarianism became a new political religion for the Age of Anxiety. Thanks to improved technology, it was possible in the twentieth century for governments to embrace total control. It is possible that totalitarian regimes are limited only by the extent to which mass communications have been made a reality. And with mass communications comes the potential for total control. Modern totalitarian regimes made their appearance with the total effort required by the Great War, a war that required all institutions to subordinate their interests to victory at all costs. Individual freedoms were constantly reduced by increasing government intervention. The invisible hand of Adam Smith had been replaced by the visible hand of government. Beyond this, the crucial experience of World War I was Lenin, the Bolsheviks, and the Russian Civil War. Lenin had shown how a revolutionary minority—the Bolsheviks—could make a dedicated effort and achieve victory over a majority. Lenin also demonstrated how institutions and human rights might be subordinated to the needs of a single party and a single leader. So, Lenin provided a model for a single-party dictatorship, a model further improvised by Stalin as well as Hitler and Mussolini. Totalitarian society was a fully mobilized society, a society constantly moving toward some goal. The totalitarian state never reached its ultimate goal but gave the illusion of doing so. As soon as one goal was reached, it was replaced by another. Such was the case with Stalin's Five-Year Plans. Production quotas were announced well before they had been reached in order to produce the illusion that the Five-Year Plan was working.

STALIN'S "REVOLUTION FROM ABOVE"

Totalitarianism meant a permanent revolution, an unfinished revolution in which rapid and profound change imposed from above simply went on forever. The individual was constantly striving for a goal placed just slightly out of reach. Such was the case with Stalin's "revolution from above." After having suppressed his enemies on both the left and the right, as well as the center, Stalin issued the general party line. Stalin's aim was to create a new kind of society and a new human personality to inhabit that society—socialist man and socialist woman. A strong army would have to be built, as well as a powerful industrial economy. Stalinist society did have its frightening aspects, and none was more frightening than the existence of brutal, unrestrained police terrorism. First used against the wealthy peasants or kulaks during the 1920s and 1930s, terror was increasingly used against party members, administrators, and ordinary people. No one was above suspicion. One Soviet recalled that in 1931, "we all trembled because there was no way of getting out of it. Even a Communist can be caught. To avoid trouble became an exception." On December 1, 1934, the Leningrad party boss, Sergei Kirov, was assassinated in Leningrad on Stalin's orders. Using Kirov's death as an excuse, Stalin systematically purged the Party of opponents. Hundreds were shot for their alleged complicity in Kirov's death. Stalin also used the crime as an excuse to introduce severe laws against all political crimes. So, following the death of Kirov at the end of 1934, there began the Soviet witch-hunt that culminated in the Great Terror of the years 1935–1939.

In 1936, Stalin brought his old comrades, Zinoviev and Kamenev, to a staged public trial. An international press corps was invited. When their trial had ended, Zinoviev, Kamenev, and fourteen other old Bolsheviks either admitted involvement in the Kirov Affair or signed confessions that had been fabricated for them. These men had not been conspirators, but they did satisfy Stalin's paranoia and they were all executed. Many confessions were voluntary because the Party demanded it. As one survivor recalled, "serving the party was not just a goal in life but an inner need." In January 1937, a second great show trial was held in which seventeen leading Bolsheviks declared that they had knowledge of a conspiracy between Trotsky and the German and Japanese intelligence services by which Soviet territory was to be transferred to Germany and Japan. A crowd of 200,000 packed Red Square in frigid weather to hear Nikita Khrushchev read out the death sentences. All seventeen were executed. Then on June 11, 1937, the cream of the Red Army, stripped of their medals and insignia, were ushered into the courtroom and accused of spying for the Germans. They were found guilty, shot, and dumped in a trench on a construction site, all within eighteen hours. Of the 100,000 Red Army officers on active duty in 1937, perhaps 60,000 were purged. The last of the public trials took place in March 1938, as twenty-one leading Bolsheviks, including Nikolai Bukharin, confessed to similar charges and were executed. Every member of Lenin's Politburo except Stalin and Trotsky either were killed or committed suicide to avoid execution. A partial list of those who died would include:

- two vice-commissars of foreign affairs
- almost all the military judges who had sat in judgment and had condemned
- two successive heads of the NKVD
- the director of the Lenin Library
- the man who had led the charge against the Winter Palace in 1917
- a man who took down a portrait of Stalin while painting a wall

The arrests multiplied in 1936 and 1937. Anything was used as an excuse for an arrest: dancing too long with a Japanese diplomat, not clapping loudly enough or long enough after one of Stalin's speeches, buying groceries from a former kulak. People went to work one day and simply did not return. The NKVD employed millions of secret informers who infiltrated every workplace. Most academics and writers came to expect arrest, exile, and prison as part of their lives. By 1938 at least one million people were in prison, some 8.5 million had been arrested and sent to the Gulag, and nearly 800,000 had been executed. Stalin's purges baffled foreign observers. Leading Communists confessed to crimes against the state they never committed. Some were brainwashed, others tortured. Eventually, even Trotsky was murdered, killed with an ice pick in Mexico City in 1940.

Nazi Germany

Popular memory reveals that of all the totalitarian regimes of the twentieth century, none was more terrifying than that of Nazi Germany. As a product of Hitler combined with Germany's social and political situation, and the general attack on liberalism, Nazi Germany emerged rapidly after 1933 when Hitler came to power. The Nazis smashed all independent organizations, mobilized the economy, and began the systematic extermination of the Jewish and other non-German populations.

Hitler was born in Austria in 1889. He dropped out of school at age 14 and then spent four years as a tramp before he went to Vienna to become an artist. In Vienna, he came to believe that the Germans were a superior race of people. He also learned his anti-Semitism, racism, and hatred of all Slavic people. A former monk by the name of Lanz von Liebenfels inspired Hitler's twisted Darwinism, which held that the master race would be created by selective breeding and the systematic sterilization of inferior races. When war broke out in 1914, Hitler believed he had found salvation. The struggle and discipline of war gave meaning to Hitler's life. Life was struggle and so, too, was war. But when defeat came in 1918, Hitler's world was shattered. The war had been his reason for living. Back home following the war, Hitler made wild speeches to small audiences in the streets. He didn't care if many people heard him out, only that he could articulate his anti-Semitism and German nationalism. People began to take him seriously. By 1921, Hitler had become the leader of a small but growing political party. The German Workers' Party denounced Jews, Marxists, and liberals and promised national socialism. They used propaganda and theatrical rallies. They wore special badges and uniforms, and as they marched, robotlike, through the streets of Münich, they rendered their special salute. Most effective of all their tools was the mass rally. Songs were sung, slogans were cast about. It was a revivalist movement, or at least it had the atmosphere of a religious revival. Hitler was a charismatic speaker and easily worked his audiences up into a frenzy. Party membership began to grow. In 1922, Hitler launched a plot to march on Münich, a plot that eventually failed and sent Hitler to Landsburg prison for five years. At his trial, Hitler presented his own program to solve Germany's problems. The audience listened. A new wave of converts began to side with the German Workers' Party. While in prison, Hitler dictated *Mein Kampf* to Rudolph Hess. Its basic themes were:

- German racial superiority
- virulent anti-Semitism
- *lebensraum*, or living space
- pan-Germanism
- the necessity of yet another war

The Nazi Party in the 1930s

By 1928, the Nazi Party had their Bible as well as 100,000 members, but they were still a marginal political group. World events in 1929 and 1930 produced a new mania for the Hitler program. Unemployment stood at 1.3 million in 1929. The following year, it rose to 5 million while industrial production in 1932 fell by more than 50 percent. In that same year, 43 percent of all Germans were unemployed. Hitler promised Germany economic salvation as well as military and political restitution for the "war guilt clause." He focused on the middle and lower middle classes. These were the people who had barely survived through the period of wild inflation following World War I. The Nazis also made their appeal to German youth. Hitler and his aides were much younger than other leading politicians. In 1931, for instance, 40 percent of all Nazis were under thirty years of age and 70 percent were under forty. This is quite different from what we would find in Stalinist Russia at the same time.

National recovery, rapid change, and personal advancement formed the main appeal of the Nazi Party. By 1932, Hitler had gained the support of key people in the army and in big business. These individuals thought they could use Hitler for their own financial interests. They accepted Hitler's condition that he would join the government only if he became chancellor. Since the government was a coalition consisting of two Nazis and nine conservatives, they reasoned that Hitler could be used and controlled. And so, on January 30th, 1933, Hitler legally became the chancellor of Germany. Hitler moved quickly to establish a dictatorship. He used terror to gain power while maintaining an air of legality. He called for new elections to Parliament and then had the Parliament building burned to the ground. He blamed the Communists for this act, thus helping to get them out of the way and out of any possible public following. He convinced President Hindenburg to sign an emergency act that abolished the freedom of speech and of assembly. On March 23, 1933, the Nazis pushed the Enabling Act through Parliament, making Hitler dictator for a period of four years. Communist Party members were arrested, the Catholic Center Party withdrew all opposition, and the Social Democratic Party was dissolved. So it was that Germany, like Soviet Russia under Stalin, became a one-party state. In the economic sphere, all strikes were made illegal and unions were abolished. The members of professional organizations were swallowed up in Nazi-based organizations. The press was under state control. Books were burned and modern art was prohibited in an atmosphere of anti-intellectualism. Hitler promised the German people work and bread and he delivered both. He launched a massive public works program to pull Germany out of the Depression. Superhighways, office buildings, huge stadiums, and public buildings were constructed at a rapid pace. By 1936, however, government spending was now being directed almost entirely to the military, necessary for the coming war. In January 1937, unemployment stood at 7 million. By 1938, Germany witnessed a shortage of labor. The standard of living increased by 20 percent and business profits were increased.

What all this recovery proved was that Hitler was more than show. For those Germans who were not Jews, Slavs, Gypsies, communists, liberals, non-Germans, or insane or weak, Hitler's government meant greater opportunity and greater equality. Older class barriers were replaced by individuals who, like Hitler, were rootless and had risen to the top. Although economic recovery and increased opportunity won Hitler support, Nazism was totally guided by two main ideas: *Lebensraum* and race. As Germany regained economic strength and built up its military, Hitler formed alliances with other dictators. Western Europe sat back and tried to appease Hitler. When war broke out in 1939, it was for one specific reason—Hitler's ambitions were without limit.

EVIL SPIRITS

In general, the fascists and Nazis elevated all that was horrific in prewar and interwar European culture. They were the evil spirits of Western civilization. They did not create the evil—they merely exploited and heightened it. They were parasites who borrowed the ideas of others to use as the new tools of power. Fascist ideology was not restricted to Italy or Germany alone. Fascism was a European phenomenon that developed as a reaction to the perceived failure of Western-style liberal democracies and industrial capitalism. From France, Belgium, and Romania to Austria, England, and the United States, fascism did manage to receive some support. Fascism was a radicalism of the political right; it glorified the country over the city and stressed blind patriotism, the family, traditional values, and old customs. We see the same emphasis in the German *Volk*. "The world between the wars was attracted to madness," wrote the British philosopher Bertrand Russell. "Of this attraction Nazism was the most emphatic expression." Watching Hitler's chanting crowds and mass meetings, one could only get the idea that some kind of madness had come over Germany. In actual fact, most Germans cared little for fascist or Nazi propaganda. They liked Hitler because he got things done, solved unemployment, and restored the pride of all Germans. It's been said that people, not being truly rational, need ritual, romance, and religion. Perhaps these needs had been neglected in a rationalized, bureaucratic, and mechanical society. Fascism reminded these people that twentieth-century man is in search of religion and religious faith. In fascism and Nazism, they found a new faith replete with rituals, symbols, sacraments, the good book, even a messiah. In the end, of course, this new faith turned out to be a disastrous one.

SUGGESTED FEATURE FILMS

Chariots of Fire. 123 min. Color. 1981. Warner Brothers. True story of two British runners, one a devout Scottish missionary, the other a Jewish Cambridge student, competing in the 1924 Summer Olympics.

Christ Stopped at Eboli (subtitled). 120 min (cut U.S. version). Color. 1980. Franklin Media. In the fascist Italy of 1935, a painter trained as a doctor is exiled to a remote region near Eboli. (Now available in a remastered 2003 DVD version.)

Gosford Park. 137 min. Color. 2001. USA Films. A Robert Altman film set in the 1930s about an English country house where a family has invited many of their friends for a weekend.

La Grande Illusion. 117 min. B/W. 1937. Cindeis-RAC. A 1917 POW camp provides the setting for Jean Renoir's examination of the decay of the aristocracy.

The Grapes of Wrath. Color. 128 min. B/W. 20th Century Fox. John Ford's adaptation of the John Steinbeck novel about the Dust Bowl and the Joad family as they migrate to California.

This Happy Breed. 115 min. Color. 1944. Universal Pictures. David Lean's production of the Noel Coward play about ordinary Londoners between the wars in the years before World War II.

Heroes for Sale. 73 min. B/W. 1933. Warner Brothers. Film deals with a returning World War I veteran who has to deal with drug addiction, Red Squads, automation, and the Great Depression.

The Remains of the Day. 134 min. Color. 1993. Columbia Pictures. A butler's world of propriety is tested by the possibility of romance and his master's ties with the Nazi cause.

Stalin. 166 min. Color. 1992. HBO. Not-quite-historically-accurate, made-for-television epic about the life of Stalin (Robert Duvall). The film is perhaps best for its ability to capture images rather than the true essence of Stalin.

Tea with Mussolini. 117 min. Color. 1999. G2 Films. Semi-autobiographical tale from the early life of director Franco Zeffirelli in which a bastard son is raised by an Englishwoman in pre–World War II Italy.

The Tin Drum. 142 min. Color. 1979. Film Polski. Based on Günter Grass's bestseller about a boy who plays his drum to the beat of Germany's tragic history in the twentieth century.

SUGGESTED CLASSROOM FILMS

1920–1929: Boom to Bust, 1929–1936: Stormy Weather, and *1936–1941: Over the Edge*. 46 min each. Color. 1999. Films for the Humanities and Social Sciences. ABC's Peter Jennings narrates events behind the tensions and crucial questions of the interwar years. Part of *The Century: Decades of Change* series.

Between the Wars: The Economic Seeds of World War II. 25 min. Color. 1997. Films for the Humanities and Social Sciences. Film highlights Germany's inability to pay reparations, chronic inflation, and the stock market crash and its effects on the rise of fascism.

Bolshevik Victory. 20 min. B/W. 1969. Films, Inc. Granada Television documentary on the October Revolution.

Eisenstein and Stalin: When Art and Politics Clash. 60 min. Color. 1999. Films for the Humanities and Social Sciences. Presents the struggle between Stalin and film director Sergei Eisenstein, who fought for freedom of expression in a climate of executions.

Europe, the Mighty Continent: Are We Making a Good Peace? 52 min. Color. 1976. Time-Life Films. Examines the Treaty of Versailles and its results.

Fascism. 49 min. Color. 1995. Films for the Humanities and Social Sciences. This film investigates why people turned to fascism in the twentieth century and why war created the downfall for fascist regimes.

The Life and Times of Joseph Stalin. 90 min. Color and B/W. n.d. Films for the Humanities and Social Sciences. Documentary account of the man who shaped the destiny of the one of the twentieth century's superpowers.

The Russian Revolution. 36 min. Color and B/W. 1989. Insight Media. Excerpts from Eisenstein films and documentaries are used to set the revolution within the context of Russian history.

Stalin and Hitler: Dangerous Liaisons. 150 min. Color. 1996. Films for the Humanities and Social Sciences. Three-part series that examines evidence that Stalin's Russia and Hitler's Germany were closer allies than either could or would acknowledge.

CHAPTER 26

The Second World War

2. Ends—how to maintain Europe's balance of power?
    a. Soviets the greater threat, so accommodate Hitler

C. The League of Nations
  1. Japanese invasion of China turned into an invasion of the whole country
    a. The Rape of Nanjing (1937)—"kill all, burn all, destroy all"
    b. The League expressed shock but did nothing
  2. Mussolini invaded Ethiopia in 1935
    a. Avenging the defeat of 1896
    b. League imposed sanctions on Italy but without enforcement

D. The Spanish Civil War (1936–1939)
  1. A weak republican government could not overcome opposition
  2. Extreme right-wing military officers rebelled
  3. Francisco Franco (r. 1936–1975)
  4. Hitler and Mussolini sent in troops and tested new weapons; war was a dress rehearsal
  5. The Soviets sided with the republicans
  6. Britain and France failed to act decisively
  7. Volunteers from England, France, and the United States
    a. Saw the war as a test of the West's determination to resist fascism
  8. Blum and the Popular Front—limited support
    a. Feared intervention would polarize France
  9. April 1937: The destruction of Guernica
  10. Hitler's lessons
    a. Britain, France, and the Soviet Union would have a hard time containing fascism
    b. Britain and France would do anything to avoid another war

E. German rearmament and the politics of appeasement
  1. Hitler played on Germans' sense of shame and betrayal
  2. Removed Germany from the League of Nations in 1933
  3. Tore up disarmament provisions of Versailles in 1935
  4. The unification of all ethnic Germans
  5. Reoccupied the Rhineland in 1936
    a. France and Britain did nothing
  6. The annexation of Austria (1938)
    a. No response from the West

7. Hitler declared his intention to occupy the Sudetenland (Czechoslovakia)
    a. Neville Chamberlain
      i. With the Sudetenland, Germany's ambitions would be satisfied
      ii. Believed Germany could not commit to a sustained war
      iii. Eastern Europe ranked low in British priorities
8. Munich: September 29, 1938
    a. Daladier (France), Chamberlain, Mussolini, and Hitler met
      i. The capitulation of France and Britain
    b. Chamberlain proclaimed "peace in our time"
    c. March 1939: Germany invaded Czechoslovakia
    d. Convinced public of the futility of appeasement
9. Stalin's response
    a. Feared the West might strike a deal with Hitler
    b. August 1939: the Nazi-Soviet pact of nonaggression
      i. Stalin promised a share of Poland, Finland, and the Baltic States

IV. The Outbreak of Hostilities and the Fall of France
A. Poland
  1. Hitler demanded the abolition of the Polish Corridor
  2. Poland stood firm, but Hitler attacked on September 1, 1939
  3. Britain and France sent a warning to Germany
    a. Germany ignored the demand
    b. Britain and France declared war on September 3, 1939
  4. The *Blitzkrieg* (lightning war)
  5. Soviet troops invaded from the east
  6. Poland fell in four weeks
B. The phony war
C. Scandinavia—Germans took Denmark in one day (spring 1940)
D. May 10, 1939: Germans moved through Belgium toward France
E. The fall of France
  1. French army overwhelmed by the German advance
  2. French army poorly organized
  3. French refugees fled south

4. Dunkirk—300,000 British and French troops evacuated to England
5. June 18, 1939: the Germans reached Paris
6. June 18, 1939: French surrendered
    a. Germans occupied northern France
    b. Southern France fell under the Vichy regime, headed by Marshall Pétain
7. The Free French movement

V. Not Alone: The Battle of Britain and the Beginnings of a Global War
  A. The Battle of Britain (July 1940–June 1941)
    1. Forty thousand civilians dead
    2. Stalemate in the air
    3. British resistance
  B. Winston Churchill (1940–1945, 1951–1955)
    1. Talented but arrogant
    2. Language and personal diplomacy
    3. Convinced FDR to break with American neutrality
    4. Lend-Lease
  C. A global war
    1. The Battle of the Atlantic
      a. German submarines ("wolf packs") sank millions of tons of merchant shipping
      b. British development of sonar and aerial reconnaissance
      c. Breaking the German codes
    2. North Africa
      a. British needed to protect the Suez
      b. British humiliation of Italian invasion force in Libya
        i. Forced Germany to intervene
      c. Afrika Korps and Erwin Rommel
      d. British defeated Italian navy in the Mediterranean
      e. Rommel's invasion of Egypt defeated at El Alamein (1942)
      f. United States landed in French territories of Algeria and Morocco
    3. Conference at Casablanca
      a. Allies discussed the course of the war
      b. Fate of French territories in North Africa
    4. Japan
      a. December 7, 1941: Japanese attack on Pearl Harbor
      b. Set out to destroy U.S. fleet
        i. Most American ships were out to sea

      c. Japanese swept through British protectorate of Malaya
      d. Singapore fell in December 1941
      e. The invasion of the Philippines
      f. Corregidor and the "Death March"
      g. Japanese pressed on to Burma
        i. William Slim reorganized imperial defenses
        ii. British and Indian troops defeated the Japanese invasion of India
    5. The American navy
      a. Rapid production of planes and ships
      b. Chester Nimitz and William Halsey
      c. Coral Sea, Midway, and Guadalcanal
        i. "Island hopping"

VI. The Rise and Ruin of Nations: Germany's War in the East and the Occupation of Europe
  A. German victories
    1. 1940: Germany took Yugoslavia
      a. Established a Croatian puppet state
    2. Romania, Hungary, and Bulgaria sided with Germany
    3. Greece ultimately fell to the Germans
    4. By the summer of 1941, Germany dominated the continent
  B. Hitler's ultimate goal
    1. Russia and the Ukraine
      a. Ethnically inferior Slavs and Jews, governed by communists
      b. Nazi-Soviet Pact as a matter of convenience for Hitler
    2. June 22, 1941: Hitler authorized Operation Barbarossa—the invasion of the Soviet Union
      a. Stalin's purges had gotten rid of Russia's most capable commanders
      b. Germans took thousands of prisoners
    3. War against the Soviets pitted one ideology against another
      a. Racial hatred
      b. Cleansing occupied territories of "undesirable elements"
    4. Hitler diverted his attack from Moscow to the industrial south
  C. The Nazi New Order
    1. A patchwork affair
      a. Military governments (Poland and Ukraine)
      b. Collaborators (France)
      c. Allied fascists (Hungary)

2. The empire was meant to feed Germany and maintain morale and support
3. Occupied countries paid "occupation costs" in taxes, food, industrial production, and manpower
4. Puppet regimes
    a. Norway and the Netherlands
        i. Dedicated party of Nazis governed
        ii. At the same time, well-organized resistance movement
5. France
    a. Collaboration ranged from simple survival tactics to active Nazi support
        i. The isolation or deportation of French Jews
    b. Communist activists
        i. Long tradition of smuggling and resisting government
        ii. Became active guerillas and saboteurs
    c. The Free French and Charles de Gaulle
6. Yugoslavia
    a. Fascist Croats against most Serbs
    b. The *Ustasha*
    c. Josip Broz (Tito) emerged as the leader of the Yugoslav resistance
        i. Communist guerilla army
        ii. Gained support of the Allies
7. Moral issues facing the occupied countries
    a. The enemies of the Nazis—the "undesirables"
VII. Racial War, Ethnic Cleansing, and the Holocaust
    A. World War II as a racial war
        1. Hitler had already outlined his war against the *Untermensch* (subhuman)
            a. Jews, Gypsies, and Slavs
            b. The purification of the German people
        2. Fall 1939: Himmler directed massive population transfers
            a. Ethnic Germans moved into the Reich
            b. Poles and Jews were deported
                i. A campaign of terror
                ii. Poles deported to forced-labor camps
                iii. Special death squads shot Jews in the streets
        3. *Rassenkampf* (racial struggle)
            a. Radicalized by the war itself

    b. 1938–1941: Nazis had no concerted plan to deal with undesirables
        i. Forced emigration
        ii. Deportation to Madagascar
    c. June 1941: The turning point— Barbarossa
        i. Nazis directed hatred against Slavs, Jews, and Marxists
        ii. A "war of extermination"
    B. From systematic brutality to atrocities to murder
        1. More than five million military prisoners marched to camps to work as slave labor
        2. The *Einsatzgruppen* (death squads)
            a. 1941: "Pacification" had killed 85,000
            b. April 1942: 500,000 killed
            c. 1943: 2.2 million Jews killed
        3. The Warsaw and Lodz ghetto—death and terror
    C. The Holocaust
        1. Nazis discussed plans for mass killings in death camps
        2. The ghettos were sealed
        3. Poison gas vans
        4. Auschwitz-Birkenau
            a. Systematic annihilation of Jews and Gypsies
            b. 1942–1944: one million killed
        5. Anonymous slaughter?
            a. People were tortured, beaten, and executed publicly
            b. Death marches
            c. Reserve Police Battalion 101 from Hamburg
                i. Ordinary Germans obeying orders
        6. Who knew?
            a. Extermination involved the knowledge and cooperation of many not directly involved in killing
            b. Most who suspected the worst were terrified and powerless
            c. The Jewish Problem
                i. Many Europeans believed there was a problem to be solved
                ii. Nazis tried to conceal the death camps
            d. What of other governments?
                i. Vichy France required Jews to wear special identification
                ii. Italians participated less actively

iii. Hungarian government dragged its feet when it came to deportation

e. Little resistance seemed to be possible

f. Rebellions at Auschwitz and Treblinka

g. Warsaw ghetto uprising (1943)

   i. 80 percent of the residents had been deported

   ii. Small Jewish underground movement

   iii. 56,000 Jews were killed

7. Human costs

a. 4.1–5.7 million Jews killed

b. Some long-standing Jewish communities were annihilated

8. A new Europe?

VIII. Total War: Home Fronts, the War of Production, Bombing and "the Bomb"

A. War demanded massive resources and a national commitment

1. Wartime profits and the "dance of the millions"

2. Germany and Japan robbed local areas of resources

3. United States, Britain, and Soviet Union

a. Long work shifts

b. Effects on women and the family

4. Rationing

5. Production

a. Propaganda campaigns encouraged the production of war equipment

b. Patriotism, communal interests, and a common stake in winning the war

c. Allies built tanks, ships, and airplanes by the tens of thousands

d. Germany was less efficient in the use of workers and resources

   i. Pet projects of the Nazis expended time and money

B. New targets

1. Centers of industry as military targets

2. American and British strategic bombing

a. For the British, a war of retribution

b. For the Americans, grinding down Germany without sacrificing too many Allied lives

3. The Dresden fire-bombing

C. The race to build the bomb

1. Nuclear fission and the chain reaction

2. British passed technical information on to American scientists

3. Enrico Fermi (1901–1954)

a. Built the first nuclear reactor at the University of Chicago in December 1942

4. German experiments

a. Best specialists were Jews or anti-Nazis now working for the Allies

b. Lacked crucial bits of technical information

5. The Manhattan Project

a. Managing the effort to build an American atomic bomb

6. Los Alamos, New Mexico (1943)

a. Laboratory that brought together most capable nuclear physicists

b. J. Robert Oppenheimer (1904–1967) placed in charge of the project

7. First atomic test on July 16, 1945, near Los Alamos

IX. Great Crusades: The Allied Counterattack and the Dropping of the Atomic Bomb

A. The Nazi penetration of the Soviet Union

B. The siege of Leningrad

C. The Eastern Front

1. Changes in the character of war

a. War to save the Russian motherland (rodina)—the Russian will to survive

b. Victory during the "General Winter"—took its toll on Nazi supplies

c. Astonishing recovery of Soviet army

   i. Whole industries were rebuilt

   ii. Whole populations moved to work in new factories

d. Soviets found the Blitzkrieg predictable

2. The turning point—1943

a. Germans aimed an all-out assault on Stalingrad

b. Drawn into bitter house-to-house fighting with Soviet snipers

c. Stalingrad destroyed

d. With supplies low, the Russian armies surrounded the Germans in the city

e. January 1943: German surrender

   i. Six thousand of 250,000 Germans survived

   ii. One million Soviet deaths

3. Soviet offensives
   a. Kursk (1943)
      i. Six thousand tanks and two million men in battle lasting six weeks
      ii. German army was crushed
      iii. The leadership of Grigori Zhukov
   b. Ukraine back in Soviet hands, Romania knocked out of the war
   c. Soviet victories in Yugoslavia and Czechoslovakia
D. The Western Front
   1. Stalin pressured the Allies to open a second front in the west
   2. The Allied invasion of Sicily
      a. Mussolini surrendered in summer 1943
   3. The Normandy invasion (June 6, 1944)
   4. The liberation of Paris (August 14, 1944)
   5. The Battle of the Bulge (December 1944)
   6. Allies crossed the Rhine in April 1945
      a. Germans preferred to surrender to the Americans or British rather than face the Russians
   7. Soviets entered Berlin on April 21, 1945
   8. Hitler commited suicide in his bunker beneath the Chancellery on April 30, 1945
   9. Germany surrendered unconditionally on May 7
E. The war in the Pacific
   1. British, Indian, and Nepalese troops liberated Rangoon (Burma)
   2. Australians recaptured Dutch East Indies
   3. Okinawa fell to the Americans (June 1945)
   4. Chinese communists and nationalists pushed the Japanese back on Hong Kong
   5. Soviet forces marched through Manchuria to Korea
   6. United States, Britain, and China called on Japan to surrender or be destroyed on July 26
      a. *B-29*s began systematic bombing of Japanese cities
      b. Japan refused to surrender
   7. The decision to drop the bomb
      a. Was it necessary? Japan had already been beaten
      b. Harry Truman
   8. August 6, 1945: Hiroshima, August 9: Nagasaki
   9. Japan surrendered unconditionally on August 14, 1945

X. Conclusion
   A. A new world ravaged by war
   B. Western imperialism
   C. Mass killing
   D. Technology, genocide, and global war

GENERAL DISCUSSION QUESTIONS

1. The First and Second World Wars are sometimes discussed as the "Thirty Years' War of the Twentieth Century." Yet our authors state that "The Second World War did not follow directly from where the First stopped." What are some arguments for each case?

2. What political and economic troubles contributed to the tense atmosphere of Europe in the 1930s? Why was it hard to solve these problems through friendly negotiations?

3. European nations disputed their borders and wanted to adjust them, but one historian (Gerhard Weinberg) argues that only Nazi Germany saw another world war as a solution to its problems. Would documentation of this point establish that Nazi Germany deserves the blame for starting World War II? Is this view generally accepted today?

4. What motives lay behind the policy of appeasement? Why did Britain and France pursue such a policy? Were there alternatives?

5. The Eastern Front of the Second World War has been described as "a war of ideologies overlaid loosely on a war of racial hatred." Why is this so? Which ethnic groups and nations were most actively involved?

6. In some areas of eastern Europe, local populations welcomed Hitler's German troops as their liberators from Stalin's Soviet dictatorship. Yet as the Nazi regime pursued policies of racial warfare and genocide in occupied territories, what kinds of support or resistance did the locals offer to those acts?

7. How did decisions made by the victorious Allies during the war lead to tensions afterward? Why was there a new kind of war, and how did it shape the United Nations?

8. Why did no Western nation intervene to stop the extermination of the Jews during the Holocaust? What is the meaning of the Holocaust today?

9. How did the great superpowers—the United States and the Soviet Union—deal with the question of Germany both during and after the war? And what of Poland?

10. Discuss the origins of the Cold War. Do you think the Cold War was inevitable considering the sorts of

tensions unleashed by World War II, or are the origins of the Cold War to be found in another historical period?

DOCUMENT DISCUSSION QUESTIONS

The Holocaust: Massacres in the Ukraine

1. During the war, the SS tried to limit public knowledge of its extermination of Jews, Gypsies, Jehovah's Witnesses, dissidents, and other "undesirables." In 1943, SS leader Heinrich Himmler told his men that this glorious page in their history would never be written, and that only those who had taken part would know the full horror. Why? Even before death camps such as Auschwitz went into operation, special squads accompanied German armies in Ukraine and Russia. They killed their victims in rural areas and buried the bodies in mass graves. The Nazis abandoned this method because it produced psychological disturbances in the killers; for their purposes, "factories of death" using poison gas and cremation were more efficient. How was this shift characteristic of the Nazi ethos? How was it unusual even for Nazis?

2. Why did Gräbe talk about what he saw at Dubno, when others kept silent? What could Gräbe have done to stop the massacre? Perhaps he could testify, clear his conscience, and help prevent future massacres? Or do you judge him more harshly?

3. What ethical obligations do we have as individuals when we learn about massacres of innocent people? What obligations do governments and nations have?

The Holocaust: Two Perspectives from the SS

4. The SS officer and camp inspector at Belzec, Poland, in 1945 left a sickeningly detailed description of killing masses of people using diesel engine exhaust gases. How do you interpret his subsequent suicide?

5. In a 1943 speech, Himmler praised SS men for their heroic acts in "the Jewish evacuation programme, the extermination of the Jewish people. . . . Most of you will know what it means when a hundred corpses are lying side by side, or five hundred or a thousand are lying there." Does this text establish that top Nazis knew about the extermination plan and approved it. No direct written or recorded evidence has surfaced showing that Adolf Hitler personally ordered the Holocaust, but the *Führer* made war against the Jews his top priority, and his lieutenants never made strategic decisions or engaged in major military actions without his approval. How does this influence your view of history in terms of evidence?

The Atomic Bomb and Its Implications

6. To express their fears about how the atomic bomb would be used, scientists circulated petitions. Look at the outcomes the scientists proposed. Which came closest to subsequent events? Which was the most prudent? The most honest?

7. Is it permissible or proper for scientists to propose how new weapons should be used? Are they overreaching in trying to give advice in foreign affairs and military strategy? Or are they obligated to voice moral qualms?

SAMPLE LECTURE 26: AN OVERVIEW OF THE SECOND WORLD WAR

Lecture Objectives

1. To show that in the 1930s, dictatorships were ascendant, democracy in decline

2. To describe Hitler's goals for Germany: space for expansion and purification of race

3. To place primary responsibility for World War II on the aggressive acts of Nazi Germany

4. To place secondary blame on Britain, France, the United States, and the Soviet Union, all of whom favored appeasement and tolerated Nazi tactics

THE DRIFT TOWARD WAR

In 1933, Hitler implemented a set of foreign policy objectives that violated the provisions of the Versailles Treaty. His aim was to make Germany the most powerful state in all of Europe. This goal was fairly consistent with German war plans during the Great War. At that time, German generals tried to conquer extensive regions in Eastern Europe. With the Treaty of Brest-Litovsk (1918) between Germany and Russia, Germany took Poland, the Ukraine, and the Baltic States from Russia. However, where Hitler departed from this traditional scenario was his total obsession with racial supremacy. His desire to annihilate whole races of peoples marked a break from the outlook of the old order who wanted to Germanize German Poles, not enslave them. But Hitler was an opportunist—and a man possessed and driven by a fanaticism that saw his destiny as identical to Germany's. With his propaganda machine intact, Hitler was able to successfully undermine his opponent's will to resist. And after winning the minds of the German people, propaganda became an instrument of German foreign policy as a whole. There were upwards of 27 million German people living outside the borders of the Reich, and to force these millions into Hitler's camp:

• The Nazis utilized their propaganda machine.
• The Nazis exported anti-Semitism internationally.

- They fed off prejudices of other nations.
- Hitler began to promote himself as Europe's best defense against Stalin.
- The Nazis convinced thousands of Europeans that Hitler was also Europe's best defense against all communists.

Hitler anticipated that the British and French would back down when faced with his direct violations of the Versailles treaty. He knew that any threat of war would drive the Anglo-French into a defensive posture, since Britain and France would do anything to avoid another conflict.

APPEASEMENT

The British believed that Germany had been treated too harshly by the provisions of Versailles, and because of this, they were willing to make concessions. The French refused to contemplate an offensive war and decided instead to protect their borders at all costs. The United States stood isolated from any European conflict because of the Great Depression. And the British and French no longer trusted Russia. So the British introduced their policy of appeasement. They hoped that by making concessions to Hitler, war would be avoided. They also held on to the illusion that Hitler was Europe's best defense against the Soviets. The British appeasers certainly missed the boat—even with *Mein Kampf* in their hands, they failed to understand Hitler's foreign policy aims. Hitler could be reasoned with, they argued.

Hitler needed a strong army to realize his war aims. According to the provisions of the Versailles Treaty, the Germany army was to be limited to 100,000 soldiers. The size of the navy was limited as well. Germany was also forbidden to produce military aircraft, tanks, and heavy artillery, and the General Staff was dissolved. In March 1935, Hitler declared that Germany was no longer bound by the provisions of the Versailles Treaty. He began conscription and built up the air force. France issue a weak protest, and Britain negotiated a naval agreement with Germany. One year later, on March 7, 1936, Hitler marched his troops into the Rhineland, a clear violation of Versailles. His generals cautioned him that such a move would provoke an attack. Again, Hitler judged the Anglo-French response correctly. The British and French took no action. The British sat back. The French saw the remilitarization of the Rhineland as a grave threat to their security. But with 22,000 German soldiers standing along the French border, the French did not act.

- France would not act alone.
- Britain offered no help at this point.
- The French overestimated German forces who marched into the Rhineland.
- French public opinion was strongly opposed to any confrontation with Hitler.

Meanwhile, between 1936 and 1937 European fascism was winning another war in Spain. Mussolini and Hitler both supported Franco's right-wing dictatorship. The Spanish Civil War was decisive for Hitler, for it was here that he was able to test new weapons and new aircraft, which would eventually make their appearance in World War II.

In 1938, Hitler ordered his troops to march into Austria. The Austrians celebrated by ringing church bells, waving swastikas, and attacking Jews. The *Anschluss* was yet another violation of Versailles, and once again nonintervention paved the way for Hitler's foreign policy aims. Hitler used the threat of force to obtain Austria and a similar threat would give him the Sudetenland. More than three-quarters of the population of the Sudetenland were ethnic Germans. The area also contained key industries and was vital to the protection of Czechoslovakia. Sudetenland Germans, encouraged by the Nazis, began to denounce the Czech government. Meanwhile, Hitler's propaganda machine accused the Czech government of hideous crimes. He ordered his generals to plan an invasion of Czechoslovakia. At this point, Neville Chamberlain decided to intervene, and Hitler agreed to a conference. The British statesmen argued that the Sudetenland, like Austria, was not worth another war. Once the Germans were living under the German flag, the British argued, Hitler would be satisfied. And so the fate of Czechoslovakia was sealed by the Münich Pact (September 29, 1938). Chamberlain, Hitler, Mussolini, and Daladier (prime minister of France) signed the pact and agreed that all Czech troops in the Sudetenland would be replaced by German troops. The British hailed Chamberlain; the French hailed Daladier. With the Sudetenland annexed, Hitler plotted to annihilate the independent existence of Czechoslovakia. And so, in March 1939, Czechoslovakian independence came to an end.

FROM APPEASEMENT TO WAR

After Czechoslovakia, Germany turned to Poland. Hitler demanded that the Polish port town of Danzig be returned to Germany. Poland refused to hand over Danzig because it was vital to their economy. Meanwhile, France and Britain warned Hitler that they would come to the assistance of Poland. On May 22, 1939, Hitler and Mussolini signed the Pact of Steel and promised one another mutual aid. One month later, the German army presented Hitler with battle plans for the invasion of Poland. While all this was going on, negotiations were under way between Britain, France, and Russia. The Soviets wanted mutual aid, but they also wanted military bases in Poland and Romania. Britain would not give in to their demands. Meanwhile, Russia conducted secret talks with Germany that resulted in the Nazi-Soviet Pact of nonaggression (August 23, 1939). One section of this pact—even more secret than the Nazi-Soviet Pact itself—called for the partition of Poland between Germany and Russia. On September 1, 1939, German troops marched into Poland. Britain and France demanded that Hitler stop his forces. Hitler ignored them, and so Britain and France declared war on Germany. After facing the *Blitzkrieg* (lightning war), Poland succumbed to Germany on September 27, 1939. The period of six months following the fall of Poland has been called "the phony war." But in the spring of 1940:

- Hitler struck at Denmark and then Norway.
- Hitler needed to establish naval bases in these countries, from which his submarines could attack England.
- Denmark surrendered in only one day, and Norway soon followed.
- Hitler then attacked Belgium, Holland, and Luxembourg.
- Surrenders followed quickly.

Meanwhile, French troops rushed to Belgium to prevent a German breakthrough. The German forces converged on the French port of Dunkirk, the last point of escape for the Allies. Hitler called off his tanks and planned to use air strikes to annihilate the Allies, but fog and rain prevented Hitler from using the full force of his airplanes. 340,000 British and French forces were ferried across the English Channel to England while Germany bombed the beaches.

By late spring 1940, there was every indication that France was about to fall to the Nazis. Numerous French divisions were cut off and in retreat. Millions of French refugees were making their way south, and on June 10, 1940, Mussolini declared war on France. The French government sent out an appeal for armistice, and so on June 22, 1940, French and German officials met in a railway car and signed the agreement.

With France fallen, Hitler assumed that Britain would make peace. The British rejected such an offer, and in August 1940, Hitler ordered his *Luftwaffe* to conduct massive airstrikes against Britain. The Battle of Britain raged for almost five months. On September 15, the British RAF shot down sixty German aircraft and Hitler was forced to postpone his invasion of Britain. By the end of 1941, Hitler had begun Operation Barbarossa, the invasion of the Soviet Union. Germany was now waging a war on two fronts. By early 1942:

- Nazi Germany ruled virtually all of Europe.
- Some territories were annexed under German military authority.
- Others, like France, collaborated with the Nazis.
- Hitler intended to superimpose a New Order.
- The Germans expropriated and exploited every country that they conquered.
- The Germans took gold, art, machinery, and food supplies back to Germany.

The Germans took whatever they wanted, including seven million people from all over occupied Europe who were enslaved and transported to Germany to work in forced-labor camps. The Nazis ruled by terror and fear. The New Order meant torture, prison, firing squads, and concentration camps. For example, in Poland, priests and intellectuals were jailed and killed and most schools and churches were closed. In Russia, political officials were immediately executed and prisoners of war were herded into camps and worked to death. Germany ended up taking 5.5 million Russian POWs, 3.5 million of which were killed or died in captivity.

THE HOLOCAUST

The task of imposing what came to be known as "the final solution of the Jewish Problem" was outlined at a conference held on January 20, 1942. One result of the Wannsee Protocol was that a portion of the responsibility for the extermination of European Jewry was given to Himmler's SS. The SS responded with fanaticism and bureaucratic efficiency. According to the Nazis, the Jews had no *Kultur*. Though perhaps German born, they were not a people of the *Volk*. The SS regarded themselves as idealists who were writing the most glorious of chapters in the history of Germany. In Russia, special squads of the SS—the *Einsatzgruppen*, trained for genocide—entered captured towns and cities and rounded up Jewish men, women, and children, herded them into groups, and shot them *en masse*. About two million Russian Jews perished as a result. In Poland, Hitler established ghettoes where some 3.5 million Jews were forced to live, sealed off from the rest of the population.

To expedite the Final Solution, the Nazis began to use concentration camps. These camps were already in existence for the use of political prisoners. Jews from all over Europe were rounded up under the notion that they were to be resettled. Although the Jews knew something about plans for their eventual extermination, they could not believe that any twentieth-century nation would resort to such a crime against humanity. Cattle cars full of Jews and other undesirables traveled days without food or water. When the doors opened, they found themselves in the unreal world of the concentration camp. SS doctors then inspected the "freight." Rudolf Hoess (1900–1947), commandant at Auschwitz, described the procedure in the following way:

> I estimate that at least 2,500,000 victims were executed and exterminated [at Auschwitz] by gassing and burning, and at least another half million succumbed to starvation and disease, making a total dead of about 3,000,000. This figure represents about 70 percent or 80 percent of all persons sent to Auschwitz as prisoners, the remainder having been selected and used for slave labor in the concentration camp industries. . . . The final solution of the Jewish Question meant the complete extermination of all Jews in Europe. I was ordered to establish extermination facilities at Auschwitz in June 1941. It took from three to fifteen minutes to kill people in the death chamber, depending upon climatic conditions. We knew when the people were dead because their screaming stopped. We usually waited about one-half hour before we opened the doors and removed the bodies. After the bodies were removed our special commandos took off the rings and extracted gold from the teeth of corpses. . . . The way we selected our victims was as follows. . . . Those who were fit to work were sent into the camp. Others were sent immediately to the extermination plants. Children of tender years were invariably exterminated since by reason of their youth they were

unable to work. . . . We endeavored to fool the victims into thinking that they were to go through a delousing process. Of course, frequently they realized our true intentions, and we sometimes had riots and difficulties due to that fact. Very frequently women would hide their children under clothes, but of course when we found them we would send the children in to be exterminated.

Auschwitz was more than a death factory. It also provided I. G. Farben with slave laborers. Workers worked at a pace that even the healthiest of workers would have found intolerable. And because Germany now had somewhat of an unlimited labor supply, working prisoners as fast as possible would solve two problems at the same time: increased production and the extermination of inmates.

Auschwitz also allowed the SS to shape themselves according to Nazi ideology. For instance, the SS amused themselves with pregnant women, having them beaten with clubs, attacked by dogs, dragged by the hair and then thrown into the crematory, still alive. The purpose of such inhuman behavior was to rob the victim of any shred of human dignity. In this way, the SS and the Nazis could demonstrate—to themselves, of course—that Jews were clearly an inferior race of people. What was unique about the Holocaust was the Nazis' intention to murder, without exception, every single Jew they found. Also unique was the fanaticism and cruelty with which they pursued this goal. The Holocaust was the culmination of Nazi *Rassenkampf*. Using modern technology and bureaucratic machinery, the Nazis systematically killed at least six million Jews. This figure represents nearly 65 percent of Europe's Jewish population. 1.5 million of these were children. Another six to seven million non-Jews were also exterminated, meaning that the Holocaust resulted in the deaths of at least 13 million people. Could man ever return to the felicific idea of progress as advocated by the eighteenth or nineteenth centuries?

RESISTANCE

Across the occupied territories of the Third Reich there were Nazi collaborators who welcomed the fall of democracy and who still saw Hitler as the best defense against communism. But each country also produced a resistance movement that grew stronger as Nazi atrocities increased. The resistance movement rescued downed pilots, radioed military movements to London, and sabotaged German railway depots. The Danish underground managed to smuggle eight thousand Jews into Sweden while the Polish resistance, estimated to number 300,000, reported on German positions and interfered with the movement of supplies. Russian partisans sabotaged railways, destroyed trucks, and killed hundreds of Germans in ambush. The Yugoslav resistance army, led by Marshall Tito, was a disciplined fighting force that ultimately liberated the country from the Germans. European Jews were specifically active in the French resistance movement. But in eastern Europe, Jewish resisters received little or no support. The Germans responded harshly to Jewish resistance—in some instances, two hundred Jews were killed for every one Nazi. However, in the spring of 1943, the surviving Jews of the Warsaw ghetto managed to fight the Germans for several weeks. Also in 1943, and after the Allies had landed in Italy, Italian resisters managed to liberate the country from the fascists and German occupation. And on July 20, 1944, Colonel Stauffenberg planted a bomb under Hitler's table at staff conference meeting—the bomb exploded but Hitler escaped serious injury. The Nazis responded by torturing and executing five thousand suspected anti-Nazis. Although the European resistance was proof that some people refused to accept Hitler and the Nazis, their efforts did not bring an end to the war. Japan's imperialist endeavors from the early 1930s on, including the attack on Pearl Harbor on December 7, 1941, forced the United States to enter the war.

THE END OF THE WAR

Meanwhile, Hitler had made the same blunder as had Napoleon by attacking Russia in winter. In February 1943, almost 300,000 soldiers died in the battle of Stalingrad, and another 130,000 were taken prisoner. In the fall of 1943, Allied forces liberated Italy. Mussolini was dismissed and eventually shot and hung by his ankles in April 1945. Finally, on D-Day (June 6, 1944) the Allies landed two million men on the beachhead at Normandy. By August, the Allies had liberated Paris and then Brussels and Antwerp. Meanwhile, the Allies were conducting massive bombing raids on German industrial cities. The Russians drove across the Baltic states, Poland, and Hungary, and by February 1945, they were one hundred miles from Berlin. By April, American, British, and Russian troops were moving toward Berlin from all sides. On April 30, 1945, Hitler and Eva Braun committed suicide, and one week later, May 7, a demoralized and near-destroyed Germany surrendered unconditionally. Finally, on August 6, 1945, the United States dropped an atomic bomb on Hiroshima—78,000 perished within fifteen minutes of the blast. Three days later, another bomb fell on Nagasaki, and on August 14, Japan surrendered.

The legacy of World War II was dramatic. Fifty million lost their lives, twenty million Russians alone. Thousands of people left Europe for either England or the United States. Hundreds of cities were destroyed, some of them centuries-old. Only 5 percent of Berlin remained intact, 70 percent of Dresden, Hamburg, Munich, and Frankfurt were destroyed. The war also revealed the existence of two superpowers—the United States and the Soviet Union, countries that would determine the fate of Europe and the world for the next four decades. The world now had the atomic bomb. Vast imperialist empires were destroyed. And then there was the Holocaust.

In the intellectual realm and in the world of art, the European war created a second Lost Generation with its own philosophy: existentialism.

SUGGESTED FEATURE FILMS

The Battle of Britain. 54 min. B/W. 1943. Warner Brothers. An account of Great Britain's last stand against the forces of Nazi Germany. An installment of the "Why We Fight" propaganda film series, directed by Frank Capra.

Breaking the Code. 75 min. Color. 1996. BBC and WGBH. Film about the English mathematician Alan Turing, who was one of the inventors of the digital computer and a key figure in breaking the German Enigma code, used to send orders to their U-boats.

Cabaret. 123 min. Color. 1972. ABC Pictures. A memorable picture of the collapse of the Weimar Republic and cultural life in Berlin in the 1930s.

Captain Corelli's Mandolin. 131 min. Color. 2001. Universal. The year is 1941 and on a remote Greek island, an Italian artillery garrison is established to maintain order. Captain Corelli adopts an attitude of mutual coexistence with the Greeks and courts the daughter of a local doctor.

Casablanca. 102 min. B/W. 1942. Warner Brothers. Drama about expatriate Rick Blaine coming to grips with war, romance, resistance, and the Nazis.

Enemy at the Gates. 131 min. Color. 2001. Paramount Pictures. Film about the Russian sniper, Vassili Zaitsev, who stalked the Germans and took them out one by one, thus hurting the morale of the German troops during the Battle of Stalingrad.

The English Patient. 160 min. Color. 1996. Miramax. The film's location is a crumbling villa in Italy during the final days of the World War II, where a young, shell-shocked war nurse remains behind to tend a horribly burned pilot.

The Great Dictator. 129 min. B/W. 1940. United Artists. Charlie Chaplin's indictment of fascism in the 1930s.

Judgment at Nuremberg. 178 min. Color. 1961. United Artists. Film about the trial and four judges who used their offices to conduct Nazi sterilization and cleansing policies.

The Pianist. 150 min. Color. 2002. Beverly Detroit. True story of Wladyslaw Szpilman, an accomplished Polish pianist who was subject to the anti-Jewish laws imposed by the conquering Germans. Excellent images of the Warsaw ghetto uprising and the Warsaw city revolt of 1945.

Saving Private Ryan. 170 min. Color. 1998. Amblin Entertainment. Steven Spielberg film about the U.S. government's attempt to locate the missing brother of three soldiers who were killed in action.

Schindler's List. 197 min. B/W and color. 1993. Amblin Entertainment. Steven Spielberg directed this true story of the Czech-born Oskar Schindler, a greedy German businessman who became compelled to turn his factory into a refuge for Jews.

Shoah. 544 min. Color. 1985. New Yorker Films. Nine-hour documentary of the Holocaust that interviews survivors, witnesses, and ex-Nazis and presents a horrifying portrait of the events of Nazi genocide.

This Land is Mine. 103 min. B/W. 1943. RKO Radio Pictures. Charles Laughton plays a teacher living in occupied France who, although a coward, is drawn into the resistance movement.

The Triumph of the Will. 120 min. B/W. 1934. Leni Riefenstahl's propagandist documentary of the 1934 Nuremberg Rallies.

There are literally hundreds of other World War II films that can be useful as classroom exercises. Here is a brief sample: *Anzio* (1968); *Back to Bataan* (1945); *Band of Brothers* (2001); *Battle Cry* (1955); *The Battle of Midway* (1942); *Battle of the Bulge* (1965); *The Best Years of Our Lives* (1946); *Bridge on the River Kwai* (1957); *A Bridge Too Far* (1977); *Charlotte Gray* (2001); *Comrade X* (1940); *Dark Blue World* (2001); *Das Boot* (1981); *Day After Trinity* (1980); *Destination Tokyo* (1943); *Enigma* (2001); *Fat Man and Little Boy* (1989); *Fighting Seabees* (1944); *Flying Tigers* (1942); *Foreign Correspondent* (1940); *The Longest Day* (1962); *The Memphis Belle* (1943); *Midway* (1976); *Mission to Moscow* (1943); *Mrs. Miniver* (1942); *Patton* (1970); *PT 109* (1963); *Ramparts We Watch* (1940); *Sands of Iwo Jima* (1949); *They Were Expendable* (1945).

SUGGESTED CLASSROOM FILMS

Adolf Hitler, Part I: The Rise to Power. 27 min. B/W. 1963. Contemporary Films. Newsreel footage tells the story of Hitler's rise.

Benito Mussolini. 26 min. B/W. 1978. Contemporary Films. A biographical account.

The End of the Old Order 1900–1929. 26 min. Color. 1985. Insight Media. A survey of political and social changes in both Europe and America.

Europe, the Mighty Continent: Form, Rifleman, Form! 52 min. Color. 1976. Time-Life Films. Growing desperation and militarism in Europe in the 1930s.

Expressionism. 26 min. Color. 1971. International Film Bureau. Explores German expressionism from its Dresden beginnings to the "Blue Rider" group in Munich.

Franklin D. Roosevelt: The New Deal. 26 min. B/W. 1973. McGraw-Hill. Uses documentary footage to relate the life of Roosevelt through his third term.

Hitler and Mussolini, 1937. 18 min. B/W. 1937. Obern. Nazi and fascist propaganda footage; no English subtitles.

The Life and Times of Bertrand Russell, Parts I and II. 50 min. B/W. 1967. BBC/Time-Life Films. Includes interviews with Russell as well as his contemporaries.

The Making of the German Nation, Part III: The Weimar Republic. 20 min. Color. n.d. Insight Media.

From the Versailles Treaty through Hitler's rise to power.

Memories of Berlin: Twilight of the Weimar Culture. 72 min. Color. 1977. Insight Media. A look at the intellectual and cultural ferment of interwar Berlin.

Minister of Hate: Goebbels. 25 min. B/W. 1959. McGraw-Hill. Interviews with historian H. R. Trevor-Roper and producer Fritz Lang on the Nazis' mastery of propaganda.

Part VIII: The West and the World

IDEAS FOR USING THE WESTERN CIVILIZATIONS DIGITAL HISTORY CENTER

The following Map Exercises and Digital History Features at *www.wwnorton.com/wciv* focus on post-1945 world of decolonization, the Cold War, and the collapse of the Soviet Union and Soviet-style communism in Europe.

- Map Exercise 19: The Cold War (Chapter 27)
- Map Exercise 20: After the Cold War (Chapters 27–29)
- Digital History Feature 8: Revolutionary Paris (Chapter 28)
- Digital History Feature 10: The Olympics—Past and Present (Chapters 27–29)
- Digital History Feature 11: The Cold War and Popular Culture (Chapters 27–28)
- Digital History Feature 12: War and Technology (Chapters 27–29)

Use Map Exercise 19 to help students understand how the geopolitical map of Europe and much of the world was rewritten by the outcome of World War II and the Cold War that followed. These exercises also emphasize the global struggles that the Cold War unleashed. Digital History Feature 12, "War and Technology," contains a discussion of the battle at Ia Drang in 1965, the first major confrontation between American forces and the People's Army of Vietnam. The global battle between American and Soviet ideologies in the post-1945 world is documented in Digital History Feature 12, "The Cold War." Use the "Revolutionary Paris" Digital History Feature to examine the events of May 1968, when university students and the people of Paris brought the city and the French government to a temporary standstill. Map Exercise 20 highlights the ways in which the great powers of Europe have lost portions of their empires over the past fifty years.

CHAPTER 27

The Cold War World: Global Politics, Economic Recovery, and Cultural Change

OUTLINE

I. Introduction
  A. Wasteland
    1. Europe as land of wreckage and confusion
    2. Refugees returned home
    3. Housing now scarce, food in short supply
  B. Trauma
    1. The brutality of war
    2. Civil war
    3. Liberation and betrayal
  C. Recovery
    1. Government authority
    2. Functioning bureaucracies
    3. Legitimate legal systems
    4. Memories
  D. The emergence of the superpowers and the Cold War
  E. Collapse of the European empires
II. The Cold War and a Divided Continent
  A. The Iron Curtain
    1. Teheran (1943) and Yalta (1945) Conferences
      a. Soviets argued they had a legitimate claim to eastern Europe
    2. Churchill, Stalin, and the percentages agreement (1944)
      a. Dividing eastern Europe into spheres of influence
    3. For the Soviets, eastern Europe was "a sphere and a shield"
  B. The Soviets and Eastern Europe
    1. The "people's republics"
      a. Sympathetic to Moscow
      b. One party took hold of key positions of power
    2. Churchill's "Iron Curtain" speech (Fulton, Missouri, 1946)
    3. Communist governments in Poland, Hungary, Romania, Bulgaria, and Czechoslovakia (1948)
    4. Yugoslavia
      a. Tito declared his government independent of Moscow in 1948
      b. Drew support from Serbs, Croats, and Muslims in Yugoslavia
      c. Expelled from Communist countries' economic and military pacts
    5. Soviet purges in the parties and administrations of satellite governments
      a. Began in the Balkans
      b. Extended through Czechoslovakia, East Germany, and Poland
      c. Renewed anti-Semitism
    6. Greece
      a. Local communist-led resistance
      b. British and United States determined to keep Greece in their sphere of influence
      c. Greece as touchstone for escalating American fear of Communist expansion
    7. The two Germanys
      a. Four occupied zones became two hostile states
      b. Berlin divided as well

c. Three Western allies created a single government for their territories in 1948
  i. Passed reforms to ease economic crisis
  ii. Introducd a new currency
d. Soviets retaliated with the Berlin Blockade (June 1948–May 1949)
  i. Cut all roads, trains, and river access from the western zone to West Berlin
e. The Berlin airlift
f. The Federal Republic (West Germany)
g. The German Democratic Republic (East Germany)

C. The Marshall Plan
1. U.S. response to Soviet expansion was massive economic and military aid
2. The Truman Doctrine (1947)
  a. Military assistance to anticommunists in Greece
  b. Tied the contest for political power to economics
3. The Marshall Plan (1948)
  a. $13 billion of aid for industrial development over four years
  b. Encouraged states to diagnose their own problems and develop solutions
  c. Founded on the idea of coordination between European countries
  d. The building block of future European economic unity
4. North Atlantic Treaty Organization (NATO, April 1949)
  a. United States, Canada, and representatives from Western European states
  b. Greece, Turkey, and West Germany added later
  c. Armed attack against one is an armed attack against all
  d. Eisenhower as senior military commander (1950)

D. Two worlds and the race for the bomb
1. Soviet response
  a. Council for Mutual Economic Assistance (COMECON)
  b. Communist Information Bureau (COMINFORM, 1947)
  c. Warsaw Pact (1955)
    i. Albania, Bulgaria, Czecho-slovakia, Hungary, Poland, Romania, East Germany

2. The nuclear arms race
  a. Soviets tested an atom bomb in 1949
  b. Soviets and United States both had the hydrogen bomb in 1953
    i. One thousand times more powerful than the Hiroshima explosion
  c. Intercontinental missiles and delivery systems
  d. Atomic-powered submarines
  e. The "nuclearization of warfare"
    i. Polarized the Cold War
    ii. Forced other countries to join United States or Soviets
    iii. Generated fears that local conflicts might trigger a general war
  f. The bomb as symbol of an age
    i. Science, technology, and progress
    ii. The threat of mass destruction
3. Was the Cold War inevitable?
  a. Stalin's ambitions fueled the Cold War
  b. United States feared Soviet expansion
    i. Unwilling to give up military, economic, and political power
  c. Trust was impossible
  d. A new balance of power
  e. George Kennan and the policy of containment
  f. Domestic intensification of the Cold War
    i. Anxiety
    ii. Air raid drills, spy trials, "the menacing other"

E. Khrushchev and the thaw
1. Death of Stalin (March 1953)
2. Nikita Khrushchev (1894–1971) came to power in 1956
  a. Agreed to summit with Britain, France, and the United States
3. The Secret Speech (1956)
  a. Denounced Stalinist excesses
  b. Allowed rehabilitation of some of Stalin's victims
  c. "Destalinization"
  d. The thaw (1956–1958)
    i. Camps released thousands of prisoners
    ii. The rehabilitation of relatives of those executed or imprisoned under Stalin

e. Cultural expression freed up

f. Aleksandr Solzhenitsyn

    i. *One Day in the Life of Ivan Denisovich* (1962)

    ii. *The First Circle* (1968)

    iii. *The Gulag Archipelago* (Paris, 1973)

    iv. Arrest and exile

F. Repression in Eastern Europe

  1. East German government faced economic crisis in 1953

    a. 58,000 East Germans left for the West

    b. Strikes and unrest

    c. Walter Ulbricht used fears of disorder to solidify one-party rule

  2. Poland

    a. Demands for more independence to manage their own economy (1956)

    b. Government responded with military repression and promises of liberalization

    c. Wladyslaw Gomulka pledged Poland's loyalty to the Warsaw Pact

  3. Hungary

    a. Imre Nagy: nationalist and communist

    b. Much broader anticommunist struggle

    c. Attempted to leave Warsaw Pact

    d. Soviet troops entered Budapest on November 4, 1956

    e. Hungarian citizens resorted to street fighting

    f. The Soviets installed Janos Kadar

      i. Staunch (Moscow) Communist

      ii. The repression continues

G. Khrushchev and "peaceful coexistence"

  1. NATO placed nuclear weapons in West Germany

  2. East Germans continued to flee (2.7 million between 1949 and 1961)

  3. Khrushchev demanded a permanent division of Germany with a free city of Berlin

  4. The Berlin Wall (1961)

III. Economic Renaissance

A. The "economic miracle"

  1. War provided technologies with practical and immediate applications

  2. Improved communications

  3. Manufacture of synthetic materials, aluminum, and alloy steels

  4. Advances in techniques of prefabrication

  5. High consumer demand and high levels of employment

B. The role of government

  1. The necessity of planning

  2. West Germany provided tax breaks to encourage business investment

  3. Britain and Italy offered investment allowances

  4. Broad experiments with the nationalization of industry and services

    a. "Mixed economies" providing public and private ownership

    b. France—electricity, gas, banking, radio, television, and auto industry are state-managed

    c. Britain—coal, utilities, road and rail transport, and banking are nationalized

  5. West Germany experienced unprecedented economic growth

    a. Production increased sixfold (1948–1964)

    b. Unemployment reached 0.4 percent (1965)

    c. New housing units built

    d. German demand for labor attracted foreign workers

  6. France

    a. Government played direct role in industrial reform

      i. Capital, expertise, shifts in national labor pool

    b. Priority to basic industries

  7. Italy

    a. heavy subsidies from Marshall Plan

    b. Olivetti, Fiat, and Pirelli became household names

    c. By 1954, real wages 50 percent higher than they had been in 1938

    d. Poverty continued to remain high in agrarian south

  8. Britain

    a. Harold Macmillan, "You've never had it so good" (1959)

    b. The economy remained sluggish

    c. Obsolete factories and methods

    d. Unwillingness to adopt new techniques

C. European economic integration

  1. European Coal and Steel Community (ECSC, 1951)

    a. Coal accounted for 82 percent of Europe's primary energy consumption

    b. Key to relations between West Germany and France

2. European Economic Community (EEC or Common Market)
    a. France, West Germany, Italy, Britain, Holland, and Luxembourg
    b. Abolition of trade barriers
    c. Committed to common external tariffs
    d. The free movement of labor
    e. A unified wage structure and social security systems
    f. The "Eurocrats"
    g. Britain
        i. Feared effects of ECSC on declining coal industry
        ii. Continued to rely on economic relations with the Empire and Commonwealth
    h. EEC became the world's largest exporter (1963)
        i. Total production 70 percent higher than it had been in 1950
3. Bretton Woods (July 1944)
    a. Aimed to coordinate movements of the global economy
    b. Created the International Monetary Fund (IMF) and the World Bank
    c. All currencies pegged to the dollar
D. Economic development in eastern Europe
    1. National income rose and output increased
    2. Poland and Hungary strengthened their economic connections with the West
    3. 30 percent of Eastern European trade done outside the Soviet bloc (1970s)
    4. COMECON compelled other members to trade with the Soviet Union
E. The welfare state
    1. Economic expansion promised more comprehensive social programs
    2. "Welfare state" coined by Clement Atlee (British Labour Party)
    3. Britain
        a. Free medical health care through the National Health Service
        b. Assistance to families
        c. Guaranteed secondary education
    4. Welfare relief as entitlement and not poor relief
    5. T. H. Marshall, social rights, and social democracy
F. European politics
    1. Pragmatism

2. Konrad Adenauer
    a. West German chancellor (1949–1963)
    b. Despised German militarism
    c. Remained apprehensive about German parliamentary government
3. General Charles de Gaulle and the Fifth French Republic
    a. Retired from politics in 1946
    b. Returned to office after Algerian War (1958)
    c. Insisted on a new constitution
    d. Strengthened executive branch of government
    e. France withdrew from NATO in 1966
    f. Cultivated better relations with Soviet Union
    g. Modern military establishment, with atomic weapons
IV. Revolution, Anticolonialism, and the Cold War
    A. The Third World
        1. Avoiding alignment with either superpower
    B. The Chinese Revolution (1949)
        1. Civil war since 1926
        2. Chiang Kai-shek (1887–1975)— nationalist
        3. Mao Zedong (1893–1976)—communist
        4. Nationalists and communists defeated Japan
            a. Mao refused to surrender northern provinces
        5. U.S. intervention
        6. The Revolution was the act of a nation of peasants
        7. Mao adapted Marxism to Chinese conditions
        8. The "fall of China" provoked fear in the West
        9. United States considered China and the Soviet Union to be a "communist bloc"
    C. The Korean War
        1. A Cold War hot spot
        2. Korea under Japanese control during World War II
        3. Post-1945: Soviets controlled north (Kim Jong II) and United States controlled south (Syngman Rhee)
        4. North Korean troops attacked across the border (June 1950)
        5. United States brought invasion to the attention of the UN Security Council

a. UN permitted an American-led "police action"
b. General Douglas MacArthur (1880–1964)
    i.. Former military governor of occupied Japan
    ii. Led amphibious assault behind North Korean lines
    iii. Wanted to press assault into China
    iv. Relieved of duty by Truman
c. Chinese troops supported North Koreans
6. Stalemate
7. The end of the Korean conflict (June 1953)
8. Korea remained divided
D. Decolonization
  1. The decline of older empires
  2. Nationalist movements and independence
E. The British Empire unravels
  1. India
    a. Post-1945: waves of Indian protest for Britain to quit India
    b. Mohandas K. Gandhi (1869–1948)
      i. Pioneered anticolonial ideas and tactics
      ii. Advocated *swaraj* (self-rule), nonviolence, and civil disobedience
    c. Jawaharlal Nehru (1889–1964)
      i. Led the pro-independence Congress Party
    d. Ethnic and religious conflict
      i. The Muslim League
    e. British India partitioned into India (majority Hindu) and Pakistan (majority Muslim)
      i. Brutal religious and ethnic warfare
    f. Gandhi assassinated in January 1948
    g. Nehru as prime minister of India (1947–1964)
      i. Program of industrialization and modernization
      ii. Steered a course of non-alignment with Soviet Union and United States
  2. Palestine
    a. Balfour Declaration (1917)
      i. Promised a "Jewish homeland" in Palestine for European Zionists

b. Rising conflict between Jewish settlers and Arabs (1930s)
c. British limited further immigration (1939)
d. A three-way war
    i. Palestinian Arabs—fighting for land and independence
    ii. Jewish settlers determined to defy British rule
    iii. British administrators with divided sympathies
e. United Nations partitioned territory into two states
f. Israel declared independence in May 1948
g. Palestinian Arabs clustered in refugee camps
    i. Gaza strip
    ii. West bank of the Jordan River
h. Israel recognized by United States and Soviet Union
3. Africa
    a. Several west African colonies moved toward independence
      i. Britain left constitutions and a legal system but no economic support
      ii. Ghana seen as model for African free nations (1960)
    b. More African colonies gained independence
      i. Could not redress losses from colonialism
    c. Mau Mau Rebellion (Kenya)
      i. Killing of civilians
      ii. British set up internment camps
    d. Britain tolerated apartheid in South Africa
      i. Required Africans to live in designated "homelands"
      ii. Forbade Africans to travel without permits
      iii. The management of labor
      iv. Banned political protest
    e. Rhodesia declared independence (1945)
4. Crisis in Suez and the end of an era
    a. Britain found the cost of maintaining naval and air bases too high
    b. Protected oil-rich states of the Middle East

c. Nationalists forced British to withdraw troops from Egypt within three years (1951)

d. King Farouk (1921–1965) deposed by nationalist officers and a republic is proclaimed (1952)

e. Gamal Abdel Nasser (1918–1970)
   i. Became Egyptian president
   ii. Nationalization of the Suez Canal Company
   iii. Financing the Aswan Dam
   iv. Pan-Arabism
   v. Willing to take aid and support from the Soviets

f. Israel, France, and Britain found pan-Arabism threatening

g. Egypt attacked by Israel, France, and Britain (1956)

h. United States inflicted financial penalties on Britain and France, forced to withdraw

F. French decolonization

1. The French Experience
   a. Decolonization was bloodier, more difficult, and more damaging to French prestige

2. The first Vietnam War, 1946–1954
   a. The French in Indochina—one of France's last imperial acquisitions
   b. Nationalist and communist independence movements
   c. Ho Chi Minh (1890–1969)
      i. Hoped for independence at Versailles (1919)
      ii. Marxist peasants organized around social, agrarian, and national issues
   d. Allies supported communist independence movement
   e. Vietnamese guerilla war against the French
   f. French pressed on for total victory
   g. French established a base at Dien Ben Phu (fell in May 1954)
      i. French began peace talks at Geneva
      ii. The Geneva Accords
   h. Indochina divided into four countries
      i. North Vietnam—taken over by Ho Chi Minh's party
      ii. South Vietnam—taken over by pro-Western politicians
   i. A virtual guarantee that war would continue

3. Algeria
   a. Since the 1830s, a settler state of three social groups
      i. One million Europeans (farmers, vintners, working class, small merchants)
      ii. Muslim Berbers (formal and informal privileges)
      iii. Muslim Arabs (largest and most deprived sector)
   b. Post-1945: Algerian nationalists called on the Allies to recognize their independence
   c. Public demonstrations
      i. Violence against settlers
      ii. French repression
   d. France granted limited enfranchisement
      i. Settlers and Berber Muslims
      ii. Arabs
   e. Arab activists form the National Liberation Front (FLN) in the mid-1950s
   f. Civil war on many fronts
      i. Guerilla war between regular French army and FLN
      ii. FLN terrorism in Algerian cities
      iii. Systematic torture by French security forces
   g. De Gaulle declared that Algeria would always be French
   h. Algeria declared its independence by referendum in 1962
   i. The war divided French society
      i. The identity of France

V. Postwar Culture and Thought

A. The black presence

1. *Présence Africaine* (published at Paris, 1947)
   a. Aimé Césaire (b. 1913) and Léopold Senghor (1906–2001)
   b. Both men were the exponents of "Negritude" (black consciousness)
   c. Assimilation was a failure
   d. Powerful indictments of colonialism

2. Frantz Fanon (1925–1961)
   a. Withdrawing into black culture was not an answer to racism
   b. A theory of radical social change
   c. *Black Skin, White Masks* (1952)
   d. *The Wretched of the Earth* (1961)

3. Pointed to the ironies of Europe's "civilizing mission"

4. The reevaluation of blackness

B. Existentialism
1. Jean-Paul Sartre (1905–1980) and Albert Camus (1913–1960)
   a. Individuality, commitment, and choice
2. "Existence precedes essence"
   a. Meaning in life is not given, it is created
   b. Individuals are condemned to be free
   c. "Bad faith"—denying one's freedom
3. Camus: *The Stranger* (1942), *The Plague* (1947), and *The Fall* (1956)
4. Existentialism and race
   a. Race derived meaning from lived experience
5. Simon de Beauvoir (1908–1986)
   a. *The Second Sex* (1949)
   b. "One is not born a woman, one becomes one"
   c. Asked why women dream the dreams of men?
   d. Marx, Freud, and the "woman question"
C. Memory and amnesia: the aftermath of war
1. Individual helplessness in the face of state power
   a. George Orwell (1903–1950)— *Animal Farm* (1946) and *Nineteen Eighty-Four* (1949)
   b. Samuel Beckett (1906–1989)— *Waiting for Godot* (1953)
   c. Harold Pinter (b. 1930)—*The Caretaker* (1960) and *Homecoming* (1965)
   d. J. R. R. Tolkien (1892–1973)— *The Lord of the Rings* (1954–1955)
2. The Frankfurt School
   a. Theodore Adorno (1903–1969) and Max Horkheimer (1895–1973)
      i. *Dialectic of Enlightenment* (1947)
      ii. Indictment of the "culture industry" for depoliticizing the masses
3. Hannah Arendt (1906–1975)
   a. Nazism and Stalinism should be understood as a form of totalitarianism
   b. *The Origins of Totalitarianism* (1951)
      i. Totalitarianism worked by mobilizing mass support
      ii. Used terror to crush resistance
      iii. The atomization of the public
      iv. Made collective resistance impossible
   c. *Eichmann in Jerusalem* (1963)
      i. Refused to demonize Nazism
      ii. Genocide as simply one more Nazi policy
4. Reaching a larger audience
   a. Jerzy Kosinski, *The Painted Bird* (1965)
   b. Czeslaw Milosz, *The Captive Mind* (1951)
   c. Günter Grass, *The Tin Drum* (1959)
   d. *The Diary of Anne Frank* (1947)
5. Repressing the past
   a. War crimes and trials
   b. Few executions led to cynicism
   c. Mythologizing the resistance movement
6. The Cold War and the burying and distortion of memory
VI. Conclusion
A. Fidel Castro
B. The Bay of Pigs (1961)
C. The Cuban Missile Crisis (1962)
1. *Dr. Strangelove* (1964)
D. Eisenhower and the military-industrial complex

GENERAL DISCUSSION QUESTIONS

1. Was the Cold War an ideological conflict or was it the result of misunderstandings, animosities, and differences of style rather than substance? During World War II, did anyone see that the gulf between the United States and the Soviet Union was great, and that their alliance against fascism was only temporary?

2. Differing ambitions and misperceptions certainly contributed to the Cold War, especially the partition of Germany and the division of Europe into opposing alliances. How did the four occupying powers relate to each other and to the Germans in 1949, during the Berlin airlift and the early years of NATO and the two republics?

3. After World War I, Germany was briefly visited by foreign troops and was forced to give up territory to its neighbors, pay reparations, and accept the war guilt clause. How different was the situation of Germany after World War II? When did the NATO allies decide that the "good Germans" could be trusted and allowed to rearm?

4. How did the Soviet Union's foreign policy in the 1950s and 1960s reflect its competition with the United States

and its concerns about the loyalty of Soviet allies in Europe? What signs of unrest were seen in East Germany, Poland, Hungary, Czechoslovakia, and Yugoslavia—and how did Soviets respond?

5. How did the West Germans achieve their economic recovery (*Wirtschaftwunder*)? What effects did their prosperity have on their neighbors and trading partners? How did it further the cause of European unity?

6. Novelists, philosophers, and poets throughout Europe have written about the legacy of the Second World War, among them Albert Camus, Jean-Paul Sartre, and Czeslaw Milosz. How much freedom does an individual have in a society overshadowed by the Cold War, occasional riots and shooting incidents, and ultimately a defective system? How can one create meaning in life through criticism and resistance?

DOCUMENT DISCUSSION QUESTIONS

The War That Refuses to Be Forgotten

1. What did Kovály mean when she remarked that World War II was "a war that no one had quite survived"? Can such an argument be made about all wars? What makes Kovály's argument so profound?

2. Although we are not survivors of Nazi concentration camps, we are, in a way, survivors of the Holocaust. Why does the Holocaust continue to matter to us today?

The Cold War: Soviet and American Views

3. Whom did Churchill blame for building the Iron Curtain between the Soviet sphere and the Western sphere? Was such a development perhaps inevitable, considering the sort of tensions that had clearly developed between the West and the Soviets?

4. Was the Soviet Union actively trying to create international communism? And the United States, was it too trying to spread the Western way of life on a global scale?

Mohandas Gandhi and Nonviolent Anticolonialism

5. Was Gandhi prepared to become a martyr to his cause? Can anyone use passive resistance and willingness to sacrifice to win support for an important cause?

6. What did Gandhi mean when he said that " it is contrary to our manhood if we obey laws repugnant to our conscience"? How might a man like Socrates have responded to such an argument?

The Vietnam War: American Analysis of the French Situation

7. Explain how the author of this CIA report has used George Kennan's policy of containment to describe the situation in Vietnam if the French military forces withdrew. Why was Southeast Asia such a hot spot in the decade following World War II?

8. Did the French or American military, just coming off a European theater of war, have any idea what it would be like to wage war in a place like Southeast Asia? Historically, what happens when a nation or nations fight war with a mentality and techniques inherited from the previous war?

SAMPLE LECTURE 27: THE UNITED STATES AND THE ORIGINS OF THE COLD WAR, 1945–1950

Lecture Objectives

1. To understand how wartime decisions affected postwar Europe

2. To highlight the origins of the Cold War in the immediate postwar world

POSTWAR TO COLD WAR

There are now two great nations in the world, which starting from different points, seem to be advancing toward the same goal: the Russians and the Anglo-Americans. . . . Each seems called by some secret design of Providence one day to hold in its hands the destinies of half the world. (Alexis de Tocqueville, *Democracy in America*, 1835)

The immediate cause of the Cold War was World War II itself. On July 25, 1945, two months after Germany had surrendered, Winston Churchill, Joseph Stalin and Harry Truman met at Potsdam in order to discuss the fate of Germany. Stalin was the veteran revolutionary. Truman had been President barely three months. The crucial issue at Potsdam, as it had been at Versailles after the Great War, was reparations. The Soviet Union wanted to rebuild their economy using German industry. The United States feared it would have to pay the whole cost of rebuilding Germany, which in turn would help rebuild the Soviet Union. So, after all the discussions had ended, a compromise was reached. Germany would be partitioned into four occupied zones. Britain, France, and the United States would occupy parts of western Germany while the Soviet Union would occupy eastern Germany. The main issue for the next two years was the control of Europe. Britain had had its chance; so too had France and Germany. Was it now the turn of the Soviet Union? Or perhaps the United States? The Soviets wanted Poland. Historically, Poland had always been the key state needed, geographically, to launch an attack against the Soviet Union. The United States upheld the principles of self-determination, principles declared in Woodrow Wilson's Fourteen Point Plan. For Wilson, nations should have the right to choose their own form of government. The Soviets viewed this demand as unacceptable, believing it indicated that the United States was taking too heavy a hand in determining what government a nation ought to adopt. Stalin went on to create what Winston Churchill dubbed the Iron Curtain. "From what I have seen of our Russian friends and allies during the war," Churchill cautioned, "I am convinced that there is nothing they admire so much as strength and nothing for which they have less respect than military weakness." By 1946, the United States and Britain were trying to unify Germany under Western rule. The Soviets responded by consolidating their grip on Europe by creating satellite states in 1946 and 1947. One by one, communist governments, loyal to Moscow, were set up in Poland, Hungary, Romania, and Bulgaria. The climax came in March 1948, when a communist coup in Czechoslovakia overthrew a democratic government and the Soviet Union gained a foothold in central Europe. Given the experience of World War II, this division of Europe was perhaps inevitable. Both sides wanted their values and economic and political systems to prevail in areas that their soldiers had helped to liberate.

The United States knew that the Soviet economy was in a state of near-collapse. The Soviet Union had lost at least 20 million souls during the war alone and millions more from Stalin's decade of purge trials. Thirty thousand factories and forty thousand miles of railroad tracks had been destroyed. All the industrialization that Stalin had promised and delivered to his people with the Five-Year Plans had been lost. Truman realized this and remained confident that the United States was in the stronger bargaining position. He surmised that the Soviets had to come to the United States for much-needed economic aid. In the spring of 1945, Congress agreed that they would not allow Lend-Lease for any postwar reconstruction in Russia. This was a major shift in policy, for under the Lend-Lease Act of 1941, the United States had shipped enormous quantities of war material to the Soviets, including 15,000 planes, 7,000 tanks, 52,000 jeeps, and 400,000 trucks.

THE BOMB

The new weapon used at Hiroshima and Nagasaki in early August presented a whole new category of problems. Even friendly nations would have had difficulty resolving their problems, but given the state of American and Soviet affairs in 1945, the situation was positively explosive. The Germans, with their V1 and V2 rockets, were far in advance of any Allied developments.

From the early 1930s onward, there was a steady exodus of Germany's greatest scientific minds. They came to Cambridge in England or to the United States. Albert Einstein, Max Planck, and Werner Heisenberg pioneered the new physics upon which nuclear fission rested. Hungarian Leo Szilard and Danish Niels Bohr worked on uranium fission in Germany before the war, but they left as well. In August 1939, Einstein wrote a letter to FDR urging him to start work on a new superweapon before the Germans developed one themselves. The Cavendish Laboratory at Cambridge became the most important British research center. It was at Cavendish that Ernest Rutherford first achieved atomic disintegration in 1919 and where James Chadwick identified the neutron in 1932. The first chain reaction uranium fission was achieved at the University of Chicago in 1942. A huge nuclear plant built at Oak Ridge, Tennessee, produced fissionable material in large quantities. Under the direction of J. Robert Oppenheimer, the actual weapons development took place at Los Alamos in New Mexico. During World War II, Roosevelt and Churchill followed a policy that would ensure a nuclear arms race at war's end. Still, Stalin found out about the Manhattan Project (begun August 1942) and by 1943 had already begun the development of a Soviet bomb. After the surrender of Japan, the United States developed a disarmament plan based on turning over all fissionable materials, plants, and bombs to an international regulatory agency. The Soviets responded quickly with their own plan: a total ban on the production of all fissionable material and the destruction of all existing bombs. The United States continued to stress regulation and inspection by an independent agency. But the Soviets, in the hopes of neutralizing any United States advantage, insisted on immediate disarmament. Eventually an agreement of sorts was reached: the two sides agreed to disagree.

CONTAINMENT

At the beginning of 1946, Truman decided that he was "tired of babysitting the Soviets who understand only an iron fist and strong language." Stalin responded in February with a speech stressing the basic incompatibility between Soviet Communism and Western democracy. A frustrated Washington found meaning in a crucial document known as the "Long Telegram." In 1946, the Soviet expert George Kennan—a foreign service officer who knew Russia well—sent an 8000-word telegram to Washington from Moscow. Kennan explained the communist mentality in the following way.

- The Soviet's hostility to the West is rooted in the need to legitimize their bloody dictatorship.
- They believed in the inevitable triumph of communism over the beast capitalism.
- The Soviets would exploit every opportunity to extend their system.
- The Soviets would not be converted to a policy of harmony and cooperation.

According to Kennan, the policy of the Soviet Union was "to undermine the general and strategic potential of major Western powers by a host of subversive measures to destroy individual governments that might stand in the Soviet path, to do everything possible to set the major Western powers against each other." But since the Soviets believed they had history on their side, the Communists were in no hurry and would not risk major war. Met with firmness, Kennan went on, the Soviets will back off. Eventually published as "The Sources of Soviet Conduct" in the journal *Foreign Affairs* and signed by "X," Kennan's observations gave Washington its own hard line. For the next three decades American foreign policy would be expressed by one word: containment.

THE UNITED STATES AND EUROPE

European communist parties were at a peak in the years immediately following World War II. The French Communist Party, for instance, won almost 30 percent of the vote in the November 1946 elections. In Greece, communist-led guerrillas from Yugoslavia, Bulgaria, and Albania, threatened the uninspired government of Greece. Greek communists attempted to seize power in late 1944, when their tactics of mass slaughter turned off a majority of Greeks. But the communists fought back, aided by Tito, and not Stalin. Civil war eventually broke out in Greece in 1946 amid economic crisis. By January 1947, the British informed the United States that they could no longer supply economic aid to Greece or Turkey. Believing that the Soviet Union was responsible for Britain's pullout, the United States decided that they had to assume the role of supplying aid. The Truman Doctrine (March 12, 1947) promised aid to Greece and Turkey in the context of a general war against communism. $400 million was approved by the House and Senate by a margin of three to one. The Truman Doctrine marked the formal declaration of the cold war between the United States and the Soviet Union and solidified the United States' position regarding containment. The Soviets accepted the Truman Doctrine's "two rival worlds" idea. It went along with the Marxist-Leninist notion of a world divided into two hostile camps. For Stalin, a final class struggle, determined by the laws of historical development, would mean certain Soviet victory. In May came the American decision to "reconstruct the two great workshops," Germany and Japan. And on June 5, Secretary of State George C. Marshall gave a speech at Harvard that hardened the United States' position toward the Soviets. Marshall proposed a scheme of extensive aid to all European nations if they could agree on how to revive a working economy, "so as to permit," he wrote, "the emergence of political and social conditions in which institutions can exist." Marshall included the Soviets in his plan, but at a meeting in Paris the following month, the Soviets gave their response to the Marshall Plan by walking out. Neither Russia nor its satellite states would take up the offer. Meanwhile, as the Marshall Plan pumped U.S. dollars into Europe, West German economic recovery began to trigger a general European recovery. The Soviets viewed this development as a capitalist plot to draw the nations of eastern Europe into the American

sphere of influence. 1947 was a crucial year in Cold War history.

- The forces of the free world, it seemed, were rallying to resist Soviet aggression.
- The defenses of the noncommunist world needed to be built up.
- The problem of European economic recovery would be met with massive assistance from the United States.
- Assistance grew to something like $20 billion before 1951.

THE NORTH ATLANTIC TREATY ORGANIZATION

Soviet containment was also played out in 1949 with the creation of NATO. The idea for something like NATO grew from general European fears of renewed Soviet aggression. Western Europe needed a guarantee from the United States that they would be protected from any aggression while they began the slow process of economic recovery. England, France, and the Benelux countries (Belgium, Netherlands and Luxembourg) formed the Western Union in March 1948. The main force behind the creation of NATO was not Truman but the British Foreign Secretary, Ernest Bevin. In January 1949, Truman called for an even broader pact which eventually would involve the United States, Canada, and ten European nations. The North Atlantic Treaty was signed on April 4, 1949. NATO was created:

- with the sole aim of protecting Europe from Soviet aggression
- "to safeguard the freedom, common heritage and civilization of their peoples founded on the principles of democracy, individual liberty, and the rule of law"
- on the idea that the United States would make a firm commitment to protect and defend Europe
- to uphold the principle that "an armed attack against one shall be considered an attack against all"

The United States would honor its commitment to defend Europe, and in 1950, Truman selected Dwight D. Eisenhower as the Supreme Commander of NATO forces. Four United States divisions were stationed in Europe to serve as the nucleus of NATO forces. The American public embraced NATO because it offered a way of participating in world affairs and opposing Soviet power in a more indirect way. Americans no longer believed that world security would come through the United Nations, but they still held on to the idea of collective security. The Atlantic nations were said to be held together by both common interests as well as a common commitment to democracy and industrial capitalism. For western Europe, NATO provided a much-needed shelter of security behind which economic recovery could take place. NATO was the political counterpart of the Marshall Plan. In the end, NATO meant that European affairs were now American affairs as well. There were problems with NATO right from the start.

- Neither Britain nor France provided much in the way of immediate military strength.
- France was too heavily committed overseas, especially in Indochina and Algeria.
- The British were in the midst of losing even more territories of their Empire.
- West German military presence in NATO was next to nothing.

The United States provided the entire muscle behind NATO in a clearly unequal partnership. But what eventually counted, at least in the context of the late 1940s and early 1950s, was not the ground forces under NATO control but the American "nuclear umbrella" acting as a deterrent against any Soviet temptation to attack. As it turned out, Eisenhower returned to Europe with tens of thousands of American GIs for the second time in a decade, this time to guard the enemy of World War II against one of America's former allies. While this buildup continued, NATO forces remained outnumbered by Russian ground forces. But what sustained Europe's spirit and perhaps deterred the Soviets was the assurance that such an attack would bring the United States, with is massive resources, into the war. The Western alliance embodied in NATO had the effect of escalating the Cold War. Historians are pretty much agreed—NATO was an overreaction of the Western world to perceived Soviet aggression. Hitler was on everybody's mind. But Stalin was not Hitler and the Soviets were not Nazis. All NATO really did was intensify Soviets fears of the West, which produced even higher levels of international tension.

THE NATIONAL SECURITY ACT

Following World War II, American leaders reformed the military forces. There were two main goals policy makers had in mind.

- In the aftermath of Pearl Harbor, the armed forces had to be unified into an integrated system.
- There was also a need for entirely new institutions to coordinate all military strategy.

In 1947, Congress solved both issues by creating the National Security Act. The act created the Department of Defense, which would serve as an organizing principle over all branches of the armed forces. The act also created the National Security Council, a special advisory board to the executive office. And lastly, it created the Central Intelligence Agency, or CIA, which was in charge of all intelligence.

In 1949, American military planners received a rather profound shock: the Soviets had just succeeded in exploding an atomic bomb of their own. The bomb was a fission bomb, created by the disintegration of plutonium 239 mixed with uranium 235. By this time, however, nuclear technology had advanced so far that this sort of bomb, like the one that leveled Hiroshima, was obsolete. In 1952, the United States detonated a 10.4 megaton bomb named "Mike" over the Enewetak Atoll, in the Marshall Islands (By the end of October 1958, the United States had conducted forty-two tests on Enewetak Atoll.) The Soviets announced the detonation of a similar thermonuclear device in August of the following year. This fusion bomb, the product of fusion at extreme temperatures of heavy isotopes of hydrogen, is many times more powerful than the A-bomb, and since it operates by chain reaction, the only limit to its size is determined by the size of the aircraft that carries it. The Hiroshima bomb, which killed more than 75,000 souls in fifteen minutes, was about 1/700th as large as a 100 megaton bomb. Because the H-bomb was manufactured from one of the most common elements, enough bombs could be readily produced to destroy the planet several times over. This was possibly the most dangerous period for nuclear war. The vast growth in the kinds and number of long-range nuclear weapons meant that neither the United States nor the Soviet Union could hope to escape the destruction of thermonuclear war. Of course, the massive numbers of nuclear warheads produced actually resulted in a stalemate. The world shuddered at the thought that the destiny of the globe was in the hands of two superpowers, yet the logic of the "balance of terror" worked right from the start. Total war was too dangerous. It would destroy everything. In the wake of all these developments, the United States needed a new national defense policy, and it came up with a policy document known as NSC-68. NSC-68 was based on two premises: first, that the Soviets were trying to impose absolute authority over the world, and second, that the United States had to face that challenge. What all this boiled down to was this: no more appeasement and no more isolation. Instead, upwards of 50 percent of the GNP of the United States was directed to defense spending. NSC-68 proposed increasing the defense budget from $13 billion to $45 billion annually. Approved in April 1950, NSC-68 stands as a symbol of America's determination to win the Cold War regardless of cost.

SUGGESTED FEATURE FILMS

The Bridges of Toko-ri. 102 min. Color. 1954. Paramount Pictures. Story of war-weary World War II veteran who must leave his family to fight again, this time in Korea.

Dr. Strangelove, or: How I Learned to Stop Worrying and Love the Bomb. 93 min. B/W. 1963. Stanley Kubrick's black comedy about human malfunction and the paranoia and megalomania of the cold warrior.

Fail-Safe. 112 min. B/W. 1964. Columbia Pictures. Sidney Lumet's film about a computer malfunction that sends American *B-52*s toward Moscow.

High Noon. 85 min. B/W. 1952. United Artists. Anti-McCarthyist allegory or celebration of the lone marshal who must stand up to a tyrant and the cowardice of a town.

The Invasion of the Body Snatchers. 80 min. B/W. 1956. Allied Artists Pictures. Don Siegel's science-fiction classic about an alien threat that dehumanizes people by enslaving them to a group-mind. The Communist threat of indoctrination is too powerful to overlook in this Cold War–era film.

The Manchurian Candidate. 126 min. B/W. 1962. United Artists. Remarkable film directed by John Frankenheimer about U.S. soldiers captured in Korea who are taken to Manchuria and brainwashed to assassinate an American politician.

My Son John. 122 min. B/W. 1952. Paramount Pictures. Subversion is everywhere in this film about a son who turns to communism and destroys his life.

On the Beach. 135 min. B/W. 1959. United Artists. Radioactive fallout has destroyed the northern hemisphere with the exception of Australia. With fallout only a month away, everyone reviews their lives and prepares for the end in this Stanley Kramer *tour de force*.

Seven Days in May. 118 min. B/W. 1964. Paramount Pictures. John Frankenheimer film about disgruntled leaders of the military establishment who plan a coup to overthrow the government and wage the Cold War in the right way.

The Spy Who Came in From the Cold. 112 min. B/W. 1965. Paramount Pictures. Alec Leamas, a disillusioned British spy is sent to East Germany supposedly to defect, but in fact to create disinformation. Based on the novel by John le Carre.

SUGGESTED CLASSROOM FILMS

Atomic Cafe. 92 min. Color and B/W. The Archives Project. Documentary that compiles films about the 1960s and what to do in case of a nuclear attack.

Brave New World: The Cold War Begins. 60 min. Color. 1998. WGBH Boston Video. The major events of the Cold War are covered in this video, and interviews with participants and archival footage show the real dangers of the times.

The Cold War. 51 min. Color. 1995. Films for the Humanities and Social Sciences. Part of the "Great American Speeches" series. Includes the "Kitchen Debate" between Nixon and Khrushchev, the "Checkers" speech, and the Army-McCarthy hearings.

The Cold War. Color and B/W. 1998. CNN/Turner Home Video. Eight volumes cover the fifty-year history of the Cold War.

Korea: The Forgotten War. 300 min. Color and B/W. 1987. Seven-volume series of archival footage documenting the military and diplomatic history of American efforts to contain Soviet communism in Korea.

Point of Order. 91 min. B/W. 1964. Point Films. Television footage of the 1954 Army-McCarthy hearings, in which the Army accused Senator McCarthy of improperly pressuring the Army for special privileges for Private David Schine, resulting in McCarthy's eventual censure for conduct unbecoming a senator.

CHAPTER 28

Red Flags and Velvet Revolutions: The End of the Cold War, 1960–1990

D. Mass culture
1. Music and youth culture
   a. New spending habits
   b. The prolongation of adolescence
   c. Music as the cultural expression of the new generation of youth (1950s)
   d. Radio and magazines
   e. Technological changes
      i. Record players
      ii. Music as the soundtrack of everyday life
   f. Rock and roll
      i. Rockabilly
      ii. British invasion
      iii. Beatles
      iv. Woodstock (1969)
E. Art and painting
1. The art market boomed
   a. New York as center of modern art
   b. Immigration of European artists
2. Abstract expressionists
   a. William De Kooning (1904–1997)
   b. Mark Rothko (1903–1970)
   c. Franz Kline (1910–1962)
   d. Jackson Pollock (1912–1956)
   e. Helen Frankenthaler (b. 1928)
   f. Robert Motherwell (1915–1991)
3. Abstract expressionists experimented with color, texture, and technique
   a. The physical act of painting (Pollock)
   b. "Action painting"
4. Pop art
   a. Did not distinguish between the artistic and the commercial
   b. Borrowed from graphic design
   c. The everyday visual experience
   d. Jasper Johns (b. 1930)
   e. Andy Warhol (1928–1987)
   f. Roy Lichtenstein (1923–1997)
F. Film
1. Italian neorealists
   a. Capturing "life as it was lived"
   b. Loneliness, war, and corruption
   c. Shot on location
   d. Nonlinear plots, unpredictable characters
   e. Robert Rossellini, *Open City* (1945)
   f. Vittorio de Sica, *The Bicycle Thief* (1948)
   g. Frederico Fellini, *La Dolce Vita* (1959) and *8 1/2* (1963)
2. French New Wave
   a. Unsentimental, naturalistic, and enigmatic social vision

b. Francois Truffaut (b. 1932)
   i. *400 Blows* (1959), *The Wild Child* (1969)
c. Jean-Luc Godard (b. 1930)
   i. *Breathless* (1959), *Contempt* (1963)
d. Raised the status of the director
   i. The real art was in the director's hands, not the script
e. Cannes Film Festival
G. Hollywood and the Americanization of culture
1. By the 1950s, Hollywood was making five hundred films a year
2. Innovations
   a. Conversion to color
   b. Widescreen
3. House Un-American Activities Committee (HUAC)
   a. Hunting communist sympathizers
4. Breakdown of American censorship
5. Television
   a. Marketing and advertising
6. *Rebel Without a Cause* (1955)
7. Exporting American values
   a. Anticommunism
   b. Rebellious teenagers
   c. America as an idea
H. Gender roles and sexual revolution
1. Less censorship and fewer taboos
2. Kinsey reports (1949 and 1955)
   a. Made sexuality and morality front page news
3. Was the family crumbling?
   a. The focus of government attention
   b. Higher expectations in marriage
   c. Paid more attention to children
   d. The erosion of paternal authority
4. The centrality of sex and eroticism
   a. Magazines and sexiness
   b. Health and personal hygiene
   c. Sexuality as self-expression
5. Contraception
   a. First approved for development in 1959
   b. Simple and could be used by women themselves
   c. Western countries legalized contraception (1960s) and abortion (1970s)
   d. Soviet Union legalized abortion in 1950
6. Feminism
   a. Family, work, and sexuality

    b. Women in the workplace
        i. Few jobs outside secretarial jobs
        ii. Received lower pay for equal work
        iii. Had to rely on husbands to establish credit
    c. Self-expression and narrowing horizons
    d. Betty Friedan, *The Feminine Mystique* (1963)
        i. Exploding cultural myths
        ii. The media shaped (lowered) women's expectations
        iii. Founded National Organization of Women in 1966

III. Social Movements During the 1960s
  A. International social unrest
  B. The civil rights movement in the United States
    1. African American migration from the south to northern cities
    2. Rights, dignity, and independence
    3. National Association for the Advancement of Colored Peoples (NAACP, founded 1909)
    4. National Urban League (founded 1910)
    5. Congress of Racial Equality (CORE, founded 1942)
      a. Boycotts and demonstrations directed against discrimination
    6. Martin Luther King, Jr. (1929–1968)
      a. A philosophy of nonviolence and civil disobedience
    7. Malcolm X (1925–1965)
      a. Black nationalism
      b. Spokesman for Black Muslim movement
    8. Civil rights legislation (1964)
      a. Some measure of equality in voting rights and school desegregation
      b. White racism continued in housing and job opportunities
  C. The antiwar movement
    1. John F. Kennedy (1917–1963)
      a. Fight communism
      b. Free markets and representative governments for developing nations
      c. The Peace Corps
    2. South Vietnam
    3. Escalation of the war under Lyndon Johnson
    4. Stalemate
    5. Magnified problems at home
    6. Student protest and violence

  D. The student movement
    1. Protest movements had roots in postwar changes in education
      a. France: 400,000 high school students in 1949, two million by 1969
      b. Similar numbers in Italy, Britain, and West Germany
      c. Lecture halls overwhelmed with students
      d. The university as "knowledge factory"
  E. 1968
    1. The collective identity of youth
    2. Points of contention
      a. The consumer culture
      b. Vietnam
      c. Cold bureaucracy
      d. The human cost of the Cold War
      e. The military-industrial complex
    3. Paris
      a. University of Paris
      b. Students demanded reforms that would modernize the university
      c. Authorities closed down the university
      d. Students took to the streets
      e. Parisians and workers sided with the students
      f. Police repression and violence
      g. Trade unions went on strike in support
      h. A weakened Charles de Gaulle
    4. Elsewhere
      a. Student protests in Germany, Italy, England, and Mexico
      b. 1968 Olympics
      c. The Tet Offensive
      d. Assassinations of Martin Luther King, Jr. and Robert F. Kennedy
      e. Democratic National Convention (Chicago)
    5. Prague Spring
      a. Alexander Dubcek (1921–1992)
        i. "Socialism with a human face"
        ii. Encouraged debate within the party, artistic freedom, and less censorship
        iii. Protest overflowed traditional party politics
      b. Leonid Brezhnev (1906–1992)
        i. More conservative than Khrushchev

ii. Less inclined to bargain with
the West
iii. Protecting the Soviet sphere
of influence
c. Prague Spring seen as directed
against Warsaw Pact and Soviet
security
d. Soviets sent tanks into Prague in
August 1968
e. The Brezhnev doctrine
i. No socialist state to adopt
policies endangering the
interests of international
socialism
ii. Soviets could intervene
if Communist rule was
threatened
6. Effects of 1968
a. De Gaulle's government recovered
b. Nixon won U.S. election
c. United States withdrew from
Vietnam (1972–1975)
d. Brezhnev doctrine
e. Eastern European and Soviet dissent
defeated but not eliminated
f. Second-wave feminism
i. "The personal is political"
g. Environmental movement
h. Voters' loyalties to traditional
parties became less reliable
IV. Economic Stagnation: The Price of Success
A. Roots of the problem
1. West Germany
a. Slowing economic growth
b. Demand for manufactured goods
declined
2. France
a. Persistent housing shortage
b. Increased cost of living
3. Britain
a. Introduction of new technology
b. Crisis in the foreign-exchange
value of the pound
c. Continued low levels of growth
4. Common Market problems
B. Oil
1. OPEC countries instituted oil embargo
against Western powers in 1973
2. Inflationary spiral
a. Interest rates rose along with prices
b. Rising costs produced demands
for higher wages
3. Europe faced stiff competition from
Japan, Asia, and Africa

C. Soviet Union
1. Sluggish economic growth despite
promises of high production
2. Eastern Europe shackled by high debt
3. Poland: cut back on production for
domestic consumption
D. The turn to the right
1. Britain under Margaret Thatcher
(b. 1925)
a. Curbing trade union power
b. Cutting taxes to stimulate the
economy
c. Privatizing publicly owned
companies
d. The economy remained weak
E. European Economic Community (now the
Economic Union, EU)
1. Program of integration
a. Monetary union with a central
European bank
b. Single currency
c. Unified social policies
F. Polish Solidarity (1980)
1. Worker's demands
a. Improved working conditions
b. Lower prices
c. Independent labor unions
2. Gdansk shipyards and Lech Walesa
(b. 1943)
V. Europe Recast: The Collapse of Communism and
the End of the Soviet Union
A. The beginning of the end
1. Mikhail Gorbachev (b. 1931) assumed
leadership of Communist Party in 1985
a. Critical of repressive aspects of
communism and the sluggish
economy
b. *Glasnost* (intellectual candor)
and *perestroika* (economic
restructuring)
c. Called for the shift from a centrally
planned economy to a mixed
economy
d. Freed a number of Soviet dissidents
e. Revoked Brezhnev doctrine
2. Gorbachev and perestroika
a. Competitive elections to official
positions and term limits
b. Shift to a mixed economy
c. Integrating the Soviet Union into
the international economy
3. Too little, too late
a. Ethnic unrest
b. Secession movements

B. Eastern Europe after Gorbachev
  1. Poland—Solidarity launched new wave of strikes in 1988
  2. Hungary—new reform government under the Hungarian Socialist Workers' Party
     a. Purged of Communist members in 1989
  3. Czechoslovakia
     a. Demonstrations against Soviet domination
     b. The Civic Forum—opposition coalition
        i. Free elections
        ii. Mass demonstrations
        iii. Threats of a general strike
     c. Václav Havel (b. 1936) elected president
  4. East Germany
     a. Severe economic stagnation and environmental degradation
     b. Massive illegal emigration of East Germans to the West
     c. November 4, 1989: East Germany opened its border with Czechoslovakia
     d. November 9, 1989: The Berlin wall was breached
  5. A united Germany (October 3, 1990)
C. The velvet revolution
  1. Romania under Nicolae Ceauşescu (1918–1989)
  2. Single-party governments collapsed
     a. Albania, Bulgaria, and Yugoslavia claimed independence from Moscow
     b. Lithuania and Latvia proclaimed their independence in 1991
D. The Soviet Union
  1. The failure of perestroika
  2. The rise of Boris Yeltsin (b. 1931)
     a. Elected president of the Russian Federation
     b. Anti-Gorbachev platform
  3. Mounting protests against slow change (1991)
  4. Hardline Communists planned a coup against Gorbachev (August 1991)
     a. Gorbachev incarcerated
  5. The Soviet Union ceased to exist on December 8, 1991
  6. Gorbachev resigned on December 25, 1991
E. After the fall of the Soviet Union
  1. Food shortages and the falling value of the ruble
  2. Free enterprise brought crime, corruption, the black market, and a lower standard of living
  3. Yeltsin dissolved parliament in September 1993
  4. The attempted conservative coup
  5. Communist resurgence and the nationalists
  6. Ethnic and religious conflict
     a. Chechnya (1994)
        i. Guerilla warfare and atrocities
  7. The end of the Cold War
     a. Ethnic conflict
     b. Diplomatic uncertainty about the new Russian government
     c. The Russian "Wild West"
VI. Postrevolutionary Troubles: Eastern Europe after 1989
  A. The Velvet Revolution: the dream
     1. Raised hopes
     2. Economic prosperity and pluralism
     3. Joining the West as capitalist partners
  B. The Velvet Revolution: the reality
     1. Uncertainty after German unification
     2. Difficult to maintain economic and cultural unity
     3. Free market brought inflation, unemployment, and protest
     4. Minorities waged campaigns for autonomous rights
     5. Continued racial and ethnic conflicts
  C. The "velvet divorce"
     1. Slovakia declared its independence from the Czechs
        a. Havel resigned
  D. Yugoslavia
     1. Federalist structure began to unravel after Tito's death (1980)
     2. Uneven economic growth benefited Belgrade, Croatia, and Slovenia
        a. Serbia, Bosnia-Herzegovina, and Kosovo lagged behind
     3. Slobodan Milosevic (b. 1941)—Serb nationalist
     4. Croatia
        a. Declared its independence from Yugoslavia as a free, capitalist state
     5. Catholic Croats v. Orthodox Serbs
     6. Bosnia-Herzegovina
        a. Ethnically diverse population
        b. Sarajevo home to several ethnic groups
        c. Bosnia attempted to secede from Yugoslavia in 1992
        d. Ethnic cleansing

> e. UN intervention
> f. American air strikes (fall 1995)
> > i. Forced Bosnian Serbs to negotiate
> g. The Dayton Accords
> > i. Bosnia divided
> > ii. Majority of land went to Muslims and Croats
> h. Three years of war meant 200,000 dead

7. Kosovo
   a. Homeland of Christian Serbs, now occupied by Albanian Muslims
   b. Terrorist tactics
   c. Talks between Milosevic and Albanian rebels fell apart in 1999
   d. American-led bombing against Serbia and Serbian forces in Kosovo
   e. More ethnic cleansing

8. The fall of Yugoslavia (2000)

VII. Conclusion

GENERAL DISCUSSION QUESTIONS

1. In the 1950s there appeared a new style of drama that seemed almost tailor-made for the twentieth century— the Theater of the Absurd. One of its leading practitioners was the Irish writer, Samuel Beckett. In 1952 Beckett wrote *Waiting for Godot*, a drama in which there is no action and no meaning. What social forces may have created this heightened attention to meaninglessness and absurdity?

2. One of the most provocative books of the 1960s was *One-Dimensional Man* (1964). In this book, the philosopher Herbert Marcuse presented a chilling social theory of repression, domination, and what he called the "irrationality of rationality." What did the generation of students weaned on the 1960s hope to get out of Marcuse?

3. On August 20, 1968, 500,000 Warsaw Pact troops invaded Czechoslovakia in order to stop a reform movement known as the Prague Spring. Alexander Dubcek's attempt to create "socialism with a human face" was no match for Soviet tanks. What effect did the Prague Spring and Soviet invasion of Czechoslovakia have in the West?

4. Do changes in the standard of living not only transform everyday life but also affect cultural and political attitudes? Is the nature of work likely to remain the same if new technologies are adopted? If people can afford televisions and computers, will they necessarily spend less time reading newspapers and listening to the radio?

5. How much credit should Mikhail Gorbachev receive for ending the Cold War? Why were his actions so significant? On the other hand, in what ways did perestroika result in both success and failure for Gorbachev?

6. Since its erection in August 1961, the Berlin wall stood as a testimony to the ideological divide between East and West. On November 9, 1989, the wall was breached and East Germans flooded into West Berlin for the first time. What was the major catalyst for the destruction of the wall? Why are the events of 1989 often referred to as the "velvet revolution"? What is the legacy of the Berlin wall?

7. On November 21, 1995, three Bosnian leaders signed a peace agreement known as the Dayton Accords, the purpose of which was to bring an end to four years of terror and killing in Yugoslavia. Why had Yugoslavia become fertile grounds for conflict and war? What did the Accords establish? Was the crisis in Yugoslavia something new or renewed?

8. There is little doubt that the United States exports ideological values along with automobiles and Big Macs. What have been the successes and failures in the Americanization of the world?

DOCUMENT DISCUSSION QUESTIONS

The "Woman Question" on Both Sides of the Atlantic

1. Analyze Beauvoir's feminist text in terms of the "clear and distinct" reasoning of Descartes. How does her rational approach affect her argument and its reception?

2. Beauvoir is certain that "a man would never get the notion of writing a book" on the male situation. How has the world changed since 1949, so that books on maleness as well as femaleness have become commonplace?

3. How does Friedan use historical evidence to support her claim that the image of women in American culture changed between 1939 and 1949? Does she make a convincing case that the position of women worsened, especially after the war?

4. Does Friedan deny the possibility of happy housewife-mothers? Or is her concern that every woman will be forced to accept this new image? In what ways has the history of the feminist movement since 1963 made this less or more so?

60s Politics: The Situationists

5. Why did students at elite universities in the 1960s suddenly attack their society with posters, graffiti, and protests, many of which were violent in nature? Did they have a program of action? Were they willing to take over university administration or the government?

6. Why has 1968 often been called "the Year of the Barricades"?

7. Why do you think the working classes of Paris joined together with students in the protests of May 1968? Why did such a joining never occur in the United States? How were the aims of American students so at variance with those of the working class?

8. Are there similarities to be noted between the revolutions of 1848 and the student protests of 1968? What were the end results of both movements?

Ludvik Vaculik, "Two Thousand Words"

9. Does it sound as if Vaculik wanted to believe in socialism? Why were popular hopes for progress subordinate to the rulers' whims? Why were dissident opinions censored? Who was blamed when things went wrong?

10. According to Vaculik's manifesto for action, how can society and government be changed? What techniques or methods were at his disposal? What techniques or methods are available today?

SAMPLE LECTURE 28:
1968 AND 1989: BARRICADES AND WALLS

Lecture Objectives

1. To suggest the origins of the student protest movements of 1968

2. To highlight the origins and significance of the "year of the barricades"

3. To outline the collapse of Soviet-style communism

THE POSTWAR WORLD

The 1950s, thanks in large part to the role played by the United States, became an era of affluence and plenty. Germany recovered so quickly that today historians refer to its rebound as the "German economic miracle." The status quo of Europe and America seemed restored if not actually rejuvenated. Hitler and the Nazis had been defeated and the policy of mutually assured destruction (MAD) kept the Americans and Soviets from initiating a thermonuclear war. The armed forces returning to their homes wanted to put the war behind them and get their lives back to normal. The children of this generation, especially as they became university students, remained basically quiet. This calm was deceptive—it was the calm before the storm. The 1950s, whether we look to Europe or the United States, was characterized by consensus—there was little need to see the world continually engaged in battle. And these quiet times were good for morale. The generation that had fought in World War II had to get back on their feet. And so, Germany, France, and England were rebuilt. Material wealth seemed to be increasing for most middle-class members of American and European society. Technology had created an automatic society, and unemployment became less of an issue. But suddenly, in 1967 and 1968, a wave of student protest movements broke out across Europe, Japan, and the United States. As it turned out, 1968, often dubbed the "year of the barricades," became one of the most turbulent years in Western history since World War II.

1968: OLD LEFT AND NEW LEFT

In 1968, the entire postwar order was challenged by a series of insurrections from Berkeley to London, from New York to Prague. Oddly enough, the challenge was not successful, at least not in the period in which it actually took place. 1968 was a year of revolution. That's the year that Grace Slick and the Jefferson Airplane sang, "Now it's time for you and me to have a revolution" on their album *Volunteers*. In a period of unprecedented material prosperity and cultural activity, the sons and daughters of the most privileged sections of the United States and Europe decided to make their own revolution. 1968 was, among many other things, a moral revolt—it was a revolt of passion in the interests of humanity. This revolt was generated by what they, the New Left, perceived to be their alienation from dominant social values, from the values of the power elites, the Establishment." Alienation is the key word here. The Old Left did not understand alienation.

- They recognized only exploitation, the exploitation of the working classes.
- The Old Left had strong Marxist and socialist roots.
- Many also had strong Leninist and, in some cases, Stalinist, roots as well.
- The Old Left exhibited a passionate desire to end the exploitation of one social class by another.
- But they were no longer willing to change the social order entirely.

The New Left believed the Old Left had run out of steam. To use the lingo of the 1960s, the Old Left had copped out, sold out to the Establishment. So the Old Left, rather than act as a direct stimulus to social change, had by the 1960s become an obstacle to such change. The New Left was indeed new.

- They believed in spontaneity and action.
- They distrusted the system.

- They hated the corporate world.
- The New Left were almost existentialist by nature.
- They wanted to unite humanity.
- Alienation was their motto.
- They were revolutionary rather than reformist.

In the vanguard of the year of the barricades were college students. But what were these students rebelling against? Why had the typically quiet 1950s suddenly burst forth with the student protest movements of the 1960s? What were they protesting?

- representative democracy
- big business
- capitalist technocracy and the rule by experts
- the Vietnam War
- the effects of a media-manipulated society
- all authority

What had all of these things produced? Was the world a better place in which to live? Or was something dreadfully wrong? The year of the barricades served as a symbol of everything an entire generation of young people detested about their parents' generation. They hated the late-twentieth-century hypocrisy of material, bourgeois, liberal, consumerist, Western society. They hated their parents for consuming it. They hated their universities for teaching it. They hated their governments for murdering for it. These students wanted their voices heard—they were not content to let their hearts and minds be controlled. The real danger was not the class struggle, as it had been for their parents. The real danger came from the establishment of consensus that their parents accepted. So these students marched, demonstrated and occupied administration buildings across Europe and the United States.

"The Whole World is Watching"

Who were these students? Were they courageous visionaries or romantic utopians? Were they genuine revolutionaries whose battles cries were "make love, not war," "the whole world is watching," and "never trust anyone over 30"? Or were they nothing more than spoiled brats who, with their ids denied, simply stamped their feet in unison as some sort of collective tantrum? Was 1968 a genuine challenge to authority in the pattern of 1789 or 1848 or 1917? Or was it nothing more than clever rhetoric designed for immediate hedonistic consumption? Who were these kids? A bunch of white middle-class American and European kids—kids who had little knowledge of poverty, deprivation, the Depression, unemployment, or World War II. They were, collectively, a cross-section of Western society that had missed the major events of the 1930s and 1940s: Stalin, Hitler, the Depression, fascism, and World War II. They were a generation for whom history had literally begun in 1960. The psychologists of the late 1960s attributed the student protest movement to something that Eric Erikson had called an identity crisis. Most kids were trying to find themselves; they were trying to create a unique

identity for themselves and others like themselves. The only way they could do this was to rebel against everything that mainstream Western society had deemed holy.

The most important factor for the students of either Europe or America was the Vietnam War. Worse than a blunder, it was a crime. Kennedy, Johnson, and, afer 1968, Nixon were to share near-total responsibility for this war. While young men burned their draft cards on the steps of their local Selective Service office, crowds chanted, "Hell no, we won't go," or "Hey, hey, LBJ, how many kids did you kill today?" The governments of Europe were to blame as well—after all, Vietnam was a French problem before it became an American problem inherited by the United States. The cold warrior mentality viewed Southeast Asia as a breeding ground for international communist aggression. 1968 was a year of violence. And the violence of the Vietnam War was echoed in the violence that emerged in Europe and America.

- Bobby Kennedy and Martin Luther King, Jr. were assassinated.
- The Democratic National Convention in Chicago erupted in violence between protestors and the police.
- The My Lai Massacre occurred in Vietnam.
- The French government was temporarily paralyzed by the most severe social protest movement since the days of the Paris Commune in 1871.
- Administration buildings at the London School of Economics were occupied by protesting students.
- Soviet tanks rolled into Prague, an event known as the Prague Spring.
- In Central Park in New York City, a 92-year-old woman, a Quaker, set herself on fire in protest of the war in Vietnam.
- There were thirty-eight arson attacks in Detroit, shootings in Pittsburgh, a four-hour gun battle at Tennessee State University, and riots in Trenton, New Jersey.
- Viet Cong opened the Tet Offensive by attacking major cities of South Vietnam.

What was wrong? Why all this violence and protest? Why did it appear to European and American youth that revolution was the only way out? During the 1950s and into the 1960s, the United States witnessed an era of conformity, prosperity, affluence, and material plenty. Television fashioned a new generation of media-manipulated consumers as the governments of Europe and America became the "State," a Leviathan—monster whose power was without limit. The universities, whether in New York, California, London, Prague, Berlin, Rome, or Paris became knowledge factories and independent critical thought suffered a profound yet temporary setback. "These are your courses! Take them and obey!" Why else would so many administration buildings be occupied across Europe and the United States?

The Soviet Union After Stalin

For the Soviet Union, World War II was yet another cruel landmark. After 1945, many returning soldiers hoped for a relaxation of Stalin terror. After all, they had helped to defeat Hitler and the Nazis during the Great Patriotic War. It was not to be. Stalin became even more ruthless and after the war he found no reason to relax his control. Wherever he looked, he saw problems that demanded his control. The government, the Party, the army, the economy, and communist ideology were all on the verge of collapse. Stalin's answer was more Five-Year Plans, and with their return came the tightening of ideological control. The target was Western influence upon Soviet society. Thousands of soldiers who had seen too much of the West during World War II were sent to the Gulag and the intelligentsia were terrorized by the KGB. Before he died, Stalin believed that his doctors had conspired against him, and so they were all tortured and one of them died as a result. When he died of a stroke on March 5, 1953, his assistants were relieved. Yet many people wept. What shape would the Soviet Union now take, now that its dictator was dead? Leadership was assumed by a team headed by Nikita Khrushchev, who became the Premier of the Soviet Union until 1964. It was Khrushchev who introduced the first Soviet "thaw." Most of the gulags were emptied and ethnic groups that had been resettled under Stalin were gradually allowed to return to their homeland. In his speech at the twentieth Party Congress in February 1956, Khrushchev denounced Stalin and the crimes Stalin had committed against his own people. Without criticizing Soviet communism, Khrushchev managed to reject the excesses of Joseph Stalin. Khrushchev's speech caused a profound stir around the world. Card-carrying Communists defected from the Party in large numbers. Meanwhile, in Eastern Europe, 1956 found Poland on the brink of rebellion. In that same year, a Hungarian uprising against Moscow might have succeeded had not the Soviets sent in their tanks. In foreign policy, Khrushchev proposed peace but threatened the West by blocking Western access to Berlin and by placing missiles in Cuba. He also gave Russia a new Party program and pressed for reforms in industry, agriculture, and party organization. In October 1964, the Politburo comrades removed him from power. The international press reported that Khrushchev had been replaced for reasons of ill-health.

THE SOVIET UNION IN THE 1970S AND 1980S

Khrushchev was replaced by Leonid Brezhnev, an elderly man who required massive doses of stimulants in order to appear active. Under Brezhnev, the Soviet government turned from personal dictatorship to oligarchy. A new class had been born in a supposedly classless society. In the 1970s, U.S.-Soviet relations entered a period of détente, or peaceful coexistence. The Soviets achieved parity in atomic weapons with the United States. Slowly, the country was opened up to the outside world: young people were allowed access to Western music and fashion, issues were open to debate, and there was some artistic freedom as well as a revival of religious belief and practice. For Russian intellectuals who criticized the state, however, the story was much different. By the 1980s, political life was suffocating and the political system had ossified. Marxist-Leninist ideology had long since turned into what one Soviet official called "stale bread." The condition of the leadership was a metaphor for a system that was itself dying. Brezhnev, Andropov, and Chernenko all died between 1982 and 1985.

GORBACHEV: "A MAN WITH WHOM WE CAN DO BUSINESS"

Mikhail Gorbachev took over in 1985. He had good health and relative youth on his side. At fifty-four years old, Gorbachev represented a generation that had begun their political and party careers after 1953. Self-confident and energetic, Gorbachev talked freely to people from all walks of life. The Soviets had to catch up to the rising prosperity and high technology of the Europe and North America. The Soviet Union had to concentrate on domestic development and promote international peace. However, it could only accomplish such a goal by giving up any global ambitions. So Gorbachev abandoned the traditional Soviet anti-western orientation. He wanted to integrate the Soviet Union into the main currents of modern life. *Time* magazine went on to vote "Gorby" Man of the Year and British Prime Minister Margaret Thatcher pronounced that Gorbachev was "a man with whom we can do business."

Gorbachev gave the Soviet Union and the world two slogans. *Perestroika* (restructuring) held out the promise of reorganizing the state and society. Perestroika was the corrective held up to Stalinist excesses. *Glasnost* (openness) would permit the open discussion of the nation's problems and it would rid public thinking of propaganda and lies. Soviet society would be transformed. Academics, writers, intellectuals, and artists responded enthusiastically, as did most Western politicians. New histories began to appear and light was shed on the recent past. Surviving participants of the Stalinist purges were interviewed, and long-suppressed documents were published for the first time. A good deal of archival material on the Stalinist purges and the Great Terror was published. Some statistics were located but an accurate count of those who suffered will probably never be known. In 1989, Soviet responsibility was finally acknowledged for the Katyn mass murders of Polish soldiers in 1939. To Gorbachev's way of thinking, the Russian Communist Party would serve as the vanguard of perestroika. It was the Party that would stimulate civic activity and responsibility. In 1988, a Soviet Congress was formed, including elected members, which in 1989 chose the smaller Supreme Soviet. In 1990, the Supreme Soviet elected Gorbachev as the country's president for a term of five years. At the time, Gorbachev was still the leader of the increasingly unpopular Communist Party. Economic changes accompanied these political reforms. Industrial enterprise was encouraged, which in turn fostered private initiative and loosed the stranglehold of decades of central planning. Religious freedoms were restored, and in 1988, the Russian Orthodox Church celebrated its millenial anniversary. Meanwhile, contacts with the outside world, especially the West, began to intensify.

However, there was a downside as well. For instance, glasnost released decades of bitterness that had accumulated over the fifty years of Stalinist repression and terror. Perestroika and glasnost also revealed the widespread ecological damage the Soviets had caused on the environment. Gorbachev's reforms also polarized opinion in ways that even Gorbachev and his stalwart supporters could never have foreseen. All that restructuring and all that openness had increased the diversity of opinions and, in the end, led to more nationalist and ethnic in-fighting. In an effort to preserve unity by compromise, Gorbachev quarreled with Boris Yeltsin. The weakening of traditional Soviet authority and the release of history brought about by the reforms of Mikhail Gorbachev brought, in the end, discord. Meanwhile, Lithuanians, Latvians, and Estonians all demanded independence, which in turn set off similar demands among Ukrainians, Georgians, Beylorussians, Armenians, and the various peoples of central Asia. By the late 1980s, interethnic violence had escalated. And in 1990, the Russian Republic, the largest republic of the Soviet Union, declared its limited independence under Yeltsin. Gorbachev, caught in an avalanche he himself had helped to create, was willing to establish a new federal union of Soviet sovereign republics but remained opposed to the outright dissolution of the Soviet Union. The production and distribution of consumer goods collapsed. Local governments hoarded essential commodities and the black market flourished. The spiritual rebirth and the revolution that Gorbachev had hoped for had not materialized. In response to a crisis produced by Gorbachev, the liberals of Moscow and Leningrad pressed Yeltsin for even quicker modernization. This included a multiparty system, a flourishing market economy, and increased civil liberties for all Soviet citizens. But on the opposite side were the Communist hardliners who were willing and eager to revive the old order, the Stalinist order, which depended on the army for restoring order. Gorbachev viewed all this with an eye toward compromise. On August 19, 1991, the conservatives acted. They imprisoned Gorbachev in his Crimean vacation home and deposed him as president of the Soviet Union. They declared a state of emergency and began preparations for a new Communist dictatorship. The problem was, the conservative faction was completely out of touch with popular opinion. Even the KGB defected over to Yeltsin's side. Emotions were high and the outburst spread to Moscow, Leningrad, and other cities. The coup collapsed in three days and the chief victims, never to recover, were the Communist Party and the unity and existence of the Soviet Union.

The Walls Came Tumbling Down

Outside the Soviet Union, perestroika and glasnost spread among people who were resentful of Soviet domination and worried about economic collapse. In 1989 and 1990, these people showed their dislike of communist leadership and demanded democratic reforms. Eastern European communist leaders either resigned their office or agreed to reform. Poland took the lead. Here the population was traditionally anti-Russian. The slightest relaxation of Soviet control only encouraged Polish nationalism, which had always been expressed with the support of the Roman Catholic Church. With the selection of Pope John Paul II in 1978, Polish nationalism surged ahead. In 1980, workers under the leadership of Lech Walesa succeeded in forming an independent labor union called Solidarity. Pressured by a series of strikes, the Polish government recognized Solidarity, despite threats of Soviet intervention. In 1981, more radical members of Solidarity began to talk about the necessity of free elections. But in December, a military dictatorship was formed and martial law was declared. Walesa and others were jailed and protesting workers were dispersed by force. Walesa appeared on Polish television pleading for pluralism and freedom. In January 1989, Solidarity was legalized and the Communist Party retired. In December 1990, the Polish people elected Walesa as their president. In May 1989, the communist bureaucracy was abolished in Hungary.

By year's end there were more than fifty political parties in existence. Democracy and free enterprise were introduced and the result, as it had been in Poland, was inflation. In East Germany, the upheaval in 1989 was even more momentous. Within a month after celebrating the fortieth anniversary as a socialist workers state, the Communist Party collapsed. Almost 400,000 people left East Germany through the opened borders of Hungary and Czechoslovakia. Meanwhile, the streets of Berlin were full of protest. On November 6, 1989, the walls came tumbling down. Three days later, on November 9, the first hole was made in the Berlin wall and East Germans crossed into West Berlin. The East German police stood by nervously, but the wall had fallen. Gorbachev eventually approved. The breach of the Berlin wall had wide ramifications. In Bulgaria, the Communists still maintained their authoritarian rule. Todor Zhikov was the longest-serving Communist dictator in the Soviet bloc. Under his rule, Bulgaria was a docile state until Gorbachev's message of glasnost and perestroika penetrated the nation. On November 10, 1989, one day after the fall of the Berlin wall, Zhivkov resigned. By mid-December, a multiparty system was in place. The end of the year was the final spurt of the "revolution of 1989."

Romania's Nicolae Ceauşescu paid no attention to Gorbachev's reforms or the events of 1989. He imposed poverty on his people and strengthened his power with the assistance of his wife and family. In 1988, he began to systematically level peasant villages to build "agrotowns." Meanwhile, his government brutally suppressed all opposition in gross violation of human rights. On December 17, 1989, he ordered his troops to fire upon antigovernment demonstrators, but four days later, the tide had turned against him. A staged mass demonstration on his behalf in Bucharest was disrupted by student protesters. The crowd followed the students—even the army turned against Ceauşescu. On Christmas Day,

Ceauşescu and his wife were tried and executed—the last Stalinist dictator had fallen.

Czechoslovakia also joined the crusade against Soviet communism. The hardline Czech Communists had held power since the Prague Spring. But events in Poland and Hungary, coupled with the nation's economic decline, increased public pressure for change. Strikes, public demonstrations, and the circulation of *samizdat*, or self-printed books, made the situation positively explosive. Early in 1989, antigovernment demonstrations escalated. Government repression followed. Vaclav Havel was jailed. But when protests again erupted in the fall, the government faltered. Havel was released and became the leader of the opposition group, the Civic Forum. Faced with massive demonstrations in Prague—all shown on television—the Czech communist leaders resigned on November 24. A month later Vaclav Havel was elected president of Czechoslovakia.

The events of 1989 in the Soviet Union and in Eastern Europe had taken a surprisingly peaceful course. Gorbachev himself was partly responsible for this. He was willing to admit that Soviet satellite states had to go their own way. Under the leadership of intellectuals and priests, the people were unified against foreign domination and economic turmoil. Like Gorbachev, Eastern European Communist rulers had lost all confidence in Marxist-Leninist ideology. Finally, the material plenty of the West appeared in sharp contrast to the depravity of the East. And the people knew it! Communist regimes could not offer an alternative to Western television.

SUGGESTED FEATURE FILMS

A Clockwork Orange. 137 min. Color. 1971. Warner Brothers. Stanley Kubrick's futuristic film about good, evil, and violence in human society.

At the River I Stand. 58 min. Color. 1993. California Newsreel. A portrait of the sanitation workers' strike that drew Martin Luther King, Jr., to Memphis, where he was assassinated.

Before the Rain. 114 min. Color. 1994. Gramercy Pictures. This look at post-Yugoslavia Macedonia was nominated for the 1995 Academy Award for Best Foreign Picture.

If. 111 min. Color. 1968. Paramount. Public-school rebellion in Britain in the 1960s. With Malcolm McDowell.

Nixon. 192 min. Color. 1995. Buena Vista Home Video. Anthony Hopkins and Joan Allen star in this controversial Oliver Stone film about the American president.

The Promise. 115 min. Color. 1995. NL Home Video. Separated by the Berlin wall, a young couple experiences the two sides of German life from the early 1960s through 1989.

We Were Soldiers. 138 min. Color. 2002. Wheelhouse Entertainment. Mel Gibson's powerful film about Colonel Hal Moore and four hundred soldiers who fought at the Battle of Ia Drang in 1965.

Weekend. 105 min. Color. 1968. Lira Films. Godard's violent attack on capitalist society.

Welcome to Sarajevo. 103 min. Color. 1997. Miramax Films. Chilling film about journalists covering the beginning of the Bosnian war in Sarajevo.

SUGGESTED CLASSROOM FILMS

The Battle of Chicago. 22 min. B/W. 1968. Footage from the Democratic National Convention in 1968.

Berlin: A Study of Two Worlds. 43 min. Color. n.d. Gertrude Purple Gorham Agency. Comparison of East and West Berlin both before and after the building of the Berlin wall.

Conversation with Gorbachev. 90 min. Color. 1994. Films for the Humanities and Sciences. Historian Stephen Cohen interviewed Gorbachev after he fell from power.

The Germans: Portrait of a New Nation. 58 min. Color. 1995. Films for the Humanities and Sciences. Includes profiles of families and individuals from both the former West and East Germanies.

The History of the European Monetary Union. 60 min. Color. 2002. Films for the Humanities and Social Sciences. Discusses the hopes and fears of the new citizens of "Euroland."

Oh! Woodstock! 26 min. Color. 1969. Films, Inc. Two groups, young Woodstock participants and older professionals, comment on film clips from the Woodstock Rock Festival.

Soviets: The True Story of Perestroika. 5 parts, 53 min. each. Color. 1991. Films for the Humanities and Sciences. Documentary series that focuses on the concerns, such as the degradation of the environment, that led to grassroots protests and political awakening.

Solidarity. 23 min. Color. 1991. Films for the Humanities and Social Sciences. Film highlights the struggle of Polish workers at the Gdansk shipyards to create Poland's first trade union in twenty-five years.

Vietnam: The Ten Thousand Day War. 360 min. B/W and color. 1980. Public Broadcasting System. Six-part comprehensive documentary covering military, social, cultural, and diplomatic aspects of the Vietnam War. Good on European antiwar protest movements.

A Woman's Place. 52 min. Color. 1973. Xerox Films. The changing roles of American women.

CHAPTER 29

A World without Walls: Globalization and the West

B. Ideas
1. Widespread flow of information
2. New commercial and cultural importance of information itself
3. Proliferation of devices to create, store, and share information
4. The personal computer
   a. Instant communication
   b. New cultural and political settings
   c. The "global village"
5. The Internet
   a. Entrepreneurs with utopian ambitions
   b. Publishing all kinds of information quickly and easily
   c. Grassroots activism
   d. Political struggles
      i. Satellite television—revolts in Eastern Europe in 1989
      ii. Fax machines—Chinese demonstrators at Tiananmen Square
6. Entertainment
   a. Producing entertainment as well as the technology to enjoy entertainment
7. Bill Gates and Microsoft
8. Corporate headquarters remained in the West
C. Peoples
1. Free flow of labor as central aspect of globalization
2. After 1945, a widespread migration of peoples
   a. Changes in everyday life
   b. Europe, Arabic states, and the United States
3. Multiculturalism
   a. New blends of music, food, language, and other forms of popular culture
   b. Raised tense questions of citizenship
   c. Effects
      i. Xenophobic backlash and bigotry
      ii. New conceptions of civil rights and cultural belonging
4. Successful and disadvantaged players
   a. Production of illegal drugs
      i. A thriving industry in Columbia, Myanmar, and Malaysia
   b. Organized crime
      i. Grew out of violence and economic breakdown of postcolonial states

A. Demographics and global health
1. Population
   a. 1800–1950: population tripled to three billion people
   b. 1960–2000: population doubled to six billion people
   c. Causes for growth
      i. Improvements in basic standards of health
      ii. Improving urban-industrial environment in postcolonial regions
   d. Strained social services, public health facilities, and urban infrastructures
2. Demographic crisis
   a. Longer life spans, welfare pro grams, rising healthcare costs, easily obtainable divorces
   b. Reliable birth-control methods
   c. A new sense of choice
   d. Population decline: Italy, Scandinavia, and Russia
3. Public health and medicine
   a. New threats and new treatments
   b. Exposure to epidemic diseases a new reality of globalization
      i. Increased cultural interaction
      ii. Exposure of new ecosystems to human development
      iii. Speed of intercontinental transportation
   c. Acquired Immune Deficiency Syndrome (AIDS) first appeared at the end of the 1970s
   d. Severe Acute Respiratory Syndrome (SARS) appeared in 2003
4. Medical research
   a. Discovery of DNA (1953)
   b. Mapping the human genome
   c. Genetic engineering
   d. Dolly (1997)
   e. New questions
      i. Legal and moral issues of cloning
      ii. Who governs genetic advances?
      iii. Saving lives and cultural preferences
      iv. Ethics, citizenship, and humanity
III. After Empire: Postcolonial Politics in the Global Age
   A. Postcolonial relationships
      1. Former colonies gained independence and new kinds of cultural and political authority

2. "Postcolonial"—underlines the fact that colonialism's legacies outlasted independence
3. Varied results
    a. Industrial success and democratization
    b. Ethnic slaughter and new forms of absolutism
B. Emancipation and ethnic conflict in Africa
    1. Most colonies obtained independence while their infrastructure was deteriorating
    2. Cold War brought few improvements
        a. Homegrown and externally imposed corruption, poverty, and civil war
    3. South Africa
        a. The politics of apartheid sponsored by the white minority government
        b. Nelson Mandela led the African National Congress (ANC)
            i. Imprisoned since 1962
        c. Intense repression and violent conflict
        d. Mandela was released from prison in 1990
            i. Resumed leadership of the ANC
            ii. Turned toward renewed public demonstrations and negotiation
        e. F. W. de Klerk succeeded Pieter Botha
        f. De Klerk and Mandela began direct talks to establish majority rule in March 1992
        g. Mandela chosen as country's first black president in May 1994
            i. Defused the climate of organized racial violence
            ii. Popular among blacks and whites
            iii. A living symbol of a new political culture
    4. Rwanda
        a. Conflict between Hutu and Tutsi populations
        b. Highly organized campaign of genocide directed at the Tutsi
        c. 800,000 dead in a matter of weeks
        d. International pressure
            i. Forced those who had participated in the genocide to flee to Zaire
            ii. Became hired mercenaries in a many-sided civil war
        e. Public services, normal trade, and basic health collapsed in Zaire

C. Economic power on the Pacific rim
    1. East Asia as a center of industrial and manufacturing production
    2. China
        a. World's leading heavy-industrial producer by 2000
        b. State-owned companies produced cheaply and in bulk for sale in the United States and Europe
        c. Established commercial zones around Shanghai
            i. Hong Kong reclaimed from Britain in 1997
            ii. Intended to encourage massive foreign investment
    3. The "Tigers"
        a. Japan led the way—an "economic miracle"
            i. Most influential model of success
            ii. Firms concentrated on efficiency and technical reliability of their products
            iii. State subsidies supported the success of Japanese firms
            iv. Well-funded programs of technical education
            v. Collective loyalty among civil servants and managers
        b. South Korea and Taiwan
            i. Treated prosperity as a fundamental patriotic duty
        c. Malaysia and Indonesia
            i. Parlayed natural resources and expansive local labor pools into industrial investment
    4. Boom and bust
        a. 1990s showed enormous slow down in growth and near-collapse of several currencies
        b. Japan: rising production costs, overvalued stocks, rampant speculation in real estate markets
            i. Launched monetary austerity programs
        c. Indonesia
            i. Inflation and unemployment
            ii. Reignited sharp ethnic conflicts
IV. A New Center of Gravity: Israel, Oil, and Political Islam in the Middle East
    A. The Middle East as crossroad
        1. Western military, political, and economic interests
        2. Deep-seated regional conflicts and transnational Islamic politics

B. The Arab-Israeli conflict
 1. National aspirations of Jewish immigrants clash with anticolonial nationalist pan-Arabists
 2. American mediated peace efforts in the late 1970s, Soviet leaders remained neutral but supportive
 3. Anwar Sadat (1918–1981) argued coexistence with rather than destruction of Israel
 4. Sadat and Carter broker a peace with Israel's Menachem Begin (1913–1992)
 5. Israel and Palestinian Arabs
   a. A blend of ethnic and religious nationalism on both sides
   b. Younger Palestinians turned to the PLO and radical Islam
 6. *Intifada* ("throwing off" or uprising)
   a. Fights escalated into cycles of Palestinian terrorism
   b. International peace brokering
   c. Yasser Arafat
   d. Assassination of Yitzhak Rabin (1922–1995)
 7. The second *intifada*
C. Oil, power, and economics
 1. Postwar demand for oil skyrocketed
 2. Automobiles and plastics
 3. Needs, desires, and profits
   a. Drew Western corporations and governments to the oil-rich states of the Middle East
   b. Vast oil reserves discovered in the 1930s and 1940s
 4. Oil a fundamental tool in new struggles over political power
 5. Organization of Petroleum Exporting Countries (OPEC)
   a. Founded in 1960
   b. Arab, African, and Latin American nations
   c. Regulating production and pricing of crude oil
   d. Militant politics of some OPEC leaders wanted to use oil as a weapon against the West
   e. 1973 oil embargo
 6. The West looks East
   a. Treated Middle Eastern oil regions as vital strategic center of gravity
   b. Constant great-power diplomacy
   c. The West always ready to intervene
     i. 1991 Gulf War
 7. Growing energy demands of postcolonial nations
   a. China and India

 b. Violent conflict inside Middle Eastern oil-producing states
     i. Haves and have-nots
     ii. Deep resentments
     iii. Continued official corruption
     iv. New wave of radical politics
D. The rise of political Islam
 1. North Africa and the Middle East
   a. Shared characteristics of "kleptocracies"
     i. Corrupt state agencies
     ii. Cronyism based on ethnic or family kinship
     iii. Decaying public services
     iv. Rapid population increase
     v. State repression of dissent
   b. Criticism of Nasser's Egypt
     i. Powerful new political movement in revolt against foreign influence and corruption
     ii. Denounced Egypt's government as greedy, brutal, and corrupt
 2. The roots of the Arab world's moral failure: centuries of colonial contact with the West
 3. Sayyid Qutb (1906–1966)
   a. Arrested several times by Egyptian authorities, ultimately executed
   b. Ruling Arab elites were at fault
     i. Frayed local and family bonds
     ii. Abandoned government's responsibility for charity and stability
     iii. The nation's elites were morally bankrupt
   c. Arab elites lived in the pockets of Western imperial and corporate powers
     i. Caused cultural impurity
     ii. Eroded authentic Muslim faith
     iii. Poisoning from without and within
   d. Arab societies should reject all Western political and cultural ideas
   e. Building a new world upon conservative Islamic government
 4. Radical Islam
   a. Combined popular anger, opposition to Western forces, and an idealized vision of the past
   b. The Muslim Brotherhood
     i. Put Qutb's policies into practice

ii. Secretive society rooted in anticolonial politics, charity, and fundamentalist Islam

c. More liberal Islamists were fragmented and easier to silence

E. Iran's Islamic revolution

1. An example of modernization gone sour

2. Shah Reza Pahlavi—installed by Britain and the United States in 1953

    a. Received oil contracts, weapons, and development aid

    b. Thousands of Westerners introduced foreign influences

    c. Challenged traditional local values

    d. New economic and political alternatives

    e. The shah kept these alternatives out of reach

        i. Denied democratic representation to middle-class Iranian workers and students

        ii. Governed through a small aristocracy divided by religious infighting

        iii. Secret police and campaign of repression

    f. Supported by Richard Nixon as a strategic ally

    g. Retired from public life in 1979 and his provisional government collapsed

3. Ayatollah Ruhollah Khomeini

    a. Returned from exile in France

    b. Supported by nation's unemployed, deeply religious university students

    c. Joined by radical Islamists

    d. The new regime

        i. Limited economic and political populism

        ii. Strict constructions of Islamic law

        iii. Restrictions on women's public life

        iv. Prohibition of ideas linked to Western influence

    e. Attacked Sunni religious establishment and atheistic Soviet communists

    f. Attacked Israel and the United States

    g. Teheran and the hostage crisis

F. Iran, Iraq, and unintended consequences of the Cold War

1. Iran-Iraqi War (1980–1988)

    a. Iraq attacked Iran over control of oil fields

    b. Chemical weapons

c. Iran defeated—left Iranian clerics more entrenched at home

    i. Used oil reserves to back grassroots radicals in Lebanon

    ii. Engaged in anti-Western terrorism

d. Threats to Iranian regime came from within

    i. New generations of young students and disenfranchised service workers

2. Iraq as the new problem for the West

    a. France, Saudi Arabia, the Soviet Union, and the United States supported Iraq in 1980

    b. Coalition patronage supported the dictatorship of Saddam Hussein

    c. Hussein invaded Kuwait in 1990

        i. Coalition forces conducted a six-week air campaign and then a ground war

        ii. Iraq forced out of Kuwait

    d. Results of the Gulf War

        i. Encouraged closeness between coalition forces

        ii. Encouraged anti-American radicals angry at a new Western presence

3. Afghanistan

    a. Socialist government of Afghanistan turned against its Soviet patrons in 1979

    b. Moscow overthrew the Afghan president and installed a pro-Soviet faction

    c. Soviets at war with militant Islamists (*mujahidin*)

    d. Conflict became a holy war

    e. *Mujahidin* assisted by advanced weapons and training given by Western powers

    f. Soviets withdrew in 1989

    g. Hardline Islamic factions took over the country

V. Violence Beyond Bounds: War and Terrorism in the Twenty-First Century

A. Terrorist organizations

1. 1960s: Organized terrorist tactics as a part of political conflict

    a. Middle East, Europe, and Latin America

    b. Specific goals

        i. Ethnic separatism

        ii. Establishment of revolutionary governments

2. 1980s and 90s: A new brand of terrorist organization
    a. Apocalyptic groups called for decisive, world-ending conflict
    b. Eliminating enemies and martyrdom
    c. Origins
        i. Groups from social dislocations of the postwar boom
        ii. Radical religion
    d. Divorced themselves from local crises
B. Al Qaeda
    1. Radical, Islamist umbrella organization
    2. Created by leaders of the foreign *mujahidin* who fought against the Soviets in Afghanistan
        a. Osama bin Laden (b. 1957): official leader and financial supporter
        b. Ayman al-Zawahri (b. 1951): linked directly to Sayyid Qutb
    3. Organized broad networks of self-contained terrorist cells around the world
    4. Goals
        a. Did not seek territory or to change governments of specific states
        b. To destroy Israel and America and European and other non-Islamic systems of government
        c. To create an Islamic community held together by faith alone
    5. Terrorist attacks on American embassies in Kenya and Tanzania in 1998
    6. September 11, 2001
        a. Hijacked airliners hit the Pentagon, leveled the World Trade Center in New York
        b. Fourth plane crashed in Pennsylvania
        c. A new brand of terror
            i. Deeply indebted to globalization
            ii. Extreme, opportunistic violence of marginal groups
    7. United States' response
        a. Attacked Afghanistan, central haven for al Qaeda
        b. Routed Taliban forces
        c. Did not capture bin Laden
        d. Rebuilding Afghanistan
    8. Persistent fears
        a. Chemical and biological weapons
        b. Weapons of mass destruction (WMD)

9. New arms race
    a. Israel
    b. India and Pakistan
10. America-led invasion of Iraq (2003)
    a. Hussein deposed and captured in December 2003
    b. No WMD found
11. North Korea
    a. Loss of Soviet patronage (1991)
    b. Economic disasters
    c. Pursued development of nuclear arsenal as bargaining chip
VI. Conclusion

GENERAL DISCUSSION QUESTIONS

1. Was postwar decolonization and independence always beneficial to colonial peoples and nations? Which nations have benefited the most from decolonization? Which regions of the world remain as "hot spots"?

2. How did the loss of empire affect the mother country? Are the former colonial peoples and possessions linked forever to the former great powers of Europe?

3. How do British, French, and Soviet approaches to decolonization differ?

4. Can globalization exist without decolonization? That is, was the granting of independence of former colonies a requirement of globalization?

5. Is the United States the only superpower? Or, have the requirements for being a superpower changed?

6. Explain how the Internet has contributed to the current revolution in information technology. What is so revolutionary about the Internet?

SAMPLE LECTURE 29: GLOBALIZATION AND THE NETWORKED WORLD

Lecture Objectives

1. To explain the events behind the terrorist bombings of the past decade.

2. To define and understand the ramifications of globalization.

3. To grasp the significance of the current revolution in information technology.

TOWARD OUR FUTURE

Although the history of Western civilizations has illustrated the enormous advances made in the arts, the sciences, literature, philosophy, and a hundred other things, as we stand at the beginning of the twenty-first century it seems we are also faced with numerous problems of an almost insurmountable nature—global warming, AIDS and SARS, ethnic cleansing, racism, bigotry, terrorism, and war. Many of these problems not only seem outside our direct control, but also our comprehension. One can only wonder just how a Sumerian high priest, or Pericles, or Charlemagne, or Louis XIV, or even an unemployed worker living on the streets of Chicago during the Great Depression may have responded to a world gone mad. But this is our world, and thanks to a revolution in information technology, we are confronted with it more directly than ever before. We must come to some kind of understanding of these problems of a "world-historical" nature. All these centuries of progress seem to have come before us, and now, with all our technological know-how, we must once again begin with fundamental questions: Why? What am I supposed to do? What is my place in the world? How do I understand the world? The twin processes of decolonization and globalization have perhaps resulted in a double-edged sword: as with any other development of a revolutionary nature, with much good necessarily comes much bad. Our task is to understand the world, grasping the manifold diversity of the world while at the same time maintaining our sense of self, as well as our sense of history.

102 MINUTES THAT CHANGED THE WORLD

The world will not soon forget the events that unfolded on Tuesday, September 11, 2001. At 8:46 in the morning, American Airlines Flight 11 crashed into the north tower of the World Trade Center in New York City between the ninety-fourth and ninety-eighth floors. Seventeen minutes later, United Airlines Flight 175 crashed into the south tower between the seventy-eighth and eighty-fourth floors. Thanks to the Internet, CNN, and satellite television, the images made stark reality immediately known around the world. At 9:25, the U. S. Federal Aviation Agency ordered all domestic flights grounded. At 9:45, and as the two towers burned, American Airlines Flight 77 crashed into the west wall of the Pentagon. Twenty minutes later, the south tower of the World Trade Center collapsed. The world watched as the unimaginable became reality. At 10:10, news services received reports that United Airlines Flight 93 had crashed in a remote area near Shanksville, Pennsylvania. At 10:28, the north tower of the World Trade Center collapsed. In a period of time lasting 102 minutes, the United States had been struck by terrorists using products—commercial airlines and highly flammable jet fuel—created by the technological wizardry of the twentieth century.

This terrorist attack was masterminded by the radical Islamist umbrella organization known as al Qaeda. Its official leader and financial supporter was the Saudi multi-millionaire, Osama bin Laden. Together with the Egyptian radical Ayman al-Zawahari, himself a follower of Sayyid

Qutb, these leaders organized global networks of largely self-contained terrorist cells from the Islamic regions of Southeast Asia, Europe, east Africa, and the United States. The organization of al Qaeda is global and as such, it defies any national boundary. These terrorist cells did not seek to obtain new land. Nor were they that interested in changing the governments of the world—they were not concerned with creating Islamic governments worldwide. Instead, they spoke about destroying the state of Israel as well as American, European, and other non-Islamic forms of government. They set out to destroy, not create. However, they did call for a united revolt by fundamentalist Muslims around the world to create an Islamic community of believers, based on faith alone. The enemy, as the leaders of al Qaeda saw it, was the United States, the symbolic seat of globalization. So, al Qaeda set out to cripple the focal point of American economic might—the World Trade Center—as well as the focal point of American military might, the Pentagon. Had the passengers on United Airlines Flight 93 not fought back against their captors, it was highly likely that the airplane would have crashed into the United States Capitol building.

The United States responded to these events by attacking al Qaeda's central place of refuge in Afghanistan, a state already in disarray after three decades of warfare. The Taliban government, which sponsored al Qaeda, was quickly routed and the remnants of the terrorist organization scattered. Osama bin Laden was not captured. The United States then began the difficult task of rebuilding Afghanistan. The war against al Qaeda prompted fears about the availability of new weapons—chemical and biological substances as well as nuclear weapons. After all, an arms race had spread beyond the borders of the great powers. By the end of the century, Israel had nuclear capability as did India and Pakistan. Then North Korea stepped into the picture, using nuclear weapons as a bargaining chip against other nations. The fear that the Iraqi dictator Saddam Hussein might have used chemical weapons during its war with Iran, as well as against his own people, prompted the West to disarm Iraq during the Gulf War of 1991. Coalition forces conducted a six-week air campaign and then sent in ground forces. Kuwait was liberated and the Iraqi Red Guard pushed to Baghdad. The government of Saddam Hussein remained intact. But then came September 11. The picture changed. The United Nations sent teams of weapons inspectors into Iraq, looking for weapons of mass destruction (WMD). The evidence of WMD in Iraq was inconclusive. However, in the spring of 2003, the Americans led another invasion of Iraq. Once again, an air and ground campaign crippled Iraq, and this time, Hussein was deposed. Then, in December 2003, Saddam Hussein was captured by American forces. In July 2004, Hussein was brought to trial by a special tribunal by Iraqi authorities. He was charged with ethnic cleansing of the Kurds (1988), the invasion of Kuwait (1990), and the execution of Iraqi political activists following the Gulf War.

THE "CULT" OF GLOBALIZATION

We live in an age of globalization. In many respects, the terrorist attacks on the United States on September 11, 2001, which killed more than 2,800 people, served as a horrible commentary that globalization certainly has its negative side. And the bombing of the World Trade Center and Pentagon by radical Islamists was only the most recent terrorist act.

- February 23, 1993: A rental van drove into the basement of the WTC. A timer detonated a 1,500-pound urea-nitrate bomb. Six were killed and more than one thousand injured.
- August 7, 1998: Terrorist bombs exploded at the American embassies in Nairobi, Kenya, and Dar es Salaam, Tanzania, leaving 258 people dead and more than 5,000 injured. The terrorists have been linked to the al Qaeda network.
- October 12, 2000: An explosives-laden boat rammed the U.S.S. *Cole* while it was taking on fuel in the port of Aden, Yemen. Seventeen members of the crew were killed and thirty-nine wounded in an attack linked directly to Osama bin Laden.

How can it be argued that globalization created the seeds for this kind of terrorism? What is globalization? The Internet, the fall of the Berlin wall, Wal-Marts in Mexico—these are all images of globalization as it appears today. Globalization means integration in that numerous networks have been created that bind together different nations and cultures. The driving force behind this development was perhaps the Internet. The idea of instant communication and the creation, storage, and distribution of "knowledge as information" has led to a situation in which goods, money, and ideas move with a frequency and speed that would have been inconceivable a generation earlier. Exchange is now global and entirely independent of national control. Globalization has altered industry and trade around the world. The IMF and International Criminal Court serve as evidence of the globalization of finance and justice. And national boundaries themselves seem to have eroded as well. Although peace, stability, and homogeneity may be the unspoken goal, globalization has not resulted in a better world for everyone. Its results are uncertain and uneven. Wealth remains unequally distributed and inequalities have increased. We still inhabit a world of "haves" and "have-nots." Then again, globalization has brought us the "global village," and new sources of cultural blending as well as new forms of sociability. But there has also been a backlash against such tendencies. Globalization has transformed the world economy in profound ways. Producers and consumers remain necessary, of course. But since the 1970s, international markets have been integrated as the international agreements made after World War II have been overturned. The movement of people, goods, and money are no longer regulated. And the market in ideas and information is now

in the midst of a revolution whose end result is not yet in sight. The personal computer is perhaps one of the most revolutionary devices of our time. Not only are millions of people using a technology that three decades ago was the province of the government, the military, and industry alone, they are also using the technology in provocative ways. The ability to process words, numbers, images, and sounds in milliseconds has perhaps produced subtle changes in our expectations and aspirations as individuals and as members of the human community. And then there is the Internet.

THE REVOLUTION IN INFORMATION TECHNOLOGY: A NEW PARADIGM

At the beginning of the twenty-first century, we have arrived at an interval in human history characterized by a new technological model organized around information technology. Around this nucleus of information technologies—microelectronics, computers, telecommunications, and genetic engineering—major technological breakthroughs took place in the last twenty years. We now have the ability to create an interface between technological innovations and a common digital language. We have become partners in a new communications network, all driven by technology. In such a world, information is generated, stored, retrieved, processed, and transmitted. We live in a world that has become digital. The creation of a digital world is a historical event as profound as the eighteenth-century industrial revolution and is characterized by its penetration into human activity itself. The digital revolution is the fabric of our lives. The core of such a revolution refers to the technologies of information processing and communication. What new sources of energy were to the eighteenth century, information technology is to our own time. Information technology is an extension of the human mind. What we think, and how we think, become expressed in goods, services, and intellectual output. The growing integration between minds and machines has fundamentally altered our existence.

Major technological breakthroughs in electronics took place during World War II. The transistor, invented in 1947 at Bell Laboratories in New Jersey, made possible the processing of electric impulses in a binary mode of interruption and application, thus allowing communication with and between machines. These processing devices are called semiconductors, or chips. The widespread use of semiconductors required new manufacturing technologies and the use of a new material—silicon. And then the integrated circuit was invented at Texas Instruments in 1957, thus triggering a technological explosion. In 1971 came the invention by an Intel engineer of the microprocessor—the computer on a chip. Microelectronics changed everything. In 1975, an engineer by the name of Ed Roberts built a computing box he called Altair. The machine was primitive but it was built as a small-scale computer around the microprocessor. It eventually became the basis for the design of Apple I and then Apple II, the first commercially successful microcomputer. Launched in 1976 with three partners and $91,000 in capital, Apple Computers had by 1982 reached almost $600 million in sales. IBM reacted quickly. In 1981 it introduced its own version of the microcomputer with a brilliant name—the personal computer, or PC. A fundamental condition for the diffusion of microcomputers was met with the development of software in the 1970s. Two young Harvard drop-outs, Bill Gates and Paul Allen, adapted the BASIC programming language for operating the Altair machine. They went on to found Micro Soft in Albuquerque and then as Microsoft in Seattle.

By the mid-1980s, computers needed to perform in networks. Not only did the whole technological system change, but social and organizational interactions changed as well. All of this was made possible by the network of all networks. The Internet originated at the U.S. Defense Department's Advanced Research Projects Agency, or ARPA. In 1957, the Soviet Union's launching of Sputnik alarmed the U.S. military. The problem was quite simple. If the Soviets bombed the United States, how would the lines of communication be kept open? It fell to Paul Baran of the Rand Corporation to design a communications system independent of any central control that would remain invulnerable to nuclear attack. ARPANET went online September 1, 1969, with four nodes of the network established at UCLA, the Stanford Research Institute, UC Santa Barbara, and the University of Utah. It was open to research centers cooperating with United States Defense Department, but scientists started to use it for their own communication purposes. ARPANET was closed down on February 28, 1990, and NSFNET took over as the backbone of the Internet. Commercial pressure and the growth of private corporate networks led to the closing of this last government-operated Internet backbone in April 1995. The Internet was fully privatized, and as a result, did not have any overseeing authority. Some institutions created by the development of the Internet took some of the informal responsibility for coordinating technical configurations, but there is no controlling authority. The Internet today is unregulated and anarchic, perhaps a testimony to the role of countercultural ideas that shaped the Internet itself.

The first step in enabling computers to talk to each other was the creation of a communications protocol that could be used by all kinds of networks. In the summer of 1973, Vinton Cerf and Robert Kahn designed TCP/IP, the basic architecture of the Internet. From that point on computers were able to encode and decode data packages traveling at high speed on the Internet network. Behind the development of the Internet there were the scientific, institutional, and personal networks cutting across the Defense Department, National Science Foundation, major research universities (Harvard, MIT, UCLA, and Stanford), and specialized think tanks (MIT's Lincoln Labs, the Palo Alto Research Center funded by Xerox, AT&T's Bell Labs, and the Rand Corporation). Computer scientists moved back and forth between these institutions and created a network of innovation—these were the technological crusaders who were convinced that they were changing the world.

What really caught fire was e-mail communication between network participants. But this is only one side of the story. A computer counterculture emerged in the United States, a movement that seemed to echo the student movements of the 1960s. An important element of the system was one of the technological breakthroughs emerging from the pioneers of this counterculture (originally called "hackers"). The modem for PCs was invented by two Chicago students in 1978 who were tired of driving to one another's house to exchange programs. In 1979, three students at Duke University and the University of North Carolina, created a modified version of the UNIX protocol that made it possible to link up computers over the regular telephone line—they called it USENET, which became a forum for discussion groups of all kinds. This countercultural approach made technological means available to whoever had the technical knowledge and a computer. Meanwhile, the PC began to increase in power as its cost decreased. People began talking about the creation of "virtual communities."

By 1990 the Internet was still difficult for novices to use. There was very limited graphic transmission capability and it was hard to locate and retrieve information. The creation of the World Wide Web took place in Geneva in 1990 at the European Center for Nuclear Research (CERN). The Web was invented by a group of researchers led by Tim Berners-Lee, a physicist. What Berners-Lee and others imagined was a new system of organizing information which was called hypertext. They created a format for documents—hypertext markup language (HTML)—as well as a hypertext transfer protocol (HTTP) to guide communications between Web browsers and Web servers. Then came a standard address format, the uniform resource locator (URL). CERN distributed its browser software for free over the Internet, and the first Web sites were established by major scientific research centers around the world. One of the centers was the National Center for Supercomputer Applications (NCSA), located at the University of Illinois. It was from there that Marc Andreessen distributed a Web browser called Mosaic, which was designed to run on personal computers. By the spring of 1994 several million copies were in use. Together with Jim Clark, formerly of Silicon Graphics, Andreessen eventually created Netscape Navigator, which was released in October 1994. The rest became history as nearly the whole world has now embraced the Internet, literally creating a World Wide Web.

In the late 1990s, information technology shifted from decentralized, stand-alone microcomputers and mainframes to computing by interconnected information-processing devices. Computer power is distributed in a network built around Web servers using common Internet protocols. Users access the network from a variety of devices distributed in all spheres of life and activity. These devices can communicate among themselves without needing their own operating system. New software programs such as Java (1995) enabled the network to become the actual information processing system. In effect, the networking logic epitomized by the Internet became applicable to every domain of activity and to every location that can be electronically connected. The extraordinary increase in transmission capacity with broadband communication technology provided the opportunity to use the Internet to transmit voice as well as data, thus revolutionizing the telecommunications industry.

Technological visionaries have suggested a future in which billions of devices are attached to the Internet. There are also those who see the application of a chemically-based or biologically-based nanotechnology approach to chip-making. In 1999, researchers discovered a way to make electronic switches using chemical processes instead of light, thus shrinking the switches to the size of a molecule. This would make it possible to pack the computing power of one hundred computer workstations into a space the size of a grain of salt. How might the past have grasped that development?

SUGGESTED FEATURE FILMS

A.I.: Artificial Intelligence. 146 min. Color. 2001. Warner Brothers. Stanley Kubrick film (finished by Steven Spielberg), about the not-too-distant future and a realistic robot "mecha" named David who wants to become real.

Fahrenheit 9/11. 122 min. Color. 2004. Miramax Films. Michael Moore's controversial film about American involvement in Iraq post–9/11.

The Gate of Heavenly Peace. 180 min. Color. 1995. Independent Television Service. Lengthy documentary about the 1989 Tiananmen Square student protests.

Gattaca. 101 min. Color, 1997. Columbia Pictures. Film depicting a near-future society of "Valids" and "In-Valids" in which one's personal and professional destiny is determined by one's genes.

Mandela. 118 min. Color. 1996. Island Pictures. Documentary highlighting the life of Nelson Mandela.

The Net. 114 min. Color. 1995. Columbia Pictures. Film about a software engineer type who has few friends outside of cyberspace and who becomes embroiled in computer espionage.

Promises. 106 min. Color. 2001. Cowboy Pictures. Three filmmakers follow seven Jewish and Palestinian children with totally different backgrounds growing up in Jerusalem between 1995 and 1998.

Witness to Apartheid. 58 min. Color. 1986. Developing News Inc. An objective look at apartheid in South Africa. Many of the film's black contributors were imprisoned or killed by the South African government after this film's release.

SUGGESTED CLASSROOM FILMS

9/11 Through Saudi Eyes. 53 min. Color. 2002. Films for the Humanities and Social Sciences. A broad cross-section of Saudis give their perceptions of events and issues involving September 11.

Al Qaeda 2.0. 46 min. Color. 2003. Films for the Humanities and Social Sciences. Film covers the period from 9/11 to the start of Gulf War in 2003 and tracks al Qaeda and its allies from London, where their Internet traffic is monitored, to recent operational areas, including Pakistan, Hong Kong, Singapore, Indonesia, Thailand, and Bangladesh.

The End of Empires. 48 min. Color. 1995. Films for the Humanities and Social Sciences. David Frost hosts this film about the end of European imperialism in Asia and Africa.

Fighting on Both Sides of the Law: Mandela and His Early Crusade. 51 min. Color. 2003. Films for the Humanities and Social Sciences. Traces Mandela's life up to the point when he was convicted of treason and began serving a life sentence in a South African jail.

The Global Generation: The Human Face Behind Globalization. 156 min. Color. 2000. Films for the Humanities and Social Sciences. Six-part series exploring the various issues and concerns about globalization. Includes *A World Without Borders: What Is Happening with Globalization*; *The Global Marketplace: The Benefits of Globalization*; *Global Partnerships: The Effects of Globalization*; *The Global Neighborhood: What Can Happen with Globalization*; *Global Grassroots: The Ramifications of Globalization*; and *The Global Dimension: The Risks of Globalization*.